Álvaro

THINKING GLOBALLY

THINKING GLOBALLY

A Global Studies Reader

EDITED BY
Mark Juergensmeyer

UNIVERSITY OF CALIFORNIA PRESS

Berkeley   Los Angeles   London

University of California Press, one of the most distinguished university presses in the United States, enriches lives around the world by advancing scholarship in the humanities, social sciences, and natural sciences. Its activities are supported by the UC Press Foundation and by philanthropic contributions from individuals and institutions. For more information, visit www.ucpress.edu.

University of California Press
Berkeley and Los Angeles, California

University of California Press, Ltd.
London, England

Library of Congress Cataloging-in-Publication Data

Thinking globally : a global studies reader / edited by Mark Juergensmeyer.
    pages cm.
  Includes bibliographical references and index.
  ISBN 978-0-520-27844-8 (pbk. : alk. paper)
  1. Globalization—Textbooks.   I. Juergensmeyer, Mark.

JZ1318.T456   2014
303.48'2 — dc23   2013022129

23   22   21   20   19   18   17   16   15   14
10   9   8   7   6   5   4   3   2   1

In keeping with a commitment to support environmentally responsible and sustainable printing practices, UC Press has printed this book on Natures Natural, a fiber that contains 30% post-consumer waste and meets the minimum requirements of ANSI/NISO Z39.48-1992 (R 1997) (*Permanence of Paper*).

CONTENTS

PREFACE
A Friendly Introduction to Global Studies

I have a lot of friends on Facebook, and they live in all parts of the world. If I post something about global trade, I get responses from friends in China and Brazil. If I put up a link about interfaith harmony, I get appreciative "likes" from friends in Indonesia, India, and Northern Ireland. When I comment about domestic politics in the United States, I'm often politely ignored by my friends in the other part of the world, who find my local obsessions as arcane as I view their postings on Eritrean political squabbles. But when I post a link to a website that portrays nothing but pictures of bouncing cats, I receive appreciative notices from around the world. Everyone, it seems, loves bouncing cats.

It is not just the bouncing cats that are global, however. It's everything. The very process of interaction and communication beyond national borders is a feature of our globalized world. And it is not just Facebook. Every time you go online, you go global.

When you turn off the computer and go to the store, chances are you will encounter not just your local milieu. A trip to Walmart is a journey into the global arena. And when you bring home all that stuff made not only in China but also in myriad countries around the world, you are literally bringing globalization home. Try this simple party game with your friends. Guess the country on everyone's clothing labels, then check to see where the t-shirts and jackets and everything else you and your friends are wearing were made—Bangladesh, Trinidad, Cambodia, Yemen, or wherever. See how many countries are represented. And then imagine the journey that the clothing had to make, from cotton fields to textile factories to seaports and cargo containers to distribution centers to retail stores and eventually to the closets of you and your friends. Perhaps the most global area of your house is that closet.

In some cases, you do not have to go anywhere to find examples of globalization because they come to you. Globalization permeates the air that you breathe—including tiny particles emitted from volcanic eruptions half a world away. It affects your weather, as cycles of warming and cooling air react to global climate change. And globalization is part of the food that you eat. This is obvious if you have a taste for Chinese take-out or pad Thai noodles or Mexican burritos. But even if you are a meat-and-potatoes kind of person who likes a little tomato salad on the side, you are enjoying the effects of globalization about five hundred years ago. It was then that potatoes and tomatoes, plants originally found only in South America, were taken elsewhere by explorers to become a part of the food habits in North America, Europe, and around the world. Their dissemination was part of the extraordinary global diffusion of plants, germs, and cultures that followed European contacts with the Western Hemisphere, beginning with Columbus in 1492.

So globalization is woven into the fabric of our daily lives. To study it is to focus on the central feature of life in the twenty-first century. But how do you go about studying globalization? Is it really possible to study the whole world? Doesn't this mean studying almost everything? And if so, where do you begin?

These were the questions in the minds of a group of scholars who met in Tokyo in 2008. They had met the year before in Santa Barbara, California, to explore the possibility of creating a new international organization for representatives of graduate programs in global studies—a whole new academic field that had been created in various universities around the world. The first college programs to be called "global studies" were formed in the mid-1990s, and within a decade there were hundreds. Students flocked to the new programs, intuitively knowing that this was something important. By the end of the first decade of the twenty-first century, graduate programs had been established in dozens of universities in Asia, Europe, and North America, including Japan, South Korea, China, India, Germany, Denmark, Russia, the United Kingdom, Australia, Canada, and the United States. The field of global studies had arrived.

But what was in this new field of study? When the scholars came together in Tokyo in 2008, their main goals were to answer this question and to define the major features of the field of global studies. They came expecting to have something of a fight. After all, each of these programs had developed independently from the others. When representatives of all these different programs came together, they did not know what they would find, thinking that the field of global studies would be defined vastly differently in Tokyo, Leipzig, and Melbourne. But as it turned out, this was not the case. Happily, there was a great deal of agreement at the outset regarding what the field of global studies contained and how to go about studying it.

The five characteristics of global studies that the scholars agreed on at that memorable founding meeting of the international Global Studies Consortium in Tokyo are discussed below.

Transnational.   The scholars in Tokyo agreed that the field of global studies focuses primarily on the analysis of events, activities, ideas, trends, processes, and phenomena that appear across national boundaries and cultural regions. These include activities such as economic distribution systems, and ideologies such as nationalism or religious beliefs. The scholars used the term *cultural regions* as well as *nations,* since these kinds of global flows of activity and ideas transcend the limitations of regions even when they are not the same as national boundaries. Historically, much of the activity that we call "transnational" might more properly be called "transregional," since it occurred before the concept of nation was applied to states.

Interdisciplinary.   Since transnational phenomena are complex, these are examined from many disciplinary points of view. In general, the field of global studies does not keep strict disciplinary divisions among, for instance, sociological, historical, political, literary, or other academic fields. Rather, it takes a problem-focused approach, looking at situations such as global warming or the rise of new religio-political ideologies as specific cases. To make sense of these problem areas requires multiple perspectives, which may be economic, political, social, cultural, religious, ideological, or environmental. Scholars involved in global studies often work in interdisciplinary teams or freely use terms and concepts across fields of study. These scholars come from all fields of the social sciences (especially from sociology, economics, political science, and anthropology). And many of the fields are also related to the humanities, including particularly the fields of history, literature, religious studies, and the arts. Some scholars have expertise in areas of science, such as environmental studies and public health.

Contemporary and Historical.   We think of globalization as being primarily contemporary, something unique to our time. But it is also historical. True, the pace and intensity of globalization have increased enormously in the post–Cold War period of the twentieth century and even more so in the twenty-first century. But transnational activities have had historical antecedents. There are moments in history—such as in the ancient Mediterranean world during the Roman and Greek Empires—when there was a great deal of transnational activity and interchange on economic, cultural, and political levels. The global reach of European colonialism from the sixteenth century to the twentieth century provides another example of a global stratum of culture, education, technology, and economic activity upon which are based many aspects of the globalization of the twenty-first century. Thus, to fully understand the patterns of globalization today, it is necessary to probe their historical precedents.

Critical and Multicultural.   The American and European view of globalization is not the only one. Although many aspects of contemporary globalization are based on European colonial precedents, most global studies scholars do not accept uncritically the notion that people in the West should be the only ones to benefit from economic, political, and cultural globalization. Some global studies scholars avoid using the term *globalization* to describe their subject of study, since the term sometimes is interpreted to imply the promotion of a Western-dominated hegemonic project aimed at spreading the acceptance of laissez-faire liberal economics throughout the world. Other scholars describe their approach as "critical globalization studies," implying that their examination of globalization is not intended to promote or privilege Western economic models of globalization, but rather to understand it.

To understand globalization well requires viewing it from many cultural perspectives—from African and Asian, as well as European and American, points of view. Scholars of global studies acknowledge that globalization and other global issues, activities, and trends can be viewed differently in different parts of the world and from different socioeconomic levels within each locality. For that reason, scholars of global studies sometimes speak of "many globalizations" or "multiple perspectives on global studies." This position acknowledges that there is no dominant paradigm or perspective in global studies that is valued over others.

Globally Responsible. Scholars who work in global studies often advance an additional criterion for what they do: to help make the world a better place in which to live. By focusing on global problems, scholars imply that they want to help solve those problems. They also hope to foster a sense of global citizenship among their students. They like to think that they are helping to create "global literacy"—the ability to function in an increasingly globalized world—by understanding both the specific aspects of diverse cultures and traditions and the commonly experienced global trends and patterns. Other teachers assert that they are providing training in "global leadership," giving potential leaders of transnational organizations and movements the understanding and skills that will help them to solve problems and deal with issues on a global scale.

In this book we will embrace all of these aspects of global studies. In Part 2, we will move around the world from region to region—from Africa, the Middle East, South and Central Asia, East Asia, and Southeast Asia and the Pacific area to Europe and bicontinental Russia and the Americas. We explore readings that show how globalization is viewed from the perspective of each region, both historically and today. We will consider how global factors have affected each region and how each region has contributed to the larger currents of globalization during different historical periods.

In Part 3, we will look at major transnational issues today, including the decline of the nation-state, the rise of new religious politics, and several economic issues—such as finance, currency, and labor in the global economy; problems of development and the role of women in the world's workforce; and the hidden economy involving trade in sex and illicit drugs. We will also explore global environmental problems, including climate change, transnational diseases and other global health issues, and global communications and new media, and end with a section on the role of civil society in the global future. In choosing the readings to explore these issues, I have tried to achieve a balance among disciplinary and cultural perspectives. And I hope for my readers to not only understand the nature of global problems, but also to consider some of the possibilities in solving them.

So when you enter the field of global studies, you are encountering some of the most significant aspects of our contemporary world. You are engaging with the transnational issues that have shaped the regions of the world from ancient times to the present and that are among the most pressing issues of our contemporary era. Like the Internet, global studies draws you into this wider world. But global studies, at its best, does more than that. As these readings will show, the scholars engaged in these studies have honed their analytic skills to make critical assessments and reasoned judgments about the character of the global transformations that are occurring around us. This does not make these scholars infallible; in fact, they frequently disagree with one another. But their insights do make them friends—not only to be liked, but also to be challenged by, to be emulated, and to be known.

PART I

INTRODUCTION

1

THINKING GLOBALLY

Your friends may have peeked over your shoulders at this book and asked why you are interested in global studies. And they might have added, just what is that, anyway? So what do you tell them? You could say that you are studying what goes on in the world that knits us all together—but that sounds sort of soft and squishy. Or you could tell them that you are studying the economic and technological networks that interact on a global plane. But that's only part of the story.

The honest truth is that "global studies" can mean a lot of different things, both the hard and the squishy. It is usually defined as the analysis of events, activities, ideas, processes, and flows that are transnational or that can affect all areas of the world. These global activities can be studied as one part of the established disciplines of sociology, economics, political science, history, religious studies, and the like. Or global studies can be a separate course or part of a whole new program or department.

As an academic field, global studies is fairly new. It blossomed largely after the turn of the twenty-first century. But the intellectual roots of the field lie in the pioneering work of the many different scholars who have thought globally over many decades. These thinkers have attempted to understand how things are related and have explored the connections among societies, polities, economies, and cultural systems throughout the world.

One could argue that the first global studies scholars were among the founders of the social sciences. Over a hundred years ago the pioneering German sociologist Max Weber (1864–1920) wrote a series of works on the religions of India, China, Judaism, and Protestant Christianity. Weber was interested in finding what was distinctive about each of them, and what was similar among all of them. Weber also attempted to discern universal elements in the development of all societies. He showed, for example, that a certain kind of rational and legal authority and its associated bureaucratization was a globalizing process. Though his intellectual interests were Europocentric, his curiosity spanned the globe.

Other early social scientists were also global thinkers. The French sociologist Émile Durkheim (1858–1917) focused first on something very local: case studies of tribal societies. What he found, however, was something he regarded as quite global: the rise of organic solidarity based on functional interdependence. The German philosopher and social critic Karl Marx (1818–1883) likewise assumed that his theories were universal. Marx showed that capitalism was a globalizing force, one that would cause both production systems and markets to expand to encompass the entire world.

Ideas in Europe, North America, and the rest of the Westernized world were influenced by thinkers such as these. At the same time, significant thinking about intercultural commonalities and global awareness was being developed in intellectual centers in other parts of the world. The tolerant ideals of the Muslim thinker Ibn Khaldun were influential in North Africa and the Middle East, and notions of universal brotherhood advocated by the Indian philosopher Rabindranath Tagore had an impact on the intellectual circles of South Asia as well as on his admirers in Western societies.

All of these early thinkers, both European and non-European, focused on two ways of thinking globally: comparison and universality. In some cases, they looked at comparative and non-Western examples to determine differences and similarities. In other studies, they adopted intellectual positions that assumed a universal applicability. Hence early European theorists such as Weber and Marx thought that the social forces that were transforming Europe in the nineteenth century would eventually have relevance globally. Current scholarship in all areas of the humanities and social sciences—including global studies—is indebted to these pioneering scholars.

But the specific focus on globalization itself is fairly new. Only recently have scholars begun to examine transnational and global networks, flows, processes, ideologies, outlooks, and systems both historically and in the contemporary world. In fact, the first explicitly global works of scholarship of this sort only emerged a few decades ago, at the end of the twentieth century.

One of the pioneers of contemporary global studies was the sociologist Immanuel Wallerstein, who helped to formulate world systems theory. He incorporated insights from political economy, sociology, and history in order to understand global patterns of hegemonic state power. Other sociologists, including Roland Robertson, Saskia Sassen, and Manfred Steger, explicitly examined the concept of the global, as opposed to local, points of view.

Perspectives from other disciplines have also contributed to global studies. The anthropologist Arjun Appadurai broadened the understanding of global perspectives from landscape to a variety of "scapes"—culturally shaped understandings of the world. The political scientist David Held helped to formulate theories of politics in relation to globalization. William H. McNeill, Akira Iriye, and Bruce Mazlish, among other historians, helped to develop the subfields of world history and global history. Economists such as Joseph Stiglitz and Jagdish Bhagwati have analyzed economic interactions and changes in global terms. And in the field of religious studies, Wilfred Cantwell Smith and Ninian Smart moved beyond the study of particular religious traditions to the study of world theology and worldview analysis, respectively. Other scholars developed analytic approaches to describe new forms of global society: Mary Kaldor examined an emerging global civil society while Kwame Anthony Appiah and Ulrich Beck have described what they regard as a cosmopolitan strand in the new global order.

By the first decade of the twenty-first century, an imposing body of scholarly literature and a flurry of new journals, book series, and scholarly conferences and associations emerged under the label of global studies. The field had arrived. This book provides a road map to the emerging field. At the same time—to mix metaphors—it provides a sampling of the intellectual feast that the current field provides.

Global studies uses the term *transnational* a lot. What this means is that global studies focus not just on the activities and patterns that are international—among nation-states—but also on those that exist beyond the borders of nations and regions and stretch across the various areas of the world. This is one way of thinking of global activity—not that it is universal, found everywhere on the planet, but that it transcends the usual boundaries that separate nation from nation. Transnational relations can be confined largely within a particular area of the world (such as economic cooperation within Europe, for instance, or among the nations along the Pacific Rim) and not necessarily occur throughout the whole world.

At the same time, there are phenomena that are truly global in that they are found everywhere, such as satellite communication systems that can be accessed anywhere on the planet. These are by definition transnational, since they occur beyond the limitations of national boundaries or control. All global phenomena encompass transnational linkages, but not everything that is transnational is global. Terms can be confusing, but it's useful to try to be as clear as possible about what we mean.

In the field of global studies, we tend not to use the term *international* very often, since it implies interactions between nation-states. In common, everyday language, however, many transnational phenomena are described as international, as in the description of some environmental issues as international problems, even though the phenomena themselves—such as the pollution of the oceans and global warming—are transnational. The wording gets tricky when one considers that many of the efforts to deal with transnational problems like global climate change are international—such as the collaboration of nations in efforts to agree on limiting carbon emissions into the atmosphere.

Global studies has to do with globalization, of course, but what does that mean? Often, *globalization* is defined as the process of bringing the world together in more intense interaction through all of the transnational activity that we have been talking about—economic, demographic, social, cultural, technological, and so on. Scholars such as Roland Robertson began using the term *globalization* in the 1980s. And a book by Martin Albrow and Elizabeth King used the term *globalization* in its title in the early 1990s. What they meant by the term was the process of social change that involved transnational interactions in all aspects of social, economic, and technological relationships. Thus, the word *globalization* describes a process.

The result of globalization is a more unified and interactive planet—a globalized world. Some scholars have called this globalized society "globality" or the era of "the global." The attitude that people adopt in this more intensely interactive world can be said to be one of "globalism," or "global consciousness," or one embracing the "global imaginary." These are all ways of thinking about the new state of global awareness in a world where transnational activity is the norm and everyone is affected by everyone else everywhere on the planet.

These broad global trends seem vast, and they are. But they also are felt on a very local level. There are pockets of globalism, for example, in neighborhoods that are multicultural and contain different immigrant communities that interact with one another. Some cities are described as "global cities," both because of their importance as global nodes of economic and cultural networks and because their own populations are a tapestry of peoples from different parts of the world. In Los Angeles, for instance, you can find areas that are entirely Filipino, and other areas where only Vietnamese is spoken. Los Angeles contains one of the largest Mexican populations in the world and also one of the largest groups of Iranians. In many ways, it is a social microcosm of the world, and yet all of these immigrant neighborhoods interact in a common urban locale.

Roland Robertson coined the term *glocal* to describe these examples of globalism in a local setting. In his description, *glocalization* is a logical extension of globalization. It is the way that local communities are affected by global trends. The appearance of big-box stores selling Chinese-manufactured products in sleepy rural towns of Arkansas is one example of glocalization. An Internet café that I found on a remote segment of the Inca trail near Machu Picchu in Peru is another.

At the same time that global trends influence local settings, the reverse can also happen: global patterns can be reinterpreted on a local level. The spread of the McDonald's fast-food franchise around the world is an example. When I visit the McDonald's in Delhi, I find that none of the hamburgers are, in fact, beef burgers; they are chicken or veggie burgers, reflecting the predominantly vegetarian eating customs of people in India. In Kyoto's McDonald's, you can get a Teriyaki McBurger; and in the McDonald's restaurant in Milan, the sophisticated Italians may choose pasta rather than fries. So when globalization is glocalized, global patterns can adapt to local situations.

In the readings in this section, these concepts of globalization and globalism are explored by several influential scholars in the field of global studies. The first essay is by Manfred Steger, a native Austrian who helped to create the School of Global, Urban and Social Studies at RMIT University in Melbourne, Australia. Steger's book *Globalization: A Very Short Introduction* is one of the most widely read books on the topic. In an excerpt from this book, Steger describes the phenomenon of globalization in the post–Cold War era—that is, since roughly 1990. He argues that globalization has increased even more since the turn of the century in 2000 and takes as his example the terrorist act on September 11, 2001. Steger shows that this incident, and the technology, media, and ideological elements related to it, exhibit the global interconnectedness of our contemporary world.

The New York Times columnist Thomas Friedman also agrees that the era of globalization is relatively recent. In his calculation, however, it begins around 1989, at the end of the Cold War, when the Berlin wall tumbled and the ideological confrontation between socialist and capitalist societies was replaced by a more fluid and varied concept of world order. In Friedman's view, the wrestling matches between two huge lumbering superpowers has been replaced by the sprints to economic success by leaner independent economies. And though previous periods of globalization in history have shrunk the world from a size "large" to a size "medium," the current era shrinks the world to a size "small."

Paul James, a sociologist who helped develop the global studies program at RMIT University in Melbourne, Australia, tries to put this global phenomenon in order. He describes the various aspects of globalization and the different approaches to studying it. In James's comprehensive survey of the field, he shows that the study of globalization comes from all the major disciplines of the social sciences and humanities.

Globalization is a basic feature of modern life. But is it always good? In an essay from *Foreign Policy,* Steven Weber, a professor of political science and director of the Institute for International Studies at the University of California, Berkeley, argues that globalization often seems to have gone bad. This is especially true for those who expected America's military and economic superiority in a post–Cold War era to give it unbridled control over the rest of the world. But Weber argues that globalization may not be such a bad thing after all. America's security—and the world's—depends not on just one superpower exerting its authority, but also on an interconnected set of relationships that reduces conflict through cooperation. Perhaps, Weber suggests, the best approach to dealing with a globalized world is not for one country to try to control it, but to let the political interconnectedness of the world provide for a mutual, collective security.

GLOBALIZATION: A CONTESTED CONCEPT

Manfred Steger

In the autumn of 2001, I was teaching an undergraduate class on modern political and social theory. Still traumatized by the recent terrorist attacks on the World Trade Center and the Pentagon, most of my students couldn't quite grasp the connection between the

violent forces of religious fundamentalism and the more secular picture of a technologically sophisticated, rapidly globalizing world that I had sought to convey in class lectures
and discussions. "I understand that 'globalization' is a contested concept that refers to
sometimes contradictory social processes," a bright history major at the back of the room
quipped, "but how can you say that the TV image of a religious fanatic who denounces
modernity and secularism from a mountain cave in Afghanistan perfectly captures the
complex dynamics of globalization? Don't these terrible acts of terrorism suggest the opposite, namely, the growth of parochial forces that undermine globalization?" Obviously,
the student was referring to Saudi-born Al Qaeda leader Osama bin Laden, whose video-
taped statement condemning the activities of "international infidels" had been broadcast
worldwide on 7 October.

Struck by the sense of intellectual urgency that fuelled my student's question,
I realized that the story of globalization would remain elusive without real-life examples
capable of breathing shape, colour, and sound into a vague concept that had become
the buzzword of our time. Hence, before delving into necessary matters of definition
and analytical clarification, we ought to approach our subject in less abstract fashion.
I suggest we begin our journey with a careful examination of the aforementioned
videotape. It will soon become fairly obvious why a deconstruction of those images
provides important clues to the nature and dynamics of the phenomenon we have come
to call "globalization."

DECONSTRUCTING OSAMA BIN LADEN

The infamous videotape bears no date, but experts estimate that the recording was made
less than two weeks before it was broadcast. The timing of its release appears to have
been carefully planned so as to achieve the maximum effect on the day the United States
commenced its bombing campaign against Taliban and Al Qaeda ("The Base") forces in
Afghanistan. Although Osama bin Laden and his top lieutenants were then hiding in a
remote region of the country, they obviously possessed the hi-tech equipment needed to
record the statement. Moreover, Al Qaeda members clearly enjoyed immediate access to
sophisticated information and telecommunication networks that kept them informed—
in real-time—of relevant international developments. Bin Laden may have denounced
the forces of modernity with great conviction, but the smooth operation of his entire
organization was entirely dependent on advanced forms of technology developed in the
last two decades of the 20th century.

To further illustrate this apparent contradiction, consider the complex chain of global
interdependencies that must have existed in order for bin Laden's message to be heard
and seen by billions of TV viewers around the world. After making its way from the
secluded mountains of eastern Afghanistan to the capital city of Kabul, the videotape
was dropped off by an unknown courier outside the local office of Al-Jazeera, a Qatar-
based television company. This network had been launched only five years earlier as a

state-financed, Arabic-language news and current affairs channel that offered limited programming. Before the founding of Al-Jazeera, cutting-edge TV journalism—such as free-ranging public affairs interviews and talk shows with call-in audiences—simply did not exist in the Arab world. Within only three years, however, Al-Jazeera was offering its Middle Eastern audience a dizzying array of programmes, transmitted around the clock by powerful satellites put into orbit by European rockets and American space shuttles.

Indeed, the network's market share increased even further as a result of the dramatic reduction in the price and size of satellite dishes. Suddenly, such technologies became affordable, even for low-income consumers. By the turn of the century, Al-Jazeera broadcasts could be watched around the clock on all five continents. In 2001, the company further intensified its global reach when its chief executives signed a lucrative cooperation agreement with CNN, the leading news network owned by the giant multinational corporation AOL-Time-Warner. A few months later, when the world's attention shifted to the war in Afghanistan, Al-Jazeera had already positioned itself as a truly global player, powerful enough to rent equipment to such prominent news providers as Reuters and ABC, sell satellite time to the Associated Press and BBC, and design an innovative Arabic-language business news channel together with its other American network partner, CNBC.

Unhampered by national borders and geographical obstacles, cooperation among these sprawling news networks had become so efficient that CNN acquired and broadcast a copy of the Osama bin Laden tape only a few hours after it had been delivered to the Al-Jazeera office in Kabul. Caught off guard by the incredible speed of today's information exchange, the Bush administration asked the Qatari government to "rein in Al-Jazeera," claiming that the swift airing of the bin Laden tape without prior consultation was contributing to the rise of anti-American sentiments in the Arab world and thus threatened to undermine the US war effort. However, not only was the perceived "damage" already done, but segments of the tape—including the full text of bin Laden's statement—could be viewed online by anyone with access to a computer and a modem. The Al-Jazeera website quickly attracted an international audience as its daily hit count skyrocketed to over seven million.

There can be no doubt that it was the existence of this chain of global interdependencies and interconnections that made possible the instant broadcast of bin Laden's speech to a global audience. At the same time, however, it must be emphasized that even those voices that oppose modernity cannot extricate themselves from the very process of globalization they so decry. In order to spread their message and recruit new sympathizers, antimodernizers must utilize the tools provided by globalization. This obvious truth was visible even in bin Laden's personal appearance. The tape shows that he was wearing contemporary military fatigues over traditional Arab garments. In other words, his dress reflects the contemporary processes of fragmentation and cross-fertilization that globalization scholars call "hybridization"—the mixing of different cultural forms and styles facilitated by global economic and cultural exchanges. In fact, the pale colours of bin

Laden's mottled combat dress betrayed its Russian origins, suggesting that he wore the jacket as a symbolic reminder of the fierce guerrilla war waged by him and other Islamic militants against the Soviet occupation forces in Afghanistan during the 1980s. His ever-present AK-47 Kalashnikov, too, was probably made in Russia, although dozens of gun factories around the world have been building this popular assault rifle for over 40 years. By the mid-1990s, more than 70 million Kalashnikovs had been manufactured in Russia and abroad. At least 50 national armies include such rifles in their arsenal, making Kalashnikovs truly weapons of global choice. Thus, bin Laden's AK-47 could have come from anywhere in the world. However, given the astonishing globalization of organized crime during the last two decades, it is quite conceivable that bin Laden's rifle was part of an illegal arms deal hatched and executed by such powerful international criminal organizations as Al Qaeda and the Russian Mafia. It is also possible that the rifle arrived in Afghanistan by means of an underground arms trade similar to the one that surfaced in May 1996, when police in San Francisco seized 2,000 illegally imported AK-47s manufactured in China.

A close look at bin Laden's right wrist reveals yet another clue to the powerful dynamics of globalization. As he directs his words of contempt for the United States and its allies at his hand-held microphone, his retreating sleeve exposes a stylish sports watch. Journalists who noticed this expensive accessory have speculated about the origins of the timepiece in question. The emerging consensus points to a Timex product. However, given that Timex watches are as American as apple pie, it seems rather ironic that the Al Qaeda leader should have chosen this particular chronometer. After all, Timex Corporation, originally the Waterbury Clock Company, was founded in the 1850s in Connecticut's Naugatuck Valley, known throughout the 19th century as the "Switzerland of America." Today, the company has gone multinational, maintaining close relations to affiliated businesses and sales offices in 65 countries. The corporation employs 7,500 employees, located on four continents. Thousands of workers—mostly from low-wage countries in the global South—constitute the driving force behind Timex's global production process.

Our brief deconstruction of some of the central images on the videotape makes it easier to understand why the seemingly anachronistic images of an antimodern terrorist in front of an Afghan cave do, in fact, capture some essential dynamics of globalization. Indeed, the tensions between the forces of particularism and those of universalism have reached unprecedented levels only because interdependencies that connect the local to the global have been growing faster than at any time in history. The rise of international terrorist organizations like Al Qaeda represents but one of the many manifestations of globalization. Just as bin Laden's romantic ideology of a "pure Islam" is itself the result of the modern imagination, so has our global age with its obsession for technology and its mass-market commodities indelibly shaped the violent backlash against globalization.

Our deconstruction of Osama bin Laden has provided us with a real-life example of the intricate—and sometimes contradictory—social dynamics of globalization. We are now in a better position to tackle the rather demanding task of assembling a working definition of globalization that brings some analytical precision to a contested concept that has proven to be notoriously hard to pin down.

THE WORLD IS TEN YEARS OLD

Thomas Friedman

On the morning of December 8, 1997, the government of Thailand announced that it was closing 56 of the country's 58 top finance houses. Almost overnight, these private banks had been bankrupted by the crash of the Thai currency, the baht. The finance houses had borrowed heavily in U.S. dollars and lent those dollars out to Thai businesses for the building of hotels, office blocks, luxury apartments and factories. The finance houses all thought they were safe because the Thai government was committed to keeping the Thai baht at a fixed rate against the dollar. But when the government failed to do so, in the wake of massive global speculation against the baht—triggered by a dawning awareness that the Thai economy was not as strong as previously believed—the Thai currency plummeted by 30 percent. This meant that businesses that had borrowed dollars had to come up with 30 percent more Thai baht to pay back each $1 of loans. Many businesses couldn't pay the finance houses back, many finance houses couldn't repay their foreign lenders and the whole system went into gridlock, putting 20,000 white-collar employees out of work. The next day, I happened to be driving to an appointment in Bangkok down Asoke Street, Thailand's equivalent of Wall Street, where most of the bankrupt finance houses were located. As we slowly passed each one of these fallen firms, my cabdriver pointed them out, pronouncing at each one: "Dead! . . . dead! . . . dead! . . . dead! . . . dead!"

I did not know it at the time—no one did—but these Thai investment houses were the first dominoes in what would prove to be the first global financial crisis of the new era of globalization—the era that followed the Cold War. The Thai crisis triggered a general flight of capital out of virtually all the Southeast Asian emerging markets, driving down the value of currencies in South Korea, Malaysia and Indonesia. Both global and local investors started scrutinizing these economies more closely, found them wanting, and either moved their cash out to safer havens or demanded higher interest rates to compensate for the higher risk. It wasn't long before one of the most popular sweatshirts around Bangkok was emblazoned with the words "Former Rich."

Within a few months, the Southeast Asian recession began to have an effect on commodity prices around the world. Asia had been an important engine for worldwide economic growth—an engine that consumed huge amounts of raw materials. When that engine started to sputter, the prices of gold, copper, aluminum and, most important, crude oil all started to fall. This fall in worldwide commodity prices turned out to be the mechanism for transmitting the Southeast Asian crisis to Russia. Russia at the time was minding its own business, trying, with the help of the IMF, to climb out of its own self-made economic morass onto a stable growth track. The problem with Russia, though, was that too many of its factories couldn't make anything of value. In fact, much of what they made was considered "negative value added." That is, a tractor made by a Russian factory was so bad it was actually worth more as scrap metal, or just raw iron ore, than it was as a finished, Russian-made tractor. On top of it all, those Russian factories that were making products that could be sold abroad were paying few, if any, taxes to the government, so the Kremlin was chronically short of cash.

Without much of an economy to rely on for revenues, the Russian government had become heavily dependent on taxes from crude oil and other commodity exports to fund its operating budget. It had also become dependent on foreign borrowers, whose money Russia lured by offering ridiculous rates of interest on various Russian government-issued bonds.

As Russia's economy continued to slide in early 1998, the Russians had to raise the interest rate on their ruble bonds from 20 to 50 to 70 percent to keep attracting the foreigners. The hedge funds and foreign banks kept buying them, figuring that even if the Russian government couldn't pay them back, the IMF would step in, bail out Russia and the foreigners would get their money back. Some hedge funds and foreign banks not only continued to put their own money into Russia, but they went out and borrowed even more money, at 5 percent, and then bought Russian T-bills with it that paid 20 or 30 percent. As Grandma would say, "Such a deal!" But as Grandma would also say, "If it sounds too good to be true, it usually is!"

And it was. The Asian-triggered slump in oil prices made it harder and harder for the Russian government to pay the interest and principal on its T-bills. And with the IMF under pressure to make loans to rescue Thailand, Korea and Indonesia, it resisted any proposals for putting more cash into Russia—unless the Russians first fulfilled their promises to reform their economy, starting with getting their biggest businesses and banks to pay some taxes. On August 17 the Russian economic house of cards came tumbling down, dealing the markets a double whammy: Russia both devalued and unilaterally defaulted on its government bonds, without giving any warning to its creditors or arranging any workout agreement. The hedge funds, banks and investment banks that were invested in Russia began piling up massive losses, and those that had borrowed money to magnify their bets in the Kremlin casino were threatened with bankruptcy.

On the face of it, the collapse of the Russian economy should not have had much impact on the global system. Russia's economy was smaller than that of the Netherlands. But the system was now more global than ever, and just as crude oil prices were the transmission mechanism from Southeast Asia to Russia, the hedge funds—the huge unregulated pools of private capital that scour the globe for the best investments—were the transmission mechanism from Russia to all the other emerging markers in the world, particularly Brazil. The hedge funds and other trading firms, having racked up huge losses in Russia, some of which were magnified fifty times by using borrowed money, suddenly had to raise cash to pay back their bankers. They had to sell anything that was liquid. So they started selling assets in financially sound countries to compensate for their losses in bad ones. Brazil, for instance, which had been doing a lot of the right things in the eyes of the global markets and the IMF, suddenly saw all its stocks and bonds being sold by panicky investors. Brazil had to raise its interest rates as high as 40 percent to try to hold capital inside the country. Variations on this scenario were played out throughout the world's emerging markets, as investors fled for safety. They cashed in their Brazilian, Korean, Egyptian, Israeli and Mexican bonds and stocks, and put the money either under their mattresses or into the safest U.S. bonds they could find. So the declines in Brazil and the other emerging markets became the transmission mechanism that triggered a herdlike stampede into U.S. Treasury bonds. This, in turn, sharply drove up the value of U.S. T-bonds, drove down the interest that the U.S. government had to offer on them to attract investors and increased the spread between U.S. T-bonds and other corporate and emerging market bonds.

The steep drop in the yield on U.S. Treasury bonds was then the transmission mechanism which crippled more hedge funds and investment banks. Take for instance Long-Term Capital Management, based in Greenwich, Connecticut. LTCM was the Mother of All Hedge Funds. Because so many hedge funds were attracted to the marketplace in the late 1980s, the field became fiercely competitive. Everyone pounced on the same opportunities. In order to make money in such a fiercely competitive world, the hedge funds had to seek ever more exotic bets with ever larger pools of cash. To guide them in placing the right bets, LTCM drew on the work of two Nobel Prize–winning business economists, whose research argued that the basic volatility of stocks and bonds could be estimated from how they reacted in the past. Using computer models, and borrowing heavily from different banks, LTCM put $120 billion at risk betting on the direction that certain key bonds would take in the summer of 1998. It implicitly bet that the value of U.S. T-bonds would go down, and that the value of junk bonds and emerging market bonds would go up. LTCM's computer model, however, never anticipated something like the global contagion that would be set off in August by Russia's collapse, and, as a result, its bets turned out to be exactly wrong. When the whole investment world panicked at once and decided to rush into U.S. T-bonds, their value soared instead of fell, and the value of junk bonds and emerging market bonds collapsed instead of soared. LTCM was like a wishbone that got pulled apart from both ends. It had to be bailed out by its bankers to prevent it from engaging in a fire sale of all its stocks and bonds that could have triggered a worldwide market meltdown.

Now we get to my street. In early August 1998, I happened to invest in my friend's new Internet bank. The shares opened at $14.50 a share and soared to $27. I felt like a genius. But then Russia defaulted and set all these dominoes in motion, and my friend's stock went to $8. Why? Because his bank held a lot of home mortgages, and with the fall of interest rates in America, triggered by the rush to buy T-bills, the markets feared that a lot of people would suddenly pay off their home mortgages early. If a lot of people paid off their home mortgages early, my friend's bank might not have the income stream that it was counting on to pay depositors. The markets were actually wrong about my friend's bank, and its stock bounced back nicely. Indeed, by early 1999 I was feeling like a genius again, as the Amazon.com Internet craze set in and drove my friend's Internet bank stock sky high, as well as other technology shares we owned. But, once again, it wasn't long before the rest of the world crashed the party. Only this time, instead of Russia breaking down the front door, it was Brazil's turn to upset U.S. markets and even dampen (temporarily) the Internet stock boom.

As I watched all this play out, all I could think of was that it took nine months for the events on Asoke Street to affect my street, and it took one week for events on the Brazilian Amazon (Amazon.country) to affect Amazon.com. *USA Today* aptly summed up the global marketplace at the end of 1998: "The trouble spread to one continent after another like a virus," the paper noted. "U.S. markets reacted instantaneously. . . . People in barbershops actually talked about the Thai baht."

If nothing else, the cycle from Asoke Street to my street and from Amazon.country to Amazon.com served to educate me and many others about the state of the world today. The slow, stable, chopped-up Cold War system that had dominated international affairs since 1945 had been firmly replaced by a new, very greased, interconnected system called globalization. We are all one river. If we didn't fully understand that in 1989, when the Berlin Wall came down, we sure understood it a decade later.

. . . From the mid-1800s to the late 1920s the world experienced a similar era of globalization. If you compared the volumes of trade and capital flows across borders, relative to GNPs, and the flow of labor across borders, relative to populations, the period of globalization preceding World War I was quite similar to the one we are living through today. Great Britain, which was then the dominant global power, was a huge investor in emerging markets, and fat cats in England, Europe and America were often buffeted by financial crises, triggered by something that happened in Argentine railroad bonds, Latvian government bonds or German government bonds. There were no currency controls, so no sooner was the transatlantic cable connected in 1866 than banking and financial crises in New York were quickly being transmitted to London or Paris. I was on a panel once with John Monks, the head of the British Trades Union Congress, the AFL-CIO of Britain, who remarked that the agenda for the TUC's first Congress in Manchester, England, in 1868, listed among the items that needed to be discussed: "The need to deal with competition from the Asian colonies" and "The need to match the educational and training standards of the United States and Germany." In those days, people also migrated more than we remember, and, other than in wartime, countries did not require passports for travel before 1914. All those immigrants who flooded America's shores came without visas. When you put all of these factors together, along with the inventions of the steamship, telegraph, railroad and eventually telephone, it is safe to say that this first era of globalization before World War I shrank the world from a size "large" to a size "medium."

This first era of globalization and global finance capitalism was broken apart by the successive hammer blows of World War I, the Russian Revolution and the Great Depression, which combined to fracture the world both physically and ideologically. The formally divided world that emerged after World War II was then frozen in place by the Cold War. The Cold War was also an international system. It lasted roughly from 1945 to 1989, when, with the fall of the Berlin Wall, it was replaced by another system: the new era of globalization we are now in. Call it "Globalization Round II." It turns out that the roughly seventy-five-year period from the start of World War I to the end of the Cold War was just a long time-out between one era of globalization and another.

While there are a lot of similarities in kind between the previous era of globalization and the one we are now in, what is new today is the degree and intensity with which the world is being tied together into a single globalized marketplace. What is also new is the sheer number of people and countries able to partake of this process and be affected by it. The pre-1914 era of globalization may have been intense, but many developing countries in that era were left out of it. The pre-1914 era may have been large in scale relative to its time, but it was minuscule in absolute terms compared to today. Daily foreign exchange trading in 1900 was measured in the millions of dollars. In 1992, it was $820 billion a day, according to the New York Federal Reserve, and by April 1998 it was up to $1.5 trillion a day, and still rising. In the last decade alone total cross-border lending by banks around the world has doubled. Around 1900, private capital flows from developed countries to developing ones could be measured in the hundreds of millions of dollars and relatively few countries were involved. According to the IMF, in 1997 alone, private capital flows from the developed world to all emerging markets totaled $215 billion. This new era of globalization, compared to the one before World War I, is turbocharged.

But today's era of globalization is not only different in degree; in some very important ways it is also different in kind. As *The Economist* once noted, the previous era of globalization was built around falling transportation costs. Thanks to the invention of the railroad, the steamship and the automobile, people could get to a lot more places faster and cheaper and they could trade with a lot more places faster and cheaper. Today's era of globalization is built around falling telecommunications costs—thanks to microchips, satellites, fiber optics and the Internet. These new technologies are able to weave the world together even tighter. These technologies mean that developing countries don't just have to trade their raw materials to the West and get finished products in return; they mean that developing countries can become big-time producers as well. These technologies also allow companies to locate different parts of their production, research and marketing in different countries, but still tie them together through computers and teleconferencing as though they were in one place. Also, thanks to the combination of computers and cheap telecommunications, people can now offer and trade services globally—from medical advice to software writing to data processing—that could never really be traded before. And why not? According to *The Economist,* a three-minute call (in 1996 dollars) between New York and London cost $300 in 1930. Today it is almost free through the Internet.

But what also makes this era of globalization unique is not just the fact that these technologies are making it possible for traditional nation-states and corporations to reach farther, faster, cheaper and deeper around the world than ever before. It is the fact that it is allowing individuals to do so. I was reminded of this point one day in the summer of 1998 when my then seventy-nine-year-old mother, Margaret Friedman, who lives in Minneapolis, called me sounding very upset. "What's wrong, Mom?" I asked. "Well," she said, "I've been playing bridge on the Internet with three Frenchmen and they keep speaking French to each other and I can't understand them." When I chuckled at the thought of my card-shark mom playing bridge with three Frenchmen on the Net, she took a little umbrage. "Don't laugh," she said, "I was playing bridge with someone in Siberia the other day."

To all those who say that this era of globalization is no different from the previous one, I would simply ask: Was your great-grandmother playing bridge with Frenchmen on the Internet in 1900? I don't think so. There are some things about this era of globalization that we've seen before, and some things that we've never seen before and some things that are so new we don't even understand them yet. For all these reasons, I would sum up the differences between the two eras of globalization this way: If the first era of globalization shrank the world from a size "large" to a size "medium," this era of globalization is shrinking the world from a size "medium" to a size "small."

. . . This new era of globalization became the dominant international system at the end of the twentieth century—replacing the Cold War system—and . . . it now shapes virtually everyone's domestic politics and international relations. The body of literature that has been attempting to define the post–Cold War world [includes] four books: Paul M. Kennedy's *The Rise and Fall of the Great Powers: Economic Change and Military Conflict from 1500 to 2000*, Francis Fukuyama's *The End of History and the Last Man*, the various essays and books of Robert D. Kaplan and Samuel P. Huntington's *The Clash of Civilizations and the Remaking of World Order*.

While all of these works contained important truths, I think none of them really captured the post–Cold War world in any holistic way. Kaplan's reporting was vivid and honest, but he took the grimmest corners of the globe and overgeneralized from them to the fate of the rest of the world. Huntington saw cultural conflicts around the world and wildly expanded that into an enduring, sharply defined clash of civilizations, even proclaiming that the next world war, if there is one, "will be a war between civilizations." I believe both Kaplan and Huntington vastly underestimated how the power of states, the lure of global markets, the diffusion of technology, the rise of networks and the spread of global norms could trump their black-and-white (mostly black) projections.

Both Kennedy and Huntington tried to divine the future too much from the past and the past alone. Kennedy traced (quite brilliantly) the decline of the Spanish, French and British empires, but he concluded by suggesting that the American empire would be the next to fall because of its own imperial overreaching. His implicit message was that the end of the Cold War not only meant the end of the Soviet Union but would also herald the decline of the United States. I believe Kennedy did not appreciate enough that the relative decline of the United States in the 1980s, when he was writing, was part of America's preparing itself for and adjusting to the new globalization system—a process that much of the rest of the world is going through only now. Kennedy did not anticipate that under the pressure of globalization America would slash its defense budget, shrink its government, and shift more and more powers to the free market in ways that would prolong its status as a Great Power, not diminish it.

Huntington's view was that, with the Cold War over, we won't have the Soviets to kick around any more, so we will naturally go back to kicking the Hindus and Muslims around and them kicking us around. He implicitly ruled out the rise of some new international system that could shape events differently. For Huntington, only tribalism could follow the Cold War, not anything new.

Fukuyama's pathbreaking book contained the most accurate insight about what was new—the triumph of liberalism and free-market capitalism as the most effective way to organize a society—but his title (more than the book itself) implied a finality to this triumph that does not jibe with the world as I find it.

In a way, each of these works became prominent because they tried to capture in a single catchy thought "The One Big Thing," the central moving part, the underlying motor, that would drive international affairs in the post–Cold War world—either the clash of civilizations, chaos, the decline of empires or the triumph of liberalism.

. . . I believe that if you want to understand the post–Cold War world you have to start by understanding that a new international system has succeeded it—globalization. That is "The One Big Thing" people should focus on. Globalization is not the only thing influencing events in the world today, but to the extent that there is a North Star and a worldwide shaping force, it is this system. What is new is the system; what is old is power politics, chaos, clashing civilizations and liberalism. And what is the drama of the post–Cold War world is the interaction between this new system and these old passions. It is a complex drama, with the final act still not written. That is why under the globalization system you will find both clashes of civilization and the homogenization of civilizations, both environmental disasters and amazing environmental rescues, both the triumph of liberal, free-market capitalism and a backlash against it, both the durability of nation-states and the rise of enormously powerful nonstate actors.

. . . The publisher . . . Jonathan Galassi called me one day and said, "I was telling some friends of mine that you're writing a book about globalization and they said, 'Oh, Friedman, he loves globalization.' What would you say to that?" I answered Jonathan that I feel about globalization a lot like I feel about the dawn. Generally speaking, I think it's a good thing that the sun comes up every morning. It does more good than harm. But even if I didn't much care for the dawn there isn't much I could do about it. I didn't start globalization, I can't stop it—except at a huge cost to human development—and I'm not going to waste time trying. All I want to think about is how I can get the best out of this new system, and cushion the worst, for the most people.

APPROACHES TO GLOBALIZATION

Paul James

There are many different approaches to the study of globalization, testifying to the diversity and vitality of the field of global studies. The diversity of these approaches is not easy to categorize, however, in part because of the intellectual climate in which most of the studies of globalization have emerged.

Studies of globalization and, more generally, studies in the broad and loosely defined field of global studies did not become conscious of themselves as such until the 1990s; and by then the direct-line lineages of classic social theory had either been broken or segmented. The social sciences and humanities were in the midst of a retreat from grand theory. There was a growing suspicion, in part influenced by a poststructuralist turn, of any generalizing theoretical explanations of particular phenomena. This suspicion was paralleled by a claim made by some that the postmodern condition could be characterized by the end of grand narratives of all kinds: nationalism, socialism, liberalism, and by implication, globalism. Although in the past, approaches to any theoretical field could be comfortably organized according to three foundational considerations—theoretical lineage, scholarly discipline, and normative orientation—this was changing. By the end of the 20th and into the early 21st century, those kinds of considerations remained useful by way of background orientation, but the pattern of approaches was becoming less obvious and with more crossovers.

There is an irony in this retreat from generalizing theory that is important to note. It concerns a paradox that is yet to be explained. At the same time that generalizing theory lost its hold, a generalizing category of social relations gripped the imagination of both academic analysts and journalistic commentators—this, of course, was the category of "the global." In this emerging imaginary, globalization was understood as a process of social interconnection, a process that was in different ways connecting people across planet Earth. Globalization as a practice and subjectivity connecting the (global) social whole thus became the standout object of critical enquiry. In other words, globalization demanded generalizing attention at the very moment that residual ideas that an all-embracing theory might be found to explain such a phenomenon was effectively dashed. This has profound consequences for the nature of globalization theory and how we might understand different approaches. . . .

EARLY APPROACHES TO GLOBALIZATION

Although there were some isolated articles across the 1960s to 1980s directly referring to globalization—with the most prominent of these being by Theodore Levitt on the globalization of markets in 1983—more elaborate academic approaches to globalization lagged by a decade or so. The burgeoning and dominant journalistic and business discourses of the first wave of intense attention into the 1980s tended to be thin on analysis and thick on hyperbole. Most suggested that globalization was a completely new phenomenon symbolized by the triumph of the capitalist market. Levitt's writing signaled the rise of the global corporation carried by a worldwide communications revolution.

It took a sociologist of religion and a couple of anthropologists and social theorists in the 1990s—scholars such as Roland Robertson, Jonathan Friedman, Arjun Appadurai, and Mike Featherstone—to write or edit the first major explorations of globalization-as-such, contributions that moved beyond hyperbole or thin description. Journals such as *Theory, Culture and Society* were in the vanguard of the new thinking of this second wave of attention. Earlier work, such as that of Immanuel Wallerstein and the world-systems theorists, or Andre Gunder Frank and the dependency theorists, had signaled a shift away from classic imperialism studies as the major carrier of work on globalizing relations. However, in relation to understanding globalization itself, this did not lead to significant developments in theory, except in the recognition that globalization was a centuries-old process.

The work of Wallerstein in the discipline of international political economy can here be used as an indication of the difficulty of coming to terms with issues of globalization. Instead of exploring the consequences of processes of globalization—economic, ecological, cultural, and political—for understanding the complexities of capitalism, Wallerstein reworked the verities of a world system's understanding: namely, that capitalism had gone through two major overlapping cycles of development: from 1450, and from 1945 to the present, suggesting that capitalism was now entering a transition phase of terminal crisis. What others called globalization, he said, was just the epiphenomenon of the transition. Here the sophisticated critic of mainstream modernization theory thus reduced globalization to a reflection of the phases of capital. He limited its consequences to the domain of economics or the nexus between capital and everything else.

Alternatively and more productively, the work of Roland Robertson took a cultural turn. Like the critical political economists, Robertson recognized the long-term and changing history of globalization. However, unlike the dominant trend that for a time defined globalization in terms of the demise of the nation-state, perhaps most prominently surfacing in the writings of Arjun Appadurai and Ulrich Beck, Robertson recognized the complex intersection and layering of nationally and globally constituted social relations. One of his major contributions was to show how globalization across its long uneven history contributed to a relativization of social meaning and social practice, including the notion of a "world system." His work still stands up to scrutiny today, and he continues to be a major figure in the field.

Another key figure of this time, Arjun Appadurai, also followed the cultural turn, but instead of taking a critical modernist position on the changing order of things as Robertson did, he headed down the postmodern path to emphasize fluidity. The key contribution for which he is known is the notion of global "scapes," unstructured formations with no boundaries or regularities. He distinguished different formations of what he called ethnoscapes, mediascapes, technoscapes, financescapes, and ideoscapes.

This approach was avidly used for a period before it lost its standing as different writers realized that, apart from the categories of ethnoscapes and perhaps ideoscapes, his global landscape focused too narrowly on the cultural present and the recent past. Broader categories of analysis were needed to understand the unevenness of social continuities and discontinuities.

APPROACHES UNDERSTOOD IN TERMS OF THE DOMAIN OF ENQUIRY

A third wave of attention emerged across the turn of the century into the present. Journals such as *Globalizations, Global Society,* and *Global Governance* emerged as the number of publications exploded in number. One of the most important broader renderings of globalization came from a jointly written book called *Global Transformations* (1999) by David Held, a political philosopher; Anthony McGrew, an international relations theorist; David Goldblatt, a theorist of environmental politics; and Jonathan Perraton, an economist. Interdisciplinary studies had become the key. As signaled in the subtitle of the book, *Politics, Economics and Culture,* and extended in the chapter structure to include a focus on globalization and environment, this approach worked across the broad domains of economy, ecology, politics, and culture. Similarly Jan Aart Scholte worked across a broad series of domains. In his case, the domains were production, governance, identity, and knowledge. And, when Chamsy el-Ojeili and Patrick Hayden came to write their book *Critical Theories of Globalization* (2006), looking back on more than a decade of developing approaches to globalization they returned to the useful categorization of economics, politics, and culture. In all of these cases, however, there was no attempt to develop a theory of globalization as such. Rather these and other related writers—writers as diverse as James Mittleman, George Ritzer, Ulf Hannerz, and Heikki Patomaki— sought to explore the complexity of globalization across different domains.

In the domain of culture, for example, a penetrating critique of the dominant ideology of globalization by Manfred Steger joined with others in introducing the notion of "globalism." In its midrange use, globalism can be defined as the ideologies and/or subjectivities associated with different historically dominant formations of global extension. Steger in his earlier writings from the early 1990s focused on globalism as neoliberalism, but as his analysis developed, he came to distinguish different kinds of globalism, including justice globalisms, imperial globalisms, and religious globalisms. He helped us to understand that globalism is therefore much more than the ideology associated with the contemporary dominant variant of globalism—market globalism and ideas of a borderless world.

APPROACHES UNDERSTOOD IN TERMS OF NORMATIVE ORIENTATION

Other ways to differentiate approaches to globalization include their normative or ethical orientation and their political descriptive stance. The most cited categorization of different kinds of approaches to globalization, which comes from *Global Transformations,* a book mentioned earlier, combines both of these categorizations and posits what it calls "three broad schools of thought": the hyperglobalists, the sceptics, and the transformationalists. They are not actually schools at all but orientations. The hyperglobalizers include writers such as Kenichi Ohmae (a neoliberal) and Martin Albrow (a critical theorist) who argue that a wave of globalization is changing the world fundamentally and supplanting older national sovereignties. The sceptics include Paul Hirst and Grahame Thompson who argue that with contemporary so-called globalization what we are witnessing is just another wave of internationalization. The transformationalists, including James Rosenau and Saskia Sassen, who suggest that while intensifying globalization is changing the nature of world politics, culture, and economy, the process is uneven.

APPROACHES UNDERSTOOD IN TERMS OF SCHOLARLY DISCIPLINE

With the realization in the 1990s that "the global" required direct attention, the taken-for-granted assumptions of fields of study such as international relations, politics, and sociology came under direct challenge. In international relations, the realist emphasis on nation-states as black-box entities in political inter-relation came under considerable pressure, as did the emphases of its critical counterparts, including even Marxism and rationalism that had long recognized the long reach of both material processes and ideas across the world. International relations as a discipline had profound problems dealing with globalization, but into the new century, books started to come out by writers crossing the boundaries of the discipline, including international critical theorist Jan Aart Scholte and international political economist Mark Rupert.

One discipline that saw a sea change in its approach was anthropology. It maintained its classical emphasis on ethnographic depth, but it shifted its orientation from internally focused microstudies of remote locales to attempting to understand communities, whether they be remote or metropolitan, in terms of their place in a globalizing world. New subfields of history developed, including "big history" and "world history." The field of global studies itself emerged during this period as an interdisciplinary approach to understanding the relation between the local and the global across the domains of social life.

APPROACHES UNDERSTOOD IN TERMS OF THEORETICAL LINEAGE

A developing aversion to grand theory did not mean that the old theoretical lineages became completely irrelevant, although it did mean that approaches associated with the classical social theories of Karl Marx, Émile Durkheim, and Max Weber tended either to draw more loosely on those past writings or to work across them synthetically. Out of a critical reading of the Durkheimian–Weberian tradition came the work of such writers as Roland Robertson and American sociologist of global religion,

Mark Juergensmeyer—although it should be said that Robertson was also influenced by an open version of neo-Marxist historical materialism. Out of the neo-Marxist lineage came the varied work of Paul Hirst, Mark Rupert, Christopher Chase-Dunn, Tony McGrew, and via Karl Polanyi, Ronnie Munck. Third, several writers explicitly set out to formulate a postclassical synthesis. The most prominent of these writers was British sociologist Anthony Giddens. He had been working across the 1980s and 1990s on a grand theoretical approach to the social called structurationism; however, by the time that he wrote in an elaborated way on globalization, his approach had become less theoretically integrated and more descriptive. His major point became that globalization is complex, shapes the way that we live, and is linked to the expansive dynamic of late modernity.

Marxist writer Justin Rosenberg immediately took Giddens to task for theoretical incoherence. In particular, he criticized a tendency in Giddens's writing (and in many other writers on globalization) to treat globalization and the extension of social relations across world space as both the explanation and the outcome of a process of change. That is, he asked how if globalization involves spatial extension can it be explained by invoking the claim that space is now global. The explanation and the thing-being-explained, he rightly says, are thus reduced into a self-confirming circle. Taking into account his critique, it is still legitimate to treat globalization as a *descriptive* category referring to a process of extension across a historically constituted world-space as we have been doing across this entry, but it is problematic to posit globalization as the simple cause of other phenomena, much less of itself.

CONCLUSION

Now, after three decades of writing on globalization, we have made some extraordinary gains in understanding. The historically changing and uneven nature of globalization is now generally understood. In the various scholarly approaches, much of the hyperbole has tended to drop away and the normative assessment of globalization has become more sober and qualified. Scholarly approaches have tended to move away from essentializing the phenomenon as necessarily good or bad. Similarly, at least in the scholarly arena, there has been a significant move beyond the reductive tendency to treat globalization only in terms of economic domain.

On the other side of the ledger, our central weakness of understanding goes back to the central paradox of globalization studies—the emergence of an aversion to generalizing theory at a time when the importance of a generalizing category of relations came to the fore. Globalization may simply be the name given to a matrix of processes that extend social relations across world-space, but the way in which people live those relations is incredibly complex, changing, and difficult to explain. Thus, we remain in search of generalizing methodologies (not a singular grand theory) that can sensitize us to those empirical complexities while enabling us to abstract patterns of change and continuity.

HOW GLOBALIZATION WENT BAD

Steven Weber

The world today is more dangerous and less orderly than it was supposed to be. Ten or 15 years ago, the naive expectations were that the "end of history" was near. The reality has been the opposite. The world has more international terrorism and more nuclear proliferation today than it did in 1990. International institutions are weaker. The threats of pandemic disease and climate change are stronger. Cleavages of religious and cultural ideology are more intense. The global financial system is more unbalanced and precarious. It wasn't supposed to be like this. The end of the Cold War was supposed to make global politics and economics easier to manage, not harder.

What went wrong? The bad news of the 21st century is that globalization has a significant dark side. The container ships that carry manufactured Chinese goods to and from the United States also carry drugs. The airplanes that fly passengers nonstop from New York to Singapore also transport infectious diseases. And the Internet has proved just as adept at spreading deadly, extremist ideologies as it has e-commerce. The conventional belief is that the single greatest challenge of geopolitics today is managing this dark side of globalization, chipping away at the illegitimate co-travelers that exploit openness, mobility, and freedom, without putting too much sand in the gears. The current U.S. strategy is to push for more trade, more connectivity, more markets, and more openness. America does so for a good reason—it benefits from globalization more than any other country in the world. The United States acknowledges globalization's dark side but attributes it merely to exploitative behavior by criminals, religious extremists, and other anachronistic elements that can be eliminated. The dark side of globalization, America says, with very little subtlety, can be mitigated by the expansion of American power, sometimes unilaterally and sometimes through multilateral institutions, depending on how the United States likes it. In other words, America is aiming for a "flat," globalized world coordinated by a single superpower.

That's nice work if you can get it. But the United States almost certainly cannot. Not only because other countries won't let it, but, more profoundly, because that line of thinking is faulty. The predominance of American power has many benefits, but the management of globalization is not one of them. The mobility of ideas, capital, technology, and people is hardly new. But the rapid advance of globalization's evils is. Most of that advance has taken place since 1990. Why? Because what changed profoundly in the 1990s was the polarity of the international system. For the first time in modern history, globalization was superimposed onto a world with a single superpower. What we have discovered in the past 15 years is that it is a dangerous mixture. The negative effects of globalization since 1990 are not the result of globalization itself. They are the dark side of American predominance.

A straightforward piece of logic from market economics helps explain why unipolarity and globalization don't mix. Monopolies, regardless of who holds them, are almost always bad for both the market and the monopolist. We propose three simple axioms of "globalization under unipolarity" that reveal these dangers.

Axiom 1: Above a certain threshold of power, the rate at which new global problems are generated will exceed the rate at which old problems are fixed. Power does two things in international politics: It enhances the capability of a state to do things, but it also increases the number of things that a state must worry about. At a certain point, the latter starts to overtake the former. It's the familiar law of diminishing returns. Because powerful states have large spheres of influence and their security and economic interests touch every region of the world, they are threatened by the risk of things going wrong—anywhere. That is particularly true for the United States, which leverages its ability to go anywhere and do anything through massive debt. No one knows exactly when the law of diminishing returns will kick in. But, historically, it starts to happen long before a single great power dominates the entire globe, which is why large empires from Byzantium to Rome have always reached a point of unsustainability. That may already be happening to the United States today, on issues ranging from oil dependency and nuclear proliferation to pandemics and global warming. What Axiom 1 tells you is that more U.S. power is not the answer; it's actually part of the problem. A multipolar world would almost certainly manage the globe's pressing problems more effectively. The larger the number of great powers in the global system, the greater the chance that at least one of them would exercise some control over a given combination of space, other actors, and problems. Such reasoning doesn't rest on hopeful notions that the great powers will work together. They might do so. But even if they don't, the result is distributed governance, where some great power is interested in most every part of the world through productive competition.

Axiom 2: In an increasingly networked world, places that fall between the networks are very dangerous places—and there will be more ungoverned zones when there is only one network to join. The second axiom acknowledges that highly connected networks can be efficient, robust, and resilient to shocks. But in a highly connected world, the pieces that fall between the networks are increasingly shut off from the benefits of connectivity. These problems fester in the form of failed states, mutate like pathogenic bacteria, and, in some cases, reconnect in subterranean networks such as al Qaeda. The truly dangerous places are the points where the subterranean networks touch the mainstream of global politics and economics. What made Afghanistan so dangerous under the Taliban was not that it was a failed state. It wasn't. It was a partially failed and partially connected state that worked the interstices of globalization through the drug trade, counterfeiting, and terrorism. Can any single superpower monitor all the seams and back alleys of globalization? Hardly. In fact, a lone hegemon is unlikely to look closely at these problems, because more pressing issues are happening elsewhere, in places where trade and technology are growing. By contrast, a world of several great powers is a more interest-rich environment in which nations must look in less obvious places to find new sources of advantage. In such a system, it's harder for troublemakers to spring up, because the cracks and seams of globalization are held together by stronger ties.

Axiom 3: Without a real chance to find useful allies to counter a superpower, opponents will try to neutralize power, by going underground, going nuclear, or going "bad." Axiom 3 is a story about the preferred strategies of the weak. It's a basic insight of international relations that states try to balance power. They protect themselves by joining groups that can hold a hegemonic threat at bay. But what if there is no viable group to join? In today's unipolar world, every nation from Venezuela to North Korea is looking for a way to constrain American power. But in the unipolar world, it's harder for states to join together to do that. So they turn to other means. They play a different game. Hamas, Iran, Somalia, North Korea, and Venezuela are not going to become allies anytime soon. Each is better off finding other ways to make life more difficult for Washington. Going nuclear is one way. Counterfeiting U.S. currency is another. Raising uncertainty about oil supplies is perhaps the most obvious method of all. Here's the important downside of unipolar globalization. In a world with multiple great powers, many of these threats would be less troublesome. The relatively weak states would have a choice among potential partners with which to ally, enhancing their influence. Without that more attractive choice, facilitating the dark side of globalization becomes the most effective means of constraining American power.

SHARING GLOBALIZATION'S BURDEN

The world is paying a heavy price for the instability created by the combination of globalization and unipolarity, and the United States is bearing most of the burden. Consider the case of nuclear proliferation. There's effectively a market out there for proliferation, with its own supply (states willing to share nuclear technology) and demand (states that badly want a nuclear weapon). The overlap of unipolarity with globalization ratchets up both the supply and demand, to the detriment of U.S. national security. It has become fashionable, in the wake of the Iraq war, to comment on the limits of conventional military force. But much of this analysis is overblown. The United States may not be able to stabilize and rebuild Iraq. But that doesn't matter much from the perspective of a government that thinks the Pentagon has it in its sights. In Tehran, Pyongyang, and many other capitals, including Beijing, the bottom line is simple: The U.S. military could, with conventional force, end those regimes tomorrow if it chose to do so. No country in the world can dream of challenging U.S. conventional military power. But they can certainly hope to deter America from using it. And the best deterrent yet invented is the threat of nuclear retaliation. Before 1989, states that felt threatened by the United States could turn to the Soviet Union's nuclear umbrella for protection. Now, they turn to people like A.Q. Khan. Having your own nuclear weapon used to be a luxury. Today, it is fast becoming a necessity. North Korea is the clearest example. Few countries had it worse during the Cold War. North Korea was surrounded by feuding, nuclear-armed communist neighbors, it was officially at war with its southern neighbor, and it stared continuously at tens of thousands of U.S. troops on its border. But, for 40 years, North Korea didn't seek nuclear weapons. It didn't need to, because it had the Soviet nuclear umbrella. Within five years of the Soviet collapse, however, Pyongyang was pushing ahead full steam on plutonium reprocessing facilities. North Korea's founder, Kim Il Sung, barely flinched when former U.S. President Bill Clinton's administration readied war plans to strike his nuclear installations preemptively. That brinkmanship paid off. Today North Korea is likely a nuclear power, and Kim's son rules the country with an iron fist. America's conventional military strength means a lot less to a nuclear North Korea. Saddam Hussein's great strategic blunder was that he took too long to get to the same place.

How would things be different in a multipolar world? For starters, great powers could split the job of policing proliferation, and even collaborate on some particularly hard cases. It's often forgotten now that, during the Cold War, the only state with a tougher nonproliferation policy than the United States was the Soviet Union. Not a single country that had a formal alliance with Moscow ever became a nuclear power. The Eastern bloc was full of countries with advanced technological capabilities in every area except one—nuclear weapons. Moscow simply wouldn't permit it. But today we see the uneven and inadequate level of effort that non-superpowers devote to stopping proliferation. The Europeans dangle carrots at Iran, but they are unwilling to consider serious sticks. The Chinese refuse to admit that there is a problem. And the Russians are aiding Iran's nuclear ambitions. When push comes to shove, nonproliferation today is almost entirely America's burden. The same is true for global public health. Globalization is turning the world into an enormous petri dish for the incubation of infectious disease. Humans cannot outsmart disease, because it just evolves too quickly. Bacteria can reproduce a new generation in less than 30 minutes, while it takes us decades to come up with a new generation of antibiotics. Solutions are only possible when and where we get the upper hand. Poor countries where humans live in close proximity to farm animals are the best place to breed extremely dangerous zoonotic disease. These are often the same countries, perhaps not entirely coincidentally, that feel threatened by American power. Establishing an early warning system for these diseases—exactly what we lacked in the case of SARS a few years ago and exactly what we lack for avian flu today—will require a significant level of intervention into the very places that don't want it. That will be true as long as international intervention means American interference. The most likely sources of the next ebola or HIV-like pandemic are the countries that simply won't let

U.S. or other Western agencies in, including the World Health Organization. Yet the threat is too arcane and not immediate enough for the West to force the issue. What's needed is another great power to take over a piece of the work, a power that has more immediate interests in the countries where diseases incubate and one that is seen as less of a threat. As long as the United States remains the world's lone superpower, we're not likely to get any help. Even after HIV, SARS, and several years of mounting hysteria about avian flu, the world is still not ready for a viral pandemic in Southeast Asia or sub-Saharan Africa. America can't change that alone.

If there were rival great powers with different cultural and ideological leanings, globalization's darkest problem of all—terrorism—would also likely look quite different. The pundits are partly right: Today's international terrorism owes something to globalization. Al Qaeda uses the Internet to transmit messages, it uses credit cards and modern banking to move money, and it uses cell phones and laptops to plot attacks. But it's not globalization that turned Osama bin Laden from a small-time Saudi dissident into the symbolic head of a radical global movement. What created Osama bin Laden was the predominance of American power. A terrorist organization needs a story to attract resources and recruits. Oftentimes, mere frustration over political, economic, or religious conditions is not enough. Al Qaeda understands that, and, for that reason, it weaves a narrative of global jihad against a "modernization," "Westernization," and a "Judeo-Christian" threat. There is really just one country that both spearheads and represents that threat: the United States. And so the most efficient way for a terrorist to gain a reputation is to attack the United States. The logic is the same for all monopolies. A few years ago, every computer hacker in the world wanted to bring down Microsoft, just as every aspiring terrorist wants to create a spectacle of destruction akin to the September 11 attacks inside the United States. Al Qaeda cells have gone after alternate targets such as Britain, Egypt, and Spain. But these are not the acts that increase recruitment and fundraising, or mobilize the energy of otherwise disparate groups around the world. Nothing enhances the profile of a terrorist like killing an American, something Abu Musab al-Zarqawi understood well in Iraq. Even if al Qaeda's deepest aspirations lie with the demise of the Saudi regime, the predominance of U.S. power and its role supporting the house of Saud makes America the only enemy really worth fighting. A multipolar world would surely confuse this kind of clear framing that pits Islamism against the West. What would be al Qaeda's message if the Chinese were equally involved in propping up authoritarian regimes in the Islamic, oil-rich Gulf states? Does the al Qaeda story work if half its enemy is neither Western nor Christian?

RESTORING THE BALANCE

The consensus today in the U.S. foreign-policy community is that more American power is always better. Across the board. For both the United States and the rest of the globe. The National Security Strategy documents of 2002 and 2006 enshrine this consensus in phrases such as "a balance of power that favors freedom." The strategy explicitly defines the "balance" as a continued imbalance, as the United States continues "dissuading potential competitors . . . from challenging the United States, its allies, and its partners." In no way is U.S. power inherently a bad thing. Nor is it true that no good comes from unipolarity. But there are significant downsides to the imbalance of power. That view is hardly revolutionary. It has a long pedigree in U.S. foreign-policy thought. It was the perspective, for instance, that George Kennan brought to the table in the late 1940s when he talked about the desirability of a European superpower to restrain the United States. Although the issues today are different than they were in Kennan's time, it's still the case that too much power may, as Kennan believed, lead to overreach. It may lead to arrogance. It may lead to insensitivity to the concerns of others. Though Kennan may have been prescient to voice these concerns, he couldn't have predicted the degree to which American unipolarity would lead to such an unstable overlap with modern-day globalization.

America has experienced this dangerous burden for 15 years, but it still refuses to see it for what it really is. Antiglobalization sentiment is coming today from both the right and the left. But by blaming globalization for what ails the world, the U.S. foreign-policy community is missing a very big part of what is undermining one of the most hopeful trends in modern history—the reconnection of societies, economies, and minds that political borders have kept apart for far too long. America cannot indefinitely stave off the rise of another superpower. But, in today's networked and interdependent world, such an event is not entirely a cause for mourning. A shift in the global balance of power would, in fact, help the United States manage some of the most costly and dangerous consequences of globalization. As the international playing field levels, the scope of these problems and the threat they pose to America will only decrease. When that happens, the United States will find globalization is a far easier burden to bear.

FURTHER READING

Albrow, Martin, and Elizabeth King. 1990. *Globalization, Knowledge, and Society*. London: Sage.

Appadurai, Arjun. 1996. *Modernity at Large: Cultural Dimensions of Globalization*. Minneapolis: University of Minnesota Press.

Chase-Dunn, Christopher. 1989. *Global Formation: Structures of the World Economy*. Oxford, UK: Blackwell.

Featherstone, Mike, ed. 1990. *Global Culture: Nationalism, Globalization and Modernity*. London: Sage.

Friedman, Thomas. 2012. *The Lexus and the Olive Tree: Understanding Globalization*. New York: Picador.

Fukuyama, Francis. 1992. *The End of History and the Last Man*. New York: The Free Press.

Held, David, Anthony McGrew, David Goldblatt, and Jonathan Perraton. 1999. *Global Transformations*. Cambridge, UK: Polity Press.

Friedman, Jonathan. 1994. *Cultural Identity and Global Process*. London: Sage.

Giddens, Anthony. 1999. *Runaway World: How Globalisation Is Reshaping Our Lives*. London: Profile Books.

James, Paul. 2006. *Globalism, Nationalism, Tribalism: Bringing Theory Back In*. London: Sage.

Robertson, Roland, "Religion, Global Complexity and the Human Condition," in *Absolute Values and the Creation of the New World*, Volume 1. New York: International Cultural Foundation, 1983; and "Interpreting Globality," in *World Realities and International Studies Today*. Glenside, PA: Pennsylvania Council on International Education, 1983.

Robertson, Roland. 1992. *Globalization: Social Theory and Global Culture*. London: Sage.

Rosenberg, Justin. 2000. *The Follies of Globalization Theory*. London: Verso.

Rupert, Mark. 2000. *Ideologies of Globalization: Contending Visions of a New World Order*. London: Routledge.

Scholte, Jan Aart. 2000. *Globalization: A Critical Introduction*. Basingstoke, UK: Palgrave Macmillan.

Steger, Manfred. 2009. *Globalization: A Very Short Introduction*. Oxford, UK: Oxford University Press.

2

GLOBALIZATION OVER TIME

When did globalization begin? If you wanted to trace the history of globalization, where would you start? Well, you could begin with the end of the Cold War and the breakup of the Soviet Union. If you get a bit more reflective, you might go back to a period of history several centuries earlier, when ships plied the oceans with cargoes of silver, spices, and sugar, or when the reach of European colonialization extended throughout the world. You might even reach back earlier in time, when great empires dominated huge stretches of land, such as the Mongol empire in Central Asia, the Incan and Aztec empires in South and Central America, respectively, and the Greek and Roman empires that shaped the Mediterranean world and united the peoples and cultures of North Africa, Southern Europe, and the Middle East. An argument could be made for each of these events as the emergence of globalization.

In a sense, though, the world has had a global history from the very beginning. Scientists tell us that the time–space continuum that informs our understanding of the world is a product of a unity of existence from the moment of the big bang some 13.75 billion years ago. When our planet began to cool and oceans and land masses appeared millions of years ago, there was only one continent. This singular land mass, which scholars call "Pangea," was racked with deep volcanic eruptions and fissures in the earth's thin crust that led to the continental drift that began 200 million years ago. South America parted from Africa, North America broke away from Europe, and the South Asian subcontinent floated from Africa across the open sea to smash into the Asian land mass, creating the high Himalayan mountain range. This process of continental drift continues today, as evidenced by the volcanic actions along the Pacific Rim from Japan and Indonesia to California.

Early species of what became humans evolved in Africa. So we might imagine that we have a great-great-great- (and so forth) grandmother who once lived in what is now Kenya or Tanzania, and who is the equivalent of the Bible's Eve—the mother of us all. The various racial distinctions came later, as humans changed and adapted to the various parts of the planet they eventually called home.

So we begin our planetary and human history with common beginnings. In that sense, we were global from the start. The history for which we have written texts and drawings is only a few thousand years old, of course, but even these manuscripts show a global awareness. Early maps, though terribly parochial from our point of view, show particular regions, such as the ancient Mediterranean area, as if they were at the center of the world. Early Incan and Chinese writers were convinced that their lands were earthly centers as well. In their own ways, they were coming to terms with the vastness of the world and their place in it.

Some ancient texts describe the origins of the world, and these creation myths provide another insight into the global consciousness of ancient peoples. In the ancient Babylonian legend, the *Enuma Elish,* the world begins when chaos, imagined as a lumbering cow-like animal, is conquered by the gods. This image of chaos conquered reverberates through the ancient world and appears in altered form in the opening chapters of Genesis in the Bible and is revered by Jews, Christians, and Muslims. Thus, even the ancient ideas of the nature of the world are themselves transported globally from culture to culture.

The readings in this section look at the span of history to determine what role globalization has played in it—the far-reaching spread of cultures and economies and political power. They ask whether globalization itself has a history: What are the roots of our present moment of globalization? They also ask whether the study of history can be done in a global way.

In the first reading, one of the great historians of our time, William McNeill, asks whether globalization is a long-term process or a new era in human affairs. McNeill, retired after years teaching at the University of Chicago, is regarded as one of the founders of world history, and his book, *The Rise of the West,* is regarded as a landmark in understanding the history of the modern world. McNeill answers his own question in the excerpt provided here, indicating that the vast intercultural reach of globalization is a long-term process that has been a part of world history from ancient times to the present.

Jane Burbank and Frederick Cooper take a distinctive approach to global history, arguing that the most significant stages of political history were built on great empires. Both of these historians teach at New York University. Cooper specializes in African studies, particularly the effects of European colonialism on African labor practices, and Burbank works on Imperial Russia from the eighteenth to the twentieth centuries.

In their book, they challenge the notion that nations are the natural configurations of societies through history and claim instead that the norm is transnational—or rather transcultural—imperial powers. Beginning with Rome and China in the third century BCE, they show how people of different cultural and language backgrounds have lived peaceably together under the rule of great empires.

The next reading is an excerpt from volume 1 of the influential book *The Modern World System,* by Immanuel Wallerstein, a sociologist and economic historian who has taught at Columbia, McGill, and the State University of New York–Binghamton. He began his academic career as a specialist on African affairs, but as he explains in the excerpt that follows, he became intrigued with the idea that the economic history of any one country, or even any one region of the world, is inextricably linked with other parts of the world. For this reason, it is important to see the interconnected relationships in a world system in order to understand how some regions benefit and develop economically while others become dependent and undeveloped based on the economic and political ties that bind them together in a global network.

The last excerpt in this section takes a different approach. It looks at historiography—the way history is conceived as a subject to be studied. The author of this excerpt, Dominic Sachsenmaier, is a German historian who has studied Chinese history and taught at Harvard, the University of California–Santa Barbara, Duke, and Jacobs University in Germany. In this excerpt, he observes that there is a tendency to look at the world from a local perspective—for European historians to think of history as dominated by Europe and for Chinese and Muslim historians to see the world centered in China and the Middle East, respectively. Even so, the political effect of the global spread of European colonialism and Western notions of academic scholarship has imposed a Eurocentric view of history on historians studying other parts of the world. Sachsenmaier shows that global forces can affect the very perception of global history.

GLOBALIZATION: LONG TERM PROCESS OR NEW ERA IN HUMAN AFFAIRS?

William McNeill

Globalization refers to the way recent changes in transport and communication have tied humankind in all parts of the earth together more closely than ever before. One effect, the widespread breakup of older forms of village life after 1950, changed the daily experience of innumerable persons so drastically that those years may plausibly claim to mark a new era in human history. New and more capacious transport and communication were primarily responsible for that change, powerfully seconded by population growth that made older ways of life unsustainable in many rural landscapes. Massive migrations from village to city were the principal manifestations of the new order, and affected all the inhabited parts of the earth.

Yet sporadic increases in the capacity of transport and communication are age-old among humankind and have always changed behavior. That process began when our proto-human ancestors learned to control fire and to dance. Fire eventually allowed humans to accelerate the recycling of organic vegetation by deliberately setting grass and brush alight in dry seasons of the year; and to survive sub-freezing temperatures even in the Arctic. Control of fire was so valuable that all surviving humans acquired that skill, beginning as long ago as 400,000 BCE.

Dancing aroused a different kind of warmth by communicating a sense of commonality to participants that dissipated inter-personal frictions. That, in turn, allowed human bands to expand in size beyond the limits our chimpanzee relatives sustain today. The advantages of larger numbers of cooperating individuals were so great that all surviving humans learned to dance. But dancing leaves no archaeological trace, so dating is completely unknowable. Yet like control of fire, all humans learned to dance; and in all probability it was among bands enlarged and sustained by dancing on festival occasions that language, the principal vehicle of subsequent human communication, developed between 90,000 and 50,000 BCE. Language, too, was so advantageous that it also became universal among humankind.

These three capabilities remain unique to our species; and of the three, language is the most amazing. It proved capable of sustaining agreed upon meanings among indefinite numbers of persons—by now even among hundreds of millions. More particularly, it freed humans from the limitations of acting in response to sense experience in a rather narrow present as other animals do. By talking about things remembered and about what might happen in times to come our ancestors became able to agree on what to do tomorrow and even further into the future. Moreover, when planned actions met disappointment, they were stimulated, indeed required, to talk things over again, seeking to change what they had done in hope of achieving better results.

That process of trial and error induced systematic change in human behavior as never before, since discrepancy between hopes, plans and actual experience was perennial and only increased as new skills and knowledge enlarged human impact on the diverse environments into which they soon penetrated. We live with the result—an ever accelerating pace of social change that strains our capability for successful adjustment.

The subsequent human past can plausibly be understood as a series of thresholds when new conditions of life rather abruptly accelerated the pace of resulting change. Control of fire, which antedated language, had particularly drastic effects, allowing humans to transform local plant life by deliberately burning grass and brush wherever they went. Mastery of movement across water by use of rafts and boats much facilitated human dispersal from their ancestral cradle in Africa. The earliest clear evidence for this capability is the initial occupation of Australia in about 40,000 BCE, which required crossing miles of open water.

Resort to agriculture was the next major accelerant of social change. As they spread to different parts of the earth, humans discovered a wide variety of different plants to feed on. Ways to multiply the number of such plants by weeding and seeding and transplant-ing roots that grew naturally may well have been familiar to many hunters and gatherers long before they ever thought of settling down in a single spot and raising food crops in fields where they did not grow of their own accord.

Why our ancestors did so remains unsure. Hunters and gatherers enjoyed a more variegated and more dependable diet than early farmers; and tilling fields was far more laborious than wandering in search of game and wild-growing plant foods. But farming did produce far more food per acre and sustained far denser populations than hunt-ing and gathering could do. That meant that wherever farmers settled down, superior numbers soon assured them against attack by hunter-gatherers and allowed them to encroach upon hunting grounds wherever cultivable land attracted their attention.

Dense populations raising different crops in diverse landscapes arose independently in several parts of the earth between 8000 BCE and 4000 BCE. From the start, deliber-ate selection of seeds and roots prevailed, sometimes changing food plants radically, as when wild teosinte turned into maize in Mexico. As food supplies increased, farming populations multiplied and established new villages wherever suitable land lay within reach. More people distributed over varying landscapes soon generated divergences of local customs and skills, so that even sporadic contacts with strangers, arriving on foot or by sea, brought attractive novelties to the attention of local communities more and more often.

Consequently, the pace of social change accelerated systematically within each of the major centers of agriculture because more people made more inventions; and some ad-vantageous inventions and discoveries traveled well—new varieties of seeds for example and preciosities like mood-altering drugs, gems for decoration, and obsidian or flint to give cutting tools a sharp edge.

In Eurasia, an impressive array of domesticated animals diversified the agricultural complex of evolving plants and people still further—dogs, cats, donkeys, cattle, horses, water buffalo, camels and still others. Cattle, horses and camels were particularly signifi-cant, for their size and strength far surpassed that of human beings and could be used to plow the soil and to transport heavy loads. The Americas lacked a comparable array of large-bodied domesticable animals and much of Africa was inhospitable to them. Overland transport in those parts of the earth therefore remained more slender than in Eurasia.

Accordingly, in the Americas and sub-Saharan Africa social change in general, largely dependent on contacts with strangers, fell behind the pace of Eurasian developments. Other factors, especially the prevalence of lethal infectious diseases in much of Africa, also handicapped human populations more than in Eurasia, which therefore remained the principal setting for further advances of human power and skill.

The appearance of cities and civilizations after 3500 BCE accelerated social changes still further. Cities existed only by virtue of occupational differentiation and systematic exchanges of goods and services between urban populations and their rural hinterlands.

Urban specialists persistently improved their skills and extended their reach further and further, as professional traders began to spend their lives traveling to and fro across long distances.

When cities started to arise in Eurasia, merchants were already sailing overseas in ships and traveling overland with caravans of pack animals. It was not accidental that where land and sea transport routes met in the land of Sumer (southernmost Iraq) was where the first cities and civilizations appeared. Other civilizations too arose at locations where strangers mingled more than usual, exchanging skills and ideas coming from extensive hinterlands. Consequently, wherever they existed, cities and civilizations circulated goods, skills and ideas more quickly and more widely than before.

The earliest civilizations of Mesopotamia and Egypt were in slender contact from the start; and successive West Asian empires and civilizations remained constantly in touch with Mediterranean cities and civilizations thereafter. Indian and Chinese civilizations were geographically distant; and climate as well as cultural differences limited what could travel from western Asia and Europe to India and China, and vice versa, even after merchant, military and missionary contacts did begin to connect them loosely together. That became a reality by about 100 BCE and made all of Eurasia into a single interacting web, with tentacles reaching into sub-Saharan Africa, the frozen north and among the far-flung Pacific islands off South East Asia.

The vastness and variety of peoples and landscapes within that circle far exceeded similar interacting webs in other parts of the earth. It is therefore not surprising that the Eurasian web evolved levels of skill and power superior to what people elsewhere had at their command when new advances in transport and communication exposed them to Old World accomplishments after 1500 CE.

Biological resistance to a long array of infectious diseases, from the common cold to small pox, measles, plague and others, was the single most decisive factor in compelling previously isolated populations to submit to intruders from the disease-experienced Eurasian web. The most lethal of these diseases were transfers from animal herds. Eurasia's uniquely complex array of domesticated—and some wild—animals had exposed civilized Eurasian peoples to these diseases across millennia, not without wreaking serious damages along the way. But when one epidemic after another started to rage in rapid succession among inexperienced populations in America and other newly-contacted lands, resulting die-offs were crippling. The newcomers remained little affected, thanks to immunities in their bloodstreams, partly inherited, and partly acquired or reinforced by exposure in early childhood.

The human destruction that followed the opening of the oceans to sustained navigation in the decades immediately after Columbus's famous voyage of 1492 was greater than ever before, since European explorers and conquistadors encountered populous, civilized lands in both Mexico and Peru where millions of persons died of new diseases within a few decades. That massive die-off in turn provoked the trade in African slaves that carried millions of Africans across the Atlantic in subsequent centuries.

Accordingly, Europeans, Africans and Amerindians mingled in the Americas earlier and more extensively than anywhere else.

In Eurasia itself after 1500 the pace of change also accelerated. New phenomena, like the flood of silver from American mines, upset prices and social-political patterns in China as well as in Europe, and the spread of new crops from America—especially maize, potatoes and sweet potatoes—enlarged food supplies very significantly as well.

The global pace of change accelerated yet again with the introduction of steam transport on both land and sea, together with instantaneous electrical communication after 1850. One manifestation was the spread of European empires across much of Asia and Africa. Everywhere weavers and other artisans suffered severely from a flood of cheap, machine-made goods coming from newfangled European factories, powered first by flowing water, then by steam and later by electricity. But before very long Asian factories, especially in Japan, China and India, began to produce cheaper and, more recently, also better goods than Europeans (and Americans) did; and European empires all collapsed soon after World War II.

From the long term point of view, therefore, recent mass migrations and widespread disruption of village patterns of life by roads, trucks, buses, radio, TV and computers look more like another wave of intensified human interaction, comparable to its predecessors and far from unique.

Argument about whether continuity or uniqueness prevails among us today is really pointless. Each moment is unique in every human life; yet continuities are strong and undeniable, both privately and publicly. It is always tempting to exaggerate the unprecedented character of the problems we face. My personal cast of mind prefers to seek commonality; and one such indisputable commonality is that in recent centuries, as social change accelerated, each generation felt uniquely challenged, yet survived in greater numbers than before. No clear end of that process is yet in view, unsustainable though it is sure to be across any lengthy future.

. . . I conclude that the world is indeed one interacting whole and always has been. Human wealth and power have sporadically increased, spurting towards unexampled heights lately. Limits to that spurt may now be close at hand. But ingenuity and invention remain alive among us as much as ever. So we and our successors may perhaps continue to stumble onward like all preceding human generations, meeting with painful disappointments and changing behavior accordingly, only to provoke new risks and meet fresh disappointments. That has always been the human condition, and seems likely to last as long as we do.

IMPERIAL TRAJECTORIES

Jane Burbank and Frederick Cooper

We live in a world of nearly two hundred states. Each flaunts symbols of sovereignty—its flag, its seat in the United Nations—and each claims to represent a people. These states, big and small, are in principle equal members of a global community, bound together by international law. Yet the world of nation-states we take for granted is scarcely sixty years old.

Throughout history, most people have lived in political units that did not pretend to represent a single people. Making state conform with nation is a recent phenomenon, neither fully carried out nor universally desired. In the 1990s the world witnessed attempts by political leaders to turn the state into an expression of "their" nationality: in Yugoslavia—a country put together after World War I on terrain wrested out from the Ottoman and Habsburg empires—and in Rwanda, a former Belgian colony. These efforts to create homogeneous nations led to the slaughter of hundreds of thousands of people who had lived side by side. In the Middle East, Sunnis, Shi'ites, Kurds, Palestinians, Jews, and many others have fought over state authority and state boundaries for more than eighty years since the end of the Ottoman empire. Even as people struggled for and welcomed the breakups of empires over the course of the twentieth century, conflicts over what a nation is and who belongs within it flared around the world. . . .

. . . The endurance of empire challenges the notion that the nation-state is natural, necessary, and inevitable, and points us instead toward exploring the wide range of ways in which people over time, and for better or worse, have thought about politics and organized their states. Investigating the history of empires does not imply praising or condemning them. Instead, understanding possibilities as they appeared to people in their own times reveals the imperatives and actions that changed the past, created our present, and perhaps will shape the future.

. . . Not that every significant state was an empire, but . . . for most of human history empires and their interactions shaped the context in which people gauged their political possibilities, pursued their ambitions, and envisioned their societies. States large and small, rebels and loyalists and people who cared little for politics—all had to take empires, their ways of rule, and their competitions into account. Whether this imperial framework has come to an end is a question we [will] address. . . .

We begin with Rome and China in the third century BCE, not because they were the first empires—their great predecessors include Egyptians, Assyrians, Persians, Alexander the Great's enormous conquests, and more ancient dynasties in China— but because these two empires became long-lasting reference points for later empire-builders. Rome and China both attained a huge physical size, integrated commerce and production into economies of world scale (the world that each of them created), devised institutions that sustained state power for centuries, developed compelling cultural frameworks to explain and promote their success, and assured, for long periods, acquiescence to imperial power. Their principal strategies—China's reliance on a class of loyal, trained officials, Rome's empowerment, at least in theory, of its citizens—had lasting and profound effects on how people imagine their states and their place in them.

We next consider empires that tried to move into Rome's place—resilient Byzantium, the dynamic but fissionable Islamic caliphates, and the short-lived Carolingians. These rivals built their empires on religious foundations; their histories display the possibilities and limits of militant monotheism as an arm of state power. The drive to convert or kill the unfaithful and to spread the true faith mobilized warriors for both Christianity and Islam, but also provoked splits inside empires over whose religious mantle was the true one and whose claim to power was god-given.

In the thirteenth century, under Chinggis Khan and his successors, Mongols put together the largest land empire of all time, based on a radically different principle—a pragmatic approach to religious and cultural difference. Mongol khans had the technological advantages of nomadic societies—above all, a mobile, largely self-sufficient, and hardy military—but it was thanks to their capacious notions of an imperial society that they rapidly made use of the skills and resources of the diverse peoples they conquered. Mongols' repertoire of rule combined intimidating violence with the protection of different religions and cultures and the politics of personal loyalty.

The Mongols are critical to our study for two reasons. First, their ways of rule influenced politics across a huge continent—in China, as well as in the later Russian, Mughal, and Ottoman empires. Second, at a time when no state on the western edge of Eurasia (today's Europe) could command loyalty and resources on a large scale, Mongols protected trade routes from the Black Sea to the Pacific and enabled cross-continental transmission of knowledge, goods, and statecraft. Other empires—in the region of today's Iran, in southern India or Africa, and elsewhere—are not described in any detail here, although they, too, promoted connections and change, long before Europeans appeared on the great-power scene.

It was the wealth and commercial vitality of Asia that eventually drew people from what is now thought of as Europe into what was for them a new sphere of trade, transport, and possibility. The empires of Spain, Portugal, France, the Netherlands, and Great Britain do not enter our account in the familiar guise of "the expansion of Europe." In the fifteenth and sixteenth centuries Europe was unimaginable as a political entity, and in any case, geographical regions are not political actors. We focus instead on the reconfiguration of relations among empires at this time, a dynamic process whose consequences became evident only much later.

"European" maritime extensions were the product of three conditions: the high-value goods produced and exchanged in the Chinese imperial sphere; the obstacle posed by the Ottoman empire's dominance of the eastern Mediterranean and land routes east; and the inability of rulers in western Eurasia to rebuild Roman-style unity on a terrain contested by rival monarchs and dynasts, lords with powerful followings, and cities defending their rights. It was this global configuration of power and resources that brought European navigators to Asia and, later, thanks to Columbus's accidental discovery, to the Americas.

These new connections eventually reconfigured the global economy and world politics. But they were a long way from producing a unipolar, European-dominated world. Portuguese and Dutch maritime power depended on using force to constrain competitors' commercial activity while ensuring that producers and local authorities in southeast

Asia, where the riches in spices and textiles came from, had a stake in new long-distance trade. The fortified commercial enclave became a key element of Europeans' repertoire of power. After Columbus's "discovery," his royal sponsors were able to make a "Spanish" empire by consolidating power on two continents and supplying the silver—produced with the coerced labor of indigenous Americans—that lubricated commerce in western Europe, across southeast Asia, and within the wealthy, commercially dynamic Chinese empire.

In the Americas, settlers from Europe, slaves brought from Africa, and their imperial masters produced new forms of imperial politics. Keeping subordinated people— indigenous or otherwise—from striking out on their own or casting their lot with rival empires was no simple task. Rulers of empires had to induce distant elites to cooperate, and they had to provide people—at home, overseas, and in between—with a sense of place within an equal but incorporate polity. Such efforts did not always produce assimilation, conformity, or even resigned acceptance; tensions and violent conflict among imperial rulers, overseas settlers, indigenous communities, and forced migrants appear throughout. . . .

Empire, in Europe or elsewhere, was more than a matter of economic exploitation. As early as the sixteenth century, a few European missionaries and jurists were making distinctions between legitimate and illegitimate forms of imperial power, condemning Europeans' assaults on indigenous societies and questioning an empire's right to take land and labor from conquered peoples.

It was only in the nineteenth century that some European states, fortified by their imperial conquests, gained a clear technological and material edge over their neighbors and in other regions of the world. This "western" moment of imperial domination was never complete or stable. Opposition to slavery and to the excesses and brutality of rulers and settlers brought before an engaged public the question of whether colonies were places where humans could be exploited at will or parts of an inclusive, albeit inequitable, polity. Moreover, the empires of China, Russia, the Ottomans, and Habsburgs were not imperial has-beens, as the conventional story reads. They took initiatives to counter economic and cultural challenges, and played crucial roles in the conflicts and connections that animated world politics. . . .

. . . [I]mperial expansion across land—not just seas—produced distinct configurations of politics and society. In the eighteenth and nineteenth centuries, the United States and Russia extended their rule across continents. Russia's repertoire of rule—inherited from a mix of imperial predecessors and rivals—relied on bringing ever more people under the emperor's care—and of course exploitation—while maintaining distinctions among incorporated groups. American revolutionaries invoked a different imperial politics, turning ideas of popular sovereignty against their British masters, then constructing an "Empire of Liberty" in Thomas Jefferson's words. The United States, expanding as Americans conquered indigenous peoples or acquired parts of others' empires, created a template for turning new territories into states, excluded Indians and slaves from the polity, and managed to stay together after a bitter civil war fought over the issue of governing different territories differently. In the late nineteenth century the young empire extended its power overseas—without developing a generally accepted idea of the United States as a ruler of colonies.

Britain, France, Germany, and other European countries were less reticent about colonial rule, and they applied it with vigor to new acquisitions in Africa and Asia in the late nineteenth century. These powers, however, found by the early twentieth century that actually governing African and Asian colonies was more difficult than military conquest. The very claim to be bringing "civilization" and economic "progress" to supposedly backward areas opened up colonial powers to questioning from inside, from rival empires, and from indigenous elites over what, if any, forms of colonialism were politically and morally defensible.

Empires, in the nineteenth and twentieth centuries, as in the sixteenth, existed in relation to each other. Different organizations of power—colonies, protectorates, dominions, territories forced into a dominant culture, semi-autonomous national regions—were combined in different ways within empires. Empires drew on human and material resources beyond the reach of any national polity, seeking control over both contiguous and distant lands and peoples.

In the twentieth century it was rivalry among empires—made all the more acute by Japan's entry into the empire game and China's temporary lapse out—that dragged imperial powers and their subjects around the world into two world wars. The devastating consequences of this interempire conflict, as well as the volatile notions of sovereignty nourished within and among empires, set the stage for the dissolution of colonial empires from the 1940s through the 1960s. But the dismantling of this kind of empire left in place the question of how powers like the United States, the USSR, and China would adapt their repertoires of power to changing conditions.

What drove these major transformations in world politics? It used to be argued that empires gave way to nation-states as ideas about rights, nations, and popular sovereignty emerged in the west. But there are several problems with this proposition. First, empires lasted well beyond the eighteenth century, when notions of popular sovereignty and natural rights captured political imagination in some parts of the world. Furthermore, if we assume that the origins of these concepts were "national," we miss a crucial dynamic of political change. In British North America, the French Caribbean, Spanish South America, and elsewhere, struggles for political voice, rights, and citizenship took place *within* empires before they became revolutions *against* them. The results of these contests were not consistently national. Relationships between democracy, nation, and empire were still debated in the middle of the twentieth century.

Other studies of world history attribute major shifts to the "rise of the state" in the "early modern period," two terms tied to the notion of a single path toward a normal and universal kind of sovereignty—the "western" kind. Scholars have advanced different dates for the birth of this "modern" state system—1648 and the Treaty of Westphalia, the eighteenth century with its innovations in western political theory, the American and French revolutions. But expanding our outlook over space and back in time and focusing on empires allows us to see that states have institutionalized power for over two millennia in different parts of the world. A story of European state development and other people's "responses" would misrepresent the long-term dynamics of state power in both Europe and the rest of the world.

To the extent that states became more powerful in England and France in the late seventeenth and eighteenth centuries, these transformations were a consequence of empire, rather than the other way around. As powers trying to control large spaces, empires channeled widely produced resources into state institutions that concentrated revenue and military force. War among empires in the eighteenth, nineteenth, and twentieth centuries set the stage for revolutionary movements that challenged Europe's empire-states.

In other words, this study of empire breaks with the special claims of nation, modernity, and Europe to explain the course of history. It is an interpretive essay, based on analyses of selected imperial settings. It suggests how imperial power—and contests over and within it—have for thousands of years configured societies and states, inspired ambition and imagination, and opened up and closed down political possibilities.

ON THE STUDY OF SOCIAL CHANGE

Immanuel Wallerstein

Change is eternal. Nothing ever changes. Both clichés are "true." Structures are those coral reefs of human relations which have a stable existence over relatively long periods of time. But structures too are born, develop, and die.

Unless we are to use the study of social change as a term synonymous to the totality of social science, its meaning should be restricted to the study of changes in those phenomena which are most durable—the definition of durability itself being of course subject to change over historical time and place.

One of the major assertions of world social science is that there are some great watersheds in the history of man. One such generally recognized watershed, though one however studied by only a minority of social scientists, is the so-called neolithic or agricultural revolution. The other great watershed is the creation of the modern world.

This latter event is at the center of most contemporary social science theory, and indeed, of the nineteenth century as well. To be sure, there is immense debate as to what are the defining characteristics of modern times (and hence what are its temporal boundaries). Furthermore, there is much disagreement about the motors of this process of change. But there seems to be widespread consensus that some great structural changes did occur in the world in the last several hundred years, changes that make the world of today qualitatively different from the world of yesterday. Even those who reject evolutionist assumptions of determinate progress nonetheless admit the difference in structures.

What are the appropriate units to study if one wishes to describe this "difference" and account for it? In a sense, many of the major theoretical debates of our time can be reduced to arguments about this. It is the great quest of contemporary social science. It is therefore appropriate to begin . . . with an intellectual itinerary of one's conceptual search.

I started with an interest in the social underpinnings of political conflict in my own society. I thought that by comprehending the modalities of such conflict, I might contribute as a rational man to the shaping of that society. This led me into two great debates. One was the degree to which "all history is the history of the class struggle." Phrased another way, are classes the only significant operating units in the social and political arenas? Or, as Weber argued, are they only one of a trinity of units—class, status-group, and party—which exist, the interactions among which explain the political process? Although I had my prejudices on the subject, I found, like others before me, that neither the definition of these terms nor the description of their relations was easy to elucidate. I felt increasingly that this was far more a conceptual than an empirical problem, and that to resolve the debate, at least in my own mind, I would have to place the issues within a larger intellectual context.

The second great debate, which was linked to the first, was about the degree to which there could or did exist a consensus of values within a given society, and to the extent that such a consensus existed, the degree to which its presence or absence was in fact a major determinant of men's actions. This debate is linked to the first because it is only if one rejects the primordial character of social struggle in civil society that the question can even be raised.

Values are of course an elusive thing to observe and I became very uneasy with a great deal of the theorizing about values, which seemed often to combine the absence of a rigorous empirical base with an affront to common sense. Still it was clear that men and groups did justify their actions by reference to ideologies. Furthermore, it seemed clear also that groups became more coherent and hence more politically efficacious to the extent that they were self-conscious, which meant that they developed a common language and a *Weltanschauung* ["worldview"].

I shifted my area of empirical concern from my own society to Africa in the hope either that I would discover theories confirmed by what I found there or that a look at distant climes would sharpen my perception by directing my attention to issues I would otherwise have missed. I expected the former to happen. But it was the latter that came to pass.

I went to Africa first during the colonial era and I witnessed the process of "decolonization," and then of the independence of a cascade of sovereign states. White man that I was, I was bombarded by the onslaught of the colonial mentality of Europeans long resident in Africa. And sympathizer of nationalist movements that I was, I was privy to the angry analyses and optimistic passions of young militants of the African movements. It did not take long to realize that not only were these two groups at odds on political issues, but that they approached the situation with entirely different sets of conceptual frameworks.

In general, in a deep conflict, the eyes of the downtrodden are more acute about the reality of the present. For it is in their interest to perceive correctly in order to expose the hypocrisies of the rulers. They have less interest in ideological deflection. So it was in this case. The nationalists saw the reality in which they lived as a "colonial situation," that is, one in which both their social action and that of the Europeans living side by side with them as administrators, missionaries, teachers, and merchants were determined by the constraints of a single legal and social entity. They saw further that the political machinery was based on a caste system in which rank and hence reward was accorded on the basis of race.

African nationalists were determined to change the political structures within which they lived. I have told this story elsewhere and it is not relevant to refer to it here. What is relevant here is that I thereby became aware of the degree to which society as an abstraction was heavily limited to politico-juridical systems as an empirical reality. It was a false perspective to take a unit like a "tribe" and seek to analyze its operations without reference to the fact that, in a colonial situation, the governing institutions of a "tribe," far from being "sovereign," were closely circumscribed by the laws (and customs) of a larger entity of which they were an indissociable part, the colony. Indeed this led me to the larger generalization that the study of social organization was by and large defective because of the widespread lack of consideration of the legal and political framework within which both organizations and their members operated.

I sought to discover the general attributes of a colonial situation and to describe what I thought of as its "natural history." It quickly became clear to me that I had to hold at least some factors of the world-system constant. So I restricted myself to an analysis of how the colonial system operated for those countries which were colonies in the nineteenth and twentieth centuries of European powers and which were "overseas possessions" of these powers. Given this constant, I felt I could make generally applicable statements about the impact on social life of the imposition of colonial authority, the motives and modalities of resistance to this authority, the mechanisms by which colonial powers entrenched and sought to legitimate their power, the contradictory nature of the forces that were able to operate within this framework, the reasons why men were led to form organizations that challenged colonial rule, and the structural elements that made for the expansion and eventual political triumph of anticolonial movements. The unit of analysis in all of this was the colonial territory as legally defined by the administering power.

I was interested equally in what happened to these "new states" after independence. As the study of colonial territories seemed to focus on the causes of the breakdown of existing political order, the study of the postindependence period seemed to focus on the opposite issue: How legitimate authority is established and a sense of membership in the national entity spread among the citizenry.

This latter study ran into problems, however. In the first place, to study the postindependence politics of Afro-Asian states seemed to be a process of running after the headlines. There could perforce be relatively little historical depth. Furthermore, there was the tricky question of Latin America. There were many ways in which the situations there seemed parallel, and more and more people began to think of the three continents as a "Third World." But Latin American countries had been politically independent for 150 years. Their cultures were far more closely linked with the European tradition than anything in Africa or Asia. The whole enterprise seemed to be wavering on very shaky ground.

In search for an appropriate unit of analysis, I turned to "states in the period after formal independence but before they had achieved something that might be termed national integration." This definition could be taken to include most or all of Latin America for all or almost all of the time up to the present. But it obviously included other areas as well. It included for example the United States of America, at least in the period before say the Civil War. It surely included eastern Europe, at least up until the twentieth century and possibly up to the present. And it even included western and southern Europe, at least for earlier periods of time.

I was therefore forced by this logic to turn my attention to early modern Europe. This led me first into the question of what I would take as the starting point of this process, a process I provisionally formulated, for want of a better conceptual tool, as the process of modernization. Furthermore, I had not only to consider the issue of starting points but of terminal points, unless I wished to include twentieth-century Britain or Germany as instances of this same social process. Since that seemed prima facie dubious, terminal points had to be thought about.

At this point, I was clearly involved in a developmental schema and some implicit notion of stages of development. This in turn posed two problems: criteria for determining stages, and comparability of units across historical time.

How many stages had there been? How many could there be? Is industrialization a turning point or the consequence of some political turning point? What in this context would the empirical meaning of a term like "revolution" mean, as in the French Revolution or the Russian Revolution? Were these stages unilinear, or could a unit go "backward"? This seemed to be a vast conceptual morass into which I had stepped.

Furthermore, getting out of the conceptual morass was very difficult because of the absence of reasonable measuring instruments. How could one say that seventeenth-century France was in some sense equivalent to twentieth-century India? Laymen might consider such a statement absurd. Were they so wrong? It was all very well to fall back on textbook formulae of the virtues of scientific abstraction, but the practical difficulties of comparison seemed immense.

One way to handle the "absurd" idea of comparing two such disparate units was to accept the legitimacy of the objection and add another variable—the world context of any given era, or what Wolfram Eberhard has called "world time." This meant that while seventeenth-century France might have shared some structural characteristics with twentieth-century India, they were to be seen as very different on the dimensions of world context. This was conceptually clarifying, but made measurement even more complicated.

Finally, there seemed to be another difficulty. If given societies went through "stages," that is, had a "natural history," what of the world-system itself? Did it not have "stages," or at least a "natural history"? If so, were we not studying evolutions within evolutions? And if that, was not the theory getting to be top-heavy in epicycles? Did it not call for some simplifying thrust?

It seemed to me it did. It was at this point that I abandoned the idea altogether of taking either the sovereign state or that vaguer concept, the national society, as the unit of analysis. I decided that neither one was a social system and that one could only speak of social change in social systems. The only social system in this scheme was the world-system.

This was of course enormously simplifying. I had one type of unit rather than units within units. I could explain changes in the sovereign states as consequent upon the evolution and interaction of the world-system. But it was also enormously complicating. I probably only had one instance of this unit in the modern era. Suppose indeed that I was right, that the correct unit of analysis was the world-system, and that sovereign states were to be seen as one kind of organizational structure among others within this single social system. Could I then do anything more than write its history?

I was not interested in writing its history, nor did I begin to have the empirical knowledge necessary for such a task. (And by its very nature, few individuals ever could.) But can there be laws about the unique? In a rigorous sense, there of course cannot be. A statement of causality or probability is made in terms of a series of like phenomena or like instances. Even if one were to include in such a series those that would probably or even possibly occur in the future, what could be proposed here was not to add a series of future possible instances to a network of present and past ones. It was to add a series of future possible instances to a single past-present one.

There had only been one "modern world." Maybe one day there would be discovered to be comparable phenomena on other planets, or additional modern world-systems on this one. But here and now, the reality was clear—only one. It was here that I was inspired by the analogy with astronomy which purports to explain the laws governing the universe, although (as far as we know) only one universe has ever existed.

MOVEMENTS AND PATTERNS: ENVIRONMENTS OF GLOBAL HISTORY

Dominic Sachsenmaier

In a general sense, it is certainly possible to speak of long "traditions" of global or world historical thought and refer to such renowned figures as Herodotus or Ibn Khaldun as forefathers of the field. In many cultures and world regions there were earlier forms of world historical scholarship, which in some cases reach even back almost to the beginnings of history writing. However, when referring to "traditions" in a more concrete sense, that is, as trajectories reaching from the past into the present, the problem becomes far more complex. The crux of the matter lies in the mere fact that acknowledging the antecedents of modern border-crossing historiography does not answer questions about conceptual, social, or even institutional continuities. For example, in the Chinese case it would certainly be very problematic to hurriedly construct the idea of a rather timeless scholarly culture that would be characterized by distinct methodological features lasting from the days of Sima Qian up until the present. Blindly assuming such epistemological permanence from "classical" texts to today's global historical scholarship would, in fact, move us dangerously close to a cascade of problematic intellectual positions ranging from new versions of Orientalism to the belief in pristine national cultures.

Indeed, in almost all world regions university-based historiography is at least partly an outcome of epistemological discontinuities, outside influences, and shared transformations. . . . These also had an impact on the conceptions of space underlying world historical scholarship in the widest sense. Prior to the spread of history as a modern academic field, forms of border-crossing histories were typically written from a clear perspective of cultural, religious, or even ethical centricity, which means that they tended to be tied to distinct value claims. This situation changed decisively during the nineteenth and twentieth centuries, when either colonial rule or nation-building efforts had a profound impact on what elements were selected into the canon of academic historiography and many earlier forms of knowledge were rendered subaltern. Particularly in many countries outside of the West, geopolitical circumstances and domestic transformations no longer allowed for historians to define the cultural self as the center of "world" historical inquiry. This, however, should not make us assume that the dualism of centricity and marginality disappeared from the main currents of world historical thinking. In Dipesh Chakrabarty's words, now a "hyperreal Europe" came to hold a strong position in many scholars' imaginations during and after the global spread of academic historiography. As a general tendency, during the nineteenth and twentieth centuries many scholars from different continents began to share similar mental maps and core assumptions about world historical centers and peripheries. During that time period, significant parts of historical scholarship may have become more globally aware but they did not become more cosmopolitan in the sense of allowing for the idea of multiple, different, and equal centers of enunciation.

A brief look at early forms of historiography reaching across civilizational boundaries will help us fill this rather rough sketch with some more detail and further accentuate the changing conceptions of space that became foundational to modern historiography in many different parts of the world. This in turn will allow us to reflect upon the specific challenges, dangers, and opportunities that the current institutional and conceptual landscapes of historiography present for today's global historical trend. A well-known

European example of early versions of transcultural history writing is the Greek historian Herodotus, who—along with Ephoros (d. 330 BCE), Polybios, and Diodorus—often figures prominently in recent histories of world historical writing. In his account of the Greco-Persian War, Herodotus tried to depict different conditions and traditions from a superordinate perspective, yet at the same time his master narrative was structured around a clear division of the Greek polis as the harbor of freedom, and the Persian Empire as a stronghold of tyranny. An arguably still more centered perspective was taken in the genre of Christian universal histories, which emerged during the later Roman Empire with scholars such as Eusebius (d. 340) or Orosius (d. 417) as leading protagonists. Here important histories of the known world such as the famous works by Otto von Freising (d. 1158) or, centuries later, Jacques Bossuet (d. 1704) were ordered along Christian timelines, and biblical events such as the creation, the deluge, or the incarnation of Christ figured as the main beats in world historical rhythms.

Outside of Europe, world historical outlooks were also usually written from the belief in the normative authority of one's own cultural experience. For example, this was the case with the main works ascribable to the Chinese genre of "universal histories," which dates at least back to the Han dynasty (c. 206-220 BCE). Likewise, the renowned Arabic historian Ibn Al Athir (d. 1233) wrote his "Complete History" covering information about the outside world largely from an Islamic perspective, following a religious chronology. Furthermore, Islamic accounts of the crusades or the Mongol conquests were—like their Christian counterparts—typically not written in the spirit of multiperspectivity. The famed historical work of the Islamic traveler Ibn Khaldun (d. 1406), whose wide range of studies included comparative explorations and was unsurpassed in his time, described the Islamic world as unique and exemplary. Even though he emphasized the rise and fall of civilizations, Ibn Khaldun maintained that only Islam had a universal mission, and according to him one of its great assets was to unite the religious and the secular realms, whereas all other civilizations supposedly separated the two. Similarly, important Ottoman schools that emerged during the expansion of the empire in the sixteenth and seventeenth centuries often included accounts of non-Muslim communities, but did not abandon narratives centered on the primacy of Islam.

Of course, culturally centrist outlooks of world history during the pre-modern period were neither globally uniform nor did they remain completely unchallenged. For example, in the East Asian context Korean and Japanese scholarship often needed to negotiate tropes of cultural belonging and related normative claims with the idea of China's dominant position in the region. However, also here outlooks on the world which acknowledged other but equal cultural centers outside of East Asia were extremely rare. This is not to say that counter-currents of this kind did not exist in premodern Asia. Even in cases like imperial China, challenges to Sinocentric world visions could emerge, particularly during times of political crises. At the same time, throughout Chinese history the main strands of world historical thought had not been written based on the assumption that a distant continent such as, later, "Europe" constituted a key reference culture—a reference culture, which defined many important categories when thinking about history.

Concomitant with the global spread of modern universities and profound changes in historiographical cultures, the belief in Europe as the sole cradle of modern scholarship came to be adopted in many parts of the world. This was certainly less so because European historiography was indeed more advanced or universalizable than other ways of conceptualizing the past. Rather, a complex nexus of global power constellations and rapid transformations led to the emergence of an international academic system that marginalized many local traditions of writing history and privileged "scientific" forms of historical scholarship. The latter were seemingly emanating from long European traditions. The word "seemingly" is important in this context because Western historiography underwent significant transformations at the same time as European academia began to heavily influence historical research elsewhere. Also in Europe the establishment of modern academic historiography marginalized other ways of writing history, many of which could look back at long traditions.

Given these massive changes in Europe itself, many globally influential character traits of modern academic historiography need to be seen not as export products of an allegedly pristine European tradition but rather as byproducts of wider, global transformations and entanglements. This is also true for the fundamental conceptions of space, which came to frame much of historical scholarship in many different parts of the world. After all, the idea of the nation as the main container of local history and the notion of West as the source of dynamism in world history had been rather unusual in Europe prior to the late eighteenth century. Such new historical outlooks reflected forms of political order and global power formations during the nineteenth and twentieth centuries. For this reason they became widely influential in conjunction with the global spread of university-based historical scholarship and surrounding sociopolitical transformations.

For these reasons it would be erroneous to treat the global spread of Eurocentric themes in history as the result of diffusion from the West to the rest. Yet even though such outlooks became very influential both in the centers and on the margins of the evolving academic system, their wider implications were rather different inside and outside of the Western world. In Europe it was possible to portray historical scholarship as the outgrowth of a shared Occidental heritage that reached back to the ancient Greeks. On the contrary, the formation of modern academic disciplines in regions such as India, China, or the Middle East was visibly part of changing geopolitical dynamics, despite the fact that many indigenous traditions were being continued at universities and particularly outside of them. In many parts of the emerging Global South and Global East, the reality of imperialism, European intellectual dominance, and the inevitability of understanding nationalization at least partly as Westernization made it impossible to posit the indigenous past and local scholarship as standards for the rest of the world. Rather, familiarity with the West and other supposedly advanced nations came to be regarded as a precondition for new and timely ways of writing history. In many parts of Africa, Latin America, and the

Middle East, a highly constructed "West" or "Europe" thus necessarily occupied a large part of the methodologies, concepts, and commonly shared background knowledge of the emerging academic communities. By contrast, a majority of scholars in the West were never forced to face the idea that their own conceptual worlds and cultures of rationality were at least partly the products of global interactions and outside influences.

In conclusion, the transformations of nineteenth- and twentieth-century scholarship had great implications for the spatial parameters within which historians in different parts of the world would think about local and translocal history. For example, whereas thinkers ranging from Sima Qian to Ibn Khaldun could still conceive of themselves as rooted in their own cultural universes and regard the outside world accordingly, the situation had been dramatically different for Chinese and Middle Eastern historians during the previous one or two centuries. Even for radically nationalistic or culturally chauvinistic scholarship, it then became impossible to adopt world historical perspectives based on the idea of allegedly unbroken Confucian, Islamic, or other traditions of conceptualizing the past. Local intellectual outlooks as well as the institutional frameworks of universities had too obviously been influenced by exogenous developments. In other words, for many parts of the world, the history of transfers and outside influences has long not constituted an additional perspective that complemented the largely autochthonous tropes of national history; rather, it stood at the very foreground of modern history and historiography.

FURTHER READING

Bayly, C.A. 2004. *The Birth of the Modern World: 1780–1914*. Oxford, UK: Blackwell.

Burbank, Jane, and Frederick Cooper. 2010. *Empires in World History: Power and the Politics of Difference*. Princeton, NJ: Princeton University Press

Chanda, Nayan. (2008). *Bound Together: How Traders, Preachers, Adventurers, and Warriors Shaped Globalization*. New Haven, CT: Yale University Press.

Iggers, Georg G., Q. Edward Wang, and Supriya Mukherjee. 2008. *A Global History of Modern Historiography*. Edinburgh Gate: Pearson Education.

Iriye, Akira. 2012. *Global and Transnational History: The Past, Present, and Future*. New York: Palgrave.

Kennedy, Paul. 1989. *The Rise and Fall of the Great Powers: Economic Change and Military Conflict from 1500 to 2000*. New York: Vintage.

McNeill, John R., and William McNeill. 2003. *The Human Web: A Bird's-Eye of World History*. New York: Norton.

McNeill, William. 1963. *The Rise of the West: A History of the Human Community*. Chicago: University of Chicago Press.

Sachsenmaier, Dominic. 2011. *Global Perspectives on Global History: Theories and Approaches in a Connected World*. Cambridge, UK: Cambridge University Press.

Wallerstein, Immanuel. 2011. *The Modern World System*. In 4 vols. Berkeley: University of California Press.

PART II

THE MARCH OF GLOBALIZATION, BY REGION

3

AFRICA
The Rise of Ethnic Politics in a Global World

In this and the next seven chapters of this book, we will explore the way that global forces have affected different regions of the world and the way that these areas have contributed to global culture, society, economy, and political life. You might call this the "global-in" and "global-out" approach. We are interested in the global currents that have flowed into a particular region at different moments in history (global in) and the way that elements of those societies have gone out into other areas of the world (global out).

We begin with Africa. It is a logical place to start, since the African continent is the birthplace of all humanity. In Ethiopia, bones have been discovered from precursors of ancient African *Homo sapiens* who roamed the earth 190,000 years ago. Archeologists have found evidence of our human predecessors in the Olduvai Gorge in Tanzania that are over a million years old. Eventually, the descendants of these ancient Africans—humans, or *Homo sapiens*—spread out from Africa to the Middle East, Europe, Asia, and everywhere else. What we think of as ethnic differences of skin and hair color and eye shapes are all later adaptations to the environmental conditions in different parts of the world. So the propagation of the human species from Africa throughout the planet is Africa's first global out.

In more recent history—the past thousand years or so—Africa has continued to play a global role. In the thirteenth century, a great empire was established in West Africa, based in what is now the country of Mali, extending over much of the adjacent region. The wealth of this Manden Kurufaba empire was based on three huge gold mines; other resources included copper, salt, and profits from overland trade. For several centuries, it was one of the richest and most influential empires in the world.

Beginning in the sixteenth century, Africa began to feel the effects of European maritime trade. Initially, this was a case of global in, as European ships plied their wares along the West African coast and traded their goods for local resources. But soon this trade turned into a global out of disastrous proportions—the slave trade, called by some the "African holocaust."

The slave trade involved the buying and selling of Africans. Some local African leaders rounded up individuals from their enemies and sold the captured men and women to European traders. The Europeans, in turn, loaded them onto boats and sailed across the Atlantic in what was called "the Middle Passage." Crowded into cargo holds like cattle, many of these unfortunate Africans died en route of disease, starvation, and brutality. Those who survived found themselves in Havana and other slave ports of the New World, where they were sold as workers for cotton fields in the United States and for sugar plantations in the Caribbean islands and the northeast coast of South America—from the three Guianas (Dutch, French, and British) all the way down to Brazil. Exact figures are hard to come by, but it is estimated that ten million to twenty million Africans were exported from the continent before the trade in enslaved Africans—and later, slavery itself—came to an end in the nineteenth century.

This wretched trade had a crippling effect on Africa both economically and socially. Not only did it rob the continent of some of its most able workers, but it also disrupted traditional social patterns and cultural homogeneity. At the same time, it enriched the European countries—especially Portugal, Spain, and England—that were involved in the trade. Some historians claim that the wealth gained from the trade of enslaved Africans helped to fuel the economies that made the Industrial Revolution possible. Others argue that the slave trade provided the excess wealth—the capital—to develop European capitalism into a formidable economic engine. Though other historians dispute these assertions, there is no question that the slave trade had a global economic impact.

There were also cultural effects from the global diaspora of Africans following the years of the slave trade. In some areas of North and South America and the Caribbean basin, the numbers of enslaved Africans were vastly greater than those of white European settlers. Descendants of the African diaspora became leading citizens of countries such as Haiti, Cuba, Jamaica, the Dominican Republic, Trinidad and Tobago, Guyana, Brazil, and the United States. African music, religion, and customs became integral parts of the cultures of these areas of the New World, creating a new synthesis of African, European, and Native American cultures in the Western hemisphere.

In time, the trade with European commercial interests led to further plundering of African resources and political control of African regions. By the nineteenth century, the map of Africa began to look like a crazy quilt of different European-controlled colonies, including those ruled by Spain, France, England, Germany, and Belgium. In the twentieth century, when the colonial powers retreated and these regions gained their independence, what remained were the nation-states of contemporary Africa. Thus, the colonial period of global-in European control resulted in the African nationalisms of the latter part of the twentieth century.

The old colonial divisions that created the new boundaries of nation-states did not always follow the cultural boundaries of traditional ethnic and linguistic groups. In Rwanda, for example, the Hutus and Tutsis warred over which group would dominate the independent nation. In other places, such as the countries of South Africa and what was Rhodesia—later renamed Zimbabwe—the issue was the role of the European settler communities that controlled the politics and economy of the countries, even though they were in the minority numerically as compared with the indigenous African populations. In both countries, the white Europeans have learned to live with black majority rule.

In the twenty-first century, African resources have again become an important aspect of the global economy. In the contemporary situation, however, it is unlikely that these resources will be exploited from the outside without providing substantially greater benefit to Africans than was the case in preceding centuries. The new situation is one in which investment in the region and extraction of its resources come not from Europe but from Asian countries, especially China.

In the readings that follow, several of these aspects of global influences in, and global impact out, will be explored. In the first reading, the African origin of global humanity is described by Nayan Chanda. Chanda was born in India and trained in history in Kolkata and in international relations at the Sorbonne in France. He then became a foreign correspondent during the Vietnam War and served as an editor of the *Far East Economic Review* in Hong Kong before launching a new career in the emerging field of global studies. Based at Yale University, where he edits the Internet journal YaleGlobal Online, Chanda has written an introductory book of global history, *Bound Together,* from which this excerpt is taken.

The next excerpt is also by a journalist and historian born in South Asia. Dilip Hiro, based in London, writes on historical themes and issues of contemporary global politics, including jihadi activism in South Asia. In the excerpt below, he puts the trade of enslaved Africans into global and historical context. The diaspora of African culture and society as a result of the forced dispersion of Africans to the Western hemisphere is described in the succeeding excerpt by Jeffrey Haynes, a political scientist studying the relation of religion and politics in Africa and the Middle East who teaches in London. Following it is an excerpt from an essay by Jacob Olupona, who explores the cultural aspects of Africa's experiences with globalization. Olupona traces the development of Christianity and Islam in the continent and shows how these traditions have become intertwined with traditional religious cultures. Olupona, originally from Nigeria, is a scholar of comparative religion who specializes in West African society. He taught at the University of California, Davis, before becoming a professor of African Studies at Harvard.

The final excerpt in this chapter is from an essay by Okwudiba Nnoli, an African political scientist who focuses on one of the enduring problems created by the nation-state system left behind by retreating European colonial powers. This is the problem of the relationship between national identity and ethnic communities. Because colonialism and nationalism are worldwide, this is a global problem, a continuing issue that confounds Africa, the Middle East, Southeast Asia, and other parts of the world where the idea of nationalism is still an unfinished project. ❧

 THE HIDDEN STORY OF A JOURNEY

Nayan Chanda

How do we know that we all are originally from Africa? Twenty years ago the proposition was mostly guesswork. In his work on human evolution *The Descent of Man, and Selection in Relation to Sex* (1871), Charles Darwin suggested that because Africa was inhabited by humans' nearest allies, gorillas and chimpanzees, "it is somewhat more probable that our early progenitors lived on the African continent than elsewhere." Although voluminous biological and paleoanthropological evidence gathered since this statement has fortified the evolutionary history of life on earth, it has been a long wait to validate Darwin's insight about Africa. Opportunity emerged with our new ability to look deep into our cells and decode the history written there. The first step was taken in 1953 when British scientist Francis S. Crick and his American colleague James D. Watson discovered the structure of DNA. "We've discovered the secret of life," Crick announced with justifiable pride. With the discovery of the double helix structure of DNA—the complex molecules that transmit genetic information from generation to generation—we received the most powerful tool to dig into our ancestral history. As Watson wrote, "We find written in every individual's DNA sequences of a record of our ancestors' respective journeys." Since these early days, sequencing DNA has gotten much easier, faster, and cheaper. With help from archaeologists, climatologists, and linguists, geneticists and paleoanthropologists have been able to reconstruct the histories of human populations—a reconstruction that was unimaginable only two decades ago.

The discovery of fossils of *Homo erectus* in Indonesia and China—the so-called Java and Peking men—showed that the ancestors of *Homo sapiens,* or anatomically modern humans, had begun to travel and colonize Asia and the Old World about two million years ago. The dedicated work of paleoanthropologists like Louis and Mary Leakey in the 1950s and a slew of researchers in the following thirty years established that ancestors of modern humans lived in East Africa's Rift Valley. The remains of a hundred-thousand-year-old *Homo sapiens* were found in Israel, but that species met a biological dead-end, blocked perhaps by the more robust Neanderthals who then inhabited the area. Amazingly, so far the only other remains of modern man dating back to forty-six thousand years have been found in Australia. Did these anatomically modern humans—*Homo sapiens*— have multiple origins, or did they evolve as a single species in Africa? The first intriguing evidence that those fossil finds in Africa were, not just the earliest humans, but our direct ancestors, came to light, not in some ancient fossils, but in the history contained in cells of modern women. This startling discovery was built on the earlier discovery of the structure of DNA. By analyzing the DNA of living humans from different parts of the world, geneticists can reconstruct the movement of their ancestors and track the prehistoric human colonization of the world. We now know that around sixty thousand years ago, a small group of people—as few as perhaps one hundred fifty to two thousand people from present-day East Africa—walked out. Over the next fifty thousand or so years they moved, slowly occupying the Fertile Crescent, Asia, Australia, and Europe and finally moving across the Beringia land bridge to the American continent. The rising waters at the end of the Ice Age separated the Americas from the Asian continent. It was not until Christopher Columbus's encounter with the Arawak on the shores of San Salvador in 1492 that the long-separated human cousins from Africa would meet each other. . . .

A MOTHER IN AFRICA

The discovery that all humanity stems from the same common parents came in 1987. The New Zealand biochemist Allan Wilson and his American colleague Rebecca Cann reached this conclusion at the University of California, Berkeley, by looking into a so-far ignored part of human DNA. Wilson and Cann's team collected 147 samples of mitochondrial DNA from baby placentas donated by hospitals around the world. Unlike the DNA that is recombined as it is passed from one generation to the next, mitochondrial DNA (abbreviated mtDNA) has tiny parts that remain largely intact through the generations, altered only occasionally by mutations that become "genetic markers." MtDNA is maternally inherited, transmitted only from a mother to her offspring, and only daughters can pass it on to the next generation. The mtDNA leaves intact all the mutations that a daughter inherits from her maternal ancestors, thus allowing one to find the traces of the earliest mutation. Since the rate of mutation is roughly constant, the level of variation in mutations allows us to calculate the age of the family tree created by the mtDNA string passed down through the generations. The result of Wilson and Cann's research was a bombshell. Going down the human family tree of five geographic populations, they found that all five stemmed from "one woman who is postulated to have lived about 200,000 years ago, probably in Africa." The press inevitably, if misleadingly, called her the "African Eve." She indeed was, as James Watson put it, "the great-great-great . . . grandmother of us all," who lived in Africa some two hundred thousand years ago. Obviously, she was not the only woman alive at that time: she was just the luckiest because her progenies survived to populate the world, while the lines of descendants of other women became extinct. Or, in genealogical terms, their lines suffered a "pedigree collapse." Children of the three surviving lines of daughters—identified by mtDNA markers L1, L2, and L3—now populate the world. While the first two lines mostly account for the African female population, the non-African women of the world all carry in their cells the inheritance of the two daughters of L3 line—M and N. A scientist has given these lines the nicknames Manju and Nasrin based on the assumption of where the two mutations are likely to have occurred: India and the Middle East.

Our most recent common mother may have been African, but what about the father? Significant recent progress in elucidating the paternal Y chromosome has filled in the gap. In a groundbreaking research paper in 2000, Italian geneticist Luigi Luca Cavalli-Sforza and his colleague Peter Underhill established that the Y chromosome that determines male sex also has an African ancestry. Just as mtDNA is transmitted only from a mother to her children, the Y chromosome that is passed on from a father to his son also does not undergo the shuffling—or recombination—that the rest of the chromosomes do. But there are mutations just like mtDNA. The result is that the history of our fathers is carried in perpetuity by sons. Human ancestors who left Africa all carried in their cells either the African Adam's Y chromosome, which has been given the prosaic label "M168," or the mtDNA of one of the African Eve's daughters. Based on extensive study of the world's population, geneticists now say that the most recent common ancestor of us all left Africa just fifty thousand years ago.

Wilson and Cann's thesis of the human out-of-Africa origin was, of course, not unchallenged by some anthropologists and geneticists. The school that believed in multiregional evolution of the modern human refused to accept a recent or unique origin of *Homo sapiens*. Its proponents argued that the abundant *Homo erectus* fossils found in China and other regions in East Asia (such as Peking Man and Java Man) demonstrate a continuity, and to these researchers it was evident that *Homo sapiens* emerged out of frequent gene exchanges between continental populations, since the earlier species *Homo erectus* came out of Africa about a million years ago. Besides, they argued, the archaeological evidence does not mesh with the out-of-Africa hypothesis, thus making this conclusion at best premature. At least in the case of Chinese critics, one also suspects that the disclaimer about African origins may be linked to national pride about the antiquity of the Chinese civilization. However, as research in the migration of the human genome has continued to produce more and more evidence of African origins, the scientific opinion has increasingly tilted toward the out-of-Africa school. Some Chinese objections have been countered with a large new body of research based on a massive DNA database collected by both Chinese and international geneticists. In 1998 a consortium of seven major research groups from China and the United States, funded by the National Natural Science Foundation of China, conducted a DNA analysis of twenty-eight of China's official population groups and concluded that "modern humans originating in Africa constitute the majority of the current gene pool in East Asia." Several other researchers, including Chinese, have since sampled a large number of Chinese from all over China and reached the same conclusion. Interestingly, research on both mtDNA and the Y chromosome has shown evidence even in Africa of the early colonization by the original group within Africa. The remaining cousins left in East Africa also spread out to the interior of the continent in search of survival. A strong school of thought in South Africa actually suggests the possibility that the ancestors of the Bushmen also are our ancestors and that the spread of those humans who all became our ancestors was from south to north. Whichever way they moved, their imprint is left in the DNA of the Bushmen or Khoisan of the Kalahari Desert and in certain pygmy tribes in the central African rain forest.

The genome revolution and the discovery of the African Eve have sparked a new interest in finding one's roots. The dark-haired *New York Times* columnist Nicholas Kristof thought he knew who he was. His father came to the United States from Europe, so Kristof assumed himself to be of a typical American-European heritage. But he wanted to find out who he really was under the skin and learn more about his origins, and so he sent his DNA sample for analysis. He was in for a surprise. A mere two thousand generations ago his great-great-great-grandmother was an African, possibly from Ethiopia or Kenya. Under his white skin and Caucasian features, exclaimed Kristof, "I am African-American!" After the publication of his column he received a flood of e-mails. One particularly droll one read, "Welcome to the club. But look out while driving in New Jersey." However, the African continent alone cannot lay sole claim to Nicholas Kristof. The genetic markers found in his DNA showed he was also related to people who now inhabit Finland, Poland, Armenia, the Netherlands, Scotland, Israel, Germany, and Norway. "The [DNA] testing just underscored the degree to which we're all mongrels," Kristof told me.

One trait of the human community makes it possible to track the genomic journey. Humans prefer to settle down in one place if conditions permit, but they are equally ready to migrate in search of a better life. The result has been that people who settled along the path of the human journey are marked by a lineage associated with geographic regions. The fact that humans have mostly practiced patrilocality—in which women come to their husband's homes after marriage—enables one to associate the Y chromosome with a particular location. Looking at my DNA, geneticists could tell I was from the Indian subcontinent. My M52 Y chromosome, shared by a large number of Indians, was a giveaway. This ability has allowed geneticists and anthropologists to sketch out a better picture of when and how the progenies of the African Eve left the old continent and found themselves in their current habitat. DNA shows that this migration, spanning forty to fifty thousand years, came in successive waves, mostly in gentle ripples and sometimes in large swells. The Wilson team found that all the world populations they examined, except the African population, have multiple origins, implying that each region was colonized repeatedly.

THE BEACHCOMBER EXPRESS TO AUSTRALIA

The lack of archaeological evidence does not allow us to answer with certainty why our ancestors left Africa. Probably a dry spell of the late Ice Age shrank the forests and dried the savannas that provided game for the hunter-gatherer population. When a small group took the momentous step of crossing the Red Sea into the southern Arabian coast, the whole world was open. Following game herds up into the Middle East or following the shellfish beds around the Arabian Peninsula and on into India, the humans were launched on a journey that would result in populating the entire planet.

One of the most striking of those journeys was the arrival of the ancestral population from Africa to Australia in just seven hundred generations. Some have called this journey an "express train" to Australia. Of course, the ancestors did not know they were headed to Australia: they were just following food. But the eastward movement of generations of people along the Indian and Southeast Asian coasts brought them to a continent twelve thousand miles from their East African origins.

SLAVERY

Dilip Hiro

Slavery has had an enormous impact on the history of the global economy in the past five centuries and has a long checkered history dating back to antiquity. It evolved differently in war and peace: In armed conflicts, victors sometimes turned their prisoners of war into slaves. During peace, it became a form of punishment for crimes or failure to discharge loans.

HISTORY

Records show the existence of slavery in such ancient civilizations as Assyria, the Nile Valley, Greece, and the Roman Empire. In their expanding realm, the Roman conquerors resorted to enslaving large groups in the vanquished territories, and the slave trade became commonplace in the empire. The Romans' captured territories included land that is now known as England, Wales, and Scotland. When Roman Emperor Septimius Severus (ruled 193–211 CE), a North African, governed Britain, he once remarked that the British made "bad slaves." . . .

The capture of slaves and slave trading thrived in the Christian world, where the pope had authority in religious and moral affairs. After taking an equivocal position on slavery and slave trading, the Pope in the mid-15th century allowed the Portuguese ruler to make slaves of pagans and other nonbelievers. Because the Portuguese, known for their maritime skills, had been exploring West Africa since 1415, the papal clearance opened the gate for taking West Africans first as servants and then as slaves. In 1444, the port of Lagos in southern Portugal saw the establishment of the first slave market for Africans in Europe. In a little over a century, 1 out of 10 residents of the capital, Lisbon, was an African slave.

When, in the latter half of the 16th century, the Iberian kings ended their slave trading monopoly, private slave traders transported slaves to the Iberian colonies in the Western Hemisphere, where there were vast plantations producing labor-intensive products, such as cotton, sugar cane, and tobacco, for export to Europe. The pace of development depended on the availability of labor, consisting of native Indian tribes, poor Whites, and African slaves. As the supply of American Indians and poor Whites dwindled, the Iberian plantation owners began to lean more heavily on the expediency of securing slave labor from Africa.

Meanwhile, England, an important European maritime nation, was busily developing contacts with West Africa and Asia through trade by sea. In 1554, John Locke, an English trader, brought slaves from West Africa to England and sold them as household servants. Sir John Hawkins, a British mariner, transported the first "cargo" of 500 slaves from West Africa to the Western Hemisphere in 1562. Later, during the early 1600s, as England established its own plantation colonies on the North American mainland and Barbados, its economic and political interests in slave trading and slavery increased. In 1655, Oliver Cromwell gave a further boost to this development by seizing Jamaica from Spain.

The rise of vast plantations, worked by slaves who cost their owners the bare minimum of maintenance, marked a qualitative change in the history of slavery. Previously, the relationship between a slave and his or her master had feudal characteristics. Now, it turned capitalist in an agrarian environment, with the plantation owner extracting maximum profit out of slave labor by spending just enough to maintain the slaves in a fit state to work. In another context, in the British plantation colonies in the Western Hemisphere, race relations emerged in their starkest form: Whites, as masters, were conceptualized as the superior race, and the Blacks, as slaves, as the inherently inferior race.

Under the Treaty of Utrecht in 1713, Britain acquired from France the contract to supply African slaves to the Spanish colonies from its Caribbean territories. As a result, within 50 years, Britain became the leading slave trading nation in the world, the foremost slave carrier for other European nations, and the center of the triangular trade: British ships ferried manufactured goods to West Africa, transported slaves to the New World, and brought back sugar, tobacco, and cotton to Britain. The slaves' transatlantic journey of 9 to 13 weeks became known as the Middle Passage.

JUSTIFYING SLAVERY

As the British involvement in, and the profits from, slavery and the slave trade increased, the concept of the slave as a commodity began to emerge. Aboard ship, Africans were considered items of cargo. On plantations, African slaves were catalogued along with livestock and treated as work animals, to be worked to the maximum at the minimum cost.

A similar view of slaves as property was taken by the courts in England where, by the mid-18th century, thousands of households of English aristocrats and retired planters used African slaves as serving boys and menservants. They and slave traders had a strong vested interest to maintain the status quo of slavery and slave trade and often rationalized these practices. To counter criticism from liberal, humane quarters, slave masters and merchants argued that African slaves were subhuman. In other words, essentially to justify their economic gain, while simultaneously exorcizing themselves of any guilt they might have felt, slave masters and merchants argued that slaves were subhuman and received the treatment they (naturally) deserved. The fact that slaves were of a different race led many British masters and traders to apply their beliefs to the whole race. They ceased to call slaves African and, instead, referred to them by a racial label—negro. Generalizations about negroes proliferated and became part of popular beliefs and myths in Britain.

Religious and cultural justifications were often advanced to establish the inherent inferiority of negroes, as a race. It was argued that they were the descendants of Ham, the Black son of Noah. As such, they were natural slaves, condemned for ever to remain "hewers of wood and drawers of water" (Joshua 9:23). This justification reasoned that negroes were not only physically black, the color of Satan, but also morally black. They were, in short, savage creatures, who jumped from tree to tree in the steamy jungles of Africa and ate one another. Thus, from this perspective, to transport these supposedly subhuman, biologically inferior, mentally retarded creatures from the hell of African jungles to the tranquility and order of the plantations of the New World, where they were assured of protected existence, was an act of Christian charity.

ABOLISHING SLAVERY

Among small pockets of European settlers in North America, however, arose objections to slavery. In 1688, the Quakers in Pennsylvania were the first to air such views. Yet it was not until 1777 that Vermont, then an independent nation, declared slavery illegal. In Europe, the First Republic of France outlawed slavery in 1794. Britain outlawed the slave trade in 1807 throughout its empire. It then set out to pressure others to follow suit. The Netherlands, the last European nation to do so, abolished slave trading in 1814. In South America, Brazil did so in 1826.

The law abolishing slavery in the British Empire was passed in London in 1833 and enforced the following year; yet, slavery continued elsewhere. Slavery was abolished in Brazil in 1853. The end to slavery in the United States came only at the end of the 1861–1865 Civil War between the proslavery South and the antislavery North. In 1863, U.S. President Abraham Lincoln signed the Proclamation of Emancipation, liberating slaves in the United States.

Between 1518 and 1853, European nations filled their Western Hemisphere–bound slave ships with an estimated 20 million Africans, of which only about 15 million survived the grueling conditions of the overcrowded African ports and the months-long Middle Passage across the Atlantic in tightly packed ships, leading to outbreaks of fatal diseases. As a result, many more Africans arrived in the New World during those 335 years than Europeans.

SLAVERY AND RELIGION

During slavery, knowledge of Christianity was often withheld from the slaves, although one of the earliest justifications for embarking on the slave trade and slavery given by

Europeans in general, and Sir John Hawkins in particular, was to "Christianize the Africans." (The first ship that Hawkins used as a slave carrier was named *The Jesus*.) With the development of a plantation economy in the West Indies, planters tended to consider it imperative to deprive their slaves of any knowledge that might lead to their "enlightenment" and possible disobedience. That included knowledge of Christian doctrine.

Furthermore, by intermingling slaves from different tribes to form work gangs, and banning the practice of their respective language and religious rituals, slave owners encouraged the decline of African religions. Over generations, through "house slaves"—slaves that worked in the owner's house and were sometimes allowed to stand in at the rear of their owner's church on Sundays—and through periodic, distant observation of the Whites at church, field slaves were exposed to Christian ritual and doctrine. The result was an amalgam of orthodox Christianity and African beliefs in witchcraft, spirits, and the supernatural.

Several slave masters in Jamaica considered this development disturbing and attempted to formalize it by importing, in 1745, Moravian missionaries from America to instruct the slaves in Christian doctrine. Later, Baptist ministers from America and England were brought in to preach the gospel. By the time all slaves were emancipated in Jamaica, for instance, almost all had been exposed to Christian doctrine in one form or another.

The African belief in the supernatural was blended with the Christian concept of Jesus the Savior. Out of the marriage of Baptist fundamentalist gospel and African belief grew the Baptize, or Pentecostal school of Christian doctrine which, in the post-emancipation period, attracted thousands of ex-slaves, and which today claims the allegiance of about 20% to 25% of the Jamaican population. The participatory approach to service at a Pentecostal church—consisting of congregational singing and incorporating the spiritualist practices of trances, spirit possession, and "speaking in tongues"—proved particularly popular with the rural and/or poor African Americans and Afro-Caribbeans.

The claim that slavery, which underwent profound changes during the past millennia, is now extinct must be qualified. It persists in its feudal form in remote pockets of the Arabian Peninsula. Some argue that an indirect form of slavery—being bound to an economic role from which one cannot be easily extricated—is an unfortunate by-product of the 21st-century global economy.

✗ AFRICAN DIASPORA RELIGIONS

Jeffrey Haynes

As many as 10 million Africans were transported from West and Central Africa to the Americas and the islands of the Caribbean between the 16th and 19th centuries, creating one of the largest and most jarring events of forced population change in global history. This Atlantic slave trade involved their removal from familiar customs and practices, and separation from families and communities. As a result of this diaspora, Africans were scattered and dispersed around the world. Yet they often managed to retain both traditions and identities in their new environments. As a result, important elements of African cultures—including religions, languages, and folklore—survived the traumatic dislocation, serving as crucial links to their past lives.

The term African diaspora religions (ADRs) refers to various African-based religions relocated to the Americas as a consequence of Africans' enslavement. ADRs highlight religious traditions originally from Africa which not only were able to survive cultural and ideological assault but also proved to be robust enough to provide spiritual resources for people whose identities were rooted in African cosmologies. ADRs are both urban and rural phenomena, emerging and developing as a direct result of the existential impacts of slavery and the associated belittling of African spirituality in the Americas.

ADRs can be grouped into various types. First, there are the neo-African religions—including Candomblé in Brazil; Santería in Cuba, the Dominican Republic, and Puerto Rico; and Vodun (Voodoo) in Haiti. Despite differences, they draw on similar ideas and concepts, often borrowing practices from Catholicism that reminded adherents of religious themes already encountered in Africa. The second type is ADRs influenced by Protestant missionary activity. Examples include Cumina and the Convince cult in Jamaica, the Big Drum Dance of Carriacou (Grenada), and St. Lucia's Kele. Third, there are ADRs influenced by Pentecostal groups from the United States, especially found in Jamaica. A fourth type of ADR includes religions that emphasize divination, healing, and spirit mediumship. Examples include Umbanda in Brazil, the Maria Lionza cult in Venezuela, and Puerto Rico's Espiritismo. The final type of ADR examined here is Rastafarianism, found primarily in Jamaica, a religion with a pronounced sociopolitical agenda.

NEO-AFRICAN RELIGIONS

Three representative examples are briefly discussed here: Candomblé (Brazil), Santería (Cuba), and Vodun (Voodoo; Haiti, Dominican Republic). Candomblé is practiced mainly in Brazil. Transported from Africa by indigenous priests and adherents, it developed in Brazil, during the era of slavery (1549–1888). The religion was originally confined to the slave population and, as a result, persecuted both by the dominant Catholic Church and the state. After slavery was ended, Candomblé grew to become a major, established religion. Now, about 2 million Brazilians (1.5% of the total population) are followers of Candomblé. Adherents come from all social classes. There are tens of thousands of temples in Brazil.

Candomblé is a religion of the body, focusing on emotions and expressions. Undertaken with blood sacrifice, trance, music, and dance, it does not have a clear code of ascetic conduct. These characteristics differentiate Candomblé from another fast-growing religion in Brazil: Pentecostalism. In short, Candomblé is a festive religion, where notions central to Western theology—including, sin, guilt, and expiation—play little or no role.

Santería, also called Regla de Ocha or Regla Lucumi, is practiced widely in Cuba. It is also found among people of Cuban extraction in the United States. Emanating from the Yoruba tradition of West Africa, Santería is, like Candomblé, a complex of divination, spirit possession, and sacrifice. To become a member of the Santería religion, one must undertake initiation, where the principal ceremony is the asiento (placing of the divinity in the initiate). The focal point of Santería is Babalawo, regarded by adherents as the diviner of the future. He also seeks causes of sicknesses, in both the past and the present, and is the officiating priest at initiations.

Vodun (or Voodoo) is traceable to an African word for "spirit." The term can be traced back to the West African Yoruba people, who lived in what is now Benin (historically, Dahomey). Slaves brought their religion with them when they were forcibly shipped to Haiti and other islands in the Caribbean.

RELIGIONS INFLUENCED BY PROTESTANT MISSIONARY ACTIVITY

All such ADRs derive from West Africa. Cumina, for example, has its traditions in those of the Ashanti-Fanti people of the Gold Coast (now, Ghana), transported in millions to the Americas during the slave trade. It was in the Ashanti-Fanti religious cult of ancestral reverence that many slaves in Jamaica discovered a medium through which to express their religious and political sentiments.

Cumina is a purely African religious cult, and elements of it remain in the rural communities of Jamaica. In times of rebellion, and there were many such times in Jamaica during colonial rule, Cumina was thought to protect followers from colonialists' bullets. An adherent possessed by the spirit of the ancestors would be swept up in dynamic dancing and would not recover from an altered state of consciousness until awakened later from the trance. The individual would be entirely ignorant of anything that had transpired. This possession trance is still found in all the ADRs of the Caribbean.

GROUPS INFLUENCED BY PENTECOSTAL GROUPS FROM THE UNITED STATES

Jamaica has many Pentecostal churches, including the Jamaica Pentecostal Church of God Trinity and the United Pentecostal Church. Such churches reflect both an intersection and a lack of fit between Western and West African religiously grounded "moral orders," which surfaced during recent Jamaican acceptance and transformation of North American Pentecostalism. Today, Jamaica's many Pentecostal churches highlight the current social/political significance of religious morality into the context of local/global transnational interconnections. Such Jamaican churches are bolstered by organizational and economic links to the transnational—mainly North American—Pentecostal movement, which not only informs and helps amend beliefs and practices of many ordinary Jamaicans followers but also helps to insulate them from pressures toward secularization.

Jamaica's Pentecostal churches were built on syncretistic ingredients of Jamaica's "moral inheritance." This was informed by various factors, including British missionary revivalism and Calvinist moralizing, introduced to enslaved peoples in Jamaica, who primarily emanated from West Africa's Gold Coast. The European moral order centered on acceptance of a single, transcendent God, with personal sin to be overcome by rigorous self-discipline. Death would lead to salvation. Such beliefs dovetailed with a suspicion of expressive ritual practice, bolstered by the missionary practice of stressing the desirability of ordered domesticity, hard work, and sexual morality as indicative of social worth. This could be contrasted with the perceived moral order of the slaves, which rested on a belief in an immanent world populated by multiple spirits, where both good and evil reside. So-called tricksters (exemplified by Anansi, the clever spider, hero of West African folktales) could make evil become good, and good turn into evil, through mediation of moral practices centering on rites of spirit possession linked to healing.

In Jamaica, acceptance of North American Pentecostalism converged with elements of the African-derived moral order. Central among these were glossolalia (speaking in tongues) and the doctrine of perfectionism leading toward individuals becoming saints. These ritually embodied signs of transformation by the holy ghost were interpreted by Jamaican converts as "tricks." The Pentecostal advent was seen as a swift, unsuspected (rather like an unpredictable turn of events in an Anansi story) transformation. It was not understood as the product of systematic and "ethical rationalism," which characterized pre-Pentecostal missionization.

RELIGIONS THAT EMPHASIZE DIVINATION, HEALING, AND SPIRIT MEDIUMSHIP

Examples include the Afro-Brazilian religion Umbanda. It is characterized not only by African religious elements but also draws on Catholicism and Kardecist Spiritualism. Although it has its own identity, Umbanda is similar in some respects to other Afro-Brazilian religions, including Candomblé, Macumba, Batuque, and Quimbanda. Umbanda emerged in Rio de Janeiro in the 1920s, a time of significant industrialization, before spreading to São Paulo and southern Brazil. It is also found in Argentina and Uruguay. Its emergence and development is linked with the name of Zélio Fernandino de Moraes, a psychic, who worked among the poor. Leaders of the religion are known as pai-de-santo and mãe-de-santo. For many adherents, one of the purposes of belonging to the religion is to seek upward mobility.

While followers of Umbanda are linked by certain beliefs, it is also the case that there are various branches of the religion, each with their own beliefs and practices. Adherents have the following in common: belief in a One Supreme Creator God (known as the Orixá Olorum) and in lesser deities called Orixás. The latter are believed to act as the Orixá Olorum's helpers. They are the spirits of the deceased believed to counsel and guide the living through their lives on earth. They are also believed to be psychics who can channel messages from the spirit world having to do with reincarnation and spiritual evolution through successive lives. Adherents of Umbanda are under a religious obligation to practice charity, to aid the less fortunate.

RASTAFARIANISM

In Jamaica, where economic downturn and political polarization are well-established phenomena, a syncretistic religious cult emerged, known as Rastafarianism. For decades, Rastafarianism has epitomized the desire of many Jamaicans for redemption from, initially, colonial rule and now a poor postcolonial socioeconomic situation.

Jamaica's 2.8 million people, mostly descendants of West African slaves, are predominantly Christian, although about 100,000 describe themselves as Rastafarians. The emergence of Rastafarianism in the 1930s was fueled by the unacceptability for many Jamaicans of the image of a white-skinned God promulgated by the British Christian colonists. Rastafarians regard the last Ethiopian emperor, Haile Selassie ("Ras Tafari"), who ruled from 1932 until his overthrow and death in 1974, as God. Rastafarians recognize the Black American, Marcus Garvey (1887–1940), as the religion's greatest prophet. Garvey's militant message of liberation, which he preached until his death in the early 1940s, was highly influential in helping to spread Rastafarianism as the route to spiritual and political emancipation from British rule.

Following Jamaica's independence in 1962, serious riots occurred in 1965 and again in 1968, reflecting the polarization of society between a small rich elite and the mass of poor people. At this time, the Rastafarians' idea of a new type of society based on equality and communitarian ideals offered a radical alternative to the status quo. Rastafarianism enjoyed a period of growing popularity, underpinned by the popularity of the great reggae artist, Bob Marley, a member of the Rastafarian faith. Following the death of Marley in 1980, however, the influence of the Rastafarian movement declined precipitously. It lost much of its direct political influence and is currently of only marginal significance in Jamaica.

CONCLUSION

ADRs are variable and various. What they have in common is that they emerged and developed during the long period during which Africans were taken against their will from Africa to Europe and the Americas, between the 16th and 19th centuries. ADRs were persecuted in the African diaspora, regarded with suspicion by authorities as having the potential to serve as vehicles of political challenge. Conventional expressions of Christianity condemned ADR practices as both heathen and demonic. During colonial times, ADR followers faced legal challenges in many countries, including Jamaica.

Laws were passed restricting Africans' right to preach and teach their religions. In Haiti, Catholic priests taught that Vodun was not a religion from God. Instead, it was said to come from the Devil.

Today, many ADRs still face problems as a consequence of their practice of sacrifice. In a recent case in the United States, however, the U.S. Supreme Court made the judgment that preventing them from undertaking sacrifices in the context of religious ceremonies violated their religious freedoms. Undeterred by both historical and contemporary setbacks, ADRs collectively continue to exhibit growth. One of their main attractions is that they evoke a world where the gods' power and strength helps to forge human destiny. Moreover, they typically celebrate family, community, and life's blessings, and offer adherents ways to understand the world and to deal with its trials and tribulations.

THINKING GLOBALLY ABOUT AFRICAN RELIGION

Jacob K. Olupona

The global dimensions of African religion sweep across the plains of the African continent and into the African diaspora. Contemporary "African religion" is itself a product of globalization, for it is less a single tradition than a sociological context in which the elements of a variety of indigenous religious experiences are combined with Islam and Christianity. All three of these dimensions—indigenous religion, Africanized Islam, and Africanized Christianity—are part of the interactive, globalized African religious experience.

Some of the products of this growing interconnectedness of African and Africanized religions are new religions. As Max Weber has observed, the charismatic becomes routinized, and new faiths become accepted as established traditions. Following Ernst Troeltsch's categories, a breakaway sect can be characterized by the presence of doctrinal or ritual differences among the church's membership, and the new African religions have elements of both. These new religious structures reflect emerging values and the adoption of new practices in a changing social context. In the case of the African religions, this process reflects a growing pluralism among African religious institutions.

As globalization affects African religion both within Africa and throughout the African diaspora, new identities emerge. In the African Christian church, the Islamic mosque and the Santería temple, a new pluralism in African identity links the values, memories and civil associations of a variety of African worldviews and moral systems. These are affected by their interactions with each other and with the cultures of the Western world.

The very language we use to describe the diverse religious experiences of people of African origin and descent is not only recent but also heavily dependent upon non-African paradigms and Eurocentric views. Terms such as Africa, Black and Pan-Africa, all derive from recent conceptual periods in history, where parts of the geographical area we now so readily call Africa interacted with Europe. It is this interaction beginning with trade and followed by the latter horrors of the slavery and colonialism, that led to the Eurocentric idea of African religious cultures and worldviews.

As a consequence, it is difficult to come up with a distinct notion of African religion that is independent of the shaping tendencies of the paradigms and terms of the Western world. A truly indigenous understanding must include not only the history of Africa before colonialism, but also aspects of living African communities that have derived from diverse heritages. Although the effort to define "African religion" can be challenging, a number of scholars, writers and theologians have made the attempt. Writers associated with the "Pan-African" movement, for instance, which dates back for over three centuries, have sought to refine their sense of common being by looking at the totality of African religions within the global environment.

GLOBALIZATION

In looking at the relationship between African religion and globalization, we should not assume that globalization is an inevitable force that will one day replace all traditional values within the world with one common consumerist mass culture. In Africa globalization has had a significant impact upon traditions and cultural values but at the same time African traditionalism retains a resiliency and adaptability that enables it to maintain cohesion both in non-Western environments and in the context of faiths such as Christianity and Islam.

African traditions are adaptable. Instead of offering inflexible dogmatic beliefs, often they provide frameworks for viewing and processing information. If a new piece of information does not fit an existing framework, it can modify but not necessarily reject the framework. For example, a form of taboo observed by an African people can be maintained until the old framework adapts, and it changes. What is interesting to ask about African immigrant religions is not so much what aspects of their traditions have been abandoned as how the frameworks of the traditions have adapted.

To some extent these churches were separated from other African churches. They had difficulty in expanding their efforts beyond their original ethnic base. They were plagued with many of the same ethnic and political divisions that have separated the wider African society and created a series of contemporary political crises. . . .

CONCLUSION

The globalization of African religion, therefore, entails not only the death of African traditional values but also in many cases their expansion and promotion. This is the product of an innovative and somewhat unpredictable reshuffling of many of Africa's cultures, faiths and traditions—which have become a force for change in both Western and non-Western societies. This is nowhere more evident than in the crosscurrents between contemporary religious communities in the Americas and the expansion of African religions within the African continent itself. These movements are sources of cultural continuity, stability and authority, and demonstrate the remarkable resiliency and strength of character of African cultures. They have also at times been sources of tension, division, and conflict. These characteristics of innovation and diversity will continue to evolve as African religions expand from their roots in the three pivotal traditions of Christianity, Islam and indigenous faiths.

THE CYCLE OF "STATE-ETHNICITY-STATE" IN AFRICAN POLITICS

Okwudiba Nnoli

The genocide in Rwanda in 1994 radically changed the attitudes of Africans and non-Africans alike toward ethnicity in Africa. The extent of the bloodletting shocked the whole world. In spite of the numerous cases of ethnic violence on the continent in the past, no one expected the carnage and brutality that attended the genocide. Worse still its perpetrators have shown no remorse. Both Rwanda and Burundi are still locked in genocidal wars in which the Tutsi are pitted against the Hutu. People are asking questions about the contribution of ethnicity to the state of affairs in African politics. Of particular interest is the reason why ethnic conflict in Africa has been so destructive.

This essay seeks to answer these questions. It suggests that past attempts to answer them failed because they are based on inadequate understanding of ethnicity in Africa. They tend to see ethnicity everywhere and to conceive it in a self-explanatory manner. They view ethnicity essentially as given and take very little account of its substratum. From this point of view interests arising from ethnic identities differ from one another because of socio-cultural and economic differences among the relevant ethnic groups. Hardly any serious thought is given to how and why individuals embrace ethnic identity in the first place, and the origin of the ethnic group interests.

Our view is that ethnicity in Africa arises from the projection of state power by those who control the state. The undemocratic character of the state means that in extending political authority throughout the country and organizing economic and social activities in the society those who control the state often inflict direct or structural violence on peoples and communities. Direct violence occurs when a punitive expedition is sent to perpetrate violence against a community for past misdeeds. A good example is the military expedition sent by the Nigerian government in 1999 to sack the town of Odi in Bayelsa state. This action was punishment for the disappearance of some policemen in the area. Structural violence occurs when decisions are imposed on communities without consulting them, and often against their will. An example is the imposition of the structural adjustment program (SAP) on the various communities in Africa.

As Ake argues, what occurs for the most part in Africa is violent aggression by the state against communities, ethnic groups, minorities, workers, peasants, religious groups and the political opposition in the routine business of projecting power to realize vested interests and to sustain domination. . . . In other words, the violence does not need to arise from any articulated or perceived differences between the state and its victims. It is not necessarily related to any explicit struggle for state power. The differences and struggles emerge ex post facto from the unilateral actions of the state. A reckless abuse of power is often involved. This gradually builds up a critical mass of desperate enemies among the victims of state action. Ethnicity emerges as an inclusive framework for responding to this violence of the state.

For example, the resort to arms by the Banyamulenge ethnic group in the Congo (DRC) emerged ex post facto from the unilateral state policy of the Mobutu regime to divest them of their citizenship of the country. The result was a series of violent actions, reactions and coalitions that swept Mobutu Sese Seko from power and turned the Congo into a theatre of violent political struggles among local and foreign forces that are yet to be resolved. In Northern Ghana, the Konkomba-Nanumba war of 1981 is traceable to the generalized state-imposed structural violence that attended the country's policy of SAP during the period 1980–1983. Those fleeing this violence to their ethnic homeland found themselves engaged in destructive socio-economic competition with neighboring ethnic groups that could not be resolved by other than violent means.

This state-ethnicity nexus dates back to the colonial period. The colonial state was undemocratic, ruthless and arbitrary. As a rule, it projected its power without consulting the people; invariably it acted against their will. Its policies completely changed the African political, economic and socio-cultural landscape. They produced a massive population shift, especially from the rural to the urban areas; alienated community land; destroyed local institutions; created new public institutions; redefined notions of physical and political space; and created new notions of citizenship. Unilateral and coercive actions of the colonial state played the leading role in forcing through these changes. This was the beginning of virulent ethnicity.

This ethnicity was reinforced by the ruthless projection of state power during the early post-colonial period. These were the heydays of the one-party state and military rule. Increased centralization of state power, a widening of the scope of corruption, increased repression, the expansion and intensification of the process of class formation, the emergence of class factions, and massive changes in the agrarian sector formed the context for the evolution of new identities, redefinition of pre-colonial and colonial identities, and the manipulation of these identities for political and other purposes. Added to all this is the impact of the political, economic and ecological crises of the state on ethnicity and its growth.

Furthermore, the growth of ethnicity is promoted by the tendency of globalization to bring everyone into close proximity by shrinking everything into one small intimate space that has to be fought for incessantly. Shrinking physical space, increasing proximity and enforced intimacy cause tension and anxiety because they crowd people into ever-smaller space with all their differences and mutual suspicions intact. Even when globalization tries to induce common values, as for example through the global market, it does not reduce the tensions; if anything it increases them by inducing convergence on the same values and focusing demand on the same scarce resources. . . .

Such tensions are compounded by the increasing openness of state boundaries spawned by globalization. Everyone everywhere is exposed to the unblinking view and judgment of a global society. There is no place to hide, no respite from scrutiny and assessment. One result of this trend is the tendency towards undermining the state. As the state is undermined it decomposes into its constituent linguistic, religious or ethnic components. The dismemberment of the Soviet Union, Yugoslavia and Czechoslovakia is illustrative. Globalization produces tensions, uncertainties and ruptures that cause serious changes in attitudes and orientations. The abstract universalism of civil identity in the nation-state is unable to contain these changes. This is because such changes elicit particularistic but holistic cultural identities such as religious or ethnic identities.

By all indications, African peoples have sought to resist oppressive state presence by embracing new identities, sometimes different from their pre-colonial identities. They have overwhelmingly embraced primary identities such as ethnic and religious identities. Their preference for primary identities is because of the generalized and cultural nature of the threat. Such a threat demands nothing but the crystallization of the self holistically. This is precisely what primary identities do. However, as self-reflexivity this type of primary identity takes itself and all its claims for granted but does not take rival identity claims seriously except in the confrontation by which it determines and invigorates itself by negation. Therefore and unfortunately, when the struggle against the threat (state violence) is waged (ethnic conflict) it is sometimes directed against the wrong enemies, other ethnic groups rather than the rampaging undemocratic state.

Unlike pre-colonial ethnicity, the ethnicity that emanates from these rapidly changing national and global conditions is fiercely competitive and intolerant of ethnic minority views and feelings. It is not aimed at promoting production and commerce as in the pre-colonial past but the control and monopolization of power and material resources. It seeks advantage in the socio-economic and political scheme of things. These characteristics are reinforced by the partisan nature of the African state in factional disputes, the extensive intervention of the state in economic and social life that makes the state a strategic instrument for power and wealth in Africa. Thus, one can understand the intensity of the struggle among ethnic groups to control and dominate the state.

FURTHER READING

Ake, Claude. 1996. *Democracy and Development in Africa*. Washington, DC: Brookings Institution.

Blackburn, Robin. 1998. *The Making of New World Slavery: From the Baroque to the Modern, 1492–1800*. London: Verso.

Blackburn, Robin. 1998. *The Overthrow of Colonial Slavery, 1776–1848*. London: Verso.

Buxton, Thomas Fowell. 2011. *The African Slave Trade*. Cambridge, UK: Cambridge University Press.

Haynes, Jeffrey. 2013. *Religion and Politics in Europe, the Middle East and North Africa*. London: Routledge.

Hiro, Dilip. 1991. *Black British, White British: A History of Race Relations in Britain*. London: HarperCollins.

Hopkins, Dwight N. 2005. *Being Human: Race, Culture, and Religion*. Minneapolis: Fortress

McCarthy Brown, Karen. 2001. *Mama Lola: A Voudou Priestess in Brooklyn* (revised edition). Berkeley: University of California Press.

Morgan, Kenneth. 2011. *Slavery, Atlantic Trade and the British Economy 1660–1800*. Cambridge, UK: Cambridge University Press.

Northrup, David(Ed.) 2010. *The Atlantic Slave Trade*. Oxford, UK: Oxford University Press.

Olmos, Marguerite Fernández, and Lizabeth Paravisini-Gebert. 2003. *Creole Religion of the Caribbean: An Introduction from Vodou and Santería to Obeah and Espiritismo*. New York: New York University Press.

Redkey, Edwin. 1969. *Black Exodus: Black Nationalism and Back to Africa Movements*. New Haven, CT: Yale University Press.

Rodney, Walter. 2011. *How Europeans Underdeveloped Africa*. Washington, DC: Howard University Press.

Russell-Wood, A.J.R. 2002. *Slavery and Freedom in Colonial Brazil*. Oxford, UK: Oneworld.

Thomas, Hugh. 2006. *The Slave Trade: History of the Atlantic Slave Trade, 1440–1870*. London: Phoenix.

Williams, Eric. 1994. *Capitalism and Slavery*. Chapel Hill: University of North Carolina Press. (Originally published in 1964.)

4

THE MIDDLE EAST
Religious Politics and Antiglobalization

The Europeans who gave the Middle East its name thought of it as the crossroads of West and East, at the intersection of the main overland routes between Africa and Asia and Europe. All of these areas influenced the Middle East, of course, but the Middle East has made its own enormous contributions to global culture and the transnational economy as well. Three of the world's great religious traditions began there—Judaism, Christianity, and Islam—and its natural resources, including oil, have made parts of the Middle East prosperous. The world's tallest building is in Dubai, and one of the world's great news networks, al Jazeera, is based in the emirate of Qatar.

As we begin to put the Middle East into a global context, however, we have to figure out exactly what we're talking about. The term originated with Europeans, who looked from Europe toward the Far East of China and Japan and found a lot of real estate in between, including Southwestern Asia. The fabled "Orient Express" of European railroads—the train from Paris that headed south and east—ended in Istanbul, making Turkey the gateway to the "Orient" of the Middle East.

What these Europeans had in mind when they talked about the Middle East was primarily the area east of the Mediterranean Sea, including all of the Arabian Peninsula and the land north of it, up to the Black and Caspian seas. (This might be a good time to check your Middle Eastern map to see for yourself how difficult it is to define the area.) If the northern and southern boundaries of the region are relatively clear, how far east should we go—Is Iran a part of the Middle East? Afghanistan? Pakistan? And how far west do the boundaries of the Middle East extend? Egypt is often considered part of the Middle East, and it is in Africa, of course (though a bit of Egypt extends to the eastern side of the Red Sea and is thus a part of the Arabian Peninsula). Other North African countries, such as Libya, Tunisia, Algeria, and Morocco, at times have also been considered to be part of the Middle East.

The region is not defined just by territory, but also by two other important cultural factors: language and religion. Arabic is the dominant language, and since the residents of North African countries speak Arabic, along with local languages, that would explain why Egypt (and often other North African countries) is included. The other cultural feature of the Middle East is the religion of Islam. Since most Turks and Iranians are Muslim, their countries are often also brought into the Middle Eastern circle even though their languages are Turkish and Farsi, respectively, not Arabic. And there are some other anomalies. Israel, for example, is predominantly Jewish and its language Hebrew, and Lebanon contains a significant Christian population, but both are squarely in the Middle East. There are also old Christian communities in Egypt, Syria, and Iraq, while the Jewish community in Iran is likewise centuries old.

The Middle East has been at the intersection of civilizations from very ancient times. Over two thousand years ago it was caught between great Persian empires to the East, Egyptian dynasties to the West, and Greek and Roman imperial powers to the Northwest. It was situated in the middle of the ancient Mediterranean world. Greek and Roman ideas intermingled with Egyptian and Persian thought, and locations such as Ephesus, Tyre, Alexandria, and Carthage—cities that are now in the nations of Turkey, Lebanon, Egypt, and Tunisia, respectively—were important trade and political centers. Hence, the ancient Middle East was in the center of the global culture of its age. Global currents flowed into and through it.

The Middle East contributed enormously to global culture as well. Perhaps most significant are the ancient cultural traditions of the Mesopotamian and Nile River civilizations. Babylonian mythology—including the creation of the earth out of chaos and the story of surviving the great flood—became a part of the world's literary heritage. The Semitic culture of ancient Israel was influenced by these traditions, and from these roots came Judaism and later Christianity. The Middle East is also the cradle of the Islamic tradition, which recalls that the line of prophecy reaches back to Christian and Jewish forebears.

These Middle Eastern religious cultures have influenced the world. The diaspora of Jewish communities were scattered from Europe to China to South America. Christianity became the dominant religion of the Roman Empire; it became so entrenched in Europe that many have thought of it as a European religion—even though in the twenty-first century there are more Christians in Africa, Asia, and South America than there are in Europe and North America. Islam also has become a global religion, having spread rapidly throughout the Middle East and beyond, from Spain to Indonesia. In the mobile demographics of the global era, significant communities of Muslims have taken root in Europe, North America, Africa, Asia, and elsewhere.

What holds Muslim culture together is the centrality of a tradition rooted in the Middle East. The Middle Eastern language of Arabic is the textual base of the tradition, and all pious Muslims must learn enough Arabic to read and even memorize the Holy Qur'an and to recite the daily prayers. The central pilgrimage place is Mecca, on the Western side of the Arabian peninsula, and undertaking a pilgrimage—the *haj*—at least once is an obligation of every Muslim who is able to afford it. The great legal and textual traditions of Islam are preserved in the Middle East, while the theological scholarship of al Al-Azhar University in Cairo serves the entire Muslim world.

Thus, although Islam reaches out to the most distant corners of the world, it is also a global center. Perhaps for this reason, strident new movements of Islamic politics that challenged secular Western notions of globalization emerged at the end of the twentieth century and the first decades of the twenty-first. In some cases, these movements were local and nationalist, resenting the foreign intrusion of Western secular ideologies. In other cases, such as the jihadi activism associated with the al Qaeda network, they were transnational in scope. In a sense, they were fighting for their own vision of an alternative globalization, one conceptualized as a global Islam.

The readings in this section begin with an evocative image of the Middle East, describing the great sweep of desert landscapes and their impact on the breadth of Muslim political visions. This excerpt is by Mohammed Bamyeh, a sociologist of Palestinian background who teaches at the University of Pittsburgh and from whose award-winning book, *The Social Origins of Islam,* this excerpt is taken. It is followed by an excerpt from an essay by Said Arjomand on the global reach of the Islamic tradition. The sociologist Arjomand was born in Iran and trained at the University of Chicago and now teaches at the State University of New York, Stony Brook.

The next selection raises the question of whether Middle Eastern conflicts are more religious than are conflicts in other parts of the world. The author, Jonathan Fox, examines empirical evidence to find the answer. His conclusion is that Middle Eastern conflicts are more intense but that religion is not the cause of this increased fervor. Rather, he suggests that historical and social conditions of the region may have led to this situation. Fox is a political scientist trained at the University of Maryland, who teaches at Bar-Ilan University in Israel.

The final reading is on the relation of religion and politics in the Middle East in a post–Arab Spring world. The author, Barah Mikaïl, argues that religion continues to be a factor in political organization in the second decade of the twenty-first century, though he contends that it now appears through democratic processes and not through the violent means that some oppositional religious politics took at the end of the twentieth century and the beginning of the twenty-first. Mikaïl is a senior researcher at the European think tank FRIDE (Fundacion para las Relaciones Internacionales y el Dialogo Exterior), with degrees in political science and international relations from universities in Paris.

✗ THE IDEOLOGY OF THE HORIZONS

Mohammed Bamyeh

We are speaking of a terrain in which life repeats itself both endlessly and precariously. Here, the eyes of the inhabitant open daily to a topography of solemn solitude, far more imposing to the soul than the minuscule islets of social life encountered thereupon. The desert is a sphere of absolute speechlessness. What is strange in the desert is speaking, thinking in words, dialogizing, communicating. In this vast expanse, ridiculing all notions of paramount subjectivity, profuse wilderness covers all visible destinations between the here and all horizons; the human actor is but an insignificant footnote to the space; to think of presence in dogmatic terms of space—where space as a *habitat* is at best a seasonal interruption—is to practically annul oneself. Only a perennially visible enigma, the *horizon,* sets the boundaries of knowable nature. Like the sea, the horizon of the desert stands out in contrast to the landscape as the unreachable terminus of nature, its inconclusive conclusion.

The Arabian Peninsula—the cradle of Islam—is dominated by the two vast deserts that occupy the bulk of the land. The great Nufud wilderness claims much of the north, while the Empty Quarter, one of the most arid and impassable deserts on earth, stretches over half a million square kilometers in the south. Such immense horizons confound the ideas of beginning and end, depositing the concept of eternity in the heart of the concrete present. This ideology of the horizons . . . is oblivious to human structures of presence as a purposeful progression of moments where one constructs for oneself a path in time, periodizes existence, valorizes destination. In other words, such an ideology sees in the spectacle of the horizon not so much an inviting mirage as the most fundamental picture of the emptiness of grandiose human quests.

There are notable exceptions, of course, to this story. The recurrent Semitic migrations *outside* of the peninsula during the four millennia preceding Islam were clearly intended to free population groups from such a magnitude of resourcelessness. But we are concerned with those who stayed and developed sedentary societies and sedentary ways of looking that challenged the desert's inhospitability to any other life than one of permanent wandering. The story of Islam, along with many contemporaneous theological and cosmological experiments, rotates around such tensions in the ways of seeing and assessing the outside—and by extension the inside—of human society.

But before such a permanent encampment, the concreteness of existential emptiness could be derived purely by looking. No exceptional ability to see into the nature of things was required. The eternity of the same readily revealed itself to all those who had the patience to pause long enough to appreciate the horizons, the boundaries of the magnificent desert, and long enough to allow the horizon to fully transform itself into an idea, to become a part of seeing in the most fundamental way, in other words, to become an "ideology." The ideology of horizons is a peculiar production of this form of wilderness. And it is an ideology that sustains wandering. Here, the horizon, consisting of visible sameness, visible emptiness, visible lack of any promise whatever, nullifies the quest after it. But on the other hand, such a horizon speaks of the conclusion of the desert and promises an unknown beyond, a different nature that cannot be seen without wandering toward the horizon. And in this other capacity, the horizon instigates the quest for that beyond.

This perplexing appeal of the horizon situates it exactly at the borderline, between two modes of wandering. One mode is to wander as a *natural fate,* preordained by the indifference of the desolate landscape to ordinary human needs. The other mode is to invest in the wandering a teleological scheme of crossing over into a land of lush riverbanks, where the horizon would gradually disappear as an invitation, goal, or boundary of permanent wandering. In both cases, the desert itself only promises traces, ruins, and betrayals of past loves and lives; nothing more. One wanders, and one forgets through wandering—in effect eliminating from view—the desert's failure to sustain other than its own overpowering expanse, eternal and normative as it seems. Here, if there is a destination, one reaches it by simply moving. No elaborate schemes are required. No scheming subject is required. In fact, no subject at all is required. Until poetic, cosmological, and thematic discourses about that nature began to be produced, valued, and preserved, there were no forms imposed on it. For the wanderer, the desert formed itself and dissipated along the way, with no everlasting images. Such a nature formed itself in the mode of interruptions, as though to encourage existence a little longer, precisely when the wanderer was about to perish. This is how the nomadic ode itself proceeded until exhaustion (and *not* conclusion) consumed its energy. But until the regular production and preservation of discourse and sedentarism, such interruptions were no more than erasable bursts of life. There was wandering, but there were no roads, no pathways, no passages into an alternative ideology or life, no meaning for time or direction. Unless one ceased to be a nomad, nothing altered that eternal presence.

Throughout the peninsula, movement was the norm and halting the exception. Agriculture, the primary precondition for settlement, was possible as a large-scale activity only in Yemen and the Green Mountain in Uman. Some isolated agricultural colonies also developed in some elevated regions of Hijaz and Najd, the most important of which was in and around Ta'if, which supplied Mecca with much of its food. Mecca itself, the birthplace of Islam, was far from being an agricultural community. In fact, it grew like a wild thorn amid an arid environment of solid rock. It survived only because of the growing world trade that passed through it. . . . But in spite of its world connection, Mecca, as a particular form of settlement, was left to determine its own ideology with reference to its own preconditions and surroundings, where nomadism and wandering predominated for enormous distances in all directions. With the exception of Yemen, the great powers of the time—the Romans, the Sassanids, the Abyssinians—displayed little interest in any part of the Arabian Peninsula.

Thus, the particular story of permanent halting in Mecca contains simultaneous elements of knowledge of and independence from all the great powers of the epoch (including peninsular powers such as Yemen). Mecca's location deep in the desert insulated the city from the fate of the other nascent trading centers that were annexed to such powers. Palmyra and Petra were annexed by Rome, Aden was dominated by the Abyssinians and Sassanids. But it was also the relations with such powers that stabilized a form of halting, which would otherwise have been devoured by a nature that does not usually allow it. The Qur'an itself registers a profound awareness of Mecca's precarious exceptionalism, nestled as it is in a resourceless terrain that under normal circumstances would not have allowed it to survive beyond a season or two. Such an exception, in turn, could be available only to foundational projects associated with prophetic effort—Abraham's in this case: "Abraham said: 'Lord, I have settled some of my offspring in a barren valley near Your Sacred House. . . . Put in the hearts of men kindness towards them, and provide them with the earth's fruits, so they may give thanks.'"

In this case, an act of halting—indeed, an expression of an intention to halt forever—was seen to depend on God's leave and bounty. This is not to say, however, that a wandering nomad had no need for deities or that the sedentary God's credentials consisted in his assistance in a mere earthly and immediate task. The story is far more complex than that. . . . [T]he decision and capacity to halt involve major metaphysical reorientations. Much of the dilemmas of Abraham's descendants, indeed, consisted of the question of how to overcome the ideology of the horizons, with all of its underpinnings. Such underpinnings had involved an attenuation of the idea of displacement, a cyclical vision of nature, a materialist rather than spiritualist contextualization of the idea of fate, an understanding of human and logical finitude in terms of processional exhaustion rather than of summary verdict or unifying conclusion, a suspicion of subjective construction and planning, a tendency to mock abstract authority, and an almost reflexive antipathy to grand political schemes in general. In an important sense, the idea of a monotheistic God exemplified a sustained attack on the ideology of the horizons and an effort to place the experiences of halting and wandering under a different order of regulation than those the nomad was willing to tolerate. . . . [There is a] rich dialectic interaction between that ideology of the horizons and the emergent faith and the resulting metamorphoses in all social and discursive spheres affected by both. But first, where does the story begin? If halting had accentuated for Abraham the necessity of God, what did that same halting signify for a more resilient nomad?

THINKING GLOBALLY ABOUT ISLAM

Said Amir Arjomand

Virtually from its inception, Islam has been a global religion. It is the youngest of what Max Weber calls the world religions of salvation. Far more than with Christianity, the old dynamics of the expansion of Islam as a world religion have remained in full vigor, even in the twenty-first century when Islam now has a billion adherents around the world. In the last quarter of the twentieth century a new variety of religious movements arose in Islam—as in Christianity and Judaism—that have been called "fundamentalist." Although such movements have been a distinctive aspect of contemporary Islamic society they by no means comprise all aspects of the contemporary expansion of Islam as a universalist religion of salvation. . . .

THE UNIVERSALIST EXPANSION OF ISLAM

The Islamic era begins with the migration of Muhammad from Mecca to Medina in 622. It was in Medina that Muhammad built a society on the basis of Islam, the new religion he had preached to a small number of Meccan followers as the final revelation in the Abrahamic tradition of monotheism. In the last years of his life, Muhammad conquered Mecca and unified the tribes of Arabia. After his death in 632, his successors, the Caliphs, fought the refractory tribes in Arabia, and conquered vast territories of the Persian and Roman empires. The major step in the institutionalization of Islam after Muhammad's death was the establishment of the text of the Qur'an under the third Caliph. The canonization of the text of the Qur'an as the Word of God made Islam the religion of the book, even more than the other Abrahamic religions. As the literal Word of God, recited by his Prophet, the Qur'an was a holy scripture *par excellence*. Its transcendent authority made possible the development of sectarian and mystical variants of Islam that diverged in their interpretation of the faith from the mainstream.

In addition to studying the Qur'an, several schools of pious learning began to collect and transmit the Traditions—reports of the sayings and deeds—of the Prophet. The influence of this pious religious learning on legal practice grew during the first two centuries of Islam. Consequently, the institution that emerged as the main embodiment of Islam by the end of its second century was neither a church, as in Christianity, nor a monastic system, as in Buddhism, but the Islamic law (*shari'a*). The law became the central institution in Islam, as had been the case with Rabbinical Judaism. The Islamic law was in principle based on the Qur'an, the Traditions of the Prophet and the consensus of the jurists, and remained, in Weber's terms, a "jurists' law." The jurists formed schools of law, and engaged both in teaching students and in legal consultation. Their compiled opinions acquired the force of law. With the consolidation of Islamic law as the main institutional embodiment of Islam, the scholar-jurists, the *ulema,* emerged as its guardians and authoritative interpreters.

The contribution of sects and heterodoxies to social transformation in the Islamic civilization has been considerable. Modern historical scholarship of the past hundred years has significantly altered our picture of the expansion of Islam in the seventh century and its penetration into the ancient societies that became parts of a vast Arab empire of conquest. As a result of modern scholarship, we know that Islam, as distinct from Arab domination, was not spread swiftly by the sword, but rather gradually and by popular missionary movements, often in defiance of the fiscal interest of the state.

During the first three centuries of Islamic history, three important groups of sectarian movements—Kharijism, Murji`ism (which later merged with mainstream Islam) and Shi`ism—played a very important role in the conversion of the non-Arab subjects of the empire to Islam.

The Arab confederate tribes which ruled a vast empire of conquest were not keen on the conversion of its subject populations. It was only with the Abbasid revolution—Islam's social revolution beyond Arabia in the mid-eighth century—that the universalist potential of Islam as a world religion of salvation was fully released from the superordinate interest of Arab imperial domination. With the Abbasid revolution, a society based on the equality of Arab and non-Arab Muslims came into being. It was in this society and during the first century of Abbasid rule that the institutionalization of Islamic law was achieved. Meanwhile, from the mid-ninth century onward, a movement known as Hanbalism sought to unify sundry traditionalist groups, first against philosophical and theological rationalism and later against Shi`ism. Among the movements that account for the spread of Islam in the formative period, Hanbalism acted as an important force in the intensive penetration and consolidation of Islam among the urban population. It opposed rationalism in matters of faith and insisted on the unconditional acceptance of the Qur'an and the Prophetic Traditions as its unalterable scriptural fundamentals. Hanbalism can therefore be regarded as the prototype of Islamic fundamentalism. Furthermore, by branding sectarian movements as heretical, the Hanbalites accelerated the process of mutual self-definition between the sects and the mainstream. The mainstream Muslims increasingly came to see themselves as standing against all schism and division, and advocating the unity of the Muslim community on the basis of the Tradition (*Sunna*) of the Prophet, hence the term Sunnism as the designation for the mainstream Islam.

In the subsequent centuries, however, the pattern of institutionalization of Islam through Islamic law showed its definite and rather rigid limits. Intensive Islamicization through the law could not facilitate Islam's missionary expansion, nor could it penetrate deeply into society. The mission to convert the population of the frontier and rural areas increasingly fell upon a new mass movement, Sufism (Islamic mysticism). Popular Sufism became the instruments of the spread of Islam both into the geographical periphery of the Muslim world and into the lower ranks of Muslim society, especially in the rural areas. For centuries, popular Sufism offered a distinct variant of Islam that was in many ways the opposite of the scriptural fundamentalism of the Hanbalites. From the fifteenth century onward, popular Shi`ism adopted many of the practices of the Sufis such the veneration of the holy Imams and their descendants, in place of the Sufi saints, and pilgrimages to the shrines.

Since the beginning of the early modern period, a number of Islamic movements have responded to the challenge of popular religiosity by advocating the revival or renewal (*tajdid*) of Islam by returning to the Book of God and the pristine Islam of the Prophet. These movements can be classified as orthodox reformism, as their aim was the reform and purification of religious beliefs and practices with close attention to the Qur'an and the Prophetic Tradition as the scriptural foundations of Islam. An important movement grew from within the Hanbalite fundamentalist tradition in Arabia to take up this challenge of popular Sufism and Shi`ism in the eighteenth century. It is known as the Wahhabi movement, after its founder Muhammad b. Abd al-Wahhab (d. 1792) who had visited Shi`ite Iran and come into contact with popular Sufism in Arabia and considered both as disguised polytheism. His followers sacked the Shi`ite holy shrines in Iraq and destroyed the Sufi orders in Arabia. Wahhabi fundamentalism rejected popular religious practices as polytheistic and aimed at returning to the pure monotheism of early Islam with the cry, "Back to the Book and the Tradition of the Prophet!"

Since the nineteenth century, Islam has faced the political and cultural challenge of the West. The Muslim response to this challenge can be simplified into three main types of reaction: secularism, Islamic modernism and Islamic fundamentalism. Since World War II, this cultural and institutional response to Western domination has been deeply affected by an increasing vitality of Islam that has been firmly rooted in processes of social change. Throughout this time, the evolution of Islam as a universalist religion has continued. This evolution has been quite obvious in conversions to Islam in Black Africa and Southeast Asia but much less obvious in the form of intensive penetration of Islam within Muslim societies. The vitality of Islam caused by the social change of the last half-century has created major advantages for scriptural fundamentalism over Sufism in popular religion, with the consequence of greater penetration of scriptural Islam into the social lives of the Muslims. . . .

ISLAM AND GLOBALIZATION

Continuous improvement and declining cost of transportation since World War II has greatly increased the number of pilgrims to Mecca, and of missionaries from Africa and Asia to the main centers of Islamic learning in the Middle East. It should be noted that this aspect of globalization reinforces Islam's old universalism institutionalized around the Hajj—pilgrimage to Mecca. In fact, improved sea transportation since the seventeenth century had encouraged international contact among Muslims and stimulated transnational movements for orthodox reformism and renewal (*tajdid*).

The post-colonial era has witnessed massive immigration of Muslims into Western Europe and North America where sizeable Muslim communities were formed. Meanwhile, there has been unprecedented global integration of Muslims through the mass media. The media contributed to the success of the Islamic revolution in Iran by enabling the Iranian opposition abroad to orchestrate widespread mass mobilization inside of Iran. Khomeini's aides abroad and his followers in Iran were able to coordinate their nationwide protests by using telephone lines. Khomeini's revolutionary speeches were disseminated by cassettes through the networks of mosques and religious associations. The Persian program of the British Broadcasting Corporation sympathetically reported Khomeini's activities and proclamations, and these reports were avidly received by millions of households in Iran to the dismay of the Shah and his political elite.

The international repercussions of the Rushdie case also illustrates the impact of the media on a globally integrated Muslim world. The protests and burning of his *Satanic Verses* by indignant Muslims began in Bradford, England. These were broadcast throughout the world and stimulated violent protests in Pakistan, which were in turn internationally broadcast. This media exposure gave Khomeini the opportunity to reassert his claim to revolutionary leadership of the Muslim world in the last year of his life. Only a few months after accepting the cease-fire in the war with Iraq, which had been like "drinking a cup of poison," he had the final satisfaction of issuing, on February 14, 1989, an injunction (*fatwa*) sanctioning the death of Salman Rushdie, a non-Iranian writer who lived in England, for apostasy.

The effects of globalization on Islam are interpreted variously. Eickelman (1998) sees the combined effect of globalization, the growth of education and vigorous discussion of Islam in books and in public debates as the making of an Islamic Reformation. According to Eickelman, the Islamicization of social life has been far reaching but also dispersed, lacking any focus or single thrust. Barber, by contrast, puts Islam in the front line of the global clash between "Jihad vs. McWorld." He sees the effect of globalization concentrated in a sharply focused and vehement "anti-Western anti-universalist struggle" (Barber 1995: 207). Barber obliterates the distinction between Islamic fundamentalism and Islam. It is not just Islamic fundamentalism but Islam, *tout court,* that nurtures conditions favorable to Jihad: "parochialism, anti-modernism, exclusiveness and hostility to 'others'" (Barber 1995: 205).

I believe Barber's view on Islam and globalization, which is widely shared by journalists and commentators, is fundamentally mistaken. Not only is there variety in Islamic fundamentalism . . . , but Islamic fundamentalism is by no means identical with all the contemporary manifestations of Islam as a universalist religion. Urbanization, development of roads and transportation, the printing revolution and other contemporary processes of social change, including globalization, all reinforce trends toward expansion and intensive penetration of society that are typical of Islam as a universalist religion. These trends are not exclusively fundamentalist. One would therefore have to agree with Eickelman on the dispersion of the current trends in Islamicization, whether or not one concurs with his value-judgement that they constitute Reformation. One important question remains to be answered, however: How does globalization affect the old forms of Islamic universalism?

An interesting feature of globalization is the unfolding of anti-global sentiments in particularistic, variety-producing movements that seek local legitimacy but nevertheless have a global frame of self-reference. Global integration induces Muslims to emphasize their unique identity within their own frames of reference—cultures that can be at once universal and local. There can be no doubt that global integration has made many Muslims seek to appropriate universalist institutions by what might be called Islamic cloning. We thus hear more and more about "Islamic science," "Islamic Human

Rights," and "the Islamic international system." There are also a variety of organizations modeled after the United Nations and its offshoots, most notably the Organization of the Islamic Conference, which was founded in 1969 and whose meeting in Tehran in December 1997 was attended by the representatives of the fifty-five member countries, including many Muslim heads of state. This phenomenon is a direct result of globalization. To confuse it with fundamentalism is a grave mistake. It is, however, a reactive tendency and I would call it defensive counter-universalism.

The dynamics of Islam as a universalist religion therefore includes a fundamentalist trend, alongside many others, that has been reinforced by some of the contemporary processes of social change, including globalization. Islam also has acquired a new and sharply political edge under the impact of political modernization. It would be misleading, however, to speak simply of a shift from universalism to fundamentalism. For one thing, missionary traditional Islam continues to flourish, and has adopted modern technology to its growth. More importantly, the main impact of globalization on the Islamic world has not been the growth of fundamentalism but what I call defensive counter-universalism. Fundamentalism can reasonably be characterized as selectively modern and electively traditional; it is therefore assimilative despite its intent. The assimilative character of defensive counter-universalism is more pronounced. It has already resulted in the assimilation of universal organizational forms, and albeit restrictively, of universal ideas such as human rights and rights of women. It is difficult to escape the conclusion that, despite its intent, defensive counter-universalism is inevitably a step toward the modernization of the Islamic tradition.

ARE MIDDLE EAST CONFLICTS MORE RELIGIOUS?

Jonathan Fox

If, as many believe and scholarship confirms, religion is particularly important in ethnic conflicts involving Muslims, how does this affect the nature of conflict in the Middle East?

This is a simple question, but finding an accurate answer is not at all simple. It is complicated by two interrelated factors. First, due to differing perspectives and differing political agendas, interpretations of events in the region vary wildly, and accuracy is often lost. This problem is not limited to the study of the Middle East and, in fact, has been a central issue in political science since its inception. For instance, Karl Deutsch points out that comparative methodology, which consists of analyzing cases using introspection, intuition, and insight, while a powerful tool for analysis, is limited by our imaginations and preconceived notions. That is, a researcher who uses the method of familiarizing himself with as many facts as possible as well as with the insights of other scholars can easily be influenced by his own preconceptions.

This can be problematic because due to such preconceptions we often think we see relationships that we expect to see even if they do not exist, and we often fail to see relationships that do exist but that we never expected to exist or even imagined might exist. Applied to the issue at hand, we must ask ourselves if the perception that religion is particularly important in the Middle East and is the driving force behind many of the region's conflicts is accurate, or merely a reflection of what we expect to see. To some extent, this is true of the study of religion and ethnic conflict in the Middle East.

Second, the issue of Islam's role in generating conflict has become especially controversial since Samuel Huntington asserted that Islam has "bloody borders" and predicted that the dynamics of civilizational conflict in the post-Cold War era would reinforce and intensify this phenomenon. His analysis is part of a larger notion that conflicts are increasingly defined by a "clash of civilizations." Huntington holds three points: that post-Cold War conflict is mostly between world civilizations defined primarily by religion; that conflicts involving Islamic civilization will be particularly common and violent; and that Islamic civilization will be the greatest threat to Western civilization. While many, if not all, aspects of Huntington's theory are controversial, his arguments concerning Islam have found acceptance among some policymakers. And that may, as some maintain, make Huntington's analyses self-fulfilling. That is, if many Westerners expect Islam to be a threat and are disposed to perceive such a threat, whether it exists or not, then the expectations may wind up influencing policy.

Thus can political agendas, preconceptions, and popular academic theories obfuscate and perhaps even alter the role of religion in the Middle East. These complications make an accurate assessment of Islam's role in Middle Eastern conflict all the more essential.

This study uses an empirical method to provide a perspective on the issue different from the comparative approach. While the empirical method has its limitations—primarily, it can analyze only what can be measured and measurements of social, political, and economic factors are often imperfect—it also has three advantages. It allows us to test and perhaps falsify theories. It makes clear what factors produce its results, and anyone analyzing the same data will get the same results. Also, it often produces surprising findings that would have never resulted from the comparative approach because no one would have looked for them.

This analysis proceeds in two stages. First, the results from previous empirical analyses are summarized. Second, we examine data on ethnic conflict to assess the extent and nature of the influence of religion in the Middle East.

PREVIOUS FINDINGS

Empirical analyses, several by this author, have established that the relationship between religion and conflict in general can be summed up as follows:

Religious differences make conflict more likely and more intense. The more diverse a country's religious population, the more violent its domestic conflicts tend to be. Similarly, when religious issues are important in ethnic conflicts, political, economic, and cultural discrimination, and rebellion all tend to increase. Religious differences also make international wars more likely.

Religious issues influence the dynamics of conflicts.   When religious issues are important in an ethnic conflict, religious institutions tend to facilitate unrest; but they tend to suppress conflict when religious issues are not important. Similarly, in countries where it is more legitimate to invoke religion in political discourse, ethnic conflicts generally focus more on religious issues as opposed to other political, cultural, and economic issues. Also, religious differences between combatants and religious affinities between minorities and those likely to intervene make foreign intervention in ethnic conflicts more probable.

Religion shapes discrimination against ethnic minorities.   Religious and non-religious discrimination is more likely in states where it is legitimate to use religion in political discourse and in conflicts where religious issues are important. Religious discrimination is likely against minorities that are otherwise culturally similar to the majority group—that is, where religion is the chief differentiating characteristic between the majority and the minority. Perhaps connected, religious minorities seeking autonomy are more likely to suffer non-religious discrimination than ethnic minorities who are not distinguished by religion.

Autocratic regimes are more likely than non-autocratic regimes to discriminate against religious minorities.   Autocracies engage in higher average levels of discrimination against ethno-religious minorities than do democracies, but it is those regimes that are somewhere between full autocracies and full democracies (and that are known as semi-democracies), that discriminate the least. At the same time, regime track type seems not to be correlated with discrimination against ethnic minorities that are not religiously different from the majority group in their states.

Regimes in Muslim states are more autocratic.   One study finds that Muslim states are the most autocratic states in the world, based on a measure of the extent to which a state is a liberal democracy as well as on a separate measure of institutional democracy. However, this study finds no relationship between Islam and a third measure which focuses on political rights.

Another study, which uses the measure for institutional democracy, finds these trends particularly pronounced in the Middle East.

Taken together, these five results suggest that Middle Eastern conflicts should be particularly frequent and intense. One would expect religious factors to be particularly important and to exacerbate ethnic conflict in that region; religious discrimination to be high; and political behavior to be particularly influenced by religious differences between groups. This is especially true given the region's high level of autocracy combined with the particular importance of religion in the region. Is this in fact the case?

The Minorities at Risk (MAR) dataset, with information on 267 politically active ethnic minorities throughout the world, plus additional data collected by this author, provides insight into the nature of the Middle East's ethno-religious conflicts.

Three preliminary points: (1) The MAR dataset, developed by the MAR project headed by Ted R. Gurr, is particularly useful for our purposes. It documents all instances of ethnic conflict between 1945 and 1998 and contains a reasonably accurate list of all ethnic groups that are actively pursuing political agendas, violently or otherwise, or that suffer from high levels of discrimination. The dataset has been in existence since the mid-1980s and has received considerable attention and criticism which, over time, have led to a fairly accurate list of the groups that meet the stated criteria. Along with data collected separately on religion for use with the dataset, it constitutes one of the few aggregate-level datasets on religion and conflict that does more than simply measure whether the groups involved are of different religions.

(2) For the purposes of this study, an ethnic minority is considered to be of a different religion than the majority group in that state if 80 percent of the population of the minority group is of a religion different from the majority group. Protestant and Catholic Christianity are considered separate religions, as are the Sunni and Shi'i branches of Islam.

(3) MAR's data refer only to conflicts involving ethnic minorities within states and not to conflicts within the same ethnic group. This means, for example, that the conflict between Egypt's Coptic minority and Muslim majority is included but the same country's conflict between the Islamist movement and the Egyptian state is not.

Are ethnic conflicts between religiously differentiated groups particularly prevalent in the Middle East? Yes: . . . 54 percent of the politically significant ethnic minorities in the Middle East are also religious minorities. Only Asia scores higher and then only slightly so. In the rest of the world, ethnic minorities are considerably less often religious ones.

An examination of religious factors in ethno-religious conflicts reinforces this picture. Religious factors are considered to be present when any, and especially all, of the following conditions are fulfilled: religion is a significant issue in the conflict; religious discrimination exists; a minority group demands more religious rights; and religion is invoked in political discourse.

Comparing the results for the Middle East to other world regions and Muslim-majority states outside of the Middle East allows us to see something important: whether the Middle East is unique in the intensity of conflicts with religious factors—or whether such conflicts exist in other world regions or are common to all Muslim states. That, in turn, allows us to say whether the explanation for such conflicts is regionally based (unique to the Middle East) or religiously based (common to states with Muslim majorities).

It turns out that all four religious factors surface considerably more often in the Middle East than in other regions. From this, one can conclude that religion is indeed particularly important in the Middle East's ethno-religious conflicts.

Comparisons involving non-Middle Eastern states with Muslim majorities are particularly interesting. In such states, all four religious factors occur more often in ethno-religious conflicts than in non-Middle Eastern states lacking Muslim majorities—but less often than in Middle Eastern states. Turning this around, ethnic conflicts in Middle Eastern states more often involve religious factors than similar conflicts in non-Middle Eastern states with Muslim majorities. The latter conflicts, in turn, more often involve religious factors than do similar conflicts in non-Middle Eastern states lacking Muslim majorities. Based on these findings, Islam provides a partial explanation for the unique importance of religion in Middle East conflicts but it cannot be considered a full explanation. Other factors must be at work.

To assess whether the Middle East's ethno-religious conflicts are particularly violent or intense, [I measure] . . . the presence of seven factors important in ethnic conflict: political discrimination, economic discrimination, cultural discrimination, repression, an expressed desire by a minority for autonomy, political demonstrations, and rebellion (terrorism, guerrilla warfare, or armed insurrection). Except for political discrimination, the Middle East scores near the world average on these measures. This permits us to conclude that the Middle East is unique in the importance that religion plays in its ethno-religious conflicts, but those conflicts are otherwise mostly similar to the ones occurring elsewhere.

Under what type of regimes do ethno-religious conflicts mostly take place—autocratic, semi-democratic, or democratic? [I find] . . . that 86 percent of Middle Eastern ethno-religious conflicts occur in autocratic states. This is a particularly strong finding considering that all of the 14 percent of cases of Middle Eastern ethno-religious conflict occurring in non-autocratic states occur in Israel. However, it is not a particularly surprising finding given that the Middle East is the world's most autocratic region. Be that as it may, these results show that all Muslim majorities in the Middle East involved in ethno-religious conflicts, as documented by the MAR dataset, preside over autocratic states. As with the presence of religious factors, Islam can provide a partial explanation for this thorough-going autocracy in the Middle East, but not a full explanation. Non-Middle Eastern Muslim majorities involved in ethno-religious conflicts are not uniformly autocratic, although they do rule autocratic states more than twice as often as non-Muslim majorities (52 percent as compared to 20 percent). More importantly, these results imply that there may be a link between Islam's, and particularly the Middle East's, association with autocracy and the finding that in Islam and the Middle East religion tends to be particularly important.

This brings up a final question: do Islam and autocracy in the Middle East combine to make religion particularly important in the region's ethno-religious conflicts? This requires a comparison of the Middle East with the non-Middle East. If the disproportionate importance of religion in Middle Eastern ethno-religious conflicts is due to a combination of Islam and autocracy, we would expect the religious factors to be similarly important outside of the Middle East in states that are both Muslim and autocratic.

To measure this, conflicts in countries outside the Middle East are broken down into five categories (with some overlap between the categories): all autocratic states; states that are both autocratic and Muslim; states that are autocratic but not Muslim; semi-democratic states; and democratic states. . . . [E]thnic conflicts in Muslim autocracies outside the Middle East include religious factors less often than within the Middle East. Ethnic conflicts in non-Muslim autocracies outside the Middle East include three of the four factors less often than do non-Middle Eastern Islamic autocracies. Most notably, outside of the Middle East, Muslim autocracies discriminate against religious minorities less often than do non-Muslim autocracies. These results rule out Islam as an explanation for the disproportionate importance of religion in Middle East ethno-religious conflicts. After all, if Islam resulted in the increased importance of religion, we would have expected to find that religion was considerably more important in non-Middle Eastern Islamic autocracies than in other non-Middle Eastern autocracies as measured by at least a majority of the variables. In fact, the reverse is true and the non-Islamic autocracies scored considerably higher on two of four variables and slightly higher on a third.

Autocracy is also ruled out as an explanation: if autocracy were the sole explanation for the disproportionate importance of religious factors in the Middle East, we would expect it to have a uniform impact outside of the Middle East, which is not the case.

What about the Middle East's combination of Islam and autocracy? Well, outside of the Middle East, the combination is associated with results quite different from the same combination in the Middle East.

CONCLUSIONS

This study has both expected and surprising results.

Religion is more important in Middle Eastern ethnic conflicts than elsewhere. Religion is important in the ethnic conflicts of all Muslim states, and it is more important in the Middle East than in Muslim states outside the region. This means that while Islam may provide a partial explanation for the particular importance of religion in the region, it cannot provide a full explanation. One potential explanation for this is the historical importance of religion in the Middle East, a region that gave birth to three of the world's major religions. On the other hand, this historical importance may also mean that whatever it is that makes religion particularly important in the Middle East is not a new phenomenon, and the findings presented here are simply the latest manifestation of an age-old phenomenon.

The Middle East is the most autocratic and least democratic region in the world. Muslim states outside of the Middle East are found to be more autocratic than other non-Middle Eastern states but less autocratic than Middle Eastern states. Again, Muslim states outside the Middle East are more often autocratic than their non-Muslim counterparts but considerably less often autocratic than those in the Middle East. Thus, Islam may provide no more than a partial explanation for the autocracy of the region.

In this case, history may provide an alternate explanation. Democracy and the liberal ideologies upon which it is based were developed in the West. Accordingly, it is not surprising that the West is the most democratic region of the world. Other regions particularly influenced by the West, such as the states of Latin America—which began as colonies of the West and whose inhabitants speak almost exclusively Western languages—also tend to be highly democratic, at least of late. Most of the former Soviet bloc is considered European but can be distinguished from the West in that it had limited historical exposure to central European experiences including the Reformation, Renaissance and Enlightenment. For nearly a century it followed another Western ideology, Marxism, and is now in the process of democratization. Other than the Middle East, the regions that are the most autocratic are Asia and Africa, regions that have retained much of their own cultures despite Western influences. Thus, the link between the Middle East and autocracy may be due more to cultural and historical momentum than anything else. Also, the link between Islam and autocracy may be due to the fact that most Islamic states are in the Middle East, Asia, and Africa, the regions that appear to have the highest levels of rejection of Western styles of government.

The level of ethnic conflict in the Middle East is about average.   This comes as a surprise, given that religion is disproportionately important in the Middle East and that the region is disproportionately autocratic. It may be due to a feeling among the region's inhabitants that religion and autocracy are normal, at least within the Middle Eastern context, and therefore do not deserve any special response. Perhaps expectations in the Middle East are lower. In the rest of the world, participants in ethnic conflicts are more sensitive to the presence of religious issues and more likely to respond to them than in the Middle East. To be specific, perhaps the Shi'i minority in Saudi Arabia, the Copts in Egypt, and the Christian and Baha'i minorities in Iran understand that religious discrimination by the autocratic governments of the region is par for the course. Because of this, even though they suffer from high levels of religious discrimination, they engaged in no protest or rebellion in 1998 (the most recent year for which data [are] currently available). By contrast, in eastern Europe, where religion was suppressed by communist regimes until the 1990s, groups that suffered from religious discrimination tended to react more forcibly in 1998: the Turks in Bulgaria engaged in large demonstrations; the Abkhazians in Georgia rebelled against the state; the Chechnians in Russia have been continuously rebelling against the state; and the Albanians in Kosovo both demonstrated and rebelled.

Islam is not an explanation for the Middle East's uniqueness.   As expected, religion is particularly important in the Middle East, and the region is the most autocratic in the world. Yet Islam cannot fully explain these findings; and the disproportionate importance of religion and the presence of autocracy in the region do not lead to the increased levels of ethnic conflict one would expect.

These findings show that the obvious explanations for phenomena are not always the correct ones. It is easy to assume that the prevalence of religious conflict in the Middle East is due to the region's Islamic and autocratic character. It is also easy to assume that the region's high concentration of autocracy is due to the region's Islamic character. Yet neither of these assumptions appear[s] to be correct. Furthermore, the findings of this study show that, except for the finding that religion is particularly important in the region, ethnic conflicts which take place in the Middle East are not considerably different from similar conflicts elsewhere.

In sum, ethno-religious conflict in the Middle East is unique but not in the way many believe. Yes, religion is disproportionately important in the region's ethnic conflicts and the region is the most autocratic in the world. But neither of these findings is explained by Islam. Furthermore, most Middle Eastern ethnic conflicts are otherwise similar to ethnic conflicts elsewhere.

IMPLICATIONS

These findings have several implications. First, they contradict Huntington's notion of Islam's "bloody borders," for ethno-religious conflict in the Middle East between Muslims and non-Muslims is not more violent than other ethnic conflicts. And Islam is not the cause of differences between ethnic conflicts in the Middle East and those taking place elsewhere. Despite this, Huntington's theory remains popular, and if it prevails, it can become a self-fulfilling prophecy in which Western fears of Islam cause threats to be seen where they do not exist and small threats to be exaggerated into large ones. This can lead to reactions that will provoke the very conflicts and threats that at first were only imagined.

That the issues involved in the Middle East's ethnic conflicts are particularly religious does not bode well for conflict resolution, for such conflicts are among the most long-lasting, violent, and difficult to settle. One possible avenue may be to apply the growing literature on religious-based conflict resolution, which advocates using those aspects of religious traditions that emphasize compromise and accommodation to prevent, settle, and mitigate conflict.

The Middle East's remaining the world's most autocratic place means that the post-Cold War trend of democratization has hardly reached it. While this may change, there is no reason to believe that that will happen any time soon—as symbolized by the fact that the region's newest political entity, the Palestinian Authority, has been vigorously repressing dissension. In all likelihood, the region's ethnic conflicts will continue to flourish in an autocratic setting and the peaceful political avenues available to ethnic groups in democratic settings do not have a bright future in the Middle East. Opposition activity is likely to be violent. Political discrimination against minorities will probably continue.

RELIGION AND POLITICS IN ARAB TRANSITIONS

Barah Mikaïl

Islamist parties, excluded from the political sphere for much of the last decade, are now coming to the forefront of Arab politics. The electoral victories of Ennahda in Tunisia and the Muslim Brotherhood in Egypt suggest that the future of Arab politics will be dominated by decision-makers with faith-based political agendas. But the part that religion should play in the new political orders of Tunisia, Egypt and Libya, and how its involvement might be shaped in law and practice, remains the subject of controversy and debate.

The role of religion in Arab politics will be determined by the people of the region. Religious parties and movements cannot be excluded from the political process. But the success of faith-based movements at the polls can exacerbate social tensions. Recent electoral results seem to indicate that strict secularism will not be an option for the new Arab states in the near future. It is yet to be seen which formula of faith-based politics emerging democracies will adopt, on the spectrum between Iranian-style theocracy or Turkish religion-inflected secularism.

The line between religion and ethnicity, culture and tradition is not always clear. It is important, however, to distinguish between religions, such as Islam and Christianity, and faith-based political ideologies, such as Islamism and fundamentalist Christianity. Whereas religion is a matter of personal identity, ideologies serve a political agenda. This policy brief will explore the role of religion and faith-based ideology in Arab transitions. And it will try to draw some lessons from other countries and regions on the different roles religion can play in a society's path towards democracy.

RELIGION IN NORTH AFRICAN TRANSITIONS

Long before the "Arab Spring," religion was recognised as a major force in Arab politics. The electoral results of 2011 confirm that (relatively) free elections in the Arab world show strong public support for political Islam, as already seen in Algeria in 1990, Egypt in 2005 and the Palestinian territories in 2006.

In 2011, new Islamist parties emerged and previously established ones consolidated their positions. In Tunisia, Ennahda won the greatest number of parliamentary seats. In Egypt, the Muslim Brothers and several Salafist parties together accounted for two thirds of the Legislative Assembly. The role of Islamist forces in Yemen remains uncertain, but their influence in Libya is clear. In Jordan and Morocco, Islamist political actors are gaining in importance. The victory of Morocco's Justice and Development Party (PJD) in the country's 2011 elections led to the appointment of the country's first Islamist prime minister.

The fact that it has a Muslim majority does not mean that the Arab world must automatically embrace Islamist rule or reject secularism. Islamists are benefiting from their former exclusion and/or persecution by ousted leaders. The search for strong alternatives to the old regime has encouraged people to support faith-based parties. Islamist movements' history of opposition to and persecution by the recently toppled authoritarian regimes has given them credibility and legitimacy, which they used effectively during their electoral campaigns. Meanwhile, liberal and secular parties may have lost ground for not opposing the former leaders strongly enough.

For decades, leaders from the Middle East and North Africa (MENA) controlled the religious sphere in their countries, either by influencing religious leaders, as in the case of al-Azhar in Egypt and the Muftis in Saudi Arabia and Syria, or by direct interference, as in Iraq under Saddam Hussein, as well as in Jordan, Algeria, Morocco and Libya. But efforts to eradicate religious-based political parties and the instrumentalisation of religion did not diminish religion's popular appeal. In the public imagination, religion became the trademark of movements that challenged authoritarian rulers, who persecuted them out of fear. These religious groups' defiant stance brought them a popularity that was further augmented by their charity and social work. Islamists presented their charity activities as filling the gaps left by the government's neglect. For them, this was evidence that religious movements were best able to provide relief for social and economic ills, as expressed in the Brotherhood slogan *"Al-Islam Houa al-Hall,"* "Islam is the solution." So, when the Arab Spring began to sweep through the region, Islamist parties could make a case that they were the only credible alternatives to authoritarian power. This image, combined with access to foreign funds mostly from Qatar and Saudi Arabia, gave the Islamists an advantage in the ensuing elections.

The current Islamist momentum does not necessarily mean that religious precepts are set to dominate the Arab world. In Tunisia, Egypt and Libya, tensions between secular and Islamist actors still exist. Many secularists and liberals doubt the Islamists' democratic commitment, while Islamist parties continue to try to reassure their domestic opponents and the international community of their democratic credentials. In Tunisia, Ennahda insists on a fundamental role for religious rules in the country, even as secular parties reject this direction. But parliamentary debates on the future Tunisian Constitution must begin before concrete issues are decided. In Egypt, too, efforts to draft a new framework for governance are under way. The Muslim Brothers control the parliamentary committees for external affairs (diplomacy, defence and energy) and Salafis are at the head of the committees for economy, education and religious affairs. This suggests that Egypt will most likely evolve towards more conservative rules and an Islamisation of social life. In Libya, the National Transitional Council (NTC) has insisted from the outset on the importance of Sharia for the country, which may give some indication of the influence Islamists are likely to have on Libya's future.

Drafting a new constitution gives new deputies the chance to determine the degree to which religion will affect their country's future political, legal and social system. New provisions will have to comply with international law as well as taking into account the rules of Islam. This should allow a break with former authoritarian laws while ensuring, as far as democratically possible, compliance with Islamic values. Achieving this balance will be a very tough challenge. Even under previous nominally secular regimes, some social issues were based on the rules of Islam, for example, inheritance, polygamy, family code and minority rights, with particular implications for women's rights. In the current debates, the most contentious issues include the right to sell and drink alcoholic beverages, women's wearing of the veil, suspension of activities during prayers, religious instruction and respecting freedom of belief.

Western partners typically view a strict separation between state and religion as a necessary prerequisite for a democratic political system. But this vision is not viable in the MENA context, where religion cannot at the moment be excluded from the public sphere. The divide between faith-based and secular political actors in the Middle East is an illusion. Progressive and nominally secular parties do not isolate themselves from religious beliefs. Any attempt to definitively exclude religion from public and political life would be met with harsh public criticism. Neither is secularism necessarily desirable for the region, since religion can serve as a powerful force for national cohesion, for example, in providing common ground between conservatives and liberals. This is due in part to the fact that, in Islamic belief, affiliation to the Islamic community (*Ummah*) transcends any ties to a nation-state.

RELIGION AND TRANSITION: INTERNATIONAL EXPERIENCES

Past international experiences provide some lessons on how to balance the democratic rule of law with religious norms and traditions. They can also shed some light on the underlying pitfalls of this process. But drawing conclusions from past transition processes is risky, since countries in transition rarely undergo exactly analogous processes. So, while some common points can be identified, it is important to be aware of the specificity of each individual nation.

Transition to democracy often leads to modernisation, but modernisation does not have to come through secularisation. In former Yugoslavia, excluding religion from the political sphere did not lead people to abandon their religiously informed political views. When the Socialist Republic of Yugoslavia disintegrated, formerly coexisting communities found in religion a common marker to fuel their mutual animosity. In Bosnia and Herzegovina, Croats were automatically identified as Catholics, Orthodox as Serbs, and Muslims as Bosnians. Indonesia, Malaysia and Singapore all went through transition processes without completely excluding religion from the political sphere. In Turkey, despite Ataturk's secular orientation, Islam remains a strong reference point both for the population and for the incumbent AK party.

The degree of religiosity of a society will influence the role religion plays in a transition. But a strong role for religion does not necessarily impede the consolidation of a democratic order. Authoritarian regimes abolished ideological trends informed by religion, but a healthy democracy allows for a wide range of views. In Indonesia, the post-Suharto period since 1998 has enabled greater tolerance of religious beliefs, including in politics, even though the situation remains fragile due to regular violence and the marginalisation of some religious communities. But pluralism, however imperfect, lets Indonesian political parties refer to religious beliefs. In South Africa, political parties take account of Christian (African Christian Democratic Party) and Muslim (al-Jama'ah) values in defining their programmes. In Poland, Catholicism plays an important role in society and the Catholic Church has popularity and prestige. Some political parties, such as the Catholic-National Movement and the National People's Movement, refer specifically to Christian values. A high degree of religiosity in some societies, for instance Mauritania and Pakistan, has enabled a greater number of parties with platforms based on religion to appear during transition. Even in predominantly non-practicing societies, parties with religious perspectives can have some appeal (see for example the Albanian Christian Democratic Party, the Slovenian People's Party, or the Christian Democratic Union in Latvia). But the chances of success for such parties are higher in very religious and/or conservative countries. In Turkey, a politically secular country, it took eight decades before a religious-based party took power.

Minorities' attempts to achieve political gains during transition processes may lead to segregation into religiously defined communities, including through territorial fragmentation. This can increase the risk of sectarian tensions. The risk of segregation is especially high when minorities and communities are based on religion (such as Shi'a groups in a mostly Sunni environment or Protestants in a Catholic environment), on language (like Berber languages and Arabic, or Flemish and French), or on ethnicity (Kurds in an Arab or Turkish environment, or Tutsis among Hutus). This situation has occurred in Iraq, where the transition process since 2003 has brought about a territorial separation between mostly Sunni Kurds and Sunni and Shi'a Arabs. In Turkey, Kurds are still fighting for their rights and have formed their own political parties. The Turkish State continues to refuse their demand for recognition of their distinctive ethnic identity. In Northern Ireland, tensions still exist between Catholics and Protestants. In Afghanistan, the current chaotic transition period has not allowed national ethnic and religious communities, like the Shi'a Hazaras and Sunni Pashtuns, to build shared perspectives. In Nigeria, violent confrontation between Christians and Sunni Muslims is common. The more a country opens itself to pluralism, the more its communities are likely to try to strengthen their positions. This can eventually result in animosity and mutual tension. So, to allow pluralism to succeed and avoid sectarian conflict, it is important that countries spend sufficient time on mutual confidence-building and take determined political steps to ensure peaceful coexistence.

Religious issues are often closely linked with power politics. Various actors use religion to enhance their own political power. In the 1980s in Latin America, the Catholic Church played a key role in transitions from authoritarian regimes to democracy. The Church initially supported the National Reorganisation Process in Argentina (1976–1983). It kept its distance from Pinochet's rule in Chile, but stayed closer to popular movements for change in El Salvador. National churches even mediated between conflict actors in Argentina, Chile, El Salvador and Guatemala. In Turkey, the ascendency of the Gülen movement, an influential Sufi Islamic brotherhood, shows religion as a powerful prop for the political ambitions of theologians.

Some conservative governments provide financial support to religious institutions in order to enhance their countries' influence through these groups' proselytising activities. Evangelical organisations in Latin America have converted 30 per cent of Guatemalans, 20 per cent of Brazilians and 10 per cent of Venezuela's inhabitants to Evangelical Protestantism. Many of these groups receive funds from the US and other governments. Saudi Arabia funds Islamic religious centres and mosques around the world, for example in Argentina, Afghanistan, Pakistan and Kosovo. Iran is said to be developing its influence through financing Shi'a-related initiatives in, for instance, Senegal, Iraq and Afghanistan.

Cultural and religious determinism is a myth, Prosperity and strong religiosity are not incompatible, and no religion or belief is more favourable to peaceful transition to democracy than another. Genuine democratisation does not unavoidably mean the triumph of secularism. Similarly, theories that consider Islam as by nature incompatible with progress, pluralism and democracy are mistaken. Political parties that base their programmes on religious considerations are not opposed to wealth, prosperity, the free market or liberalism. Christian Democrats in Chile, Germany, Ireland, Poland and Spain as well as Islamic parties in Indonesia, Malaysia and Turkey generally promote healthy economic perspectives and growth. With globalisation, economies have become interconnected and countries have had to minimise the impact religious considerations have on their political and economic decisions. Some predominantly Christian Western European countries like Greece, Portugal and Spain and some Eastern European countries, such as Poland and the Czech Republic, performed well during and after their transition periods. Other similarly religious European societies, such as Albania, Bulgaria and Romania, encountered more difficulties. Israel's economy does well, independently of religious considerations. In the Muslim world, the economies of Bangladesh, Egypt and Tunisia are struggling, whereas Indonesia and Malaysia are thriving. In Christian Brazil, Shinto/Buddhist Japan and Muslim Singapore, transition and modernity have succeeded without any direct link to the country's majority religion.

CONCLUSION

Religion has a big part to play in the MENA region. Religious leaders and influences dominate in Tunisia and Egypt, and the same thing could occur in Libya and Yemen. Elections in Morocco have confirmed the ascendancy of Islamist leadership in that country. Lebanon may stand as an exception, even though religion is a strong referent for its 18 coexisting communities. For now, Western-style secularism is not a realistic option in these countries. Integrating religious principles into a genuinely democratic order will be among the greatest challenges for these societies in the decades to come.

This does not mean, however, that religion will remain the dominant political factor in the long run. Religious parties have benefited from their status as strong alternatives to former regimes, but without the contrast of the authoritarian regimes they have replaced, they will be judged on their results. If they succeed in charting a better path for their countries, they may hold power for years. But if they fail, they will be held accountable. The next round of elections in the young Arab democracies will be a strong indicator of the likely longevity of the Islamist political current. The funds that the international community makes available to countries in transition may also determine the success of the currently emerging Islamist rulers. And it could affect their policies, depending on whether the international community insists on conditionality in return for its aid.

The objectives and ideological and political influences of these parties may cause them to adopt any of a range of political models, from the so-called "Turkish model," where religious freedom is guaranteed even though a religious party is in power, to a theocratic model such as that of Iran. That said, in the decades since the Iranian Revolution, societies have evolved considerably, and so has Islamist ideology itself. Popular demands for change have been based on standards that include the recognition of religious and political pluralism. An increasing majority of the population in many Arab countries is young, and few of these young people seem eager to merge politics and religion at an institutional level. So, evolution towards a Saudi or Iranian model is possible, but rigid theocratic structures seem unlikely to prevail in the long term.

The most urgent challenge for the MENA region is building new and modern states that guarantee citizenship and human rights, including freedom of belief. To ensure the success of this endeavour, the new leaders need to aim for transparent and fair parliamentary debates. And they must heed the international community's advice and recommendations on peaceful transition and good governance, the maintenance of free and open democratic processes and the improvement of economic conditions.

FURTHER READING

Akram, Susan M., Michael Dumper, Michael Lynk, and Lain Scobbie(Eds.) 2011. *International Law and the Israeli-Palestinian Conflict: A Rights Based Approach to Middle East Peace*. London: Routledge.

An Naim, Abdullahi. 2010. *Islam and the Secular State: Negotiating the Future of Shari'ah*. Cambridge, MA: Harvard University Press.

Arjomand, Said Amir. 2010. *The Shadow of God and the Hidden Imam: Religion, Political Order, and Societal Change in Shi'ite Iran from the Beginning to 1890*. Chicago: University of Chicago Press.

Bamyeh, Mohammed A. 2012. *Intellectuals and Civil Society in the Middle East: Liberalism, Modernity and Political Discourse*. London: Tauris Academic Studies

Bamyeh, Mohammed. 1999. *The Social Origins of Islam: Mind, Economy, Discourse*. Minneapolis: University of Minnesota Press.

Barber, Benjamin. 1995. *Jihad vs. McWorld: Terrorism's Challenge to Democracy.* New York: Ballantine Books.

Eickelman, Dale. 1998. *The Middle East and Central Asia: An Anthropological Approach.* New York: Pearson.

Elver, Hilal. 2012. *The Headscarf Controversy: Secularism and Freedom of Religion.* New York: Oxford University Press.

Gellner, Ernst. 1981. *Muslim Society.* Cambridge, UK: Cambridge University Press.

Hefner, Robert. 2000. *Civil Islam.* Princeton, NJ: Princeton University Press.

Kamrava, Mehran. 2008. *The Modern Middle East.* Berkeley: University of California Press.

Keddie, Nikki. 2003. *Modern Iran: Roots and Results of Revolution.* New Haven, CT: Yale University Press.

Kepel, Gilles. 2004. *The War for Muslim Minds: Islam and the West.* Cambridge, MA: Harvard University Press.

Kennedy, Hugh. 2007. *The Great Arab Conquests: How the Spread of Islam Changed the World We Live In.* New York: De Capo Press.

Lawrence, Bruce. 2004. *New Faiths, Old Fears: Muslims and Other Asian Immigrants in American Religious Life.* New York: Columbia University Press.

Mandaville, Peter. 2007. *Global Political Islam.* London: Routledge

Roy, Olivier. 2006. *Globalized Islam: The Search for a New Ummah.* New York: Columbia University Press.

Wright, Robin. 2013. *The Islamists Are Coming.* Washington, DC: United States Institute of Peace.

5

SOUTH AND CENTRAL ASIA
Global Labor and Asian Culture

Like the Middle East, South Asia has been at the crossroads of civilizations over the centuries. Outsiders came from the West, transforming Indian culture and bringing Islam, Christianity, and ancient Indo-European cultures and languages to the subcontinent. Some of Asia's most important cultural traditions have flowed out of South Asia. Buddhism was born in India, and it spread from there around the world. Hinduism and Sikhism, which also had their origins in India, have had a global reach as well. The current interaction of South Asia with the world culturally, economically, and demographically has historical precedents.

When we talk about South Asia, we are talking about a region that is, in a narrow sense, easy to define—it is the subcontinent extending south from the huge continental mass of Eurasia, a wedge of land surrounded by the Indian Ocean to the southeast and southwest, by the world's highest mountain range to the north, by deserts to the west, and by jungles to the east. It is the land of India, Pakistan, and Bangladesh; the island nations of Sri Lanka and the Maldives; and the mountain nations of Bhutan and Nepal. It is so self-contained that for centuries the region had no name; indeed, a name was not necessary, since this region's inhabitants were scarcely aware that other people existed. However, from ancient times to the present, there have been busy trade routes both overland and over sea, and it was outsiders, in fact, who gave a name to the people living beyond the Indus River. They named them for the river—they were Indoos, or Hindus, and their land was Indu-land, or India.

Outsiders indeed discovered India. But, perhaps because it was so isolated, each incursion into the region—by ancient Aryans, medieval Mughals, colonial British, and contemporary globalization—has had a significant impact. At the same time, culture and trade has flowed out of the subcontinent to other parts of the world. The trails led over water to Southeast Asia and over land to Central Asia and beyond. Because of the land connection through Central Asia's Silk Road, Central Asia has been linked to South Asia, culturally as well as economically, for most of the world's history. During the colonial period, British India was an entity unto itself, and in the twentieth century, Central Asia was dominated by the Soviet Union and thus was cut off from the subcontinent. But there has always been a South Asian–Central Asian connection.

South Asia is, like the Middle East, the spawning ground for great religious cultures. In the case of South Asia, these religious cultures are Hinduism and Buddhism, along with the religious traditions of Jains and Sikhs. Hence, it is culturally a region of global-out impact. From the very beginning, however, the global-in influences of other cultures have challenged and changed the region.

One of the first of these global flows of influence from the outside came around 1500 BCE from peoples and cultures from the West. This is the Indo-European culture often referred to as Aryan, though scholars debate who these people were and the actual nature of the incursion, whether it was a gradual intermingling or a series of sudden occupations. These people came from what is now Central Asia and Iran and were part of a large cultural interchange thousands of years ago that spread from Europe to South Asia. The Aryans brought with them the linguistic structure of Indo-European languages that, merged with indigenous languages, became ancient Sanskrit. Their gods also traveled to South Asia and became, in a somewhat different form, the gods of the ancient Vedic religion.

In the fourth century BCE, the Greek warrior Alexander the Great conquered the lands from the Mediterranean to the Indus River. Much of Afghanistan, Pakistan, and Indian Punjab were under Alexander's influence. Some scholars think the name of the Afghan city, Kandahar, is etymologically linked to the name of Alexander. In any event, there were cultural interchanges from this meeting of Europe and South Asia, including influences on Buddhist iconography. Some of the earliest representations of the Buddha in the Greek-dominated South Asian region of Gandhara portray him in robes and with physical features that look distinctively Greek.

Buddhist religious images and ideas traveled up the trade routes from India to the region of Bactria, in what is now Afghanistan, which was ruled by Alexander's generals and descendants, and then to the great cities of Bukhara and Samarkhand, in what is present-day Uzbekistan. These were hubs in the overland commercial trails that comprised the Silk Road, uniting regions of the Middle East and the Middle East with India and China. It was the route that Mahayana Buddhism followed in spreading throughout Asia, making South Asian religious and philosophical ideas the dominant cultural stratum of the whole Asian region.

In the thirteenth and fourteenth centuries, Central Asia was almost literally at the center of the world. Through extraordinary horse-mounted military conquests, the great Genghis Khan and his grandson Kublai Khan ruled over an empire that stretched from Europe to China. It was the largest land empire in history, and for a time it united Eurasia politically. But the union was not a cultural one, since the Khans did not impose their own indigenous religion or customs on the areas they conquered. Later the ties established by Mongol rule allowed Tibetan Buddhism to become the religion of Genghis Khan's old homeland, Mongolia, and the political networks created by the Mongols facilitated the spread of Islam throughout much of Central and South Asia.

Beginning in the tenth century CE, Muslim rulers came to the Indian subcontinent to establish an empire culminating in the Mughal dynasty. They left behind some of the region's most magnificent architecture—including the elegant Taj Mahal—and the Muslim faith, which was adopted by a quarter of the population. From the seventeenth to the twentieth centuries, the British came from the West by sea, replacing the Mughal empire with a British one, and it too left its mark, although Indians disagree over whether the impact of British rule was, in the end, more helpful or harmful. Among the positive legacies of British rule in India were political institutions, education, railways, and roads. These, more than architecture and religion, connected the Indian subcontinent to the wider world.

In the global era of the twenty-first century, the Indian subcontinent is very much in a wider world. Through its development of sophisticated information technology systems, India has become a leader in computer technology and systems support. Once again, the subcontinent is linked to the world's shifting currents, and like its connections through the ancient Silk Road, the ties are both economic and cultural.

In the readings in this section, we begin with an excerpt from a book on the religions of the Silk Road by historian of religion Richard Foltz, an American who has lived in the Central Asian region and currently teaches in Montreal, Canada. Central Asia's moment of global centrality in the time of the Mongol emperors is described in an excerpt from a book on Kublai Khan by Morris Rossabi, a historian who teaches at City University of New York.

The next reading is an essay that explores the global aspects of Hindu religion and the influence that Hindu ideas have had in America, Europe, and other parts of the world. The author of this essay, Vasudha Narayanan, was born in India, received her Ph.D. from Harvard, and teaches religious studies at the University of Florida. In the next excerpt, two historians, Barbara and Thomas Metcalf, discuss the impact of British colonial rule on India, outlining its positive as well as its negative features. For most of his career, Thomas Metcalf has taught at the University of California, Berkeley, and Barbara Metcalf has taught at the University of Michigan and the University of California, Davis.

The final reading is an excerpt from a book on the latest aspect of India's relationship to the global world, its role in the global information economy. The authors of this excerpt, Carol Upadhya and A.R. Vasavi, are both social anthropologists who specialize in South Asia and globalization and are located at the National Institute of Advanced Studies in India's technological center, Bangalore.

RELIGIONS OF THE SILK ROAD

Richard Foltz

It is no coincidence that throughout history ideas and technologies have spread along trade routes, and that merchants have been among their prime transmitters. One only has to think about it to realize that traveling businessmen do not simply convey, sell, and acquire goods, and move on. They socialize, interact, and observe while on the road, and they take their impressions home with them.

Nor are businessmen the only utilizers of trade routes; many other kinds of travelers benefit from the networks fostered by commercial activity. In the modern world business travelers are the driving force behind the airline industry, even if the average flier thinks little about that connection. Likewise, the interstate highway system in the United States was devised as a means to encourage trucking—a thought to temper one's curses when struggling to control the steering wheel in the wake of a passing eighteen-wheeler!

Increasing attention has been given in recent years to the role of long-distance trade in the cross-pollination of cultures and ideas. . . . Religions accompanied merchants and their goods along the overland Asian trade routes of pre-modern times. It is a story of continuous movement, encounters, mutual reactions and responses, adaptation and change. This is part—though, the reader is cautioned, only a part—of a much broader historical dynamic of cultural interaction, exchange, and cultural conversion. While long-distance trade is not in and of itself an "explanation" of how religions spread across Asia or why Asians converted to them, a case will be made here that it is an important factor. . . .

Although some of the religious traditions in this story (Christianity, Islam, Judaism, and Buddhism) are familiar to us living today, it would be misleading to project too much of what we know of their modern manifestations into the Silk Road context. Religions are not monolithic, fixed institutions existing each in their own realm of dominance, although we often speak of "Christendom," "the Islamic World," and so on. In reality, religions are like organisms: They are born into this world at a point in time, they grow, develop, undergo diverse influences, and adapt to their environment. They quibble with their neighbors, experience periods of painful soul-searching, have good days and bad. At some point they may split like cells, each taking on a new life. Over time, having proven themselves, they may settle into the self-confident stasis of maturity. Sometimes, eventually, they die. In China, especially, they are more often simply absorbed. Nothing could better illustrate the organic nature of religious traditions than the example of their experiences along the Silk Road.

The Silk Road was more than just a conduit along which religions hitched rides East; it constituted a formative and transformative rite of passage. No religion emerges unchanged at the end of that arduous journey. Key formative influences on the early development of the Mahayana and Pure Land movements, which became so much a part of East Asian civilization, are to be sought in Buddhism's earlier encounters along the Silk Road. Manichaeism, driven underground in the West, appears in the eighth century as a powerful political force in East Turkestan, then gradually blends into the amorphous mass of Chinese popular religion. Nestorian Christianity, expelled as a heresy from the Byzantine realm, moves eastward, touches hundreds of thousands among the Eurasian steppe peoples, and appears centuries later like a bad dream to the first Catholic missionaries in China, who find it comfortably entrenched there as the recognized resident Christianity of the East.

Islam, carried along by the momentum of the Arabs' military success, makes its appearance on the Silk Road in the eighth century but comes to a temporary halt halfway, following the Battle of Talas in 751. Directly and indirectly, Islam would be carried east through trade, just like its predecessors. Nor would the new tradition remain Arab property: It would belong instead to the Persians, the Turks, the Chinese—and it would feed from their cultures. Ideas, after all, like individuals, need to acquire new tastes and new sponsors if they are to thrive in foreign climes.

The existence of trade routes and constant commercial activity linking diverse cultures from ancient times meant that religious ideas (like technology and other aspects of culture) could spread easily along trade networks which spanned Eurasia. Indeed, like running water finding open channels, this spread was probably inevitable. But the religion-trade relationship was mutually reinforcing. For example, the expansion of Buddhism brought an increased demand for silk, which was used in Buddhist ceremonies, thereby further stimulating the long-distance trading activity that had facilitated the spread of Buddhism in the first place.

THE EARLY MONGOLS

Morris Rossabi

Khubilai Khan lived during the height of Mongol power. He was born at the beginning of the Mongol expansion and grew up as Mongol armies spread far to the north and west. Khubilai and his grandfather Chinggis were the most renowned of the Mongols in this glorious period of their and indeed Eurasian history. Eurasian history begins with the Mongols. Within a few decades in the thirteenth century, they had carved out the most sizable empire in world history, stretching from Korea to Western Russia in the north and from Burma to Iraq in the south. Their armies reached all the way to Poland and to Hungary. In the process, they destroyed some of the most powerful dynasties of their age: the Abbāsid rulers of the Middle East and Persia, the Chin and Southern Sung dynasties of China, the Khwārazmian khanate of Central Asia. For a generation, the Mongols were masters of much of Eurasia and terrorized the rest.

Though their empire lasted less than a century, it inextricably linked Europe to Asia, ushering in an era of frequent and extended contacts between East and West. And, once the Mongols had achieved relative stability and order in their newly acquired domains, they neither discouraged nor impeded relations with foreigners. Though they never abandoned their claims of universal rule, they were hospitable to foreign travelers, even those whose monarchs had not submitted to them. They expedited and encouraged travel in the sizable section of Asia that was under Mongol rule, permitting European merchants, craftsmen, and envoys, the first time, to journey as far as China. Asian goods reached Europe along the caravan trails, and the ensuing European demand for these products eventually inspired the search for a sea route to Asia. Thus, the Mongol era indirectly led to the European age of exploration of the fifteenth century, which culminated in the discovery of the sea route around the Cape of Good Hope to Asia and in Christopher Columbus's unsuccessful effort to find a western route to the Indies.

The Mongols accomplished much more than simply linking Europe and Asia. They governed many of the territories they had seized. With the indispensable help of Chinese, Persian, and Turkic advisers and administrators, they progressed from plunderers to rulers. They set up governments and bureaucracies, devised systems of taxation, and promoted the interests of farmers, herdsmen, and merchants. Since most of the Khans were either tolerant of or indifferent to foreign religions, active persecution of any sect in the Mongol realm was rare. Some of the Mongol leaders encouraged the various native cultures, patronizing artists, writers, and historians. Chinese drama, Persian historical writing, and Tibetan Buddhist art and architecture all flourished during the Mongol occupation.

Yet the dark side of Mongol rule ought not to be ignored. Their armies so devastated some of the regions they conquered that recovery took years, even decades. Toward those who dared to resist them, they showed no mercy. A thirteenth-century Persian historian writes of their "massacring, plundering, and ravaging" and adds that in one of their campaigns, "with one stroke a world which billowed with fertility was laid desolate, and the regions thereof became a desert, and the greater part of the living dead, and their skin and bones crumbling dust; and the mighty were humbled and immersed in the calamities of perdition." Modern writers have often been equally harsh in assessing the Mongols, one implying that the Mongols increased the brutality of Chinese court life, that they "brought violence and destruction to all aspects of China's civilization," and that they were "insensitive to Chinese cultural values, distrustful of Chinese influences, and inept heads of Chinese government."

The victorious Mongols have scarcely left us their own versions of their campaigns and of the rule and administration of their empire, unfortunately, since they did not develop a written language until the time of Chinggis. Thus the Mongol written sources of the thirteenth century are meager, and most of our knowledge of them derives from the chronicles of the peoples they subjugated: the Chinese, the Persians, the Koreans, the Armenians, the Arabs, and various others. It is only natural, then, that they were often depicted as brutal and tyrannical. Certainly some of the more outlandish tales of Mongol cruelty, even monstrousness, must be discounted.

HINDUISM

Vasudha Narayanan

Hinduism is a global religion in at least three ways: First, there is a sizable number of Hindus who are from (or descended from immigrants from) the Indian subcontinent in almost every part of the world; second, people from local populations in various countries have adopted and still accept teachers, doctrines, beliefs, or practices of one of the many Hindu traditions, whether it is the Khmer aristocracy in the 9th century CE or members of the International Society of Krishna Consciousness (ISKCON, more popularly known as "Hare Krishnas"); and third, ideas and practices derived from Hindu traditions are decontextualized from their sociocultural milieu, distanced from the name "Hindu," and integrated into the cultures outside of India. Although the word Hindu has been popular only since the 19th century to designate the diverse and dominant philosophies, beliefs, and practices that form the faith of approximately 80% of the Indian subcontinent, the ideas, texts, sectarian movements, rituals, as well as expressive and visual arts connected with the religion that we now call "Hinduism" have traveled along with material culture to many parts of the world for more than two millennia.

An example of the last point is found in America; starting approximately with the time of the New England Transcendentalists in the 19th century and all the way into the 21st century, we see American engagement with ideas, philosophies, and practices connected with the many Hindu traditions in the Indian subcontinent; however, these ideas or practices (like yoga) are called "universal," "spiritual," or even just as "stress-relief techniques" and not connected with Hinduism. In general, one can say that Hinduism comes both in brand names and as a generic mode with a "universal" message. One can seldom find a generic Hindu in India; they belong to a caste, community, and sectarian group, all of which are further subdivided along linguistic and geographic lines. However, the texts and practices of Hinduism have been mined for "universal" messages that have been disseminated as not belonging to any one religion but to all human beings. Thus, Hindu teachers beginning with leaders like Vivekananda and Yogananda, who came to America in the late 19th and early 20th centuries, stress the "timeless" truths and practices of Hinduism that are not bound by sectarian belief, dogma, or ethnic fences. Examples of these include contemplative practices and meditation, yoga, recitation of simple mantras, and even concepts like the immortality and reincarnation of the soul.

The term Hindu has been contested and is used here as a fluid, shorthand term to refer to the diverse philosophies, practices, arts, and branches of knowledge connected with people and communities who have geographic, biological, intellectual, or spiritual connections, whether it be through an ancestor or religious teachings, with the Indian subcontinent but excludes those faiths that explicitly reject the exalted status of the Vedas, the earliest compositions in India. Although millions of people in India may have never heard of the Vedas, they are assumed to be Hindu unless they belong to a faith tradition that explicitly rejects, denies, or self-consciously bypasses their status as supreme sources of knowledge.

The names Hindu and India have geographic origin and are linked to the Indus river, which was known as Sindhu in Sanskrit literature, and thus, the global understanding of the traditions have to be observed in a localized context where the sacred land of the Indian subcontinent has been valorized periodically. Historically, and from certain political and legal perspectives, Hindu has also been used to denote people of other religious traditions if they are domiciled in India, but this entry will not deal with the Jain, Buddhist, or Sikh traditions. There are other issues to make this more complex: The boundaries among some Hindu, Jain, and Sikh communities are porous; the Buddha is sometimes revered as an incarnation of the Hindu deity Vishnu; and social divisions known as the "caste system" are prevalent among Christians and members of other faith groups in India. Thus, some features identified strongly with the Hindu traditions may be shared by other faith communities in India but not in other places in the world.

According to some estimates, there are approximately 1 billion Hindus in the world today, which translates to approximately 13–15% of the world's population. Most Hindus live in South Asian countries, particularly India, but there are sizable numbers in other countries in the region, especially Nepal and Bangladesh, as well as in Singapore and Indonesia in Southeast Asia, South Africa, and elsewhere in the African continent, Sri Lanka, Mauritius, and other island nations in the Indian ocean, Fiji in the South Pacific, Trinidad in the Caribbean Islands, and throughout Europe and the Americas. Because Hinduism is not a congregational religion and Hindus are not necessarily affiliated with a temple for membership and regular worship, their numbers in other parts of the world remain approximations. Estimates in 2007 indicate upward of 500,000 Hindus in the United Kingdom and approximately 1.5 million in the United States, but Hindus believe that these estimates are low.

Although Sanskrit texts, including the Manu Smriti or the Code of Manu, composed around the beginning of the common era frowned on travel outside the northern part of the Indian subcontinent and some notion of ritual pollution was connected in practice with traveling abroad even to the beginning of the 20th century, Hindus have traveled and settled in Africa, parts of Europe, and more extensively, Southeast Asia, from before the Common Era. Much of this was connected with economic and professional reasons for men, as some in Southeast Asia may have been linked with invitations from and patronage by aristocracy. The economic reasons include trade, indentured work, and more recently, in the late 20th century, professional opportunities in western Europe, Australia, North America, and the Middle East. With a few significant exceptions, particularly after the 20th century, and then restricted largely to a few charismatic leaders, sharing of religious ideas does not seem to be the primary force for Hindus to be traveling outside of India. . . .

RECENT AMBASSADORS AND RELATED MOVEMENTS

Although Hinduism does not have a significant history of proselytizing, there have been several ambassadors of Hindu traditions to Western countries after the late 19th century. Preachers such as Vivekananda and Yogananda have emphasized the universal and intellectual dimensions of Hinduism, such that the traditions can be adopted by followers without their changing their faith traditions. Others like A.C. Bhaktivedanta Swami Prabhupada (1896–1977), founder of ISKCON, have taught a highly regulated lifestyle connected with a very specific sectarian faith tradition in India. ISKCON communities and temples dedicated to the Hindu deities Krishna and Radha are found all over the world. Among other observances, ISKCON devotees are noted for their strict adherence to not just a vegetarian diet but to avoidance of many foods, including onions and garlic.

Apart from the impact of Hindu immigrants as well as those who have chosen to adopt Hinduism as their faith around the world, we may also note the presence of ideas and practices derived from Hinduism. Ideas and practices with Hindu roots have become popular globally without being considered "Hindu." Examples are the Self-Realization Fellowship, The Art of Living, Siddha Yoga, Transcendental Meditation, and organizations started by followers of religious teachers such as Amritandandamayi or Karunamayi. The teachings in these movements cluster around a Hindu charismatic leader who in many cases comes from India, and they focus on self-transformation or the transformation of society. To a large extent, these "universal" or "spiritual" movements underplay, ignore, or distance their connections with Hinduism. A second way in which ideas and practices with Hindu origins have become pervasive in global cultures is through the large-scale co-opting or the secularization of Hinduism-based practices such as yoga as part of "self-help" programs. Some of these are popular because of the physical exercise with which they are associated and are taught in gyms and exercise centers; some are advertised as stress reduction techniques; and others are promoted as leading to spiritual enlightenment.

CONCLUSION

Hindu traditions continue to operate on two registers globally: the explicit practice by immigrants or their descendents, and parts of the tradition adopted either by spiritual teachers or through practices such as yoga. Temple building and performing arts continue to be the primary signifiers of Hindu immigrants. Cultural markers such as names and dress, as well as sectarian and community diversity, are retained by first-generation immigrants, while a more homogenized version of beliefs is emerging among second-generation Hindus in the diaspora. Along with immigrant-derived Hinduism, new religious movements such as ISKCON continue to flourish. One of the greatest booms, however, in global Hinduism can be found in another register through the silent, disembedded traditions, the universalistic themes presented by global gurus who connect the ideas and practices with spirituality or health benefits, rather than with cultural or religious Hindu traditions.

REVOLT, THE MODERN STATE, AND COLONIZED SUBJECTS, 1848–1885

Barbara D. Metcalf and Thomas R. Metcalf

The revolt of 1857–8, which swept across much of north India in opposition to British rule, has conventionally been taken as the dividing point that marks the beginning of modern India. Historical periodization is, however, always somewhat arbitrary. With greater distance from the colonial period, when the searing chaos of the uprising was understood either as "Mutiny" to the colonial rulers or as the "First War of Independence" to many nationalists, it is possible to focus on substantial, long-term transformations rather than on a single event. Such an emphasis, moreover, places India in the context of changes taking place in the larger world, not just in terms of events and personalities in India itself. Far from modernity "happening" in Europe and then being transplanted to a country like India, many of these changes took place in relation to each other.

Modern technological changes, among them canals, railways, and telegraph, were introduced into India within years of their introduction in Europe. Changes essential to the modern state, including the unification of sovereignty, the surveying and policing of the population, and institutions meant to create an educated citizenry were also, broadly speaking, introduced during the same period in India and in parts of Europe. Indeed, certain modern practices and institutions were either stimulated by the Indian experience or originated in India itself. Municipal cemeteries, as noted above, appeared in India before they did in England; the same is true of English literature as a curricular subject, and of state-sponsored scientific and surveying institutions. The colonial relationship with India was essential, moreover, as Gauri Viswanathan recently argued, to one of the fundamental characteristics of modern states, namely the practice of state secularism. At the same time, new religious organizations in both India and Britain shared the common pattern of an unprecedented involvement of the laity. In both countries too, the spread of electoral politics was accompanied by debate over the place of religion in public life. Above all, the economic lives of both countries were profoundly, and increasingly, intertwined.

The date 1848 as starting point for the "modern state" in India is a reminder, however, of a key difference in the nature of the state in India. In Europe during 1848 a wave of protests swept across the continent demanding expansion of the suffrage and other political reforms. In Britain, the Chartist movement, gaining support from economic depression and the limited expansion of suffrage brought about by the Reform. Act of 1832, brought the working classes on to the streets in an effort to secure political power for themselves. The opportunities for a public voice and public life varied greatly among regions in India, but even in Bengal, where modern voluntary associations and publications were most widespread, relatively few voices could be raised to demand such political reforms before the end of the century. In politics, as in economic life, an authoritarian colonial state constrained Indian aspirations.

Most historians now agree that the rigidities introduced by colonial policy decisively shaped, even distorted, modernity in India. This approach offers a corrective to what was too easily described during the colonial era as the "blessings of British rule," namely the pacification and unification of the country, legal codification, the use of the English language, public works, and a range of social reforms. Critics of European modernity, among them Britons as well as Indians, even at the time saw the dark side of these changes, among them racism, militarism, and the economic exploitation that was part of the colonial relationship. What colored those "blessings" above all was a mentality that discounted Indian abilities and aspirations to self-rule, an attitude the historian Francis Hutchins termed the British "illusion of permanence." British rule in the 1830s and 1840s had been founded in Enlightenment notions of universal human destiny and expectations of progress, although, to be sure, even then an authoritarian strain was evident in evangelical and utilitarian reform. But by the 1870s the mood was different, above all in an explicitly authoritarian attitude among colonial officials. They were, for the most part, convinced of an essential difference between British and Indian that justified indefinite control of political power by a "superior race."

OUTPOSTS OF THE GLOBAL INFORMATION ECONOMY: WORK AND WORKERS IN INDIA'S OUTSOURCING INDUSTRY

Carol Upadhya and A.R. Vasavi

Over the past two decades, India has become a major outpost of the global economy, as the recipient of outsourced technology-based and mediated work mainly from the post-industrial economies of the West. The emergent information technology (IT) and IT enabled services (ITES) industries have become emblematic of India's entry and integration into the global economy and have put India at the centre of discourses about globalisation.

The emergence of these "high tech" offshore industries in India is one manifestation of the latest phase in the development of global capitalism. Aided by the spread of sophisticated computer and telecommunications technologies, systems of production are becoming ever more geographically dispersed and an increasing array of economic activities are being outsourced and offshored to new destinations, leading to the establishment of new "knowledge" industries in countries that were formerly labelled "Third

World." Today, China and India are continually under the gaze of international media, and the apparent unstoppable outflow of jobs from the US to these and other "developing" countries has sparked public outcries in the West. Although the IT and ITES industries still constitute a very small part of India's economy as a whole and employ an insignificant proportion of the working population, they have substantially enhanced India's visibility and reputation in the global cultural economy. The country's prowess in the IT field has been widely celebrated even as Indian software engineers and call centre agents are blamed for stealing American and European jobs (as seen in the use of term "Bangalored" to refer to the loss of American jobs to India).

While the state, the media and IT industry leaders hail this new sector as a model for development that will enable India to "leapfrog into a post-industrial economy" (and hence provide an opportunity to become a world superpower), and although the industry has received substantial media and academic attention, there has been till recently relatively little research on these developments from sociological or anthropological perspectives. There is substantial literature on the history, growth and structure of India's IT-ITES industries, but few critical analyses of the nature of work in this sector, the new workforces that have been created, or their significance for India's overall social and economic development. For instance, we know little about the organisational structures and work processes that have developed in these industries—are they culturally distinctive or do they simply replicate the features of their Western parent or client companies? Have IT-ITES companies introduced new forms and cultures of work into India, and if so, what are the implications of these changes? What are the characteristics of the new workforces that have been produced to cater to these industries, and how does working "virtually" in the global economy affect the lives and identities of workers? Has the IT-ITES sector provided employment to a broad cross-section of the population, expanding India's "new middle classes" or only reinforced existing caste-class-gender divisions by drawing primarily on the existing educated middle class for its workforce?

An additional set of questions concerns the wider cultural and social repercussions of the rapid growth of these offshore industries in India and the emergence of a distinctive category of global "knowledge workers." In cities where IT activity is concentrated, such as Bangalore, Chennai, NOIDA and Hyderabad, the transformations that have been wrought by this industry are starkly visible. Most IT and ITES companies are housed in hypermodern glass-and-steel structures that are often jarring against the background of their more traditional urban or semi-rural surroundings. IT professionals too have become a highly visible segment of the new middle class that has emerged in liberalising India: with their high salaries and opportunities for travel abroad, they can afford fairly luxurious lifestyles at relatively young ages, thus forming a new elite professional class. IT and ITES jobs have become the most sought after career options for Indian youth, significantly altering their educational choices and social trajectories.

Moreover, due to their sudden rise and social significance, the IT and ITES industries have been subjected to excessive media attention, and this has produced a range of popular images about these new workplaces and their workers. Narratives circulating in the media and other public spheres have helped to create the high level of visibility that these industries and their workers enjoy, and are central to the construction of a specific discourse about IT and its significance for India's development. For all these reasons, there is a need to match the dynamics of these last evolving industries with solid academic research, deploying a sociological gaze to scrutinise them and their employees, and especially to understand the ways in which outsourced IT work leaves its imprint on workers and the larger society. . . . .

POLITICAL ECONOMY OF THE INDIAN IT INDUSTRY

As already noted, the emergence of the Indian IT-ITES industries is directly linked to the process of global economic restructuring that has been underway since the 1980s. In the first phase, the shift from "Fordist" mass production to "post-Fordist" networked flexible production forged new links among countries and economies across the globe. Under the regime of "flexible accumulation" that emerged, economic activity was increasingly organised through complex transnational production networks rather than through vertically integrated multinational companies. Since the 1980s, the regime of flexible accumulation has been taken a step further. Work is increasingly performed through the manipulation of symbols in computer systems rather than of material objects—what Zuboff has called textualisation of work. As a result, production and services have become dematerialised, disembodied, and divided among workers located in geographically distant sites. Modern information and communication technologies (ICTs) have facilitated the vertical disintegration of the production process within large companies, which are then reaggregated into specialised industries and relocated in various global production centres.

The globalisation of services is a key feature of this phase in the development of global capitalism. The "servitisation" of the advanced economies and increasingly sharp competition have led companies to prioritise customer service and satisfaction even while they attempt to reduce their costs by centralising and outsourcing routine services such as customer support. These shifts, together with the integration and spread of new digital and communication technologies, have given rise to global commodity chains of service provision. While in the earlier stage of globalisation manufacturing jobs moved from the industrialised economies to low-cost locations in the "Third World," now it is primarily service jobs that are migrating—both "high tech" professional jobs such as computer programming and software development as well as "low-end" back office services such as insurance claims processing and telemarketing (IT-enabled services and business process outsourcing or BPO). Thus, a range of white and "pink collar" work has been outsourced or offshored to sites where cheaper labour enables large amounts of clerical work to be carried out round the clock. Work carried out in these dispersed sites is managed and coordinated through the use of the new ICTs. These economic shifts have created a global informational economy based on complex production and services networks that create and support information technology systems and provide remote backend services, linking together workers, managers, and customers located across multiple sites and borders. In this "new economy," information or "knowledge" has become the key resource and factor of production as well as the primary product.

The emergence and growth of India's IT industry coincided with an acceleration in the internationalisation of the production, distribution, and management of goods and services in the 1990s. Companies located in the advanced industrial economies are outsourcing and offshoring an increasing proportion and range of their business activities to places where skilled human resources are more easily available and at lower cost. India has seen the setting up of offshore software development centres by MNCs (multinational corporations) and the burgeoning of international call centres and other back office operations. In tandem with these developments has been the emergence and spectacular growth of Indian-owned IT services companies (now being transformed into transnational corporations) to cater to the global demand for these services. India now accounts for 65 per cent of the global market for offshore IT services and 46 per cent of global business process outsourcing. . . . The Indian software and services industry (often simply referred to as the "IT industry") grew at a rate of about 50 per cent per year in the 1990s and in 2005–06 generated total earnings of $17.8 billion. Riding on the back of the software industry's success, ITES (which includes BPO or business process outsourcing and call centres) has become the new boom industry, generating revenues of $7.2 billion in 2005–06. . . . Although accurate employment figures are difficult to obtain, current official estimates place total direct employment generated by the industry at 1.3 million in 2005–06—representing a rapid expansion from the figure of 284,000 in 1999–2000.

While global economic restructuring provided the space for the emergence of the IT-ITES industries in India, their rapid growth can also be attributed to specific political and economic processes that have unfolded in the country since the 1980s. These include the deepening policy of liberalisation that has exposed India to global economic forces; the push towards technological modernisation, especially in the computer and telecom sectors, that began under Rajiv Gandhi's regime; and the emergence of a class of indigenous "middle class" entrepreneurs in the IT sector who represent a new model for Indian business. . . . The IT industry right from its inception has enjoyed significant state support, both directly and indirectly, and at both national and state levels. In addition, it has drawn on the large pool of skilled manpower (especially engineering graduates) that was produced during the long period of Nehruvian state-led development policies. The industry's requirement for a steady supply of "knowledge workers" has shaped both public policy and the production of the IT workforce in particular ways.

The export-oriented nature of the IT-ITES industries in India also has significant implications for the nature of work and the modes of organisational control employed. Despite frequent claims that it is "moving up the value chain" towards the provision of end-to-end software development, consultancy and "knowledge process outsourcing," the IT industry continues to rely on labor cost arbitrage. Its profitability is based largely on its ability to marshal sufficient and well-qualified human resources, to deploy them onto projects as and when needed, and to maximise labor productivity. Similarly, the ITES industry needs to hire and manage large numbers of English-speaking educated youth. The labor market and modes of control over the labour process are largely structured by the need to recruit, deploy, and manage this army of "knowledge workers."

FURTHER READING

Boulnois, Luce. 2005. *Silk Road: Monks, Warriors, and Merchants*. Hong Kong: Odyssey Books

Chaudhuri, K.N. 1985. *Trade and Civilisation in the Indian Ocean: An Economic History from the Rise of Islam to 1750*. Cambridge, UK: Cambridge University Press.

Demspey, C. (2005). *The Goddess Lives in Upstate New York: Breaking Convention and Making Home at a North American Hindu Temple*. New York: Oxford University Press.

Foltz, Richard. 2010. *Religions of the Silk Road: Premodern Patterns of Globalization*. New York: Palgrave MacMillan.

Golden, Peter. 2012. *Central Asia in World History*. New York: Oxford University Press.

Jacobsen, K.A. (2008). *South Asian Religions on Display: Religious Processions in South Asia and in the Diaspora*. London: Routledge.

Jacobsen, K.A., and P. Pratap Kumar (2004). *South Asians in the Diaspora: Histories and Religious Traditions*. Leiden, the Netherlands: Brill.

Kearney, Milo. 2004. *The Indian Ocean in World History*. London: Routledge.

Kurien, P. (2007). *A Place at the Multicultural Table: The Development of an American Hinduism*. New Brunswick, NJ: Rutgers University Press.

Mann, Gurinder Singh, Paul Numrich, and Raymond Williams. 2007. *Buddhists, Hindus, and Sikhs in America*. New York: Oxford University Press.

Metcalf, Barbara D., and Thomas R. Metcalf. 2012. *A Concise History of Modern India*. Cambridge, UK: Cambridge University Press.

Narayanan, V. (2007). "Creating the South Indian 'Hindu' Experience in the United States." In J. S. Hawley and V. Narayanan (Eds.), *The Life of Hinduism*. Berkeley: University of California Press.

Raghuram, P. (2008). *Tracing an Indian Diaspora: Contexts, Memories, Representations*. Thousand Oaks, CA: Sage.

Rossabi, Morris. 2010. *The Mongols and Global History*. New York: Norton.

Singh, Pashaura. 2012. *Sikhism in Global Context*. New York: Oxford University Press.

Upadhya, Carol, and A.R. Vasavi, 2011. *In an Outpost of the Global Economy: Work and Workers in India's Technology Industry*. London: Routledge.

6

EAST ASIA
Global Economic Empires

Whether a region is east or west or at the center depends, of course, on one's point of view. To whom is "East Asia" east, or even "far east," and to whom is it "the Orient"? The answer is Europeans, of course. For centuries, they thought of the area at the other end of the Eurasian land mass as mystical and foreboding, as forbidden as the Forbidden City adjacent to Tiananmen Square in Beijing. And yet East Asia has never been that remote. Even though Japan and Korea were sometimes reclusive, China always interacted economically with the rest of the world. In the global era of the twenty-first century, all of East Asia is at the center.

East Asia is fairly easy to define. It generally refers to China, Japan, and the two Koreas. In recent decades, however, scholars have begun to recognize that there are other countries that can also be said to be part of East Asia, including Mongolia and the Asian part of Russia. Asian Russia is, in fact, much larger than European Russia. A new name has been proposed to include all of these areas—Northeast Asia. Even in the larger definition of the region, however, China is major.

China has dominated much of the world's history. It has consistently been the world's most populous country, and for many centuries it had the most developed and highly commercialized economy. It was not eclipsed by western Europe until the industrialization of the late eighteenth century. Yet over the centuries, China and Europe have been connected. From the second century BCE to the second century CE, the Han dynasty in China and the Roman Empire in Europe were like two bookends bracketing the vast Eurasian land mass. Trade linked the two empires. Luxurious Chinese silk and elegant porcelain found their way to the Roman Empire, while manufactured glass, amber from the resin of trees in the Baltic region, woolen textiles and linen, coral and pearls from the Red Sea, and various precious stones went eastward from Roman lands to China.

The arteries that facilitated this trade were the "Silk Road(s)." This name was conjured up by a German geographer to refer to a series of caravan routes that ran from Xi'an, once China's capital, westward to the fabled cities of Samarkand and Bukhara (in today's Uzbekistan). There they branched out, one route traversing Persian lands south of the Caspian Sea and another turning northward toward the Black Sea, ending in the Middle East and Europe. What the Chinese desired above all else from these western territories were horses—especially the "heavenly horses" from the Fergana Valley (in today's eastern Uzbekistan).

Then there is the cultural transmission of food. Scholars still argue over whether it was Italian pasta that traveled east over the Silk Road to China or whether Chinese noodles were in the baggage of traders who went west from China to Italy. I once ate at a café in Honolulu that specialized in Chinese and Italian cuisine that called itself "Ciao Mein," thus giving a nod of respect to both of those possibilities of cultural origin. There are ancient forms of Italian pasta, however, and in 2005, Chinese archeologists discovered a 4000-year-old bowl of noodles, indicating that perhaps both cultures long ago independently thought up what was, after all, a pretty edible idea.

Along the Silk Road came not only goods and food but also religion. Buddhism traveled from India to China, Korea, and Japan; Christianity, primarily in its Nestorian form, came from the Roman empire; while Islam spread from the Arabian peninsula first to greater Syria, then Mesopotamia (today's Iraq), Persia (today's Iran), Central Asia, and China. As each religious tradition spread, it was transformed by local cultures, a fact that helps to explain why Buddhism is distinctively different in China, Mongolia, Japan, and Korea. Moreover, as one wave after another of religions made their way through a region, people converted to each one in turn. Thus, the Uighurs in western China first became Buddhists, then Christians, and finally Muslims. They are among the 23 million Muslims living in China today—almost as many as the number of Muslims in Saudi Arabia, making them one of the largest Muslim communities in the world. Though the dominant ethnic group in China is Han, the country officially recognizes 55 ethnicities, making China a multiethnic, multicultural, multireligious, and multilingual nation.

In the sixteenth century, a different trade pattern emerged. Silver became king. The Ming dynasty rulers decided to stop using paper currencies, and instead used silver as the basis of China's monetary system. Now everybody, including the poorest peasants, had to acquire silver to pay their taxes. This fueled an increasingly enormous demand for silver, especially as the population grew. China got its silver from other countries, including from the New World. From the mid-sixteenth century to the mid-seventeenth, Japan and the Spanish-colonized regions of South America mined the bulk of the world's silver. The most fabulous area of all was a veritable silver mountain named Potosí in Peru (located in today's southern Bolivia); it produced more than 40,000 metric tons of silver from the sixteenth century through the eighteenth, enabling the Spanish crown to pay for its colonial administration all over Latin America and to fight decades of war in Europe. A significant part of those shipments ended up in China by way of northern Europe (carried in Dutch ships) as well as via reexport from India. But silver was also smuggled through the "back door" of the Andes from the port of Acapulco, Mexico, across the Pacific to Manila, the capital of Spain's colony in the Philippines. From Manila, the silver was shipped to southern China. Even though in most years only one ship made that voyage, the Manila galleon trade was important in global history because it was sustained for two and a half centuries, shipping more than 50 tons of silver to China every year and forming a regular physical link between the Americas and Europe and Asia. Silver was not just a form of money; it was traded as a commodity itself. As such, it played a significant role in creating a truly global financial market from the mid-sixteenth century onward. This picture of widespread Chinese trade by land and by sea over several millennia belies the stereotypical image of China as an insulated, inward-looking country.

In contrast, Japan did seal itself off from the outside world, especially during the Tokugawa shogunate period from the seventeenth century through the nineteenth. But with the Meiji Restoration, in which the emperor was nominally returned to power in 1868, Japan opened itself to the world and quickly imported technical, scientific, financial, and military advisors from the West. It industrialized, especially in military hardware, at an amazing speed. As Japan's economy grew, so too did its imperial ambitions. It acquired the island of Taiwan, which it renamed Formosa, at the conclusion of the Sino-Japanese War in 1895. Ten years later, it astonished the world when it sank the Russian ships that had sailed all the way from the Baltic Sea to Japanese waters to try to protect Russian interests in the region. Japan annexed Korea in 1910 and invaded Manchuria in northeastern China in 1931, turning it into a puppet state. Ten years later, as Japan bombed the U.S. fleet in Pearl Harbor, it also invaded and occupied all the countries in Southeast Asia except for Thailand. Following World War II, Japan arose from the ashes of war and defeat to become, within just a few decades, the second largest capitalist economy in the world. It pioneered a form of economic development based on the export of manufactured goods—a model followed first by the "four tigers" (South Korea, Taiwan, Singapore, and Hong Kong) and later by Malaysia, Indonesia, Thailand, and Vietnam.

Before it was colonized by Japan, Korea had also been a "hermit kingdom" for many years, though it was greatly influenced by Chinese culture and, in the nineteenth century, by American Christian missionaries. The Japanese treated the Koreans harshly. They forced Koreans to change their names to Japanese ones, speak only Japanese, and attend schools where Japanese was the medium of instruction. At the end of World War II, Russians accepted the Japanese surrender in the northern part of Korea, while Americans accepted the surrender in the southern part, thereby producing a division that lasts to this day. The Korean War (1950–1953) caused the enmity between Communist North Korea and pro-Western South Korea to become even more firmly entrenched.

In the twenty-first century, China is seen as the world's rising economic star. New political leadership in the country after the death of legendary Marxist leader Mao Zedong (also spelled Mao Tse-Tung) altered China's domestic economic policies and opened up the country to global trade. Another leader, Deng Xiaoping, took a realistic, solution-oriented approach to economic policies. "It doesn't make any difference if the cat is black or white," he is famously said to have remarked, "as long as it catches mice." China has become not only an economic superpower but also a growing, and ultimately formidable, military power.

The readings in this section trace the globalization of East Asia over the centuries. The first reading, by Kenneth Pomeranz, a historian of China teaching at the University of Chicago, discusses how and why silver became such a vital factor in China's economic history and, indeed, in world history. The other readings focus on the present day and East Asia's role in recent global economic activities. The late Andre Gunder Frank was an economic historian and sociologist born in Germany who received his Ph.D. from the University of Chicago, taught at the University of Chile, served as an advisor to the social-ist government of Salvador Allende, and eventually moved from South America to the University of Amsterdam. In the excerpt below, he argues that the rise of the East Asian economies portend the eclipse of American and European hegemony over global trade.

The next selection is from a report for the Asian Development Bank written by three economists—Steven Radelet, Jeffrey Sachs, and Jong-Wha Lee—who at the time they wrote this were all affiliated with Harvard's Institute for International Development. In this report, they ask whether East Asia's rapid economic development can continue and whether it can be a model for countries elsewhere in the world. They answer "yes" to both questions. Radelet became the chief economist for the U.S. Agency for Interna-tional Development in the Barack Obama administration, and Sachs became director of the Earth Institute at Columbia University, authoring best-selling books on sustainable development. Lee became head of the Asian Development Bank's Office of Regional Economic Integration.

The final selection, by Ho-Fung Hung, a sociologist at Johns Hopkins University who specializes in global political economy, asks whether the Chinese economy's extraordi-narily rapid growth can be sustained. He believes it can if the government is willing to carry out some restructuring, not only to remain economically vibrant, but also to be-come more equitable and more protective of the environment in the future.

THE GREAT DIVERGENCE

Kenneth Pomeranz

From roughly 1400 on, China was essentially remonetizing its economy after a series of failed experiments with paper and a grossly mismanaged copper coinage under the Yuan dynasty (1279–1368) had left the country without any widely accepted monetary medium. In this process, silver was becoming the store of value, the money of account (and often the actual medium) for large transactions, and the medium of state payments for this huge and highly commercialized economy. The enormous demand for silver this created made it far more valuable in China (relative to gold and to most other goods) than anywhere else in the world; and China itself had few silver mines. Consequently, China was already importing huge amounts of silver (mostly from Japan, and to some extent from India and Southeast Asia) in the century *before* Western ships reached Asia.

When Westerners did arrive, carrying silver from the richest mines ever discovered (Latin America produced roughly 85 percent of the world's silver between 1500 and 1800), they found that sending this silver to China (whether directly or through intermediaries) yielded large and very reliable arbitrage profits—profits so large that there was no good reason for profit-maximizing merchants to send much of anything else. (The tribute missions to Beijing, which Marshall Sahlins has analyzed to understand "Chinese" attitudes, were unaffected by this, since they were essentially symbolic exchanges between sovereigns at administered prices. Profit-seeking often played a decidedly secondary role in these exchanges, though the missions were generally accompanied by profit-seeking "private" trade.)

Various Western intellectuals and politicians, who would have rather kept this silver at home (as a stockpile to pay for wars, for instance), were constantly arguing that other goods should be sent to Asia instead. The prominence of their protests in the written record has often made it appear that "the West" was desperately trying to get "Asians" to buy other foreign goods, while the Chinese were simply too ethnocentric (or Westerns artisans too unskillful) for this to work. But to focus on these polemics is to mistake the opinions of a few political leaders for the preferences of a whole society, just as focusing on the pronouncements of Chinese emperors about the proper forms and limits of tribute trade does. And in both cases, the actual decisions about what to trade were made by merchants embedded in markets.

The tendency to see China's import preferences as a sign of cultural conservatism has been further reinforced by treating silver as modern "money"—in other words, a residual store of abstract value transferred to make up Europe's "trade deficit." Instead, we need to see silver itself as a good: a refined product with a mineral base, which was well suited to an important function and which the West could produce far more cheaply than any place in Asia (excepting, in certain periods, Japan); the accidents of geology were such that China could barely produce it at all. It was, moreover, one of the few manufactured goods in which the West had an advantage not only in its supply of raw materials but in the technology of further production: European minting produced better and harder-to-copy coins than anything available in Asia. Since the Chinese used silver in bar form, this advantage in minting mattered little to them, but it mattered a great deal to south Asian and other users who were often the initial purchasers of European silver, subsequently sending much of it to China through their own trade networks.

The arbitrariness of treating silver as "money" in the modern sense, which was sent to east Asia *in lieu of goods,* rather than as a good the Chinese used as a monetary medium, becomes obvious once the issue is raised. After all, many prestige goods—silk, pepper, opium, cocoa beans—have also performed monetary functions in one place or another but are nonetheless treated as goods. Moreover, much silver went back and forth between being used as money and as decoration (when jewelry was pawned or melted down, for instance). Treating silver as one more specific good, rather than as the equivalent of modern dollar bills, helps us make sense of the fact that significant amounts of gold flowed from China to both Europe and India during the same period that silver was flowing in. Finally, the tendency to see silver as a residual store of value sent to China to pay for consumer goods has been reinforced by a long-standing tendency among Western scholars to see the West as the active (and desiring) agent in the knitting together of the world. But once we think about the dynamic created by changing the monetary base of perhaps as much as 40 percent of the world's economy in this period (once we add in China's tributary states, which were also "silver-izing"), it becomes hard not to see China's silver demand as every bit as much an "active" force in creating a global economy as was the West's demand for porcelain, tea, and so on.

. . . The West's huge comparative advantage in the export of silver sucked in trendsetting prestige goods from Asia. This helps explain why so many other exotic goods flooded into Europe—they paid for silver and made the wheel of fashion spin faster here than elsewhere. . . . It roots this unique influx in an economic conjuncture spanning Europe, Asia, and America, rather than in any uniquely European "materialism" or "curiosity." And, given the way Europe acquired and ran the American silver mines, it reminds us of the tremendous significance of coercion in generating Europe's economic edge. (Advances in technology also mattered, but they would not have without the seizure of the mines and the imposition of labor obligations on the population.) In this particular case, the fruits of external coercion may have been significant for the way in which they accelerated changes in fashion and thus a consensual market-based trade within Europe; but it is crucial that the direction of explanation runs from coercion abroad to an extra boost to Smithian dynamics (and later to import-substituting industrialization) at home, *not* from more efficient marketing and industrial production at home to the power to coerce people abroad. . . .

Those metals probably did little for Europe's economic development, since they financed numerous wars, including Spain's nearly successful assaults on the emerging core economies of northwest Europe. Nonetheless, the metals may have helped grease the wheels of European trade, and they certainly played a role in the growth of more effective militaries. Meanwhile, much New World treasure went further east, bringing other commodities to Europe. It can be roughly divided into three separate streams.

One substantial stream of New World gold and silver exports went to various ecologically rich small market zones in the Old World—from Southeast Asia to parts of the Near East to eastern Europe—making it possible for Europe to expand its imports of real resources from these peripheries. In these cases, silver or (less often) gold were used like modern currency reserves: they were a residual store of value transferred to cover an otherwise unbalanced trade with areas that had limited demand for the goods Europe sold.

But one could also see these metals, which were usually coined before transshipment from Europe, as the one European manufactured good for which these zones had fairly large markets and (lacking the proper raw materials) limited local production. In economies that were monetizing rapidly (e.g., much of Scandinavia), this manufactured good was at least partially an item of popular use; in the least marketized peripheries, such as eastern Europe, it was essentially a luxury good. Either way, it made it possible to obtain more primary products from these areas than would have been possible otherwise.

But, since precious metals do not wear out or get used up (unlike cloth, or grain), it was hard to create an *expanding* (or perhaps even enduring) market for them if only a tiny part of the society used them. True, wealthy people could add to their silver or jewelry hoards; but at some point they had enough for all conceivable obligations, and silver as a form of conspicuous consumption must have begun to lose value relative to silk, porcelain, paintings, and so on. Thus, New World silver helped western Europe obtain more raw materials than they could have had the fifteenth-century "bullion famine" continued, but could not by itself indefinitely expand western Europe's trade with less-monetized Old World economies.

The second stream also helped Europe obtain land-intensive goods, but less directly. This flow was exchanged for various Asian (mostly Indian) manufactured products, which then covered much of the cost of procuring slaves for the Americas. Indian cloth alone made up roughly one-third of all the cargo by value exchanged by English traders for African slaves in the eighteenth century and may have made up over half of the goods that French traders (whose industries were slower to produce good imitations of Indian fabrics) used to acquire slaves. Much Portuguese imperial trade went directly from Asia to Africa to Brazil, stopping in the mother country only to deliver New World goods. In other words, this portion of the metals flow facilitated the process we have already described, in which New World slave areas became an important complement to labor and capital-rich, land-poor Europe.

In India, as we have seen, there is a strong case for seeing much of the flow of gold and silver coins as meeting a broadly based transactions demand, rather than as a store of wealth that covered a "trade deficit." But despite impressive evidence of ongoing monetization in India, it does not necessarily follow that in the absence of New World metals, India would simply have imported more of other Euro-American goods. Much of the population still only entered the market to obtain a few necessities, meet occasional ceremonial expenses (e.g., for weddings), and raise cash to pay taxes and other dues; and to the extent that they did purchase other goods, it is not clear that European manufactures would have been competitive. And the greater prestige of Chinese fabrics and ceramics, Southeast Asian delicacies, and specifically Islamic goods from the Middle East meant that European luxury goods would not have found a large market either. So even if we treat precious metals flowing to India as just another product, they were probably special in another sense: they were about the only European good that one could imagine India buying on such a huge scale. (The one possible alternative that comes to mind is arms; it is unclear what effect a large further increase in this already substantial trade might have had in the period spanning Mogul decline and British ascendancy.)

Finally, the third stream of metals was for decades the largest of all; but this flow of silver probably did the least to ease pressures on Europe's land. It went to densely populated, heavily commercialized parts of Asia, where it was used as a medium for transactions involving every class in society; and in return, various consumer goods flowed to Europe and to the Americas themselves. This description, as we have seen, may fit some of the Indian trade, but it refers above all to the enormous flow of silver to China, where millions of ordinary people used silver to pay their taxes and for many ordinary purchases.

Here silver was clearly a good, not residual wealth used to settle unbalanced accounts. Indeed, while silver flowed into China between 1500 and 1640, gold and copper left China, often ending up in Europe. And though silk, the most important "real good" among China's exports, was a fabric rather than a metal, it, too, was used as money in some places. Thus, New World silver in this trade was just one of many goods being arbitraged: items that were more plentiful in China than elsewhere (gold, porcelain, silk) were exchanged for silver, which was comparatively scarce in China but in very high demand as it became the monetary and fiscal base of the world's largest economy. By about 1640, this trade had brought silver to gold ratios in China and Europe into rough equilibrium; thus, having lost its raison d'être, this trade went into a sharp decline, recovering only in the eighteenth century. In its first incarnation, the trade did little to supply land-intensive commodities to Europe. It had, however, been enormously profitable and yielded goods that (unlike more and more silver) could be used to make exchanges elsewhere.

In China, as in India, it may be difficult to imagine another good that would have been imported on such a massive scale had silver not been available. Thus in this case, too, New World mines were important to Europe's capacity to obtain goods in the rest of the Old World. But the Chinese case differs from the Indian one, from the importer's side, in that it is far harder to see much of the silver it imported as nonessential; thus, in the absence of that flow, we must imagine either other imports of monetary media or a large reallocation of China's own productive resources, perhaps in turn expanding demand for other imports. From the European side, meanwhile, the difference between this flow of metals and that which went to India is that this one did relatively little, even indirectly, to ease pressure on the land.

These distinctions among various uses of New World treasure are post hoc and highly imperfect, and the association of different uses with different final destinations for the metals must be seen as tendencies, not absolute rules. Even in eastern Europe—perhaps the periphery in which the general population was the least involved in the cash economy—not all imported metals represent abstract "wealth" hoarded by the elite in a stagnant economy. At the other end of the scale, there was surely some hoarding of silver even in China. What we need to recognize is that some of this behavior went on everywhere; there are no grounds for the sharp distinction some scholars have seen between western "spenders" and Asian "hoarders." Moreover, the line between hoarding and transactions demand was itself vague in a world in which ordinary people did not have savings accounts, and in which jewelry and other items of display were often a crucial part of securing the marriages that reproduced productive units.

But despite the approximate and fluid nature of these categories, they do show us something: New World metals were not simply "money" that Europeans turned into "real" resources by distributing them around the Old World, with European needs always driving the story. The internal dynamics of other regions could create "needs" no less real than those of Europe, such as China's need for a more usable currency, or the desire of eastern European elites to turn their grain surpluses into something easily stored and shipped and thus usable for provisioning their troops on campaign. It was the *intersection* of European and other regional dynamics that determined the extent and nature of these metals' flows: the world economy remained polycentric, and forces emanating from elsewhere could shape it just as much as those emanating from Europe.

Indeed . . . had China in particular not had such a dynamic economy that changing its metallic base could absorb the staggering quantities of silver mined in the New World over three centuries, those mines might have become unprofitable within a few decades. The massive inflation of silver-denominated prices in Europe from 1500 to 1640 indicates a shrinking value for the metal there even with Asia draining off much of the supply, and the less-monetized parts of the Old World would not have indefinitely kept absorbing precious metals without also devaluing them. This is one more way in which early modern silver and gold were not quite like contemporary "money": today those who have hard currency to spend will never have trouble obtaining more resources, since contemporary peripheries have staggeringly large needs for capital.

Nonetheless, the transshipment of New World metals did allow western Europe to expand its imports of real resources far beyond what it could have obtained otherwise. Some New World silver may have had to have been converted to cloth, porcelain, or spices to keep expanding the flow of resources from some of the less-monetized Old World peripheries; but thanks to Chinese demand, this option was available, too. And as we have already noted, the combination of New World metals themselves, transshipped Asian goods that had often been obtained with silver, and exotica from the New World itself (such as sugar and tobacco) paid for more of western Europe's imports from the rest of the Old World than did manufactures created wholly within Europe.

THE 21ST CENTURY WILL BE ASIAN

Andre Gunder Frank

The 21st century will be Asian. Recent research, including my book *ReOrient: Global Economy in the Asian Age*, overturn Eurocentric historiography and show that Asia was dominant in the world until at least 1800. However, my forthcoming book, *ReOrient the 19th Century*, shows that, except for colonial India, much of West, Central, Southeast and East Asia, as well as Latin America and Africa, prospered until at least the mid-19th century. China did not really "decline" until after the 1850s Taiping Rebellion and the Second Opium War in 1860. The Great Divergence, as Kenneth Pomeranz, professor of history at University of California at Irvine, calls it, between East and West became so only after 1870. A major factor in Asian decline was the weakness of the state and colonialism. Japan, falsely called "feudal" in the Tokugawa period (1603–1867) and still independent after the Meiji Restoration in 1868, avoided these problems and so was the first to develop in the second half of the 19th century.

In the 20th century, though starting from a lower level than before, the Asian growth rate has been faster than that in the West, and in the last half century since the liberation of China and the end of colonialism the rate of economic growth in East Asia has been double that of the West. Led first by Japan, then in the "flying geese" pattern by the First Four Tigers or little Dragons, and then by the next four, and for two decades now the Big Rising Dragon of China has had a nearly 10% annual growth rate. That is enough to double income every six years and is more even than the Japanese miracle. All that means that Western dominance in the world lasted only about a century and now it appears to become only temporary as well, contrary to the Eurocentric allegations of a half or even a whole millennium.

The East Asian financial and economic crisis, starting in Japan and in 1997 in Thailand, was misunderstood and greeted in the West as proof of Asian weakness. But it was really the result and proof of Asian productive strength.

This was the first time that an economic crisis started in the East and moved West rather than the other way around. That was because East Asian industry had begun to produce so well and so much that it swamped the world industrial export market. So the East Asian balance of trade declined and made debt service difficult. That scared speculative financial capital, both foreign and domestic, to take flight to what seemed an American safe haven in Wall Street and U.S. Treasury certificates. It was this Asian, and also Russian, capital and not some "new economy" non-existent productivity rise that created the American prosperity of the Clinton 1990s.

To examine the present and future, it will be useful to consider some alternative scenarios. The first is continued American prosperity and dominance, which speaks for itself, but not truthfully. Another is that we are living in a financial and debt economy in which U.S. dollar debt instruments are the primary basis of what is being bought and sold in the world, 20 times as much money as goods every year. But the debt is the counterpart of credit, especially the foreign credit that is keeping the U.S. economy afloat and also finances the Pentagon, which the U.S. then also uses to dominate and blackmail the rest of the world to accept policies in its own interest. The U.S trade deficit is now $550 billion a year and growing. Every year about $100 billion is supplied by Europeans, $100 billion by China and about $100 billion by the Japanese, though this year it is already over $120 billion. The rest is supplied by others, especially other East Asians but now also by India. Americans save nothing and spend far more than they produce by drawing on the savings, and thereby the production, of others who lend their savings to the Americans.

Also, because world reserves and principal payments—especially for oil and gold—are in dollars, the U.S. can and does simply print dollars and uses them to buy up the rest of the world's production for American consumption and investment. Yet in the end, these U.S. paper dollars, Treasury bonds, electronic accounts and funds, are all only paper and totally worthless, i.e., have no value beyond their acceptance by others, because the U.S. will not and cannot make good on them. The U.S. foreign debt is said to be already equivalent to one quarter of the U.S. gross domestic product (in reality it is even more), and foreigners already own 45% of U.S. government debt and a significant portion of U.S. assets. That is already an indication that it is economically and politically impossible to pay that debt. We, especially Asia and America, are playing in a "casino economy," but with worthless paper chips with imaginary value. In fact it is a gigantic Ponzi scheme, continually fed by contributions of real goods produced at the bottom of the pyramid, until they stop coming and the entire paper tiger house of cards comes crashing down, especially in America. Yet for the first time in history, this permits an uncompetitive world's largest debtor to call the shots.

One resulting scenario is that this situation offers an opportunity for more productive and competitive Europeans to step in and replace the dollar with the euro and/or another as the world's reserve currency. However, the Europeans lack a strong state to do so. But a major step would be for Russia, OPEC and other oil exporters to price their oil in euros instead of dollars, thus increasing demand for the euro and sending the dollar crashing down. Iraq priced its oil in euros, and an important reason for the U.S. war against it was to keep others from doing the same.

My alternative scenario is Asian, including a possible Asian currency basket. Let us examine especially the Chinese connection today and its possible future. First, low cost Chinese workers produce real goods, and are already the world's leading producers of 100 manufactured goods, and export $350 billion worth a year, mostly to rich American consumers, who buy them essentially for free with printed paper dollars. China is already the No. 4 world exporter with an over 5% share of the export market (but only 4% of imports).

But that is only the half of it, because the Chinese use these paper dollars to purchase paper Treasury certificates paying only 4–5% yearly interest. Still, what a bargain! Of the $700 billion Treasury bonds outstanding, the Chinese central bank already holds $300 billion, and the Bank of Japan and European and other central banks, including oil exporters, most of the rest. Why do the Chinese, Japanese, Europeans and others do this?

About Japan, my friend Jeff Sommers writes, "Japan has to keep the export game going, even if it means subsidizing the U.S. Until then, Japan has no choice but to play the U.S. game and both extend free loans to the U.S. through purchasing its bonds, and also to send real goods to the U.S. for (worthless) dollars. The Asian market is not yet large enough to replace the U.S." I may be misinformed, but I disagree.

The main reason the Chinese give to keep the dollar up against the Chinese yuan—and other dollar-linked currencies—down in order to be able to sell to the U.S. market. Only recently has China begun to use some of its dollars to buy Southeast Asian goods. But why in dollars? That need not be. Instead, as Henry C. K. Lui [of Lui Investment in New York] writes: "China has the power to make the yuan an alternative reserve currency in world trade by simply denominating all Chinese export in yuan. This will set off a frantic scramble by importers of Chinese goods around the world to buy yuan instead of dollars. OPEC would accept yuan for payment for their oil."

Why only China? What about "Greater China," including Hong Kong, Taiwan and especially the overseas Chinese who are now the source of the largest capital investment in mainland China? Mainland China already receives the most direct investment in the developing world. And why not more Asians, e.g., ASEAN+3 [Japan, South Korea and China], which China is already "organizing," and India? In the 1997 financial crash Japan proposed an Asian Fund to bail the economies out but the U.S. squashed that and in so doing taught the Asians a bitter lesson—never be caught unprepared again and next time have an Asian Fund to get out from under the IMF/U.S. Treasury and its blackmail and organize its own East Asian economy.

Finally, returning to a longer historical perspective, it is noteworthy that the economically most dynamic regions of East Asia today are exactly the same ones as before 1800, which survived into the nineteenth century.

1. In the south, Lingnan, centered on the Hong Kong-Guangzhou corridor
2. Fujian, centered on Amoy/Xiamen and focusing on the Taiwan Straits and all of Southeast Asia in the South China Sea
3. The Yangtze Valley, centered on Shanghai, whose trade with Japan is again taking the lead
4. Northeast Asia, including Northeast China, Manchuria, Mongolia, Siberia/Russian Far East, Japan and the Korean Peninsula. The region's ample mineral, forestry, agricultural and petroleum resources and abundant low-cost Chinese and North Korean labor can permit Chinese, Japanese and South Korean capital to again develop the area into an important regional growth center in itself and a region that is highly competitive on the world market.

ECONOMIC GROWTH IN ASIA

Steven Radelat, Jeffrey Sachs, and Jong-Wha Lee

The countries of East and Southeast Asia grew extremely rapidly during the last quarter century. The eight best performers—Hong Kong, Singapore, Taiwan, Korea, China, Malaysia, Thailand, and Indonesia—grew at an average of over 5.5% per year in per capita terms between 1965 and 1990. With the exception of several European countries in the immediate post World War II period, growth rates of this magnitude and duration are unprecedented in human history. But as remarkable as was the growth performance of these eight core economies, not all Asian developing countries were able to follow their lead. South Asia, the Philippines, Burma, Central Asia, and many of the Pacific Island nations all recorded average or below average growth in comparison with developing countries in other regions of the world.

In this section we explore the Asian growth patterns by quantifying the empirical relationships between long-term growth and various structural and policy variables. We base the analysis on a general framework of cross-country regression analysis that allows us to put the Asian experience in a global context. Our objective is to understand the critical dimensions in which the East Asian countries differed from other countries that allowed them to achieve rapid growth, and to explore the extent to which those dimensions are unique to these fast-growing economies.

Our approach does not identify all of the specific factors associated with economic growth across countries, nor does it in every case clarify the precise channels through which certain variables affect growth. Rather, it is an attempt to distill the vast amounts of information available on dozens of countries into a tractable, parsimonious framework that identifies a small set of variables that stand out as the most important factors influencing rates of growth around the world. This approach allows us to discern broad trends across countries that illuminate some of the key differences between fast and slow growing economies. Most importantly, this exercise provides strong clues to what lies ahead for Asian countries during the next thirty years. It provides a foundation to understand the likelihood of continued rapid growth in the "tiger" economies, as well as insights to the most appropriate steps that other countries in Asia can take to accelerate growth.

THE BASIC GROWTH FRAMEWORK

The basic empirical framework is based on an extended version of the neoclassical growth model. . . . This model predicts conditional convergence of income: a country with a low initial income relative to its own long-run (or steady-state) potential level of income will grow faster than a country that is already closer to its long-run potential level of income. The basic idea is that the farther an economy is located from its steady-state income level, the greater is the gap of reproducible (physical and human) capital and technical efficiency from their long-run levels. The gap of existing capital and technology from steady-state levels offers the chance for rapid "catching up," via high rates of capital accumulation as well as the diffusion of technology from more technically advanced economies. Hence, the lower is the initial level of per capita income relative to steady state, the higher will tend to be the subsequent growth. This framework presumably helps to explain why wealthier countries, with relatively large capital stocks and already operating near the world's technological frontier, tend to grow more slowly than some lower-income countries that are catching up with the leaders.

If we could presume that all countries have the same steady-state income levels, then the neoclassical approach would imply, simply, that poorer countries would grow faster than richer countries. In fact, such a pattern is not generally observed. Over the period 1965–90, poorer countries did not, on average, narrow the income gap with the richer economies. The cross-country growth framework therefore builds in a crucial assumption, that countries have *distinctive* long-term levels of per capita income to which each is converging. Crucially, the long-term levels depend on two main kinds of variables: economic policies and economic structure. Countries with favorable economic policies (as identified below) tend to have a higher steady-state level of income, and therefore faster growth at any given initial level of income. Similarly, countries with a favorable economic structure . . . tend to experience faster growth, on a path of convergence to a higher long-term level of income. . . .

DIFFERENT PATHS TO DEVELOPMENT WITHIN EAST ASIA

We should point out that in searching for these common traits across successful economies, we are not suggesting that there has been only one path to sustained development. The East and Southeast Asian countries differ widely in their resource endowments, human capital accumulation, population densities and structures, and political systems. They have faced different opportunities and challenges during the last thirty years, and chosen different economic strategies to achieve their goals. Among the eight rapidly growing economies, at least four different paths to development are apparent.

Hong Kong and Singapore are small, urban, very open economies that have relied heavily on commerce and a free port service as the foundation for growth. They have few natural resources, but have well-educated workforces. Their basic strategy was to rely on free and open markets, backed by a competent civil service and a strong legal system. Both governments consistently welcomed and encouraged foreign direct investment. Of course, there are important differences between the two—Singapore features many more state owned enterprises (generally operating profitably in competitive markets), and the government has been more active in encouraging the development of new technologies and promoting manufactured exports.

Korea and Taipei, China are also relatively small economies with few natural resources and a well educated workforce. Agricultural growth, spurred in part by land reform and green revolution technologies, contributed significantly to aggregate growth in the early stages of the take-off period. Both countries initially followed a strategy of import substitution for consumer goods. They kept the level of protection low and the duration of protection relatively brief, and did not extend protection to capital goods sectors. Both countries switched course to aggressively promote export production, with governments at times intervening forcefully in the market with subsidies, special lines of credit, and controls on international capital flows. Both countries discouraged foreign direct investment. Again, there are important differences in their strategies—Taipei, China encouraged small and medium enterprise development, while Korea relied on a small number of large conglomerates to meet its export goals.

Indonesia, Malaysia, and Thailand are larger countries with abundant natural resources and a smaller human capital base. As with Korea and Taipei, China, agriculture has played a critical role in reducing poverty and contributing to aggregate economic growth. These countries adopted much more protectionist industrial policies than the Four Tigers, with more extensive and longer lasting import substitution policies. Many sectors have remained under the control of state enterprises or heavily protected from competition for long periods of time, even when they have performed poorly. Nevertheless, each of these countries established mechanisms through which exporters could avoid the high costs associated with protection and become competitive on international markets. Once again, there are important differences: Malaysia welcomed foreign direct investment more than the other two countries, and concentrated more on exports of consumer electronics rather than textiles and apparel.

China's path to development has differed dramatically from other developing countries. The period of total state control and near autarky prior to 1978 was followed by a dramatic decollectivization of agriculture and gradual privatization and opening of the economy. The majority of the population continues to live in rural areas and depends on agricultural production. The government maintains a heavy hand in the economy through extensive state ownership of enterprises and widespread price and quantity controls. Nevertheless, the government has actively encouraged the development of privately owned export oriented firms by establishing facilities to allow exporters to avoid the most serious price distortions in the economy. Foreign direct investment, once completely banned, is now encouraged along the coastal areas.

These differences suggest that the road to sustained growth and development has differed in important ways across the region, with each country facing different obstacles, complications, and opportunities. Yet, despite these differences, there are several striking similarities in each country's economic strategy. This analysis of controlled averages in this section, combined with the earlier cross country growth regressions point to four key areas that are associated with rapid growth across all countries, and in which East and Southeast Asia differed from other countries:

· openness and manufactured exports;
· higher savings and investment;
· strong macroeconomic management, especially government fiscal policy; and
· education.

In our view, these common elements are the key to understanding rapid growth in East and Southeast Asia, and slower growth elsewhere in the region.

IS THE RISE OF CHINA SUSTAINABLE?

Ho-Fung Hung

It is doubtful whether China's formidable export engine, so far the economy's single most profitable component as well as one that neutralizes the risk of an overaccumulation crisis, will last indefinitely. In the three decades following the Second World War, the success of the export-led development strategy of the Asian Tigers rested mainly on the fact that there were so few small developing economies pursuing the strategy. The exports of these economies were easily absorbed in the world market. But when many more developing countries adopted the strategy in the 1980s and 1990s, the world market, flooded with cheap manufactured exports, became ever more volatile. Given how great its economic size and export volume are, China is exceptionally vulnerable. Worse, China's exporting trade is highly concentrated in the U.S. consumer market, which currently absorbs more than 30 percent of China's total exports (including reexports via Hong Kong).

The expansion of the U.S. consumer market has hinged on an unsustainable, debt-financed consumption spree and has created a mega-current account deficit. As has been long anticipated, the U.S. economy has started to readjust via the bursting of its real-estate bubble and collapse of its debt-financed consumerism since 2007. This readjustment of China's main export outlet is occurring along-side a substantial appreciation of the Chinese yuan and the rise of protectionist measures in the U.S. and other economies. This conjuncture of events puts great pressure on the profitability of China's export sector. If the current economic adjustment of the United States escalates into a full-blown and protracted crisis that spreads to the entire global economy, and the gap between domestic production capacity and domestic consumption in China is not sufficiently narrowed in time, the outbreak of an overaccumulation crisis in China is certain.

Just at the moment when an economic slowdown is looming, the environmental cost of three decades of reckless development has begun to exact a toll on the Chinese economy. For example, it is estimated that 40 percent of China's water supply is now so polluted that it is unusable for any purpose, a circumstance that substantially increases the cost of industrial production in many sectors. Pollution-related diseases are also escalating, and this also diminishes the labor productivity of the country. It is therefore not an exaggeration for a report on the state of the Chinese environment to claim that:

> China's environmental problems are reaching the point where they could constrain its GDP growth. . . .

In light of these possible constraints on China's economic growth in the future, the prospect for China to perpetuate its rapid economic expansion can no longer be taken for granted.

The highest echelon of China's party-state elite has long been aware of the vulnerability of the economy, and they have been actively devising preemptive policies to redress the economic imbalance. Following the Asian Financial Crisis of 1997–98, China's State Council launched a series of income redistribution programs to boost domestic demand, with an expectation that they could end China's precarious dependence on export and debt-financed investment for economic growth. These initiatives included directing state investment into the impoverished, rural Western interior as well as increasing peasants' disposable income through tax and fee reduction. They aimed to open up China's rural market, a vast and uncharted frontier for many consumer goods, in contrast to the more or less saturated urban markets. They also included the institutionalization of a comprehensive social security system that would encourage urbanites and villagers alike to spend more in the present and save less for future uncertainty. Beginning in late 2003, the central government launched a series of macroeconomic adjustment measures to curb excessive investment via administrative orders and tightening of credit supply to local governments and state-owned enterprises. On the environmental front, the central government strengthened regulations on polluting industrial enterprises, hoping that tougher measures would lead to a phase-out of low-value-added sectors more detrimental to the environment and speed up the rise of cleaner, more technologically intensive industries.

The ambition of these high-sounding measures notwithstanding, the key question is how the central government could ensure their full implementation by local governments. Some optimistically see these measures as the beginning of a great shift in China's developmental model for good, although this shift will take time to unfold. . . . Others pessimistically see them as no more than yet another series of ineffective reforms on paper fiercely resisted by local officials, whose obsession with maximizing their short-term private gains contradicts Beijing's concern about the economy's long-term stability. . . .

Given the strong resistance to these economic and environmental regulations on the part of local vested interests, preventing an overaccumulation crisis through these regulations will inevitably involve more than technical policy change. A restructuring of China's sociopolitical order is necessary. The state could recentralize state power all the way to the central government to strengthen its capacity in coordinating the hitherto anarchic local developments. To break the resistance of the entrenched local interests that frequently hijacked the making or implementation of central government's policy, the party-state could mobilize the support of the downtrodden peasants and workers by installing institutional protection of their rights. There are signs that the current leaders of the CCP have been moving in this direction, as the implementation of the New Labor Contract Law in 2008 suggests. . . . On the other hand, it is doubtful whether these sociopolitical restructurings can be accomplished soon, as the sociopolitical order underlining the current economic expansion and its imbalance has taken root during three decades of market transition.

Given the great imbalance of the Chinese economy and the delay in its sociopolitical restructuring, China is increasingly vulnerable to any protracted global economic slump that can curtail China's capability of exporting its excess capacity to the world. On the other hand, we have reason to believe that China is likely to be able to emerge from such a crisis in the long run. Provided with the massive financial resources that the Chinese government has accumulated for the last two decades, it enjoys plentiful leeway to resort to large-scale fiscal stimulus and social spending to shore up consumption demand should the economy run into trouble. If the crisis lingers, the pains of economic collapse and the subsequent sociopolitical conflicts will probably generate an impetus that helps clear the vested interests' resistance to social reform and the restructuring of China's developmental model once and for all, hence accelerating the current half-hearted, incremental restructuring. It is reminiscent of how the Great Depression empowered the progressive reformers in the United States to break the resistance of big business to redistributive and regulatory reforms and introduce the New Deal, which hastened the transition of the economic growth of the United States from a reckless and unstable path dominated by robber barons at the turn of the twentieth century to the more sustainable course of Keynesian-Fordist growth in the mid-twentieth century.

Thus, despite the increasing likelihood of an economic slowdown or contraction in China in the short to medium run due to its overaccumulation tendency and environmental crisis, it is quite possible that the shift of the center of gravity of global capitalism to Asia in general and to China in particular will sustain in the long run, creating a new global order in the twenty-first century. The key determinant of whether this possibility can become reality is whether China can eventually transform its developmental model into a more egalitarian, more coordinated, and less environmentally destructive one.

FURTHER READING

Bunker, Stephen G., and Paul S. Ciccantell. 2007. *East Asia and the Global Economy: Japan's Ascent, with Implications for China's Future.* Baltimore: Johns Hopkins University Press.

Frank, Andre Gunder. 1998. *ReOrient: Global Economy in the Asian Age.* Berkeley: University of California Press.

Goodman, Roger, Ceri Peach, Ayumi Takenaka, and Paul White (Eds.). 2009. *Global Japan: The Experience of Japan's New Immigrant and Overseas Communities.* London: Routledge.

Huffman, James. 2010. *Japan in World History.* New York: Oxford University Press.

Hung, Ho-Fung. 2011. *Protest with Chinese Characteristics: Demonstrations, Riots, and Petitions in the Mid-Qing Dynasty.* New York: Columbia University Press.

Jacques, Martin. 2012. *When China Rules the World: The End of the Western World and the Birth of a New Global Order.* New York: Penguin.

Lardy, Nicholas R. 2000. *Sustaining China's Economic Growth after the Global Financial Crisis.* Washington, DC: Peterson Institute for International Economics.

Lee, Jongsoo. 2007. *The Partition of Korea after World War II: A Global History.* New York: Palgrave Macmillan.

Mahbubani, Kishore. 2008. *The New Asian Hemisphere: The Irresistible Shift of Global Power to the East.* New York: Perseus Books.

Pomeranz, Kenneth. 2001. *The Great Divergence: China, Europe, and the Making of the Modern World Economy.* Princeton, NJ: Princeton University Press.

Rigger, Shelley. 2011. *Why Taiwan Matters: Small Island, Global Powerhouse.* Lanham, MD: Rowman and Littlefield

Ropp, Paul S. 2010. *China in World History.* New York: Oxford University Press.

Shambaugh, David. 2013. *China Goes Global: The Partial Power.* New York: Oxford University Press.

Tudor, Daniel. 2012. *Korea: The Impossible Country.* Tokyo: Tuttle.

Wang, Chi. 2013. *The United States and China Since World War II.* New York: M.E. Sharp.

Westad, Odd Arne. 2012. *Restless Empire: China and the World Since 1750.* New York: Basic Books.

7

SOUTHEAST ASIA AND THE PACIFIC
The Edges of Globalization

Southeast Asia has been on the edges of great civilizations of Asia such as China and India. But also, its strategic geographic location has put the mainland and islands of Southeast Asia at the crossroads of commercial traffic and cultural interaction, leading it to have formidable transnational empires of its own. As a result, Southeast Asia has been a mélange of competing influences from ancient times to the present.

Southeast Asia consists of the land and islands east of India, south of China, and north of Australia. A distinction is often made between mainland and insular areas. Mainland Southeast Asia consists of Myanmar (also known as Burma), Thailand, Cambodia, Laos, and Vietnam; and island Southeast Asia is made up of Indonesia, Singapore, East Timor, Brunei, and the Philippines. Malaysia can be placed in either category. One part of it is the Malay Peninsula that juts southward from the mainland, while two other parts, Sabah and Sarawak, are located in northern Borneo—a large island that Malaysia shares with Indonesia and the small, oil-rich country of Brunei.

Like most of the regions of the world, it is not always clear where Southeast Asia starts and where it ends. What about Papua New Guinea, for instance? It is on the island of New Guinea at the eastern end of Indonesia and is sometimes included in Southeast Asia and sometimes in Oceania. In the other direction is the island of Sri Lanka, next to India. It is at times listed with Southeast Asia because of the Theravada Buddhist culture it shares with Thailand, Burma, Laos, and Cambodia, but usually it is linked with South Asia, since it was under British South Asian colonial control. Taiwan is sometimes grouped with Southeast Asia as well, though since it is ethnically and historically associated with China, it is far more often counted as a part of East Asia.

Australia and New Zealand could be considered to be within Southeast Asia, but they are often considered separately because of their predominantly European immigrant populations. They are sometimes regarded as part of Oceania, a term that encompasses the South Pacific island nations in the vast oceanic regions of Micronesia, Melanesia, and Polynesia. Many of the peoples of these islands retain traditional cultural customs, though they are affected by the demographic, cultural, and economic winds of globalization as well.

The original people of Southeast Asia were Austronesian, similar to Australian aboriginal people and residents of contemporary New Guinea. But from the third century BCE, and perhaps earlier, cultural, ethnic, and economic influences came from the West. These influences arrived along with seafaring traders from India and from traveling Hindu Brahmans. Chinese also discovered the wealth of Southeast Asia, including its spices and abundant forest products. The Chinese particularly valued the sea cucumbers gleaned from warm tropical waters and the nests of swallows where the bird's secretions glue the nests together, thus providing the key ingredient for bird's nest soup, a delicacy in Chinese cuisine.

From very ancient times, Hindu and Buddhist temples were established on both the mainland and island areas of Southeast Asia. The most famous of these structures that are still standing are the magnificent twelfth-century Hindu and Buddhist temple complex in Angkor Wat, Cambodia; the remarkable ninth-century Buddhist monument with its profusion of stupas at Borobudur, Indonesia; and the ninth-century Prambanam Hindu Temple in the nearby city of Yogyakarta in Indonesia. The Champa civilization—originally Hindu and later Muslim—dominated the central area of Vietnam in the ninth and tenth centuries. Although only a small number of people in Southeast Asia today are Hindu— the Hindu community in Indonesian Bali is the rare exception—Hinduism has left its mark on Southeast Asian culture. Ancient Hindu legendary figures and Sanskrit terms are inextricably woven into the fabric of Indonesian culture. The famous Indonesian performances of shadow puppets, *wayang kulit,* recounts the stories of the classic Hindu epic, the Ramayana; and the name of the national airlines, Garuda, evokes the image of the great bird that the Hindu god Vishnu rode like a stallion and which in the Hindu epic, the Mahabharata, is identified with the avatar of Vishnu, Lord Krishna. Muslim traders sailed to the Southeast Asian region, and from the thirteenth century on, Muslim settlements were established in the region. Eventually, the Indonesian population became predominantly Muslim, and today, Indonesia is the largest Islamic country in the world. More than forty percent of nearby Malaysia is also Muslim, and so is the nation of Brunei, which shares space on the island of Borneo along with parts of Malaysia and Indonesia.

Beginning in the sixteenth century, a parade of European ships sailed into Southeast Asian ports, looking for spices and other products to buy and take back to Europe for sale. The Portuguese were the first, followed by the Spanish, Dutch, British, and French. Remarkably, the tiny European country of the Netherlands was able to colonize the whole of Indonesia and its 17,803 islands. In fact, the Dutch colonial government gave Indonesia the elements of administrative and political unity that eventually made an independent country out of what the anthropologist Benedict Anderson called "an imagined community."

The Philippine islands were America's only colony in Southeast Asia. Initially, the islands were colonized by the Spanish, who named them after their monarch, Philip II. At the end of the Spanish-American War in 1898, the Philippine islands were sold to the United States for the monumental sum of $20 million dollars. Philippine nationalists thought that they would soon proclaim the Philippines' independence, but the country became an American colony, and it remained so until 1935, when it achieved commonwealth status; it finally received its full independence in 1946.

Hence, the global effects of colonialization that gave Southeast Asia its political boundaries also set the stage for the twentieth-century form of political globalization—the emergence of independent nation-states. Independence was the goal of the Vietnamese as they struggled first against the French colonial government and then against a local one supported by the United States. The United States was involved in Vietnam not because it wanted to replace the French in colonizing Vietnam, but rather because of another aspect of global politics in the latter half of the twentieth century—the worldwide Cold War. Fearing that the Marxist government of North Vietnam would want to take over the whole country and make it part of the Communist world, the American military was brought in to defend the fledgling South Vietnamese government and protect its Catholic supporters. According to the "domino theory" of the prevailing American Cold War policy at the time, the march of communism had to be halted in Vietnam; otherwise, like dominoes lined up in a row, one Southeast Asia country after another would fall into Communist hands until the whole of the region was a part of the Marxist world.

Eventually, the U.S. military retreated from Vietnam and, as it turned out, the domino theory was wrong: the rest of Southeast Asia did not become Communist. The end of the war did contribute to another aspect of globalization, however—the growing spread of immigrant and refugee Southeast Asia communities to the United States and around the world.

The selections in this section begin with an excerpt from a famous book on the "Indianization" of Southeast Asia by the French historian and archeologist Georges Coedès. He had lived for a time in Thailand and traveled frequently to Indochina, where he uncovered significant sites indicating the ancient spread of Hindu culture throughout the region. In this excerpt, Coedès writes about the various Hindu influences—cultural and legal—that persist in Southeast Asia. In the next excerpt, the American anthropologist Benedict Anderson writes about how the Dutch colonialists in Indonesia prepared the way for that country's independence as a single political entity when it was transformed into "the spectacular butterfly called Indonesia."

The next essay in this section shows how two significant processes in globalization are related in the Vietnam War and its aftermath. The author, Sucheng Chan, is a social scientist and historian who was born in China and became a Chinese American, teaching at the Berkeley, Santa Cruz, and Santa Barbara campuses of the University of California, where she helped to develop the field of Asian American studies. In this essay she shows how the Vietnam War was a product of the global wave of decolonialization and the ideological conflict of the Cold War. At the end of thirty years of war in 1975, waves of Vietnamese refugees fled the country; many of them found their way to the United States. Thus, the war contributed to another global trend at the end of the twentieth century and the rise of the twenty-first: the worldwide diffusion of cultures and peoples in global diaspora communities.

The final selections focus on Australia and New Zealand and the island countries of the Pacific. Australia was settled by the British and identified with the West until after the end of World War II. After that, leading citizens began to identify more with Southeast and East Asia as Australia's economic partners. Eventually, the country became more ethnically and culturally diverse as well. The author of this selection, Celeste Lipow MacLeod, is an American writer who lives in Berkeley, California, but frequently travels to Australia, where she observes its changing role within the region. The final selection looks eastward to the vast ocean stretches of the Southern Pacific, where island nations make up the distinctive Micronesian, Melanesian, and Polynesian regions. Joel Robbins, the author of this essay, is an anthropologist at the University of California, San Diego, who has researched the changing cultural patterns of the indigenous people of Papua New Guinea, who have converted to Christianity. Robbins shows how the effects of globalization have a profound cultural effect on the traditional societies of these island ocean countries.

THE INDIANIZED STATES OF SOUTHEAST ASIA

~~Georges Coedès~~

The importance of studying the Indianized countries of Southeast Asia—which . . . were never political dependencies of India, but rather cultural colonies—lies above all in the observation of the impact of Indian civilization on the primitive civilizations. [My] work has no other object than to provide the historical and chronological framework of the implantation of Indian culture and its continued transformation on contact with the native societies. We can measure the power of penetration of this culture by the importance of that which remains of it in these countries even though all of them except Siam passed sooner or later under European domination and a great part of the area was converted to Islam.

Except on the island of Bali and among some Cham groups, the Indian cults in their old form—Sivaism, Vishnuism, the Theravada Buddhism that used the Sanskrit language, and Mahayana Buddhism—have disappeared, but not without leaving traces. In Phnom Penh and Bangkok, Brahmans of very mixed blood, Brahmans who follow Buddhism but wear chignons and the Brahman thread, officiate at all the great royal ceremonies, the ritual of which is an inheritance from the Indian epoch. But these ceremonies are holdovers that interest only the court and do not affect the general population.

In the twelfth and thirteenth centuries the common people received a new contribution from India in the form of Singhalese Buddhism. The penetration of this new faith to the masses cannot be doubted: in Cambodia, Siam, Laos, and Burma, Buddhist cosmogony and cosmology and the doctrines of retribution for one's acts and of transmigration have been deeply implanted in the humblest classes by the teaching of the Buddhist monks.

It is difficult to say what would have happened in Indonesia if Islam had not come to cut the spiritual ties with Brahmanic India. The mildness and tolerance of Islam in Java are often attributed to the character of the Javanese population. But Javanese peoples are not fundamentally different in origin from the other Indonesian peoples, the Bataks of Sumatra, the Dayaks of Borneo, and the mountain people of the Indochinese cordillera, none of whom are known for the gentleness of their ways. So we may ask ourselves if the particular aspect assumed by Islam in Java was not due rather to the influence that Indian religions exercised over the character of the inhabitants of the island for more than ten centuries.

The literary heritage from ancient India is even more apparent than the religious heritage. Throughout the entire Indian period, the *Rāmāyana* and the *Mahābhārata,* the *Harivamśa,* and the *Purānas* were the principal, if not the only, sources of inspiration for local literature. In all of the Indianized mainland, in Malaysia, and on Java, this epic and legendary literature, to which was added the Buddhist folklore of the *Jātakas,* still makes up the substance of the classical theater, of the dances, and of the shadow-plays and puppet theater. From one end of Farther India to the other, spectators continue to weep over the misfortunes of Rāma and Sītā and to be moved by the virtues of the Bodhisattva, and the theatrical performances they attend have retained their original character of pantomime: the positions and the movements of the arms and legs and the gestures of the hands constitute a silent language capable of suggesting a subject, evoking an action, or expressing a sentiment, exactly as in Indian choreography.

The influence of Indian law has been no less profound. The *dharmaśāstras,* and especially the most famous of them known as the "laws of Manu," have formed the framework for the ordering of local customs of the Indianized countries in somewhat the same fashion that Latin law served the barbarian societies that were constructed on the ruins of the Roman Empire.

The *arthaśāstras,* or political treatises, have also had an influence. They have contributed to the fashioning of the hierarchical administration of the states of Farther India, an administration that is dominated by the person of the king, whose conduct is still theoretically guided by the precepts of the *rājanīti,* or "royal conduct."

Although the Indian colonists undoubtedly spoke Prakrit dialects or Dravidian languages, it was the scholarly language, Sanskrit, that served and still serves to enrich the vocabulary of the native languages with a considerable number of words. . . . Technical terms referring to the material world were also borrowed. And so were grammatical particles, which had the important effect of making the native isolating languages more flexible, enabling them to express thoughts natural to the vehicle of flexible languages.

The native languages have not only been enriched and made more flexible by India; they have above all been stabilized, thanks to the use of Indian script. The common origin of the Mon, Burmese, Thai, Khmer, Cham, Javanese, and Balinese systems of writing is still recognizable.

To turn to another area of knowledge: in spite of the virtually universal adoption of the Gregorian calendar for official purposes, the Indian lunar-solar year is still in popular use; and the dating systems in use, including both the Buddhist era system based on 543 BC and the "little era" system based on AD 638, are also of Indian origin.

Finally, the beneficial influence of a superior civilization freely accepted was strikingly felt in the realm of the arts. In fact, as Sylvain Lévi has said, India "produced its definitive masterworks only through the activity of the foreigner or on foreign soil. . . . In architecture, it is in distant Cambodia and Java that we must seek the two marvels born of the Indian genius: Angkor and the Borobudur."

How did the Indian aesthetic, transplanted to Cambodia, Java, and the other countries of Farther India, give birth to Khmer art, Javanese art, and the other Indian arts of the Far East? This is one of the most delicate problems facing archaeologists. In the study of the common Indian origin of these arts, we must not forget that there is an enormous gap in documentation for the period from the start of Indianization around the beginning of the Christian Era to the first known monuments, which do not date back any farther than the sixth century. The very remarkable differences that clearly distinguish the oldest architectural and sculptural monuments of Champa, Cambodia, and Java from those of India proper would undoubtedly surprise us much less if we had the intermediaries we lack, intermediaries that in architecture were undoubtedly made of perishable materials.

The influence of the native substratum on Indian art was mostly formal, external; that is why, from the very first, it is more striking than the internal ties that unite the plastic arts of Farther India to India. We know no monument in India resembling even remotely the Bayon of Angkor Thom or the Borobudur. And yet these monuments are pure productions of the Indian genius, the deep meaning of which is apparent only to the eyes of the Indianist.

Much the same thing is true in the other domains: religious, literary, and legal. Underneath the diversity of the civilizations of Farther India, underneath their apparent uniqueness . . . lies the imprint of the Indian genius, which gives the countries . . . a family likeness and produces a clear contrast between these countries and the lands that have been civilized by China.

IMAGINED COMMUNITIES

Benedict Anderson

In 1913, the Dutch colonial regime in Batavia, taking its lead from The Hague, sponsored massive colony-wide festivities to celebrate the centennial of the "national liberation" of the Netherlands from French imperialism. Orders went out to secure physical participation and financial contributions, not merely from the local Dutch and Eurasian communities, but also from the subject native population. In protest, the early Javanese-Indonesian nationalist Suwardi Surjaningrat (Ki Hadjar Dewantoro) wrote his famous Dutch-language newspaper article "Als ik eens Nederlander was" (If I were for once to be a Dutchman).

> In my opinion, there is something out of place—something indecent—if we (I still being a Dutchman in my imagination) ask the natives to join the festivities which celebrate our independence. Firstly, we will hurt their sensitive feelings because we are here celebrating our own independence in their native country which we colonize. At the moment we are very happy because a hundred years ago we liberated ourselves from foreign domination; and all of this is occurring in front of the eyes of those who are still under our domination. Does it not occur to us that these poor slaves are also longing for such a moment as this, when they like us will be able to celebrate their independence? Or do we perhaps feel that because of our soul-destroying policy we regard all human souls as dead? If that is so, then we are deluding ourselves, because no matter how primitive a community is, it is against any type of oppression. If I were a Dutchman, I would not organize an independence celebration in a country where the independence of the people has been stolen.

With these words Suwardi was able to turn Dutch history against the Dutch, by scraping boldly at the weld between Dutch nationalism and imperialism. Furthermore, by the imaginary transformation of himself into a temporary Dutchman (which invited a reciprocal transformation of his Dutch readers into temporary Indonesians), he undermined all the racist fatalities that underlay Dutch colonial ideology.

Suwardi's broadside—which delighted his Indonesian as much as it irritated his Dutch audience—is exemplary of a world-wide twentieth-century phenomenon. For the paradox of imperial official nationalism was that it inevitably brought what were increasingly thought of and written about as European "national histories" into the consciousnesses of the colonized—not merely via occasional obtuse festivities, but also through reading-rooms and classrooms. Vietnamese youngsters could not avoid learning about the *philosophes* and the Revolution, and what Debray calls "our secular antagonism to Germany." Magna Carta, the Mother of Parliaments, and the Glorious Revolution, glossed as English national history, entered schools all over the British Empire. Belgium's independence struggle against Holland was not erasable from schoolbooks Congolese children would one day read. So also the histories of the USA in the Philippines and, last of all, Portugal in Mozambique and Angola. The irony, of course, is that these histories were written out of a historiographical consciousness which by the turn of the century was, all over Europe, becoming nationally defined. (The barons who imposed Magna Carta on John Plantagenet did not speak "English," and had no conception of themselves as "Englishmen," but they were firmly defined as early patriots in the classrooms of the United Kingdom 700 years later.)

Yet there is a characteristic feature of the emerging nationalist intelligentsias in the colonies which to some degree marks them off from the vernacularizing nationalist intelligentsias of nineteenth-century Europe. Almost invariably they were very young, and attached a complex political significance to their youth—a significance which, though it has changed over time, remains important to this day. The rise of (modern/ organized) Burmese nationalism is often dated to the founding in 1908 of the Young Men's Buddhist Association in Rangoon; and of Malayan by the establishment in 1938 of the Kesatuan Melayu Muda (Union of Malay Youth). Indonesians annually celebrate the *Sumpah Pemuda* (Oath of Youth) drawn up and sworn by the nationalist youth congress of 1928. And so on. It is perfectly true that in one sense Europe had been there before—if we think of Young Ireland, Young Italy, and the like. Both in Europe and in the colonies "young" and "youth" signified dynamism, progress, self-sacrificing idealism and revolutionary will. But in Europe "young" had little in the way of definable sociological contours. One could be middle-aged and still part of Young Ireland; one could be illiterate and still part of Young Italy. The reason, of course, was that the language of these nationalisms was either a vernacular mother-tongue to which the members had spoken access from the cradle, or, as in the case of Ireland, a metropolitan language which had sunk such deep roots in sections of the population over centuries of conquest that it too could manifest itself, creole-style, as a vernacular. There was thus no necessary connection between language, age, class, and status.

In the colonies things were very different. Youth meant, above all, the *first* generation in any significant numbers to have acquired a European education, marking them off linguistically and culturally from their parents' generation, as well from the vast bulk of their colonized agemates. . . . Burma's "English-language" YMBA, modelled in part on the YMCA, was built by English-reading schoolboys. In the Netherlands Indies one finds, *inter alia,* Jong Java (Young Java), Jong Ambon (Young Amboina), and Jong Islamietenbond (League of Young Muslims) — titles incomprehensible to any young native unacquainted with the colonial tongue. In the colonies, then, by "Youth" we mean "Schooled Youth," at least at the start. This in turn reminds us again of the unique role played by colonial school-systems in promoting colonial nationalisms.

The case of Indonesia affords a fascinatingly intricate illustration of this process, not least because of its enormous size, huge population (even in colonial times), geographical fragmentation (about 3,000 islands), religious variegation (Muslims, Buddhists, Catholics, assorted Protestants, Hindu-Balinese, and "animists"), and ethnolinguistic diversity (well over 100 distinct groups). Furthermore, as its hybrid pseudo-Hellenic name suggests, its stretch does not remotely correspond to any precolonial domain; on the contrary, at least until General Suharto's brutal invasion of ex-Portuguese East Timor in 1975, its boundaries have been those left behind by the last Dutch conquests (c. 1910).

Some of the peoples on the eastern coast of Sumatra are not only physically close, across the narrow Straits of Malacca, to the populations of the western littoral of the Malay Peninsula, but they are ethnically related, understand each other's speech, have a common religion, and so forth. These same Sumatrans share neither mother-tongue, ethnicity, nor religion with the Ambonese, located on islands thousands of miles away to the east. Yet during this century they have come to understand the Ambonese as fellow-Indonesians, the Malays as foreigners.

Nothing nurtured this bonding more than the schools that the regime in Batavia set up in increasing numbers after the turn of the century. To see why, one has to remember that in complete contrast to traditional, indigenous schools, which were always local and personal enterprises (even if, in good Muslim fashion, there was plenty of horizontal movement of students from one particularly well-reputed ulama-teacher to another), the government schools formed a colossal, highly rationalized, tightly centralized hierarchy, structurally analogous to the state bureaucracy itself. Uniform textbooks, standardized diplomas and teaching certificates, a strictly regulated gradation of age-groups, classes and instructional materials, in themselves created a self-contained, coherent universe of experience. But no less important was the hierarchy's geography. Standardized elementary schools came to be scattered about in villages and small townships of the colony; junior and senior middle-schools in larger towns and provincial centres; while tertiary education (the pyramid's apex) was confined to the colonial capital of Batavia and the Dutch-built city of Bandung, 100 miles southwest in the cool Priangan highlands. Thus the twentieth-century colonial school-system brought into being pilgrimages which paralleled longer-established functionary journeys. The Rome of these pilgrimages was Batavia: not Singapore, not Manila, not Rangoon, not even the old Javanese royal capitals of Jogjakarta and Surakarta. From all over the vast colony, but from nowhere outside it, the tender pilgrims made their inward, upward way, meeting fellow-pilgrims from different, perhaps once hostile, villages in primary school; from different ethnolinguistic groups in middle-school; and from every part of the realm in the tertiary institutions of the capital. And they knew that from wherever they had come they still had read the same books and done the same sums. They also knew, even if they never got so far—and most did not—that Rome was Batavia, and that all these journeyings derived their "sense" from the capital, in effect explaining why "we" are "here" "together." To put it another way, their common experience, and the amiably competitive comradeship of the classroom, gave the maps of the colony which they studied (always coloured differently from British Malaya or the American Philippines) a territorially specific imagined reality which was every day confirmed by the accents and physiognomies of their classmates.

And what were they all together? The Dutch were quite clear on this point: whatever mother-tongue they spoke, they were irremediably *inlanders,* a word which, like the English "natives" and the French "*indigènes,*" always carried an unintentionally paradoxical semantic load. In this colony, as in each separate, other colony, it meant that the persons referred to were both "inferior" *and "belonged there"* (just as the Dutch, being "natives" of Holland, belonged *there*). Conversely, the Dutch by such language assigned themselves, along with superiority, "not-belonging-there." The word also implied that in their common inferiority, the *inlanders* were *equally* contemptible, no matter what ethnolinguistic group or class they came from. Yet even this miserable equality of condition had a definite perimeter. For *inlander* always raised the question "native of what?" If the Dutch sometimes spoke as if *inlanders* were a world-category, experience showed that this notion was hardly sustainable in practice. *Inlanders* stopped at the coloured colony's drawn edge. Beyond that were, variously, "natives," *indigènes* and *indios*. Moreover, colonial legal terminology included the category *vreemde oosterlingen* (foreign Orientals), which had the dubious ring of false coin—as it were "foreign natives." Such "foreign Orientals," mainly Chinese, Arabs and Japanese, though they might live in the colony, had a politico-legal status superior to that of the "native natives." Furthermore, tiny Holland was sufficiently awed by the Meiji oligarchs' economic strength and military prowess for Japanese in the colony to be legally promoted, from 1899 on, to "honorary Europeans." From all this, by a sort of sedimentation, *inlander*—excluding whites, Dutchmen, Chinese, Arabs, Japanese, "natives," *indigènes,* and *indios*—grew ever more specific in content; until, like a ripe larva, it was suddenly transmogrified into the spectacular butterfly called "Indonesian."

VIETNAM, 1945–2000: THE GLOBAL DIMENSIONS OF DECOLONIZATION, WAR, REVOLUTION, AND REFUGEE OUTFLOWS

Sucheng Chan

Scholars, journalists, and others who write about globalization have focused mainly on the economic, technological, and cultural aspects of globalization. Far less attention has been paid to globalizing geopolitical configurations, especially those that appeared in the years after the end of the Second World War, the most consequential of which were decolonization and the Cold War and its proxy hot wars in Asia. Decolonization and the Cold War have engendered a voluminous scholarly literature, but these two topics have been treated as separate historical developments. In fact, the two were concurrent and intertwined phenomena. One way to see the connections between them is to examine the history of Vietnam from the end of the Second World War to the turn of the twenty-first century.

Decolonization, the process that transformed colonies into independent nation-states either by bloody wars of national liberation or by nonviolent transfers of political power, occurred unexpectedly fast. In just four decades after 1945, virtually all the lands in Asia and Africa that had been colonized by Britain, France, the Netherlands, Portugal, and the United States over four and a half centuries gained their independence, in the process changing an earth that had been divided into competing western European colonial powers and their (often territorially huge) overseas colonies into a world with some two hundred sovereign countries. (Two other European empires had disintegrated earlier: Spain lost its empire in Latin America, the Philippines, and several Pacific Ocean islands during the nineteenth century while Germany lost its colonies in Africa and in islands in the Pacific Ocean as a result of its defeat during the First World War.) The two post-World War II superpowers, the United States and the former Union of Soviet Socialist Republics (USSR), pressured the new nations to ally with them as they broke free from European colonial control. Some did so but a significant number refused to be sucked into the superpowers' spheres of influence. Instead, they launched a non-aligned, neutralist movement that gained global visibility at the 1955 Bandung Conference held in Indonesia and attended by representatives from twenty-nine Asian and African nations that contained half of the world's total population at the time.

The USA-USSR confrontation called the Cold War developed concurrently as the decolonization process. Both countries possessed atomic and hydrogen bombs, which meant that any "hot" conflict might have led to mutual nuclear annihilation. So the war had to be kept "cold," to be fought over political, ideological, economic, and cultural grounds, with a gigantic buildup of armaments intended to prevent, rather than carry on, a war. The war began in 1946 as the USSR tightened its grip on Eastern Europe and ended in 1989-1991 when it lost control over its satellite or client states in Poland, East Germany, Hungary, Czechoslovakia, Romania, Bulgaria, Yugoslavia, and Albania. This was a falling-dominos scenario that culminated in the dissolution of the former Soviet Union itself into fifteen separate countries—Estonia, Latvia, Lithuania, Belarus, Ukraine, Moldova, Georgia, Armenia, Azerbaijan, Kazakhstan, Kyrgyzstan, Turkmenistan, Uzbekistan, Tajikistan, and the Russian Federation. It can be argued that the breakup of the Russian/Soviet empire was the last stage of decolonization in the modern world. The Cold War was not entirely cold, however. Hot "limited" wars raged in China, Korea, Vietnam, Laos, and Cambodia that killed millions of people and devastated the lands on which they were fought. These conflicts were simultaneously civil wars and proxy wars of the Cold War because the opposing belligerents within each country were supported militarily, politically, economically, and diplomatically either by the Communist camp or by the "Free World" camp. The Cold War was waged in three theaters of operation: 1) in an European continent divided into a Communist-dominated Eastern Europe and a pro-American Western Europe, a Germany divided into East (Communist) and West (anti-Communist) Germany, and the city of Berlin divided into East and West Berlin until 1990; 2) in Asia where the wars resulted in a divided China (between a Communist mainland and an anti-Communist regime on the island of Taiwan since 1949), in Korea (between a Communist North Korea and an anti-Communist South Korea since 1948), and in Vietnam (between a Communist North Vietnam and an anti-Communist South Vietnam from 1954 until 1975); and 3) in scattered locales in Latin America and Africa.

France colonized Vietnam, Cambodia, and Laos, situated on the eastern part of mainland Southeast Asia, between 1862 and 1889. The French dubbed their new colonies "French Indochina," made up of Cochinchina (southern Vietnam), Annam (central Vietnam), Tonkin (northern Vietnam), Cambodia, and Laos. The French governed them indirectly, with the exception of Cochinchina, which they ruled directly. In the four indirectly governed colonies, native rulers were allowed to remain on their thrones but they had no real power. Vietnam, especially Cochinchina, was always of the greatest importance to the French, who had a much more positive view of the abilities of the Vietnamese than of Cambodians and Laotians. The lower echelons of the French colonial administration, not only in the three regions of Vietnam, but also in Cambodia and Laos, were staffed by Vietnamese civil servants.

Beginning in the 1920s, a nationalist movement based on traditional patriotism emerged in Vietnam to challenge French rule. A small number of politically conscious Vietnamese also became attracted to Marxism— an ideology that, along with its organizational blueprint for carrying out socialist revolutions around the world, might prove useful for their own anti-colonial struggles even though Karl Marx's original analysis dealt with capitalism and not colonialism. To make Marxism applicable to Czarist Russia, Vladimir Lenin propounded that a vanguard Communist Party could lead a revolution in the name of workers even when the number of industrial workers in a country was small—an insight proven correct with the success of the Bolshevik Revolution in 1917. In China, Mao Zedong further expanded Marxist theory to argue that peasants could also play a significant revolutionary role as he "creatively" applied Marxism to China's specific conditions.

Ho Chi Minh, the scion of a respected but impoverished scholar-gentry family in central Vietnam, likewise found revolutionary inspiration in Marxism-Leninism. He left Vietnam in 1911, serving as a cook's assistant on a ship that enabled him to visit many ports in Africa and Europe. Next he lived for several years each in Great Britain and France. In 1920, he participated in the founding of the French Communist Party. During his sojourn in France, he wrote and published many articles and pamphlets. Then he went to Moscow to study Marxism, especially its Leninist exegesis, more deeply and worked for the Comintern—the Communist organization founded in 1919 dedicated to the overthrow of the "international bourgeoisie." Ho established the Vietnamese Revolutionary Youth Association in 1925; it was the first explicitly Marxist organization among Vietnamese. He then founded the Indochinese Communist Party in 1930 while he was in Hong Kong. During the next decade, he moved stealthily from one place to another to elude the dragnet of the French *sûreté* (undercover police) and finally returned to Vietnam three decades after he had left.

After Nazi Germany invaded France in 1940 and set up a collaborationist government under Philippe Pétain located in the town of Vichy, anti-Nazi French resistance fighters under General Charles de Gaulle established a French government-in-exile in London and began building an armed force, the Free French, with headquarters in the North African French colony of Algeria. Neither the Free French nor the Vichy government was able to maintain contact with French colonial administrators in Indochina; the latter were thus left to fend for themselves.

Meanwhile, Japan, which was intent on enlarging its empire in Asia beyond the Korean peninsula, the island of Taiwan, and the northeastern provinces of China that it had acquired between 1910 and 1937, made an agreement with the French Vichy government to allow Japanese troops to be stationed in and to transit through Vietnam as

Japan prepared to invade the British colonies of Malaya, Singapore, and Burma; the U.S. colony in the Philippines; and the Dutch colony in the Netherlands East Indies (today's Indonesia). Japan also pressured Thailand, the only Southeast Asian country that was never colonized, to accede to Japanese troop movements through that country. The planned Japanese conquests began in December 1941 (simultaneously with the Japanese bombing of the U.S. fleet anchored in Pearl Harbor, Hawaii) and were carried out with lightning speed. Given the agreement between Japan and the French Vichy government, the colonial administrative apparatus in Vietnam, Cambodia, and Laos was left intact. No fighting occurred in Indochina (or Thailand), thereby sparing the land and people from wartime destruction. However, more than a million Vietnamese died from a severe famine during the war because Japanese troops had forcibly requisitioned the region's rice harvests, leaving peasants with little to eat.

As the war turned against Japan in the Pacific, Japanese authorities decided to turn over control of Southeast Asia to native political leaders. The Japanese arrested the French on March 9, 1945 and imprisoned them. They urged the local leaders to declare their independence because Japan did not wish to see the British, French, Dutch, and American colonial regimes return to Southeast Asia even as its own dream of establishing a Greater East Asia Co-Prosperity Sphere vanished. Emperor Bao Dai of Vietnam promptly abrogated the treaties that the French had imposed on his ancestors and declared that Vietnam was once again a unified and independent country. At the same time, the Indochinese Communist Party, with a ragtag army of about three thousand men, under the cloak of a broad coalition it had formed called the Viet Minh, began seizing weapons and ammunition from French armories and started taking over villages in northern Vietnam. Japan's unconditional surrender, after the United States dropped atomic bombs on Hiroshima and Nagasaki on August 6 and 9, 1945, respectively, brought World War II to a sudden end. A year before that, the Free French, along with U.S. forces under General George S. Patton, had liberated Paris. Soon thereafter, General Charles de Gaulle ordered some French paratroopers to be parachuted into Vietnam to prepare the ground for an eventual French return to Indochina.

After Japan's surrender, with the help of the British, whose navy transported French military officers and civilian officials to Saigon in October, all the French people whom the Japanese had imprisoned were released from prison. The French then fought their way northward, trying to reclaim territory that the Viet Minh's forces had taken. Before the French arrival, Ho Chi Minh had proclaimed the establishment of the Democratic Republic of Vietnam (commonly called "North Vietnam") on September 2, 1945 in Hanoi. Three days earlier, Emperor Bao Dai had abdicated the throne and turned a golden sword and the imperial seal—royal insignia of the Nguyen dynasty—over to a Viet Minh delegation. As French and Vietnamese forces fought, with the French dominating the cities and the Viet Minh the countryside, Ho's comrade, Pham Van Dong, negotiated with the French government in Paris for a political settlement but without success. In late November 1946, after Viet Minh shore batteries fired shots at a French boat in Haiphong harbor, the French bombarded Haiphong, killing six thousand civilians. The First Indochina War, an anti-colonial war of independence, began in December and lasted eight long years. The French colonial regime ended in 1954 after Vietnamese Communist forces dealt French forces a decisive defeat in a valley called Dien Bien Phu in northwestern Vietnam near the Vietnamese-Laotian border. The 1954 Geneva Conference divided Vietnam into two at the seventeenth parallel with the stipulation that elections be held in 1956 to determine the political future of the country. The Geneva settlement allowed people in the north to migrate south and vice versa. U.S. Navy ships helped transport about a million people, many of them Catholics who feared persecution under Communist rule, from the north southward to the Republic of Vietnam (commonly known as "South Vietnam"). Viet Minh adherents in the south simultaneously moved north.

The Geneva Agreements did not end fighting in Vietnam, however. Between 1954 and 1965, the anti-colonial war morphed into a sporadic civil war between North and South Vietnam. The 1956 elections mandated by the Geneva accords never took place because the South Vietnamese government under President Ngo Dinh Diem refused to hold nationwide elections, fearing that the Communists might win. The U.S.-supported Diem regime launched a campaign to hunt down, imprison, and kill suspected Communists as well as members of two religious sects. Opposition against the repressive Diem government grew. Even Buddhist monks, a few of whom immolated themselves, participated in the protests. In response, North Vietnam created Group 559 in May 1959 to infiltrate weapons and political cadres into South Vietnam, transporting heavy loads on bicycles moving via a complex web of paths dubbed the Ho Chi Minh Trail that ran along the Laotian-Vietnamese and Cambodian-Vietnamese borders, hidden from view by thick canopies of trees. North Vietnam also organized Group 759 in July of the same year to send supplies southward by sea. In December 1960, the National Liberation Front (Communists in South Vietnam), whom President Diem called the "Viet Cong," came into being. In November 1963, several South Vietnamese generals, with the connivance of the U.S. Central Intelligence Agency, murdered President Diem and his brother. There followed a period of great political instability. Eventually, South Vietnam came to be controlled by two generals-turned-politicians, Nguyen Van Thieu and Nguyen Cao Ky.

U.S. involvement in Vietnam had begun quietly during the First Indochina War. Even though the United States was not eager to see the French re-colonize Indochina, the administration of President Harry S Truman decided it had to support the French because it was important that France exert maximum effort to help hold back Soviet advances in Europe. To secure U.S. involvement, the French characterized their war in Vietnam as an anti-Communist campaign—a crucial component of the Cold War. To reduce American uneasiness over aiding a re-colonization campaign, the French government used U.S. aid to pay for its domestic expenditures while appropriating revenues it collected itself to pay for the cost of the war in Vietnam. By 1954, U.S. aid to France equaled four-fifths of the total cost of that war.

As Americans entered the scene, the nature of the war between North and South Vietnam changed once again—this time from a civil war to a proxy war of the Cold War. The United States and its allies fought on the side of South Vietnam, while the Soviet Union and China supported North Vietnam with military supplies and a large number of advisors. In the United States, during the administration of President John F. Kennedy, 12,000 military advisors, including members of the U.S. Army Special Forces, were sent to South Vietnam. After Kennedy's assassination, President Lyndon B. Johnson augmented that number to 23,000, composed of both military and civilian advisors. Johnson also authorized commando raids into the areas where the Ho Chi Minh Trail ran in an effort to disrupt Communist supply lines, air and naval surveillance of North Vietnam, and increased U.S. economic aid to South Vietnam. After the North Vietnamese allegedly torpedoed the U.S. destroyer, the *Maddox*, in the Gulf of Tonkin in July 1964, Congress voted overwhelmingly for the Tonkin Gulf Resolution to allow the president to take "all necessary measures to repel any armed attacks against the forces of the United States and to prevent further aggression." In December 1964, the United States initiated bombing raids over the Ho Chi Minh Trail and in March 1965, the first two U.S. marine brigades landed in Danang, South Vietnam. The American Vietnam War (sometimes called the Second Indochina War) lasted from 1965 to 1973.

At its peak, more than half a million U.S. troops were fighting in Vietnam at a time. Ever larger and more destructive bombing raids, dropping not only bombs but also napalm and defoliants, destroyed huge areas of Vietnam, including all of North Vietnam's industrial and transportation infrastructure. More than a million tons of bombs were dropped over North Vietnam and four times that number over South Vietnam. Together with the one and a half million tons of bombs dropped over Laos, and half a million tons over Cambodia, the total tonnage greatly exceeded the combined tonnage of bombs dropped on Nazi Germany and the countries it occupied during World War II. Still, Communist troops managed to persevere. American combat casualties included more than 58,000 killed, more than 303,600 wounded (about half of whom required hospitalization), plus more than 2,600 missing in action, and 779 prisoners of war of whom 600 were freed with the rest dying in captivity. Casualty numbers for Vietnamese, in both South and North Vietnam, are less precise. Conservative estimates of South Vietnamese combat casualties give a figure of over 250,000 while that for North Vietnamese and Viet Cong troops was over a million. A 1995 Vietnamese government report claimed that the total civilian casualties in both parts of Vietnam was about two million. American military involvement finally ended in early 1973 after years of tortuous secret negotiations between President Richard M. Nixon's national security advisor, Henry Kissinger, and Le Duc Tho, a representative of North Vietnam. After all American forces withdrew from Vietnam in March 1973, the war continued as a civil war once again. It ended on April 30, 1975, when Saigon fell. Launching the Ho Chi Minh Campaign on March 31, 1975, North Vietnamese forces took only a month to rout ARVN (Army of the Republic of Vietnam) soldiers, chasing them all the way from central Vietnam to the Mekong

Delta in the country's southernmost region. In 1976, the two Vietnams were formally re-unified; the new name of the country is the Socialist Republic of Vietnam, a Communist regime. Thus, the 30-year long armed conflict in Vietnam entwined an anti-colonial war with two periods of civil war, a proxy war of the Cold War, and a Communist revolution.

These wars generated streams of refugees. The first group left in 1975 just before the fall of Saigon. They consisted mostly of government officials, wealthy people, well-educated professionals, white-collar workers, and some women who had worked in bars and brothels who had become acquainted with American troops—all of them fearing potential Communist persecution. The United States helped evacuate about 130,000 people, who were resettled in places large and small around the United States with the help of newly created, as well as existing, government agencies. Private voluntary agencies likewise played a crucial role. Once in power, the Communist regime that now ruled all of Vietnam rounded up former South Vietnamese government officials, military officers, and other prominent persons who had not escaped and sent them to "re-education camps," where the prisoners were taught Marxist doctrine, assigned to hard labor, and severely disciplined or even killed for even small infractions. The government also confiscated and nationalized the businesses, both wholesale and retail, owned by Vietnam's ethnic Chinese and forced some of them to move to New Economic Zones in the wilderness where they were expected to survive as farmers but without being given shelter, food, farm tools, seeds, or draft animals. In the late 1970s, hundreds of thousands of "boat people," so called because they escaped in small boats, many of which were not seaworthy, fled from southern Vietnam to neighboring countries in Southeast Asia. An estimated seventy percent of them were ethnic Chinese whose families had lived in Vietnam for generations in some cases. In northern Vietnam, almost a quarter million ethnic Chinese fled across the mountainous Vietnamese-Chinese border into China and were resettled on collective farms in four southern provinces.

The "boat people" exodus created an international crisis as neighboring countries of first asylum (mainly Thailand, Malaysia, Indonesia, the Philippines, and the then-British crown colony of Hong Kong) tried to stem the influx by towing boats back out to sea. Countries of second asylum or resettlement—primarily the United States, France, Canada, and Australia—screened the refuge-seekers huddled in refugee camps set up by the United Nations High Commissioner of Refugees (UNHCR) to determine whom to take in but they could not do so fast enough to prevent the number of refuge-seekers from increasing almost exponentially. Dozens of other countries also admitted small numbers. The attitude toward the "boat people" hardened when large ships each carrying thousands of refuge-seekers appeared on the shores of countries of first asylum. An investigation discovered that the passengers had paid large sums to the Vietnamese government and had been forced to hand over all their property before they were allowed to leave. Unlike the small boats that formed the first stage of the "boat people" exodus, this new stage appeared to be a well-organized, large-scale "ethnic cleansing" project carried out by the Vietnamese government. This fact led to a loud outcry against the Communist regime.

Two international conferences, the first convened in 1979, the second in 1989, resulted in efforts to bring some order to the chaotic situation. Under the aegis of the UNHCR, an Orderly Departure Program (ODP) was set up to allow would-be refugees to apply for admission into countries of second asylum while they were still in Vietnam. People in refugee camps who did not meet the United Nations definition of "refugee" were repatriated, often against their will. To be accepted as bona fide refugees, people had to demonstrate that they had a well-founded fear of being persecuted because of their membership in certain ethnic, social, or political groups. Between 1989 and 1992, more than 300,000 Vietnamese left the country legally via the ODP for resettlement abroad. About three-quarters of them came to the United States. By the end of 1996, all the refugee camps except a number in Hong Kong were closed.

As a gesture of its acceptance of responsibility for the war and its consequences, Congress passed special legislation to admit Amerasians (the children of American fathers and Vietnamese mothers) and their mothers and minor siblings, as well as former inmates of re-education camps who had been imprisoned for three years or longer and their immediate family members. The two groups together, admitted into the United States between 1989 and 1999, numbered about a quarter million persons.

Even though the two major post-World War II geopolitical forces of globalization—decolonization and the Cold War—are no longer salient, their combined legacies have created a new engine for globalization in the form of some two million refugees from Vietnam, Laos, and Cambodia. By maintaining transnational ties and interactions with their kin and compatriots scattered around the world in more than sixty countries where they have been resettled, they have created, and continue to create, socio-cultural, economic, and political networks with the aid of information technologies, as well as older methods of contact, to help bind ever more peoples and lands together in a globalized world.

ASIAN CONNECTIONS

Celeste Lipow MacLeod

Australia woke up to find itself in the right place at the right time. As countries such as Japan, South Korea, Taiwan and Hong Kong prospered, Australia's location at the tip of Southeast Asia meant it could readily supply them with many of the raw materials, products and services they needed for their development. Singapore, Malaysia and Indonesia also became buyers. The financial collapse of some Asian nations in 1997 caused a slowdown in sales but not as much as expected; by 2000, these countries were on the road to recovery and Australia was selling to many of them, especially its mining and agricultural products. In time China emerged as the biggest buyer of them all.

In building relationships with countries in the region, however, Australia faces a delicate situation because of the past. Memories of the former European occupation of much of that region, and of Australia's past exclusion of immigrants from Asia, have made nearby countries sensitive to any signs of the old colonial attitudes and prejudices. Mistrust decreased in the decades after the Second World War as immigration from Asian countries swelled, Australia's policies stressed tolerance and inclusion and the government made special efforts to cement friendships with neighboring nations. But events in the second half of the 1990s, especially the backlash against Asian immigrants fomented by MP Pauline Hanson soon after a new administration came to power in 1996, put some nations on guard; and the country's treatment of boat refugees seeking asylum has brought international criticism. Still, the momentum has been toward Asia.

After World War II, many political analysts, economists, historians and other specialists in Australia realized that their country's future would be tied to that of its neighbors. When the government opened Australia National University (ANU) in Canberra in 1947, Professor Brij V. Lal pointed out, a major reason for the new university was to provide a research center where Australians could learn more about their region. Lal, director of the Centre for the Contemporary Pacific at ANU's Research School of Pacific and Asian Studies, is one of many academics specializing in Asian countries. His input has helped Australia interact with its region. An Indian Fijian Australian, his grandfather came to Fiji from India in 1906 as a *girmitiya* (indentured servant) and Lal grew up in Fiji. His continued interest in that country led the Fijian government to invite Lal to help write its 1997 constitution.

If government interest in Asia waned in the 1950s after Robert Menzies returned to power, at the nation's universities that interest continued. Librarians kept building up their Asia collections, while scholars quietly initiated contacts and exchanges with professors and students in the Asian countries they studied. More universities opened Asian studies departments and the number of Asian languages offered at Australian universities continued to grow. By 2003 ANU's National Institute for Asia and the Pacific offered intensive language study in Arabic, Chinese, Hindi, Indonesian, Japanese, Javanese, Korean, Lao, Persian, Sanskrit, Thai, Urdu, and Vietnamese.

Some Asian countries, in turn, began studying about Australia. Japan, a major trading partner, was the first. In 1967, Otemon Gakuin University outside Osaka opened a Center for Australian Studies; more followed in Tokyo and other cities. In China, which has had considerable interaction with Australia for 30 years, by 1998 there were Australia Studies Centres at universities in Beijing, Shanghai and Guangzhou, and courses on Australia in half a dozen provinces. In Indonesia, Petra Christian University in Java has an Australian Studies Centre, while Nanyang Technical University in Singapore offers several courses on Australia.

The Australian government began actively reaching out to Asian nations in the 1970s. The pace accelerated after Bob Hawke became prime minister in 1983. Noting the success of the European Economic Community (forerunner of the European Union), Hawke helped organize a trade alliance of Pacific countries, the Asia Pacific Economic Cooperation Forum (APEC), now a 21-member group of countries on both edges of the Pacific Rim. Paul Keating, who succeeded Hawke as prime minister in 1991, made building stronger relationships with Asian nations a top priority. During his first year in office, he visited Indonesia, Papua New Guinea, Japan, Singapore, Cambodia and the Solomon Islands. His foreign minister Gareth Evans told the *New York Times:* "What has got to change in Australia's relationship with Asia is not just the substance, but the perception. We have to create the environment in which we are perceived by our Asian neighbors as having made that psychological transition," that is, away from identifying mainly with Britain and Europe.

Keating championed the movement for a republic. He told a Canadian reporter: "Australia will be taken more seriously as a player in regional affairs if we are clear about our identity. I think that in the area in which we live, which is an area of ancient cultures, there'll be a greater willingness to include us in the affairs of the region if we are of an independent mind."

The country's new policies and practices bore fruit. After it promoted ethnic diversity and encouraged services to help immigrants, many Asian leaders and their people began changing their image of Australia. Asian students attended Australian universities in record numbers and Asian tourists came in droves. By the early 1990s, more than a million tourists a year were coming from Asian countries. If one excludes New Zealand, whose citizens come and go frequently, Asian tourists outnumbered those from all other countries combined.

Australia also forged strategic agreements with nearby countries such as Indonesia, Malaysia, Singapore, and Papua New Guinea. "As never before Australia's economic, strategic, and political interests now coalesce in the region around us . . . and importantly, finding a place for ourselves in Asia is also about finding our own identity," Paul Keating wrote in *Asiawatch.* Then early in 1996, after a campaign that centered more on domestic than international issues, the Labor Party was defeated in federal elections. John Howard became prime minister of a coalition government of his Liberal Party and the National Party. Their opponents feared that Howard might revert to the old policy of ignoring Asia.

Howard, however, swiftly scheduled meetings with leaders of several nearby Asian countries to reassure them that his government wanted continued trade and friendly relations. An astute politician, he surely realized that ignoring Asia in 1996 would be tantamount to political suicide. Large blocs in both coalition parties relied increasingly on sales to Asian countries: the Liberal Party had a strong city-based business constituency while the National Party, whose stronghold was in rural areas, attracted ranchers, farmers, and miners.

At the same time, the new prime minister made no secret of his strong support for retaining Britain's monarch as Australia's head of state. He looked for ways to bolster friendships with Britain, other European countries and the United States, while summarily dismissing any suggestion that Australia was part of Asia. His opponents, however, saw danger in this approach, coupled as it was with his distaste for multiculturalism.

As James Jupp, Director of the Centre for Immigration and Multicultural Studies, has pointed out: "It is impossible to have fruitful trade, tourism, and foreign relations with neighboring states while discriminating against their citizens on a racial or ethnic basis." There was another consideration as well, Jupp wrote: "It is already hard enough to persuade some states of the region that Australia is part of Asia.'" Just as a remnant of the old guard in Australia remained fixated on the past, so some Asian leaders could not put the colonial period in perspective and see the whole region as part of a new geopolitical bloc in the world.

Malaysia's prime minister Mahathir Mohamad was one such leader. After several Asian and European Union nations formed the Asia-Europe Meeting (ASEM), a group that met annually to discuss common interests, Mahathir insisted that Australia and New Zealand were not Asian countries. He managed to bar them from the first two meetings and urged their permanent exclusion. Likewise his opposition was crucial in excluding Australia and New Zealand from a meaningful role in the Association of Southeast Asian Nations, or ASEAN, the region's most important coalition group. But a new breed of leaders in Asia appeared to have a different view. "We regard Australia and New Zealand as Asian," Thailand's foreign minister Prachuab Chaiyasan said in 1997. Thailand pledged to sponsor the country's admission to the next meeting of ASEM. A year later, Surin Pitsuwan, the new Thai foreign minister, described Australia as the third leg of a tripod supporting the Southeast Asian economies. (The other two legs were Japan and China.) "You belong to the region," he told participants at a business seminar in Sydney.

After the Asian economic plunge, some other countries looked to Australia. On a visit early in 1998, British trade minister Lord Clinton-Davis said Australia was a critical link between Asian and European countries. In June, the *Herald* reported, "The World Bank yesterday called on Australia to take a leading role in communication between crisis-ridden Asian countries and major industrialized nations." Jean-Michel Severino, the Bank's vice-president for the Asia Pacific region, said: "There are very few countries that can be credibly heard in the region. . . . The role for Australia is critical." And in October, Chris Patten, the last British governor of Hong Kong, who became the EU's minister for external affairs, told a group of foreign correspondents in Singapore: "Australia is in a better position than almost anybody to help give a lead in Asia . . . (it) can provide a very useful bridge for Asia and can march over that bridge a lot of ideas about good government and sensible economic management."

Nearby Indonesia also weighed in. After One Nation's gains in the 1998 Queensland election, Indonesia's new president downplayed its significance. B.J. Habibie, who had recently replaced Suharto, told reporters that the election "will not damage Australia's standing in Asia." He had visited Australia, he said, and did not believe its people, who were "very cultivated, very open" would choose the isolationism advocated by Hanson.

The next year, however, troubles in East Timor caused a rift between Australia and Indonesia. Timor, an eastern island of the Malay Archipelago, has been divided for more than four centuries. The Dutch held the western half until 1950 when it became part of the new Republic of Indonesia, while East Timor was under Portuguese rule from the sixteenth century until 1975 when Portugal withdrew. The country declared its independence but as rival factions fought for control, the Indonesian army annexed the country in a bloody coup. But violence continued. The East Timorese, more than 90 percent Roman Catholic, resisted becoming part of predominantly Muslim Indonesia.

After a United Nations-brokered referendum was held in East Timor in 1999 and its people voted overwhelmingly to become an independent nation, Indonesian military forces and their local supporters went on a rampage there. When Australia led a United Nations peacekeeping mission into East Timor, Indonesians reacted with anger. Although Habibie had agreed to both the referendum and the peacekeepers, Australia's participation set off protests in Jakarta. The Indonesian government canceled a joint security agreement between the two nations. Gradually the countries mended fences.

Over the years, as more Australians became engaged with Asian countries through diplomacy, business, development projects, academic studies and tourism, the call for closer identification with the region has increased. Stephen FitzGerald has been one of the strongest advocates of this view. He served as ambassador to China during the Whitlam administration and later became chair of the Department of Far Eastern History and the Contemporary China Centre at ANU. He has also headed the Asia-Australia Institute at the University of New South Wales in Sydney and worked as a consultant for Australian companies doing business in Asian countries, principally China.

FitzGerald's book, *Is Australia an Asian Country?* (1997), gave a new picture of Asian nations. After getting to know top political, intellectual, and business leaders in several Asian countries, he saw a growing consciousness there "of confidence and pride in achievement, a sense of being 'empowered,' of being Asian' in the way that elites in Europe have of being 'European.'" He used the term "elites" to mean a country's government and business leaders as well as its professionals and specialists. FitzGerald, who is fluent in Mandarin Chinese, urged Australians to learn the languages of its neighbors along with more about their cultures. He saw these steps as crucial prerequisites to effective participation in the region.

PACIFIC ISLANDS RELIGIOUS COMMUNITIES

Joel Robbins

When one considers processes of globalization in the Pacific Islands, one is struck by the extent to which religion has been central. Indeed, if we define globalization both as the movement of cultural ideas and institutions (including cultural constructions of politics, economics etc.) and as the processes by which people come to construe themselves as acting in larger worlds and relating to people across vaster distances than they have in the past, then there are grounds to argue that religion, and Christianity in particular, has been the single most powerful globalizing force throughout the Pacific Islands.

Although the region is comprised of such social, cultural, and historical diversity among the islands of Melanesia, Polynesia and Micronesia that generalization is rendered treacherous, this claim about the importance of religion to globalization is one that holds very broadly. Urban politics are almost everywhere carried out in rhetoric rich in Christian allusions and assumptions; the sound of church bells can be heard daily even in rural areas that the capitalist market has hardly penetrated; and Pacific Island migrants to New Zealand, Australia, and the United States as often construct diasporic communities around shared Christian faiths as they do around traditional beliefs and practices.

There are at least two reasons why Christianity and religion more generally have been so important in the Pacific Island experience of globalization. First, the carriers of Western culture to the Pacific Islands have elaborated its religious aspects more fully than other aspects. This was of course true of the missionaries who from the outset took a leading role in bringing Western culture to Pacific Islanders, often arriving before or alongside government representatives. But it was also in many cases true of the colonial administrators as well. Seeing little economic potential in most areas, colonial officers were relatively uninterested in training rural people in the secular aspects of Western culture. With little incentive to spread their secular culture, and cash-strapped as well, colonial officers often left oversight of key secular institutions such as health care and schooling to missionaries. The missionaries responded to having the colonial field so much to themselves by conveying a version of Western culture in which Christianity was capable of grounding the social world in its entirety.

For their part, Pacific Islanders were in many cases quick to grasp the explanatory value of Christianity as a key to the new global world they were coming to inhabit, and this is the second reason it has played such an important part in their experience of globalization. The cultures of the region, both traditionally and still today, generally give religion a prominent place, and none of them holds it separate from other domains such as politics or economics: all of social life in the Pacific Islands has religious aspects and most situations, whatever else they demand, require that people take religious considerations into account in formulating their responses. These are cultures that have neither been nor understood themselves to be disenchanted.

Coming from this background, Pacific Islanders who encountered missionaries were inclined to make the effort needed to construct versions of Christianity that they could comprehend and use to fashion lives appropriate to their changing worlds. And as they encountered other aspects of Western ideology—for example, those surrounding politics and economics—they were inclined to understand them as much as possible in terms shaped by their religious commitments. It is this indigenous tendency to elaborate religious understandings of all domains of life, as much as the predominance of missionaries among those who have brought Western culture to the Pacific Islands, that has put religion at the center of globalization in the region.

The statistical data display a stunning record of missionary success. Melanesia, the most recently colonized sub-region of the Pacific Islands, and one which contains 75% of the region's population, is 90% Christian. The rest of the Pacific Islands, not including the settler societies of New Zealand and Hawaii, are 99% Christian. Yet it is also true that scholars rarely report such figures without qualifying them by noting that many people who identify themselves as Christian are Christian only in a "nominal" sense. The criteria scholars use in making this judgment are rarely specified, and the scholarly politics of such attributions demand study in their own right. Yet in the present context it is perhaps best to let the nominalism charge stand. For the cultural terrain that that charge opens onto, a terrain whose features consist of various kinds of syncretism, is a very fertile one for those interested in the globalization of culture.

One can find all kinds of syncretism in the Pacific Islands. In some Polynesian societies one can find people who are committed to various brands of mission Christianity that look in many doctrinal and ritual respects quite orthodox, except where Islanders have modified them to make them fit with the elaborate traditional social hierarchies that are still a fundamental part of their social lives. Elsewhere, too, one finds situations in which people committed to change can yet be found to be carrying over much of their traditional belief. In other parts of the Pacific, by contrast, one can find self conscious movements back to tradition or *kastom* ("custom") that are unselfconsciously shot-through with Christian beliefs and practices. And beyond these straightforward examples of syncretism, one finds that even those cases that seem to approach a kind of purity of traditional or Christian expression usually contain some mixtures.

FURTHER READING

Anderson, Benedict. 1983. *Imagined Communities: Reflections on the Origins and Spread of Nationalism.* London: Verso.

Anderson, Benedict. 1990. *Language and Power: Exploring Political Cultures in Indonesia.* Ithaca, NY: Cornell University Press.

Burridge, Kenelm. 1995. *Mambu: A Melanesian Millennium.* Princeton, NJ: Princeton University Press. (Originally published in 1960.)

Chan, Kwok B., and Doreen Marie Indra(Eds.). 1987. *Uprooting, Loss and Adaptation: The Resettlement of Indochinese Refugees in Canada.* Ottawa: Canadian Public Health Association.

Chan, Sucheng. 2006. *The Vietnamese American 1.5 Generation: Stories of War, Revolution, Flight, and New Beginnings.* Philadelphia: Temple University Press.

Christie, Clive J. 2000. *A Modern History of Southeast Asia: Decolonization, Nationalism and Separatism.* London: Tauris.

Coedès, Georges. 1968. *The Indianized States of Southeast Asia.* Honolulu: University of Hawaii Press.

Dommen, Arthur J. 2001. *The Indochinese Experience of the French and the Americans: Nationalism and Communism in Cambodia, Laos, and Vietnam.* Bloomington: Indiana University Press.

Goscha, Christopher E. and Christian F. Ostermann. 2009. *Connecting Histories: Decolonization and the Cold War in Southeast Asia, 1945–1962.* Washington, DC: Woodrow Wilson Center Press.

Fitzgerald, Stephen. 1997. *Is Australia an Asian Country?* San Leonards, Australia: Allen & Unwin.

MacLeod, Celeste Lipow. 2006. *Multiethnic Australia: Its History and Future.* Jefferson, NC: MacFarland.

Reid, Anthony. 1993. *Southeast Asia in the Early Modern Era: Trade, Power, and Belief.* Ithaca, NY: Cornell University Press.

Robbins, Joel. 2004. *Becoming Sinners: Christianity and Moral Torment in a Papua New Guinea Society.* Berkeley: University of California Press.

Robinson, W. Courtland. 1998. *Terms of Refuge: The Indochinese Exodus and the International Response.* London: Zed Books.

Swain, Tony, and Garry Tromp. 1995. *The Religions of Oceania.* London: Routledge.

Thomas, Mandy. 1999. *Dreams in the Shadows: Vietnamese-Australian Lives in Transition.* San Leonards, Australia: Allen & Unwin.

8

EUROPE AND RUSSIA
Nationalism and Transnationalism

During the time of the Mediterranean civilizations some two thousand years ago, Europe was at the margins of the civilized world, However, in the past several centuries it has dominated the global order. European nations reached out to the world seeking resources and trade, and they ended up conquering vast spans of territory. When they receded from their colonial territories, they left behind Europe's distinctive contribution to global politics, the concept of the nation-state. It is something of a paradox, then, that in the current global age Europe is forming a new transnational political and economic structure, the European Union.

Everyone knows where Europe is, though exactly where it begins and ends is another matter. This is because Europe is not a separate entity but is, in fact, the westernmost portion of the Eurasian continental mass. It is usually defined as the nations north of the Caucasus mountains, west of the Ural mountains, and north of the Mediterranean, Black, and Caspian seas. The island nations of Cyprus and Malta in the Mediterranean are also considered part of Europe, as are the Northern Atlantic Ocean island nations of the United Kingdom, Ireland, and Iceland (though they are not regarded as part of "continental" Europe). Russia is also part of Europe, even though most of Russia's land mass extends eastward to the Pacific Ocean; even so, whatever is within the boundaries of the nation of Russia is usually considered European for cultural and political reasons. Turkey lies on the southern border of Europe. Most of the inhabitants of its largest city, Istanbul, live on the European side of the Bosporus—the waterway that connects the Mediterranean and Black seas—yet its longstanding interest in joining the European

Union has often been rebuffed on the grounds that it is not really European. What many Europeans may have in mind, however, is not geography, but culture; the Muslim faith that predominates in Turkey sets it apart from most other European countries, except for Albania and Kosovo.

It is a bit odd that some Europeans would regard the Christian religion as something that is distinctively European, since today the majority of the world's Christians live in Asia, Africa, and Latin America. Historically, Christianity—like Islam—was a Middle Eastern religion. Ultimately, Christianity became European, and the story of how that happened is an interesting case in cultural globalization.

Christianity emerged as a sect of Judaism and then became part of the religions of the Mediterranean world, a region that encompassed Southern Europe, Northern Africa and much of the Middle East. After the Roman Emperor Constantine converted to Christianity in 312 CE, it soon became the major religion of the Roman Empire. But the areas of Northern Europe, such as France, Germany, Britain, and the Scandinavian countries were far from Roman civilization, and it took centuries before they were Christianized. The religion of pre-Christian Europe was centered around fertility cults, rites related to the equinoxes and the changing seasons, holy men, and goddesses. As Christianity moved into these European cultural areas, it adopted many of the features of European religion. The holidays of Christmas and Easter were linked to seasonal festival days, Christian saints became as prominent as pagan European holy men, and the cult of the Virgin Mary seemed to replicate the goddess veneration of an earlier tradition. What Christianity brought to the European cultural tradition was religious organization, the transnational power of the church, and—in the Roman Catholic tradition—a central headquarters in the Vatican.

The global impact of Europe was not just cultural, however; it also changed the world's economic and political landscape. Beginning with Christopher Columbus and his famous journey to the Americas in 1492, European explorers have searched for new trade routes over the seas, in the process discovering new territories. Eventually these territories were conquered and settled by Europeans—especially Spanish, British, Portuguese, Dutch, and French—in a network of colonies spread throughout the world and encompassing much of Asia, Africa, the Middle East, and the Americas. The impact of this centuries-long period of domination is incalculable. Brazil would be unthinkable without the Portuguese language; Mexico would be hard to imagine without its Spanish culture; and in India, political and educational institutions are still modeled after those of the British.

Perhaps the quintessential European gift to the world was the idea of the nation-state and the democratic values associated with it. The ideology of rationalism and nationalism that emerged from the eighteenth-century European Enlightenment was spread throughout the world. By the middle of the twentieth century, virtually every inch of global territory was a part of, or was claimed by, a nation-state. Nationalism was one of the most influential ideologies of the twentieth century. Another was communism, the state socialism promoted by the great European social thinker, Karl Marx, and adopted by Russia, China, and many Eastern European countries. Though many people in the Eastern European and Central Asian countries that fell under Soviet domination regarded their plight as a form of Russian colonialism, they were at least officially united by a common socialist ideology. Their communism was an inheritor of European Enlightenment ideals, where the notion of democracy was applied to economic institutions. Thus, the great conflict of the latter half of the twentieth century, the Cold War, was a contest between two European ideologies.

In the twenty-first century, Europe occupies a more modest role in the global order, but its role is still an influential one. The European attempt at regional consolidation in the form of the European Union is a model of transnational organization that is closely watched by other parts of the world. The way that Europe deals with multiculturalism is also an important bellwether of how the global community will deal with an increasingly diverse population throughout the world. In an era of easy mobility, where everyone can—and does—live everywhere is a challenge to the old European notion of a nationalism based on a common, homogeneous, ancestral culture. As Europe explores ways of assimilating a diversity of populations into its national and regional identities, it will be offering examples—both good and bad—to the rest of the world.

The selections in this section begin with a consideration of the European contributions to globalization, especially in the nineteenth century, by the American historian Peter Stearns. Stearns taught at Carnegie Mellon University for some years and later became a provost at George Mason University. He helped to develop the field of world history. In this excerpt, he describes the effects of European aspects of industrialization and modern political ideas on global culture. This selection is followed by one that specifically explores an influential and transformative European notion, the idea of the nation, to which the European political culture gave birth. The author of this excerpt, Eric Hobsbawm, is one of the great economic historians of the twentieth century. Hobsbawm was British, born in Egypt and raised for a time in Austria before his Jewish family fled Hitler's Nazi regime and came to England, where Hobsbawm eventually became a student and then professor at Cambridge University.

The next selection is from an essay by Seyla Benhabib, a political philosopher who teaches at Yale; she was born in Turkey and achieved acclaim in the United States for her contributions to critical theory and feminist theory. In this selection, she observes that the European Enlightenment notion of national citizenship is challenged in an era of globalization and that a middle path needs to be found between the extremes of open borders and rigid notions of national membership. The Soviet empire during the Cold War is the subject of the next selection. It was written by Odd Arne Westad, a Norwegian historian specializing in the history of China and of the Cold War, who received his graduate training at the University of North Carolina–Chapel Hill, and is now a professor of international history at the London School of Economics and Politics (familiarly known as LSE). In this selection, Westad argues that Soviet communism was at heart an attempt to create a Russian version of modernity.

The last selection is by the great German social and political philosopher Jürgen Habermas. He writes in the tradition of Max Weber, one of the founders of the modern field of sociology, in emphasizing rational communication as a prerequisite to citizenship in what he describes as the "public sphere." In this excerpt, Habermas responds to one of the most critical issues in contemporary Europe, the flood of new immigrants from Eastern Europe to Western Europe and from North Africa and the Middle East to Germany, France, and other European nations. Habermas argues that there should be soft boundaries between nations and a continuity of a sense of citizenship between national identities and the attitude of being world citizens in a global society.

THE 1850S AS TURNING POINT: THE BIRTH OF GLOBALIZATION?

Peter Stearns

A growing group of historians specifically interested in globalization place the effective origins of the phenomenon in the middle of the 19th century. They differ from the larger cluster of world historians who add features to already-sanctioned dates like 1000 or 1500 to provide a larger historical perspective (though of course they would not deny the importance of preparatory developments prior to 1850). They certainly quarrel, if implicitly, with the advocates of 1750. But they also part ways with the "new global history" approach, which is so fascinated with the radical departures, the historical disconnects, of the past fifty years.

Thomas Zeiler puts the case this way. Admittedly, recent changes, particularly in technology, have accelerated globalization's pace beyond anything visible 150 years ago. But in terms of basic changes in transportation, new business networks and economic relationships, the real movement to globalization began earlier. The movement was "nascent and incomplete," and it was "interrupted by events of the twentieth century": "but movement existed, nonetheless." Zeiler sees changes taking shape before World War I as the "early era of globalization." It was fueled not only by new steamships but also the two great world canals, which sped commerce around the globe; and also by real breakthroughs in communications, with telegraph lines between the United States and Latin America and Europe, and British cables lines to Asia, allowing faster commercial interactions than ever before but also unprecedented exchanges of news. Great world's fairs, beginning in London in 1851, highlighted Western manufacturing, to be sure, but with growing attention to economic and cultural patterns in other parts of the world. "Global connections shrunk the world itself"—precisely the claim made about globalization more recently. It was also in this "early era" that not only the United States but also Japan made basic adjustments to globalization that have, with a few disruptions, defined basic orientations ever since. Japanese historians readily see this period, and not the more recent one, as the point at when Japan made its really fundamental global commitments, and the same could be said about North America. Global worries about

Asian competition—defined in the words of the German emperor shortly after 1900 as a new "yellow peril"—and the first stirrings of concerns about cultural and economic "Americanization" accompanied these changes.

This chapter will amplify these claims, and add others, noting changes in patterns of immigration, the onset of new kinds of global connection in popular culture, and a really new era in political globalization with the emergence of capacities to define global standards in a number of areas—beyond anti-slavery—and the formation of international conventions on a host of crucial topics.

We will also, of course, deal with limitations in globalization's "early era"—because the global processes common today were not fully sketched. Even in advance, however, we must take up a still more fundamental question: if a really good case can be made for 1850 as globalization's inception, why has this date never been widely used in world history before?

Both European and world historians have conventionally seized on a period 1750 or 1789 to 1914 as an almost self-evident chronological unit in the human experience, with 1850s and early globalization buried within this larger scheme. The great British historian Eric Hobsbawm dubbed the period the "long 19th century," and virtually every survey history, whether Western or global in focus, has followed suit. Again, there's a bit of dispute about when to begin the "long" century. The date 1750 or so captures the early stages of British and then European industrialization, undeniably (if not then, at least ultimately) a major change in human history. As we have seen, a few voices for a first globalization phase have chimed in with a similar periodization. The date 1789 highlights the revolutionary era, launched a bit earlier but gaining new urgency with the great French rising of that year. And of course, regardless of specific inception, the two developments can be put together, with a long 19th century focused ultimately on the twin phenomena of economic upheaval—industrialization—and political and social challenge through the revolutionary ideas and precedents. Interweaving with both developments, though particularly with industrialization, the long 19th century also saw the further blossoming of Western imperialism, with Africa, Oceania and new parts of southeast Asia offering new jewels to European imperial crowns.

Ending in 1914 seems even more obvious: World War I was a huge event, disrupting lives and social processes around the world, though particularly of course in Europe itself. The generation that experienced that war understandably believed that it was a true watershed, the "Great War," and even later groups of historians picked up the same basic assessment. The brutality of the war, though foreshadowed by earlier conflicts like the American Civil War, was a marker in and of itself. More recent historians have also seen the war as the beginning of the end of European imperial dominance, thanks to the weakening of the major European powers and the unintended encouragement given to nationalist movements elsewhere, from Japan through India and Turkey to Africa.

The overall result is a really powerful set of historical assumptions, into which the idea of an intervening globalization process can fit only with difficulty. It is possible, of course, to envisage a scheme that would continue to argue for the long 19th century as a basic period, but with a new surge toward globalization coming in the middle. Given the importance that globalization has assumed today, and the fact that many people were claiming new and wide-ranging global connections even by 1900, this compromise seems dubious. In fact, aspects of the argument for a break around 1850 really assume that some of the features normally assigned to the late 18th century—particularly, the earliest stages of European industrialization—really gained full global importance only after mid-century, which makes the latter date preferable in indicating a real break in trends. Though British industrial competition had impact in places like Latin America and India earlier, mainly by driving down levels of traditional manual production especially in textiles, it was really only by the 1850s that a truly global dimension emerged, embracing for example China and Japan as well as south Asia. The age of revolutions angle is trickier, for it did move out earlier from origins in North America and western Europe, to impact Haiti and Latin America in the revolutions and independence movements between the 1790s and 1820s, and through nationalism affected southeastern Europe as well. But here, too, a fuller global roll-out of revolutionary principles, often highlighting nationalism, also awaited the later 19th century.

World War I takes on a partial new role in a globalization-based periodization as well. It did encourage some powerful countercurrents to globalization, in the form of nationalist and regional reactions seeking to limit globalization's impact and develop alternative economic structures. The war's importance is in this sense confirmed, partly on rather familiar grounds. Globalization hit a really rough patch between the 1920s and 1945. But obviously the results were not permanent, and a resumption of the trajectory took shape (at least in some crucial respects) from 1945 onward. World War I is a break, then, but it did not usher in a durable new structure, at least in global mechanisms.

Fortunately, the focus on globalization does not require a full consideration of all aspects of world history chronology. It suggests the possibility, however, of beginning to rethink conventional structures, to argue for a longer early modern period—1450–1850—based on the inclusion of the Americas, a new level of global exchange, and some shifts in global power relationships including a greater role for the West. The last century of this span, after 1750, with accelerated world trade, fuller inclusion of the Pacific regions, and some other changes, expanded several key themes of the period in ways that would provide transitions to the sharper departures of the 1850s and ensuing decades. Then, with the 1850s, came the real advent of modern globalization, with an important but not permanent disruption following World War I, and then a resumption with added acceleration from the later 1940s to the present. Again, this chapter does not depend on recasting world history so completely, but if globalization is the key change in modern world history (which is at least a defendable proposition) and if the modern form of globalization began in the 1850s, the new framework can certainly be suggested.

THE NATION AS NOVELTY

Eric Hobsbawm

Given the historical novelty of the modern concept of "the nation," the best way to understand its nature, I suggest, is to follow those who began systematically to operate with this concept in their political and social discourse during the Age of Revolution, and especially, under the name of "the principle of nationality" from about 1830 onwards. This excursus into *Begriffsgeschichte* is not easy, partly because, as we shall see, contemporaries were too unselfconscious about their use of such words, and partly because the same word simultaneously meant, or could mean, very different things.

The primary meaning of "nation," and the one most frequently ventilated in the literature, was political. It equated "the people" and the state in the manner of the American and French Revolutions, an equation which is familiar in such phrases as "the nation-state," the "United Nations," or the rhetoric of late-twentieth-century presidents. Early political discourse in the USA preferred to speak of "the people," "the union," "the confederation," "our common land," "the public," "public welfare" or "the community" in order to avoid the centralizing and unitary implications of the term "nation" against the rights of the federated states. For it was, or certainly soon became, part of the concept of the nation in the era of the Revolutions that it should be, in the French phrase, "one and indivisible." The "nation" so considered, was the body of citizens whose collective sovereignty constituted them a state which was their political expression. For, whatever else a nation was, the element of citizenship and mass participation or choice was never absent from it. John Stuart Mill did not merely define the nation by its possession of national sentiment. He also added that the members of a nationality "desire to be under the same government, and desire that it should be government by themselves or a portion of themselves exclusively." We observe without surprise that Mill discusses the idea of nationality not in a separate publication as such, but, characteristically—and briefly—in the context of his little treatise on Representative Government, or democracy.

The equation nation = state = people, and especially sovereign people, undoubtedly linked nation to territory, since structure and definition of states were now essentially territorial. It also implied a multiplicity of nation-states so constituted, and this was indeed a necessary consequence of popular self-determination. As the French Declaration of Rights of 1795 put it:

> Each people is independent and sovereign, whatever the number of individuals who compose it and the extent of the territory it occupies. This sovereignty is inalienable.

But it said little about what constituted a "people." In particular there was no logical connection between the body of citizens of a territorial state on one hand, and the identification of a "nation" on ethnic, linguistic or other grounds or of other characteristics which allowed collective recognition of group membership. Indeed, it has been argued that the

French Revolution "was completely foreign to the principle or feeling of nationality; it was even hostile to it" for this reason. . . .

Indeed, if "the nation" had anything in common from the popular-revolutionary point of view, it was not, in any fundamental sense, ethnicity, language and the like, though these could be indications of collective belonging also. As Pierre Vilar has pointed out, what characterized the nation–people as seen from below was precisely that it represented the common interest against particular interests, the common good against privilege, as indeed is suggested by the term Americans used before 1800 to indicate nationhood while avoiding the word itself. Ethnic group differences were from this revolutionary-democratic point of view as secondary as they later seemed to socialists. Patently what distinguished the American colonists from King George and his supporters was neither language nor ethnicity, and conversely, the French Republic saw no difficulty in electing the Anglo-American Thomas Paine to its National Convention.

We cannot therefore read into the revolutionary "nation" anything like the later nationalist programme of establishing nation-states for bodies defined in terms of the criteria so hotly debated by the nineteenth-century theorists, such as ethnicity, common language, religion, territory and common historical memories (to cite John Stuart Mill yet again). As we have seen, except for a territory whose extent was undefined (and perhaps skin colour) none of these united the new American nation. Moreover, as the "grande nation" of the French extended its frontiers in the course of the revolutionary and Napoleonic wars to areas which were French by none of the later criteria of national belonging, it was clear that none of them were the basis of its constitution. . . .

To understand the "nation" of the classical liberal era it is thus essential to bear in mind that "nation-building," however central to nineteenth-century history, applied only to some nations. And indeed the demand to apply the "principle of nationality" was not universal either. Both as an international problem and as a domestic political problem it affected only a limited number of peoples or regions, even within multilingual and multiethnic states such as the Habsburg empire, where it clearly dominated politics already. It would not be too much to say that, after 1871—always excepting the slowly disintegrating Ottoman empire—few people expected any further substantial changes in the map of Europe, and recognized few national problems likely to bring them about, other than the perennial Polish question. And, indeed, outside the Balkans, the only change in the European map between the creation of the German empire and World War I was the separation of Norway from Sweden. What is more, after the national alarums and excursions of the years from 1848 to 1867, it was not too much to suppose that even in Austria–Hungary tempers would cool. That, at all events, is what the officials of the Habsburg empire expected when (rather reluctantly) they decided to accept a resolution of the International Statistical Congress at St Petersburg in 1873 to include a question about language in future censuses, but proposed to postpone its application until after 1880 to allow time for opinion to grow less agitated. They could not have been more spectacularly mistaken in their prognosis.

It also follows that, by and large, in this period nations and nationalism were not major domestic problems for political entities which had reached the status of "nation-states," however nationally heterogeneous they were by modern standards, though they were acutely troublesome to non-national empires which were not (anachronistically) classifiable as "multinational." None of the European states west of the Rhine as yet faced serious complications on this score, except Britain from that permanent anomaly, the Irish. This is not to suggest that politicians were unaware of Catalans or Basques, Bretons or Flemings, Scots and Welsh, but they were mainly seen as adding to or subtracting from the strength of some statewide political force. The Scots and the Welsh functioned as reinforcements to liberalism, the Bretons and Flemings to traditionalist Catholicism. Of course the political systems of nation-states still benefited from the absence of electoral democracy, which was to undermine the liberal theory and practice of the nation, as it was to undermine so much else in nineteenth-century liberalism.

That is perhaps why the serious theoretical literature about nationalism in the liberal era is small and has a somewhat casual air. Observers like Mill and Renan were relaxed enough about the elements which made up "national sentiment"—ethnicity—in spite of the Victorians' passionate preoccupation with "race"—language, religion, territory, history, culture and the rest—because politically it did not much matter, as yet, whether one or the other among these was regarded as more important than the rest. But from the 1880s on the debate about "the national question" becomes serious and intensive, especially among the socialists, because the political appeal of national slogans to masses of potential or actual voters or supporters of mass political movements was now a matter of real practical concern. And the debate on such questions as the theoretical criteria of nationhood became passionate, because any particular answer was now believed to imply a particular form of political strategy, struggle and programme. This was a matter of importance not only for governments confronted with various kinds of national agitation or demand, but for political parties seeking to mobilize constituencies on the basis of national, non-national or alternative national appeals. For socialists in central and eastern Europe it made a great deal of difference on what theoretical basis the nation and its future were defined. Marx and Engels, like Mill and Renan, had regarded such questions as marginal. In the Second International [an organization of socialist and labor parties formed in Paris in 1889] such debates were central, and a constellation of eminent figures, or figures with an eminent future, contributed important writings to them: Kautsky, Luxemburg, Bauer, Lenin and Stalin. But if such questions concerned Marxist theorists, it was also a matter of acute practical importance to, say, Croats and Serbs, Macedonians and Bulgarians, whether the nationality of Southern Slavs was defined in one way or another.

The "principle of nationality" which diplomats debated and which changed the map of Europe in the period from 1830 to 1878 was thus different from the political phenomenon of nationalism which became increasingly central in the era of European democratization and mass politics. In the days of Mazzini it did not matter that, for the great bulk of Italians, the Risorgimento did not exist so that, as Massimo d'Azeglio admitted in the famous phrase: "We have made Italy, now we have to make Italians." It did not even matter to those who considered "the Polish Question" that probably most Polish-speaking peasants (not to mention the third of the population of the old pre-1772 Rzecspopolita who spoke other idioms) did not yet feel themselves to be nationalist Poles; as the eventual liberator of Poland, Colonal Pilsudski recognized in *his* phrase: "It is the state which makes the nation and not the nation the state." But after 1880 it increasingly did matter how ordinary common men and women felt about nationality. It is therefore important to consider the feelings and attitudes among pre-industrial people of this kind, on which the novel appeal of political nationalism could build.

CITIZENS, RESIDENTS, AND ALIENS IN A CHANGING WORLD: POLITICAL MEMBERSHIP IN THE GLOBAL ERA

Seyla Benhabib

Our contemporary condition is marked by the emergence of new forms of identity/difference politics around the globe. As globalization proceeds at a dizzying rate, as a material global civilization encompasses the earth from Hong Kong to Lima, from Pretoria to Helsinki, worldwide integration in economics, technology, communication, armament, and tourism is accompanied by the collective and cultural disintegration of older political entities, in particular of the nation-state. India and Turkey, which are among the oldest democracies of the Third World, are in the throes of struggles that call into question the very project of a secular, representative democracy. Need one mention in this context ethnic wars, cleansings, and massacres in the former Yugoslavia, the Russian destruction of Chechnya, the simmering nationality conflicts between Azerbaijan and Armenia, Macedonia and Greece, the rise of militant Islamic fundamentalism, and the continuing tribal massacres in the central African states of Rwanda, Uganda, and the Congo? Displaying a social dynamic that we have hardly begun to understand, global integration is proceeding alongside sociocultural disintegration and the resurgence of ethnic, nationalist, religious, and linguistic separatisms.

With globalization and fragmentation proceeding apace, human rights and sovereignty claims come into increasing conflict with each other. On the one hand, a worldwide consciousness about universal principles of human rights is growing; on the other hand, particularistic identities of nationality, ethnicity, religion, race, and language in virtue of which one is said to belong to a sovereign people are asserted with increasing ferocity. Globalization, far from creating a "cosmopolitical order," a condition of perpetual peace among peoples governed by the principles of a republican constitution, has brought to a head conflicts between human rights and the claim to self-determination of sovereign collectivities. Because sovereignty means the right of a collectivity to define itself by asserting power over a bounded territory, declarations of sovereignty more often than not create distinctions between "us" and "them," those who belong to the sovereign people and those who do not. Historically, there is no convergence between the identity of all those "others" over whom power is asserted because they happen to reside in a bounded state territory and the sovereign people in the name of whom such power is exercised. The distinction between citizens, on the one hand, and residents and foreigners, on the other, is central to the theory and practice of democracies. In this regard, Hannah Arendt's astute observations, although formulated in a different context and with respect to the difficulties of protecting human rights in the interwar period in Europe, are more perspicacious than ever: "From the beginning the paradox involved in the declaration of inalienable human rights was that it reckoned with an 'abstract' human being who seemed to exist nowhere. . . . The whole question of human rights, therefore, was quickly and inextricably blended with the question of national emancipation; only the emancipated sovereignty of the people, of one's own people, seemed to be able to insure them."

The citizenship and naturalization claims of foreigners, denizens, and residents within the borders of a polity, as well as the laws, norms, and rules governing such procedures, are pivotal social practices through which the normative perplexities of human rights and sovereignty can be most acutely observed. Sovereignty entails the right of a people to control its borders as well as to define the procedures for admitting "aliens" into its territory and society; yet, in a liberal-democratic polity, such sovereignty claims must always be constrained by human rights, which individuals are entitled to, not in virtue of being citizens or members of a polity, but insofar as they are human beings *simpliciter*. Universal human rights transcend the rights of citizens and extend to all persons considered as moral beings. What kinds of immigration, naturalization, and citizenship practices, then, would be compatible with the commitments of liberal democracies to human rights? Can claims to sovereign self-determination be reconciled with the just and fair treatment of aliens and others in our midst?

In debates around these issues, two approaches dominate: the radical universalist argument for open borders and the civic republican perspective of "thick conceptions of citizenship." Radical universalists argue that, from a moral point of view, national borders are arbitrary and that the only morally consistent universalist position would be one of open borders. Joseph Carens, for example, uses the device of the Rawlsian "veil of ignorance" to think through principles of justice from the standpoint of the refugee, the immigrant, the asylum seeker. Are the borders within which we happen to be born, and the documents to which we are entitled, any less arbitrary from a moral point of view than other characteristics such as skin color, gender, and genetic makeup? Carens's answer is "no." From a moral point of view, the borders that circumscribe our birth and the papers to which we are entitled are arbitrary because their distribution does not follow any clear criteria of moral worth, achievement, and compensation. Therefore, claims Carens, liberal democracies should practice policies that are as compatible as possible with the vision of a world without borders.

Opposed to Carens's radical universalism are a range of communitarian and civic-republican positions, articulating more or less "thick" conceptions of citizenship, community, and belonging. These theories of citizenship, though not precluding or prohibiting immigration, will want to articulate stricter criteria of incorporation and citizenship of foreigners than the universalists. Only those immigrants who come closest to the model of the republican citizen envisaged by these theories will be welcome; others will be spurned. Of course, given how contested such thick conceptions of citizenship inevitably are, communitarian theories can easily lend themselves to the justification of illiberal immigration policies and the restricting of the rights of immigrants and aliens.

This essay steers a middle course between the radical universalism of open borders politics, on the one hand, and sociologically antiquated conceptions of thick republican citizenship, on the other. Instead, stressing the constitutive tension between universalistic human rights claims and democratic sovereignty principles, it will analyze the contemporary practices of political incorporation into liberal democracies. The essay will focus on dilemmas of citizenship and political membership in contemporary Western Europe against the background of these larger theoretical concerns. Current developments in citizenship and incorporation practices within the member states of the European Union in particular are the primary focus. There are a number of compelling historical as well as philosophical reasons for choosing European citizenship and incorporation practices as the focal point for these concerns.

Insofar as they are liberal democracies, member states of the European Union cannot form a "fortress Europe." No liberal democracy can close its borders to refugees and asylum seekers, immigrants and foreign workers. The porousness of borders is a necessary, though not sufficient, condition of liberal democracies. By the same token, no sovereign liberal democracy can lose its right to define immigration and incorporation policies.

I distinguish conditions of entry into a country (e.g., the permission to visit, work, study, and buy property) from conditions of *temporary residency,* and both in turn from *permanent residency* and *civil incorporation,* the final stage of which is naturalization and *political membership.* These are different stages of political incorporation, very often collapsed into one another in theoretical discussions, but analytically distinguishable. At each of these stages, the rights and claims of foreigners, residents, and aliens will be regulated by sovereign polities; but these regulations can be subject to scrutiny, debate, and contestation, as well as protest by those to whom they apply, their advocates, and national and international human-rights groups. No step of this process can be shielded from scrutiny by interested parties. Democratic sovereignty in immigration and incorporation policy is not an unlimited right. The right to self-assertion of a particular people must be examined and evaluated in the light of the commitment of this very same people to universal human rights. Developments of citizenship and immigration practices within contemporary Europe reflect some of the deepest perplexities faced by all nation-states in the era of globalization.

SOVIET IDEOLOGY AND FOREIGN INTERVENTIONS IN THE GLOBAL COLD WAR

Odd Arne Westad

Like the United States, the Soviet state was founded on ideas and plans for the betterment of humanity, rather than on concepts of identity and nation. Both were envisaged by their founders to be grand experiments, on the success of which the future of humankind depended. As states, both were universalist in their approaches to the world and the majority of their leaders believed that friends or enemies on the international stage were defined by proximity or nonproximity to the specific ideological premises on which each of these Powers had been founded. During the Cold War both Soviet and American leaders came to define the potential for such proximity by any country's distance from the other superpower in its foreign policy and domestic political agenda.

In historical terms, much of the twentieth century can be seen as a continuous attempt by other states to socialize Russia and America into forms of international interaction based on principles of sovereignty. In these efforts there were some successes, but many failures. The successes have mainly been connected to crises within the international system that could directly threaten Moscow or Washington themselves. For the United States, as we have seen, the Great Depression, the Second World War, and the end of the Vietnam War all led to a greater degree of accommodation to the interests of other states. For Russia, the period between the 1905 and 1917 revolutions, the aftermath of the German attack in 1941, and the Gorbachev–Yeltsin era signaled such accommodation. But the periods in which both powers have been poised to intervene unilaterally *against* the gradually developing norms of international interaction have been much more prevalent. Given the form that American and—at least during its Soviet period—Russian policy took during the twentieth century, it is reasonable to assume that the two projects—one of state sovereignty and another of global ideological predominance—cannot be reconciled, even though both Cold War superpowers at least in form came to accept alliances and international organizations. . . .

While most of the interventionist impulses in Soviet foreign policy were unique to that specific form of a Russian state, the Communists when taking power in Russia of course became successors to an old expansionist empire, in much the same way as the American revolutionaries developed out of the British empire. In both cases the ideologies that justified intervention had developed from concerns that were formed in earlier centuries, under different regimes. For the Russian Communists, this meant that not only did they inherit a multicultural space in which Russian was spoken by less than half the population, but they also took over a state in which the tsars for at least two generations had attempted a policy of Russification and modernization of their non-Russian subjects. Many Russians in the late nineteenth and early twentieth centuries, including some who became Communists, believed that their country had been endowed with a special destiny to clear the Asian wilderness and civilize the tribes of the East.

In the first decade of the twentieth century Vladimir Illich Ulianov—also known as Lenin—created a party that believed in a form of Marxist modernity that would drive away backwardness from European Russia and set the Asian peoples of the empire on the path to modern development. The Bolsheviks—later known as the All-Russia Communist Party and the Communist Party of the Soviet Union—placed the liberation of the productive potential of the people at the core of the political process. To Lenin, as a Marxist, that liberation meant their transformation from peasants to modern workers, but without the oppression that capitalist systems had inflicted on the industrial proletariat in other European countries. The small Russian proletariat could, the Bolsheviks believed, free itself from the capitalist stage of development if led by a revolutionary vanguard—the Communist Party. The party represented the proletariat and would direct Russia's historical development from a peasant society to a society of industrial workers.

While US and Soviet ideologies had much in common in terms of background and project, what separated them were their distinctive definitions of what modernity meant. While most Americans celebrated the market, the Soviet elites denied it. Even while realizing that the market was the mechanism on which most of the expansion of Europe had been based, Lenin's followers believed that it was in the process of being superseded by class-based collective action in favor of equality and justice. Modernity came in two stages: a capitalist form and a communal form, reflecting two revolutions—that of capital and productivity, and that of democratization and the social advancement of the underprivileged. Communism was the higher stage of modernity, and it had been given to Russian workers to lead the way toward it.

CITIZENSHIP AND NATIONAL IDENTITY

Jürgen Habermas

Hannah Arendt's analysis that stateless persons, refugees, and those deprived of rights would determine the mark of this century has turned out to be frighteningly correct. The displaced persons whom the Second World War had left in the midst of a Europe in ruins have been replaced by asylum seekers and immigrants flooding into a peaceful and wealthy Europe from the South and the East. The old refugee camps cannot accommodate the flood of new immigration. In coming years statisticians anticipate twenty to thirty million immigrants from Eastern Europe. This problem can be solved only by the joint action of the European states involved. This process would repeat a dialectic that has already taken place, on a smaller scale, during the process of German unification. The trans-national immigrants' movements function as sanctions which force Western Europe to act responsibly in the aftermath of the bankruptcy of state socialism. Europe must make a great effort to quickly improve conditions in the poorer areas of middle and Eastern Europe or it will be flooded by asylum seekers and immigrants.

The experts are debating the capacity of the economic system to absorb these people, but the readiness to politically integrate the asylum seekers depends more upon how citizens *perceive* the social and economic problems posed by immigration. Throughout Europe, right-wing xenophobic reaction against the "estrangement" (*überfremdung*) caused by foreigners has increased. The relatively deprived classes, whether they feel endangered by social decline or have already slipped into segmented marginal groups, identify quite openly with the ideologized supremacy of their own collectivity and reject everything foreign. This is the underside of a chauvinism of prosperity which is increasing everywhere. Thus the asylum problem as well brings to light the latent tension between citizenship and national identity.

One example is the nationalistic and anti-Polish sentiments in the new German state. The newly acquired status of German citizenship is bound together with the hope that the Republic's frontier of prosperity will be pushed toward the Oder and Neiβe. Their newly gained citizenship also gives many of them the ethnocentric satisfaction that they will no longer be treated as second-class Germans. They forget that citizenship rights guarantee liberty because they contain a core composed of universal human rights. Article Four of the Revolutionary Constitution of 1793, which defined the status of the citizen, gave to *every* adult foreigner who lived for one year in France not just the right to remain within the country but also the active rights of a citizen. . . .

These tendencies signify only that a concept of citizenship, the normative content of which has been dissociated from that of national identity, cannot allow arguments for restrictive and obstructionist asylum or immigration policies. It remains an open question whether the European Community today, in expectation of great and turbulent migrations, can and ought to adopt even such liberal foreigner and immigration policies as the Jacobins did in their time. Today the pertinent *moral-theoretical discussion* regarding the definition of "special duties" and special responsibilities is restricted to the social boundaries of a community. Thus the state too forms a concrete legal community which imposes special duties on its citizens. Asylum seekers and immigrants generally present the European states with the problem of whether special citizenship-related duties are to be privileged above those universal, trans-national duties which transcend state boundaries. . . .

Special duties are those which specific persons owe to others to whom they are obligated by virtue of being "connected" to them as dependents, thus as members of a family, as friends, as neighbors, and as co-members of a political community or nation. Parents have special obligations toward their children—and vice versa. Consulates in foreign countries have special obligations to those of their citizenry who need protection—these in turn are obligated to the institutions and laws of their own land. In this context, we think above all of positive duties, which remain undetermined, insofar as they demand acts of solidarity, engagement, and care in measures which cannot be accurately determined. Help cannot always be expected by everyone. Special duties are those which result from the relationship between the concrete community and a part of its membership, and can be understood as social attributes and factual specifications of such intrinsically undetermined duties. . . .

A special duty toward these "others" does not result primarily from their membership in a concrete community. It results more from the abstract coordinating tendencies of *judicial* institutions, which specify, according to certain attributes, certain categories of persons or agents; this process, in turn, specifies and legally enforces those positive social and factual obligations which would have been undetermined otherwise. According to this interpretation, institutionally mediated responsibilities determine those specific obligations owed to certain others active in a moral division of labor. Within such a judicially regulated moral economy, the social boundaries of a legal community only have the function of regulating the distribution of responsibilities throughout the community. That does not mean that our responsibility ends at this boundary. More must be done by the national government so that the citizenry fulfills its duties toward its nonmembers—to the asylum seekers, for example. Still, with this argument the question, "What are these duties?" has not yet been answered.

The moral point of view commits us to assess this problem impartially, and thus not just from the one-sided perspective of those living in prosperous regions, but also from the perspective of the immigrants, those who search for grace. Let us say that they seek not only political asylum but a free and dignified human existence. . . . Legitimate restrictions of immigration rights would then be established by competing viewpoints, such as consideration to avoid the enormity of claims, social conflicts, and burdens that might seriously endanger the public order or the economic reproduction of society. The criteria of ethnic origin, language, and education—or an "acknowledgment of belonging to the cultural community" of the land of migration, in the case of those who have Germanic status—could not establish privileges in the process of immigration and naturalization. . . .

The modern state also presents a political way of life which cannot be exhausted through the abstract form of an institutionalization of legal principles. The way of life builds a political-cultural context in which basic universalistic constitutional principles must be implemented. Then and only then will a population, because it is *accustomed* to freedom, also secure and support free institutions. For that reason, Michael Walzer is of the opinion that the right of immigration is limited by the political right of a community to protect the integrity of its life form. According to him, the right of citizens to self-determination implies the right of self-assertion to each particular way of life. . . .

The requisite competence "to act as citizens of a special political community (this particular polity)" is to be understood in another sense completely—namely, the *universalistic* sense—as soon as the political community itself implements universalistic basic laws. The identity of a political community, which may not be touched by immigration, depends primarily upon the constitutional principles rooted in a political culture and not upon an ethical-cultural form of life as a whole. That is why it must be expected that the new citizens will readily engage in the political culture of their new home, without necessarily giving up the cultural life specific to their country of origin. The *political acculturation* demanded of them does not include the entirety of their socialization. With immigration, new forms of life are imported which expand and multiply the perspective of all, and on the basis of which the common political constitution is always interpreted. . . . We can draw the following normative conclusion: The European states should agree upon a liberal immigration policy. They should not draw their wagons around themselves and their chauvinism of prosperity, hoping to ignore the pressures of those hoping to immigrate or seek asylum. The democratic right of self-determination includes, of course, the right to preserve one's own *political* culture, which includes the concrete context of citizen's rights, though it does not include the self-assertion of a privileged *cultural* life form. Only within the constitutional framework of a democratic legal system can different ways of life coexist equally. These must, however, overlap within a common political culture, which again implies an impulse to open these ways of life to others.

Only democratic citizenship can prepare the way for a condition of world citizenship which does not close itself off within particularistic biases, and which accepts a worldwide form of political communication. The Vietnam War, the revolutionary changes in Eastern and middle Europe, as well as the war in the Persian Gulf are the first *world political* events in a strict sense. Through the electronic mass media, these events were made instantaneous and ubiquitous. In the context of the French Revolution, Kant speculated on the role of the participating public. He identified a world public sphere, which today will become a political reality for the first time with the new relations of global communication. Even the superpowers must recognize worldwide protests. The obsolescence of the state of nature between bellicose states has begun, implying that states have lost some sovereignty. The arrival of world citizenship is no longer merely a phantom, though we are still far from achieving it. State citizenship and world citizenship form a continuum which already shows itself, at least, in outline form.

FURTHER READING

Benhabib, Seyla. 1992. *Situating the Self: Gender, Community, and Postmodernism in Contemporary Ethics.* London: Routledge.

Davies, Norman. 1998. *Europe: A History.* New York: Harper

Habermas, Jürgen. 1991. *The Structural Transformation of the Public Sphere: An Inquiry into a Category of Bourgeois Society.* Cambridge, MA: MIT Press.

Hobsbawm, Eric. 1989. *The Age of Empire: 1875–1914.* New York: Vintage Books.

Lincoln, W. Bruce. 1994. *The Conquest of a Continent: Siberia and the Russians.* New York: Random House.

Menz, Georg, and Alexander Caviedes. 2010. *Labour Migration in Europe.* London: Palgrave Macmillan.

Pinder, John, and Simon Usherwood. 2008. *The European Union: A Very Short Introduction.* Oxford, UK: Oxford University Press.

Roberts, J.M. 1998. *The Penguin History of Europe.* New York: Penguin Press.

Schierup, Carl-Ulrik, Peo Hansen, and Stephen Castles. 2006. *Migration, Citizenship, and the European Welfare State*. Oxford, UK: Oxford University Press.

Sewell, Mike. 2002. *The Cold War*. Cambridge, UK: Cambridge University Press.

Stearns, Peter N., Michael B. Adas, Stuart B. Schwartz, and Jason Mark Gilbert. 2010. *World Civilizations: The Global Experience*. Upper Saddle River, NJ: Pearson.

Tilly, Charles. 1992. *Coercion, Capital and European States: AD 990-1992*. Oxford, UK: Wiley-Blackwell.

Tolan, John, Henry Laurens, Gilles Veinstein, and John Esposito. 2012. *Europe and the Islamic World: A History*. Princeton, NJ: Princeton University Press.

Varoufakis, Yanis. 2013. *The Global Minotaur: America, Europe, and the Future of the Global Economy*. London: Zed Books.

Zubok, Vladislav. 2007. *A Failed Empire: The Soviet Union in the Cold War from Stalin to Gorbachev*. Chapel Hill: University of North Carolina Press.

9

THE AMERICAS
Development Strategies

The rest of the world has been aware of the Western hemisphere for only a little over five hundred years, but in those relatively brief years, the Americas have played a vital role in global development. Initially, the resources of the region were plundered to bring wealth to Europe and other parts of the world. Later, America's countries—particularly its leading nation, the United States—dominated the rest of the world both economically and in popular culture. But development among countries within the region has never been equal. The same region that produced one of the world's richest nations also includes some of its poorest.

The European discovery of what was called "the New World" in 1492 changed everything. Even though the Scandinavian Vikings had come to North America in the eleventh century CE and named it "Vinland," most of Europe was unaware of this discovery. The Americas remained a mystery until the Italian Christopher Columbus and the crew from his three Spanish ships came to the shores of the Caribbean islands, mistakenly thinking that they had arrived in Southeast Asia, at that time called the East Indies. What they really discovered was a whole new world.

The Americas are usually regarded as two continents, divided between North and South, with the Central American nations of the land bridge between the two and the nations on the Caribbean islands to the east. A distinction is sometimes made between North America—defined only as the English- and French-speaking nations of Canada and the United States—and Latin America, which includes Mexico and the Spanish- and Portuguese-speaking nations of Central and South America (and many, but not all, of the island nations of the Caribbean). The island nation of the Bahamas and the British colony of Bermuda off the Atlantic coast of the United States are also usually considered part of the Americas.

Even before European contact in 1492, imperial civilizations stretched over much of the landscape, including the great cultures of the Incas, the Mayans, and the Aztecs. These were as encompassing as the ancient Mediterranean World of the West. The arrival of Spanish and Portuguese Conquistadors changed all of that. In 1520, the armies of Spanish general Hernando Cortés conquered the Aztec empire of central Mexico. This ended Aztec domination over the region and ushered in a period of Spanish control that persisted for centuries. The Spanish and Portuguese plundered the continent for precious resources such as silver and gold, and they also created European settlements to develop agricultural lands and promote trade. In North America, British and French colonialists set up their own settlements. In time, some of the Europeans intermarried with the local population of native peoples, an ethnic intermixing that is seen most prominently in Mexican, Central American, and many South American countries. The importation of enslaved Africans in the seventeenth through the nineteenth centuries brought another ethnic dimension to the Americas, especially in nations that relied on large plantation crops of cotton and sugar cane, including the United States, Brazil, and Cuba and many other Caribbean islands.

At the same time that the Americas were experiencing the "global-in" effect of colonialization, the New World was also making an impact on the rest of the world. Perhaps nothing exemplifies this more than the availability of new foods. The arrival of these exotic—though now quite familiar—plants changed the eating habits of Europeans forever. Can you imagine Italian food without tomatoes? Tomatoes originally came from what are now Peru and Ecuador, and it took decades to make them edible and sweet. Can you imagine German food without potatoes? These came originally from Southern Peru. Corn, peppers, beans, squash, peanuts, pineapples, cashews, pecans—the list of New World foods goes on and on. Tobacco also originated in the Americas, and the use of it, for good or ill, has spread around the world. So have the sources of some drugs, such as the coca bush from which cocaine is derived.

The European conquerors who came to the Americas in the sixteenth and seventeenth centuries were not interested just in nice things to eat and smoke, however. They were after the wealth of the new lands—specifically, the enormous veins of silver, gold, and other precious metals that were lying beneath the surface of the earth. The mountain of Potosí, located in present-day Bolivia, was thought to be made of silver, and indeed the silver mines there created a major supply route across the Pacific and Atlantic that made Spain wealthy. European settlers, relying on enslaved Africans for their workforce, were able to raise the kind of crops that could be grown only in warm climates with abundant water, such as cotton and sugar. These were shipped throughout the world to satisfy the need for clothing and sweets. The wealth generated from the exploitation of the Americas' resources was in part squandered and in part wasted on wars. But this wealth also helped to develop European capitalism, and some argue that it provided the financial impetus behind Europe's great eighteenth- and nineteenth-century strides in industrialization.

The European settlers in the Americas eventually realized that they could profit from their continents' resources themselves, and they demanded independence from European colonial control. The American Revolution allowed the original thirteen colonies on the Eastern Seaboard of the North American continent to break free and form their own federation of "united states." Eventually, these colonists expanded their sphere of influence to much of the North American continent, purchasing land from France and Russia and conquering lands from Spanish settlers in the south. The Native American people in the way of these colonists were tragic victims. Those who were not killed or who did not die from European diseases against which they had no immunity were consigned to life on reservations on land with poor soil. Canada likewise gained its independence from Britain and extended its borders to the Pacific Ocean.

Independence movements swept through the rest of the Americas in the nineteenth century. South America's greatest hero in this regard was Simón Bolívar, who led revolutionary forces throughout the northern part of the continent. He is revered as the liberator of his native Venezuela, and also Colombia, Panama, Ecuador, Peru, and the country that now bears his name, Bolivia.

In the twentieth century, the United States emerged as the world's dominant economic power. European nations had been weakened by two exhausting wars and the economic drain of colonial control. By the end of the century, Europe had begun to revive and the relative strength of U.S. global economic influence waned as new forces of production emerged in Asia. In the meantime, some of the other countries of the Americas progressed economically as well, though not nearly as dramatically. In the twenty-first century, however, Brazil is included as one of the BRICS, countries with economic potential within the emerging global world—Brazil, Russia, India, China, and South Africa.

The readings in this section explore some of these aspects of the history of the Americas' global impact. The first section is from the book *1493*, which looks at the way that the world changed after Columbus's discovery of the New World. Not only was Europe and the rest of the world enriched by the Americas' resources, but also the Americas themselves were transformed through European conquest and development. Truly, a new world was created. The author, Charles C. Mann, is an American writer who lives in Massachusetts and focuses on scientific discoveries. An earlier book of his, *1491*, examines life in the Americas before European contact and conquest. The next reading focuses on the European conquest of the native people, including the powerful Aztec civilization, and shows how the European colonial rule in many ways replicated the imperial designs of the Aztecs. The author of this excerpt, Tzvetan Todorov, was born in Bulgaria and lives in France. He writes on literary theory and historical topics such as the conquest of the Americas and the concentration camps established in Nazi and Stalinist regimes.

The other two readings focus on the global impact of the contemporary economic situation in the Americas. An American political scientist, Francis Fukuyama, raises the question of why the United States and most of Latin America have had such different experiences in economic development. Fukuyama is best known for an earlier book, *The End of History and the Last Man* (New York: Free Press, 1982), which claimed that the end of the Cold War in 1989 signaled the triumph of global capitalism and the end of ideological clashes. Both assertions were greatly contested, and his book on Latin American economic development, *Falling Behind,* from which the excerpt in this section is taken, is also controversial. Fukuyama appears to blame Latin American political leaders for social policies that emphasize economic equality and government-supplied welfare over economic austerity and capital economic infrastructure development. Critics of Fukuyama assert that he ignores two other major factors in Latin America's slow economic growth: large landed aristocracies that have maintained a division between poor labor and a small number of wealthy owners and economic dependency on the United States, which has exploited the resources and cheap labor of Latin America for its own economic benefit.

The final reading in this section gives a different picture of Latin American development from Fukuyama's portrayal. The author, Denis Lynn Daly Heyck, teaches Latin American Literature and Culture at Loyola University in Chicago, and in this excerpt, she introduces her study of the economic aspirations of three Latin American communities: Brazil's rubber tappers, Bolivia's Guaraní Indians, and Nicaragua's women cooperativists. She finds that their development goals are different from those of many of the development experts in their countries' capitals and in Washington, D.C. In general, they desire a sustainable economy that maintains traditional customs, cultures, and values.

DISCOVERING THE NEW WORLD COLUMBUS CREATED

Charles C. Mann

Almost twenty years ago I came across a newspaper notice about some local college students who had grown a hundred different varieties of tomato. Visitors were welcome to take a look at their work. Because I like tomatoes, I decided to drop by with my eight-year-old son. When we arrived at the school greenhouse I was amazed—I'd never seen tomatoes in so many different sizes, shapes, and colors.

A student offered us samples on a plastic plate. Among them was an alarmingly lumpy specimen, the color of an old brick, with a broad, green-black tonsure about the stem. Occasionally I have dreams in which I experience a sensation so intensely that I wake up. This tomato was like that—it jolted my mouth awake. Its name, the student said, was Black from Tula. It was an "heirloom" tomato, developed in nineteenth-century Ukraine.

"I thought tomatoes came from Mexico," I said, surprised. "What are they doing breeding them in Ukraine?"

The student gave me a catalog of heirloom seeds for tomatoes, chili peppers, and beans (common beans, not green beans). After I went home, I flipped through the pages. All three crops originated in the Americas. But time and again the varieties in the catalog came from overseas: Japanese tomatoes, Italian peppers, Congolese beans. Wanting to have more of those strange but tasty tomatoes, I went on to order seeds, sprout them in plastic containers, and stick the seedlings in a garden, something I'd never done before.

Not long after my trip to the greenhouse I visited the library. I discovered that my question to the student had been off the mark. To begin, tomatoes probably originated not in Mexico, but in the Andes Mountains. Half a dozen wild tomato species exist in Peru and Ecuador, all but one inedible, producing fruit the size of a thumbtack. And to botanists the real mystery is less how tomatoes ended up in Ukraine or Japan than how the progenitors of today's tomato journeyed from South America to Mexico, where native plant breeders radically transformed the fruits, making them bigger, redder, and, most important, more edible. Why transport useless wild tomatoes for thousands of miles? Why had the species not been domesticated in its home range? How had people in Mexico gone about changing the plant to their needs?

These questions touched on a long-standing interest of mine: the original inhabitants of the Americas. As a reporter in the news division of the journal *Science,* I had from time to time spoken with archaeologists, anthropologists, and geographers about their increasing recognition of the size and sophistication of long-ago native societies. The botanists' puzzled respect for Indian plant breeders fit nicely into that picture. Eventually I learned enough from these conversations that I wrote a book about researchers' current views of the history of the Americas before Columbus. The tomatoes in my garden carried a little of that history in their DNA.

They also carried some of the history *after* Columbus. Beginning in the sixteenth century, Europeans carried tomatoes around the world. After convincing themselves that the strange fruits were not poisonous, farmers planted them from Africa to Asia. In a small way, the plant had a cultural impact everywhere it moved. Sometimes not so small—one can scarcely imagine southern Italy without tomato sauce.

Still, I didn't grasp that such biological transplants might have played a role beyond the dinner plate until in a used-book store I came across a paperback: *Ecological Imperialism,* by Alfred W. Crosby, a geographer and historian then at the University of Texas. Wondering what the title could refer to, I picked up the book. The first sentence seemed to jump off the page: "European emigrants and their descendants are all over the place, which requires explanation."

I understood exactly what Crosby was getting at. Most Africans live in Africa, most Asians in Asia, and most Native Americans in the Americas. People of European descent, by contrast, are thick on the ground in Australia, the Americas, and southern Africa. Successful transplants, they form the majority in many of those places—an obvious fact, but one I had never really thought about before. Now I wondered: Why *is* that the case? Ecologically speaking, it is just as much a puzzle as tomatoes in Ukraine.

Before Crosby (and some of his colleagues) looked into the matter, historians tended to explain Europe's spread across the globe almost entirely in terms of European superiority, social or scientific. Crosby proposed another explanation in *Ecological Imperialism*. Europe frequently had better-trained troops and more-advanced weaponry than its adversaries, he agreed, but in the long run its critical advantage was biological, not technological. The ships that sailed across the Atlantic carried not only human beings, but plants and animals—sometimes intentionally, sometimes accidentally. After Columbus, ecosystems that had been separate for eons suddenly met and mixed in a process Crosby called, as he had titled his previous book, the Columbian Exchange. The exchange took corn (maize) to Africa and sweet potatoes to East Asia, horses and apples to the Americas, and rhubarb and eucalyptus to Europe—and also swapped about a host of less-familiar organisms like insects, grasses, bacteria, and viruses. The Columbian Exchange was neither fully controlled nor understood by its participants, but it allowed Europeans to transform much of the Americas, Asia, and, to a lesser extent, Africa into ecological versions of Europe, landscapes the foreigners could use more comfortably than could their original inhabitants. This ecological imperialism, Crosby argued, provided the British, French, Dutch, Portuguese, and Spanish with the consistent edge needed to win their empires.

Crosby's books were constitutive documents in a new discipline: environmental history. The same period witnessed the rise of another discipline, Atlantic studies, which stressed the importance of interactions among the cultures bordering that ocean. (Recently a number of Atlanticists have added movements across the Pacific to their purview; the field may have to be renamed.) Taken together, researchers in all these fields have been assembling what amounts to a new picture of the origins of our world-spanning, interconnected civilization, the way of life evoked by the term "globalization." One way to summarize their efforts might be to say that to the history of kings and queens most of us learned as students has been added a recognition of the remarkable role of *exchange,* both ecological and economic. Another way might be to say that there is a growing recognition that Columbus's voyage did not mark the discovery of a New World, but its creation. . . .

Satellites map out environmental changes wreaked by the huge, largely hidden trade in latex, the main ingredient in natural rubber. Geneticists use DNA assays to trace the ruinous path of potato blight. Ecologists employ mathematical simulations to simulate the spread of malaria in Europe. And so on—the examples are legion. Political changes, too, have helped. To cite one of special importance . . . , it is much easier to work in China nowadays than it was in the early 1980s, when Crosby was researching *Ecological Imperialism*. Today, bureaucratic suspicion is minimal; the chief obstacle I faced during my visits to Beijing was the abominable traffic. Librarians and researchers there happily gave me early Chinese records—digital scans of the originals, which they let me copy onto a little memory stick that I carried in my shirt pocket.

What happened after Columbus, this new research says, was nothing less than the forming of a single new world from the collision of two old worlds—three, if one counts

Africa as separate from Eurasia. Born in the sixteenth century from European desires to join the thriving Asian trade sphere, the economic system for exchange ended up transforming the globe into a single ecological system by the nineteenth century—almost instantly, in biological terms. The creation of this ecological system helped Europe seize, for several vital centuries, the political initiative, which in turn shaped the contours of today's world-spanning economic system, in its interlaced, omnipresent, barely comprehended splendor.

Ever since violent protests at a 1999 World Trade Organization meeting in Seattle brought the idea of globalization to the world's attention, pundits of every ideological stripe have barraged the public with articles, books, white papers, blog posts, and video documentaries attempting to explain, celebrate, or attack it. From the start the debate has focused around two poles. On one side are economists and entrepreneurs who argue passionately that free trade makes societies better off—that both sides of an uncoerced exchange gain from it. The more trade the better! they say. Anything less amounts to depriving people in one place of the fruits of human ingenuity in other places. On the other side is a din of environmental activists, cultural nationalists, labor organizers, and anti-corporate agitators who charge that unregulated trade upends political, social, and environmental arrangements in ways that are rarely anticipated and usually destructive. The less trade, they say, the better. Protect local communities from the forces unleashed by multinational greed!

Whipsawed between these two opposing views, the global network has become the subject of a furious intellectual battle, complete with mutually contradictory charts, graphs, and statistics—and tear gas and flying bricks in the streets where political leaders meet behind walls of riot police to wrangle through international-trade agreements. Sometimes the moil of slogans and counter-slogans, facts and factoids, seems impenetrable, but as I learned more I came to suspect that both sides may be correct. From the outset globalization brought both enormous economic gains *and* ecological and social tumult that threatened to offset those gains.

It is true that our times are different from the past. Our ancestors did not have the Internet, air travel, genetically modified crops, or computerized international stock exchanges. Still, reading the accounts of the creation of the world market one cannot help hearing echoes—some muted, some thunderously loud—of the disputes now on the television news. Events four centuries ago set a template for events we are living through today.

THE REASONS FOR THE VICTORY

Tzvetan Todorov

The encounter between Old World and New made possible by Columbus's discovery is of a very special type: war, or rather, in the term of the period, conquest. A mystery concerning the very outcome of the combat still hovers over the conquest: why this lightninglike victory, when the inhabitants of America are so superior in number to their adversaries and fighting on their own territory as well? To confine ourselves to the conquest of Mexico—the most spectacular, since the Mexican civilization is the most brilliant of the pre-Columbian world—how are we to account for the fact that Cortés, leading a few hundred men, managed to seize the kingdom of Montezuma, who commanded several hundred thousand? I shall try to find an answer in the abundant literature to which this phase of the conquest gave rise at the time: Cortés's own reports; the Spanish chronicles, the most remarkable of which is that of Bernal Díaz del Castillo; lastly, the native accounts, transcribed by the Spanish missionaries or written by the Mexicans themselves.

The chief stages of the conquest of Mexico are well known. Cortés's expedition, in 1519, is the third to land on the Mexican coasts; it consists of several hundred men. Cortés is sent by the governor of Cuba; but after the ships leave, this governor changes his mind and attempts to recall Cortés. The latter disembarks in Vera Cruz and declares himself to be under the direct authority of the king of Spain. Having learned of the existence of the Aztec empire, he begins a slow progress toward the interior, attempting to win over to his cause, either by promises or by warfare, the populations whose lands he passes through. The most difficult battle is waged against the Tlaxcaltecs, who will nevertheless become, subsequently, his best allies. Cortés finally reaches Mexico City, where he is cordially received; shortly thereafter, he decides to take the Aztec sovereign prisoner and succeeds in doing so. He then learns of the arrival on the coast of a new Spanish expedition, sent against him by the Cuban governor; the newcomers outnumber his own forces. Cortés sets out with some of these to meet this army, the rest remaining in Mexico to guard Montezuma, under the command of Pedro de Alvarado. Cortés wins the battle against his compatriots, imprisons their leader Panfilo de Narvaez, and convinces the rest to accept his command. But he then learns that during his absence things have gone badly in Mexico City: Alvarado has massacred a group of Mexicans in the course of a religious festival, and warfare has broken out. Cortés returns to the capital and joins his troops in their besieged fortress; at this point Montezuma dies. The Aztec attacks are so insistent that Cortés decides to leave the city by night; his departure is discovered, and in the ensuing battle more than half his army is annihilated: this is the Noche Triste. Cortés withdraws to Tlaxcala, reorganizes his forces, and returns to besiege the capital; he cuts off all means of access and orders the construction of swift brigantines (at the time, the city was surrounded by lakes). After several months' siege, Mexico falls; the conquest has lasted about two years.

Let us first review the explanations commonly proposed for Cortés's victory. A first reason is the ambiguous, hesitant behavior of Montezuma himself, who offers Cortés virtually no resistance (this will therefore concern the first phase of the conquest, until Montezuma's death); such behavior may have, beyond certain cultural motivations to which I shall return, more personal reasons: in many respects, it differs from that of the other Aztec leaders. Bernal Díaz, reporting the remarks of the Cholula dignitaries, describes it thus: "They said that their lord Montezuma had known we were coming to Cholula, and that every day he was of many minds, unable to decide what to do about it. Sometimes he sent them instructions that if we arrived they were to pay us great honor and guide us on to Mexico, and at other times he said that he did not want us to come to his city and now recently the gods Tezcatlipoca and Huitzilopochtli, for whom they had great devotion, had proposed to him that we should be killed at Cholula or brought bound to Mexico." One has the impression that there is a genuine ambiguity involved here, and not mere clumsiness, when Montezuma's messengers inform the Spaniards both that the Aztec kingdom is to be given to them as a present and that they are not to enter Mexico but to return whence they had come; but we shall see that Cortés deliberately sustains this equivocation.

In certain chronicles, Montezuma is depicted as a melancholy and resigned man; it is asserted that he is a prey to his bad conscience, expiating in person an inglorious episode of earlier Aztec history: the Aztecs like to represent themselves as the legitimate successors of the Toltecs, the previous dynasty, whereas they are in reality usurpers, newcomers. Has this national guilt complex caused Montezuma to imagine that the Spaniards are direct descendants of the ancient Toltecs, come to reclaim what is rightfully theirs? We shall see that here, too, the idea is in part suggested by the Spaniards; it is impossible to declare with any certainty that Montezuma himself believed in it.

Once the Spaniards have arrived in his capital, Montezuma's behavior is even more singular. Not only does he let himself be taken captive by Cortés and his men (this captivity is Cortés's most startling decision, along with that of "burning"—in reality, scuttling— his own ships: with the handful of men under his command, he arrests the emperor, whereas he himself is surrounded by the all-powerful Aztec army), but also, once a prisoner, Montezuma's sole concern is to avoid all bloodshed. Contrary, for example, to what the final Aztec emperor, Cuauhtemoc, will do, Montezuma tries by every means in his power to keep war from breaking out in his city: he prefers to abandon his leadership, his privileges, and his wealth. Even during Cortés's brief absence, when the Spaniard has gone to face the punitive expedition sent against him, Montezuma will not attempt to take advantage of the situation in order to get rid of the invaders. "Many of those who had been with Pedro de Alvarado through the critical time said that if the uprising had been desired by Montezuma or started on his advice, or if Montezuma had had any hand in it, they would all have been killed. Montezuma had pacified his people and made them give up the attack." History or legend (though it matters little which), in this case transcribed by the Jesuit Tovar, goes so far as to describe Montezuma, on the eve of his death, as ready to convert to Christianity; but as a final mockery, the Spanish priest, busy amassing gold, does not find the time. "It is said that he asked for baptism and converted to the truth of the Holy Gospel, and although there was a priest at hand, it is presumed that the latter was much more concerned to collect wealth than to catechize the poor king."

Unfortunately, we lack the documents that might have permitted us to penetrate the mental world of this strange emperor: in the presence of his enemies he is reluctant to make use of his enormous power, as if he were not convinced he wished to conquer; as Gomara, Cortés's chaplain and biographer, says: "Our Spaniards were never able to learn the truth, because at the time they did not understand the language, and afterward no one was found alive with whom Montezuma had shared the secret." The Spanish historians of the period vainly sought the answer to these questions, seeing Montezuma sometimes as a madman, sometimes as a philosopher. Peter Martyr, a chronicler who remained in Spain, tends toward this latter solution: "He seemed to obey injunctions much harsher than the rules of grammar imposed upon little children, and with great patience endured everything in order to prevent an uprising of his subjects and his nobles. Any yoke seemed to him lighter than a revolt of his people. It was as if he sought to imitate Diocletian, who preferred to take poison than once more assume the reins of the empire he had abdicated." Gomara sometimes shows contempt for him: "Montezuma must have been a weak man of little courage, to let himself be seized and then, while a prisoner, never to attempt flight, even when Cortés offered him his freedom, and his own men begged him to take it." But on other occasions he admits his perplexity, and the impossibility of settling the question: "the cowardice of Montezuma, or the love he bore Cortés and the Spaniards . . ." or again: "in my opinion he was either very wise in disregarding the things he had to put up with, or very foolish, in not resenting them." We are still subject to the same uncertainties.

The figure of Montezuma certainly counts for something in this nonresistance to evil. Yet such an explanation is valid only for the first part of Cortés's campaign, for Montezuma dies in the middle of events, as mysteriously as he had lived (probably stabbed by his Spanish jailers), and his successors at the head of the Aztec state immediately declare a fierce and pitiless war on the Spaniards. However, during the war's second phase, another factor begins to play a decisive role: this is Cortés's exploitation of the internal dissensions among the various populations occupying Mexican territory. He succeeds very well in this endeavor: throughout the campaign, he manages to take advantage of the struggles between rival factions, and during the final phase he commands an army of Tlaxcaltecs and other Indian allies numerically comparable to that of the Aztecs, an army of which the Spaniards are now merely, in a sense, the logistical support or command force: their units often seem to be composed of ten Spanish horse and ten thousand Indian foot soldiers! This is already the perception of contemporaries: according to Motolinia, a Franciscan historian of "New Spain," "the conquistadors say that the Tlaxcaltecs deserve that His Majesty grant them much favor, and that if it had not been for them, they would all have been dead, when the Aztecs repulsed the Christians from Mexico, and that the Tlaxcaltecs offered them a haven." And indeed, for many years the Tlaxcaltecs enjoy numerous privileges granted them by the Spanish crown: exempted from taxes, they very often become administrators of the newly conquered lands.

We cannot avoid wondering, when we read the history of Mexico: why did the Indians not offer more resistance? Didn't they realize Cortés's colonizing ambitions? The answer displaces the question: the Indians in the regions Cortés first passed through are not more impressed by his imperialist intentions because they have already been conquered and colonized—by the Aztecs. Mexico at the time is not a homogeneous state, but a conglomerate of populations, defeated by the Aztecs who occupy the top of the pyramid. So that far from incarnating an absolute evil, Cortés often appears to them as a lesser evil, as a liberator, so to speak, who permits them to throw off the yoke of a tyranny especially detestable because so close at hand.

Sensitized as we are to the misdeeds of European colonialism, it is difficult for us to understand why the Indians do not immediately rebel, when there is still time, against the Spaniards. But the conquistadors merely fall into step with the Aztecs. We may be scandalized to learn that the Spaniards seek only gold, slaves, and women. "They were in fact concerned only to furnish themselves with some fine Indian women and to take a certain amount of booty," writes Bernal Díaz, and he tells the following anecdote: after the fall of Mexico, "Cuauhtemoc and all his captains complained to Cortés that some of our leaders who happened to be in the brigantines, as well as several who had fought on the highways, had carried off the wives and daughters of a great number of chieftains. They asked him to show mercy and to order that these women be returned. Cortés replied that he would have great difficulty taking them away from his comrades who already set great store by them, that he had sent for them, furthermore, and had them brought before him; that he would see if they had become Christians, declaring further that if they wished to return to their fathers and their husbands, he would make every effort to see that they did so." The result of the investigation is not surprising: "Most of the women chose to follow neither father, nor mother, nor husband; but indeed to remain with the soldiers of which they had become the companions. Others hid themselves; some, moreover, declared that they no longer wished to be idolators. Indeed there were some who were already pregnant; so that only three returned to their people, Cortés having given specific orders to let them go."

But it is precisely the same thing that the Indians complained of in the other parts of Mexico when they related the Aztecs' misdeeds: "The inhabitants of these villages . . . offered vigorous protests against Montezuma and especially against his tax-collectors, saying that they stole everything they possessed from them and that, if their wives and their daughters appeared to them worthy of attention, they violated them in the presence of the husbands and the fathers, and sometimes carried them off for good; that by their orders they were forced to work as if they were slaves, and to transport in canoes, or even overland, timber, stones, corn, without on the other hand leaving off the labor of their arms for sowing maize and other services of great number."

The gold and precious stones that lure the Spaniards were already taken as taxes by Montezuma's functionaries; it does not seem that we can reject this allegation as a pure invention of the Spaniards seeking to legitimize their conquest, even if this is also a contributing factor: too many testimonies agree in this direction. The *Florentine Codex* reports the chiefs of the neighboring tribes coming to protest to Cortés the oppression imposed by the Aztecs: "For Montezuma and the Mexicans have caused us great grief and the Mexicans have brought us evil. They have brought poverty under our very noses, for they have imposed upon us all kinds of taxes." And Diego Durán, a Dominican sympathizer and a cultural half-caste, one might say, discovers the resemblance precisely at the moment he reproaches the Aztecs: "If their hosts were inattentive or indifferent, the Aztecs pillaged and sacked the villages, despoiled the people of their clothes, beat them, stripped them of all their possessions and dishonored them; they destroyed the harvests and inflicted a thousand injuries and damages upon them. The whole country trembled before them. Wherever they came, they were given all they needed; but even when they were treated well, they behaved in this same fashion. . . . This was the cruellest and most devilish people that can be conceived, on account of the way in which they treated their vassals, which was much worse than the way in which the Spaniards treated them and treat them still. They did all the harm they could, as our Spaniards do today if they are not restrained from doing so."

There are many resemblances between old conquerors and new, as the latter themselves felt, since they described the Aztecs as recent invaders, conquistadors comparable to themselves. More precisely, and in this too the resemblance persists, the relation to the predecessor is that of an implicit and sometimes unconscious continuity, accompanied by a denial concerning this very relation. The Spaniards burn the Mexicans' books in order to wipe out their religion; they destroy their monuments in order to abolish any memory of a former greatness. But a hundred years earlier, during the reign of Itzcoatl, the Aztecs themselves had destroyed all the old books in order to rewrite history in their own fashion. At the same time the Aztecs, as we have seen, like to depict themselves as heirs of the Toltecs; and the Spaniards often choose a certain fidelity to the past, in religion or in politics; they are assimilated at the same time that they assimilate. One symbolic fact among others: the capital of the new state will be the same as that of the conquered Mexico. "Considering that Tenoxtitlan had been so great and so famous, we decided to settle in it. . . . If in the past it was the capital and the queen of all these provinces, it will be so, the same, henceforward." Cortés seeks, in a sense, to constitute his legitimacy, no longer in the eyes of the king of Spain though this had been one of his great concerns during the campaign but in the eyes of the local population, by assuming a continuity with the kingdom of Montezuma. The viceroy Mendoza will resort to the fiscal records of the Aztec empire.

The same holds true in the realm of faith: religious conquest often consists in removing from a holy place certain images and establishing others there instead, preserving— and this is essential—the cult sites in which the same aromatic herbs are burned. Cortés tells the story: "The most important of these idols and the ones in which they have most faith I had taken from their places and thrown down the steps; and I ordered those chapels where they had been to be cleaned, for they were full of the blood of sacrifices; and I had images of Our Lady and of other saints put there." And Bernal Díaz bears witness: "An order was given that the incense of their country should be burned before the holy image and the Blessed Cross."

"It is only just that what has served the worship of the demons should be transformed into a temple for the service of God," writes Fray Lorenzo de Bienvenida. The Christian priests and friars will occupy exactly the places left empty after the repression of those professing the native religious worship, whom the Spaniards, moreover, called by that overdetermined name *popes* (contamination of the Indian term designating them and the word "pope"); Cortés made the continuity quite explicit: "The respect and welcome that they give to the friars is the result of the commands of the Marqués del Valle, Don Hernando Cortés, for from the beginning he ordered them to be very reverent and respectful to the priests, just as they used to be the ministers of their idols."

To Montezuma's hesitations during the first phase of the conquest and the internal divisions among the Mexicans during the second, a third factor is frequently added: the Spanish superiority with regard to weapons. The Aztecs do not know how to work metal, and their swords, like their armor, are less effective; arrows (nonpoisoned arrows) are not as powerful as harquebuses and cannon; in their movements the Spaniards are much swifter: for land operations they have horses, whereas the Aztecs are always on foot; and on water they know how to build brigantines whose superiority over the Indian canoes plays a decisive role in the final phase of the siege of Mexico. Finally, the Spaniards also—unwittingly—inaugurate bacteriological warfare, since they bring smallpox, which ravages the opposing army. Yet these superiorities, in themselves incontestable, do not suffice to explain everything, if we take into account, at the same time, the numerical relation between the two camps. And there are in fact very few harquebuses, and even fewer cannon, whose power is not that of a modern bomb; further, the gunpowder is often wet. The effect of firearms and horses cannot be measured directly by the number of victims.

EXPLAINING THE DEVELOPMENT GAP BETWEEN LATIN AMERICA AND THE UNITED STATES

Francis Fukuyama

In 1492, on the eve of the European settlement and colonization of the New World, Bolivia and Peru hosted richer and more complex civilizations than any that existed in North America. After two centuries of colonization, in 1700, per capita income in continental Latin America was $521, and it was a marginally higher $527 in what would become the United States. During the eighteenth century, the sugar-producing island of Cuba was far wealthier than Britain's American colonies. Yet, over the next three centuries, the United States steadily pulled ahead of Latin America in economic growth, such that, by the beginning of the twenty-first century, per capita income in the United States was five times the Latin American average.

It may be that the United States is simply exceptional in its ability to sustain long-term economic growth; if true, any comparison with other parts of the world would be unfair. Yet East Asia has managed to close the gap over a relatively short period of time. For example, per capita income in East Asia was $746 in 1950, or 8 percent of that of the United States; by 1998, it had risen to 16 percent of the U.S. figure. In contrast, Latin America's per capita income in 1950 was 27 percent of that of the United States, and by 1998 it had fallen to only 21 percent. The gap would be even greater if we selected only the high-performing countries of East Asia instead of the region as a whole. . . .

The subject of Latin America's lagging performance is, of course, one that has been addressed at enormous length in the existing academic and popular literature, and there is no lack of theories for why the gap exists and no lack of recommendations for remedies. The present study cannot hope to provide definitive conclusions as to the source of the gap. Latin America is, to begin with, a huge, varied, and complex region; Haiti's problems are of an entirely different order from those of Bolivia or Peru, not to mention Argentina or Uruguay. The sources of the United States' long-term economic performance are, similarly, quite complicated when examined over a centuries-long perspective. Interpretations of the causes of the gap need to take account of the specific history, culture, conditions, and contexts of each society in question.

There is, nonetheless, some virtue in taking a bird's-eye view of the problem. It is clear, for example, that despite Latin America's diversity, there are some overarching patterns in its economic and political development that distinguish the region both from North America and from other parts of the developing world, like East Asia. . . . There was a tremendous variability in wealth across Latin America by the year 1800, but in the years following, the entire region fell behind—with no exceptions. The debt crisis of the 1980s emerged not just in one country, but in several across the region. Since many analyses and policy prescriptions tend to be shared across regions, it makes sense to look at the broad patterns and toward common policy prescriptions that have applicability beyond individual countries.

The long-term durability of the performance gap between Latin America and the United States suggests that closing it will not be an easy matter. No reader . . . should expect to find a simple answer to the question of why the gap exists, nor a set of policy prescriptions that will magically raise economic growth rates, solve deeply embedded political conflicts, or provide the key to social problems. On the other hand, Latin America's overall performance relative to that of the United States has dramatically improved in some historical periods, only to fall back again in others. Understanding the reasons for these changes in relative growth rates can help to isolate factors that have been important in keeping the gap alive.

There is another reason to think that centuries-long patterns of growth and divergence may not always persist into the future. In 1492, it is safe to say, there was virtually no contact between North and South America. Since that time, there has been a steady increase in the interchanges between the regions, punctuated by periods of greater isolation (as after the Great Depression). But the phenomenon of globalization has vastly accelerated in the last half century and shows no signs of slowing down.

Globalization is not merely the integration of markets for goods, services, and investments; it also encompasses the flow of people and ideas. In the Western Hemisphere, integration has occurred on the level of populations, with the movement of millions of individuals from Latin America to the United States (and, to a lesser extent, to Canada and Western Europe). This has resulted in a large reverse flow not only of remittances, but also of people and ideas (as in the case of *dependencia* theory). The degree of intellectual interchange and cross-fertilization has been growing far more intensely with the passage of time, and lower communications and travel costs will inevitably serve to continue the trend. Just as there has been a growing Americanization of the cultures of most Latin American countries, so too has there been an increasing Latin Americanization of U.S. culture. Under these circumstances, the prospects for greater convergence seem strong. . . .

Latin America has been a constant importer of ideas from North America and Europe. At the time of the wars of independence, the United States was seen as a model of modernity and democracy, whose political institutions (such as presidentialism and federalism) were widely imitated. But even in periods of great American prestige, there was on undercurrent of hurt and resentment, due in part to American disinterest in reciprocating the admiration or focusing properly on the region. When the United States did focus on the region, it was to expand its territory and influence, as in the case of the Mexican-American and Spanish-American wars. The power of the United States has always been more evident to Latin Americans than to others, and its dominance in a variety of realms has led to hostility in a variety of forms, from anti-American versions of Marxism during the Cold War to the . . . populism of Hugo Chávez.

THE DEVELOPMENT GAP: HISTORICAL CONTEXT

Prior to the arrival of the Europeans in 1492, many parts of Latin America were richer than North America. Colonization, it is widely agreed, had a devastating impact on the welfare of the indigenous pre-Colombian populations in Mexico and the Andean region, as the Spanish set up an empire to extract gold, silver, and other commodities, much in the same way that British and French colonization devastated the smaller numbers of indigenous peoples in North America. But initial conditions were not all that different in the two halves of the New World, in terms either of per capita income or economic structure. Both regions were predominantly agricultural economies and commodity exporters to the more-developed parts of the world. This situation persisted more or less through the end of the eighteenth century and the emergence of an independent United States of America.

The gap . . . really emerged in the first two-thirds of the nineteenth century, a period following Latin America's wars of independence from Spain and Portugal during which new states were being formed. The period from 1820 to 1870 was particularly disastrous for Latin America while U.S. per capita GDP grew at a 1.39 percent annual rate in this period, per capita GDP actually fell by .05 percent per year in Latin America. The struggle for independence was costly both for the new United States and for the countries of Latin America, but it took the latter on average much longer both to win independence and to consolidate new state institutions in their territory. The retreat of the Spanish reduced access to some markets and technology and collapsed the internal customs unions that had existed within their empire, all of which was very costly in terms of growth.

The period from 1870 to 1970 was, in contrast, a period of modest catching up for most of Latin America. In the earlier part of that period, until 1929, per capita GDP growth was actually higher there than in the United States, as it was again in the period from 1950 to 1970. Throughout the region, post-independence regimes slowly consolidated, and there were prolonged periods in which both the internal and external environments were relatively benign. Growth from 1870 to 1970 was, of course, dramatically interrupted by the Great Depression after 1929 and the outbreak of World War II. While these events had important consequences for all countries in the Western Hemisphere, their impact was arguably less severe in Latin America than in the United States.

The gap widened again in the last three decades of the twentieth century with the spread of authoritarian regimes throughout the region. In addition, many of the large countries in Latin America catastrophically failed to adjust to the rapidly changing external environment, resulting from the two oil shocks of the 1970s. Burgeoning fiscal deficits, attempts to monetize deficits through growth in money supplies, hyperinflation, and overvalued exchange rates in Mexico, Brazil, Argentina, Peru, and other countries set the stage for the debt crisis of the 1980s and the subsequent drop in real growth rates throughout Latin America. The United States, on the other hand, controlled the inflationary spiral set off by the oil crisis relatively quickly in the early 1980s and put into place a series of liberalizing economic policies that laid the groundwork for two decades of almost uninterrupted growth in per capita income. Indeed, growth in total factor productivity, which had been declining through much of the postwar period, began an upward trend in the late 1990s as a series of innovations in information and communications technology began to take root.

The 1990s and early years of the twenty-first century brought to most Latin American countries a return to economic orthodoxy and stable macroeconomic indicators. This set the stage in a number of countries for a return to growth, though not to an appreciable closing of the gap with the United States, due in part to the latter's relatively good economic performance. Moreover, results were noticeably uneven. Mexico and Argentina experienced severe currency and economic crises in 1994 and 2001, respectively. Growth, where it occurred, was steady but not spectacular. While modest progress was made toward reducing the region's levels of economic inequality, in many countries there was little political will to share the gains from growth. This situation brought about the emergence of populist and Left-leaning political leaders in several countries, including Venezuela, Ecuador, Brazil, Uruguay, and Argentina.

The gap . . . has varied over time, opening up dramatically in some decades and then closing again in others. The causes of the gap are similarly varied. . . . Those explanations that focus on geography, natural endowments of resources or other material conditions, culture in a broad sense, or a dependent relationship with the developed world are unlikely to be identifying the true reasons for lagging performance.

There are other factors, however. . . . Latin America must follow sensible economic policies that produce monetary and fiscal stability, while at the same time seeking to open the region's economies to the global trading system. Institutions are critical for formulating, implementing, and supporting good policies. These institutions include property rights and the rule of law, electoral systems, executive branches with appropriate powers, legislatures that are both representative and efficient, political parties that include society's important social actors, court systems that are independent of political authority and effective in implementing the rule of law, and an appropriate distribution of powers to the different levels of government—national, state, and local. Social inequality lies at the root of the region's lack of economic competitiveness, in addition to being a source of political instability. This suggests, then, a need to take a new look at social policy, not by returning to the entitlement politics of the past, but by seeking innovative ways of solving social problems.

It is important not to be excessively pessimistic about Latin America's overall prospects and the likelihood of closing the development gap in the future. For all of the economic turmoil that engulfed the region at the turn of the twenty-first century, there was a remarkable degree of democratic continuity throughout the region, even in its most troubled countries. Conflicts that in previous decades had been addressed through military coups or violence tended to be resolved through elections or judicial proceedings. There has been institutional and policy learning, as traumatic experiences like currency crises and hyperinflation created political incentives for reform. And the process of institutional growth and state building has proceeded, not as rapidly or evenly as one would hope, but steadily nonetheless. There is reason to hope, therefore, that the history of the gap over the next generation will be written differently than that of the past.

SURVIVING GLOBALIZATION IN THREE LATIN AMERICAN COMMUNITIES

Denis Lynn Daly Heyck

Of course, poverty existed long before globalization, but currently it seems that most local and national efforts to fight poverty are undercut by that process. Since poverty and its new global guardian are immediate dangers to the survival of these peoples, their cultures, and their livelihoods, they, unlike some intellectual observers, do not have the luxury of regarding globalization as simply a trend whose consequences can be described but probably not fundamentally altered. The people who tell their stories here must react in order to survive. They have no choice but to take action. They must at least alter the consequences, if not the trend itself. . . .

Much recent research confirms that globalization and development are having an enormous impact even in the most remote corners of Latin America, and that their effects are destructive of traditional communities and cultures. However, my research has also found that rural populations are not merely passive victims of an inexorable process; rather, they are active agents on their own behalf. For example, villagers in each setting relate the ways in which their locales have both adapted to powerful outside influences and attempted to refashion them to accommodate local realities and values. Community members detail their own efforts to develop a political, economic, and environmental awareness; to organize at the grassroots level; to form coalitions; and to raise up local leaders with the assistance of religious workers, popular education programs, and NGOs (non-governmental organizations). In other words, while some aspects of globalization have been extremely destructive, in each case analyzed here global agencies are helping the people to cope.

Two powerful constants underlie local strategies: . . . attitudes toward the land—tenure, ownership, and one's relationship to it—and religious faith—both institutional and popular. But the main story varies from place to place. In Brazil, the interviews highlight the extraordinary efforts of the progressive wing of the Catholic church to protect, organize, and raise the consciousness of the population, often at great personal risk and in the face of death threats and assassinations of base community and union members. Indeed, the rubber tappers' inspirational leader Chico Mendes was assassinated by ranchers in 1988. However, neither his work nor that of the church officials with whom he collaborated in the early years was in vain, for today the movers of both the union and the cooperative were forged in the leadership training courses at the heart of base community activities in the Amazon.

In Bolivia, the story is that of the painstaking efforts of foreign missionaries working with local Guaraní to revive the degraded Guaraní culture, helping to save their language and rescue from near extinction traditional indigenous values of community and assembly, including above all a town hall type of democracy. The Guarani themselves have placed these values in the balance as counter-weights to the corruption, racism, and rigid class stratification that characterize Bolivia's political system, debilitating its ecclesiastical hierarchy and afflicting their own traditional culture. Not surprisingly, the missionaries and the Guaraní have at times provoked the displeasure of these national institutions.

In Nicaragua, the central story is the stubborn resistance by a number of campesinas, or rural women, to the erasure of certain features of the Nicaraguan revolution, particularly, their feminist consciousness in sustaining their cooperatives and their tenacity in defending their rights, at a time when the official Catholic church, like the national government, has metamorphosed from revolutionary to reactionary. In Nicaragua, there is also the related story of relative ecumenical solidarity at the grassroots level, an unusual phenomenon in Latin America and another striking legacy of the Sandinista revolution of 1979.

In each case, then, there is a unique, central story, but there is also a common one among the three: a basic conflict over land rights. This clash arises from diametrically opposed value systems. One system—capitalist, growth-oriented, and embedded in globalizing imperatives—sees human beings as economic creatures driven by self-interest. Society is a collection of self-interested individuals, who occasionally come into conflict; for this reason, outside controls, such as government or law, are required to keep random encounters from restricting individual rights. In this view, nature is an inert object, and humankind is its master. It is the entrepreneur's right and duty to make the land productive—that is, to produce economic growth—through development by logging, cutting the forest, setting up cattle ranches, drilling for oil, and promoting export agriculture. The bigger the technology applied, the better. By this vision, destruction of habitats and cultures is an unfortunate but necessary price to pay for economic growth that will one day improve the country or region as a whole. After all, it is argued, a rising tide lifts all boats.

The other approach to the land, that of these particular communities, is long term and relational. It sees human activity as part of, and dependent on, the natural world. It is at bottom a traditional, not a capitalistic—much less a global—attitude. It is not primarily profit-oriented but, rather, is based on the idea of sufficiency. The notion of sufficiency implies an interrelatedness with nature, a recognition of human dependence on the natural world, and a future ethic, the sense that one must consider future generations in the economic and cultural choices made today. In the relational view, the scale of economic activity must be contained within the natural recuperative boundaries of the ecosystem. The tappers learn as children how to cut the bark correctly so that the tree keeps producing; the Guaraní restrict the gathering of palm fronds for basket-weaving when the supply gets low; and the Nicaraguan women find that organic agriculture improves their yield without harming the land. The technology applied is appropriate in scale and expense, what E.F. Schumacher called "appropriate technology."

The capitalist-growth and traditional-communitarian views conflict sharply, especially when placed within the broader context of rapidly accelerating economic globalization. Currently the former is in the ascendancy in all three countries of this study, but in each case there are growing pockets of resistance where communities have organized to create what they hope will be workable alternatives, breathing spaces allowing them to survive long enough to adapt. . . . In a broad sense, they are representative of diverse rural communities all across Latin America.

FURTHER READING

Bender, Thomas. 2006. *A Nation Among Nations: America's Place in World History.* New York: Hill and Wang, a division of Farrar, Straus, Giroux.

Bertola, Luis, and Jose Antonio Ocampo. 2012. *The Economic Development of Latin America since Independence*. New York: Oxford University Press.

Carrasco, David. 2009. *The History of the Conquest of New Spain by Bernal Diaz del Castillo*. Albuquerque: University of New Mexico Press.

Cumings, Bruce. 2009. *Dominion from Sea to Sea: Pacific Ascendancy and American Power*. New Haven, CT: Yale University Press.

Fukuyama, Francis. 2011. *Falling Behind: Explaining the Development Gap Between Latin America and the United States*. New York: Oxford University Press.

Heyck, Denis Lynn Daly. 2002. *Surviving Globalization in Three Latin American Communities*. Toronto: University of Toronto Press.

Friedman, Thomas L., and Michael Mandelbaum. 2011. *That Used to Be Us: How America Fell Behind in the World It Invented and How We Can Come Back*. New York: Farrar, Straus and Giroux.

Johnston, Hank, Paul Almeida, Javier Auyero, and Joe Bandy. 2006. *Latin American Social Movements: Globalization, Democratization, and Transnational Networks*. Lanham, MD: Rowman and Littlefield.

Li, Peter S. 2003. *Destination Canada: Immigration Debates and Issues*. Toronto: Oxford University Press.

Lipset, Seymour Martin. 2003. *The First New Nation: The United States in Historical and Comparative Perspective*. New York: Norton.

Maestro, Betsy. 1997. *Exploration and Conquest: The Americas after Columbus, 1500–1620*. New York: HarperCollins.

Mann, Charles C. 2012. *1493: Discovering the New World Columbus Created*. New York: Vintage.

Pease, Donald. 2003. *The New American Exceptionalism*. Minneapolis: University of Minnesota Press.

Stasiulis, Daiva, and Abigail B. Bakan. 2005. *Negotiating Citizenship: Migrant Women in Canada and the Global System*. Toronto: University of Toronto Press.

Todorov, Tzvetan. 1999. *The Conquest of America: The Question of the Other*. Norman: University of Oklahoma Press.

Trexler, Richard C. 1999. *Sex and Conquest: Gendered Violence, Political Order, and the European Conquest of the Americas*. Ithaca, NY: Cornell University Press.

PART III

TRANSNATIONAL GLOBAL ISSUES

10

GLOBAL FORCES IN THE NEW WORLD ORDER

Beginning with this section of the book, we turn from the regional explorations of glob alization to a series of contemporary issues that affect the whole world. Though many of these issues have a historical dimension and have been a feature of all parts of the world from ancient times to the present, we will focus on the contemporary period—the global era of the late twentieth and early twenty-first century.

By general consensus, something big began to happen at the end of the twentieth century. Part of what happened was obvious: the end of the Cold War. The Berlin wall came tumbling down in November 1989—the most visible symbol of the ending of an ideological war that had carved the world into two spheres of competing superpower control for most of the latter half of the twentieth century. Some observers, including Francis Fukuyama, rushed to conclude that this event was "the end of history" and that the European ideology of secular nationalism and the economic system of capitalism had triumphed throughout the world. This observation appeared premature, however, as new forces of globalization seemed to be emerging at almost precisely the same time, unleashed by transformations in technology, communications, and the global economy. These forces weakened the traditional nation-state and led to a backlash of local move-ments to protect traditional ethnic and local political ideas and to assert the possibility of religious politics as an alternative to the failures of the secular nation-state.

How do we make sense of what has happened in the world since the end of the Cold War? There were several explanations that soon emerged, including my own—that globalization has undercut the faith in secular nationalism as the basis of world order

(Juergensmeyer 1994; revised edition 2008). Other analyses focused on new technological, political, and economic developments in the world. This chapter features excerpts from several of the more influential of these writings.

The first selection presents a thesis that also focuses on globalization as the critical factor in post–Cold War developments. In an article in the *Atlantic* magazine in 1992, later developed into a book with the same title, *Jihad vs. McWorld,* Benjamin Barber describes two tendencies that were emerging around the world in a post–Cold War era. One was *McWorld,* Barber's term for the Westernized consumer culture associated with fast food, music videos, and technological gadgets. Barber opined that this was the kind of superficial culture that globalization was bringing to the far reaches of the world, and he thought of it as a kind of spiraling outward from traditional society and civil responsibilities.

The other tendency in the global era, according to Barber, was *jihad,* the term that some Muslim activists used to describe their form of radical politics. The term means "struggle" in Arabic, and most Muslims think of *jihad* as a spiritual and moral matter, as the internal struggle that everyone goes through in trying to keep true to their values and commitments. But it can also apply to struggles with injustice in the world, and this is the way that the Muslim activists have applied it. Barber uses the term in this sense, as the symbol of a certain sort of radical political ideology that defends a traditional view of faith and society. It relates to a kind of tribalism that Barber sees developing around the world in response to globalization. He thought of this as a spiraling inward away from global society and toward a new provincialism and isolation.

Neither of these tendencies, in Barber's view, promoted the concept of democratic society and responsible civil order. In fact, he thought of them both as leading to anarchism. As the director of a center for the study of democracy at Rutgers University in New Jersey at the time that the article was published, this concerned Barber. Later, while holding posts at George Mason University in Virginia and at the City University of New York Graduate Center, he continued to promote the concept of responsible global citizenship as a response to both "Jihad" and "McWorld," and he proposed the creation of an Interdependence Day to observe humanity's interdependence on each other.

The next selection is perhaps the best known—and most controversial—writing on global order in a post–Cold War world. It is from *The Clash of Civilizations and the Remaking of World Order,* by Samuel Huntington. Huntington was a professor of political science at Harvard who was greatly respected within his field and was well known for his work on theories of democracy. So it came as a shock to the fields of political science and international relations when he published an essay in 1993 in the journal *Foreign Affairs,* suggesting that in the post–Cold War world the main global competition was not between the economic ideologies of socialism and capitalism, but between differing cultures. We were moving into a world where the "clash of civilizations" described the most potent political competition.

The essay, and the book that followed, had a huge impact. Almost immediately there were admirers and critics. Admirers were pleased that Huntington was recognizing the importance of culture in political alignments, which was notable primarily because political scientists previously had focused on issues of national security and self-interest and had paid little attention to religion and other cultural aspects of society. At the same time, critics pointed out, his notion of civilizations in conflict was simplistic. There is no single political notion that unites all of "Islamic civilization," for instance, especially since the Muslim-majority nations stretch from Morocco to Indonesia and large numbers of Muslims are found in other countries, including China, Russia, European countries, and the United States. Increasingly, in fact, every country is multicultural, and it is difficult to draw lines distinguishing between Western Christian and Muslim civilizations, for instance.

Despite these criticisms within the scholarly community, what became known as the "Huntington thesis" about the clash of civilizations resonated among many members of the general public and policy makers. After 9/11, when the U.S. administration of George W. Bush declared a "War on Terror," the Huntington thesis was regarded as one of principal intellectual concepts behind it. The notion that Islamic civilization was potentially a threat to the United States and other Western countries helped to justify the broadening of the military response to the relatively small number of Islamic extremists associated with Osama bin Laden and Khalid Sheikh Mohammad and their al Qaeda network. The Huntington thesis gave credibility to the invasion and occupation of two Islamic countries—first Afghanistan and then Iraq. It is somewhat ironic that Huntington's ideas would be used by the Bush administration, since Huntington himself was a lifelong Democrat who had served in President Jimmy Carter's administration, and he was personally opposed to the U.S. military occupation of Iraq.

The third reading in this section, an excerpt from the book *Empire*, takes a historical perspective on the present changes in global politics. It argues that for most of world history, large-scale political organization was characterized by empires rather than by nation-states and that the era of globalization is ushering in a new imperial order. Empires have no borders and feast on almost endless expansion. The empire in the global era, the authors argue, is not confined to the expansive colonialization of a single country—such as the British Empire or the Spanish Empire. Rather, the modern global empire is a complex web of technological, economic, and communication networks that privilege an emerging transnational class. They predict that this empire will eventually collapse and that democratic forces will be unleashed.

The authors of *Empire* are Michael Hardt and Antonio Negri. Hardt, an American who has a background in environmental activism and received his Ph.D. from the University of Washington, teaches literary theory at Duke University. Hardt is fluent in French, Spanish, and Italian and holds a joint position as a professor of philosophy and politics at the European Graduate School in Saas-Fee, located in the Swiss Alps. His coauthor, Antonio Negri, is a noted Italian Marxist sociologist and political philosopher who was accused of being associated with the left-wing terrorist organization the Red Brigade, which was behind the assassination of Italian Prime Minister Aldo Moro in

1978. Negri escaped prison by living in France, but then decided to return to Italy to serve out a reduced sentence. It was in an Italian prison that Negri coauthored the book from which this excerpt is taken.

The final selection in this section is an essay by Saskia Sassen on the central feature of the new global topography: global cities. Sassen was raised in Buenos Aires in a family originally from the Netherlands, received her Ph.D. from Notre Dame University in Indiana, and now teaches sociology jointly at Columbia University and the London School of Economics. In this essay, as in many of her earlier writings, Sassen argues that the nation-state is being replaced by new forces of globalization that are best exemplified not in national units but in cities. It is in these cities with dense multicultural populations that the most vital economic, technological, and communication aspects of the contemporary global era occur. She claims that there are over a hundred global cities, including New York, Los Angeles, Mexico City, São Paulo, and Buenos Aires in the Americas; London, Paris, and Amsterdam in Europe; Tokyo, Shanghai, Hong Kong, Seoul, Bangkok, Taipei, and Mumbai in Asia; and Istanbul, Cairo, and Dubai in the Middle East. Each of these encapsulates a new transnational global culture, and together they participate in the strands of trade, technology, and communication that weave together in the emerging global society.

JIHAD VS. MCWORLD

Benjamin Barber

History is not over. Nor are we arrived in the wondrous land of techné promised by the futurologists. The collapse of state communism has not delivered people to a safe democratic haven, and the past, fratricide and civil discord perduring, still clouds the horizon just behind us. Those who look back see all of the horrors of the ancient slaughterbench reenacted in disintegral nations like Bosnia, Sri Lanka, Ossetia, and Rwanda and they declare that nothing has changed. Those who look forward prophesize commercial and technological interdependence—a virtual paradise made possible by spreading markets and global technology—and they proclaim that everything is or soon will be different. The rival observers seem to consult different almanacs drawn from the libraries of contrarian planets.

Yet anyone who reads the daily papers carefully, taking in the front page accounts of civil carnage as well as the business page stories on the mechanics of the information superhighway and the economics of communication mergers, anyone who turns deliberately to take in the whole 360-degree horizon, knows that our world and our lives are caught between what William Butler Yeats called the two eternities of race and soul: that of race reflecting the tribal past, that of soul anticipating the cosmopolitan future. Our secular eternities are corrupted, however, race reduced to an insignia of resentment, and soul sized down to fit the demanding body by which it now measures its needs. Neither race nor soul offers us a future that is other than bleak, neither promises a polity that is remotely democratic.

The first scenario rooted in race holds out the grim prospect of a retribalization of large swaths of humankind by war and bloodshed: a threatened balkanization of nation-states in which culture is pitted against culture, people against people, tribe against tribe, a Jihad in the name of a hundred narrowly conceived faiths against every kind of interdependence, every kind of artificial social cooperation and mutuality: against technology, against pop culture, and against integrated markets; against modernity itself as well as the future in which modernity issues. The second paints that future in shimmering pastels, a busy portrait of onrushing economic, technological, and ecological forces that demand integration and uniformity and that mesmerize peoples everywhere with fast music, fast computers, and fast food—MTV, Macintosh, and McDonald's—pressing nations into one homogeneous global theme park, one McWorld tied together by communications, information, entertainment, and commerce. Caught between Babel and Disneyland, the planet is falling precipitously apart and coming reluctantly together at the very same moment.

Some stunned observers notice only Babel, complaining about the thousand newly sundered "peoples" who prefer to address their neighbors with sniper rifles and mortars; others—zealots in Disneyland—seize on futurological platitudes and the promise of virtuality, exclaiming "It's a small world after all!" Both are right, but how can that be?

We are compelled to choose between what passes as "the twilight of sovereignty" and an entropic end of all history; or a return to the past's most fractious and demoralizing discord; to "the menace of global anarchy," to Milton's capital of hell, Pandaemonium; to a world totally "out of control."

The apparent truth, which speaks to the paradox at the core of this book, is that the tendencies of both Jihad *and* McWorld are at work, both visible sometimes in the same country at the very same instant. Iranian zealots keep one ear tuned to the mullahs urging holy war and the other cocked to Rupert Murdoch's Star television beaming in *Dynasty*, *Donahue*, and *The Simpsons* from hovering satellites. Chinese entrepreneurs vie for the attention of party cadres in Beijing and simultaneously pursue KFC franchises in cities like Nanjing, Hangzhou, and Xian where twenty-eight outlets serve over 100,000 customers a day. The Russian Orthodox church, even as it struggles to renew the ancient faith, has entered a joint venture with California businessmen to bottle and sell natural waters under the rubric Saint Springs Water Company. Serbian assassins wear Adidas sneakers and listen to Madonna on Walkman headphones as they take aim through their gunscopes at scurrying Sarajevo civilians looking to fill family watercans. Orthodox Hasids and brooding neo-Nazis have both turned to rock music to get their traditional messages out to the new generation, while fundamentalists plot virtual conspiracies on the Internet.

Now neither Jihad nor McWorld is in itself novel. History ending in the triumph of science and reason or some monstrous perversion thereof (Mary Shelley's Doctor Frankenstein) has been the leitmotiv of every philosopher and poet who has regretted the Age of Reason since the Enlightenment. Yeats lamented "the center will not hold, mere anarchy is loosed upon the world," and observers of Jihad today have little but historical detail to add. The Christian parable of the Fall and of the possibilities of redemption that it makes possible captures the eighteenth-century ambivalence—and our own—about past and future. I want, however, to do more than dress up the central paradox of human history in modern clothes. It is not Jihad and McWorld but the relationship between them that most interests me. For, squeezed between their opposing forces, the world has been sent spinning out of control. Can it be that what Jihad and McWorld have in common is anarchy: the absence of common will and that conscious and collective human control under the guidance of law we call democracy?

A MULTIPOLAR, MULTICIVILIZATIONAL WORLD

Samuel Huntington

In the post–Cold War world, for the first time in history, global politics has become multipolar *and* multicivilizational. During most of human existence, contacts between civilizations were intermittent or nonexistent. Then, with the beginning of the modern era, about AD 1500, global politics assumed two dimensions. For over four hundred years, the nation states of the West—Britain, France, Spain, Austria, Prussia, Germany, the United States, and others—constituted a multipolar international system within Western civilization and interacted, competed, and fought wars with each other. At the same time, Western nations also expanded, conquered, colonized, or decisively influenced every other civilization. . . . During the Cold War global politics became bipolar and the world was divided into three parts. A group of mostly wealthy and democratic societies, led by the United States, was engaged in a pervasive ideological, political, economic, and, at times, military competition with a group of somewhat poorer communist societies associated with and led by the Soviet Union. Much of this conflict occurred in the Third World outside these two camps, composed of countries which often were poor, lacked political stability, were recently independent, and claimed to be nonaligned. . . .

In the late 1980s the communist world collapsed, and the Cold War international system became history. In the post–Cold War world, the most important distinctions among peoples are not ideological, political, or economic. They are cultural. Peoples and nations are attempting to answer the most basic question humans can face: Who are we? And they are answering that question in the traditional way human beings have answered it, by reference to the things that mean most to them. People define themselves in terms of ancestry, religion, language, history, values, customs, and institutions. They identify with cultural groups: tribes, ethnic groups, religious communities, nations, and, at the broadest level, civilizations. People use politics not just to advance their interests but also to define their identity. We know who we are only when we know who we are not and often only when we know whom we are against.

Nation states remain the principal actors in world affairs. Their behavior is shaped as in the past by the pursuit of power and wealth, but it is also shaped by cultural preferences, commonalities, and differences. The most important groupings of states are no longer the three blocs of the Cold War but rather the world's seven or eight major civilizations. . . . Non-Western societies, particularly in East Asia, are developing their economic wealth and creating the basis for enhanced military power and political influence. As their power and self-confidence increase, non-Western societies increasingly assert their own cultural values and reject those "imposed" on them by the West. The "international system of the twenty-first century," Henry Kissinger has noted, ". . . will contain at least six major powers—the United States, Europe, China, Japan, Russia, and probably India—as well as a multiplicity of medium-sized and smaller countries." Kissinger's six major powers belong to five very different civilizations, and in addition there are important Islamic states whose strategic locations, large populations, and/or oil resources make them influential in world affairs. In this new world, local politics is the politics of ethnicity; global politics is the politics of civilizations. The rivalry of the superpowers is replaced by the clash of civilizations.

In this new world the most pervasive, important, and dangerous conflicts will not be between social classes, rich and poor, or other economically defined groups, but between peoples belonging to different cultural entities. Tribal wars and ethnic conflicts will occur within civilizations. Violence between states and groups from different civilizations, however, carries with it the potential for escalation as other states and groups from these civilizations rally to the support of their "kin countries." The bloody clash of clans in Somalia poses no threat of broader conflict. The bloody clash of tribes in Rwanda has consequences for Uganda, Zaire, and Burundi but not much further, The bloody clashes of civilizations in Bosnia, the Caucasus, Central Asia, or Kashmir could become bigger wars. In the Yugoslav conflicts, Russia provided diplomatic support to the Serbs, and Saudi Arabia, Turkey, Iran, and Libya provided funds and arms to the Bosnians, not for reasons of ideology or power politics or economic interest but because of cultural kinship. "Cultural conflicts," Vaclav Havel has observed, "are increasing and are more dangerous today than at any time in history," and Jacques Delors agreed that "future conflicts will be sparked by cultural factors rather than economics or ideology." And the most dangerous cultural conflicts are those along the fault lines between civilizations.

In the post–Cold War world, culture is both a divisive and a unifying force. People separated by ideology but united by culture come together, as the two Germanys did and as the two Koreas and the several Chinas are beginning to. Societies united by ideology or historical circumstance but divided by civilization either come apart, as did the Soviet Union, Yugoslavia, and Bosnia, or are subjected to intense strain, as is the case with Ukraine, Nigeria, Sudan, India, Sri Lanka, and many others. Countries with cultural affinities cooperate economically and politically. International organizations based on states with cultural commonality, such as the European Union, are far more successful than those that attempt to transcend cultures. For forty-five years the Iron Curtain was the central dividing line in Europe. That line has moved several hundred miles east. It is now the line separating the peoples of Western Christianity, on the one hand, from Muslim and Orthodox peoples on the other.

The philosophical assumptions, underlying values, social relations, customs, and overall outlooks on life differ significantly among civilizations. The revitalization of religion throughout much of the world is reinforcing these cultural differences. Cultures can change, and the nature of their impact on politics and economics can vary from one period to another. Yet the major differences in political and economic development among civilizations are clearly rooted in their different cultures. East Asian economic success has its source in East Asian culture, as do the difficulties East Asian societies have had in achieving stable democratic political systems. Islamic culture explains in large part the failure of democracy to emerge in much of the Muslim world. Developments in the postcommunist societies of Eastern Europe and the former Soviet Union are shaped by their civilizational identities. Those with Western Christian heritages are making progress toward economic development and democratic politics; the prospects for economic and political development in the Orthodox countries are uncertain; the prospects in the Muslim republics are bleak.

The West is and will remain for years to come the most powerful civilization. Yet its power relative to that of other civilizations is declining. As the West attempts to assert its values and to protect its interests, non-Western societies confront a choice. Some attempt to emulate the West and to join or to "bandwagon" with the West. Other Confucian and Islamic societies attempt to expand their own economic and military power to resist and to "balance" against the West. A central axis of post–Cold War world politics is thus the interaction of Western power and culture with the power and culture of non-Western civilizations.

In sum, the post–Cold War world is a world of seven or eight major civilizations. Cultural commonalities and differences shape the interests, antagonisms, and associations of states. The most important countries in the world come overwhelmingly from different civilizations. The local conflicts most likely to escalate into broader wars are those between groups and states from different civilizations. The predominant patterns of political and economic development differ from civilization to civilization. The key issues on the international agenda involve differences among civilizations. Power is shifting from the long predominant West to non-Western civilizations. Global politics has become multipolar and multicivilizational.

EMPIRE

Michael Hardt and Antonio Negri

Empire is materializing before our very eyes. Over the past several decades, as colonial regimes were overthrown and then precipitously after the Soviet barriers to the capitalist world market finally collapsed, we have witnessed an irresistible and irreversible globalization of economic and cultural exchanges. Along with the global market and global circuits of production has emerged a global order, a new logic and structure of rule—in short, a new form of sovereignty. Empire is the political subject that effectively regulates these global exchanges, the sovereign power that governs the world.

Many argue that the globalization of capitalist production and exchange means that economic relations have become more autonomous from political controls, and consequently that political sovereignty has declined. Some celebrate this new era as the liberation of the capitalist economy from the restrictions and distortions that political forces have imposed on it; others lament it as the closing of the institutional channels through which workers and citizens can influence or contest the cold logic of capitalist profit. It is certainly true that, in step with the processes of globalization, the sovereignty of nation-states, while still effective, has progressively declined. The primary factors of production and exchange—money, technology, people, and goods—move with increasing ease across national boundaries; hence the nation-state has less and less power to regulate these flows and impose its authority over the economy. Even the most dominant nation-states should no longer be thought of as supreme and sovereign authorities, either outside or even within their own borders. *The decline in sovereignty of nation-states, however, does not mean that sovereignty as such has declined* [emphasis in original]. Throughout the contemporary transformations, political controls, state functions, and regulatory mechanisms have continued to rule the realm of economic and social production and exchange. Our basic hypothesis is that sovereignty has taken a new form, composed of a series of national and supranational organisms united under a single logic of rule. This new global form of sovereignty is what we call Empire.

The declining sovereignty of nation-states and their increasing inability to regulate economic and cultural exchanges is in fact one of the primary symptoms of the coming of Empire. The sovereignty of the nation-state was the cornerstone of the imperialisms that European powers constructed throughout the modern era. By "Empire," however, we understand something altogether different from "imperialism." The boundaries defined by the modern system of nation-states were fundamental to European colonialism and economic expansion: the territorial boundaries of the nation delimited the center of power from which rule was exerted over external foreign territories through a system of channels and barriers that alternately facilitated and obstructed the flows of production and circulation. Imperialism was really an extension of the sovereignty of the European nation-states beyond their own boundaries. Eventually nearly all the world's territories could be parceled out and the entire world map could be coded in European colors: red for British territory, blue for French, green for Portuguese, and so forth. Wherever modern sovereignty took root, it constructed a Leviathan that overarched its social domain and imposed hierarchical territorial boundaries, both to police the purity of its own identity and to exclude all that was other.

The passage to Empire emerges from the twilight of modern sovereignty. In contrast to imperialism, Empire establishes no territorial center of power and does not rely on fixed boundaries or barriers. It is a *decentered* and *deterritorializing* apparatus of rule that progressively incorporates the entire global realm within its open, expanding frontiers. Empire manages hybrid identities, flexible hierarchies, and plural exchanges through modulating networks of command. The distinct national colors of the imperialist map of the world have merged and blended in the imperial global rainbow.

The transformation of the modern imperialist geography of the globe and the realization of the world market signal a passage within the capitalist mode of production. Most significant, the spatial divisions of the three Worlds (First, Second, and Third) have been scrambled so that we continually find the First World in the Third, the Third in the First, and the Second almost nowhere at all. Capital seems to be faced with a smooth world—or really, a world defined by new and complex regimes of differentiation and homogenization, deterritorialization and reterritorialization. The construction of the paths and limits of these new global flows has been accompanied by a transformation of the dominant productive processes themselves, with the result that the role of industrial factory labor has been reduced and priority given instead to communicative, cooperative, and affective labor. In the postmodernization of the global economy, the creation of wealth tends ever more toward what we will call biopolitical production, the production of social life itself, in which the economic, the political, and the cultural increasingly overlap and invest one another.

Many locate the ultimate authority that rules over the processes of globalization and the new world order in the United States. Proponents praise the United States as the world leader and sole superpower, and detractors denounce it as an imperialist oppressor. Both these views rest on the assumption that the United States has simply donned the mantle of global power that the European nations have now let fall. If the nineteenth century was a British century, then the twentieth century has been an American century; or really, if modernity was European, then postmodernity is American. The most damning charge critics can level, then, is that the United States is repeating the practices of old European imperialists, while proponents celebrate the United States as a more efficient and more benevolent world leader, getting right what the Europeans got wrong. Our basic hypothesis, however, that a new imperial form of sovereignty has emerged, contradicts both these views. *The United States does not, and indeed no nation-state can today, form the center of an imperialist project* [emphasis in original]. Imperialism is over. No nation will be world leader in the way modern European nations were.

The United States does indeed occupy a privileged position in Empire, but this privilege derives not from its similarities to the old European imperialist powers, but from its differences. These differences can be recognized most clearly by focusing on the properly imperial (not imperialist) foundations of the United States constitution, where by "constitution" we mean both the *formal constitution*, the written document along with its various amendments and legal apparatuses, and the *material constitution*, that is, the continuous formation and re-formation of the composition of social forces. Thomas Jefferson, the authors of the *Federalist*, and the other ideological founders of the United

States were all inspired by the ancient imperial model; they believed they were creating on the other side of the Atlantic a new Empire with open, expanding frontiers, where power would be effectively distributed in networks. This imperial idea has survived and matured throughout the history of the United States constitution and has emerged now on a global scale in its fully realized form.

We should emphasize that we use "Empire" here not as a metaphor, which would require demonstration of the resemblances between today's world order and the Empires of Rome, China, the Americas, and so forth, but rather as a *concept,* which calls primarily for a theoretical approach. The concept of Empire is characterized fundamentally by a lack of boundaries: Empire's rule has no limits. First and foremost, then, the concept of Empire posits a regime that effectively encompasses the spatial totality, or really that rules over the entire "civilized" world. No territorial boundaries limit its reign. Second, the concept of Empire presents itself not as a historical regime originating in conquest, but rather as an order that effectively suspends history and thereby fixes the existing state of affairs for eternity. From the perspective of Empire, this is the way things will always be and the way they were always meant to be. In other words, Empire presents its rule not as a transitory moment in the movement of history, but as a regime with no temporal boundaries and in this sense outside of history or at the end of history. Third, the rule of Empire operates on all registers of the social order extending down to the depths of the social world. Empire not only manages a territory and a population but also creates the very world it inhabits. It not only regulates human interactions but also seeks directly to rule over human nature. The object of its rule is social life in its entirety, and thus Empire presents the paradigmatic form of biopower. Finally, although the practice of Empire is continually bathed in blood, the concept of Empire is always dedicated to peace—a perpetual and universal peace outside of history.

The Empire we are faced with wields enormous powers of oppression and destruction, but that fact should not make us nostalgic in any way for the old forms of domination. The passage to Empire and its processes of globalization offer new possibilities to the forces of liberation. Globalization, of course, is not one thing, and the multiple processes that we recognize as globalization are not unified or univocal. Our political task, we will argue, is not simply to resist these processes but to reorganize them and redirect them toward new ends. The creative forces of the multitude that sustain Empire are also capable of autonomously constructing a counter-Empire, an alternative political organization of global flows and exchanges. The struggles to contest and subvert Empire, as well as those to construct a real alternative, will thus take place on the imperial terrain itself—indeed, such new struggles have already begun to emerge. Through these struggles and many more like them, the multitude will have to invent new democratic forms and a new constituent power that will one day take us through and beyond Empire.

The genealogy we follow in our analysis of the passage from imperialism to Empire will be first European and then Euro-American, not because we believe that these regions are the exclusive or privileged source of new ideas and historical innovation, but simply because this was the dominant geographical path along which the concepts and practices that animate today's Empire developed—in step, as we will argue, with the development of the capitalist mode of production. Whereas the genealogy of Empire is in this sense Eurocentric, however, its present powers are not limited to any region. Logics of rule that in some sense originated in Europe and the United States now invest practices of domination throughout the globe. More important, the forces that contest Empire and effectively prefigure an alternative global society are themselves not limited to any geographical region. The geography of these alternative powers, the new cartography, is still waiting to be written—or really, it is being written today through the resistances, struggles, and desires of the multitude.

GLOBAL CITIES

Saskia Sassen

In the global era, the city emerged as a strategic site for understanding some of the major new trends reconfiguring the social order. The city and the metropolitan region have become locations where major macrosocial trends materialize and hence can be constituted as an object of global studies. Each of those major trends has its own specific contents and consequences. The urban moment is but one moment in their often complex multisited trajectories.

The city has long been a strategic site for the exploration of many of the issues confronting society. But it has not always been a heuristic space—a space capable of producing knowledge about some of the major transformations of an epoch. In the first half of the 20th century, the study of cities was at the heart of sociology. This is evident in the work of Georg Simmel, Max Weber, Walter Benjamin, Henri Lefebvre, and most prominently the Chicago School, especially Robert Park and Louis Wirth, both deeply influenced by German sociology. These sociologists confronted massive processes—industrialization, urbanization, alienation, and a new cultural formation they called "urbanity." Studying the city was not simply studying the urban. It was about studying the major social processes of an era. Since then, the study of the city, and with it urban sociology, gradually lost this privileged role as a lens for the discipline and as a producer of key analytic categories. There are many reasons for this, most important among which are questions of the particular developments of method and data in sociology generally. Critical was the fact that the city ceased being the fulcrum for epochal transformations and hence a strategic site for research about nonurban processes. Urban sociology became increasingly concerned with what came to be called "social problems."

The worldwide resurgence in the 1990s of the city as a site for research on these major contemporary dynamics is evident in multiple disciplines—sociology, anthropology, economic geography, cultural studies, and literary criticism. In the global era, economists have begun to address the urban and regional economy in their analyses in ways that go beyond older forms of urban economics. Globalization has given rise to new information technologies, the intensifying of transnational and translocal dynamics, and the strengthening presence and voice of sociocultural diversity. All of these are at a cutting edge of change. These trends do not encompass the majority of social conditions; on the contrary, most social reality probably corresponds to older continuing and familiar trends. Yet, although these trends involve only parts of the urban condition and cannot be confined to the urban, they are strategic in that they mark the urban condition in novel ways and make it, in turn, a key research site for major urban and nonurban trends.

THE CITY AS EXEMPLAR OF THE GLOBAL INFORMATION ECONOMY

The concept of the city is complex, imprecise, and charged with specific historical meanings. A more abstract notion might be centrality, present in all cities, and, in turn, something that cities have historically given to societies. For most of known history, centrality has largely been embedded in the major city of a region or a country. One of the changes brought about by the new communication technologies of the 21st century is the reconfiguring of centrality: The central city is today but one form of centrality. Important emerging spaces for the constitution of centrality range from the new transnational networks of cities to electronic space. What are the conditions for the continuity of centrality in advanced societies in the face of major new technologies that maximize the possibility for geographic dispersal at the regional, national, and indeed, global scale, and simultaneous system integration?

A second major challenge for thinking about the city as a site for researching major (including nonurban) contemporary dynamics concerns the narratives we have constructed about the city and how this narrative relates to the global economy and to the new technologies. The understandings and the categories that dominate mainstream discussions about the future of advanced economies imply the city has become obsolete for leading economic sectors given electronic networks. We need to subject these notions to critical examination. At least two sets of issues need to be teased out if we are to understand the role, if any, of cities in a global information economy and, hence, the capacity of urban research to produce knowledge about that larger economy. One concerns the extent to which these new types of electronic formations, such as electronic financial markets, are indeed disembedded from social contexts. The second set of issues concerns possible instances of the global economy and of the new technologies that have not been recognized as such or are contested representations.

Finally, and on a somewhat more theoretical level, certain properties of power make cities strategic. Power needs to be historicized to overcome the abstractions of the concept. Power is not simply an attribute or a sort of factor endowment. It is actively produced and reproduced. Many studies on the local dimensions of power have made important contributions to this subject. One of the aspects today in the production of power structures has to do with new forms of economic power and the relocation of certain forms of power from the state to the market, partly as a result of deregulation and privatization. In the case of cities, this brings with it also questions about the built environment and the architectures of centrality that represent different kinds of power—the civic power of the grand bourgeoisies of the late 19th century and the aggressive power of the new rich of the 1990s. Cities have long been places for the spatialization of power. More generally, we might ask whether power has spatial correlates, or a spatial moment? In terms of the economy, this question could be operationalized more concretely: Can the current economic system, with its strong tendencies toward concentration in ownership and control, have a space economy that lacks points of physical concentration? It is hard to think about a discourse on the future of cities that would not include this dimension of power.

To some extent, it is the major cities in the highly developed world that most clearly display the processes discussed in this entry. However, these processes are present in cities in developing countries as well: But they are less visible because they are submerged under the megacity syndrome—sheer population size and urban sprawl create their own realities. Size and sprawl do not prevent the new power equation described; however, the spatial correlates (e.g., gentrification and the building of a new glamour zone) are less visible in a city of 20 million inhabitants. The geography of globalization contains both a dynamic of dispersal of people and activities and a dynamic of centralization. Most of the attention has gone to dispersal patterns. But the massive spatial dispersal of people and economic activities has itself contributed to a demand for new forms of territorial centralization of top-level management and control operations. The fact, for instance, that firms worldwide now have approximately 1 million affiliates outside their home countries signals that the sheer number of dispersed factories and service outlets that are part of a firm's integrated operation creates massive new needs for central coordination and servicing. This is one of the major trends leading to the emergence of global cities. In brief, the spatial dispersal of economic activity made possible by globalization and telecommunications contributes to an expansion of central functions if this dispersal is to take place under the continuing concentration in control, ownership, and profit appropriation that characterizes the current economic system.

The city enters the discourse at this point. Cities regain strategic importance because they are favored sites for the production of these central functions. National and global markets as well as globally integrated organizations require central places where the work of globalization gets done. Finance and advanced corporate services are industries producing the organizational commodities necessary for the implementation and management of global economic systems. Cities are preferred sites for the production of these services, particularly the most innovative, speculative, internationalized service sectors, but more provincial cities play this role as well, although for less complex versions of these services.

Furthermore, leading firms in information industries require a vast physical infrastructure containing strategic nodes with hyperconcentration of facilities. We need to distinguish between the capacity for global transmission/communication and the material conditions that make this possible. Finally, even the most advanced information industries have a production process that is at least partly place-bound because of the combination of resources it requires even when the outputs are hypermobile; the tendency in the specialized literature has been to study these advanced information industries in terms of their hypermobile outputs rather than the actual work processes, which include top-level professionals as well as clerical and manual service workers.

When we start by examining broader dynamics in order to detect their localization patterns, we can begin to observe and conceptualize the formation, at least incipient, of transnational urban systems. The growth of global markets for finance and specialized services, the need for transnational servicing networks as a result of sharp increases in international investment, the reduced role of the government in the regulation of international economic activity and the corresponding ascendance of other institutional arenas with a strong urban connection—all these point to the existence of a series of transnational networks of cities. These are of many different kinds and types. Business networks are probably the most developed given the growth of a global economy. But we also see a proliferation of social, cultural, professional, activist, and political networks connecting particular sets of cities.

To a large extent, the major business centers in the world today draw their importance from these transnational networks. There is no such entity as a single global city—and, in this sense, there is a sharp contrast with the erstwhile capitals of empires. A global firm, an international museum, or a global civil society organization need not be one perfect global city but many. The networks of major international business centers constitute new geographies of centrality. The most powerful of these new geographies of centrality at the global level binds the major international financial and business centers. In the 1980s, these networks were centered on New York, London, Tokyo, Paris, Frankfurt, Zurich, Amsterdam, Los Angeles, Sydney, and Hong Kong, among others. By the late 1990s, they had added Mumbai, Bangkok, Seoul, Taipei, Shanghai, São Paulo, Mexico City, and Buenos Aires. By 2011, they included more than 100 major and minor global cities.

The intensity of transactions among these cities, particularly through the financial markets, trade in services, and investment has increased sharply, and so have the orders of magnitude involved. There has been a sharpening inequality in the concentration of strategic resources and activities between each of these cities and others in the same country. This has consequences for the role of urban systems in national territorial integration. Although the latter has never been what its model tells us, the last decade has observed a subsequent acceleration in the fragmentation of national territory. National urban systems are being partly unbundled as their major cities become part of a new or strengthened transnational urban system.

But we can no longer think of centers for international business and finance simply in terms of the corporate towers and corporate culture at their center. The international character of major cities lies not only in their telecommunication infrastructure and foreign firms: It lies also in the many different cultural environments in which these workers and others exist. This is one arena where we have observed the growth of an enormously rich scholarship.

CITIES AND POLITICAL SUBJECTIVITY

It is helpful to consider Max Weber's *The City* to examine the production of political subjectivity signaled by the preceding section. In his effort to specify the ideal typical features of what constitutes the city, Weber sought out a certain type of city—most prominently the cities of the late middle ages rather than the modern industrial cities of his time. Weber sought a kind of city that combined conditions and dynamics that forced its residents and leaders into creative and innovative responses/adaptations. Furthermore, he posited that these changes produced in the context of the city-generated transformations that went beyond the city and could institute often larger fundamental transformations. In that regard, the city offered the possibility of understanding far-reaching changes that could—under certain conditions—eventually encompass society at large.

There are two aspects of Weber's *The City* of particular importance in this entry. Weber helps us understand under what conditions cities can be positive and creative influences on peoples' lives. For Weber cities are a set of social structures that encourage individuality and innovation and, hence, are an instrument of historical change. There is, in this intellectual project, a deep sense of the historicity of these conditions. Modern urban life did not correspond to this positive and creative power of cities; Weber viewed modern cities as dominated by large factories and office bureaucracies. The Fordist city that was to come much later and culminate in the 1950s and 1960s can be viewed as illustrating Weber's view in the sense that the strategic scale under Fordism is the national scale and cities lose significance. Unlike medieval times, it is not the city, but the large Fordist factory and the mines that emerge as key sites for the political work of the disadvantaged and those without or with only limited power.

Struggles around political, economic, legal, and cultural issues centered in the realities of cities can become the catalysts for new trans-urban developments in all these institutional domains—markets, participatory governance, rights for members of the urban community regardless of lineage, judicial recourse, cultures of engagement, and deliberation. For Weber, it is particularly the cities of the late Middle Ages that combine the conditions that pushed urban residents, merchants, artisans, and leaders to address them and deal with them. These transformations could make for epochal change beyond the city itself: Weber shows us how in many of these cities these struggles led to the creation of the elements of what we could call governance systems and citizenship.

Today a certain type of city—the global city—has emerged as a strategic site for innovations and transformations in multiple institutional domains. Several key components of economic globalization and digitization concentrate in global cities and produce dislocations and destabilizations of existing institutional orders and legal/regulatory/ normative frames for handling urban conditions. The high level of concentration of these new dynamics in these cities forces creative responses and innovations. There is, most probably, a threshold effect at work here.

In contrast, in the 1930s until the 1970s, when mass manufacturing dominated, cities lost strategic functions and were not the site for creative institutional innovations. The strategic sites were the large factory at the heart of the larger process of mass manufacturing and mass consumption, and the government as site for making a new social contract (e.g., legal protections for workers and the welfare state). The factory and the government were the strategic sites where the crucial dynamics producing the major institutional innovations of the epoch were located. With globalization and digitization— and all the specific elements they entail—global cities emerge as such strategic sites but with a project of concentrating power and wealth and an opposing actor consisting of a mix of immigrants, minoritized citizens, and other disadvantaged. Although the strategic transformations are sharply concentrated in global cities, many are also enacted (besides being diffused) in cities at lower orders of national urban hierarchies.

Current conditions in global cities are creating not only new structurations of power but also operational and rhetorical openings for new types of political actors that may have been submerged, invisible or without voice. A key element of the argument here is that the localization of strategic components of globalization in these cities means that the disadvantaged can engage the new forms of globalized corporate power, and second, that the growing numbers and diversity of the disadvantaged in these cities takes on a distinctive "presence." This entails a distinction between powerlessness and invisibility/ impotence. The disadvantaged in global cities can gain "presence" in their engagement with power but also vis-à-vis each other.

This is different from the period between the 1950s and the 1970s in the United States, for instance, when White flight and the significant departure of major corporate headquarters left cities hollowed out and the disadvantaged in a condition of abandonment. Today, the localization of the global creates a set of objective conditions of engagement, for example, the struggles against gentrification which encroaches on minority and disadvantaged neighborhoods and led to growing numbers of homeless beginning in the 1980s and the struggles for the rights of the homeless, or demonstrations against police brutalizing minority people. These struggles are different from the ghetto uprisings of the 1960s, which were short, intense eruptions confined to the ghettos and causing most of the damage in the neighborhoods of the disadvantaged themselves. In these ghetto uprisings there was no engagement with power, but more protest against power.

CONCLUSION

The conditions that today make some cities strategic sites are basically two, and both capture major transformations that are destabilizing older systems organizing territory and politics. One of these is the rescaling of what are the strategic territories that articulate the new politicoeconomic system. The other is the partial unbundling or at least weakening of the national as container of social process resulting from the variety of dynamics encompassed by globalization and digitization, but also by the fact of growing inequalities—the making of global elites and the impoverishment of the modest middle sectors. The consequences for cities of these two conditions are many: What matters here is that cities emerge as strategic sites for major economic processes and for new types of political actors.

What is being engendered today in terms of political practices in the global city is different from what it might have been in the medieval city of Weber. In the medieval city, we observe a set of practices that allowed the burghers to set up systems for owning and protecting property and to implement various immunities against despots of all sorts. Today's political practices may have to do with the production of "presence" by those without power and with a politics that claims rights to the city rather than protection of property. What the two situations share is the notion that, through these practices, new forms of political subjectivity (i.e., new notions of citizenship/membership) are being constituted and that the city is a key site for this type of political work. The city is, in turn, partly constituted through these dynamics. Far more so than a peaceful and harmonious suburb, the contested city is where the civic is getting made. After the long historical phase that saw the ascendance of the national state and the scaling of key economic dynamics at the national level, the city is once again today a scale for strategic economic and political dynamics.

FURTHER READING

Abu-Lughod, J.L. 1999. *New York, Los Angeles, Chicago: America's Global Cities.* Minneapolis: University of Minnesota Press.

Barber, Benjamin. 1996. *Jihad vs. McWorld: Terrorism's Challenge to Democracy.* New York: Ballantine Books.

Berger, Peter, and Samuel P. Huntington (Eds.). 2003. *Many Globalizations: Cultural Diversity in the Contemporary World.* New York: Oxford University Press.

Falk, Richard. 1999. *Predatory Globalization: A Critique.* London: Polity Press.

Fukuyama, Francis. 1992. *The End of History and the Last Man.* New York: The Free Press.

Gugler, Josef. 2004. *World Cities Beyond the West.* Cambridge, UK: Cambridge University Press.

Hardt, Michael, and Antonio Negri. 2001. *Empire.* Cambridge, MA: Harvard University Press.

Huntington, Samuel. 1995. *The Clash of Civilizations and the Remaking of World Order.* New York: Simon and Schuster.

Juergensmeyer, Mark. 2008. *Global Rebellion: Religious Challenges to the Secular State*, Berkeley: University of California Press.

Mahbubani, Kishore. 2013. *The Great Convergence: Asia, the West, and the Logic of One World.* New York: Perseus Books.

McNally, David. 2011. *Global Slump: The Economics and Politics of Crisis and Resistance.* Oakland CA: PM Press.

Narlikar, Amrita. 2005. *The World Trade Organization: A Very Short Introduction.* Oxford, UK: Oxford University Press.

Sassen, Saskia. 2001. *The Global City: New York, London and Tokyo.* Princeton, NJ: Princeton University. (Originally published in 1991.)

11

THE EROSION OF THE NATION-STATE

Before I traveled to another country, I used to carefully convert my dollars into German deutschmarks, Italian lira, and all the other currency I would need abroad. Today, I never do such a thing. For one thing, the deutschmark and lira no longer exist; they have been replaced by the European euro. For another thing, all I need is the piece of plastic in my pocket—my credit card.

The disappearance of foreign currency is an eerie symbol of the fading of the idea of the nation-state in the global era. It can be argued that the idea of the nation-state is a fairly new invention in world history, so it is no surprise that its novelty is wearing off; in the twenty-first century it is showing signs of stress, perhaps even becoming obsolete. The globalization of everything—economic production and distribution, financial markets, communications, ethnic communities, religious networks, and ideologies—challenge the notion that the nation is the primary community of reference, and that the nation-states are the only building blocks for world order.

The world has not always consisted of independent nations. For most of world history, political order was under the control of relatively small kingdoms and large empires that swept over vast reaches of topography, usually with only minimal interference with whatever local political arrangements governed the affairs of towns and villages in their precincts. The boundaries between these regions of political control were often fuzzy. The further one got from a center of power, the weaker was the authority's control, and at the frontiers between the authority of one state and that of another, often a sort of lawless anarchy reigned.

This situation began to change in Europe in the seventeenth century. The region had been ravaged by wars of religion for decades when a peace treaty in 1648 in the Westphalian city of Münster settled the matter with the proclamation in Latin, *cuius regio, eius religio* ("whose region, their religion"), meaning that the matter of religious affiliation should be linked with the preferences of the ruler. This Westphalian Treaty is often regarded as the beginning of the idea of the nation-state, since for the first time it connected the idea of state power with the culture and identity of a national community. Eventually, this led to the idea of a nationhood with borders rather than frontiers, in which all inhabitants were connected to the network of state authority.

The idea of a nation-state was developed more fully during the European Enlightenment. The eighteenth century French philosopher Jean-Jacques Rousseau thought that there was a natural "social contract" between the people of a nation and those who governed them. The implication was that if rulers abused the trust implied in that contract, they could be deposed. The British philosopher John Locke went further in describing the instruments of democratic authority by which the people could be justly represented in a government that truly represented the citizens of a nation. The idea of democracy and representative government, then, became a tacit requirement for status as a nation-state. Needless to say, there was little room for old-fashioned tyrants in this conception of political order, and monarchs, if they remained, were to adopt a more ceremonial role in the affairs of the state.

The concept took hold in Europe and the areas that it influenced around the world. The American Revolution of 1776, which freed the colonies from British rule and established the United States of America, embraced Enlightenment values; the new country strived to create a democratic state along the lines of representative government. So too did France, after the French Revolution a decade later, when it replaced a monarchy with civil order firmly based on Enlightenment democratic principles.

In the twentieth century, the three great wars of the century were concerned, in part, with the the future of the nation-state. World War I was a contest between the allies of France, Russia, and the United Kingdom, against old imperial powers. The victory of the Allies led to the breakup of the Austro-Hungarian Empire in Eastern Europe and the Ottoman Empire in the Middle East. New nation-states were created in their wake. In World War II, nation-states in Europe and the Pacific faced two imperial foes, Hitler's imperial Nazi regime and the Japanese Emperor's territorial expansion in the Pacific. The war was the deadliest in human history, with over fifty million casualties, and the eventual defeat of the Axis powers of Germany, Italy, and Japan. After the war, many of the formerly occupied lands became independent, and they invariably created their own nation-states. All these new nations were given voice through a new organization—the United Nations—that allowed every nation in the world to have representation in a parliamentary body that would make it possible for grievances to be aired and agencies to be promoted that would be conducive to world peace. The underlying premise of the United Nations was something that most political observers at the time regarded as fact: the world had become constituted of independent nation-states, and virtually every inch of the planet (except for Antarctica) was part of one nation-state or another.

The final confrontation of the twentieth century, the Cold War, provided a new challenge to the concept of the nation-state: the notion of transnational socialism as an organizing principle for political order. Formerly independent states in Eastern Europe and Central Asia were gathered under the umbrella of the Union of Soviet Socialist Republics—the USSR—which became a sort of superstate. Though theoretically the individual nations within the sphere of the USSR's influence retained their autonomy, many of the citizens of those nations regarded themselves as being under the control of Russian imperialism. After the fall of the Berlin wall in 1989 and the end of the Cold War in 1991, the USSR was disbanded, and fifteen separate nations reemerged, some of them fiercely independent of their former Russian overlords.

Hence, in the final decade of the twentieth century, it may have appeared that the last challenges to the idea of the nation-state had been overcome. Yet this was precisely the moment in history when a new phenomenon emerged as a threat to that concept: the era of globalization. Moreover, problems had begun to emerge because of the hasty creation of many nations in the twentieth century. In some cases. the retreating colonial powers had drawn lines in the sand to distinguish one nation from another—dividing Iraq, for example, from Syria—and these lines did not always follow traditional ethnic and other social configurations. Even the very idea of the nation-state was open to question. In the excitement of independence in the mid twentieth century, many of these issues were pushed under the rug, but decades later, in an era when the colonial powers themselves seemed weaker, the nature of the postcolonial nation-states was increasingly being questioned.

By the 1990s, globalization was on the rise. National economic markets were undercut by the immense power of the global economy. The flow of diasporic ethnic communities around the world often created new demands for an ethnic homeland to be carved out of existing states. Sikhs in India and Kurds in Turkey and Iraq were clamoring for nations of their own. Interethnic battles racked Rwanda, the former Yugoslavia, and elsewhere. The nation-state was under siege.

In Europe, where the nation-state was invented, a new form of regional identity was created to compete economically with the United States and the rising economic powers of Asia. The European Union (EU) established its own parliament in Brussels, created its own currency—the euro—and brought down the rigid borders and passport and visa regulations that had made commerce and travel difficult in the past. European students can easily enroll in universities in countries throughout the region, and laborers from the EU member nations can easily move from country to country in search of work. Though the individual nation-states of Europe have not been abolished, the European Union provides a new model of regional identity and governance.

In the era of globalization, is the nation-state dead? Since it has been around only for a couple of hundred years, largely in the West, there is no reason to think that the nation-state will be a permanent form of cultural and political organization. Yet it still exists, and most laws and rules are set by national governments, and it is governmental military and police that have the power to enforce them. So it is uncertain whether the nation-state is all that obsolete. And it's even less certain what forms of socioeconomic and political organization are replacing it.

The readings in this section give differing perspectives on the role of the nation-state in the era of globalization. The first reading is by a Japanese business management consultant who advises the leaders of transnational corporations. In the excerpt from his book, *The End of the Nation-State,* Kenichi Ohmae claims that it is a "cartographic illusion" that the world is constituted of individual interacting nation-states. In fact, he claims, the real economic power is in transnational organizations that sometimes operate within the framework of the nation-state and sometimes not. And their view of the world has no clear definable borders.

The next reading is by Susan Strange, a British economist who helped to develop the field of international political economy and taught for years at the London School of Economics. In this essay, written toward the end of her illustrious career, she examines the flaws in the system of nation-states that has come to be described as the Westphalian system, named after the Treaty of Westphalia in 1648, which first promoted the idea of a nation-state. According to her, the Westphalian system always had an economic component; it was created and thrived in part because it helped to nurture the global economy. In the current global era, however, the nation-state economic system has shown itself incapable of protecting the world against financial market collapse, preserving the environment, and developing equity between rich and poor.

The next selection also presumes that the nation-state is in trouble in an era of globalization. It asks whether there are any options to replacing it. The author, Zgymunt Bauman, is a Polish sociologist who left his native country in the Communist anti-Semitic campaigns in 1971 and settled in England, where he has taught at the University of Leeds and written on a variety of topics, including postmodern consumer society. In his book, *Globalization: The Human Consequences,* Bauman states that in the "new world disorder," no one seems to be in control.

It remains unclear, however, what if anything is poised to replace the nation-state. It could be Ohmae's vision of a network of powerful transnational corporations, Sassen's notion of interacting global cities, or Hardt and Negri's idea of empire. Or it could be anarchy.

The last reading in this section describes another development, the emergence of a transnational class of capitalist leaders of corporate organizations. The author, William I. Robinson, is a sociologist who for many years worked with the Sandinista government in Nicaragua and now teaches at the University of California–Santa Barbara. He argues that this new transnational corporate class is challenged in two directions: by its competitor, the wealthy corporate class based on national rather than transnational economies, and by an emerging global social movement of workers and consumers who regard themselves as exploited by the global transnational class. Robinson regards this movement as one of the great hopes for the future. It is uncertain, however, how such an emerging movement could seize control from the globally powerful or what kind of national or transnational social order this movement would install in its place.

THE CARTOGRAPHIC ILLUSION

Kenichi Ohmae

A funny—and, to many observers, a very troubling—thing has happened on the way to former U.S. President Bush's so-called "new world order": the old world has fallen apart. Most visibly, with the ending of the Cold War, the long-familiar pattern of alliances and oppositions among industrialized nations has fractured beyond repair. Less visibly, but arguably far more important, the modern nation state itself—that artifact of the 18th and 19th centuries—has begun to crumble.

For many observers, this erosion of the long-familiar building blocks of the political world has been a source of discomfort at least and, far more likely, of genuine distress. They used to be confident that they could tell with certainty where the boundary lines ran. These are our people; those are not. These are our interests; those are not. These are our industries; those are not. It did not matter that little economic activity remained truly domestic in any sense that an Adam Smith or a David Ricardo would understand. Nor did it matter that the people served or the interests protected represented a small and diminishing fraction of the complex social universe within each set of established political borders.

The point, after all, was that everyone knew—or could talk and act as if he or she knew—where the boundary lines ran. Everyone's dealings could rest, with comfortable assurance, on the certain knowledge, as Robert Reich has put it, of who was "us" and who was "them." The inconvenient fact that most of the guns pointed in anger during the past two decades were pointed by national governments at some segment of the people those governments would define as "us"—well, that really did not matter, either. Boundaries are boundaries.

Politics, runs the time-worn adage, is the art of the possible. Translated, that means it is also the art of ignoring or overlooking discordant facts: guns pointed the wrong way, democratic institutions clogged to the point of paralysis by minority interests defended in the name of the majority—and, perhaps most important, domestic economies in an increasingly borderless world of economic activity. So what if average GNP per capita in China is $317 but, in Shenzhen, whose economy is closely linked with that of Hong Kong, it is $5,695? Boundaries are boundaries, and political dividing lines mean far more than demonstrable communities of economic interest.

No, they don't. Public debate may still be hostage to the outdated vocabulary of political borders, but the daily realities facing most people in the developed and developing worlds—both as citizens and as consumers—speak a vastly different idiom. Theirs is the language of an increasingly borderless economy, a true global marketplace. But the references we have—the maps and guides—to this new terrain are still largely drawn in political terms. Moreover, as the primary features on this landscape—the traditional nation states—begin to come apart at the seams, the overwhelming temptation is to redraw obsolete, U.N.-style maps to reflect the shifting borders of those states. The temptation is understandable, but the result is pure illusion. No more than the work of early cartographers do these new efforts show the boundaries and linkages that matter in the world now emerging. They are the product of illusion, and they are faithful to their roots.

This, too, is understandable. Much of the current awareness of the decay of the modern nation state has been driven by the wrenching experiences of the former Soviet Union and Czechoslovakia, which have formally ceased to exist as single national entities. Perhaps even more frightening, of course, is the noxious brew of ancient hatred, more recent antagonism, and unbridled ambition in what used to be Yugoslavia. These are extremes, to be sure, but they are deeply representative of the kind of erosion that has at last begun to capture an important share of public attention.

In a newly unified Germany, for example, unprecedented amounts of power have been ceded to the individual *Länder*. In Canada, before the recent elections in Quebec and even before the failure of the Meech Lake accords, the French-speaking province had been moving to cut its constitutional ties with the other, English-speaking provinces. In Spain, an explicit program of devolution is transferring much of the apparatus of independent statehood to the country's 17 "autonomous communities," especially those like Catalonia with a deeply entrenched historical identity of their own. In Italy, long-preoccupied with the problems of the Mezzagiorno in the south, recent elections have shown the Lombard League in the north to be a real and growing factor on the political scene. Even in *dirigiste* France, the prefects of Mitterrand's government can no longer unilaterally veto local decisions in the country's 22 provinces.

Developments as striking as these clearly merit the attention they have received in the media and in the regular comments of opinion makers and public officials. Nearly a half century of Cold War cannot end without dramatic—and eminently noteworthy— changes on both sides. Relaxation of the long-entrenched bipolar discipline imposed by the United States and the former USSR cannot help but allow even older fault lines to spread. Equally striking, however, is the way in which such attention has been framed and articulated. To the extent these developments have been treated as evidence of a systemic challenge to traditional nation states (and not just as a challenge to this or that current policy or set of leaders), they have been interpreted for the most part in political terms. Whatever their root, the centrifugal forces now at work have been seen to be meaningful, first and foremost, as statements about the inadequacies of established modes and processes of political order—that is, as evidence of troubling realignments within previously established borders.

Thus, as today's public debate would have it, the fission represented by local autonomy and by ethnic or racial or even tribal irredentism, no less than the proposed fusion represented by

Maastricht, shows clearly that the postwar writ of central governments no longer holds with anything like the power it enjoyed even a generation ago. And as that debate would also have it, this failure of the political center is a legitimate cause for concern. When no one seems to know where we are—or should be—going, initiative stagnates, special interests reduce each other to paralysis, and the consensus necessary for effective policy moves still further out of reach. In tones of despair, the more literary pundits like to cite Yeats: "Things fall apart; The center cannot hold." But the truer message comes from Matthew Arnold: we are "wandering between two worlds,/One dead, the other unable to be born."

These lamentations at least have the virtue of taking the erosion of nation states seriously. But they view it almost entirely as the result of long-repressed political aspirations bursting into the open once the various imposed restraints of the Cold War era have been relaxed. No matter how deeply rooted, however, these aspirations are not the only—or arguably, even the primary—forces now at work. Something else is going on. The battle and the battlefield have shifted.

A QUESTION OF CULTURE?

In a recent, highly influential article, "The Clash of Civilizations?" Samuel Huntington offers an interpretation of what that "something else" is. According to Huntington, the fault lines in our new, post-Cold War world do not flow from politics or ideology, but from culture. From now on, when large masses of people join in common purpose, the primary link between them will increasingly be their shared heritage of language, history, tradition, and religion—that is, civilization. And when they stonily face each other across a divide, the unbridgeable gap between them will be the lack of just such a shared civilization. Groupings based on culture will become—in fact, have already become—the most powerful actors in world affairs.

For all the truth of these observations, Huntington's argument ignores the fact that, even within the same civilization, people have often fought against each other. From the outside, the differences between Catholics and Protestants in Northern Ireland do not seem like a good reason for intense hatred. But for political leaders and mass agitators, they are good enough. Again, from outside, it is awfully difficult to tell the Hutu from the Tutsi in Rwanda. But they have mutually created, during the past decade, one of the bloodiest clashes in the world. People usually fight when their political and/or military leaders inflate minute differences so as to stir up latent hatred—not when "civilizations" clash. If leaders are enlightened, they can make their people believe in the power of working together. This is the case today with the multiple races and cultures linked peacefully by Lee Kwan Yew in Singapore and Dr. Mahathir in Malaysia (and was true in the Yugoslavia of Josip Broz Tito and the India of Mahatma Gandhi and Jawaharlal Nehru after World War II). It is not civilizations that promote clashes. They occur when old-fashioned leaders look for old-fashioned ways to solve problems by rousing their people to armed confrontation.

Such skirmishes confuse the ground of geopolitical interpretation. But they confuse the ground of economic interpretation as well. The glue holding together older constellations of nation-based political interests has visibly begun to wear thin. In economics as in politics, the older patterns of nation-to-nation linkage have begun to lose their dominance. What is emerging in their place, however, is not a set of new channels based on culture instead of nations. Nor is it a simple realignment of previous flows of nation-based trade or investment.

In my view, what is really at stake is not really which party or policy agenda dominates the apparatus of a nation state's central government. Nor is it the number of new, independent units into which that old center, which has held through the upheavals of industrialization and the agonies of two world wars, is likely to decompose. Nor is it the cultural fault lines along which it is likely to fragment.

Instead, what we are witnessing is the cumulative effect of fundamental changes in the currents of economic activity around the globe. So powerful have these currents become that they have carved out entirely new channels for themselves—channels that owe nothing to the lines of demarcation on traditional political maps. Put simply, in terms of real flows of economic activity, nation states have *already* lost their role as meaningful units of participation in the global economy of today's borderless world.

THE WESTFAILURE SYSTEM

Susan Strange

From a globalist, humanitarian and true political economy perspective, the system known as Westphalian has been an abject failure. Those of us engaged in international studies ought therefore to bend our future thinking and efforts to the consideration of ways in which it can be changed or superseded. That is the gist of my argument.

The system can be briefly defined as that in which prime political authority is conceded to those institutions, called states, claiming the monopoly of legitimate use of violence within their respective territorial borders. It is a system purporting to rest on mutual restraint (non-intervention); but it is also a system based on mutual recognition of each other's "sovereignty" if that should be challenged from whatever quarter.

But while we constantly refer to the "international political system" or to the "security structure" this Westphalian system cannot realistically be isolated from—indeed is inseparable from—the market economy which the states of Europe, from the mid-17th century onwards, both nurtured and promoted. To the extent that the powers of these states over society and over economy grew through the 18th, 19th and 20th centuries, they did so both in response to the political system in which states competed with other states (for territory at first but later for industrial and financial power) and in response to the growing demands made on political authority as a result of the capitalist system of production and its social consequences. The label "capitalist" applied to the market-driven economy is justified because the accumulation of capital, as the Marxists put it, or the creation and trading in credit as I would describe it, was the necessary condition for continued investment of resources in the new technologies of agriculture, manufacture and services. As I put it in *States and Markets*, the security structure and the production, financial and knowledge structures constantly interact with each other and cannot therefore be analysed in isolation. The point is "kids-stuff" to social and economic historians but is frequently overlooked by writers on international relations.

When I say that the system has failed, I do not mean to say that it is collapsing, only that it has failed to satisfy the long term conditions of sustainability. Like the empires of old—Persian, Roman, Spanish, British or Tsarist Russian—the signs of decline and ultimate disintegration appear some while before the edifice itself collapses. These signs are to be seen already in the three areas in which the system's sustainability is in jeopardy. One area is ecological: the Westfailure system is unable by its nature to correct and reverse the processes of environmental damage that threaten the survival of not only our own but other species of animals and plants. Another is financial: the Westfailure system is unable—again, because of its very nature—to govern and control the institutions and markets that create and trade the credit instruments essential to the "real economy." The last area is social: the Westfailure system is unable to hold a sustainable balance between the constantly growing power of what the neo-Gramscians call the transnational capitalist class (TCC) and that of the "have-nots," the social underclasses, the discontents that the French call *les exclus*—immigrants, unemployed, refugees, peasants, and all those who already feel that globalisation does nothing for them and are inclined to look to warlords, Mafias or extreme-right fascist politicians for protection. The point here is that until quite recently the state through its control over the national economy, and with the fiscal resources it derived from it, was able to act as an agent of economic and social redistribution, operating welfare systems that gave shelter to the old, the sick, the jobless and the disabled. This made up for the decline in its role—in Europe particularly—as defender of the realm against foreign invasion. Now, however, its ability to act as such a shield and protector of the underprivileged is being rapidly eroded—and for reasons to which I shall return in a while.

In short, the system is failing Nature—the planet Earth—which is being increasingly pillaged, perverted and polluted by economic enterprises which the state-system is unable to control or restrain. It is failing Capitalism in that the national and international institutions that are supposed to manage financial markets are progressively unable—as recent developments in east Asia demonstrate—to keep up with the accelerating pace of technological change in the private sectors, with potentially dire consequences for the whole world market economy. And it is failing world society by allowing a dangerously wide gap to develop between the rich and powerful and the weak and powerless.

The fact that the system survives despite its failures only shows the difficulty of finding and building an alternative. No one is keen to go back to the old colonialist empires. And though Islam and Christian fundamentalism make good sticks with which to beat the western capitalist model, the myriad divisions within both make any kind of theocratic-religious alternative highly improbable. So the old advice, "Keep hold of nurse, for fear of worse" is still widely followed even while faith in her skill and competence is more than a little doubted. . . .

WHAT IS TO BE DONE?

The two commonest reactions to the three failures of the system I have briefly described are either to deny the failures and to defend the dual capitalism-state system in pan-glossian fashion as the best of all possible post-Cold War worlds, or else fatalistically to conclude that, despite its shortcomings there is nothing that can be done to change things. Only quite recently has it been possible to detect the first tentative indications of a third response. It is to be heard more from sociologists than from international relations writers, perhaps because sociologists tend to think in terms of social classes and social movements rather than in terms of nation-states. As a recent collection of essays around the theme, "The Direction of Contemporary Capitalism" shows, there is little consensus among them either about current trends or about possible outcomes. A good deal of this thinking has been inspired by the rediscovery of Antonio Gramsci and his concepts of hegemony, the historic bloc and social myths that permit effective political action. A common assumption is that the present system is sustained by the power of a transnational capitalist class (TCC).

I have no doubt that such a class exists and does exert its power over the market economy and the rules—such as they are—that govern it. Nearly a decade ago, I referred to it as the dominant "business civilization." I think Gill was mistaken in seeing evidence of its power in the Tripartite Commission, which was more a club of well-meaning has-beens than an effective political actor, a mirror rather than a driver. But he was right in spotlighting the emergence of a transnational interest group with powerful levers over national governments including that of the United States and members of the European Union. Recent research in telecommunications, trade negotiations concerning intellectual property rights and a number of other spheres where international organisations have been penetrated and influenced by big-business lobbies all point to the existence of such a TCC. Yet to call it a class suggests far more solidarity and uniformity than in fact exists. The more I look into the politics of international business, the more I am struck by the growing divide between big business—the so-called multinationals—and the people running and employed by small and medium business enterprises. These enjoy few of the perks and privileges of the big corporations yet have to conform to the rules and agencies created by them. For them, globalization is something to be resisted, if only because it so blatantly tramples on the democratic principles of accountability and transparency.

The environmental issue area is a good example of the fissures in the TCC. On the one side are the big oil companies, the giant chemical combines, the vested interests of the car manufacturers and associated businesses. On the other are firms in the vanguard of waste disposal and clean-up technologies and interestingly—the transnational insurance business. . . . Fear of the vast claims that might be made against their clients on environmental grounds is putting insurers increasingly in opposition to the polluters. Their opposition, of course, is predicated on legal systems that are sensitive to public opinion. The power of the latter meanwhile is also evident in the growing sensitivity of some elements in business to shareholders and consumers.

Thus, the notion tentatively posited by some of the neo-Gramscians that while there is some sort of TCC there is also an emerging global civil society is not lightly to be dismissed. To quote Leslie Sklair:

> No social movement appears even remotely likely to overthrow the three fundamental institutional supports of global capitalism . . . namely, the TNCs [transnational corporations], the transnational capitalist class and the culture-ideology of consumerism. Nevertheless in each of these spheres there are resistances expressed by social movements.

Similarly, Rodolfo Stavenhagen, writing on "People's movements, the antisystemic challenge" in the collection of essays edited by Bob Cox, finds the growth points of a nascent transnational opposition, or counterforce to Sklair's three institutional supports sustaining the Westfailure system. Not only, he says, are such social movements nongovernmental, they are popular in the widest sense of that word; they are alternative to established political systems, and therefore often at odds with national governments and political parties and they seek "to attain objectives that would entail alternative forms of economic development, political control and social organisation."

In his introduction to this collection of essays, Cox does not predict the imminent demise of the "fading Westphalian system." The future world, he observes, "will be determined by the relative strength of the bottom-up and top-down pressures." The contest may be a long one and no one should underestimate the power of big business and big government interests behind these top-down pressures. Yet at the same time there is no denying that as Cox says, "people have become alienated from existing regimes, states and political processes." Witness the recent amazing, unforeseen turn-out—a quarter of a million in Paris and the same in London—in anti-government marches by country dwellers of every class and occupation. Everywhere, in fact, politicians are discredited and despised as never before. The state is indeed in retreat from its core competences in security, finance and control over the economy; and this retreat is not inconsistent with its proliferating regulation of many trivial aspects of daily life. The new multilateralism Cox predicates "will not be born from constitutional amendments to existing multilateral institutions but rather from a reconstitution of civil societies and political authorities on a global scale building a system of global governance from the bottom up."

For international studies, and for those of us engaged in them, the implications are far-reaching. We have to escape and resist the state-centrism inherent in the analysis of conventional international relations. The study of globalisation has to embrace the study of the behaviour of firms no less than of other forms of political authority. International political economy has to be recombined with comparative political economy at the sub-state as well as the state level. It is not our job, in short, to defend or excuse the Westphalian system. We should be concerned as much with its significant failures as with its alleged successes.

AFTER THE NATION-STATE—WHAT?

Zygmunt Bauman

"In an earlier generation, social policy was based on the belief that nations, and within nations cities, could control their fortunes; now, a divide is opening between polity and economy"—observes Richard Sennett.

With the overall speed of movement gathering momentum—with time/space as such, as David Harvey points out, "compressing"—some objects move faster than others. "The economy"—capital, which means money and other resources needed to get things done, to make more money and more things yet—moves fast; enough to keep permanently a step ahead of any (territorial, as ever) polity which may try to contain and redirect its travels, in this case, at least, the reduction of travel time to zero leads to a new quality: to a total annihilation of spatial constraints, or rather to the total "overcoming of gravity." Whatever moves with the speed approaching the velocity of the electronic signal is practically free from constraints related to the territory inside which it originated, towards which it is aimed or through which it passes on the way.

A recent commentary by Martin Woollacott grasps well the consequences of that emancipation:

> The Swedish-Swiss conglomerate Asea Brown Boveri announced it would be cutting its West European work force by 57,000, while creating other jobs in Asia. Electrolux followed with the announcement that it will cut its global work force by 11 per cent, with most of the cuts in Europe and North America. Pilkington Glass also announced significant cuts. In just ten days, three European firms had cut jobs on a scale large enough to be compared with the numbers mentioned in the new French and British governments' proposals on job creation. . . .

Germany, notoriously, has lost 1 million jobs in five years, and its companies are busy building plants in Eastern Europe, Asia, and Latin America. If West European industry is massively relocating outside Western Europe, then all these arguments about the best government approach to unemployment would have to be seen as of limited relevance.

Balancing the books of what once seemed to be the indispensable setting for all economic thinking—the *Nationalökonomie*—is becoming more and more an actuarial fiction. As Vincent Cable points out in his recent *Demos* pamphlet—"it is no longer obvious what it means to describe the Midland Bank or ICL as British (or for that matter companies like British Petroleum, British Airways, British Gas or British Telecom). . . . In a world where capital has no fixed abode and financial flows are largely beyond the control of national governments, many of the levers of economic policy no longer work." And Alberto Melucci suggests that the rapidly growing influence of supranational—"planetary"—organizations "has had the effect of both accelerating the exclusion of weak areas and of creating new channels for the allocation of resources, removed, at least in part, from the control of the various national states."

In the words of G.H. von Wright, the "nation-state, it seems, is eroding or perhaps 'withering away.' The eroding forces are *transnational*." Since nation-states remain the sole frame for book-balancing and the sole sources of effective political initiative, the "transnationality" of eroding forces puts them outside the realm of deliberate, purposeful and potentially rational action. As everything that elides such action, such forces, their shapes and actions are blurred in the mist of mystery; they are objects of guesses rather than reliable analysis. As von Wright puts it,

> The moulding forces of transnational character are largely anonymous and therefore difficult to identify. They do not form a unified system or order. They are an agglomeration of systems manipulated by largely 'invisible' actors . . . [there is no] unity or purposeful co-ordination of the forces in question . . . '[M]arket' is not a bargaining interaction of competing forces so much as the pull and push of manipulated demands, artificially created needs, and desire for quick profit.

All this surrounds the ongoing process of the "withering away" of nation-states with an aura of a natural catastrophe. Its causes are not fully understood; it cannot be exactly predicted even if the causes are known; and it certainly cannot be prevented from happening even if predicted. The feeling of unease, an expectable response to a situation without obvious levers of control, has been pointedly and incisively captured in the title of Kenneth Jowitt's book—*The New World Disorder*. Throughout the modern era we have grown used to the idea that order is tantamount to "being in control." It is this assumption—whether well-founded or merely illusionary—of "being in control" which we miss most.

The present-day "new world disorder" cannot be explained away merely by the circumstance which constitutes the most immediate and obvious reason to feel at a loss and aghast: namely, by "the morning-after" confusion following the abrupt end of the Great Schism and the sudden collapse of the power-block political routine—even if it was indeed that collapse which triggered the "new disorder" alert. The image of global disorder reflects, rather, the new awareness (facilitated, but not necessarily caused, by the abrupt demise of block politics) of the essentially elemental and contingent nature of the things which previously seemed to be tightly controlled or at least "technically controllable."

Before the collapse of the Communist block, the contingent, erratic and wayward nature of the global state of affairs was not so much non-existent, as it was barred from sight by the all-energy-and-thought-consuming day-to-day reproduction of the balance between the world powers. By dividing the world, power politics conjured up the image of totality. Our shared world was made whole by assigning to each nook and cranny of the globe its significance in the "global order of things"—to wit, in the two power-camps' conflict and the meticulously guarded, though forever precarious, equilibrium. The world was a totality in as far as there was nothing in it which could escape such significance, and so nothing could be indifferent from the point of view of the balance between the two powers which appropriated a considerable part of the world and cast the rest in the shadow of that appropriation. Everything in the world had a meaning, and that meaning emanated from a split, yet single centre—from the two enormous power blocks locked up, riveted and glued to each other in an all-out combat. With the Great Schism out of the way, the world does not look a totality anymore; it looks rather like a field of scattered and disparate forces, congealing in places difficult to predict and gathering momentum which no one really knows how to arrest.

To put it in a nutshell: *no one seems now to be in control*. Worse still—it is not clear what "being in control" could, under the circumstances, be like. As before, all ordering initiatives and actions are local and issue-oriented; but there is no longer a locality arrogant enough to pronounce for mankind as a whole, or to be listened to and obeyed by mankind when making the pronouncements. Neither is there a single issue which could grasp and telescope the totality of global affairs while commanding global consent.

THE TRANSNATIONAL STATE

William I. Robinson

"Within the next hundred years . . . nationhood as we know it will be obsolete; all states will recognize a single, global authority. A phrase briefly fashionable in the mid-20th century—'citizen of the world'—will have assumed real meaning by the end of the 21st century." Thus declared President Bill Clinton's Deputy Secretary of State, Strobe Talbott, in 1992. He continued, "All countries are basically social arrangements, accommodations to changing circumstances. No matter how permanent and even sacred they may seem at any one time, in fact they are all artificial and temporary." In fact, it became fashionable for writers on globalization in the late twentieth century to produce quotes from top-level global capitalists on their views regarding the "end of the nation-state" and the stateless corporation. Remarks to this effect, such as the following one by Karl A. Gerstacker, CEO of Dow Chemical, abounded: "I have long dreamed of buying an island owned by no nation and of establishing the World Headquarters of the Dow Company on the truly neutral ground of such an island, beholden to no nation or society." In an equally oft-cited remark, Gilbert Williamson, president of the NCR Corporation, affirmed, "We at NCR think of ourselves as a globally competitive company that happens to be head-quartered in the United States." Now, if . . . the hegemonic fractions of capital on a world scale have become transnationalized, increasingly detached from particular territories and from the old political and social projects of nation-states, does this not imply that they are stateless? But are TNCs [transnational corporations] really *stateless*, or are they *nation-less*? Are *state* and *nation* the same thing? I attempt to answer these questions . . . , but first I want to approach the matter from a different angle, posing another set of questions with regard to the TCC [transnational capitalist class] and its agency. . . .

The TCC is dominant economically in the sense that it controls the "commanding heights" of the global economy. But is it also dominant politically? The economically dominant class in a society is not necessarily the political ruling class: that it is (or is not) must be demonstrated. A closely related question is, to what extent does it act collectively as a class in the exercise of power? In what sense and to what degree can the TCC be shown to be a global ruling class? There is a long debate in the literature of the social sciences, a debate that it is not possible to take up here, on "collective actors" and on whether classes can be collective actors. My view is that classes *are* collective actors. . . . The TCC, in part by virtue of its position as an "organized minority" and the resources and networks at its disposal for coordination, works through identifiable institutions and is fairly coherent as a collective actor. . . .

I shift the focus of inquiry from the economic dominance of transnational capital to possible forms of its political rule. I further develop my earlier proposition that a TCC has emerged as a class fraction of the world bourgeoisie and that this TCC is in the process of achieving its rule or becoming a global ruling class. I introduce the concept of a transnational state (TNS) and link this concept to that of the TCC. I argue that the rise of a TNS apparatus is an integral dimension of global capitalism. The emergence and consolidation of the global economy and the rise of a politically active TCC cannot be understood apart from the TNS. The TCC has articulated economic interests with political aims in pursuing the globalist project of an integrated global economy and society, what I referred to . . . as the transnational elite agenda, aimed at creating the conditions most propitious for global capitalism to function. And it has advanced that agenda through the institutions of a TNS apparatus.

I have emphasized . . . the importance of looking at both structure and agency, or the objective and subjective sides of social life. I believe it is absolutely necessary to examine these two dimensions in their interrelation if we are to understand the social world. By the *objective*, recall, I mean forces that are beyond the level of individual wills and consciousness. Our very existence requires that everyone participate in the economy independent of their will or their understanding of economic institutions. These economic forces, which shape our lives whether or not we are aware of them, constitute an objective dimension of our existence. By the *subjective* I mean our consciousness of the reality in which we are immersed and our actions in the world based on our conscious understanding and "free" will. Earlier I observed that class formation is both an objective and a subjective process, involving structural and agency levels of analysis. . . . I emphasized the objective dimensions of global capitalism and the TCC, focusing on the objective determinants of the process in the productive structure, and found that the transnationalization of the production process was key. . . . I want to focus some attention on the more subjective dimensions involved in capitalist globalization and the formation of a TCC. Examining the rise of a TNS apparatus allows us to uncover collective agency in the process of capitalist globalization, to identify crucial political and institutional dimensions of the process.

An analysis of the power of the capitalist ruling class must take into account the state and the political process. But we can proceed to analyze, first, the economic-material determination of the TCC as embodied in transnational capital . . . and second, the exercise of its class power as expressed in TNS apparatuses, to which I now turn. The social power of groups is grounded in control over wealth (the means of production and the social product) but is always exercised through institutions. Political sociologists and political scientists have long noted that a dominant class exercises its rule through political institutions, whose higher personnel must represent the class, as far as possible unifying its actions and reinforcing its control over the process of social reproduction. With regard to globalization and the TCC, this means ensuring the reproduction of global capitalist relations of production as well as the creation and reproduction of political and cultural institutions favorable to its rule, *central among which is the state*. We have seen already that one central institution is the TNC, the key institution for organizing the process of global capital accumulation. In the global capitalist system the giant TNCs that control the global economy make the key decisions affecting the lives of most, if not all, of the people on the planet. But corporations do not act alone in organizing capitalist production. Notwithstanding the prevailing market ideology, the conditions of production are not brought forth in accordance with the laws of the market. There must be some agency whose task is to produce these conditions or to regulate capital's access to them. This institution is the capitalist state. Under globalization, I suggest, the capitalist state has increasingly acquired the form of a TNS.

Here in a nutshell is my argument: The leading strata among the emergent TCC became politicized from the 1970s into the 1990s. The notion of a managerial elite at the apex of the global ruling class that controls key levers of global policymaking captures the idea of a politically active wing of the global ruling class. As part of its political protagonism, this wing set about to create or transform a set of emerging transnational institutions. These institutions constitute an incipient TNS [transnational state] apparatus. This TNS apparatus is an emerging network that comprises transformed and externally integrated national states, *together with* the supranational economic and political forums, and has not yet acquired any centralized institutional form. The economic forums include the IMF [International Monetary Fund], the WB [World Bank], the WTO [World Trade Organization], the regional banks, and so on. The political forums include the Group of Seven (G-7) countries and the larger Group of 22 countries, among others, as well as the U.N. system, the OECD [Organization for Economic Cooperation and Development], the EU [European Union], the Conference on Security and Cooperation in Europe (CSCE), and so on. The TCC has directly instrumentalized this TNS apparatus, exercising a form of TNS power through the multilayered configuration of the TNS. It is through these global institutions that the TCC has been attempting to forge a new global capitalist historic bloc. . . .

My thesis on the TNS involves three interrelated propositions:

1. Economic globalization has its counterpart in transnational class formation and in the emergence of a TNS, which has been brought into existence to function as the collective authority for a global ruling class.

2. The nation-state is neither retaining its primacy nor disappearing but is being transformed and absorbed into the larger structure of a TNS.

3. The emergent TNS institutionalizes the new class relation between global capital and global labor. . . .

I refer to the tendency to accord continued centrality to the nation-state in existing theoretical approaches in the social sciences as *nation-state centrism*. Nations are seen as discrete units within a larger system—the world system or the international system—that is characterized by external exchanges among these units. Despite their divergent theoretical principles, these nation-state paradigms share as the domain of their inquiry the nation-state and the interstate system. But nation-states are no longer appropriate units of analysis, in part because they are no longer "containers" (if indeed they ever were) of the diverse economic, political, social, and cultural processes that are the objects of study in the social sciences. Adopting a transnational, or global, perspective means moving beyond a focus on the social world that emphasizes country-level analysis or an international system made up of discrete nation-states as interacting units of comparative analysis. We need to make a break with nation-state-centered analysis if we are to understand the twenty-first-century world.

With the onset of globalization social scientists have recognized the increasing obsolescence of the nation-state as a practical unit of the global political economy and acknowledged the need for new perspectives. The new, transnational phase of capitalism is characterized by a period of major restructuring of the system, including restructuring the institutional forms of capitalism. The breakup of national economic, political, and social structures is reciprocal to the gradual breakup, starting in the 1970s, of a preglobalization world order based on nation-states. Nonetheless, given ingrained nation-state centrism, much scholarship has analyzed economic globalization from the political framework of the nation-state system and the agency therein of national classes and groups. Transnational institutions and political globalization are seen in most accounts as extensions or modifications of the nation-state system. These are national/international approaches that focus on the preexisting system of nation-states, seen as experiencing internationalization rather than globalization. Indeed, two of the most prominent theoreticians on globalization, Roland Robertson and Anthony Giddens, insist that a defining feature of the process is the "universalization" of the nation-state. *Transnational* or globalization approaches focus on how the system of nation-states and national economies, and so on, are being transcended by transnational forces and institutions grounded in the global rather than the interstate system.

To get beyond nation-state-centrist ways of thinking about globalization, we need to keep in mind that a study of globalization is fundamentally *historical analysis*. Events or social conditions can be conceived in terms of previous social processes and conditions that gave rise to them. The nation-state is not transhistorical. Good social analysis requires that we study not only the laws of motion of a given set of structures but also the *transformation* of those structures.

FURTHER READING

Anderson, Benedict. 1992. *Imagined Communities: Reflections on the Origin and Spread of Nationalism*. London: Verso.

Bauman, Zygmunt. 1998. *Globalization: The Human Consequences*. Oxford, UK: Blackwell.

Calhoun, Craig. 1998. *Nationalism*. Minneapolis: University of Minnesota Press.

Fukuyama, Francis. 2012. *The Origins of Political Order: From Prehuman Times to the French Revolution*. New York: Farrar, Strauss, Giroux.

Gellner, Ernest, and John Breuly. 2009. *Nations and Nationalism*. 2nd ed. Ithaca, NY: Cornell University Press.

Hobsbawm, Eric. 2012. *Nations and Nationalism Since 1780: Programme, Myth, Reality*. Cambridge, UK: Cambridge University Press.

Holton, Robert J. 1998. *Globalization and the Nation-State*. New York: St. Martin's Press.

Jowitt, Kenneth. 1993. *The New World Disorder: The Leninist Extinction*. Berkeley: University of California Press.

Ohmae, Kenichi. 1996. *The End of the Nation-State: The Rise of Regional Economies*. New York: HarperCollins.

Paul, T.V., G. John Ikenberry, and John A. Hall (Eds.). 2003. *The Nation-State in Question*. Princeton, NJ: Princeton University Press.

Robinson, William. 2004. *A Theory of Global Capitalism: Production, Class, and State in a Transnational World*. Baltimore: John Hopkins University Press.

Smith, Anthony D. 2010. *Nationalism*. London: Polity Press.

Strange, Susan. 1999. The Westfailure System. In *Review of International Studies*, vol. 25, 3, pp. 345–354.

Strange, Susan. 1996. *The Retreat of the State: The Diffusion of Power in the World Economy*. Cambridge, UK: Cambridge University Press.

Weiss, Linda. 1998. *The Myth of the Powerless State*. London: Polity Press.

12

RELIGIOUS POLITICS AND THE NEW WORLD ORDER

The horrendous images of the World Trade Center towers crumbling to dust in the terrorist attacks of September 11, 2001, were a shock to people around the world. They were even more surprised to find that these attacks were framed in the language of religion. These acts were not about religion in the narrow sense—they were not efforts to promote a particular set of beliefs—yet religion was part of the language that justified them.

One of the remarkable features of political life in the global era is the rise of strident new forms of religious politics. The last decades of the twentieth century and the first decades of the twenty-first have witnessed the emergence of a Hindu nationalist party in India, an antigovernment Buddhist movement in Sri Lanka, Christian militias in the United States, xenophobic Christian nationalists in Europe, Jewish extremists in Israel, and Muslim activists in Iran, Iraq, Egypt, Palestine, and throughout the Middle East. Everywhere, it seems, in every religious tradition, new forms of religious activism have been on the rise.

This activism is surprising, because only a few decades ago some of the best minds were predicting the death of religion. One of the main premises of the Enlightenment vision of the nation-state is that although religion is regarded as necessary to provide the sense of cultural homogeneity that makes a nation cohesive, it should stay out of public life. The idea of the state was a secular one, in which interests of individuals and groups could be adjudicated through reason and the secular instruments of government.

In the global era, however, traditional notions of homogeneous nationalist culture has been challenged by demographic shifts that allowed new ethnic communities to appear in the multicultural societies of many modern countries, by the global communications system that enabled everyone to be in touch with everyone else throughout the world, and by the media representations of a globalized modern culture that offers alternative images of society. At the same time, the effects of globalization were weakening the authority of nation-states economically and militarily as well as culturally. In such a climate, it is no surprise that resurgent religious groups emerged in defense of traditional values and alignments that seemed to be quickly slipping away.

One is tempted to think of these new movements of religious politics as antiglobal, in that many seem to be reacting against the forces of globalization. Some of them are indeed, fiercely nationalistic. The Hindu Bharatiya Janata Party in India and the Tea Party movement in the United States both rely on traditional religious characterizations of their countries in order to assert their own vision of a parochial nationalism. In some cases, the religious movements are fused with independence movements, such as the Hamas movement in Palestine that aims to liberate Palestine from Israeli control and establish an independent state.

Other movements are transnational in character. Rather than opposing globalization, they seem to offer their own alternative notion of globalization. After 9/11, when the Muslim extremism associated with the al Qaeda network was much in the news, Muslims in many parts of the world were puzzled. It was not clear to them—or to anyone else—exactly what the al Qaeda activists were fighting for and what kind of government they wanted to see in power. It was clear what they did not like—American domination of global society—but their own vision was less certain. The comments of Osama bin Laden referred to what had been lost since the disappearance of the great Muslim empires, and the implication seemed to be that he longed for a transnational, global Islamic rule—an alternative globalization.

In all these cases, the movements of cultural nationalism and transnationalism appear to be stridently religious. When groups such as the Taliban do not allow girls to go to school and enforce Muslim law with a ferocity that includes chopping off criminals' hands, it appears that religion has taken over in a big way. But a closer look reveals a more complicated picture, one in which social conflict and local politics are at play.

Most of the contemporary conflicts with which religion has been associated are not solely about religion, if by "religion" one means a set of doctrines and beliefs. The conflicts have been about identity and economics, about privilege and power—the things that motivate most social conflicts. When these conflicts are religionized—justified in religious terms and presented with the aura of sacred combat—they often become more intractable, less susceptible to negotiated settlement. Thus, although religion is seldom the problem—in the sense of causing the tensions that produced the conflicts in the first place—it is often poses problems by increasing the intensity and changing the character of the struggle. Since the religionization of conflict is appearing all over the planet at roughly the same time as the emergence of increased globalization, one might suspect that globalization has something to do with it. And yet religious activism is intensely local. Could the two be related?

An abundant number of new studies argue that this is the case, that religious conflict *is* a by-product of the global age (see the "Further Reading" section). In the global era, religion helps to legitimize movements of rebellion with symbolic empowerment and enables the rebels to respond with traditional cultural credibility to the challenges of globalization.

The first reading in this section provides an overview of religious politics in what the authors describe as "God's Century," meaning the twenty-first century. In this excerpt, the authors talk about how in the twentieth century religion was supposed to stay out of secular public life and how surprised many observers have been to see the eruption of religious politics in recent years. Yet, the authors advise us, the role of religion in public life is not always destructive; it can also lead to tolerance and reconciliation and provide a positive voice for social justice. The authors are all American political scientists who were graduate students together at Harvard. Monica Duffy Toft has taught at Harvard and later at Oxford; Daniel Philpott has taught at the University of California, Santa Barbara, and then at Notre Dame University; and Timothy Samuel Shah has taught at Boston University and Georgetown.

The next reading is on the rise of religious politics as a response to globalization and the weakening of the nation-state. This essay comes out of research that I have been doing since the mid-1980s, when I first began to study the rise of religious violence in the confrontation between Sikh activists and India's government in the region of the Punjab in which I had once lived and taught. I found that religious activists there saw the world as spiraling out of control, and their violent actions were, in their minds, attempts to set it right. In interviewing activists around the world, including those involved in the Hamas and al Qaeda Islamic movements, Jewish extremists in Israel, and Christian militias in the United States, I found that the pattern was repeated. Global changes had produced a violent religious response.

In the following selection, the French political theorist Olivier Roy examines the best known of these movements—the al Qaeda organization associated with Osama bin Laden. He shows how a small movement of fighters from various Muslim countries who came to Afghanistan to defend Islam from secular Soviet socialism gradually emerged into a worldwide guerilla fighting force, with global aspirations of its own. Roy studied Persian and served in Afghanistan with the United Nations, as well as being an advisor for the French Foreign Ministry. He is a professor in the European University Institute in Florence, Italy.

The final reading in this section is on the role of religion in what author Richard Falk calls "humane global governance." For many years, Falk was a professor of international law at Princeton University. He has been a Special Rapporteur on Human Rights in Palestine for the United Nations and is a Senior Fellow at the Orfalea Center for Global and International Studies at the University of California, Santa Barbara. Falk looks beyond the destructive aspects of the religious resurgence in public life in recent years and sees a longing for a more spiritual and moral civic order within the varied public expressions of religion. Though Falk himself is a rationalist, he sees the value of religious traditions in providing society with guidelines and a dimension of depth in order to make possible an emerging global society that is just and humane.

THE TWENTY-FIRST CENTURY AS GOD'S CENTURY

Monica Duffy Toft, Daniel Philpott, and Timothy Samuel Shah

Had an enterprising fortune-teller predicted four decades ago that in the twenty-first century religion would become a formidable force in global politics, educated people would have considered him a laughingstock. In 1968, Peter Berger, one of the past generation's greatest sociologists, predicted that by "the 21st century, religious believers are likely to be found only in small sects, huddled together to resist a worldwide secular culture." Similarly, in 1966 *Time* magazine printed starkly on its cover, "Is God Dead?," recalling German philosopher Friedrich Nietzsche's audacious assertions at the end of the previous century: "God is dead. God remains dead. And we have killed Him."

Global trends seemed to support these prophets of decline. Like dying supernovae, every major religion on every continent seemed to be rapidly losing its influence on politics, economics, and culture. More than that, they seemed "afloat on a receding wave of history," destined for oblivion. Surging forward with seemingly unstoppable historical momentum were instead ideologies and doctrines that sought to replace religion as the source of people's loyalties. Apostles of nationalism, socialism, and modernization—such as Fidel Castro of Cuba, David Ben-Gurion of Israel, Gamal Abdel Nasser of Egypt, and the Shah of Iran—were men of the future. Mullahs, monks, and priests, with their dogmas, rites, and hierarchies, were creatures of an increasingly irrelevant past.

What came to be known as the "secularization thesis"—the prediction that religion would wilt before the juggernauts of the modern world—seemed triumphant. Science, the thesis held, would expose the supernatural as superstition and reveal the truth of humanity's origins and makeup. Historical inquiry would explain in similar fashion the true—and entirely human—story behind events that the religious claimed to be miraculous and divinely orchestrated. Democracy, free thought, and open expression would allow ordinary citizens to challenge the myths and dogmas by which church authorities held people in servility and lent legitimacy to monarchy, aristocracy, and the favorite pastime of the powerful, war. Industrialization, economic growth, and technological progress would eradicate hunger, disease, and stunted opportunity, the forces that lead people to turn to religion for answers. All of this was hopeful. Religion's regress spelled humanity's progress.

Such thinking originated in the Enlightenment philosophical movement of seventeenth- and eighteenth-century Europe. It included Thomas Jefferson, who edited his own version of the New Testament so as to omit all reference to the supernatural—heaven, hell, cross, and resurrection—and retain only the gentle ethical wisdom of

Jesus, from which he believed readers could profit greatly. It also included Jean-Jacques Rousseau and other philosophers of the French Revolution, who sought to kill off the monarchy and the Catholic Church and replace them with a system of secular thought and culture centered on the nation. The thinking gained steam in the nineteenth and twentieth centuries in the thought of Nietzsche, Charles Darwin, Karl Marx, Sigmund Freud, Max Weber, and so many others. By the 1950s and 1960s, the secularization thesis all but dominated the university, most elite sectors in the West, and the views of Western-educated elites in Asia, Africa, and the Middle East.

But the secularization thesis has proven a poor guide to global historical reality. Contrary to its predictions, the portion of the world population adhering to Catholic Christianity, Protestant Christianity, Islam, and Hinduism jumped from 50 percent in 1900 to 64 percent in 2000. Globally speaking, most people—79 percent—believe in God (a slight increase from the late 1980s and early 1990s, which was 73 percent), and although in most countries majorities agree that religion is private and should be kept separate from government, these majorities are increasingly slim in a number of countries and the intensity of support for this separation has declined in over half of the countries polled. In India, for example, the number of people who "completely" agree on the separation of faith and government dropped from 78 percent to 50 percent in just five years, from 2002 to 2007. Thus, over the past four decades, religion's influence on politics has reversed its decline and become more powerful on every continent and across every major world religion. Earlier confined to the home, the family, the village, the mosque, synagogue, temple, and church, religion has come to exert its influence in parliaments, presidential palaces, lobbyists' offices, campaigns, militant training camps, negotiation rooms, protest rallies, city squares, and dissident jail cells. Workplaces increasingly are the sites of prayer rooms and small-group Scripture studies. Even sporting events now feature conspicuous prayers by players and coaches, huddled together in supplication to the Almighty. Once private, religion has gone public. Once passive, religion is now assertive and engaged. Once local, it is now global. Once subservient to the powers that be, religion has often become "prophetic" and resistant to politicians at every level. . . .

How and why has religion become publicly expressed and politically acceptable in so many parts of the world after a century of so many efforts to dethrone or displace faith as a source of political authority? What explains the diversity of political activities that the religious pursue? Why do some religious actors take up the gun through terrorism or civil war while others promote democracy, human rights, and reconciliation? . . . If religion is to have a seat at the political table, how big—and how elevated—should it be? . . .

If God is not dead, neither is the secularization thesis. In the past few years, a school of writers dubbed the "neo-atheists" has penned books with titles like *God Is Not Great, The God Delusion, Breaking the Spell: Religion as a Natural Phenomenon,* and *The End of Faith: Religion, Terror, and the Future of Reason.* But their version of the thesis is somewhat different from that of their predecessors. They acknowledge that religion has not disappeared— at least not yet—and are alarmed by its persistence. They still believe that religion will eventually recede and hope that it will do so sooner rather than later—before it does more damage. Where they differ from the old secularization theorists most is in their moral assessment of religion, which, if anything, is even more splenetic, leading them to insist that religion is always and everywhere hard-wired to be irrational, violent, and repressive. In the view of Christopher Hitchens, for example, religion "poisons everything."

This version of the secularization thesis fares poorly, too, however. Religion can be violent and repressive, the source of civil war, terrorism, and laws that oppress women and minorities. But the last four decades have shown religion also to be a destroyer of dictatorships, an architect of democracy, a facilitator of peace negotiations and reconciliation initiatives, a promoter of economic development and entrepreneurship, a partisan in the cause of women, and a warrior against disease and a defender of human rights. These many faces of religious politics not only elude simple description but reveal the broader reality that religion's political influence is too little understood, partly because the instruments and frameworks widely used to interpret it remain far too crude.

If scholars, journalists, educators, and public intellectuals have come to realize by now *that* religion matters, they have only begun to understand *how* religion matters and whether it is likely to bring violence or peace, division or unity, progress or decline. But such an understanding is crucial for grasping contemporary global politics. Whether one is a maker of foreign policy, a business person conducting global commerce, a scholar of politics, economics, or culture, an advocate for economic development or human rights, a doctor fighting disease overseas, a translator, a missionary, or simply a world traveler, one cannot afford to ignore religion's resurgent political power in its almost infinitely varied manifestations.

RELIGION IN THE NEW GLOBAL ORDER

Mark Juergensmeyer

The globally-televised images of the aftermath of the savage attacks on a Sikh Gurdwara in Wisconsin in 2012 and a youth camp in Norway in 2011 brought back memories of other horrific scenes—the London subways in 2005, the Madrid train bombings in 2004, the catastrophic assault on the World Trade Center and Pentagon on September 11, 2001, the many suicide bombings in Iraq and Israel, and all of the other recent examples of the explosive power of religion. Or rather, these images portray the potency of the violent political ideologies that have been in some way related to religion. It is not religion that has suddenly gone bad in the first decade of the 21st century, but rather that things in the world have. Radical religious ideologies have become the vehicles for a variety of rebellions against authority that are linked with myriad social, cultural, and political grievances.

Yet religion gives more than a voice for the dispossessed. It provides a basis for a fundamental critique of the modern nation-state. In doing so, it challenges the legitimacy of secular institutions and national identity. For this reason the religious activists involved in radical assaults on the symbols of secular society and national authority should be taken seriously. They are not only temporary social nuisances, but also potentially long-lasting threats to the twentieth-century Western vision of an international order consisting of a network of discrete national societies organized in a secular nation-state world.

Religious ideologies have emerged in the twenty-first century as new bases for political legitimacy and national identity at a time when the nation-state is vulnerable. In an era of economic globalization and the mobility of traditional populations, and in the wake of secular nationalism's failure to deliver its promises of human rights, democracy, and economic progress to countries around the world, the premises of modern secular nationalism are under attack. In the ruins of modernism, religion has risen like a Phoenix to provide the legitimacy and identity necessary for public order.

Born as a stepchild of the European Enlightenment, the idea of the modern nation-state is profound and simple: the state is created by the people within a given national territory. Secular nationalism—the ideology that originally gave the nation-state its legitimacy—contends that a nation's authority is based on the secular idea of a social compact of equals rather than on ethnic ties or sacred mandates. It is a compelling idea, one with pretensions of universal applicability. It reached its widest extent of world-wide acceptance in the mid-twentieth century.

But the latter half of the century was a different story. The secular nation-state proved to be a fragile artifice, especially in those areas of the world where nations had been created by retreating colonial powers—in Africa and the Middle East by Britain and France; in Latin America by Spain and Portugal; in South and Southeast Asia by Britain, France, the Netherlands, and the United States; and in Eurasia by the Soviet Union. In some cases boundary disputes led to squabbles among neighboring nations. In others the very idea of the nation was a cause for suspicion.

Many of these imagined nations—some with invented names such as Pakistan, Indonesia, and Yugoslavia—were not accepted by everyone within their territory. In yet other cases, the tasks of administration became too difficult to perform in honest and efficient ways. The newly-created nations had only brief histories of prior colonial control to unite them, and after independence they had only the most modest of economic, administrative, and cultural infrastructures to hold their disparate regions together.

THE CHALLENGE OF GLOBALIZATION

By the 1990s these ties had begun to fray. The global economic market undercut national economies, and the awesome military technology of the US and NATO reduced national armies to border patrols. More significantly the rationale for the nation-state came into question. With the collapse of the Soviet Union and the post-colonial, post-Vietnam critique of Western democracy, the secular basis for the nation-state seemed increasingly open to criticism. In some instances, such as in Yugoslavia, when the ideological glue of secular nationalism began to dissolve, the state fell apart.

In other places the economic promises of the Western models of modernization seemed to come up empty, especially in places where local leaders felt exploited by the global economy—as in Iran and Egypt—or believed that somehow the benefits of economic globalization passed them by. The global shifts in economic and political power that occurred following the break-up of the Soviet Union and the sudden rise and subsequent fall of Japanese and other Asian economies also had significant social repercussions.

At one time, leaders such as India's Jawaharlal Nehru, Egypt's Gamal Abdel Nasser, and Iran's Riza Shah Pahlavi tried to create their own versions of America—or in some cases a cross between America and the Soviet Union. But following after them a new, postcolonial generation no longer believed in the Westernized vision of Nehru, Nasser or the Shah. Rather, it wanted to complete the process of decolonialization by asserting the legitimacy of their countries' own traditional values in the public sphere and constructing a national identity based on indigenous culture. The need for local control seemed pressing in the global media assault of Western music, videos and films that satellite television beam around the world, and which threaten to obliterate local and traditional forms of cultural expression.

In other cases it has been a different kind of globalization—the emergence of multicultural societies through global diasporas of peoples and cultures, and the suggestion of global military and political control in a "new world order"—that has elicited fear. Perhaps surprisingly, this response has been most intense in the most developed countries, which in other ways seem to be the very paradigm of globalization. In Europe, the presence of large immigrant populations from the Middle East ignited new forms of racism and new fears of the erosion of national values. In the United States, the Christian militia organizations were animated by fears of a massive global conspiracy involving liberal American politicians and the United Nations. In Japan a similar conspiracy theory motivated leaders of the Aum Shinrikyo movement to predict a catastrophic World War III, which their nerve gas assault in the Tokyo subways was meant to emulate.

As far-fetched as the idea of a "new world order" of global control may be, there is some truth to the notion that the integration of societies, communication among disparate peoples, and the globalization of culture have brought the world closer together. Although it is unlikely that a cartel of malicious schemers has designed this global trend, its effect on local societies and national identities has nonetheless been profound. It has undermined the modern idea of the nation-state by providing nonnational and transnational forms of economic, social, and cultural interaction. The global economic and social ties of the inhabitants of contemporary global cities are linked together in a way that supercedes the Enlightenment notion that peoples in particular regions are naturally linked together in a social contract. In a global world, it is hard to say where particular regions begin and end. For that matter, it is hard to say how one should define the "people" of a particular nation.

This is where religion and ethnicity step in to redefine public communities. The fading of the nation-state and old forms of secular nationalism have produced both the opportunity for new nationalisms and the need for them. The opportunity has arisen because the old orders seem so weak; and the need for national identity persists because no single alternative form of social cohesion and affiliation has yet appeared to dominate public life the way the nation-state did in the twentieth century. In a curious way, traditional forms of social identity have helped to rescue the idea of national societies. In the increasing absence of any other demarcation of national loyalty and commitment, these old staples—religion, ethnicity and traditional culture—have become resources for national identification.

In the contemporary political climate, therefore, religious nationalism provides a solution to the problem of Western-style secular politics in a non-Western and multicultural world. As secular ties have begun to unravel in the post-Soviet and post-colonial era, local leaders have searched for new anchors to ground their social identities and political loyalties. Many have turned to religion. They often reach back in history for ancient images and concepts that will give their ideas credibility, but they are not simply resuscitating old ideas from the past. They are providing contemporary ideologies that meet present-day social and political needs.

In the modern context this is a revolutionary notion—that indigenous culture can provide the basis for new political institutions, including revived forms of the nation-state. Since they challenge secular politics in fundamental ways, movements of ethno-religious nationalism are often confrontational and sometimes violent. They reject the intervention of outsiders and their ideologies and, at the risk of being intolerant, pander to their indigenous cultural bases and enforce traditional social boundaries. It is no surprise, then, that they get into trouble with each other and with defenders of the secular state. Yet even such conflicts with secular modernity serve a purpose for the movements: it helps define who they are as a people and who they are not. They are not, for instance, secularists. And they are not pawns in the forces of globalization.

RELIGION AND GLOBALIZATION

Although the members of many radical religious and ethnic groups may appear to fear globalization, what they distrust most are the secular aspects of globalization. They are afraid that global economic forces and cultural values will undercut the legitimacy of their own bases of identity and power. Other aspects of globalization are often perceived by them as neutral, and in some instances, useful for their purposes. Global communications, for instance, provide a vital link between expatriate groups.

Some groups have a global agenda of their own, a transnational alternative to political nationalism. Increasingly terrorist wars have been waged on an international and transnational scale. Osama bin Laden, from his encampment in Afghanistan, once helped to orchestrate acts of terrorism around the world.

These world-wide attacks may be seen as skirmishes in a new Cold War between religious politics and the secular state. It might also be described more dramatically as a "clash of civilizations," as the Harvard political scientist, Samuel Huntington, once termed it. Though most intellectuals disagree with Huntington's characterization of this all-encompassing "we-they" view of the world, the use of the "clash of civilizations" phrase in policy discussions carries with it a kind of self-fulfilling prophecy. When the United States, for instance, acts as if Western civilization is at war with Islamic civilization, this attitude helps to bring about a similar kind of response.

It is interesting that one group of activists who appear to agree with Huntington are Islamic extremists. They contend that they are intrinsically part of Islamic, not Western, civilization, and it is an act of imperialism to think of them in any other way. Proponents of extreme versions of Islamic politics, therefore, often see themselves as a part of a larger, global encounter between Western and Islamic cultures. This view of a "clash of civilizations" although at present confined to the imaginations of Samuel Huntington and a small number of Islamic radicals, might become a dominant theme in the political unrest of the 21st century.

An even more troubling version of this global cultural clash is an apocalyptic one, in which contemporary politics is seen as fulfilling an extraordinary religious vision. Ideas such as this are held by extremists in many religions. Some Messianic Jews, for instance, think that the biblical age that will be ushered in at the time of the return of the Messiah is close at hand. It will occur when the Biblical lands of the West Bank are returned to Jewish control and when the Jerusalem temple described in the Bible is restored on its original site—now occupied by the Muslim shrine, the Dome of the Rock. American Christian political activists such as Jerry Falwell and Pat Robertson have been animated by the idea that the political agenda of a righteous America will help to usher in an era of global redemption. The leader of Japan's Aum Shinrikyo predicted the coming of Armageddon in 1999.

These are trans-national ideas, since they envision the world as caught up in a cosmic confrontation, one that will ultimately lead to a peaceful world order constructed through a dramatic religious transformation. The result of this process is a form of global order radically different than secular versions of globalization, yet it is an ideological confrontation on a global scale.

RELIGION IN THE GLOBAL FUTURE

Emerging movements of religious politics are therefore ambivalent about globalization. To the extent that they are nationalistic they often oppose the global reach of world government, at least in its secular form. But the more visionary of these movements also at times have their own transnational dimensions, and some dream of world domination shaped in their own ideological images. . . .

Each of these futures contains a paradoxical relationship between the national and globalizing aspects of religious politics. This suggests that there is a symbiotic relationship between religion and certain forms of globalization. It may appear ironic, but the globalism of culture and the emergence of transnational political and economic institutions enhance the need for local identities. They also create the desire for a more localized form of authority and social accountability.

The crucial problems in an era of globalization are identity and control. The two are linked, in that a loss of a sense of belonging leads to a feeling of powerlessness. At the same time, what has been perceived as a loss of faith in secular nationalism is experienced as a loss of agency as well as identity. For these reasons the assertion of traditional forms of religious and ethnic identities are linked to attempts to reclaim personal and cultural power. The vicious outbreaks of religious violence that have occurred in Amsterdam, Madrid, and elsewhere in the world in the first decade of the twentieth-first century can be seen as tragic attempts to regain social control through acts of violence. Until there is a surer sense of citizenship in a global order, therefore, religious visions of moral order will continue to appear as attractive though often disruptive solutions to the problems of identity and belonging in a global world.

AL QAEDA AND THE NEW TERRORISTS

Olivier Roy

Al Qaeda is an organisation and a trademark. It can operate directly, in a joint venture, or by franchising. It embodies, but does not have the monopoly of, a new kind of violence. Many groups (such as the Kelkal network in France) are acting along the same lines without necessarily having a direct connection with Al Qaeda. In the pages below we shall concentrate on Al Qaeda but also mention other groups and actors, focusing more on new patterns of Islam-related violence than on Al Qaeda itself.

The strength of Al Qaeda is that it is made up of veterans of the Afghan wars, who know each other and have developed an *esprit de corps* in the Afghan "trenches" (*sangar*) or training camps. This comrade-based solidarity between people from different countries has been translated into a flexible and mobile international organisation where the chain of command duplicates personal ties. The weaknesses of Al Qaeda are, first, that it needs a sanctuary to create such a spirit of brotherhood and, second, that the uprootedness of these militants makes it difficult for them to establish a social and political basis among Muslim populations in areas where they do not benefit from the support of some sort of indigenous subcontractors. . . .

The volunteers were cut off from Afghan society and organised into two categories: an infantry battalion that fought alongside the Taliban against the Northern Alliance, and more gifted Western Muslims were trained to go return to Europe and the United States to perpetrate terrorism. While the initial action of Al Qaeda was the first bombing of the World Trade Center in 1993, it was only in 1998 that it became well known in the West when the creation of the "World Islamic Front for the Struggle against Jews and Crusaders" was announced, followed by the bombings of US embassies in East Africa.

Al Qaeda's first-generation members shared common traits: all came from a Muslim country and had a previous record of political activism; almost all went directly from the Middle East to Afghanistan. They had little experience of the West, and had a traditional way of life (traditional marriages, and their women kept at home).

From the early 1990s a new breed of militants slowly emerged. The change was embodied by two leading figures who participated in anti-US terrorist attacks, namely the first World Trade Center bombing in February 1993, and the attack on the US embassy in Kenya in August 1998. Ramzi Ahmed Yousef was born in 1968 in Kuwait, of a Pakistani father (from Baluchistan) and a Palestinian mother. He did not identify with a given country (although he used to call himself a Pakistani). His name (an alias) means "secret"; it is almost a choice of identity. He was educated at a vocational training school in Wales between 1986 and 1989 under the name Adul Basit Mahmoud Kareem, graduated in electronic engineering, and then went in 1990 to Afghanistan to wage *jihad*. There he met the brother of the founder of the Philippine Abu Sayyaf Group (Janjalani), who invited him to his country. Yousef left for Baghdad, acquired an Iraqi passport, returned to Peshawar, met Ahmed Ajjaj (a Palestinian refugee in the United States), and settled in New Jersey. He left the very day of the first attack against the World Trade Center, stayed in Karachi with an extremist Pakistani anti-Shiite group, the Sipah-e-Sahaba, then returned to the Philippines, where he was involved in a plot to hijack aeroplanes and kill the Pope. Finally he was arraigned in Karachi and extradited to the United States. The second example is Mohamed Saddiq Odeh (Awadh or Howeyda), a Jordanian citizen, born in Saudi Arabia of a Palestinian family. He received a degree in architecture in the Philippines in 1990, was trained in Afghanistan in the same year, and went to Somalia in 1992 to join the Sheikh Hassan radical Islamic group. Odeh married a Kenyan wife, acquired a Yemeni passport, settled in Kenya and was involved in the bombing of the US embassy there in 1998.

This new breed was above all largely uprooted and more westernised than its predecessors, had few links (if any) to any particular Muslim country, and moved around the world, travelling from *jihad* to *jihad*. The flying *jihadi* was born, the *jihadi* jet set.

THE SECOND WAVE: WESTERN MUSLIMS

The second wave of Al Qaeda militants operating internationally was characterised by the breaking of their ties with the "real" Muslim world they claimed to represent. If we exclude most of the Saudis and Yemenis, as well as the "subcontractors" (militants from local organisations that act under the Al Qaeda label in their own country), most Al Qaeda militants left their country of origin to fight or study abroad (usually in the West), breaking with their families. They lived separate from society and rarely integrated with a new community, except around some radical mosques. They were cultural outcasts, in their home countries and their host countries. But they were all westernised in some way (again, except for the Saudis and Yemenis); none had attended a *madrasa*, and all were trained in technical or scientific disciplines and spoke a Western language. If we include the logistical networks, some held Western citizenship (the alleged 9/11 conspirator Zacarias Moussaoui was born in France). Most of them (except, again, the Saudis) became born-again Muslims in the West after living "normal" lives in their countries of origin. The mosques of Hamburg (Al Quds), London (Finsbury Park), Marseilles and even Montreal played a far greater role in their religious radicalisation than any Saudi *madrasa*.

Thus, far from representing a traditional religious community or culture, these militants broke with their past (and some with traditional Islam altogether). They experienced an individual re-Islamisation in a small cell of uprooted fellows, where they forged their own Islam—as vividly illustrated by Muhammad Atta's refusal to be buried according to tradition, which he dubbed un-Islamic. They did not follow any Islamic school or notable cleric, and sometimes lived according to non-Muslim standards. They were all far more products of a westernised Islam than of traditional Middle Eastern politics. However old-fashioned their theology may seem to Westerners, and whatever they may think of themselves, radical Euro-Islamists are clearly more a postmodern phenomenon than a premodern one.

Even if many of these militants come from the Middle East, they are not linked to or used by any Middle Eastern state, intelligence service or radical movement, as had been the case with the militants of the 1980s. With a single, transitional exception, they are part of the deterritorialised, supranational Islamic networks that operate specifically in the West and at the periphery of the Middle East. Their background has nothing to do with Middle Eastern conflicts. Their groups are often mixtures of educated middle-class leaders and working-class dropouts, a pattern common to most West European radicals of the 1970s and 1980s (Germany's Red Army Faction, Italy's Red Brigades, France's Action Directe). Many became "born-again" Muslims or gaolhouse converts, sharing a common marginal culture.

Roughly there are three main categories: students, who came from Middle Eastern countries to study in the West; second-generation Muslims, who were either born in the West or came as infants; and converts. The students (for example, the World Trade Center pilots) are usually middle or upper class, and all were educated in technical or scientific disciplines. The second-generation Muslims emanate from the working class and disfranchised urban youths. The converts are a more complex category. Most of the individuals who gravitate towards these three categories are "new Muslims," either born-again or converts.

We will now try to summarise what these new militants have in common, using a sample based on those individuals involved in or indicted for international terrorism since the 1993 World Trade Center attack. International terrorism is taken to mean attacks that are committed outside the homeland of the perpetrators, and are not state-sponsored.

DETERRITORIALISATION

Our militants operate globally, travelling widely, settling in various countries that have little connection with their homelands and learning foreign languages. Zacarias Moussaoui, a French citizen of Moroccan descent, studied in Montpellier, learnt English and settled in London, where he became a born-again Muslim. Muhammad Atta and the other 9/11 pilots came from the Middle East, settled first in Germany, learnt German, and then went to the United States. Djamel Beghal, who was living in the Paris suburb of Corbeil, settled in Leicester, in the English Midlands. Ahmed Ressam left Algeria, where he was born, for Marseilles and later for Corsica (1992-94), before settling in Montreal, where he scraped a living from casual jobs and theft. He became a born-again Muslim at the As Sunnah mosque and went to Afghanistan in 1998. Back in Montreal, he was contacted by a Mauritanian, Mohambedou Ould Slahi, who funded his preparations to attack Los Angeles International Airport in December 1999. Ould Slahi used to live in Duisburg, Germany, where he attended university and launched an import business.

Al Qaeda is an international organisation, even if its centre till 2001 was in Afghanistan. Its local networks were built with the aim of targeting a specific objective and organised around "hubs," none of which was in a Middle Eastern country. The 9/11 attacks were prepared in Hamburg, Spain and Kuala Lumpur by four students based in Hamburg (an Egyptian, Muhammad Atta; an Emirati, Marwan al-Shehhi; a Yemeni, Ramzi Binalshibh; and a Lebanese, Ziad Jarrah). The members of the Hamburg support cell for 9/11 fitted the same patterns. They met at the Al Quds mosque in Hamburg. London probably served as the main global centre for propaganda and the recruitment of would-be terrorists who were dispatched to Afghanistan.

Relations between militants and their country of origin are weak or non-existent; we are facing not a diaspora but a truly deterritorialised population. Almost none of the militants fought in his own country, or in his family's country of origin (except some Pakistanis). Two cases are especially relevant: those of the Palestinians and the Algerians. One would expect a Western-based born-again Muslim of Algerian or Palestinian origin to be eager to wage *jihad* in his country of origin, both Algeria and Palestine being battlefields. But I do not know of a single instance of such a return from the diaspora. The French Redouane Hammadi and Stephane Ait Idir, of Algerian origin, carried out a terrorist attack in Morocco (1995); Fateh Kamel and Ahmed Ressam (both Algerians) tried to blow up Los Angeles airport. None of the Algerian militants in Al Qaeda came directly from Algeria. Links with Al Qaeda were built up through Algerian immigration, not by way of the GIA's headquarters or other groups within Algeria. Conversely, the campaign of demonstrations in Algeria, from 1999 onwards, has been carried out in the name of democracy, human rights and defence of the Kabyle (Berber) identity, not of *sharia* or an Islamic state.

All of the Palestinians in Al Qaeda (such as Mohamed Odeh and Abu Zubayda) come from refugee families (either from 1948 or 1967). None of them tried to return to Palestinian-Israeli territory There is a trend among uprooted Islamic Palestinians towards a "de-Palestinisation" of their identity in favour of the *ummah,* as is obvious in the Palestinian refugee camp of Ain al-Hilweh, in Lebanon, where Salafi groups are gaining ground, as we saw previously.

The same is true of the Egyptians: how does one explain the discrepancy between the high number of Egyptians in Al Qaeda's leadership and the decrease in religious violence in Egypt? Clearly this time it is the leadership inside Egypt that has cut links with the internationalists.

Some personal trajectories are particularly instructive in highlighting the internationalisation of Islamist militants. Ramzi Ahmed Yousef's life has already been discussed. Mohammed Mansour Jabarah, who was born in Kuwait, went to Canada when he was twelve years old and later became a Canadian citizen. He was allegedly the intermediary between Al Qaeda and Jemaah Islamiah in Indonesia. It is interesting to note that (as was the case with Khalid Sheikh Mohammed and Abu Zubayda, other Al Qaeda Kuwaitis) he never attempted an operation in Kuwait. Amor Sliti, a Tunisian-born Belgian citizen, was a frequent worshipper at the Finsbury Park mosque in London, spent years in Afghanistan with Bin Laden, and helped the murderers of the anti-Taliban commander Massoud to travel to Afghanistan. Sliti married a Belgian woman and gave his very young daughter in marriage to an Afghan *mujahid.*

Wadih el-Hage, a US citizen, has been indicted for helping in the attacks on the East African US embassies in 1998. A Lebanese Christian who converted to Islam, el-Hage also lived for a while in Kuwait and went to the United States in 1978 to study city planning at South-Western Louisiana University. He married an American, fathered seven children, and went off to help the *mujahedin* fight the Soviet Union. Then, in the early 1990s, he worked in Sudan as Bin Laden's secretary. By 1994 el-Hage had moved to Kenya and helped to establish an Al Qaeda cell in Nairobi—the same unit that allegedly plotted the embassy bombing there. El-Hage returned home in 1997 and took a low-level job as manager of the Lone Star Wheels and Tires shop in Fort Worth, Texas. Also indicted in the case was Ali Mohamed, a major in the Egyptian army. He went to the United States in 1986 and continued his military career. He joined the US army and was eventually assigned to the John F. Kennedy Special Warfare Center at Fort Bragg, North Carolina. Within a year of his 1989 discharge, he was training Al Qaeda members in Afghanistan and Sudan and travelling the world for Bin Laden, delivering messages and conducting financial transactions.

Born March 1960 at El-Harrach, in the suburbs of Algiers, Fateh Kamel moved to France, and later settled in Canada in 1987. He took citizenship, married a woman (Nathalie B.) from Gaspé, Quebec, and opened a business in Montreal, importing Cuban cigars. Kamel went to Afghanistan in 1990 and then to Bosnia, where he met members of the Roubaix gang. He was extradited from Jordan to France in April 1999 for allegedly being the "*emir*" of the Roubaix network.

L'Houssaine Kherchtou, born in Morocco in 1964, went to Corsica after graduating from university, settled in Milan where he headed the Islamic cultural centre, and went to Afghanistan in 1991. He was arrested in Kenya for his role in the 1998 attack on the US embassy there.

Beyond these examples, a general rule is that, except for a few Pakistanis and Yemenis, no Al Qaeda member left Europe or the United States to fight for Islam in his homeland or that of his family. As we have seen, none of the Algerians involved in international Al Qaeda terrorism came from a GIA stronghold in Algeria; they all became radicalised in Europe (like Ahmed Ressam). The foreigners sentenced in Yemen in January 1999 for kidnapping included six British citizens of Pakistani descent (including the son-in-law of Abu Hamza, the Egyptian-born former *imam* of the Finsbury Park mosque) and two French Algerians. No Britons of Yemeni descent were involved in the case. The two young Muslims sentenced in Morocco for shooting tourists in a Marrakech hotel in 1994 were from French Algerian families. Omar Saeed Sheikh, convicted in Pakistan for the kidnapping of Daniel Pearl, is a British-born citizen of the United Kingdom. He is one of the few who returned to his family's country of origin.

All these examples bear out how activists of Middle Eastern origin have hardly ever undertaken missions in the region or with a regional objective. They have struck global targets, in most cases from the West.

RELIGION AND HUMANE GLOBAL GOVERNANCE

Richard Falk

Nothing has shocked, angered, and confused the modern, secular sensibility more than the return of religion to the mainstream of political life in an array of settings around the world. Mocking both our capacity to overcome our past and anticipate our future, this religious resurgence converges with an era of unprecedented and radical technological innovation that is also subverting the sensibility and lifeworld of modernity in ways that we are only beginning to realize. Such a start for the new millennium presents both extraordinary opportunities for enhancing the material and spiritual life of peoples inhabiting the planet and severe dangers to the well-being, and even the survival, of the human species. Among the ironies of the present is this strange mixture of technological dynamism that exceeds the most grandiose promises of the Enlightenment and a new wave of skepticism directed toward the role of science and reason in shaping our sense of reality.

The religious resurgence comes in many forms, not all welcome but certainly not all an occasion of regret, much less menace. To the extent that the new wave of religion is animated mainly by negative spiritual energy, that is, by unconditional and extreme moves to negate the modern, it tends to be destructive of human potentiality, to deny freedom, to claim an exclusive access to truth, to be regressively otherworldly in its promises of salvation, and to fail to provide humanity with positive ways forward. It revives a widespread sense among moderate sensibilities that organized religion is an obstacle to be overcome. But there are other more positive and emancipatory energies also contained in this renewal of religion that are associated with a reaffirmation of the spiritual sense of the person, a feeling for the sacred and the mystery that lies at the heart of human existence, an embrace of human solidarity, and a recognition that spiritual longing and religious tradition can take many authentic forms that offer us many evocative metaphors for truth and ultimate concern that no human agency can grasp with infallibility.

Undoubtedly, part of this recent lure of religion is as an antidote to the homogenizing impacts of the false universalism and runaway consumerism associated with a new post-Marxist economism that represents the latest phase of capitalism and is an ambitious project of the West to establish the first world megacivilization under its dominion. The United States occupies a special role in this unfolding global drama, being the main source of the most innovative market practices, the most active purveyor of a new economistic global ideology, and the toughest and most adept guarantor of "law and order" by virtue of its planetary military prowess and its interventionary diplomacy. It is in America that this battlefield among creativity, species suicide, and religious awakening is likely to be fought out in the decades ahead, for it is on its frontiers that the revolutionary transformations of biotechnology, genetic engineering, robotics, and molecular electronics are likely first to present profound and dramatic questions about identity and existence. Of course such a struggle over identities and fundamental issues will resonate throughout the world and cannot be confined, or even centered, within a particular territorial domain, however powerful.

Who are we? Can we control the machines that we have developed? Do we even want to have at our disposal such awesome power to extend life, to design human beings, to download software and hardware in such a way to fulfill dreams (and nightmares) of omnipotence and immortality? Should we impose limits on inquiry and application, thereby challenging the most basic affirmation of the Enlightenment heritage, the freedom to inquire and to know? How shall we strike a new balance between freedom and regulation? What boundaries shall identify the authority structures of the future? And what institutions shall administer laws and dispense justice? The primitive form of these questions is currently raised in relation to such matters as intellectual property rights on the Internet and off-shore money laundering and tax havens. The state is groping for new modes of regulatory effectiveness in this era of diminished territoriality, at least for money and elites. But these issues are but foretastes of what lies ahead, a time when human cloning will pose a choice between upholding the autonomy of human evolution as we have previously understood it and a societally managed evolutionary process that will almost inevitably make eugenics the queen of the sciences. We face choices also about the outer limits of artificial intelligence, the brilliant robot that can be sent on lethal missions, or worse, robot armies and air forces that can be programmed to devastate a less-developed adversary without risk or casualty. Do we not need desperately a spiritual ground from which to pose such questions before they are foreclosed by technological momentum, decisions behind closed doors, and economic/political ambition?

On one level the relation of religion to these emergent economic, political, and cultural forces is a reflexive flourish that expresses hysteria and little else. A Greek Orthodox cleric, Archbishop Christodoulos' *cri de coeur* is typical: "Resist, my dear Christians, the forces of globalization and religious marginalization are out to get you." The struggle, so conceived, is mindlessly against modernity itself rather than against its menacing extremities and an accompanying false universalism that is globe-encircling. Those who demonstrated in the streets of Seattle against the inequities of globalization, which they attributed to the World Trade Organization (WTO) (and its sibling institutions, the World Bank and the International Monetary Fund [IMF]), and who vandalized a McDonald's in France shared the simplistic view that it is possible and desirable to hold back the march of history by postures of defiance. . . . Neither the disease nor the cure are so obvious, we must look deeply into our individual and collective past, and we need to fashion visions of a preferred future that can mobilize the positive energies of humanity in whatever religious, cultural, or political form they assume. Because the globalizing reality is undeniable, the moment for a critical ethical ecumenism has arrived. The critical element ensures that only those ethical orientations that are consistent with the broad premises of a human rights culture are affirmed. Precisely because this ecumenical moment has arrived, there is widespread fear, foreboding, and a disposition to retreat into the closed and rigid structures of the past, both a traditionalist past and a blinkered secularism that represents a degeneration of the modern impulse toward freedom, reason, and autonomy.

The complexity of the challenge arises because it is not usefully reducible to either the dualisms of good and evil or the assured remedies of this or that fundamentalism. It is neither possible to affirm unconditionally the main tendencies of modernity, including ideas about sovereignty, the territorial state, and the right of self-determination on the political sensibility, nor useful to pretend that such defining categories have been superseded by such fashionable phrases as "the end of the nation-state," "the borderless world," "a new medievalism," or "the end of history." More suitable for the age are such ideas as that of "negative capability," associated with the musing of the English poet John Keats, who thought of a mature mind as one that did not press for answers prematurely. Being able to accept uncertainty as the outer limit of knowability is an emphasis that has been featured in the postmodernist insistence that most of human life consists of choices that are by their nature "undecidable." Also helpful are Eastern patterns of thought, perhaps most fully and clearly embodied in the Hindu worldview, which affirms that opposites coexist in experienced reality and cannot be eliminated without generating crippling distortions. Such notions are not easily accepted in the West, which has premised its development on a classical Greek heritage that was itself built upon an either/or foundation for knowledge, thought, action, and belief. There are two elements here that are easily confounded. The first is that the human mind, capable of so much that is ingenious, is also at a loss when it comes to grasping the fullness of reality. The second is that the rationalistic device of dividing choices into dualisms creates an illusion about the comprehension of alternatives but is reductive and essentialist in actuality, pretending that reality can be adequately understood to be either "this" or "that."

THE WAY FORWARD: EXPLORATION, COLLABORATION, AND RECONCILIATION

The historical circumstances of religious revival, postcolonial rediscoveries of identity and claims for redress of past grievance, secularist self-doubts, and a variety of ideas and practices encompassed by the terminology of globalization are conditioning our under-standing of world order and shaping alternative paths to the future. There are significant unifying circumstances arising from the global scope of telecommunications, solidarity in actions designed to reduce human suffering, a consensus about sustaining life prospects on the planet, and a willingness to affirm abstract adherence to human rights and democracy as the basis for legitimate governance.

Widespread efforts to reclaim non-Western civilizational identities involve an encouraging project to reach back in cultural history past the experiences of modernity and forward beyond the constraints of nationalism, statism, and a Western conception of progress and fulfillment. Such explorations are complemented by important experiments in regionalism, economic restructuring, and political and cultural relations on the basis of wider affinities that are rooted partly in pragmatic concerns about economic gains and security. These regional undertakings also incorporate shared ethical principles and values that provide the foundation for a political community that is wider than the statist demarcations of community under the Westphalian regime and yet narrower than the false universalism of schemes for unifying the world under a single source of authority or an exaggerated view of the impact of technology. Religions are part of this dynamic of regional self-exploration, creating transnational bonds and affinities that extend beyond state, nation, tribe, ethnic community, and language group.

In every respect, such developments partake of ambiguity and contradiction. The regional and the civilizational perspectives also create openings for exclusivist interpretations of the historical and human situation. It is plausible to construct a vision of the future based on the "West against the rest" that organizes a fragment of humanity to take part in intercivilizational warfare. It is also plausible to view the West as the "Great

Satan" that must be destroyed as the precondition for self-realization throughout the planet.

My idea . . . is to take a stand in favor of collaboration and reconciliation, but not with sentimental hopes that conflict will disappear or that humane institutions for global governance can be agreed upon in the years immediately ahead. Instead, the positive inclusive tendencies in secularism and religious outlooks need to bond, without subverting their distinctive forms of attentiveness to human suffering and aspiration, in the course of defining "humane globalization" for all peoples in the world. In this respect, the rigid separation of politics and religion that is under attack by conservatives in the West and is being supported by liberals needs to be reinterpreted at a time when various civilizations are both mingling in shared geographic space and searching for their own autonomy. Whether secularists like it or not, the questions just over the technological horizon are "religious" in character, reminding us of the dangers and temptations associated with going beyond prior limit conditions that have for centuries expressed the outer contours of human existence. These contours have included anthropocentrism in relation to natural surroundings and the products of human intelligence. What lies ahead are scenarios of blurred limitations and unavoidable soul-searching and, more mundanely, challenges about how to address current inequities, grievances, and survival risks. It is bound to be an exciting period that will shake the foundations of consumerism, the McWorld, and materialist worldviews, but it is also a menacing period that will generate idolatrous temptations to mechanize the fundaments of life itself, as well as give rise to death-oriented and salvationist cults that herald the end of the world.

At such times of turmoil, it is helpful to stand back and yet hold fast, affirming a commitment to work together while respecting the needs of the peoples of the world to consider separately what sort of future their specific heritages most favors at this point. And yet not fall into new traps of civilizational and religiously grounded essentialism. Every collective identity is itself plural in its memories, perceptions, and potentialities and needs to address inner tensions as urgently as its relations with the domineering threat of renewed Western hegemony. And of course, the West, least of all, is exempt from this imperative to reconsider its identity under the pressure of criticism from without and from explosive prospects within, especially those associated with developments on the technological frontiers. . . .

[This] depicts a starting point that is responsive to dangers, potentialities, hopes, and dreams that are not normally incorporated into the study of world politics, or even emphasized in the more normative offerings of world order studies. It implicitly questions whether the premises of international relations can any longer be usefully comprehended by a reliance on realism, liberalism, Marxism, constructivism, and idealism, even taking account of their variability in and adaptability to a changing global setting. If its own orientation must be categorized, it comes closest to being a form of *reconstructive postmodernism*, that is, a post-Westphalian perspective that is informed by ethical values and spiritual belief.

FURTHER READING

Aslan, Reza. 2009. *How to Win a Cosmic War: God, Globalization, and the End of the War on Terror*. New York: Random House.

Calhoun, Craig, Mark Juergensmeyer, and Jonathan VanAntwerpen (Eds.). 2011. *Rethinking Secularism*. New York: Oxford University Press.

Crockett, Clayton (Ed.). 2006. *Religion and Violence in a Secular World*. Charlottesville: University of Virginia Press.

Hassner, Ron. 2009. *War on Sacred Grounds*. Ithaca, NY: Cornell University Press.

Falk, Richard. 2001. *Religion and Humane Global Governance*. New York: Palgrave Macmillan.

Juergensmeyer, Mark. 2003. *Terror in the Mind of God: The Global Rise of Religious Violence*. Berkeley: University of California Press.

Juergensmeyer, Mark. 2008. *Global Rebellion: Religious Challenges to the Secular State*. Berkeley: University of California Press.

Kippenberg, Hans. 2012. *Violence as Worship: Religious Wars in the Age of Globalization*. Stanford: Stanford University Press.

Lincoln, Bruce. 2002. *Holy Terrors: Thinking About Religion after September 11, 2001*. Chicago: University of Chicago Press.

Roy, Olivier. 2006. *Globalized Islam: The Search for a New Ummah*. New York: Columbia University Press.

Toft, Monica Duffy, Daniel Philpott, and Timothy Shah. 2011. *God's Century: Resurgent Religion and Global Politics*. New York: Norton.

Wellman, James K.(Ed.). 2007. *Belief and Bloodshed: Religion and Violence across Time and Tradition*. Lanham, MD: Rowman and Littlefield.

Van der Berg, Peter. 1994. *Religious Nationalism: Hindus and Muslims in India*. Berkeley: University of California Press.

13

TRANSNATIONAL ECONOMY AND GLOBAL LABOR

When the term *globalization* is used, it often means economic globalization—and not just economic globalization in general. Those who use the term often have a certain kind of globalization in mind—the spread of corporate capitalism around the world. So when people argue about whether globalization is a good thing, often what they're really talking about is whether global corporate capitalism is a good thing. They are arguing about the way that transnational corporations affect society in different parts of the world. This controversial subject often does not present a very pretty picture, especially if sweatshops and environmental damage are involved.

But globalization is about much more than corporate capitalism, as the many different topics in this book show; globalization also involves culture, communications, political and ideological changes, and much more. Even economic globalization is much more complicated than simply the rise of transnational corporations. It involves the globalization of manufacturing; the distribution, ownership, and control of goods and services; and the globalization of financial instruments and investments. Ultimately, it leads to a major transformation in the way in which global business is conducted.

Let's take an example. Let's say that back in the old days, the owners of company A in country X had a factory that made something—it could be tennis shoes, for instance. They made the shoes and then looked for someone to buy a bunch of them, and that someone, in turn, would sell the shoes to their customers. Company A would sell their tennis shoes to department stores and individual shoe stores, and the stores would sell them to us. It was a pretty simple arrangement. Probably most of their business was in their home country, country X, but they might also ship some of their tennis shoes abroad to countries Y and Z to be sold there. Since everything was made in country X, anything related to the manufacturing and finances of the company would be regulated by the laws of that country.

In the new pattern, things are quite different. For one thing, company A likely doesn't have any factories. It might operate out of an office in a high-rise building in some place like Wilshire Boulevard in Los Angeles. And its owners might employ a team to design its tennis shoes. Company A will take that design and a business plan and try to get a contract from a major marketer, such as Wal-Mart Stores, Inc., that sells consumer items through retail outlets known as Walmart. Or, just as frequently, Wal-Mart may come to company A and specify what kind of tennis shoes it would like to sell, and if everyone agrees, they have a deal. As soon as company A has a contract to manufacture the shoes it will go looking for a factory somewhere in the world to make tennis shoes like the ones they designed, as cheaply and efficiently as possible. The tennis shoe factory that company A decides to use may be in its own country, the United States, for example. But it is just as likely that it will find a cheaper and more efficient factory somewhere else, say China. If it does, then it will outsource the manufacture of these tennis shoes to a factory in China. But it might also bargain with a factory in Bangladesh, which may offer even cheaper labor and a lower price to construct and ship the tennis shoes back to United States. Or part of the tennis shoes may be made in factories in China—the soles of the shoes, perhaps—and then the half-finished items are sent to Nicaragua, where the cloth and leather tops are manufactured and attached to the soles before the completely assembled tennis shoes are sent back to United States (and to other countries elsewhere around the world). Now that company A has the tennis shoes, they are ready to sell them, either by themselves online, or to a retail giant like Wal-Mart that will sell them in stores to us. Added to the complication is that company A may not be wholly owned and registered in the United States. It might be registered in Panama for tax purposes and use ocean liners registered in Liberia for shipping purposes, and its board of directors and capital investors may come from all over the world.

Sound confusing? It is. This is the nature of economic activity in an era of globalization. Everything is made everywhere, owned and controlled everywhere, and distributed everywhere. Everyone, it seems, has a hand in making and selling those innocent little tennis shoes.

Now that you understand how it works, you probably have already thought of some potential complications. How do you make sure that countries won't levy taxes on the shoes when the factories ship them back to United States? And how do you keep China and Bangladesh from creating tariffs to keep the tennis shoes from being sold in their countries? This is where trade agreements and a whole new organization—the World Trade Organization (WTO)—come in. The WTO was created to encourage agreements that will facilitate trade and provide for some kind of monitoring of the situation to make sure the agreements work. The WTO tries to regulate these things, but their enforcement mechanisms are not very strong. They don't have an army standing behind them, and they can't throw companies in jail.

A couple of other issues you may have imagined have even weaker controls. Since company A is searching the world for the cheapest way to make their tennis shoes, this means that the winning country is likely to be the one that has the cheapest labor—Bangladesh, for instance. This may be a good deal for company A and the leaders of Bangladesh, but not such a good deal for the laborers, especially if they are worked to the bone for very little return. What kind of monitoring and enforcement mechanism exists to ensure labor standards, a minimum wage, and workers' safety and health benefits and to prohibit child labor? And what kind of controls are in place to keep factories around the world from polluting the air and abusing the environment?

The answers to these questions are even less comforting than the questions themselves. The fact is that very few international agencies monitor labor and environmental standards and demand that minimum expectations be met. In a global era in general, the problems are those of accountability and control. Yet the public is often angry when they hear about sweatshops and environmental degradation. Sometimes they take out their frustration on the WTO.

To the surprise of the representatives of the WTO when they convened in Seattle in 1999, they were met by masses of protestors. And protestors have gathered outside every meeting of the WTO since then. The protests have focused on a variety of things—including workers' rights, wages and working conditions, and environmental problems that the protestors think are caused by the global economy. They protest at the meetings of the WTO—which is not an international government and is only a forum for negotiating agreements—largely because there is nowhere else for them to protest. There is no single country or center of economic control that can enforce these labor and environmental standards globally.

Transnational social movements have organized to try to counter some of these perceived excesses. The most effective ones try to mobilize consumers and the public through the news media to put pressure on companies that allow sweatshop labor and substandard conditions; others attempt to establish international standards through the United Nations and other global organizations. At times they do make a difference. Since we are speaking of tennis shoes, it is interesting to note that several years ago the Nike tennis shoe company responded to a public outcry over news about sweatshop conditions in some of the Chinese factories that made their shoes. Nike established a code of conduct for the factories and hired an independent monitoring agency to regularly check to make sure that those labor and environment standards are upheld.

The first reading in this section is on outsourcing and why it is a central part of the commodity chain production in the global marketplace. The author, Richard Appelbaum, is a professor of sociology and global studies at the University of California, Santa Barbara, and has been active in the anti-sweatshop movement. He was instrumental in getting the University of California system to require that all clothing items that used the university logo be certified as sweatshop-free. This reading is followed by an essay on Wal-Mart by Nelson Lichtenstein, a labor historian who also teaches at UC–Santa Barbara. He asserts that the marketing giant has become the emblematic company of our generation, not only because of its size—it is the largest private employer in the world—but also because of its efficient use of transnational outsourcing and commodity chains to create low-price merchandising in a highly profitable way.

The next reading raises the question of who is "us" when Americans ask whether they benefit from the global economy. Robert Reich, U.S. Secretary of Labor during the Clinton administration, argues that the "us" is the American labor force. For this reason he would rather see foreign corporations, such as Honda, employ American workers to build their automobiles in the United States than to see American companies such as General Motors make their automobiles abroad with foreign labor.

The last two readings in this section raise large issues regarding the global economic system and how to manage it. Jagdish Bhagwati, an economist who was raised in India and now teaches at Columbia University, provides a defense of globalization. Or, rather, he regards the global economic system as an inevitable development of the technological and political circumstances of our times and thinks there are benefits to be had from it as well as problems to be overcome. In this excerpt, taken from an afterword appended to his book *In Defense of Globalization*, Bhagwati argues that global trade is conducive to economic development and that the changes in demand for labor are due as much to the increased technological proficiency that is needed as to globalization. Bhagwati has been an economic advisor to the World Trade Organization and he serves on the advisory board of Human Rights Watch.

The final reading is by Joseph Stiglitz, a Nobel Prize–winning economist who teaches at Columbia University and was once the chief economist at the World Bank. The reading in this section is an excerpt from the closing section of his book, *Globalization and Its Discontents*. As the title suggests, Stiglitz is less optimistic than Bhagwati about the positive benefits accrued by economic globalization. Though he admits that it can be a force for good, he also acknowledges that the global economic system has had a negative impact on many people, lowering their standard of living and destroying traditional lifestyles. Yet he does not regard the situation as hopeless. Instead he encourages reforms in the way countries deal with global corporations and changes in the international institutions that manage them, including the World Trade Organization, the International Monetary Fund, and the World Bank. He encourages policies that would promote a sustainable, equitable, democratic growth that would allow globalization to do what it does, but to have an impact on societies "with a more human face."

OUTSOURCING

Richard Appelbaum

Outsourcing—sometimes referred to as subcontracting—involves a firm's use of an external vendor to provide a business function that would otherwise be done by the firm itself. While the practice has long been commonplace, since the 1970s outsourcing has increasingly been done on a global scale. Firms from advanced industrial countries have outsourced many of their manufacturing operations—along with services such as accounting and call centers—to lower-wage countries around the globe. Outsourcing has been facilitated both by advances in information technology, which has made it possible to coordinate suppliers of goods and services across a global space, and by containerization, which enables goods to be quickly and efficiently transported by sea and land.

Cutting labor costs is a major reason for outsourcing. In manufacturing, for example, the wage gap between advanced industrial countries such as the United States, Germany, or Japan—and an impoverished developing country in Asia, Africa, or Latin America—can be significant. In Bangladesh manufacturing workers (if paid the legal minimum wage) might earn $30–$50 a month; in the U.S., comparable minimum-wage earnings would be $1,200. Labor cost differentials, of course, do not directly equate to cost savings: workers in developing countries may be less skilled, and thus produce fewer goods per hour; quality may suffer; and transportation costs for goods shipped long distances by sea or air have to be factored in. Increased efficiency is another reason for outsourcing: a company can focus on its key competency—for example, designing cell phones—and outsource manufacturing and assembly to other firms that are more specialized in such functions. Outsourcing can also provide access to new knowledge, intellectual property, and, more generally, a global talent pool, providing access to new skills and competencies. Tax and other economic incentives can be a factor; many developing countries offer "tax holidays" and supportive infrastructure in export processing zones where foreign firms can use local factories. Finally, easier access to markets can also be an important reason for outsourcing: partly for this reason, Japanese automobile manufacturers such as Toyota have opened assembly plants in the U.S., while many multinational corporations are now manufacturing in China in hopes of selling their products to that country's large and growing middle class.

CHANGING FORMS OF GLOBAL OUTSOURCING: FROM PRODUCER- TO
BUYER-DRIVEN GLOBAL COMMODITY CHAINS

Outsourcing often involves global supplier networks that are governed or coordinated by a central firm. These activities—which typically involve low-cost manufacturing, but which may also include financial and other services—are often thought of as links in a chain; they are variously described as comprising "supply chains" or "commodity chains." The term "supply chain," which is prominent in the business literature, emphasizes the role that different firms play as suppliers of key inputs for a final product, and has given rise to a field of study concerned with supply chain management. The term "commodity chain" refers to those networks of labor and production processes that result in a finished commodity. Sociologist Gary Gereffi distinguishes between producer-driven commodity chains, characteristic of capital-intensive (heavy manufacturing) industries such as automobiles, aircraft, computers, semiconductors, and heavy machinery, and buyer-driven commodity chains, in which large retailers and larger brands set up decentralized production networks in low-wage exporting countries, characteristic of labor-intensive (light manufacturing) industries such as apparel, footwear, toys, and consumer electronics.

Producer-driven commodity chains are governed by large manufacturers: while the parent company may engage in some outsourcing, much of its production is done "in house," literally under its own roof. Such commodity chains tend to be vertically integrated, in that the parent firm centrally controls most of their operations; as a result they tended to be bureaucratically inflexible, slow to respond to changing market conditions. Large factories house large numbers of workers, who are often organized into trade unions; the ability of unions to bargain for wages and benefits—backed up by the threat (and sometimes reality) of a strike, which can shut down the entire industry—results in significant wage gains for workers in advanced industrial nations. Producer-driven commodity chains were a key organizational form during the mid-twentieth century; large automobile manufacturers, such as Ford or General Motors, were typical.

Buyer-driven commodity chains, on the other hand, are governed by large retailers (Wal-Mart is a prominent example), or large brands (Nike and Apple are prime examples). Unlike the manufacturers that govern producer-driven commodity chains, these retailers and brands do not actually make their own products; rather, they are best thought of as "branded marketers" who design products and create a market based on product image and recognition. Sociologist Gary Hamilton has aptly described such firms as "market makers"; their actual manufacturing takes place in a global network set of independently owned and operated contract factories that purchase raw materials, employ the workers, and oversee production. Such commodity chains are horizontally integrated, with the parent firm outsourcing to a large number of competing contract factories. This, in turn, provides greater organizational flexibility, in that the parent firm can respond to changing market conditions by simply changing its roster of subcontractors. Contract factories in buyer-driven commodity chains can range in size from a handful of workers, to giant firms that house a hundred thousand or more workers. (Foxcomm, a Taiwanese firm that provides electronics for Apple, Dell, Sony, Microsoft, Amazon, and Nintendo, among others, employs more than 400,000 workers in one South China factory complex.)

Producer-driven commodity chains remain important, but their importance relative to buyer-driven commodity chains has declined since the mid-twentieth century, when multinational manufacturers played the dominant role in coordinating worldwide production networks. Wal-Mart long ago surpassed General Motors and other manufacturing firms as the world's largest non energy-related corporation (the largest oil companies, Shell and ExxonMobil, are only slightly larger).

UPGRADING

Although production networks span the globe, value is not added equally at all locations. In the mid-twentieth century significant value was added during the manufacturing—value which was in part captured by factory workers, whose rising wages in the U.S. and Europe enabled many to achieve middle class status. Today, major value is added by design, branding, and marketing—activities which are located in advanced industrial economies. Manufacturing, globally dispersed to competing factories in developing economies, is no longer a principal source of added value, and therefore does not pay high wages. One 2007 Sloan Foundation study of the value-added by the Apple iPod's 451 different components concluded that more than half of the $299 retail value remained in the U.S., realized by Apple and its distributors—even though almost all of the components manufacture occurred in Asia. Although the final assembly occurred in China, Chinese workers contributed only an estimated one percent of the total value added.

One advantage of globally dispersed outsourcing is that supplier firms can sometimes upgrade their capabilities, moving into higher value-added activities. Upgrading is achieved when a firm that initially engages in the manufacture of a single component acquires the knowledge and skills to begin designing those components. Upgrading also occurs when a contractor moves from making a single component to "full package production"—providing the full range of goods and services associated with manufacturing a particular commodity. This has been especially common in production in the footwear and apparel industries, where a single firm—typically from South Korea, Taiwan, Hong Kong, or China—can take an order from a U.S. or European brand and assemble all the components necessary to produce a complete finished athletic shoe or line of clothing. Finally, upgrading occurs when a firm moves from simpler to more technologically complex products, or from simpler to more sophisticated production systems. All forms of upgrading involve "organizational learning"—the ability of a firm to learn from its experiences in a global production network, often from the firms for which it is providing inputs.

To take one example, Yue Yuen, a subsidiary of the Taiwanese company Pou Chen, is the world's largest manufacturer of athletic shoes: its factories in China, Vietnam, and Indonesia produce more than 250 million pairs a year for leading global brands such as Nike, Adidas, Reebok, New Balance, and Puma. Yue Yuen, which accounts for a sixth of the global branded athletic shoe and casual footwear market, has its own research and development facilities, produces many of the chemicals and raw materials used in its shoe components, makes many of its own tools, and even handles logistics for its customers. It has even developed a network of retail outlets throughout China. The company has "learned through doing," and some day may challenge Nike and its other clients, becoming its own designer and retailer of athletic shoes, particularly for the large and growing Chinese market.

THE CHANGING GEOGRAPHY OF PRODUCTION

While global outsourcing historically has involved networks of many small suppliers, a pattern seems to be emerging: the consolidation of suppliers into a smaller number of large, powerful East Asian firms that are better equipped to work with the larger orders placed by major brands and retailers. Nike places its athletic shoe orders with Yue Yuen, mentioned above; Polo Ralph Lauren, Liz Claiborne, Limited, Express, Victoria's Secret, Fast Retailing, Dillard's and Debenhams place apparel orders with the multinational Luen Thai Holdings, whose "supply chain city" in Dongguan, China includes a two-million square foot factory, a 300-room hotel, a dormitory for the factory's workers, and product-development centers. (Significantly, in 2004 Yue Yuen and Luen Thai announced a "strategic alliance" to develop sports apparel for the global market.) And, as noted previously, every major electronics brand sources from the Taiwanese giant Foxcomm. The emergence of giant transnational contractors, as suppliers for giant retailers and brands, is a relatively recent phenomenon; the fact that these contractors are often Taiwanese and Chinese is especially significant, since it suggests a possible change in the power dynamic between the "big buyers" and their suppliers. Large multinational contractors may come to offer a counterweight to the growing power of companies such as Wal-Mart, Nike, and Apple—and, if that proves to be the case, that will also portend a geographic economic shift to Asia. As such giant contractors engage in upgrading and knowledge acquisition, they may also develop their own brands, becoming competitors with the companies they currently supply.

IMPLICATIONS FOR LABOR RIGHTS

Critics of globalization see outsourcing as a key cause of what they term the "global race to the bottom"—the ability of firms to outsource the provision of goods and services to the lowest-wage sites in the world, such that if workers in one location achieve (or even demand) improvements in wages or working conditions, businesses will simply relocate their outsourced operations to more "business-friendly" factories elsewhere. Global competition between contractors competing for orders is a key factor in keeping labor costs down, since any factory that cannot not meet the price requirements of its buyers risks losing business to another factory down the street or around the globe. This dynamic has also discouraged efforts by workers to form independent trade unions, since unionized shops are vulnerable to losing their contracts. Furthermore, in the absence of binding international law (or even norms) governing outsourcing, firms that engage in outsourcing are not legally liable for problems that occur in their subcontracted factories.

When most production occurred "in house" in a manufacturers' home country, the government could enforce labor laws. But in a highly globalized network of contract factories, there are no comparable international bodies to monitor factories and assure that wages and working conditions are equitable. Consumers, with mixed results, sometimes put pressure on retailers and brands to require their contract factories to adhere to basic labor standards. Students in some 200 colleges and universities have developed codes of conduct designed to insure that products bearing the campus logo sold are made in a decent working environment. Such efforts are hampered, however, by the globally dispersed nature of outsourced production, which makes monitoring of thousands of factories virtually impossible. It is possible, however, that as production becomes consolidated in fewer, larger factories, it will be easier to monitor and enforce labor standards.

WAL-MART: TEMPLATE FOR 21ST CENTURY CAPITALISM?

Nelson Lichtenstein

Giant corporations are the most important institutions shaping the character of world capitalism. As Peter Drucker, the founder of modern management science, put it nearly 60 years ago, the great corporations of our time are "the representative social actuality" shaping the general condition of "modern industrial society." The "emergence of Big Business as a social reality during the past fifty years is the most important event in the recent social history of the Western world." He wrote all that in 1945, but his understanding is just as true today, if on a scale that includes not only the West, but the East and global South as well.

In each historical epoch a prototypical enterprise embodies a new and innovative set of technological advances, organizational structures, and social relationships. They become the "template" economic institutions of their time and place. By template, we mean not just the internal organization of the business, or the character of the market it taps or creates, but the entire range of economic, social, and political transmutations generated by a particularly successful form of business enterprise. These template businesses are emulated because they have perfected for their era the most efficient and profitable relationship between the technology of production, the organization of work, and the new shape of the market. Thus at the end of the 19th century the Pennsylvania Railroad declared itself "the standard of the world." In the mid-twentieth century, General Motors symbolized sophisticated, bureaucratic management, and technologically proficient mass production. When Peter Drucker wrote *The Concept of the Corporation* in 1945 it was the General Motors organization, from the Flint assembly line to the executive offices in Detroit, that exemplified corporate modernity in all its variegated aspects. And in more recent years, first IBM and then Microsoft has seemed the template for an information economy that has transformed the diffusion and production of knowledge around the globe.

At the dawn of the twenty-first century Wal-Mart has emerged as just the kind of world transforming economic institution Peter Drucker analyzed at the end of World War II. As even a casual glance at the newspapers and television makes overwhelmingly clear, Wal-Mart is an inescapable touchstone for so many of the social, urban, labor, and global issues that confront 21st century Americans. In California, where Wal-Mart's actual footprint is still tiny, the expectation that this corporation will build scores of giant new "supercenters" has generated one high profile conflict after another. A bitter, four-month grocery strike that began in the fall of 2003 was provoked by Wal-Mart's downward competitive pressure on the old-line supermarkets. In April 2004, Inglewood residents won their 15 minutes of fame when that majority black and Latino city voted down a Wal-Mart sponsored referendum, designed to pave the way for construction of a huge supercenter. Then, in August 2004, the Los Angeles city council enacted an ordinance requiring "big box" stores like Wal-Mart to fund an "economic impact" analysis to determine their effect on community wages, existing businesses, and traffic patterns. The next month the Democratically-controlled legislature passed a similar law designed to apply to the entire state, but Governor Schwarzenegger vetoed the bill. And while all this was going on, a San Francisco judge gave the Berkeley-based Impact Fund permission to seek higher pay and back pay for more than a million women workers at Wal-Mart, in the largest class action employment discrimination suit ever certified by a federal court.

Founded just over 40 years ago by Sam Walton and his brother Bud, this Bentonville, Arkansas, company is today the largest profit making enterprise in the world, with sales of more than a quarter of a trillion dollars, and 1.4 million employees. As of the end of 2003 it had 4,688 stores worldwide, about 80 percent of them in the United States. Twenty million shoppers visit its stores each day and more than four out of five U.S. households purchase at least some products from the retailer each year. It does more business than Target, Sears, Kmart, J.C. Penney, Safeway, and Kroger combined. Its trucking fleet is the largest private carrier in the United States. Wal-Mart is the single largest U.S. importer from China and the largest private employer in both the United States and Mexico. If this corporation were an independent country it would have been China's eighth largest trading partner, ahead of Russia and Britain.

In selling general merchandise and groceries, it has no real rivals. A Harvard Business School study estimates that by 2008 the company will double its sales and employ at least 2.2 million "associates" worldwide. In March 2003, *Fortune* magazine ranked Wal-Mart—for the first time—as America's most admired, as well as its largest company. Many observers expect Wal-Mart to gross a trillion dollars a year by 2013. Indeed, Wal-Mart perfectly embodies the process of "creative destruction" identified by the early twentieth century economist Joseph Schumpeter as the engine by which one mode of capitalist production and distribution is replaced by another. And as Schumpeter made clear early in the twentieth century, every set of technological and organizational innovations not only reconfigures the immediate economic landscape, but it also casts a social and political shadow across all of society.

And it is precisely Wal-Mart's enormous social, economic, and cultural weight that makes Wal-Mart not just an organizing imperative for American labor, but a subject of increasingly intense political and social scrutiny. For no company of Wal-Mart's size and influence is a "private enterprise." By its very existence and competitive success, it rezones our cities, determines the real minimum wage, channels capital throughout the world, and conducts a kind of international diplomacy with a score of nations. In an era of weak unions and waning governmental regulation, Wal-Mart management may well have more power than any other entity to "legislate" key components of American social and industrial policy.

The last time an American company had such power was 50 years ago when General Motors was the largest and most profitable American corporation, with sales that amounted to about three percent of the gross national product, which made the car maker an even larger economic presence than Wal-Mart is today. (Wal-Mart's share of the GNP is still only 2.3 percent.) Both Wal-Mart and GM are both template enterprises, but the patterns they have both done so much to establish have had a very different impact on working-class America.

In 1953 when President Eisenhower appointed General Motors President Charles E. Wilson to his cabinet, the GM executive appeared before Congress to defend his views and qualifications. When asked if there was any conflict between his career as an auto executive and his new governmental duties, Wilson famously replied, that what was "good for the country was good for General Motors, and vice versa."

Congress eventually confirmed Charles Wilson as Secretary of Defense, but his bold declaration generated a howl of outrage that has not quite lost all its voltage even after half a century. Wilson's quip might have been arrogant, but it was controversial precisely because there was a plausible case for making it. In its heyday, from the late 1920s through the 1970s, General Motors was the largest corporation in the United States, dominating the country's most important industry. And it was not just the largest manufacturer of cars, but also of heavy trucks, locomotives, and military equipment. It was a major player in aircraft production, and in household appliances, and the GM Acceptance Corporation was by far the largest retail credit institution in the United States. Like Wal-Mart today, it had no competition that could threaten its market supremacy. And also like Wal-Mart, whose ever-present TV spots claim a beneficial link between the corporation's fortune and that of workers, customers, and community, one might scoff at the claim, but no one could ignore it.

It is therefore useful to juxtapose these two corporate templates, if only to gain some purchase on how the history, economics, and sociology of these giant enterprises can generate insights and questions that may help us see what is uniquely transformative about Wal-Mart, and what is merely a function of its sheer size and market leverage. Does this compare apples and oranges? General Motors and Wal-Mart might seem to be in quite different lines of business. One is primarily the manufacturer of durable consumer goods, while the other is essentially a retailer. One firm typifies industrial America, the other "post-industrial" consumer society.

But upon closer inspection, these differences seem less salient. GM did manufacture lots of cars, but its franchised dealer system, which was always kept on a tight leash, sold them by the millions, and its wholly owned GMAC subsidiary financed them, and sometimes made as much profit as did the production side of the corporation. Wal-Mart is obviously a big retailer that buys its goods from thousands of supplier firms. But the relationship between Wal-Mart and its suppliers is an increasingly intimate one that is transforming Wal-Mart into a de facto manufacturing company. At GM the manufacturing end of the enterprise squeezed the car dealers; at Wal-Mart the retail sales operation wags the manufacturing tail, but in the end it may not matter all that much. When it comes to giant global enterprise, we still live in an industrial world. More people work in factories today than at any time in human history. Still more sell, talk, or manipulate a keyboard under assembly line conditions. The post-industrial age has not yet arrived.

Both General Motors and Wal-Mart are themselves high productivity workplaces, and both generate economies of scale that have had a substantial ripple impact throughout the rest of the economy. They did not invent the technologies and the organizational innovations that generated this productivity dividend—Ford was more creative in the early years of the 20th century, and Chrysler pioneered many of the innovative engineering breakthroughs we associate with the mid-century automobile. Likewise, the Walton brothers always acknowledged their debt to such retail innovators as Price Club, J.C. Penney, and Kmart. The Waltons took the idea of self-service from Ben Franklin, the large purchase discount store from Price Club, and the Supercenter from the French Carrefour markets. But Wal-Mart, like General Motors, perfected, integrated, and systematized technological and marketing ideas put in play by their competitors. And in doing so they both ratcheted up their own overall productivity, and made it impossible for any competitor to survive without emulating the template firm. Thus Ford imitated GM in 1946 by purging the managerial men and methods put in place by the original Henry Ford in order to make itself fit the GM template.

What makes for giganticism in big business? Why was GM so big at mid-century and why is Wal-Mart so huge today? In their theory of the firm, business economists have described the corporation as an "island of conscious power" in an "ocean of unconscious cooperation, like lumps of butter coagulating in a pail of buttermilk." Every firm has an optimal size beyond which the risk of loss from mismanagement more than offsets the chance of gain from the economies of scale it can realize. In the first half of the 20th century GM became a vertically integrated conglomerate because teletype, telephones, and good roads enabled the corporation to deploy its famous system of centralized control and decentralized operations across dozens of states and scores of major production facilities. But such highly integrated production and distribution within a single firm may not always be the most cost efficient way to make the most money. If new technologies and sociopolitical mores make it cheaper and faster to purchase rather than make these same goods and services, then executives will begin to dismantle the huge firm. According to the most savvy, technologically hip business writers, the contemporary corporation is doomed to disaggregation within a world of cheap, rapid communications and increasingly efficient markets in goods and services. The "virtual" corporation of the 21st century should consist of a few thousand highly skilled managers and professions who contract out nonessential services to cheaper, specialist firms.

Thus we have the outsourcing of both call center work and janitorial services to an ever shifting coterie of independent firms, while "branded" companies like Nike and Dell farm out virtually all the manufacturing work that goes into their core products. This has been the path followed by General Motors, which has created and spun off Delco, once a vertically integrated parts division. Except for final assembly and the manufacture of key components, GM and the other big car companies seek to outsource as much work as possible, even sharing space with suppliers under the same roof and on the same shop floor. So the GM payroll, white collar and blue, is about half the size it was in 1970. Giving all this a metahistorical punch, Forbes columnist Peter Huber declared that it was "market forces and the information age" that had beaten the Soviets and would soon force the dissolution of America's largest corporations. "If you have grown accustomed to a sheltered life inside a really large corporation," he advised, "take care. The next Kremlin to fall may be your own."

But Wal-Mart has found giganticism efficient and profitable. This is because the price of goods and services it purchases on the market has not fallen as rapidly as has the cost of "managing" within a single organization the production or deployment of those same economic inputs. The same technologies and cost imperatives that have led to the decomposition of many manufacturing firms, have enabled Wal-Mart and other retail distribution companies to vastly enhance their own managerial "span of control." . . . This is not just a tribute to Wal-Mart's clever deployment of sophisticated control technologies, but arises from the politics and culture of a business system that has arisen in the post-New Deal world. . . .

WHO IS US?

Robert B. Reich

Who is "us"? Is it IBM, Motorola, Whirlpool, and General Motors? Or is it Sony, Thomson, Philips, and Honda?

Consider two successful corporations:

- Corporation A is headquartered north of New York City. Most of its top managers are citizens of the United States. All of its directors are American citizens, and a majority of its shares are held by American investors. But most of Corporation A's employees are non-Americans. Indeed, the company undertakes much of its R&D and product design, and most of its complex manufacturing, outside the borders of the United States in Asia, Latin America, and Europe. Within the American market, an increasing amount of the company's product comes from its laboratories and factories abroad.

- Corporation B is headquartered abroad, in another industrialized nation. Most of its top managers and directors are citizens of that nation, and a majority of its shares are held by citizens of that nation. But most of Corporation B's employees are Americans. Indeed, Corporation B undertakes much of its R&D and new product design in the United States. And it does most of its manufacturing in the U.S. The company exports an increasing proportion of its American-based production, some of it even back to the nation where Corporation B is headquartered.

Now, who is "us"? Between these two corporations, which is the American corporation, which the foreign corporation? Which is more important to the economic future of the United States?

As the American economy becomes more globalized, examples of both Corporation A and B are increasing. At the same time, American concern for the competitiveness of the United States is increasing. Typically, the assumed vehicle for improving the competitive performance of the United States is the American corporation—by which most people would mean Corporation A. But today, the competitiveness of American-owned corporations is no longer the same as American competitiveness. Indeed, American ownership of the corporation is profoundly less relevant to America's economic future than the skills, training, and knowledge commanded by American workers—workers who are increasingly employed within the United States by foreign-owned corporations.

So who is us? The answer is, the American work force, the American people, but not particularly the American corporation. The implications of this new answer are clear: if we hope to revitalize the competitive performance of the United States economy we must invest in people, not in nationally defined corporations. We must open our borders to investors from around the world rather than favoring companies that may simply fly the U.S. flag. And government policies should promote human capital in this country rather than assuming that American corporations will invest on "our" behalf. The American corporation is simply no longer "us."

GLOBAL COMPANIES

American corporations have been abroad for years, even decades. So in one sense, the multinational identity of American companies is nothing new. What is new is that American-owned multinationals are beginning to employ large numbers of foreigners relative to their American work forces, are beginning to rely on foreign facilities to do many of their most technologically complex activities, and are beginning to export from their foreign facilities—including bringing products back to the United States.

Around the world, the numbers are already large—and still growing. Take IBM—often considered the thoroughbred of competitive American corporations. Forty percent of IBM's world employees are foreign, and the percentage is increasing. IBM Japan boasts 18,000 Japanese employees and annual sales of more than $6 billion, making it one of Japan's major exporters of computers.

Or consider Whirlpool. After cutting its American work force by 10% and buying Philips's appliance business, Whirlpool now employs 43,500 people around the world in 45 countries—most of them non-Americans. Another example is Texas Instruments, which now does most of its research, development, design, and manufacturing in East Asia. TI employs over 5,000 people in Japan alone, making advanced semiconductors— almost half of which are exported, many of them back to the United States.

American corporations now employ 11% of the industrial work force of Northern Ireland, making everything from cigarettes to computer software, much of which comes back to the United States. More than 100,000 Singaporians work for more than 200 U.S. corporations, most of them fabricating and assembling electronic components for export to the United States. Singapore's largest private employer is General Electric, which also accounts for a big share of that nation's growing exports. Taiwan counts AT&T, RCA, and Texas Instruments among its largest exporters. In fact, more than one-third of Taiwan's notorious trade surplus with the United States comes from U.S. corporations making or buying things there, then selling or using them back in the United States. The same corporate sourcing practice accounts for a substantial share of the U.S. trade imbalance with Singapore, South Korea, and Mexico—raising a question as to whom complaints about trade imbalances should be directed.

The pattern is not confined to America's largest companies. Molex, a suburban Chicago maker of connectors used to link wires in cars and computer boards, with revenues of about $300 million in 1988, has 38 overseas factories, 5 in Japan. Loctite, a midsize company with sales in 1988 of $457 million, headquartered in Newington, Connecticut, makes and sells adhesives and sealants all over the world. It has 3,500 employees—only 1,200 of whom are Americans. These companies are just part of a much larger trend: according to a 1987 McKinsey & Company study, America's most profitable midsize companies increased their investments in overseas production at an annual rate of 20% between 1981 and 1986.

Overall, the evidence suggests that U.S. companies have not lost their competitive edge over the last 20 years—they've just moved their base of operations. In 1966, American-based multinationals accounted for about 17% of world exports; since then their share has remained almost unchanged. But over the same period, the share of exports from the United States in the world's total trade in manufactures fell from 16% to 14%. In other words, while Americans exported less, the overseas affiliates of U.S.-owned corporations exported more than enough to offset the drop.

The old trend of overseas capital investment is accelerating: U.S. companies increased foreign capital spending by 24% in 1988, 13% in 1989. But even more important, U.S. businesses are now putting substantial sums of money into foreign countries to do R&D work. According to National Science Foundation figures, American corporations increased their overseas R&D spending by 33% between 1986 and 1988, compared with a 6% increase in

R&D spending in the United States. Since 1987, Eastman Kodak, W.R. Grace, Du Pont, Merck, and Upjohn have all opened new R&D facilities in Japan. At Du Pont's Yokohama laboratory, more than 180 Japanese scientists and technicians are working at developing new materials technologies. IBM's Tokyo Research Lab, tucked away behind the far side of the Imperial Palace in downtown Tokyo, houses a small army of Japanese engineers who are perfecting image-processing technology. Another IBM laboratory, the Kanagawa arm of its Yamato Development Laboratory, houses 1,500 researchers who are developing hardware and software. Nor does IBM confine its pioneering work to Japan: recently, two European researchers at IBM's Zurich laboratory announced major breakthroughs into superconductivity and microscopy—earning them both Nobel Prizes.

An even more dramatic development is the arrival of foreign corporations in the United States at a rapidly increasing pace. As recently as 1977, only about 3.5% of the value added and the employment of American manufacturing originated in companies controlled by foreign parents. By 1987, the number had grown to almost 8%. In just the last two years, with the faster pace of foreign acquisitions and investments, the figure is now almost 11%. Foreign-owned companies now employ 3 million Americans, roughly 10% of our manufacturing workers. In fact, in 1989, affiliates of foreign manufacturers created more jobs in the United States than American-owned manufacturing companies.

And these non-U.S. companies are vigorously exporting from the United States. Sony now exports audio- and videotapes to Europe from its Dothan, Alabama factory and ships audio recorders from its Fort Lauderdale, Florida plant. Sharp exports 100,000 microwave ovens a year from its factory in Memphis, Tennessee. Last year, Dutch-owned Philips Consumer Electronics Company exported 1,500 color televisions from its Greenville, Tennessee plant to Japan. Its 1990 target is 30,000 televisions; by 1991, it plans to export 50,000 sets. Toshiba America is sending projection televisions from its Wayne, New Jersey plant to Japan. And by the early 1990s, when Honda annually exports 50,000 cars to Japan from its Ohio production base, it will actually be making more cars in the United States than in Japan.

In an economy of increasing global investment, foreign-owned Corporation B, with its R&D and manufacturing presence in the United States and its reliance on American workers, is far more important to America's economic future than American-owned Corporation A, with its platoons of foreign workers. Corporation A may fly the American flag, but Corporation B invests in Americans.

TWO CRITIQUES OF GLOBALIZATION

Jagdish Bhagwati

In Defense of Globalization was written against the background of the massive demonstrations that erupted in Seattle in November 1999 when the World Trade Organization (WTO) was meeting to launch a new Round of multilateral Trade Negotiations. If launched, the

Seattle Round would have been the first under the auspices of the WTO as distinct from the seven Rounds that had been successfully concluded under GATT, the General Agreement on Tariffs and Trade, which was the predecessor of the WTO. The protests were about the alleged adverse social implications of the economic globalization that trade typified in the minds—or perhaps I should say the hearts—of many of the militating critics.

. . . By looking at virtually every social concern I could lay my hands on, I argued that globalization, by and large, advanced these social agendas instead of handicapping them. In short, globalization *has* a human face. I can only illustrate with one compelling example the kind of argumentation and evidence that I marshaled to arrive at this startling conclusion: the reader has the entire book to judge for herself the case I build, patiently and without an ideological straitjacket, against the entire range of current anti-globalization critiques.

Thus, take the wage differential against women. Take the phenomenon that, for the same type of work and the same qualifications, a firm pays men more than women. Using Gary Becker's theory of price and prejudice, we may hypothesize that the willingness of firms to pay more for equally qualified men will begin to shrink once they face stiff international competition. So, in traded industries, you would see the wage differential closing faster than in non-traded industries. Lo and behold, that is just what two splendid women economists found to be the case in the United States over a long period. Globalization, in the shape of trade, was a force for good, not harm.

But take the differential in pay that comes, not at the level of the firm, but because women traditionally have been confined to jobs that pay less: like teaching and nursing. But even here, take the example of Japanese multinationals. In Japan the glass ceiling beyond which women cannot go used to be so low that women could barely stand up! One went to Japan and found that, in a land that produced the world's first great female novelist (Lady Murasaki in the eleventh century), today the women typically were either housewives or in jobs such as serving tea to male executives who did all of the talking and negotiating. When Japanese multinationals started going abroad in massive numbers in the late 1980s, the men, of course, remained executives. Their wives who lived in New York, Paris, Rome, and London, suddenly saw how Western men treated their wives differently and how the women were upwardly mobile in business and other occupations. That turned them into powerful agents of change when they returned. And so now we have had Madame Ogata as the UN High Commissioner for Refugees, Madame Tanaka as the Foreign Minister and many women getting into the Diet and also rising in executive ranks. Japanese investment abroad was among the phenomena that fostered the change in attitudes that led to the promotion of equality for Japanese women.

SELF-INTEREST AND FEAR

If the concerns about globalization that proceed from altruism and empathy can be laid to rest, those arising from self-interest and fear are not so easily dismissed, though they are even less grounded in objective reality. As the Russian proverb goes: fear has big eyes. But it also has deaf ears.

The fear of trade and multinationals today particularly afflicts the rich countries, where many are afraid that economic prosperity is imperiled by trade with the poor countries. Additionally, the working classes and the unions typically fear that their wages and standards are in peril from trade with poor countries. But it was only a few decades ago that the fear was rampant among the poor countries that were in such peril from trade with the rich countries: how ironic this seems. A few economists and some cash-rich NGOs have worked hard to renew the fear among the poor countries as well. Let me, therefore, urge the reader to work through the extended analysis and empirical evidence that I have produced, on the benefits of trade for prosperity in the poor countries . . . and on the need to discount the alleged adverse effect of trade on wages and labor standards in the rich countries. . . . But let me add a few salient points here, on the question of the relationship between trade and prosperity, while dealing with the question of wages and labor standards more robustly later. I will also start with conventional worries; and then I will address worries (such as the fear of India and China) that have emerged in recent years, reinforcing the old concerns, in regard to both overall prosperity and wages.

1. *Prosperity from Trade.*   First, my colleague Professor Arvind Panagariya has noted that, if one examines the growth and trade record (where available) of rich and poor countries for nearly forty years in the postwar period, you see a remarkable phenomenon. The "economic miracle" countries which averaged a high annual growth rate of per capita income at about 3 percent, also showed similar growth in their trade; and the "economic debacle" countries that experienced negligible or even negative growth rates were also characterized by similarly dismal trade performance. Now, this does not necessarily imply that trade led to growth instead of the other way around. Anyone who has studied the experience of developing countries in depth knows—and I know because I have participated in two major projects (one where I was a country co-author and one which I co-directed) in the 1960s and 1970s on the trade and development policies of several countries—the argument that growth happened independently of trade, which simply followed as a "trickle-down" effect of growth, is little short of crazy. But this area does invite entry by crazy people, or people who are not crazy but act as if they were because the market incentives, as I argue below, are such today that they reward craziness.

Second, note that it is possible to observe periods, which may last over almost two decades in rare cases, where autarky and high growth rates may be observed together. But it is impossible to find cases where this has been a "sustainable" relationship over very long periods. The Soviet Union collapsed after making many economists, including me at one stage, believe that its autarky was no barrier. Well, just look at a chart on Soviet Russia's steadily declining growth rate in the face of huge investment rates. You see a decline in productivity that must be at least partly attributed to a virtually closed economy and rigid central planning laced with massive restrictions on production and investment. After a huge spurt in the 1920s and 1930s, these ill-advised policies finally caught up with them.

Let me also recall a funny, and true, story about my Cambridge teacher Joan Robinson. In the mid-1960s, she and Gus Ranis of Yale, one a radical and the other a mainstream economist, were overheard agreeing that Korea was an economic miracle. How could this harmony have arisen? It turned out that she was thinking of North Korea whereas Ranis was talking about South Korea! Now, after over a quarter of a century, we know who was right: North Korea simply failed to sustain its high growth rate. Autarky, and total lack of political and economic freedoms, turned the short-run miracle into a debacle.

Third, much is made these days of the cliché that "one (shoe) size does not fit all," implying that general advice that trade is good is unsound and that we must vary the prescription with each country, presumably advocating protection here and there, on an ad hoc basis, and without an overarching philosophy that progress towards freeing trade is desirable. This sounds so right; but it is downright shallow and silly. Science, and good policy, require that certain general propositions be taken as guiding principles, as distinct from reliance on ad hoc prescriptions. One has to decide whether one wants to go bare-foot or wear shoes. And once one decides to wear shoes, the shoe size will inevitably tend to vary, as the policy gets grounded in reality. Thus, one has to decide whether the central policy has to be openness or autarky. After the post-war experience, it is clearly possible to argue that good policymaking requires a policy of freer trade. But this does not mean that the actual freeing of trade must not take into account the political and economic difficulties that may attend the transition from one system to another: the transition to freer trade, and working with an open economy, require policy and institutional support that have in fact been the subject of rich analysis by trade economists for decades.

2. Globalization: Trade, Immigration and Wages. The long-standing stagnation, or at best very sluggish rise, in workers' earnings in the United States has given rise to the fear that globalization, involving trade with the poor countries and also illegal unskilled immigration from them, is at the heart of the problem. Yet, this causation should not be taken at face value, no matter how plausible it seems to many in the rich countries.

First, all empirical studies, including those done by some of today's top trade economists (such as Paul Krugman and Robert Feenstra), show that the adverse effect of trade on wages is not substantial. My own empirical investigation . . . in fact argues that the effect of trade with poor countries may even have been to moderate the downward pressure on wages that rapid unskilled-labor-saving technical change would have caused.

Second, the same goes for the econometric studies by the best labor economists today, regarding the effects of the influx of unskilled illegal immigrants into the United States. The latest study by George Borjas (no friend of illegal immigrants) and Larry Katz, both of Harvard, once necessary adjustments are made, also shows a virtually negligible impact on U.S. workers' wages.

So, despite the popular fears, globalization does not appear to be the cause of the problem. What then explains the disturbing situation regarding wages? Can it be that globalization has significantly reduced the bargaining ability of workers and thus puts a downward pressure on wages? I strongly doubt this. First, the argument is not relevant when employers and workers are in a competitive market and workers must be paid the going wage. As it happens, less than 10 percent of the workers in the private sector in the United States are now unionized. Second, if it is claimed that acceleration in globalization has decimated unionization, that is dubious. The decline in unionization has been going on for longer than the last two decades of globalization, shows no dramatic acceleration in the last two decades, and is to be attributed to the union-unfriendly provisions of the half-century-old Taft-Hartley provisions that crippled the ability to strike. Third, it seems plausible that unionization has also suffered because fewer workers now expect that unions can deliver higher wages. In the public sector, the wages are squeezed because of budget constraints: as the recent New York Transit strike showed, the public utilities are increasingly unable to raise the price of services or to get more subsidies to finance losses and therefore the ability of unions in such a situation to get more for their workers is crippled. Again, increasing numbers work at home, in no small measure due to technical change such as on-line transactions, that facilitates such decentralized work, in a return to the pre-factory-work era, and are therefore less amenable to unionization.

Again, can we turn to yet another element of globalization for an explanation? Has the outflow of Direct Foreign Investment (DFI) to the poor countries with cheap labor caused a decline in the capital which works at home with unskilled labor and hence to a decline in wages? As I look at the data, the United States has received more or less as much equity investment as it has lost over the last two decades. One cannot just look at one side of the ledger; I might add that I was once in a BBC radio debate with the Mayor of the French town, which had lost its Hoover factory to England. He was lamenting the loss and holding up multinationals as somewhat wicked in their pursuit of profits. So, I told him: Mr. Mayor, Hoover is an American firm. When it came to your town, you applauded. Now that they have traveled on, you are agitated. You cannot have it both ways. Again, as I argue below, the econometric evidence on location by multinationals does not show that cheap labor is a big draw; and many other factors producing competitiveness are at play, making the rich countries also major attractions for the inflow of equity investments by multinationals.

So, in lieu of globalization as the culprit, one has to fall back on the argument that substantial unskilled-labor-saving technical change is putting pressure on the wages of the unskilled. Technical change (except for the Green Revolution, where the new seeds led to increases in both the demand for landless labor and real wages because the application of irrigation and fertilizers to the new seeds led to more intensive land use with multiple shifts) happens to be continually economizing on the use of unskilled labor. Much empirical argumentation and evidence exists on this, coming from world-class economists such as Alan Krueger of Princeton. But, as always, anecdotes (which obviously cannot substitute for systematic evidence) can make this point come alive. The effect of technical change in increasing the demand for skilled and reducing that for unskilled labor today can be illustrated by two examples.

First, to take an example from my own professorial life, secretaries are increasingly hard to get from the university administration on campuses. Instead, universities now offer you computers. Whereas secretaries are generally semi-skilled—though in the past highly educated and gifted females often became secretaries because they had few other options—the computers have to be looked after, and fixed frequently due to failure (especially when one has a deadline), by "electronic plumbers" who are skilled and get paid much more. So the rapid spread of computers is steadily reducing demand for secretaries and increasing the demand for the electronic plumbers.

A more striking example comes from Charlie Chaplin's famous film, *Modern Times*. You will recall how he goes berserk on the assembly line, the mechanical motion of turning the spanner finally getting to him (illustrating Adam Smith's famous observation that the division of labor, and concentration on repetitive, narrow tasks could turn workers into morons and that education for them had to provide the antidote). Suppose that you take your child to see the film and she asks you: Daddy, take me to see an assembly line so I can actually see the people working at it. Well, it is going to be increasingly difficult to find such an assembly line for your child to see. Yes, there are assembly lines today; but they are without workers; they are managed by computers in a glass cage above, with highly skilled engineers in charge. The disoriented Charlie Chaplins have increasingly disappeared, at least from the assembly lines. Amusingly, this was brought home to Americans when, having decided to investigate the production of potato and semiconductor chips because of the widespread perception that potato chips were produced by primitive techniques and semiconductors were made with advanced technology, a reporter found that the facts were the other way around. He visited a factory that produced semiconductors and found that it involved moronic fitting of little wires onto small boards, whereas the Pringles factory he visited for potato chips was fully automated on its assembly line, with Pringles fitting beautifully on one another, each a total replica of the other, in the red and green boxes one finds in hotel mini-bars.

The facts are that this is rapidly occurring in the United States, and in other rich countries, as technical change is quickly spreading through the system. This naturally creates, in the short-run, pressure on the jobs and wages of the workers being displaced. But we know from past experience with technical change that we usually get a J-curve where, as productivity increase takes hold, it will (except in cases where macroeconomic difficulties may occur and are not addressed by macroeconomic remedies) result in wage increases. A Luddite response, therefore, is hardly called for. So, why has there been no such effect—or at least a significant effect—in the statistics on wages for almost two decades?

I suspect that the answer lies in the intensity of displacement of unskilled labor by IT-based technical change—its potency is dramatic, as is evident from nearly everyone's daily experience—and in the fact that it is continuous now, unlike such discrete changes as the invention of the steam engine. Before the workers get on to the rising part of the J-curve, they run into yet more such technical change, so that the working class gets to go from one declining segment of the J-curve to another, to yet another. The pressure on wages gets to be relentless, lasting over longer periods than in earlier experience with unskilled-labor-saving technical change. But this technical change, which proceeds like a tsunami, has nothing to do with globalization.

TOWARD A GLOBALIZATION WITH A MORE HUMAN FACE

Joseph Stiglitz

One of the reasons globalization is being attacked is that it seems to undermine traditional values. The conflicts are real, and to some extent unavoidable. Economic growth—including that induced by globalization—will result in urbanization, undermining traditional rural societies. Unfortunately, so far, those responsible for managing globalization, while praising these positive benefits, all too often have shown an insufficient appreciation of this adverse side, the threat to cultural identity and values. This is surprising, given the awareness of the issues within the developed countries themselves: Europe defends its agricultural policies not just in terms of those special interests, but to preserve rural traditions. People in small towns everywhere complain that large national retailers and shopping malls have killed their small businesses and their communities.

The pace of global integration matters: a more gradual process means that traditional institutions and norms, rather than being overwhelmed, can adapt and respond to the new challenges.

Of equal concern is what globalization does to democracy. Globalization, as it has been advocated, often seems to replace the old dictatorships of national elites with new dictatorships of international finance. Countries are effectively told that if they don't follow certain conditions, the capital markets or the IMF will refuse to lend them money. They are basically forced to give up part of their sovereignty, to let capricious capital markets, including the speculators whose only concerns are short-term rather than the long-term growth of the country and the improvement of living standards, "discipline" them, telling them what they should and should not do.

But countries do have choices, and among those choices is the extent to which they wish to subject themselves to international capital markets. Those, such as in East Asia, that have avoided the strictures of the IMF have grown faster, with greater equality and poverty reduction, than those who have obeyed its commandments. Because alternative policies affect different groups differently, it is the role of the political process—not international bureaucrats—to sort out the choices. Even if growth *were* adversely affected, it is a cost many developing countries may be willing to pay to achieve a more democratic and equitable society, just as many societies today are saying it is worth sacrificing some growth for a better environment. So long as globalization is presented in the way that it has been, it represents a disenfranchisement. No wonder then that it will be resisted, especially by those who are being disenfranchised.

Today, globalization is being challenged around the world. There is discontent with globalization, and rightfully so. Globalization can be a force for good: the globalization of ideas about democracy and of civil society have changed the way people think, while global political movements have led to debt relief and the treaty on land mines. Globalization has helped hundreds of millions of people attain higher standards of living, beyond what they, or most economists, thought imaginable but a short while ago. The globalization of the economy has benefited countries that took advantage of it by seeking new markets for their exports and by welcoming foreign investment. Even so, the countries that have benefited the most have been those that took charge of their own destiny and recognized the role government can play in development rather than relying on the notion of a self-regulated market that would fix its own problems.

But for millions of people globalization has not worked. Many have actually been made worse off, as they have seen their jobs destroyed and their lives become more insecure. They have felt increasingly powerless against forces beyond their control. They have seen their democracies undermined, their cultures eroded.

If globalization continues to be conducted in the way that it has been in the past, if we continue to fail to learn from our mistakes, globalization will not only not succeed in promoting development but will continue to create poverty and instability. Without reform, the backlash that has already started will mount and discontent with globalization will grow.

This will be a tragedy for all of us, and especially for the billions who might otherwise have benefited. While those in the developing world stand to lose the most economically, there will be broader political ramifications that will affect the developed world too.

If the reforms . . . are taken seriously, then there is hope that a more humane process of globalization can be a powerful force for the good, with the vast majority of those living in the developing countries benefiting from it and welcoming it. If this is done, the discontent with globalization would have served us all well.

The current situation reminds me of the world some seventy years ago. As the world plummeted into the Great Depression, advocates of the free market said, "Not to worry; markets are self-regulating, and given time, economic prosperity will resume." Never mind the misery of those whose lives are destroyed waiting for this so-called eventuality. Keynes argued that markets were not self-correcting, or not at least in a relevant time frame. (As he famously put it, "In the long run, we are all dead.") Unemployment could persist for years, and government intervention was required. Keynes was pilloried—attacked as a Socialist, a critic of the market. Yet in a sense, Keynes was intensely conservative. He had a fundamental belief in the markets: if only government could correct this one failure, the economy would be able to function reasonably efficiently. He did not want a wholesale replacement of the market system; but he knew that unless these fundamental problems were addressed, there would be enormous popular pressures. And Keynes's medicine worked: since World War II, countries like the United States, following Keynesian prescriptions, have had fewer and shorter-lived downturns, and longer expansions than previously.

Today, the system of capitalism is at a crossroads just as it was during the Great Depression. In the 1930s, capitalism was saved by Keynes, who thought of policies to create jobs and rescue those suffering from the collapse of the global economy. Now, millions of people around the world are waiting to see whether globalization can be reformed so that its benefits can be more widely shared.

Thankfully, there is a growing recognition of these problems and increasing political will to do something. Almost everyone involved in development, even those in the Washington establishment, now agrees that rapid capital market liberalization without accompanying regulation can be dangerous. They agree too that the excessive tightness in fiscal policy in the Asian crisis of 1997 was a mistake. As Bolivia moved into a recession in 2001, caused in part by the global economic slowdown, there were some intimations that that country would not be forced to follow the traditional path of austerity and have to cut governmental spending. Instead, . . . it looks like Bolivia will be allowed to stimulate its economy, helping it to overcome the recession, using revenues that it is about to receive from its newly discovered natural gas reserves to tide it over until the economy starts to grow again. In the aftermath of the Argentina debacle, the IMF has recognized the failings of the big-bailout strategy and is beginning to discuss the use of standstills and restructuring through bankruptcy, the kinds of alternatives that I and others have been advocating for years. Debt forgiveness brought about by the work of the Jubilee movement and the concessions made to initiate a new development round of trade negotiations at Doha represent two more victories.

Despite these gains, there is still more to be done to bridge the gap between rhetoric and reality. At Doha, the developing countries only agreed to begin discussing a fairer trade agenda; the imbalances of the past have yet to be redressed. Bankruptcy and standstills are now on the agenda; but there is no assurance that there will be an appropriate balance of creditor and debtor interests. There is a lot more participation by those in developing countries in discussions concerning economic strategy, but there is little evidence yet of changes in policies that reflect greater participation. There need to be changes in institutions and in mind-sets. The free market ideology should be replaced with analyses based on economic science, with a more balanced view of the role of government drawn from an understanding of both market and government failures. There should be more sensitivity about the role of outside advisers, so they support democratic decision making by clarifying the consequences of different policies, including impacts on different groups, especially the poor, rather than undermining it by pushing particular policies on reluctant countries.

It is clear that there must be a *multipronged* strategy of reform. One should be concerned with reform of the international economic arrangements. But such reforms will be a long time coming. Thus, the second prong should be directed at encouraging reforms that each country can take upon itself. The developed countries have a special responsibility, for instance, to eliminate their trade barriers, to practice what they preach. But while the developed countries' responsibility may be great, their incentives are weak: after all, offshore banking centers and hedge funds serve interests in the developed countries, and the developed countries can withstand well the instability that a failure to reform might bring to the developing world. Indeed, the United States arguably benefited in several ways from the East Asia crisis.

Hence, the developing countries must assume responsibility for their well-being themselves. They can manage their budgets so that they live within their means, meager though that might be, and eliminate the protectionist barriers which, while they may generate large profits for a few, force consumers to pay higher prices. They can put in place strong regulations to protect themselves from speculators from the outside or corporate misbehavior from the inside. Most important, developing countries need effective governments, with strong and independent judiciaries, democratic accountability, openness and transparency and freedom from the corruption that has stifled the effectiveness of the public sector and the growth of the private.

What they should ask of the international community is only this: the acceptance of their need, and right, to make their own choices, in ways which reflect their own political judgments about who, for instance, should bear what risks. They should be encouraged to adopt bankruptcy laws and regulatory structures adapted to their own situation, not to accept templates designed by and for the more developed countries.

What is needed are policies for sustainable, equitable, and democratic growth. This is the reason for development. Development is not about helping a few people get rich or creating a handful of pointless protected industries that only benefit the country's elite; it is not about bringing in Prada and Benetton, Ralph Lauren or Louis Vuitton, for the urban rich and leaving the rural poor in their misery. Being able to buy Gucci handbags in Moscow department stores did not mean that country had become a market economy. Development is about transforming societies, improving the lives of the poor, enabling everyone to have a chance at success and access to health care and education.

This sort of development won't happen if only a few people dictate the policies a country must follow. Making sure that democratic decisions are made means ensuring that a broad range of economists, officials, and experts from developing countries are actively involved in the debate. It also means that there must be broad participation that goes well beyond the experts and politicians. Developing countries must take charge of their own futures. But we in the West cannot escape our responsibilities.

It's not easy to change how things are done. Bureaucracies, like people, fall into bad habits, and adapting to change can be painful. But the international institutions must undertake the perhaps painful changes that will enable them to play the role they *should* be playing to make globalization work, and work not just for the well off and the industrial countries, but for the poor and the developing nations.

The developed world needs to do its part to reform the international institutions that govern globalization. We set up these institutions and we need to work to fix them. If we are to address the legitimate concerns of those who have expressed a discontent with globalization, if we are to make globalization work for the billions of people for whom it has not, if we are to make globalization with a human face succeed, then our voices must be raised. We cannot, we should not, stand idly by.

FURTHER READING

Anderson, Saraj, John Cavanaugh, and Thea Lee. 2005. *The Field Guide to the Global Economy.* New York: The New Press.

Appelbaum, Richard P. 2008. "Giant Transnational Contractors in East Asia: Emergent Trends in Global Supply Chains," *Competition and Change 12*(1): 69–87.

Appelbaum, Richard P., and Nelson Lichtenstein. 2006. "A New World of Retail Supremacy: Supply Chains and Workers' Chains in the Age of Wal-Mart," *International Labor and Working-Class History* 70(fall):106–125.

Berger, Suzanne, and Ronald Dore. 1996. *National Diversity and Global Capitalism.* Ithaca, NY: Cornell University Press.

Bhagwati, Jagdish. 2007. *In Defense of Globalization: With a New Word.* New York: Oxford University Press.

Chandler, Alfred D., and Bruce Mazlish (Eds.). 2005. *Leviathans: Multinational Corporations and the New Global History.* Cambridge, UK: Cambridge University Press.

Desai, Radhika. 2013. *Geopolitical Economy: After US Hegemony, Globalization and Empire.* London: Pluto Press.

Esbenshade, Jill (2004) *Monitoring Sweatshop: Workers, Consumers, and the Global Apparel Industry.* Philadelphia: Temple University Press.

Hung, Ho-Fung (Ed.). 2009. *China and the Transformation of Global Capitalism.* Baltimore: Johns Hopkins University Press.

Gilpin, Robert. 2000. *The Challenge of Global Capitalism: The World Economy in the 21st Century.* Princeton, NJ: Princeton University Press.

Kaletsky, Anatole. 2010. *Capitalism 4.0: The Birth of a New Economy in the Aftermath of Crisis.* New York: Perseus.

Oshri, Ilan, Julia Kotlarsky, and Leslie P. Willcocks. 2009. *The Handbook of Global Outsourcing and Offshoring.* New York: Palgrave Macmillan.

Reich, Robert B. 2012. *Beyond Outrage: Expanded Edition: What Has Gone Wrong with Our Economy and Our Democracy, and How to Fix It.* New York: Vintage.

Rodrik, Dani. 2012. *The Globalization Paradox: Democracy and the Future of the World Economy.* New York: Norton.

Stiglitz, Joseph. 2003. *Globalization and Its Discontents.* New York: Norton.

14

GLOBAL FINANCE AND FINANCIAL INEQUALITY

If someone asked you to name the most widely traded thing in the world, what would your answer be? Would you say oil? Arms? Illegal drugs? If you said any of these, you would be wrong. The most frequently traded thing is money—lots of money. Every day currency of every denomination is traded back and forth, some $4 trillion dollars' worth daily.

The value of most currencies fluctuates from day to day according to how much people in other countries are willing to pay to buy them, using their own currency or one that is commonly accepted around the world, such as the U.S. dollar or the European euro. Because currencies "float" in this way, you can speculate on how much the value of a particular currency is going to be in the future and buy and sell it accordingly, just as you would speculate on any other commodity.

It didn't always work this way. Not too long ago, most currencies were "fixed." This meant that their value did not change from day to day. Usually, the value of the currencies were secured by being tied to something else, like the value of a precious metal like gold or silver. If you look at a dollar bill from sixty or seventy years ago, it might have the words "silver certificate" printed on it, meaning that you were entitled to exchange that dollar bill for a certain fixed amount of silver. In 1971, the United States abandoned that practice—called the "silver standard," and before that, the "gold standard"—and ever since, the value of the U.S. dollar has floated. The same is true of currencies in the world. Their absolute value is literally worth the paper the money is printed on, but in practice people accept it as being worth a certain value, and that value fluctuates from day to day.

The buying and selling of currency is big business, and it can have significant political consequences. For this reason, an international conference was convened in 1944 at Bretton Woods, New Hampshire, to create a system with regulations for the orderly exchange of currency. The Bretton Woods agreement also established the International Monetary Fund (IMF) as a transnational agency to stabilize currencies, especially in times of crisis. In some cases, the crisis has involved a run on a particular currency and a sudden drop in its value.

In 1997, many people around the world thought that the Thai baht was overvalued and artificially propped up by its government. When the Thai government allowed its currency to float, it sank like a stone. Investors around the world began to sell off large quantities of the Thai currency. Panic set in, and there was a global race among financial companies to get rid of their Thai baht, as well as many other currencies from the same region, including the Malaysian ringgit, the Indonesian rupiah, the South Korean won, the Vietnamese dong, and the Japanese yen. The IMF had to intercede to help stabilize the currencies of Indonesia, Thailand, and South Korea. Economies were collapsing in an international house of cards.

Speculation like this is particularly volatile with currencies from smaller countries, as these can fluctuate wildly. Some countries and companies try to stabilize their financial situation by relying on a more international currency. The U.S. dollar is the most widely used currency around the world, and for this reason there is more printed U.S. money in circulation outside the U.S. than in it. But most money that is bought and sold does not involve the actual exchange of paper bills and coins, of course; it is really a matter of digits on electronic screens.

This brings up the interesting question of what money is, especially in the global era, when so many transactions are done electronically by computer or by credit cards. Ultimately, these digits have to be tied to real cash, and anyone who promises payment digitally has to be able to back up that promise with hard currency. Though, of course, "hard currency" is just printed paper.

What makes that paper into money is the common acceptance that it really is worth something. Currency is traditionally a way of measuring and storing the value of something for the purpose of exchanging it for something of like value—goods, services, or other kinds of money. Its other purposes are helping to stabilize a nation's economy and give the nation a sense of identity. In some ways, national money became the symbol of the nation-state. If you were in Japan, you used yen; if you were in Mexico, you used pesos; if you were in Russia, you used rubles.

The European euro was the first attempt to create a transnational currency. Germans abandoned the deutschmark, Italians let go of the lira, and the French said adieu to the franc. Instead they took on a new currency that for a time seemed to challenge the U.S. dollar as the international currency of choice. Although the euro was not the currency of any particular country, it was the currency of the region. The euro became identified with a growing European consciousness of a cultural and political unity that was bigger than any single country within it, but not quite a global entity. Recently, other forms of currency have emerged that are not tied to nations or to regions. Frequent flier miles, for instance, do all of the things that traditional currency does—measure and store value and act as an instrument for exchanges—and they are not issued by particular countries, but by airline carriers.

The value of currency is different in each country, and the total amount of currency that is circulated by each country varies as well. This brings up another matter—the unequal distribution of wealth in countries around the world. This is to some degree a development problem, since wealth is dependent in large part upon international trade, which requires a country to have something of value—natural resources, labor, or manufactured products—that it can sell and receive money for in an open market. But it can also be affected by currency policy. China, for instance, has been accused of keeping its currency artificially low in order to make the value of its labor and manufactured goods cheaper on the international market and thus more attractive to trade and investment. The result of this practice is that China can undersell other countries and increase its own national wealth.

In a global era, however, the distribution of wealth around the world is not measured solely by country. There are still rich nations and poor nations, of course, though in an era of globalization, companies and individuals can plug into the global economy and do very well regardless of where they live. For this reason, there are some interesting anomalies. The richest person in the world, according to *Forbes* magazine's 2012 list, is from Mexico—telecom magnate Carlos Slim Helu, whose $69 billion fortune topped that of Microsoft founder Bill Gates and U.S. financier Warren Buffett. Also in the top 20 richest people in the world were Eike Batista, a mining and oil investor from Brazil, and Mukush Ambani from India, whose wealth stems from petrochemicals, oil, and gas. Mexico, Brazil, and India are not usually thought of as rich societies: Mexico ranks 60th, Brazil 75th, and India 126th among the world's nations in terms of per capita share of their nation's gross domestic product (GDP). The United States, one of the richest countries in the world, had a per capita GDP in 2011 of $48,000 (according to World Bank statistics), whereas India's was only $3,627. Even China, touted as one of the most vibrant economies in the world, is comparatively quite poor, with its wealth amounting to only $8,400 per person (though, of course, it has a huge population—two billion people). Still, the point remains: the world's wealth is quite unevenly distributed.

The readings in this section focus on different aspects of the international financial scene. The first reading is by economist Benjamin J. Cohen of the University of California, Santa Barbara, who teaches in the department of political science. In this excerpt from his book *The Geography of Money*, Cohen explains how the concept of national currency is changing in a global age, when money is used not just to protect the economies of individual countries but also to facilitate a global financial market. The next reading focuses specifically on the role of electronic cash in undercutting the traditional role of nation-states in creating and protecting the interests of the currency. The author,

Stephen J. Kobrin, is professor of Multinational Management in the Wharton School of Business at the University of Pennsylvania.

The other two readings in this section discuss the world's unequal distribution of wealth. Glenn Firebaugh, a professor of sociology at Pennsylvania State University, looks at global income inequality and suggests that the situation may not be getting any better in the global age. The final selection is by Dani Rodrik, a Turkish economist who is a professor of international political economy at the John F. Kennedy School of Government at Harvard. Rodrik looks at the larger picture of economic globalization and asks, "globalization for whom?" The answer may not be surprising: globalization does not benefit all persons in the world equally.

MONEY IN INTERNATIONAL AFFAIRS

Benjamin J. Cohen

How should we think about money in international affairs? Ask the proverbial man or woman in the street, and the answer will be straightforward. All currencies are national: One Nation/One Money. America has its dollar, the British their pound, Japan the yen, each money exclusive within its own sovereign domain. The geography of money coincides precisely with the political frontiers of nation-states.

Even professionals who should know better, like the late Fred Hirsch, a noted international economist, share the One Nation/One Money myth. Economists in particular find it difficult to think of currency relations in anything other than traditional territorial terms. In the words of the research director of the International Monetary Fund: "Virtually all of the world's nations assert and express their sovereign authority by maintaining a distinct national money and protecting its use within their respective jurisdictions. Money is like a flag; each country has to have its own. . . ." The vice president of the Federal Reserve Bank of Boston concurs: "Currency independence rules the waves. . . ."

In fact, nothing could be further from the truth. Currency use is by no means confined by the territorial limits of individual states. Quite the contrary. As a French economist, Pascal Salin, writes, in a rare dissent from the conventional wisdom: "The production of money, like the production of law, is not an essential attribute of state sovereignty, despite what the mythology says. . . ." The geography of money is far more complex than we generally assume.

As a practical matter, a surprising number of moneys have come to be employed outside their home country for transactions either between nations or within foreign states. The former is usually called "international" currency use or currency "internationalization"; the latter is typically described as "currency substitution" and may be referred to as "foreign-domestic use." An even larger number of moneys now routinely face domestic competition from currencies that originate abroad. It is simply wrong to deny that several currencies may circulate in the same state; the phenomenon has become commonplace. The time has come to adjust our thinking to the new reality of cross-border currency competition.

Both international and foreign-domestic currency use result from intense market rivalry—a kind of Darwinian process of natural selection, driven by the force of demand, in which some moneys such as the U.S. dollar and German mark (the Deutschemark) come to seem more attractive than others for various commercial or financial purposes. Once, before the emergence of the modern nation-state system, cross-border circulation of currencies was quite common. The phenomenon has now reappeared as barriers to market exchange have come down since World War II, greatly expanding the array of currency choice. Competition between national moneys, a market-driven process in which transactors are free to choose among alternative currencies, is accelerating rapidly. As a result, the domains within which individual currencies serve the standard functions of money now diverge ever more sharply from the legal jurisdictions of issuing governments.

Does it matter? Again ask the person in the street, and the answer may be no more than a shrug of the shoulders. For national governments, however, intensely jealous of their sovereign authority, the question is anything but uninteresting. To those responsible for public policy, currency competition poses a clear and present danger. The production of money may not in fact be an essential attribute of state sovereignty, but along with the raising of armies and the levying of taxes it has long been regarded as essential. Genuine power resides in the privilege that money represents. The ability to monopolize monetary issue, excluding all other currencies from circulation, promises abundant access to real resources—goods and services of all kinds—and a powerful instrument of command over the operation of the national economy. Such advantages are lost when a government no longer exercises effective control over the creation and management of money. As one observer has argued, with only a touch of sarcasm: "A government that does not control money is a limited government. . . . No government likes to be limited. . . . Governments simply must monopolize money if they are to control it and they must control it if they really are to be governments. . . ."

Like it or not, the changing geography of money *does* matter—for governments, whose powers are diluted, and hence for those in whose name the state ostensibly rules. Political regimes differ, of course. The relationship between state and society, the public sector and the private sector, runs the gamut from purest democracy to the most arbitrary forms of authoritarianism. A government may act solely as agent for the electorate or as a principal in its own right. Public policy may serve the interests of the many or merely line the pockets of a few. The nature of the political regime, however, is not the issue here. Whatever the political regime—however representative or unrepresentative it may be—private citizens are vitally affected when public decisionmaking is compromised. Indifference to cross-border currency competition is a luxury that people in the street simply cannot afford.

[My aim] is to reconsider the role that money plays in today's world. This means looking beyond finance in the conventional sense of the term—the processes and institutions responsible for the mobilization of savings and allocation of credit—to focus on the underlying supplies of currency in which investments and other transactions are conducted. My starting point is the widespread and growing use of currencies outside their country of origin. My central thesis is that international relations, political as well as economic, are being dramatically reshaped by the increasing interpenetration of national monetary spaces. Market-driven currency competition alters the distribution of resources and power around the globe. It generates mounting tensions and insecurities—potential threats to global stability as well as promising opportunities for cooperation.

The impact on public policy is visible everywhere: from the European Union's heated debates about a new common currency to the still-unresolved fallout from the breakup of the old Soviet ruble zone; from Latin American concerns about the hegemonic implications of "dollarization" to anxieties sparked by the looming possibility of a yen bloc in the Asian Pacific. The United States worries about how to preserve the privileges associated with global use of the greenback; the British worry about whether to preserve the pound itself. Former Soviet republics seek to establish credible new currencies to go with their newfound political independence; inflation-prone developing economies struggle to sustain confidence in old currencies threatened with displacement from abroad. Governments on every continent fret about the risks involved in increased dependence on other states; even more, policymakers fear a growing vulnerability to unpredictable pressures from the market. A fresh wind is blowing across traditional boundaries, dramatically altering established patterns of global wealth and influence. The stakes could not be higher.

Analytically, what we need is a new understanding of the spatial organization of currency relations—the geography of money. To date, monetary geography has been woefully underexplored in the social sciences. Indeed, the very term "monetary geography" remains unknown to all but a few academic specialists. In a world of increasingly competitive currencies, such thoughtless disregard is inexcusable.

The issues are clear. If currency domains are no longer confined by territorial frontiers, what shape do they take? How are they determined? And what are their economic and political effects? If national monetary sovereignty can no longer be assured, how in practice are monetary affairs governed, and what can or should we do about it? Such questions affect us all. One does not have to be a geographer to appreciate the need for a better grasp of monetary geography.

TOWARD A NEW MENTAL MAP

. . . The traditional myth of One Nation/One Money inaccurately privileges the interests of governments in relation to other societal actors, perpetuating a misleading image of the structure of power in global currency relations. In reality, competition across borders transforms the role of the state in monetary governance, threatening a major crisis of legitimacy in this vital realm of political economy.

At issue is a growing gap between image and fact: between the way we conceive monetary geography in our minds—the imaginary landscapes that make up our mental maps of money—and the way currency spaces have come to be configured in actual practice. Representations of space are socially constructed. Such cognitive images matter because they embody specific understandings of underlying political relationships—who has power and how it is exercised. Our choice of particular spatial images automatically lends legitimacy to particular forms of dominion or authority. Clinging to an outmoded vision of monetary geography makes it more difficult for us to come to grips with the real problems of currency relations today.

One Nation/One Money is derived from the conventions of standard political geography which, ever since the seventeenth-century Peace of Westphalia, has celebrated the nation-state, absolutely sovereign within its own territory, as the basic unit of governance in world politics. Just as political space was conceived in terms of those fixed and mutually exclusive entities we call states, so currency spaces came to be visualized in terms of the separate sovereign territories where each money originated. I call this the Westphalian model of monetary geography.

In this state-centered model, national governments exercise monopoly control over the issue and management of their own money. As a result, power in monetary matters is concentrated decisively in the hands of the state. Not every government may be able to avail itself of all the advantages of monetary monopoly; compromises may be required that lead to either a subordination or a sharing of currency sovereignty among states. But even then, monetary governance remains, it is assumed, the privileged mandate of governments.

The Westphalian model may have been largely accurate once upon a time—but no longer. What was once a reasonable approximation of reality has now become an outmoded and misleading caricature. Today, market-driven competition has greatly altered the spatial organization of monetary relations, significantly eroding the monopoly powers of the state. We need an updated model, in order to bring perceptions more in line with contemporary developments. At a time when currencies increasingly are employed outside their country of origin, penetrating other national monetary spaces, we need an image defined not by political frontiers but rather by the full range of each money's effective use and authority. Monetary geography needs to be reconceptualized in functional terms, to focus on evolving networks of currency transactions and relationships. Seen in this light, the traditional Westphalian model is in fact a very special case. A strictly territorial money is a transactional network confined exclusively to the borders of a single state. We need to comprehend a much wider range of possible currency configurations.

In this new imaginary landscape, power has been redistributed not only between states but, even more important, from states to market forces. Government is no longer automatically privileged in relation to societal actors. States remain influential, of course, through their continuing jurisdiction over the supply of national moneys. But their role in monetary governance has been transformed, evolving in effect from Westphalian monopolist to something more akin to an industrial oligopolist. Now authority must be shared with other market agents, in particular the users on the demand side of the market. Currency spaces now are shaped not by political sovereignty but by the invisible hand of competition—governments interacting together with societal actors in the social spaces created by money's transactional networks.

The principal advantage of this new system of governance is that it provides a check on the arbitrary exercise of governmental authority. The state now, as oligopolist, is far less likely to abuse or mismanage its monetary powers than it was when it enjoyed a monopoly. The main disadvantage is also clear: market actors are less accountable than politicians to the general electorate, raising serious questions about legitimacy and representation in decisionmaking. Should markets be permitted to rule without the formal consent of the governed? Governments have not entirely lost their capacity to act on behalf of their own citizens. But without an accurate mental map to guide them, politicians may be unable to respond effectively to the many problems they face in making public policy today.

ELECTRONIC CASH AND THE END OF NATIONAL MARKETS

Stephen J. Kobrin

Twenty-six years ago, Raymond Vernon's *Sovereignty at Bay* proclaimed that "concepts such as national sovereignty and national economic strength appear curiously drained of meaning." Other books followed, arguing that sovereignty, the nation-state, and the national economy were finished—victims of multinational enterprises and the internationalization of production. While sovereign states and national markets have outlasted the chorus of Cassandras, this time the sky really may be falling. The emergence of electronic cash and a digitally networked global economy pose direct threats to the very basis of the territorial state.

Let us begin with two vignettes. Fact: Smugglers fly Boeing 747s loaded with illicit drugs into Mexico and then cram the jumbo jets full of cash—American bills—for the return trip. Fiction: Uncle Enzo, Mafia CEO, pays for intelligence in the digital future of Neal Stephenson's novel *Snow Crash:* "He reaches into his pocket and pulls out a hypercard and hands it toward Hiro. It says 'Twenty-Five Million Hong Kong Dollars.' Hiro reaches out and takes the card. Somewhere on earth, two computers swap bursts of electronic noise and the money gets transferred from the Mafia's account to Hiro's."

The 747s leaving Mexico are anachronisms, among the last surviving examples of the physical transfer of large amounts of currency across national borders. Most money has been electronic for some time: Virtually all of the trillions of dollars, marks, and yen that make their way around the world each day take the form of bytes—chains of zeros and ones. Only at the very end of its journey is money transformed into something tangible: credit cards, checks, cash, or coins.

Hypercards are here. Mondex, a smart card or electronic purse, can be "loaded" with electronic money from an automatic teller machine (atm) or by telephone or personal computer using a card-reading device. Money is spent either by swiping the card through a retailer's terminal or over the Internet by using the card reader and a personal computer. An electronic wallet allows anonymous card-to-card transfers.

It is not just the current technology of electronic cash (e-cash) or even what might be technologically feasible in the future that presents policymakers with new challenges. Rather, policymakers must confront directly the implications of this technology—and, more generally, the emergence of an electronically networked global economy—for economic and political governance. As the U.S. comptroller of the currency, Eugene Ludwig, has noted, "There is clearly a freight train coming down the tracks. . . . Just because it hasn't arrived yet doesn't mean we shouldn't start getting ready."

GOVERNANCE IN THE DIGITAL WORLD

E-cash and the increasing importance of digital markets pose problems for central government control over the economy and the behavior of economic actors; they also render borders around national markets and nation-states increasingly permeable—or, perhaps, increasingly irrelevant. In a world where true e-cash is an everyday reality, the basic role of government in a liberal market economy and the relevance of borders and geography will be drastically redefined.

While at first glance this concern appears to reflect a traditional break between domestic and international economic issues, in fact the advent of e-cash raises serious questions about the very idea of "domestic" and "international" as meaningful and distinct concepts. The new digital world presents a number of governance issues, described below.

· Can central banks control the rate of growth and the size of the money supply?

Private e-currencies will make it difficult for central bankers to control—or even measure or define—monetary aggregates. Several forms of money, issued by banks and nonbanks, will circulate. Many of these monies may be beyond the regulatory reach of the state. At the extreme, if, as some libertarians imagine, private currencies dominate, currencies issued by central banks may no longer matter.

· Will there still be official foreign exchange transactions?

E-cash will markedly lower existing barriers to the transfer of funds across borders. Transactions that have been restricted to money-center banks will be available to anyone with a computer. Peer-to-peer transfers of DVUs [digital value units] across national borders do not amount to "official" foreign exchange transactions. If you have $200 worth of DVUs on your computer and buy a program from a German vendor, you will probably have to agree on a mark-to-dollar price. However, transferring the DVUs to Germany is not an "official" foreign exchange transaction; the DVUs are simply revalued as marks. In fact, national currencies may lose meaning with the development of DVUs that have a universally accepted denomination. Without severe restrictions on individual privacy—which are not out of the question—governments will be hard-pressed to track, account for, and control the flows of money across borders.

· Who will regulate or control financial institutions?

The U.S. Treasury is not sure whether existing regulations, which apply to both banks and institutions that act like banks (i.e., take deposits), would apply to all who issue (and create) e-cash. If nonfinancial institutions do not accept the extensive regulatory controls that banks take as the norm, can reserve or reporting requirements be enforced? What about consumer protection in the event of the insolvency of an issuer of e-cash, a system breakdown, or the loss of a smart card?

· Will national income data still be meaningful?

It will be almost impossible to track transactions when e-cash becomes a widely used means of payment, online deals across borders become much easier, and many of the intermediaries that now serve as checkpoints for recording transactions are eliminated by direct, peer-to-peer payments. The widespread use of e-cash will render national economic data much less meaningful. Indeed, the advent of both e-cash and e-commerce raises fundamental questions about the national market as the basic unit of account in the international economic system.

· How will taxes be collected?

Tax evasion will be a serious problem in an economy where e-cash transactions are the norm. It will be easy to transfer large sums of money across borders, and tax havens will be much easier to reach. Encrypted anonymous transactions will make audits increasingly problematic. Additionally, tax reporting and compliance relies on institutions and intermediaries. With e-cash and direct payments, all sorts of sales taxes, value-added taxes, and income taxes will be increasingly difficult to collect. More fundamentally, the question of jurisdiction—who gets to tax what—will become increasingly problematic. Say you are in Philadelphia and you decide to download music from a computer located outside Dublin that is run by a firm in Frankfurt. You pay with e-cash deposited in a Cayman Islands account. In which jurisdiction does the transaction take place?

· Will e-cash and e-commerce widen the gap between the haves and the have-nots?

Participation in the global electronic economy requires infrastructure and access to a computer.

· Will e-cash and e-commerce further marginalize poorer population groups and even entire poor countries?

This widened gap between the haves and the have-nots—those with and without access to computers—could become increasingly difficult to bridge. Will the loss of seigniorage be important as governments fight to balance budgets? Seigniorage originally referred to the revenue or profit generated due to the difference between the cost of making a coin and its face value; it also refers to the reduction in government interest payments when money circulates. The U.S. Treasury estimates that traditional seigniorage amounted to $773 million in 1994 and that the reduction in interest payments due to holdings of currency rather than debt could be as much as $3.5 billion per year. The Bank for International Settlements reports that the loss of seigniorage for its 11 member states will be more than $17 billion if smart cards eliminate all bank notes under $25.

· Will fraud and criminal activity increase in an e-cash economy?

At the extreme—and the issue of privacy versus the needs of law enforcement is unresolved—transfers of large sums of cash across borders would be untraceable: There would be no audit trail. Digital counterfeiters could work from anywhere in the world and spend currency in any and all places. New financial crimes and forms of fraud could arise that would be hard to detect, and it would be extremely difficult to locate the perpetrators. The task of financing illegal and criminal activity would be easier by orders of magnitude. E-cash will lower the barriers to entry and reduce the risks of criminal activity.

Most of the issues raised in the recent National Research Council report on cryptography's role in the information society apply directly to electronic cash. Secure, easily authenticated, and anonymous e-cash requires strong encryption technology. Anonymous transactions, however, cannot be restricted to law-abiding citizens. Encryption makes it as difficult for enforcement authorities to track criminal activity as it does for criminals to penetrate legitimate transmissions. Should privacy be complete? Or should law enforcement authorities and national security agencies be provided access to e-cash transactions through escrowed encryption, for example? What about U.S. restrictions on the export of strong encryption technology? E-cash is global cash; how can governments limit its geographic spread? Can they even suggest that strong encryption algorithms be restricted territorially?

THE RISE IN INCOME DISPARITIES OVER THE NINETEENTH AND TWENTIETH CENTURIES

Glenn Firebaugh

There are two big stories about world income trends over the past two centuries. The first story is the remarkable growth in the world's average income. . . . The second story is that the growth has disproportionately benefited different regions of the world, with richer regions generally benefiting much more than poorer regions. As a result global income inequality has worsened dramatically since the early nineteenth century. (The terms "global income inequality" and "world income inequality" are used as synonyms to refer to the total level of income inequality across all the world's people.) . . . The enormous growth in global inequality occurred during the period of Western industrialization, that is, during the nineteenth century and the first half of the twentieth century. Today, during the period of Asian industrialization, global inequality is no longer growing.

. . . The remarkable rise in average income over the past two centuries has produced massive global income inequality, as income growth in the world's richer regions and nations has outpaced growth in poorer regions and nations. The practical implication for individuals is that in today's world, one's income is determined largely by one's residence. . . . [T]he data in [the table] . . . reveal . . . not only the striking growth in world per capita income over the past two centuries but also the striking unevenness of that growth across space. Incomes have surged ahead in Europe and lagged behind in Africa and (until recently) in Asia. So the eightfold increase in average world income since 1820 is easy to misinterpret, because it masks huge differences in income growth across the world's major regions.

An important part of the global inequality story is that the world has divided into three income camps. As [the table] shows, although the three camps were discernible in 1820, the divisions are much sharper today. It is important to note, however, that the divisions are no longer becoming more and more distinct, because the era of global "trifurcation" in income occurred during the period of Western industrialization and now appears to be behind us. Compare the two columns under Income Growth in [the table]. If we rank regions on the basis of their estimated income levels in 1820, we find that over the course of the nineteenth century and first half of the twentieth century the initially richer regions got richer much faster than the poorer regions did (first column under Income Growth). From 1820 to 1950—the period of Western industrialization— per capita income increased by a multiple of 4.0–7.7 for the initially higher-income regions, by a multiple of 2.5–3.7 for the middle-income regions, and by a multiple of 1.8 or less for the lower-income regions. Since 1950—the period of Asian industrialization— income growth rates no longer line up with initial incomes. Some regions in the low-income group have been growing faster than some regions in the high-income group. These results point to the possibility that the era of big-time growth in global income inequality may be ending.

In the meantime the legacy of the big-time growth in inequality remains. To appreciate the unevenness of the income growth across regions during the period of Western industrialization, compare income growth in the Western offshoots (Australia, Canada, New Zealand, and the United States) to income growth in Africa from 1820 to 1950. Average income is estimated to have been about $2000 in the Western offshoots in 1820 compared with about $450 in Africa in 1820—a ratio of less than 3

World "Trifurcation" Since 1820

Average income in major regions of the world in 1820, 1950, and 1990

Region	Income per capita			Income growth	
	1820	1950	1990	1950/1820	1990/1950
High-income group					
Western Europe (23 nations)	$1,292	$5,126	$17,272	4.0	3.4
Western offshoots (4 nations)	1,205	9,255	21,261	7.7	2.3
Middle-income group					
Southern Europe (7 nations)	804	2,021	8,092	2.5	4.0
Eastern Europe (9 nations)	772	2,631	6,397	3.4	2.4
Latin America (44 nations)	679	2,487	4,735	3.7	1.9
Low-income group					
Asia (56 nations)					
China	523	614	2,700	1.2	4.4
India	531	597	1,316	1.1	2.2
Rest of Asia	625	1,081	4,745	1.7	4.4
Africa (56 nations)	450	830	1,336	1.8	1.6
WORLD TOTALS	651	2,138	5,204	3.3	2.4

to 1 at the early stages of Western industrialization. By 1950 the ratio had ballooned to $9,255 versus $830. Unless income estimates are wildly off the mark . . . , regional differences in average incomes are profound.

In sum, the world income pie has expanded greatly over the past two centuries, but not everyone's piece has expanded at the same rate. Because incomes tended to grow more rapidly in the richer regions in the nineteenth and early twentieth centuries, income inequality has increased across the world's major regions. . . . I emphasize between-nation income inequality, first, because most of the world's total income inequality lies between nations and, second, because there has been a historic turnaround in between-nation income inequality that has gone virtually unnoticed.

GLOBALIZATION FOR WHOM?

Dani Rodrik

Globalization has brought little but good news to those with the products, skills, and resources to market worldwide. But does it also work for the world's poor?

That is the central question around which the debate over globalization—in essence, free trade and free flows of capital—revolves. Antiglobalization protesters may have had only limited success in blocking world trade negotiations or disrupting the meetings of the International Monetary Fund (IMF), but they have irrevocably altered the terms of the debate. Poverty is now *the* defining issue for both sides. The captains of the world economy have conceded that progress in international trade and finance has to be measured against the yardsticks of poverty alleviation and sustainable development.

For most of the world's developing countries, the 1990s were a decade of frustration and disappointment. The economies of sub-Saharan Africa, with few exceptions, stubbornly refused to respond to the medicine meted out by the World Bank and the IMF. Latin American countries were buffeted by a never-ending series of boom-and-bust cycles in capital markets and experienced growth rates significantly below their historical averages. Most of the former socialist economies ended the decade at *lower* levels of per-capita income than they started it—and even in the rare successes, such as Poland, poverty rates remained higher than under communism. East Asian economies such as South Korea, Thailand, and Malaysia, which had been hailed previously as "miracles," were dealt a humiliating blow in the financial crisis of 1997. That this was also the decade in which globalization came into full swing is more than a minor inconvenience for its advocates. If globalization is such a boon for poor countries, why so many setbacks?

Globalizers deploy two counter-arguments against such complaints. One is that global poverty has actually decreased. The reason is simple: while *most* countries have seen lower income growth, the world's two largest countries, China and India, have had the opposite experience. (Economic growth tends to be highly correlated with poverty reduction.) China's growth since the late 1970s—averaging almost 8 percent per annum per capita—has been nothing short of spectacular. India's performance has not been as extraordinary, but the country's growth rate has more than doubled since the early 1980s—from 1.5 percent per capita to 3.7 percent. These two countries house more than half of the world's poor, and their experience is perhaps enough to dispel the collective doom elsewhere.

The second counter-argument is that it is precisely those countries that have experienced the greatest integration with the world economy that have managed to grow fastest and reduce poverty the most. A typical exercise in this vein consists of dividing developing countries into two groups on the basis of the increase in their trade—"globalizers" versus "non-globalizers"—and to show that the first group did much better than the second. Here too, China, India, and a few other high performers like Vietnam and Uganda are the key exhibits for the pro-globalization argument. The intended message from such studies is that countries that have the best shot at lifting themselves out of poverty are those that open themselves up to the world economy.

How we read globalization's record in alleviating poverty hinges critically, therefore, on what we make of the experience of a small number of countries that have done well in the last decade or two—China in particular. In 1960, the average Chinese expected to live only 36 years. By 1999, life expectancy had risen to 70 years, not far below the level of the United States. Literacy has risen from less than 50 percent to more than

80 percent. Even though economic development has been uneven, with the coastal regions doing much better than the interior, there has been a striking reduction in poverty rates almost everywhere.

What does this impressive experience tell us about what globalization can do for poor countries? There is little doubt that exports and foreign investment have played an important role in China's development. By selling its products on world markets, China has been able to purchase the capital equipment and inputs needed for its modernization. And the surge in foreign investment has brought much-needed managerial and technical expertise. The regions of China that have grown fastest are those that took the greatest advantage of foreign trade and investment.

But look closer at the Chinese experience, and you discover that it is hardly a poster child for globalization. China's economic policies have violated virtually every rule by which the proselytizers of globalization would like the game to be played. China did *not* liberalize its trade regime to any significant extent, and it joined the World Trade Organization (WTO) only last year; to this day, its economy remains among the most protected in the world. Chinese currency markets were *not* unified until 1994. China resolutely refused to open its financial markets to foreigners, again until very recently. Most striking of all, China achieved its transformation without adopting private-property rights, let alone privatizing its state enterprises. China's policymakers were practical enough to understand the role that private incentives and markets could play in producing results. But they were also smart enough to realize that the solution to their problems lay in institutional innovations suited to the local conditions—the household responsibility system, township and village enterprises, special economic zones, partial liberalization in agriculture and industry—rather than in off-the-shelf blueprints and Western rules of good behavior.

The remarkable thing about China is that it has achieved integration with the world economy *despite* having ignored these rules—and indeed because it did so. If China were a basket case today, rather than the stunning success that it is, officials of the WTO and the World Bank would have fewer difficulties fitting it within their worldview than they do now.

China's experience may represent an extreme case, but it is by no means an exception. Earlier successes such as South Korea and Taiwan tell a similar story. Economic development often requires unconventional strategies that fit awkwardly with the ideology of free trade and free capital flows. South Korea and Taiwan made extensive use of import quotas, local-content requirements, patent infringements, and export subsidies—all of which are currently prohibited by the WTO. Both countries heavily regulated capital flows well into the 1990s. India managed to increase its growth rate through the adoption of more pro-business policies, despite having one of the world's most protectionist trade regimes. Its comparatively mild import liberalization in the 1990s came a decade *after* the onset of higher growth in the early 1980s. And India has *yet* to open itself up to world financial markets—which is why it emerged unscathed from the Asian financial crisis of 1997.

By contrast, many of the countries that *have* opened themselves up to trade and capital flows with abandon have been rewarded with financial crises and disappointing performance. Latin America, the region that adopted the globalization agenda with the greatest enthusiasm in the 1990s, has suffered rising inequality, enormous volatility, and economic growth rates significantly below those of the post–World War II decades. Argentina represents a particularly tragic case. It tried harder in the 1990s than virtually any country to endear itself to international capital markets, only to be the victim of an abrupt reversal in "market sentiment" by the end of the decade. The Argentine strategy may have had elements of a gamble, but it was solidly grounded in the theories expounded by U.S.-based economists and multilateral agencies such as the World Bank and the IMF. When Argentina's economy took off in the early 1990s after decades of stagnation, the reaction from these quarters was not that this was puzzling—it was that reform pays off.

What these countries' experience tells us, therefore, is that while global markets are good for poor countries, the rules according to which they are being asked to play the game are often not. Caught between WTO agreements, World Bank strictures, IMF conditions, and the need to maintain the confidence of financial markets, developing countries are increasingly deprived of the room they need to devise their own paths out of poverty. They are being asked to implement an agenda of institutional reform that took today's advanced countries generations to accomplish. The United States, to take a particularly telling example, was hardly a paragon of free-trade virtue while catching up with and surpassing Britain. In fact, U.S. import tariffs during the latter half of the nineteenth century were higher than in all but a few developing countries today. Today's rules are not only impractical, they divert attention and resources from more urgent developmental priorities. Turning away from world markets is surely not a good way to alleviate domestic poverty—but countries that have scored the most impressive gains are those that have developed their *own* version of the rulebook while taking advantage of world markets.

The regulations that developing nations confront in those markets are highly asymmetric. Import barriers tend to be highest for manufactured products of greatest interest to poor countries, such as garments. The global intellectual-property-rights regime tends to raise prices of essential medicines in poor countries.

But the disconnect between trade rules and development needs is nowhere greater than in the area of international labor mobility. Thanks to the efforts of the United States and other rich countries, barriers to trade in goods, financial services, and investment flows have now been brought down to historic lows. But the one market where poor nations have something in abundance to sell—the market for labor services—has remained untouched by this liberalizing trend. Rules on cross-border labor flows are determined almost always unilaterally (rather than multilaterally as in other areas of economic exchange) and remain highly restrictive. Even a small relaxation of these rules would produce huge gains for the world economy, and for poor nations in particular.

Consider, for example, instituting a system that would allot temporary work permits to skilled and unskilled workers from poorer nations, amounting to, say, 3 percent of the rich countries' labor force. Under the scheme, these workers would be allowed to obtain employment in the rich countries for a period of three to five years, after which they would be expected to return to their home countries and be replaced by new workers. (While many workers, no doubt, will want to remain in the host countries permanently, it would be possible to achieve acceptable rates of return by building specific incentives into the scheme. For example, a portion of workers' earnings could be withheld until repatriation takes place. Or there could be penalties for home governments whose nationals failed to comply with return requirements: sending countries' quotas could be reduced in proportion to the numbers who fail to return.) A back-of-the-envelope calculation indicates that such a system would easily yield $200 billion of income annually for the citizens of developing nations—vastly more than what the existing WTO trade agenda is expected to produce. The positive spillovers that the returnees would generate for their home countries—the experience, entrepreneurship, investment, and work ethic they would bring back with them—would add considerably to these gains. What is equally important, the economic benefits would accrue directly to workers from developing nations. There would be no need for "trickle down."

If the political leaders of the advanced countries have chosen to champion trade liberalization but not international labor mobility, the reason is not that the former is popular with voters at home while the latter is not. They are *both* unpopular. When asked their views on trade policy, fewer than one in five Americans reject import restrictions. In most advanced countries, including the United States, the proportion of respondents who want to expand imports tends to be about the same or lower than the proportion who believe immigration is good for the economy. The main difference seems to be that the beneficiaries of trade and investment liberalization have managed to become politically effective. Multinational firms and financial enterprises have been successful in setting the agenda of multilateral trade negotiations because they have been quick to see the link between enhanced market access abroad and increased profits at home. Cross-border labor flows, by contrast, usually have not had a well-defined constituency in the advanced countries. Rules on foreign workers have been relaxed only in those rare instances where there has been intense lobbying from special interests. When Silicon Valley firms became concerned about labor costs, for example, they pushed Congress hard to be allowed to import software engineers from India and other developing nations.

It will take a lot of work to make globalization's rules friendlier to poor nations. Leaders of the advanced countries will have to stop dressing up policies championed by special interests at home as responses to the needs of the poor in the developing world. Remembering their own history, they will have to provide room for poor nations to develop their own strategies of institution-building and economic catch-up. For their part, developing nations will have to stop looking to financial markets and multilateral agencies for the recipes of economic growth. Perhaps most difficult of all, economists will have to learn to be more humble!

FURTHER READING

Calhoun, Craig, and Georgi Derluguian (Eds.). 2011. *Aftermath: A New Global Economic Order?* New York: New York University Press.

Cohen, Benjamin J. 2000. *The Geography of Money.* Ithaca, NY: Cornell University Press.

Dowd, Douglas, ed. 2009. *Inequality and the Global Economic Crisis.* London: Pluto Press.

Firebaugh, Glenn. 2003. *The New Geography of Global Income Inequality.* Cambridge, MA: Harvard University Press.

Held, David, and Ayse Kaya (Eds.). 2007. *Global Inequality: Patterns and Explanations.* London: Polity Press.

Hirsch, Fred. 1978. *Social Limits to Growth.* London: Routledge.

Kobrin, Stephen J. 1997. "Electronic Cash and the End of National Markets," *Foreign Policy,* 107: 65–77.

Milanovic, Branko. 2012. *The Haves and the Have-Nots: A Brief and Idiosyncratic History of Global Inequality.* New York: Basic Books.

Rickards, James. 2011. *Currency Wars: The Making of the Next Global Crisis.* New York: Penguin.

Rodrik, Dani. 2003. *In Search of Prosperity.* Princeton, NJ: Princeton University Press.

Siegel, Lawrence. 2009. *Insights into the Global Financial Crisis.* New York: Research Foundation of the CFA Institute.

15

DEVELOPMENT AND THE ROLE OF WOMEN IN THE GLOBAL ECONOMY

Development sounds like the kind of thing everyone would want. After all, a child is not considered to be grown up until he or she is fully developed. When our bodies are mature, our minds are more alert. So when the term is applied to countries and regions of the world, it sounds like this is the sort of thing to which all countries would aspire. No matter how rugged their roads, how tawdry their houses, how backwards their schools, they want to develop into something better, and be more like the big kids—the developed countries of the world.

All of this sounds good. But what does it mean to develop a country? The obvious answer is to increase its wealth by producing more goods and services or selling more natural resources. But wealth alone is not sufficient if everyone does not benefit from it. So a certain amount of equitable distribution of wealth is usually an element of development. And this would likely mean jobs for everyone who wants to work. But in addition to these economic forms of development, we would also expect a developed country to have an improved quality of life—good health services, schools, environmental quality, and the like. So all of these things are part of development.

And yet, all of these goals are different. Seldom does a country achieve fulfillment in all of them, for it is possible to excel at one without being very good at the other.

Take the issue of wealth. The wealth of a country is often measured by its gross domestic product (GDP), the sum total of the dollar value of all of the goods and services and natural resources that it produces in a given year. According to the 2011 statistics of the World Bank, the country with the highest GDP in the world, by far, was the United States, with a GDP of over $15 trillion. China was second with about half that amount, followed by Japan, Germany, France, Brazil, Britain, India, Italy, and Russia. If the European Union were a country it would be first, with an even higher GDP than that of the United States. The lowest GDP was earned by Somalia and a number of small island nations. Clearly, small countries are at a disadvantage in measuring GDP.

But that's a point worth considering. Since the United States and China have huge populations and tiny island countries such as Grenada and Tuvalu have small populations, a more accurate measure of GDP would be to divide the total amount by the number of persons—to come up with a figure for per capita GDP. Now the comparisons create a different picture. According to the 2011 World Bank statistics, the richest nations per capita were fairly wealthy small countries such as Luxembourg, Qatar, and Norway, each of which had a GDP of over $60,000 per person. The United States is the only large country on the top ten list for total GDP and also on the top ten list for per capita GDP. In the per capita GDP listings it is number 8, with $48,000 per year. The listing for China, with its 2 billion population, sinks like a stone, from number 2 on the total GDP list to number 94 in the per capita rankings ($8,400 per person). India, which has a fairly high total GDP, has one of the lowest listings when it is ranked according to per capita calculations—126th place ($3,600 per person).

So it would appear that the United States does fairly well, both in total GDP and per capita GDP. But wait—the fact that the per capita GDP in the United States comes to $48,000 per year does not mean that this is the average income of the American wage earner. As we know, some people make much more, and the income of a billionaire family such as the Waltons who own the Wal-Mart corporation can equal the income of the bottom 30 percent of all wage earners in America. So you need to take into account the equitability of income. There are scales to measure the distribution of wealth within a country, and according to World Bank figures for the years 2008 to 2011, the United States does not do very well at all. The most equitable income countries in the world are the Scandinavian countries of Denmark, Sweden, and Norway, followed by Austria and the Czech Republic. Most European countries are fairly high in the equality scale. India is also fairly high, in the top fourth, higher than the United Kingdom. The United States is in the bottom half, just below Guyana and Venezuela. China is even lower on the equality index, just above the Dominican Republic. So if equitability is the measure, this might indicate that India is more developed than the United States and that Northern European countries are the most developed in the world.

But money is not everything, and quality of life is also a factor. The New Economics Foundation has developed a "Happy Planet Index" that includes not only money, but also availability of jobs, health services, education, and environmental quality. The index also includes political representation and independence and an economy that is sustainable and self-reliant. On this index, small countries rate the best: Costa Rica is first, followed by Vietnam, Colombia, Belize, and El Salvador. New Zealand and Norway did fairly well, ranking 28th and 29th, respectively. The United Kingdom was 41st. Japan was 45th. The United States rated only 114 on this scale; among the lowest were Russia and many African countries. (There were no statistics available for China on this index.) It is clear that money alone does not buy happiness.

According to the Nobel Prize–winning economist Amartya Sen the goal of development should be freedom. Freedom, however, can mean quite different things depending on whether one is a worker in a factory or a captain of industry. And in a global economy, quite often the factory workers are women, and many of them feel doubly oppressed, both by their society and by their working conditions.

The issue of gender is not a trivial matter. Women work long hours in very restrictive circumstances. They are often preferred as workers by men who think that they are more reliable than male workers, more compliant, and more willing to work for low wages. All of this adds up to a virtual global exploitation of the female workforce. Women pay the price for this dark side of global development.

Discussions about development often ignore the impact of development approaches on the largest labor force in the global economy: women. An emphasis on the kind of development limited to increasing GDP often means a form of development that exploits the lowest paid workers, and these are often the women factory and farm workers. Forms of development that affect women more positively are those that aim to increase wage rates, reduce inequality, focus on living standards, and, as Amartya Sen describes it, aims at individual freedom. One of the more interesting attempts to raise women's independence and economic freedom are the microcredit schemes pioneered by Bangladesh economist Muhammad Yunus. These provide opportunities for women to receive small loans to start local business and agricultural ventures in developing areas of the world.

The readings in this section begin with a discussion of ways of thinking about development, including the modernization school, the dependency school, and the world-systems approach. The author, Alvin Y. So, also discusses the convergent approach that combines the features of each school of thought and raises the question of what the goals of development should be. Alvin Y. So is a sociologist from Hong Kong who specializes in development; he received his Ph.D. from UCLA and taught at the University of Hawaii for some years before returning to Hong Kong to teach at the Hong Kong University of Science and Technology.

The other two readings focus on women's roles in development. The essay in *Foreign Policy* by Mayra Buvinić describes "the feminization of poverty"—the way that the global economy has created a new underclass of poorly paid women. Buvinić is from Chile, received her Ph.D. from the University of Wisconsin, and works with the World Bank as the director of the gender and development group; she is also a Senior Fellow at the United Nations Foundation.

The final reading asserts that mainstream development models have largely failed in most areas of the world, particularly regarding the integration of women into the workforce. The usual development models either marginalize women or exploit them; either way, the opportunities for women to improve their roles in society and assert their leadership are limited. This selection is written by a team of scholars, including sociologists Kum-Kum Bhavnani and John Foran from the University of California, Santa Barbara. Bhavnani was raised in the United Kingdom in a family originally from India, and she received her education in England. Foran received his Ph.D. from the University of California, Berkeley. The other two authors are originally from India; Priya Kurian is a political scientist who received her Ph.D. from the University of Madras and teaches at the University of Waikato in New Zealand, where the fourth author, Debashish Munshi, is a professor in the School of Management.

SOCIAL CHANGE AND DEVELOPMENT

Alvin Y. So

Over the past four decades, the field of development has been dominated by . . . three different schools of research . . . : the modernization school, the dependency school, and the world-system school. These three schools rose up under different historical contexts and were influenced by different theoretical traditions; their empirical studies have been informed by different theoretical assumptions. Thus these schools have offered different solutions to the problems attached to Third World development. However, as I have argued . . . , the three schools themselves have had a common pattern of development—after each came under attack by other schools, it modified its basic assumptions and initiated a new research agenda in response to the arguments of its critics.

The modernization school emerged in the 1950s, when the United States became the superpower of the world. American social scientists were called upon to develop a program for the promotion of modernization in the newly independent Third World countries. Heavily influenced by the evolutionary theory, American social scientists conceptualized modernization as a phased, irreversible, progressive, lengthy process that moves in the direction of the American model. Strongly influenced by Parsons's functionalist theory, they looked upon modernity as incompatible with tradition. Subsequently, American social scientists proposed that Third World countries should copy American values, rely on U.S. loans and aid, and transform their traditional institutions. However, when the modernization school came under attack in the late 1960s, its researchers modified their basic assumptions. The latest theme of the modernization school is that tradition can play a beneficial role in development and Third World countries can pursue their own paths of development. These recent modifications of the modernization school have started a new direction of research referred to here as the "new modernization studies."

Although the modernization school was an American product, the dependency school had its roots in the Third World. Specifically, it arose as a response to the failure of the ECLA [United Nations Economic Commission for Latin America] program and the crisis of orthodox Marxism in Latin American countries in the early 1960s. Drawing heavily upon radical ECLA and neo-Marxist theories, the dependency school conceptualized the linkages between Western and Third World countries as a set of externally imposed, exploitative, dependent, economic relationships incompatible with development. Thus the dependency school advocated that Third World countries should sever their linkages with Western countries in order to promote an autonomous, independent path of development. However, when the dependency school came under attack in the early 1970s, its researchers modified their basic assumptions. The latest assertions of the dependency school are as follows: Dependency is not just an economic but also a sociopolitical process; dependency is not just an external relationship but also a historically specific internal relationship; and development can occur side by side with dependency. These recent modifications in the dependency school started a new direction of research referred to . . . as the "new dependency studies."

The world-system perspective is the latest school to emerge in the field of development. It offered a new orientation to the interpretation of major events in the 1970s, such as East Asian industrialization, the crisis of the socialist states, and the decline of the capitalist world-economy. Influenced first by the dependency school and then by the French Annales school, world-system researchers emphasized the need to examine the totality and the *longue duree*. The unit of analysis thus should be the world-economy, a historical system composed of three strata: the core, the semiperiphery, and the periphery. The world-system school contended that by the late twentieth century, the capitalist world-economy would reach a transitional stage at which real choices might be made to change the path of human history. However, when the world-system school came under attack in the late 1970s, its researchers modified some of their basic assumptions. In the modified version, the concept of the world-system is taken merely as a research tool rather than as a reified reality; studies are now conducted on both the world level and the national level; and class analysis is brought back in to supplement stratification analysis and the like. These modifications started a research trend referred to here as "world-system studies at the national level."

Although . . . I have reviewed the rise, development, and transformation of the three dominant schools of development . . . I do not profess to categorize all works in the development literature into three pigeonholes and to label each as a modernization, dependency, or world-system study. I am not interested in creating typologies and classifications about other people's theories on development. . . . My goal is to show how the changes in the theoretical assumptions of the three dominant schools of development have led to a corresponding shift in research orientations in the development literature from the 1950s to the 1980s. . . .

Given the current pluralism in the development literature, what does the future hold for theories of development? Many researchers observe that the field of development is moving in the direction of synthesis. For example, Evans and Stephens have dubbed this synthesis the "new comparative political economy." Portes notes that there is a possible convergence between the "culturalist" modernization perspective and the "structuralist" dependency and world-system perspectives. And Hermassi suggests that "disciplined eclecticism" is a better guide than overreliance on paradigmatic thinking by the "liberal, managerial, neo-Marxist" approaches to development. . . .

It seems that the three dominant schools of development have shared the following traits in the 1980s. First, each has seen a call to bring history back in. Instead of focusing on the ideal types of modernity and tradition, instead of outlining the universal pattern of dependency, and instead of constructing the totality of the world-system, researchers are now more interested in understanding historically specific concrete cases. They probe into research problems that require detailed historical analyses, such as why the Islamic Revolution occurred in Iran, how the triple alliance broke down in Brazil in the 1980s, and what caused the economic miracle of Hong Kong over the past four decades.

Second, the new studies attempt to provide a *multi-institutional* analysis. Instead of just relying on one variable such as achievement motivation, instead of treating dependency merely as an economic process, and instead of stressing the overwhelming constraints of the world-system, researchers are now examining the complex interplay among different institutions, that is, how the family, religion, ethnic groups, classes, the state, social movements, transnational corporations, the interstate system, and the world-economy interact to shape the historical development of Third World countries. Subsequently, the new studies have become more sophisticated than the old ones, and they have moved beyond the simplistic argument of whether external factors are more important than internal factors.

Third, the question of whether development is beneficial or harmful is left open. Instead of portraying modernization as a progressive process, and instead of emphasizing the damaging effects of dependency, recent studies indicate that development has *both* beneficial and harmful effects. Researchers now need to examine each concrete case against its own historical conjuncture before deciding whether development has a positive or negative effect and on which segment of the population. For example, when Japan modernized its economy, Japanese workers turned to folk religion for refuge. When China withdrew from the capitalist world-economy, the interests of the Chinese peasants and workers were developed at the expense of the interests of the Chinese capitalists and bureaucrats.

In sum, there appears to be a trend toward convergence in the literature of development. The new studies should be more satisfactory than their predecessors because they generally do less violence to historical realities. They also seem to provide a more sophisticated, multi-institutional analysis to explain the major historical events that took place in the capitalist world-economy in the 1980s.

However, the trend toward convergence is far from complete. The literature seems to be moving toward a kind of selective convergence rather than toward a wholesale convergence. Despite sharing a few similar traits, the three dominant schools of development still maintain their individual features and "trademarks," as indicated by their names. The modernization school still focuses on the relationship between modernity and tradition, although now more on the positive role of tradition than before. The dependency school still analyzes the linkages between dependency and development, although now more on the positive side of development than before. And the world-system school still examines the secular and the cyclical trends of the world-economy and their impact, although now it is more concerned with microregions than before. It seems clear that the modernization, dependency, and world-system schools will not disappear.

WOMEN IN POVERTY: A NEW GLOBAL UNDERCLASS

Mayra Buvinić

To understand the plight of poor women around the world, consider the stories of Ade, Runa, and Reina. On the outskirts of Ibadan, Nigeria, Ade cultivates a small, sparsely planted plot with a baby on her back and other visibly undernourished children nearby. Her efforts to grow an improved soybean variety, which could have improved her children's diet, failed because she lacked the extra time to tend the new crop, did not have a spouse who would help her, and could not afford hired labor. Runa, a young woman with boundless energy, piercing eyes, and a warm smile, founded and runs the Self-Employed Women's Association in the Indian city of Lucknow, one of the country's most disadvantaged regions. Until a year ago, she had been unable to obtain credit from local banks for her impressively well-organized business, which now employs about 5,000 women homeworkers who sell *chikan* embroidery in national and international markets. Reina is a former guerrilla fighter in El Salvador who is being taught how to bake bread under a post-civil war reconstruction program. But as she says, "The only thing I have is this training and I don't want to be just a baker. I have other dreams for my life."

A farmer, an entrepreneur, and a former guerrilla—the working lives of these three women have little in common, except that they, along with most women worldwide, face similar obstacles to increasing their economic power: no "slack" time to invest in additional work that could bring in needed income; lack of access to commercial credit; and training in traditionally female—and mostly low-wage—skills. These obstacles differentiate the work experiences of men and women, exacerbate women's poverty, and sustain a vicious cycle of impoverishment from one generation to the next.

They also help to account for a disturbing global trend: the "feminization" of poverty. When the yardstick used to measure the degree of people's poverty is their level of well-being, women are traditionally found to be more impoverished than men. But poverty is more commonly defined according to income, and today, although the gap between the two sexes is decreasing in terms of well-being, it is increasing in terms of income. The evidence is imperfect, but current trends suggest that women account for a growing proportion of those people who are considered poor on the basis of income, not only in industrial countries such as the United States, but also in the developing world.

POOR WOMEN, POOR WORLD

This feminization of poverty should be considered a legitimate foreign policy concern. Because women are increasingly economic actors and heads of households as well as mothers, their poverty slows global economic growth. Moreover, in poor countries, their disadvantage feeds a destructive spiral of poverty, population growth, and environmental degradation. In a world of blurring borders, women's poverty creates enclaves of want in the midst of wealth and puts rising pressures on the developed world, whether by fueling costly humanitarian crises or by unleashing—for the first time—waves of females who migrate without spouses to seek work in richer countries.

The United States and other industrial countries have much to gain by reducing the impoverishment of women in developing countries. Not only can there be no substantial easing of world poverty until the international community focuses on female well-being as a goal and widens women's economic opportunities, but in this age of shrinking foreign aid budgets, investing in women offers policymakers the highest economic and social returns at the lowest cost.

Poverty has many dimensions and is difficult to measure. Calculated in dollars and cents, it is inadequacy of income. But measured in terms of the human condition, it is inadequacy of health and nutrition, education, and other components of well-being, including leisure time.

There is broad evidence that women in developing countries seem to bear the brunt of this latter type of "capability-based" poverty. In 1996, the United Nations Development Programme (UNDP) introduced a new index in their annual *Human Development Report* that reflects the percentage of people who lack three basic, or minimally essential, capabilities: to be well nourished and healthy (measured by the proportion of children under five who are underweight); to reproduce healthily (assessed by the proportion of births unattended by trained health personnel); and to be educated (represented by rates of illiteracy). This index primarily gauges women's deprivation since two of the three measures pick up disadvantages that are specific to women. Calculations show that 37 percent of the population in developing countries, or 1.6 billion people, lack these three essentials of well-being, while only 21 percent of them, or 900 million people, are "income poor," with incomes below the poverty line defined by the World Bank. Most of the "extra" 700 million poor are women.

Four Key Indicators of Women's Quality of Life

Region	Life Expectancy[a] (years)		Fertility[b] (births per woman)		Girls Enrolled in Primary School[c] (percent)		Women Aged 15–44 Using Modern Contraception (percent)	
	1970	1990	1970	1990	1970	1990	1970	1990
Arab States	65	57	6.1	4.7	46	92	29	52
East Asia	65	72	4.4	2.2	95[d]	113[d]	69	81
Latin America and the Caribbean	64	70	5.0	3.2	89	103	39	52
OECD[e]	75	79	2.1	1.8	104	102	68	73
South Asia	49	57	5.8	4.5	53	75	30	39
Southeast Asia and Oceania	54	63	5.3	3.6	—	—	33	51
Sub-Saharan Africa	47	52	6.7	6.5	36	67	14	19

[a]Regional average weighted by each country's total female population.

[b]Regional average weighted by each country's female population aged 15–44.

[c]Girls aged 6–11. The gross enrollment ratio may exceed 100 if the actual age distribution of pupils goes outside the official school ages, e.g., because of early age at enrollment, repetition of grades, etc. Data for 1970 from UNESCO *World Education Report* 1991 (Paris: UNESCO, 1991); 1986–92 data from UNICEF 1995 *State of the World's Children* (New York: Oxford University Press, 1995); all other data from WISTAT Database, version 3, United Nations, New York.

[d]Includes figures for East Asia, Southeast Asia, and Oceania.

[e]OECD, the Organization for Economic Cooperation and Development, includes most European countries, the United States, and other developed countries around the world.

SOURCE: International Center for Research on Women, Washington, D.C. 1995.

Statistics that show women lagging behind men in terms of well-being support the idea that women bear more than their fair share of capability-based poverty.

- Global literacy statistics show that in 1990 there were only 74 literate women for every 100 literate men. Schooling statistics reveal a similar trend. Worldwide, 77 million girls of primary school age (6–11 years) are out of school, compared with 52 million boys—a gap that becomes even larger when girls' higher overall dropout rates, absenteeism, and repetition levels are taken into account.

- Contrary to the biological advantage in survival that females have over males at all ages, men outnumber women in some regions, especially in South Asia, which is home to about one-half of the world's poor. Using vital statistics on the actual ratio of women to men in a society and contrasting them with those figures on the ratio expected if there were no female disadvantage in survival, economist and philosopher Amartya Sen of Harvard University has estimated that more than 100 million females are "missing" globally—a stark figure that he attributes to the comparative neglect of female health and nutrition, especially, but not exclusively, during childhood.

- Time is perhaps the one resource that the poor have available to them, and study after study shows that in poor families males have more leisure time than their female kin. To take care of their families, women farmers wake up before dawn in Honduras to grind the corn for tortillas, in Nigeria to process cassava, and in Nepal to fetch water and firewood. Put simply, women in poor households work more hours than men, and the poorer the household, the longer women work.

- While statistics on female reproductive health tell little about gender differences in poverty levels, they help to reveal women's disadvantage in poor countries, where high fertility and maternal mortality rates are the norm. About one-half million women die every year from complications related to pregnancy and delivery, the majority in poor countries. In some countries in sub-Saharan Africa, approximately one woman in 50 dies during childbirth—a grim contrast to Scandinavia where the rate is one per 20,000. At a total fertility rate of seven or more children per woman, the odds of such a woman surviving her reproductive years is one in six. As economist Partha Dasgupta of Cambridge University observes, for these women producing children is like playing Russian roulette.

The good news is that two decades ago, the proportion of women lacking the basics of well-being would have been much higher. Between 1970 and 1990, the life expectancy at birth of the average woman in the developing world rose by as much as five to nine years. She had substantially more schooling than she had in 1970, especially in the poorest countries where the school-age population of girls almost doubled. She also had greater access to modern contraception. As a result, global fertility rates fell by 40 percent. Unfortunately, international statistics on women are not disaggregated by levels of income, and it is likely that the quality of life of better-off women improved more than that of poor ones. Still, there is evidence of substantial gains in well-being, even for women in the most impoverished countries.

The bad news, however, is that while poor women have made gains in their overall well-being, they are falling behind in terms of income. Measuring household income or consumption is intrinsically difficult; even more so is apportioning this household income by gender, or separating women's income from men's. One way to gauge gender differences in poverty levels is to compare the situation of female-headed households with that of male-headed ones in developing countries. Looking at female-headed households also makes sense because in industrial countries such as the United States, where information on individuals and households is more reliable, the feminization of poverty has been closely linked with the rise in poor households headed by women.

Using information on female-headed households, the International Fund for Agricultural Development estimated the extent of rural poverty in 41 developing countries, which together account for 84 percent of the total rural developing country population. They found that between 1965–70 and 1988, the number of women in rural communities living below the poverty line rose more than the number of rural men living below the poverty line—increasing by 47 percent for women versus 30 percent for men. While in 1965–70 women made up 57 percent of the rural poor, by 1988 they accounted for 60 percent.

Female-headed households used to be the exception in developing societies, but no longer. In recent decades, the percentage of households headed by women has risen. Women everywhere are shouldering households' economic burdens. They are farmers in southern Botswana and Uttar Pradesh, India, left behind to mind farm and family by migrant husbands who sometimes do, and sometimes do not, send remittances back home. They are abandoned wives and young widows in Bangladesh and Egypt; unwed mothers in Latin American and sub-Saharan African cities; and refugee women with children throughout the world. Data compiled by the Population Council show a rise in female-headed households in 18 out of 26 censuses and surveys reviewed globally. Tabulations by the U.N. Economic Commission for Latin America and the Caribbean (ECLAC) find this trend in 8 out of 13 countries in the region.

Another new phenomenon in some countries is households maintained by wives. Two Argentine researchers, Rosa Geldstein and Nena Delpino, report that the number of households maintained by women in Buenos Aires rose from 19 percent in 1980 to 27 percent in 1992—one in every 3.7 households. Almost one-half of these female heads of household were wives who became main earners. Wife-householders were more prevalent in the middle-income groups, and their earnings helped families through economic downturns. Unpartnered females with children were more typical of low-income households. Where wives were the main earners and had small children, one-half of the households were poor; this figure rose to two-thirds for households with unpartnered female heads (while for all Buenos Aires households the figure was 40 percent).

The available evidence suggests that most female-headed families, especially those with younger children, are overrepresented among the poor. Data from ECLAC show that they are more numerous in the lowest income (indigent) category in 9 out of 13 countries. The International Center for Research on Women reviewed 61 headship studies conducted in developing countries over the last decade and in 53 of them found greater poverty in female-headed families. And if anything, the deficiencies in how we measure poverty (including the fact that leisure time is not computed as a household resource) suggest that the poverty of female-headed households is underreported.

A main reason for the greater poverty of these families is the lower earnings of the women heading them. Trends such as lower fertility and increased female schooling, combined with the economic downturns that many countries suffered during the 1980s and 1990s, have led to more women working in both low-paid market activities and in nonmarket production. In developing countries, we have seen a feminization of agricultural work, a sector characterized by low earnings. Women seek market work to "weather" the effects of economic and environmental crises and tend to spend more time participating in unpaid activities such as community kitchens and in providing primary health care to compensate for reduced government services.

Research on the economics of poor households and families has shown that increased family burdens, including declining household income or additional children, tend to change women's and children's—but not men's—allocation of time between work and leisure. That women respond to increased external demands on the family by sacrificing more of their leisure time is a gender feature in poor families. Poor women can be caught in a vicious cycle of deprivation: Unable to cope with too much work, they hand over child-care responsibilities to older daughters, who then must drop out of school. Thus, deprivation carries from one generation of women to the next, leading to the feminization of income poverty.

It is widely known that women's access to paid employment has drastically increased in recent decades, as has their social equality in many countries. Why, then, are more and more women finding themselves in poverty? Mahbub ul Haq, principal coordinator of the 1995 UNDP *Human Development Report,* which carried a special section on women, summarized women's achievements in the last decades as "a story of expanding capabilities and limited opportunities." Social and economic progress, including the contributions of development assistance and the international women's movement, have improved the well-being of women and better equipped them for the world of paid work and public life. Women have left their homes and their farms. A few have broken barriers and risen to the top, but most have encountered limited opportunities.

The majority of women obtain low-wage work because of persistent sexual discrimination in terms of employment and wages. In Honduras, for example, coffee and tobacco farmers prefer to hire girls and women as laborers because they are willing to accept lower wages and are more reliable workers. Especially in poor countries, female labor is primarily sought for low-paid positions in services, agriculture, small-scale commerce, and in the growing, unregulated manufacturing and agribusiness industries, which pay their workers individual rather than family wages, offer seasonal or part-time employment, and carry few or no benefits. Hence, this explains the seemingly contradictory trends of women's increased economic participation alongside their growing impoverishment.

BREAKING THE VICIOUS CYCLE

The vicious cycle of poverty that unfolds when women work more and earn less and children, as a result, get less food and maternal time, is both commonplace and hard to break. But recent studies have also made clear that while households headed or maintained by women may lack resources, they are generally more "resourceful" than their male counterparts. In Brazil, for instance, economist Duncan Thomas has found that income in the hands of mothers has an effect on child health that is almost 20 times greater than income that is controlled by the father. Similar results have been reported in Chile, Guatemala, Kenya, and Malawi. The key appears to be that in households where women control resources, they prefer (whether for reasons of nature or nurture) to invest scarce resources in child well-being. In Jamaica, for instance, studies have found that female-headed households spend more on food and other family-oriented goods than male-headed households.

These differences in the way that men and women prefer to spend scarce resources in poor households suggest that the income that poor women earn can yield higher health or social benefits than that earned by men. They are a strong argument for the desirability of expanding poor women's economic opportunities—precisely the area where there has been little, if any, advancement in recent decades.

In short, the question before individual nations and the international community at large is not why they should invest more in women, but how. Nations need to take measures that reinforce the virtuous cycle between poor women's and children's well-being. They also need to avoid actions that aggravate the obstacles that women and children already face.

A good place to start would be avoiding the unintended consequences of social and economic policies that can increase women's work burdens—such as reducing those public services that cushion the impact of negative economic shocks. Taking such measures without providing complementary policies that adequately "protect" poor women in their multiple roles as producers and reproducers is likely to set in motion, or intensify, the poverty cycle. Enlightened approaches such as providing women with access to reliable credit and savings can have multiplier effects that raise poor women's productivity in the home, as well as productivity and earnings in the market.

With that in mind, policy-makers should also stop promoting well-meaning programs that ignore women's traditional productive roles, the economic value of their time, and their domestic time constraints. One project, for example, established a cooperative for rural women in western Kenya that produced potholders for sale in Nairobi at a price lower than the cost of the banana fiber that was used to make them.

There are several other specific areas of national and international policy where changes and improvements could yield great dividends for poor women and for the developing world in general. Governments should take the following measures:

·   Expand substantially the access of poor women to family-planning and reproductive health services. Many successful reproductive health programs offer women a package of health services for themselves—and sometimes their children—bundled into one visit, in one location, which saves them both time and transportation costs. Boosting women's capacities to generate income will also increase their access to higher quality health services that may be purchased through private providers.

- Adopt education reform agendas designed to increase the quantity and quality of, first primary, and then secondary, schooling for girls. With the support of international agencies, innovative efforts to increase girls' access to schools are under way in Bangladesh, Pakistan, and other countries. These include giving scholarships and engaging families and communities in the task of getting and keeping girls enrolled. As World Bank vice president Mieko Nishimizu has said, "If you educate a boy you educate a human being. If you educate a girl, you educate generations."

- Create incentives for the private sector to expand women's access to agencies that offer credit and savings services. Microfinance operations, like the well-known Grameen Bank in Bangladesh, have succeeded in providing access to reliable credit and savings services to more than 3 million female borrowers in developing countries, but such operations still reach only about 5 percent of those in need of their services. They also provide benefits in other areas. One female microcredit client in Bangladesh, for example, mentioned that the profits from her expanded business had enabled her to buy a rickshaw for her unemployed husband to use as a taxi. As a result, she mentioned in passing, he had stopped beating her.

- Increase rural women's access to agricultural extension services by modifying existing ones or by establishing separate services for them. Currently, women farmers receive fewer farm extension services than men. In western Kenya, the lack of these services accounted for about 30 percent of the productivity loss in food crops grown by women.

- Expand women's access to productive infrastructure, especially in rural areas. This requires shifting government investment priorities to favor rural roads, improving women's access to water and electricity, and designing infrastructure that will support rural women as well as men.

- Adopt labor-intensive "pro-poor" economic growth policies that expand employment opportunities. Invest in upgrading women's skills in both traditional and nontraditional occupations that can compete in national as well as export markets.

- Overhaul social security systems as a complement to pro-poor growth policies, establishing gender-friendly regulatory frameworks for industrial and agricultural growth, and legislating childcare options.

- Target agricultural policies at impoverished farmers and give women farmers access to land titles; financial policies should promote the growth of small enterprises and foster entrepreneurship among women.

- Change statistical collection systems—that which is not counted is not valued. Much of the poor's productive work worldwide takes place in the informal sector, in home-based production, petty trading, and small-holder agriculture. Such work is still mostly invisible in labor force and employment statistics. Globalization, export promotion, and deregulation have all dramatically changed the nature of labor markets, and women's participation in them, while employment statistics have lagged behind. If women are not counted as working in productive activities, and employment trends are not disaggregated by gender, it will be hard to justify the implementation of public policies designed to increase women's productivity and wages.

Women's issues are becoming more visible in U.S. foreign policy. But although Secretary of State Madeleine K. Albright has legitimized a concern for women in foreign policy, she has done so primarily within a human rights framework. A growing body of statistical evidence shows that for developing countries what makes sense in terms of human rights also makes sense in terms of economics.

If not out of altruism, then for reasons of bald self-interest, developed countries should work to expand the economic opportunities of poor women. Once upon a time, women like Reina, the former guerrilla fighter in El Salvador, only migrated to follow or find a husband. This is no longer the case. It is likely that Reina, with few opportunities in her own country, will sooner or later join the rising number of female migrants who leave families and children behind to seek better paying work in the United States and other industrial countries. Wisely spent foreign aid can give Reina the chance to realize her dreams in her *own* country. I have not met Reina but I have met Runa and Ade, and I am convinced that they represent some of the wisest and safest investments available in the developing world today.

FROM THE EDGES OF DEVELOPMENT

Kum-Kum Bhavnani, John Foran, Priya A. Kurian, and Debashish Munshi

After some six decades of circulation, *development* continues to be a contested term, referring both to the ideal of improvement in people's well-being and to a far more dystopian reality on the ground. Because of our commitment to a noneconomistic development as an important way to ameliorate poverty, we start from the premise that the post-1940s development project has clearly failed the Third World.

In the contemporary neocolonial age, the nexus of big business, financial institutions, and capitalist regimes have wreaked havoc on the Third World in the name of development, usually making the word a euphemism for the exploitation of the world's natural resources to benefit minuscule transnational elites located in all sections of the world.

Flames of death and destruction, fueled by the desire of the United States, the United Kingdom, and their allies to control the cash-rich resource of oil, have engulfed large parts of the world, most visibly in the Middle East, from Iraq to Lebanon, but also in places such as Sudan and Venezuela, which are firmly in the media gaze but whose oil resources are often not discussed at length. The battles to control water—the other vital resource—have had no less devastating consequences. Much of the strife in the Middle East has been about Israel's relentless push for a development that is based on a disproportionate control of water systems that has left Palestinians with scarce access to a vital resource. In fact, as Vandana Shiva points out in *Water Wars,* some of the most important conflicts of our time revolve around contested needs for resources that are crucial for being seen as part of this apparently modern, technologically advanced, and strongly scientific era. So obsessed have neoliberal governments and market libertarians become with their need to control water that they have systematically promoted the privatization of a resource that every living being ought to take for granted, an obsession that has had tragic consequences for the poor in regions as diverse as Bolivia, South Africa, and India. Development-driven projects funded by the World Bank in South Africa that redrew water distribution networks on commercially viable lines sparked cholera epidemics in the poorest regions of the country. State terror was unleashed on the residents of the Bolivian city of Cochabamba to quell protests against the exorbitant prices of water set by Aguas del Tunari, a subsidiary of the transnational corporation Bechtel. The government annulled the contract only after sustained public protests and rebellion.

That these regions were predominantly populated by Black people would come as no surprise to those who have followed the development agenda in much of the world. In most cases, the worst impacts are felt by Third World subaltern publics who are at the receiving end of the environmental havoc and social upheaval caused by an endless quest for resources on their lands. Some of these Third World publics include the Adivasis in India, the Ogoni peoples who bore the brunt of multinational oil exploration in Nigeria, the Kayapo in Brazil, and the Meratus Dayaks of Indonesia.

In each of these cases, development as a project that centers growth as its main goal has failed the most vulnerable people of the Third World because of a misplaced emphasis on varieties of top-down, elite-devised "modernization" strategies, a lack of attention to the central contributions of women and people of color, and a disregard for culture. For this form of development project, the Third World has been used as space for the creation of new "resource frontiers . . . made possible by Cold War militarization of the Third World and the growing power of corporate transnationalism." As Anna Tsing points out, these "resource frontiers" were places where business and the military joined hands to "disengage nature from local ecologies and livelihoods" and rebrand natural resources as commodities for trade and profit. As Tsing shows, through a powerful study of the South East Kalimantan region of Indonesia, the relentless pursuit of resources to fire the engine of development has devastated local populations not just economically but also culturally, as local ways of living and being give way to the profit-and-loss logic of capitalism. This is not totally new of course. Retelling what is a familiar story, the ravages of colonialism meant that European colonizers had embarked on what they saw as a mission to "civilize" the colonies but, as Frantz Fanon says, we now "know with what sufferings humanity has paid for every one of their triumphs of the mind." This link between the civilizing mission of colonialism and the modernization project of development is rarely discussed within mainstream publications on development. As a result, much of conventional development is founded upon a set of fictional narratives that overlook many of its exploitative practices—fictions which might suggest some reasons for its failure for the peoples of the Third World.

There is another face to development, however. For us, this is an apt moment to insistently interrogate the dominant paradigm of development that has—along with the rather different approaches in Harry S Truman's 1949 inaugural presidential address and at the 1955 Bandung Conference—served to produce the idea of the Third World. Truman, in his 1949 inaugural presidential address said: "We must embark on a bold new programme for making the benefits of our scientific advances and industrial progress available for the improvement and growth of underdeveloped areas. The old imperialism—exploitation for foreign profit—has no place in our plans. What we envisage is a programme of development based on the concepts of democratic fair dealing."

As Wolfgang Sachs says, "Two billion people became underdeveloped on that day," and, we would argue, despite Truman's insistence otherwise, that it provided a legitimation to continue the colonial relationship albeit in a more modern guise. Truman's way of thinking about development is in contrast to, for example, the notion put forward at the 1955 Bandung Conference when Third World countries emphasized the importance of Third World nations relying on each other for scientific technical assistance and expertise, rather than relying on, and thus becoming dependent on, First World nations for such knowledge. Although the thinking about development at Bandung was top-down, nonetheless, those at that conference envisioned development as having the potential to be mutually supportive through a reciprocal exchange of scientific and technological expertise. In other words, development, at Bandung, was not viewed merely as a site for the entry of capitalism.

In our interrogations, we also seek to show how a critical element of development is about access to resources by the poorest and most marginalized populations and, as Mike Keefe-Feldman says, this access is "a struggle that is at once cultural, political, and ideological" (2006). The struggles over life-sustaining "goods" such as water, land, and forests epitomize not only the ongoing process of commodification of such resources but also a reframing of essential resources, within the antiprivatization movement, "from public good to human right." In this way, new concepts of development—from below, democratically engaged, and seeking empowerment by those most affected—are constantly bubbling up. . . .

POST-DEVELOPMENT AND ITS CHALLENGES

Wide-ranging critiques of the modern development project from a variety of perspectives have been present at least since the 1970s. Perhaps the most radical of these critiques are those that have emerged since the 1990s over the rejection of the development project itself—sometimes grouped together under the umbrella term of *post-development, alternative development,* or *neo/populist development,* to name the most prominent. Post-development perspectives scrutinize the narrow rationalist thinking upon which mainstream development—its institutions and practitioners—rely. The philosophical basis for the failure of development is this rationalist approach founded on a belief in a unilinear notion of progress and the conviction that the Third World is deficient in both knowledge and information. The struggles "between global capital and biotechnology interests, on the one hand, and local communities and organizations, on the other, constitute the most advanced stage in which the meanings over development and postdevelopment are being fought over."

Arturo Escobar's post-development argument, drawing from Foucauldian thinking, identifies three major discourses—democracy, (cultural) difference, and antidevelopment—which could serve as the basis for envisioning new struggles and expanding "anti-imperialist, anti-capitalist, anti-productivist, and anti-market struggles to new terrains." Through this emphasis on discursive analyses, as well as the significance it gives local and indigenous knowledges, post-development offers a move away from "the centring of economic relations" which characterize mainstream development studies. Indeed, Foucauldian notions of discourse and power have been central to the efforts of many post-development authors in focusing on the discourses of rationality that drive mainstream development institutions and development practices.

The post-development critique of development dovetails with feminist, indigenous, and environmentalist critiques of the development project. Each of these critical trajectories has demonstrated, in varying detail, the flaws, absences, and the explicitly destructive nature of modern economistic development. There are, also, however, many who question this modern development project and simultaneously take issue with the writings of those sympathetic to post-development, who appear to simplify and homogenize mainstream development and underestimate its appeal for Third World states. Thus, in his comments on post-development, Piers Blaikie calls for "a more politically astute and practical reconstruction of certain aspects of 'development,' particularly in the neopopulist mode of developmentalism." Further, he criticizes what he considers to be a "romanticised notion of the local," the failure to question problematic "social agendas that appear at the local sites of power," and, alongside others, the absence of credible alternatives offered by post-development work. A number of other analysts have attempted to moderate post-development's argument that development is one form of colonization and have argued that such a notion not only stems from a misinterpretation of Foucauldian notions of power, but is also "a hyperbolic rhetorical device." Indeed, as Aram Ziai succinctly states, the "ambivalence of post-development" lends itself to either a "reactionary neo-populism" or an emancipatory radical democracy.

Against this background, Sally Matthews offers the argument that the African context "with its rich variety of ways of understanding and being" is a source that "can provide the seeds for thought for all those . . . who question the PWWII [post-World War II] development project." In contrast to the lamenting of the loss of African values that some argue occur in the wake of mainstream development, there are others such as Jean-Marc Ela . . . , whose argument we embrace, albeit critically. . . .

Africa is not against development. It dreams of other things than the expansion of a culture of death or an alienating modernity that destroys the fundamental values so dear to Africans. . . . Africa sees further than an all-embracing world of material things and the dictatorship of the here and now, that insists on trying to persuade us that the only valid motto is "I sell, therefore I am." In a world often devoid of meaning, Africa is a reminder that there are other ways of being.

This eloquent statement offers much food for thought, despite the fact that it homogenizes "Africa," a homogenization that is a little too close for our comfort to how colonizers and Eurocentric perspectives view the continent.

FROM THE EDGES OF DEVELOPMENT

We are mindful that some of the critiques of post-development scholarship stem partly from the desire for answers—for alternatives to existing paradigms and practices of development. [We do] not offer prescriptions or "how-to" formulae for doing development. The primary goal . . . is to reenvision development through a rigorous yet imaginative exploration of how alternative conceptualizations—many of which emerge from the edges of development—can recenter the myriad refusals to contemporary mainstream development policy and thought. These conceptualizations draw on a variety of approaches from the realms of cultural studies, postcolonial studies, critical geography, and literary criticism. Most specifically, we adopt a Third World Cultural Studies perspective that represents a political approach to culture, and a cultural approach to politics, focusing on how political discourses circulate and compete. Our approach . . . builds on the Women, Culture, Development (WCD) paradigm, which rearticulates development by centering women and viewing culture as lived experience, thereby making visible the agency of subaltern women and men in the facilitation of social change and transformation in the Third World.

Mapping these cultural, political, and ideological fault lines is a major step in demystifying development. We put forward our cartography as a way to demonstrate how the articulation of the labor, cultures, and histories of women and men outside the mainstream frame of development offers more helpful insights to ameliorate injustice and inequality, the ultimate goal for all forms of development. The subaltern women and men centered in our approach are not seen, first and foremost, as victims in a system of cruel and unjust inequalities, but rather, as leading agents of change. This emphasis on racialization, ethnicization, and gender includes, by definition, a discussion of indigenous modes of agency. That we base our thinking on cultural studies approaches means that paradigms of development can be propelled toward an active engagement with subaltern agency. This, in turn, decenters the top-down approach to development we have critiqued previously. . . .

In line with the idea that Europe is "an imaginary figure that remains deeply embedded in clichéd and shorthand forms in some everyday habits of thought," we argue that mainstream development is largely elitist, functionalist, and inclined to privilege

First World ways of being. From this it is possible to see that this unilinear or progressivist concept of development is entrenched in policymakers' and practitioners' minds along with top-down science and technology. We address this unilinearity through a series of critical interrogations. This only becomes possible when drawing on multidisciplinary perspectives which emanate beyond the borders of the mainstream development literature. In our insistence that we closely examine the edges of development rather than an epistemological core, we put forward an idea of development that focuses on the realities of people's lives in the Third World. What this means is that . . . we turn the spotlight onto the lived experiences of the largely unsung but key protagonists of the South such as "peasants, tribals, semi- or unskilled industrial workers in non-Western cities, men and women from the subordinate social groups—in short, the subaltern classes of the third world." It is this multidisciplinary approach—one that peels away the fictions of development, that centers refusals to development, and that understands the significance of science and technology as being crucial in creating greater equality as long as it is not under the control of those whose only motivation is to create greater and greater profits—that we offer here. That is, we privilege an analysis of ways in which development has been, and continues to be, refused. In so doing, [it] focuses our critical gaze on the discourses that create an inferiorized Third World and which quickly translate into forms of development that are inherently oppressive . . .

In the quest to articulate this new conception, we . . . address three questions: (1) How is mainstream development "refused," and how can such a refusal suggest ways toward a more equitable and livable development? (2) How are emergent discourses around science, sexuality, and gendered economies challenging dominant approaches to development? (3) How do fictions and other cultural productions help us to analyze mainstream development as well as envision alternatives?

FURTHER READING

Anggraeni, Dewi. 2006. *Dreamseekers: Indonesian Women as Domestic Workers in Asia.* Jakarta: Equinox.

Bhavnani, Kum-Kum, John Foran, Priya Kurian, and Debashish Munshi. 2009. *On the Edges of Development: Cultural Interventions.* London: Routledge

Braungart, Michael, and William McDonough. 2002. *Cradle to Cradle. Remaking the Way We Make Things.* New York: North Point Press.

Buvinić, Mayra. 1997. " Women in Poverty: A New Global Underclass," *Foreign Policy, 108:* 38–53.

Chang, Grace. 2000. *Disposable Domestics: Immigrant Women Workers in the Global Economy.* Cambridge MA: South End Press.

Ferguson, Kathy, and Monique Mironesco (Eds.). 2008. *Gender and Globalization in Asia and the Pacific.* Honolulu: University of Hawaii Press.

Guevarra, Anna Romina. 2010. *Marketing Dreams, Manufacturing Heroes: The Transnational Labor Brokering of Filipino Workers.* New Brunswick, NJ: Rutgers University Press.

Jackson, Tim. 2011. *Prosperity Without Growth: Economic for a Finite Planet.* London: Routledge.

McMichael, Philip. 2011. *Development and Social Change: A Global Perspective*. Thousand Oaks, CA: Sage.

McKay, Steven C. 2006. *Satanic Mills or Silicon Islands? The Politics of High-Tech Production in the Philippines*. Ithaca, NY: Cornell University Press.

Momsen, Janet. 2010. *Gender and Development*. London: Routledge

Ngai, Pun. 2006. *Made in China: Women Factory Workers in a Global Workplace*. Durham, NC: Duke University Press.

Nederveen Pieterse, Jan. *Development Theory*. Thousand Oaks, CA: Sage.

So, Alvin Y. 1999. *Social Change and Development: Modernization, Dependency, and World-System Theories*. Thousand Oaks, CA: Sage.

Visvanathan, Nalini, Lynn Duggan, Nan Wiegersma, and Laurie Nisonoff (Eds.). 2011. *The Women, Gender and Development Reader*. London: Zed Books.

16

THE HIDDEN GLOBAL ECONOMY OF SEX AND DRUGS

Most of the world's economic activity is in plain sight. You can go down to the docks at the port of Long Beach near Los Angeles, for instance, and see a line of huge container ships that have arrived from China. From there, the goods they carry are trucked throughout the country, as everyone can see. But other aspects of the global economy are less visible, such as commodities and activities that are slipped across borders in the middle of the night. They are part of the hidden economy, and they are hidden for a reason: They are illegal.

Throughout history, many things have been traded illegally. Some have been legal goods that have been traded secretly to escape taxation or tariffs. In other cases, the item or activity itself has been illegal, such as mind-altering drugs and enslaved sex workers. Trade in illegal drugs is, in fact, among the world's largest and most profitable forms of economic exchange. Though, for obvious reasons, there are no exact figures available, the trade of illegal drugs is estimated as being among the largest and most profitable in the world—as large as crude oil, the largest legal commodity that is bought and sold in global trade. The United Nations Office on Drugs and Crime (UNODC) and the International Monetary Fund (IMF) estimate profits derived from illicit drug trafficking worldwide at about $600 billion, or 7.6 percent of global trade.

Illegal drugs are big business indeed. Up to $1.5 trillion in drug money are laundered through legal enterprises, accounting for perhaps 5 percent of global GDP. Because the drug trade is such big business, large illegal organizations—gangs, cartels, and the mafia—have been created to facilitate it. Currently, criminal organizations worldwide receive

70 percent of their revenue from illicit drug trafficking. The reason that they are engaged in illegal drug trafficking is obvious: it is immensely profitable. The profit margin for drug dealing ranges from 300 percent to 2,000 percent.

Marijuana is the most common illegal drug, but it is not necessarily the one that is traded in the largest quantities globally, nor is it among the most profitable. The reason for this is that it can be grown anywhere, including in garages and the bathrooms of college dorms. Although this may not be breaking news to some of you, what might surprise you is the extent of the global networks that do ship marijuana and many other drugs around the world—particularly cocaine and opium-related drugs. The so-called Golden Triangle in northern Thailand, Vietnam, Laos, and Myanmar is one of the most productive opium-producing areas in the world. Afghanistan is also a major producer of the sap from poppies that is refined to produce opium and converted into heroin, and then these products are sold everywhere, They are brought to Europe and the United States by couriers, often flying in commercial airlines. California and Florida are frequent entry points. Much of the co-caine that is sold in the United States comes from Colombia and other areas of South and Central America. It is often smuggled to Mexico, where the Mexican drug cartels, which also deal in large exports of marijuana, ship their products to the United States. These ship-ments arrive by every means available. Some are sent by truck across the border, others by small boats that come ashore on California beaches at night, and still others by private airplanes that land in secluded airstrips far within American territory. Though some of these shipments are intercepted and the smugglers are caught, enough of the shipments come through to provide immense profits to the leaders of the cartels. In 2013, the city of Chicago named Joaquin "el Chapo" Guzman as "Public Enemy Number One," because of the enormous amounts of illegal drugs that he was shipping into the city from Mexico. It was the first time that the city had made such a designation since the 1920s, when it desig-nated crime syndicate leader Al Capone as Public Enemy Number One. Capone also made his money from the sales of an illegal substance, but in those days it was alcohol during the Prohibition years, when the U.S. government outlawed the sale of alcoholic beverages.

The penalties for drug smuggling can be severe indeed. Most countries impose lengthy prison sentences on those involved in the drug trade. The United States has one of the highest percentages of incarceration per capita, and most of these offenses are related to drugs. In some countries, the sentences can be extreme. In 2005, a young Australian man was hanged in Singapore for attempting to import marijuana, and a similar fate was imposed on drug smugglers in Malaysia in 2010.

Clearly, these attempts to try to end the illegal drug trade have not worked, though in some areas great progress has been made. In Colombia, for example, the government has had some success in breaking the control of drug cartels over the production of co-caine in the rural areas of the country. More frequently, however, government officials in many countries have begun seriously to entertain the idea of some forms of legaliza-tion that would allow some drugs to be internationally transported and sold legally, with closer government scrutiny and control.

The problem of another form of illegal trade—human trafficking for sexual purposes and other kinds of forced labor—is equally difficult to solve. While not as large as the global drug trade, human trafficking is highly profitable. The victims are mostly women and children from poorer areas of the world. According to statistics maintained by UNICEF (the United Nations Children's Fund), some 5.5 million children worldwide are peddled for sexual purposes every year. The numbers of people who are forced into sexual slavery and transported across borders are also enormous—some 2.5 million per year, according to the UN Global Initiative to Stop Trafficking. Most of them are women between the ages of 18 and 24, and over a million are children. They come from poor areas of Asia and the Pacific, including Thailand and the Philippines, and are sent to brothels in Europe and the United States.

How can these abused women and children be protected? One approach is to intercept the networks that transport people illegally, and major efforts have been launched to do just that. Cooperation between the police forces of sending and receiving countries allow Americans and Europeans to be arrested when they go to countries like Thailand and the Philippines to arrange for the illegal transportation of children and young people for sexual purposes. And nongovernmental organizations have attempted to provide better economic support in poor communities where potential victims have been lured into the sex trade out of financial desperation. Still, the problem persists as part of the dark side of the global economy.

The readings in this section cover several aspects of this hidden economy. The first two selections are about the illegal drug trade, beginning with an excerpt from a book by David Shirk about the competition between drug cartels in Mexico that has often been described as a war. Shirk is an associate professor of political science at the University of California–San Diego, where he directs the Trans-Border Institute, which is concerned with U.S.–Mexico relations. The following selection analyzes the successes and failures of the war against the illegal drug trade and determines that there are far more failures than successes. The author, Eduardo Porter, is a writer who served on the *New York Times* editorial board. He was born in Phoenix and raised in the United States, Mexico, and Belgium. He has studied in Mexico and London, and he writes on global economic issues as well as issues relating to Latin America and Hispanic communities in the United States.

The other two readings focus on the trafficking of people for illegal purposes, including sexual activity. The first of these readings is an excerpt from the book *Disposable People*, which graphically describes the degree to which enslaved labor is a major aspect of the global economy. According to author Kevin Bales, more people work in enslaved conditions now than at any other point in human history. Bales is a scholar and writer who was raised in Oklahoma and received a Ph.D. from the London School of Economics. His concern about the magnitude of the global slavery situation led him to co-found the organization Free the Slaves, which is affiliated with Anti-Slavery International, the world's oldest human rights organization. The final reading is an excerpt from the book *Global Woman,* which chronicles the way that women in subservient household roles—both legal and illegal—have been an important though exploited part of the global economy. The authors of the excerpt, Barbara Ehrenreich and Arlie Russell Hochschild, are both distinguished writers. Ehrenreich writes on economic and feminist issues in a wide range of newspapers and magazines, including the *New York Times* and *Atlantic Monthly.* She was raised in Montana and received a Ph.D. in cellular immunology. Hochschild is a sociologist who taught at the University of California–Berkeley and has written on the social aspects of economic issues.

THE DRUG WAR IN MEXICO

David Shirk

Mexico is in the midst of a worsening security crisis. Explosive clashes and territorial disputes among powerful drug trafficking organizations (DTOs) have killed more than thirty-five thousand people since President Felipe Calderon took office in December 2006. The geography of that violence is limited but continues to spread, and its targets include a growing number of government officials, police officers, journalists, and individuals unrelated to the drug trade. The Mexican government has made the war on drugs its top priority and has even called in the military to support the country's weak police and judicial institutions. Even so, few Mexican citizens feel safer today than they did ten years ago, and most believe that their government is losing the fight.

Despite the most dismal assessments, the Mexican state has not failed, nor has it confronted a growing insurgent movement. Moreover, violence elsewhere in the Western Hemisphere is far worse than in Mexico. Whereas 45,000 homicides (14 per 100,000) have occurred in Mexico since 2007. Brazil and Colombia saw more than 80,000 (20 per 100,000) and 50,000 (30 per 100,000) murders, respectively. Even so, the country's violent organized crime groups represent a real and present danger to Mexico, the United States, and neighboring countries. The tactics they use often resemble those of terrorists and insurgents, even though their objectives are profit seeking rather than politically motivated. Meanwhile, although the Mexican state retains democratic legitimacy and a firm grasp on the overwhelming majority of Mexican territory, some DTOs capitalize on antigovernment sentiments and have operational control of certain limited geographic areas. DTOs have also corrupted officials at all levels of government, and they increasingly lash out against Mexican government officials and ordinary citizens. The February 2011 killing of a U.S. immigration and customs agent signals that U.S. law enforcement officials are now in the crosshairs. If current security trends continue to worsen, the emergence of a genuine insurgent movement, the proliferation of "ungoverned spaces," and the deliberate and sustained targeting of U.S. government personnel will become more likely.

The United States has much to gain by helping strengthen its southern neighbor and even more to lose if it does not. The cumulative effects of an embattled Mexican state harm the United States and a further reduction of Mexican state capacity is both unacceptable and a clear motivation for U.S. preventive action.

First, the weaker the Mexican state, the greater difficulty the United States will have in controlling the nearly two-thousand-mile border. Spillover violence, in which DTOs bring their fight to U.S. soil, is a remote worst-case scenario. Even so, lawlessness south of the border directly affects the United States. A weak Mexican government increases the flow of both illegal immigrants and contraband (such as drugs, money, and weapons) into the United States. As the dominant wholesale distributors of illegal drugs to U.S. consumers, Mexican traffickers are also the single greatest domestic organized crime threat within the United States, operating in every state and hundreds of cities, selling uncontrolled substances that directly endanger the health and safety of millions of ordinary citizens.

Second, economically, Mexico is an important market for the United States. As a member of the North American Free Trade Agreement (NAFTA), it is one of only seventeen states with which the United States has a free trade pact, outside the General Agreement on Tariffs and Trade (GATT). The United States has placed nearly $100 billion of foreign direct investment in Mexico. Mexico is also the United States' third-largest trade partner, the third-largest source of U.S. imports, and the second-largest exporter of U.S. goods and services—with potential for further market growth as the country develops. Trade with Mexico benefits the U.S. economy, and the market collapse that would likely accompany a deteriorated security situation could hamper U.S. economic recovery.

Third, Mexican stability serves as an important anchor for the region. With networks stretching into Central America, the Caribbean, and the Andean countries, Mexican DTOs undermine the security and reliability of other U.S. partners in the hemisphere, corrupting high-level officials, military operatives, and law enforcement personnel; undermining due process and human rights; reducing public support for counter-drug efforts: and even provoking hostility toward the United States. Given the fragility of some Central American and Caribbean states, expansion of DTO operations and violence into the region would have a gravely destabilizing effect.

Fourth, the unchecked power and violence of these Mexican DTOs present a substantial humanitarian concern and have contributed to forced migration and numerous U.S. asylum requests. If the situation were to worsen, a humanitarian emergency might lead to an unmanageable flow of people into the United States. It would also adversely affect the many U.S. citizens living in Mexico.

Solving the crisis is not only in the U.S. national interest but also in part a U.S. responsibility, given that U.S. drug consumption, firearms, and cash have fueled much of Mexico's recent violence. The United States should therefore take full advantage of the unprecedented resolve of Mexican authorities to work bilaterally to address a common threat. The best hope for near-term progress is to bolster U.S. domestic law enforcement efforts to curb illicit drug distribution, firearms smuggling, and money laundering. In the intermediate term, the United States should also both make an overall commitment to preventing and treating drug abuse and other societal ills caused by drugs and reevaluate the effectiveness of current U.S. and international drug policies. Additionally, with an eye to strengthening Mexico in the longer term, the United States should redouble rule of law and economic assistance to Mexico, with an emphasis on professionalizing the judicial sector and creating economic alternatives to a life of crime. To prevent Mexico's problems from spreading to Central America and the Caribbean, the United States should also work actively to reinvigorate and adapt regional security frameworks for the transnational challenges of the post-Cold War era.

NUMBERS TELL OF FAILURE IN DRUG WAR

Eduardo Porter

When policy makers in Washington worry about Mexico these days, they think in terms of a handful of numbers: Mexico's 19,500 hectares devoted to poppy cultivation for heroin; its 17,500 hectares growing cannabis; the 95 percent of American cocaine imports brought by Mexican cartels through Mexico and Central America.

They are thinking about the wrong numbers. If there is one number that embodies the seemingly intractable challenge imposed by the illegal drug trade on the relationship between the United States and Mexico, it is $177.26. That is the retail price, according to Drug Enforcement Administration data, of one gram of pure cocaine from your typical local pusher. That is 74 percent cheaper than it was 30 years ago.

This number contains pretty much all you need to evaluate the Mexican and American governments' "war" to eradicate illegal drugs from the streets of the United States. They would do well to heed its message. What it says is that the struggle on which they have spent billions of dollars and lost tens of thousands of lives over the last four decades has failed.

There is little reason to expect the elections this year will do much to address the challenges to the bilateral relationship. Enrique Peña Nieto, elected president of Mexico . . . , is a scion of Mexico's Institutional Revolutionary Party, which was tainted by authoritarianism, corruption and fraud during seven decades in power, before it was booted out by voters. . . . In the United States, neither President Obama nor his Republican challenger, Mitt Romney, has shown much interest in the nation's southern neighbor.

Yet the presidential elections on both sides of the border offer a unique opportunity to re-examine the central flaws of the two countries' strategy against illegal narcotics. Its threadbare victories—a drug seizure here, a captured kingpin there—pale against its cost in blood and treasure. And its collateral damage, measured in terms of social harm, has become too intense to ignore.

Most important, conceived to eradicate the illegal drug market, the war on drugs cannot be won. Once they understand this, the Mexican and American governments may consider refocusing their strategies to take aim at what really matters: the health and security of their citizens, communities and nations.

Prices match supply with demand. If the supply of an illicit drug were to fall, say because the Drug Enforcement Administration stopped it from reaching the nation's shores, we should expect its price to go up.

That is not what happened with cocaine. Despite billions spent on measures from spraying coca fields high in the Andes to jailing local dealers in Miami or Washington, a gram of cocaine cost about 16 percent less last year than it did in 2001. The drop is similar for heroin and methamphetamine. The only drug that has not experienced a significant fall in price is marijuana.

And it's not as if we've lost our taste for the stuff, either. About 40 percent of high school seniors admit to having taken some illegal drug in the last year—up from 30 percent two decades ago, according to the Monitoring the Future survey, financed by the National Institute on Drug Abuse.

The use of hard drugs, meanwhile, has remained roughly stable over the last two decades, rising by a few percentage points in the 1990s and declining by a few percentage points over the last decade, with consumption patterns moving from one drug to another according to fashion and ease of purchase.

For instance, 2.9 percent of high school seniors admit to having tried cocaine in the last year, just slightly less than in 1992. About 15 percent of seniors said they abused a prescription drug last year. Twenty years ago, prescription drug abuse was not even consistently measured.

The only dimension along which the war on drugs might be conceived as a success is political. If you ask Americans how concerned they are about drugs, they will give you roughly the same answer they have given for years: not so much.

In a Gallup poll, only 31 percent of Americans said they thought the government was making much progress dealing with illegal drugs, the lowest share since 1997. But fewer people say they worry about drug abuse than 10 years ago. Only 29 percent of Americans think it is an extremely or very serious problem where they live, the lowest share in the last decade.

But the government has spent $20 billion to $25 billion a year on counternarcotics efforts over the last decade. That is a pretty high price tag for political cover, to stop drugs from becoming a prominent issue on voters' radar screen. It becomes unacceptably high if you add in the real costs of the drug wars. That includes more than 55,000 Mexicans and tens of thousands of Central Americans killed by drug-fueled violence since Mexico's departing president, Felipe Calderón, declared war six years ago against the traffickers ferrying drugs across the border.

And the domestic costs are enormous, too. Almost one in five inmates in state prisons and half of those in federal prisons are serving time for drug offenses. In 2010, 1.64 million people were arrested for drug violations. Four out of five arrests were for possession. Nearly half were for possession of often-tiny amounts of marijuana.

Harry Levine, a sociologist at Queens College of the City University of New York, told me that processing each of the roughly 85,000 arrests for drug misdemeanors in

New York City last year cost the city $1,500 to $2,000. And that is just the cost to the budget. Hundreds of thousands of Americans, mostly black and poor, are unable to get a job, a credit card or even an apartment to rent because of the lasting stigma of a criminal record for carrying an ounce of marijuana.

Cracking down hard on drug users may sound great on the stump. But Americans who inject drugs are four times as likely to have H.I.V. as British addicts and seven times as likely as drug-injecting Swiss, mainly because the United States has been much slower in introducing needle exchanges and other measures to address the impact of drug abuse on public health.

The Obama administration acknowledges the limitations of the drug wars, and has shifted its priorities, focusing more on drug abuse prevention and treatment of addicts, and less on enforcement.

Still, many critics of the current policy believe the solution is to legalize—to bring illegal drugs out of the shadows where they are controlled by criminal gangs, into the light of the legal market where they can be regulated and taxed by the government.

Jeffrey Miron, an economist at Harvard who studies drug policy closely, has suggested that legalizing all illicit drugs would produce net benefits to the United States of some $65 billion a year, mostly by cutting public spending on enforcement as well as through reduced crime and corruption.

A study by analysts at the RAND Corporation, a California research organization, suggested that if marijuana were legalized in California and the drug spilled from there to other states, Mexican drug cartels would lose about a fifth of their annual income of some $6.5 billion from illegal exports to the United States.

A growing array of Latin American presidents have asked for the United States to consider legalizing some drugs, like marijuana. Even Mr. Calderón is realizing the futility of the war against the narco-syndicates. He asked President Obama and the United States Congress last month to consider "market solutions" to reduce the cash flow to criminal groups.

Legalization may carry risks, too. Peter H. Reuter, one of the authors of the RAND study, who is now a professor of public policy in the department of criminology of the University of Maryland, said he worried that legalizing drugs would vastly expand drug abuse, leading to other potential social and health costs. Supporters of the war on drugs insist that without it, consumption would have soared to the heights of the 1980s and perhaps beyond.

There are other options. The Global Commission on Drug Policy, whose membership includes former presidents of Mexico, Colombia, Chile, Brazil and Poland, has called on national governments to "depenalize" if not necessarily legalize drug possession and sales.

This means stopping the arrest and imprisonment of people who use drugs but cause no harm to others, and going easy on small-scale dealers, whose arrest does nothing to dent the flow of illegal drugs. It means focusing enforcement efforts on reducing the violence of the drug trade, rather than eliminating the drug market itself. It may also entail giving drugs to the most addicted users, to get them into clinics and off the streets.

Such policies require a drastic change of approach in Mexico and the United States. Their governments could start by acknowledging that drug dependence is a complex condition that is not solved through punishment, and that numbers of addicts or dealers arrested, or tons of drugs seized, are hardly measures of success.

A war on drugs whose objective is to eradicate the drug market—to stop drugs from arriving in the United States and stop Americans from swallowing, smoking, inhaling or injecting them—is a war that cannot be won. What we care about is the harm that drugs, drug trafficking and drug policy do to individuals, society and even national security. Reducing this harm is a goal worth fighting for.

THE NEW SLAVERY

Kevin Bales

Slavery is a booming business and the number of slaves is increasing. People get rich by using slaves. And when they've finished with their slaves, they just throw these people away. This is the new slavery, which focuses on big profits and cheap lives. It is not about owning people in the traditional sense of the old slavery, but about controlling them completely. People become completely disposable tools for making money.

On more than ten occasions I woke early in the morning to find the corpse of a young girl floating in the water by the barge. Nobody bothered to bury the girls. They just threw their bodies in the river to be eaten by the fish.

This was the fate of young girls enslaved as prostitutes in the gold mining towns of the Amazon, explained Antonia Pinto, who worked there as a cook and a procurer. While the developed world bemoans the destruction of the rain forests, few people realize that slave labor is used to destroy them. Men are lured to the region by promises of riches in gold dust, and girls as young as eleven are offered jobs in the offices and restaurants that serve the mines. When they arrive in the remote mining areas, the men are locked up and forced to work in the mines; the girls are beaten, raped, and put to work as prostitutes. Their "recruitment agents" are paid a small amount for each body, perhaps $150. The "recruits" have become slaves—not through legal ownership, but through the final authority of violence. The local police act as enforcers to control the slaves. As one young woman explained, "Here the brothel owners send the police to beat us . . . if we flee they go after us, if they find us they kill us, or if they don't kill us they beat us all the way back to the brothel."

The brothels are incredibly lucrative. The girl who "cost" $150 can be sold for sex up to ten times a night and bring in $10,000 per month. The only expenses are payments to the police and a pittance for food. If a girl is a troublemaker, runs away, or gets sick, she is easy to get rid of and replace. Antonia Pinto described what happened to an eleven-year-old girl when she refused to have sex with a miner: "After decapitating her with his machete, the miner drove around in his speedboat, showing off her head to the other miners, who clapped and shouted their approval."

As the story of these girls shows, slavery has not, as most of us have been led to believe, ended. To be sure, the word *slavery* continues to be used to mean all sorts of things, and all too often it has been applied as an easy metaphor. Having just enough money to get by, receiving wages that barely keep you alive, may be called wage slavery, but it is not slavery. Sharecroppers have a hard life, but they are not slaves. Child labor is terrible, but it is not necessarily slavery.

We might think slavery is a matter of ownership, but that depends on what we mean by *ownership*. In the past, slavery entailed one person legally owning another person, but modern slavery is different. Today slavery is illegal everywhere, and there is no more *legal* ownership of human beings. When people buy slaves today they don't ask for a receipt or ownership papers, but they do gain *control*—and they use violence to maintain this control. Slaveholders have all of the benefits of ownership without the legalities. Indeed, for the slaveholders, not having legal ownership is an improvement because they get total control without any responsibility for what they own. For that reason tend to use the term slave*holder* instead of slave*owner*.

In spite of this difference between the new and the old slavery, I think everyone would agree that what I am talking about is slavery: the total control of one person by another for the purpose of economic exploitation. Modern slavery hides behind different masks, using clever lawyers and legal smoke screens, but when we strip away the lies, we find someone controlled by violence and denied all of their personal freedom to make money for someone else. As I traveled around the world to study the new slavery, I looked behind the legal masks and I saw people in chains. Of course, many people think there is no such thing as slavery anymore, and I was one of those people just a few years ago.

FROM KNOWLEDGE TO FREEDOM

Looking at the nature of the new slavery we see obvious themes: slaves are cheap and disposable; control continues without legal ownership; slavery is hidden behind contracts; and slavery flourishes in communities under stress. Those social conditions have to exist side by side with an economy that fosters slavery. Order sometimes breaks down in European or American communities, but slavery doesn't take hold. This is because very, very few people live in the kind of destitution that makes them good candidates for slavery. In most Western countries the extreme differential in power needed to enslave doesn't exist, and the idea of slavery is abhorrent. When most of the population has a reasonable standard of living and some financial security (whether their own or assured by government safety nets), slavery can't thrive.

Slavery grows best in extreme poverty, so we can identify its *economic* as well as social preconditions. Most obviously, there have to be people, perhaps nonnative to an area, who can be enslaved as well as a demand for slave labor. Slaveholders must have the resources to fund the purchase, capture, or enticement of slaves and the power to control them after enslavement. The cost of keeping a slave has to be less than or equal to the cost of hiring free labor. And there must be a demand for slave products at a price that makes slaveholding profitable. Moreover, the potential slave must lack perceived alternatives to enslavement. Being poor, homeless, a refugee, or abandoned can all lead to the desperation that opens the door to slavery, making it easy for the slaver to lay an attractive trap. And when slaves are kidnapped, they must lack sufficient power to defend themselves against that violent enslavement.

It may seem that I am too insistent on setting out these conditions and themes in the new slavery. But the new slavery is like a new disease for which no vaccine exists. Until we really understand it, until we really know what makes it work, we have little chance of stopping it. And this disease is spreading. As the new slavery increases, the number of people enslaved grows every day. We're facing an epidemic of slavery that is tied through the global economy to our own lives.

These conditions also suggest why some of the current strategies might not stop the new slavery. Legal remedies that enforce prohibitions against ownership are ineffective, since enslavement and control are achieved without ownership. When ownership is not required for slavery, it can be concealed or legitimated within normal labor contracts. For laws against slavery to work, there must be clear violations that can be prosecuted. To be sure, other laws make it a violation to take away basic human rights, to restrict movement, to take labor without pay, or to force people to work in dangerous conditions. Slavery is unquestionably the ultimate human rights violation short of murder, but to uncover such violations requires two things: political will and an ability to protect the victim. If a government has no motivation to guarantee human rights within its borders, those rights can disappear. If those whose rights are violated cannot find protection, they are unlikely to accuse and fight those with guns and power. Such is the case in many of the countries where slavery exists today.

This lack of protection is the main problem in trying to stop the new slavery. The United Nations calls on national governments to protect their citizens and enforce their laws. But if the governments choose to ignore the UN, there is little that the UN can do. In 1986 the United Nations received reports of families being kidnapped into slavery in Sudan. In 1996, ten years after being asked to address the problem, the government of Sudan finally announced that it would undertake an official inquiry. Its deadline for announcing the results of the inquiry, August 1996, passed without any comment. Not until 2004 did a cease-fire agreement seem to bring an end to kidnapping and enslavement by government-backed militias. If slavery continues because national governments turn a blind eye, cooperate with slaveholders, or even enslave people themselves, then the diplomatic approach will have little impact.

That is why it is necessary to ask two questions: What can make (or help) these governments protect their own citizens? And what do we know about the new slavery that can help us put a stop to it, if national governments won't? Both have economic answers. If we have learned one thing from the end of apartheid in South Africa, it is that hitting a government in the pocketbook hard enough can make it change its ways. If slavery stops being profitable, there is little motivation to enslave. But what do we really know about the economics of the new slavery? The answer, I'm afraid, is almost nothing. That is the reason I began this journey. In Thailand, Mauritania, Brazil, Pakistan, and India (all countries that have signed the United Nations agreements on slavery and bonded labor), I investigated local slavery. In each case I looked hard into how slavery worked as a *business*, and how the surrounding community protected slavery by custom or ignored it in fear. When you have met the slaves I met and come to understand their lives, when you have heard the justifications of the slaveholders and the government officials, then you will know the new slavery and, I hope, how we can work to stop it.

NANNIES, MAIDS, AND SEX WORKERS IN THE GLOBAL ECONOMY

Barbara Ehrenreich and Arlie Russell Hochschild

The lifestyles of the First World are made possible by a global transfer of the services associated with a wife's traditional role—child care, homemoo9aking, and sex—from poor countries to rich ones. To generalize and perhaps oversimplify: in an earlier phase of imperialism, northern countries extracted natural resources and agricultural products— rubber, metals, and sugar, for example—from lands they conquered and colonized. Today, while still relying on Third World countries for agricultural and industrial labor, the wealthy countries also seek to extract something harder to measure and quantify, something that can look very much like love. Nannies like Josephine bring the distant families that employ them real maternal affection, no doubt enhanced by the heartbreaking absence of their own children in the poor countries they leave behind. Similarly, women who migrate from country to country to work as maids bring not only their muscle power but an attentiveness to detail and to the human relationships in the household that might otherwise have been invested in their own families. Sex workers offer the simulation of sexual and romantic love, or at least transient sexual companionship. It is as if the wealthy parts of the world are running short on precious emotional and sexual resources and have had to turn to poorer regions for fresh supplies.

There are plenty of historical precedents for this globalization of traditional female services. In the ancient Middle East, the women of populations defeated in war were routinely enslaved and hauled off to serve as household workers and concubines for the victors. Among the Africans brought to North America as slaves in the sixteenth through nineteenth centuries, about a third were women and children, and many of those women were pressed to be concubines, domestic servants, or both. Nineteenth-century Irishwomen—along with many rural Englishwomen—migrated to English towns and cities to work as domestics in the homes of the growing upper middle class. Services thought to be innately feminine—child care, housework, and sex—often win little recognition or pay. But they have always been sufficiently in demand to transport over long distances if necessary. What is new today is the sheer number of female migrants and the very long distances they travel. Immigration statistics show huge numbers of women in motion, typically from poor countries to rich. Although the gross statistics give little clue as to the jobs women eventually take, there are reasons to infer that much of their work is "caring work," performed either in private homes or in institutional settings such as hospitals, hospices, child-care centers, and nursing homes.

The statistics are, in many ways, frustrating. We have information on legal migrants but not on illegal migrants, who, experts tell us, travel in equal if not greater numbers. Furthermore, many Third World countries lack data for past years, which makes it hard to trace trends over time; or they use varying methods of gathering information, which makes it hard to compare one country with another. Nevertheless, the trend is clear enough for some scholars, including Stephen Castles, Mark Miller, and Janet Momsen, to speak of a "feminization of migration." From 1950 to 1970, for example, men predominated in labor migration to northern Europe from Turkey, Greece, and North Africa. Since then, women have been replacing men. In 1946, women were fewer than 3 percent of the Algerians and Moroccans living in France; by 1990, they were more than 40 percent. Overall, half of the world's 120 million legal and illegal migrants are now believed to be women.

. . . The men in wealthier countries are also, of course, directly responsible for the demand for immigrant sex workers—as well as for the sexual abuse of many migrant women who work as domestics. Why, we wondered, is there a particular demand for "imported" sexual partners? Part of the answer may lie in the fact that new immigrants often take up the least desirable work, and, thanks to the AIDS epidemic, prostitution has become a job that ever fewer women deliberately choose. But perhaps some of this demand, as we see in Denise Brennan's [discussion of] sex tourism, grows out of the erotic lure of the "exotic." Immigrant women may seem desirable sexual partners for the same reason that First World employers believe them to be especially gifted as caregivers: they are thought to embody the traditional feminine qualities of nurturance, docility, and eagerness to please. Some men feel nostalgic for these qualities, which they associate with a bygone way of life. Even as many wage-earning Western women assimilate to the competitive culture of "male" work and ask respect for making it in a man's world, some men seek in the "exotic Orient" or "hot-blooded tropics" a woman from the imagined past.

Of course, not all sex workers migrate voluntarily. An alarming number of women and girls are trafficked by smugglers and sold into bondage. Because trafficking is illegal and secret, the numbers are hard to know with any certainty. Kevin Bales estimates that in Thailand alone, a country of 60 million, half a million to a million women are prostitutes, and one out of every twenty of these is enslaved. As Bales . . . shows, many of these women are daughters whom northern hill-tribe families have sold to brothels in the cities of the south. Believing the promises of jobs and money, some begin the voyage willingly, only to discover days later that the "arrangers" are traffickers who steal their passports, define them as debtors, and enslave them as prostitutes. Other women and girls are kidnapped, or sold by their impoverished families, and then trafficked to brothels. Even worse fates befall women from neighboring Laos and Burma, who flee crushing poverty and repression at home only to fall into the hands of Thai slave traders.

If the factors that pull migrant women workers to affluent countries are not as simple as they at first appear, neither are the factors that push them. Certainly relative poverty plays a major role, but, interestingly, migrant women often do not come from the poorest classes of their societies. In fact, they are typically more affluent and better educated than male migrants. Many female migrants from the Philippines and Mexico, for example, have high school or college diplomas and have held middle-class—albeit low-paid—jobs back home. One study of Mexican migrants suggests that the trend is toward increasingly better-educated female migrants. Thirty years ago, most Mexican-born maids in the United States had been poorly educated maids in Mexico. Now a majority have high school degrees and have held clerical, retail, or professional jobs before leaving for the United States. Such women are likely to be enterprising and adventurous enough to resist the social pressures to stay home and accept their lot in life.

Noneconomic factors—or at least factors that are not immediately and directly economic—also influence a woman's decision to emigrate. By migrating, a woman may escape the expectation that she care for elderly family members, relinquish her paycheck to a husband or father, or defer to an abusive husband. Migration may also be a practical response to a failed marriage and the need to provide for children without male help. In the Philippines, . . . Rhacel Salazar Parreñas tells us, migration is sometimes called a "Philippine divorce." And there are forces at work that may be making the men of poor countries less desirable as husbands. Male unemployment runs high in the countries that supply female domestics to the First World. Unable to make a living, these men often grow demoralized and cease contributing to their families in other ways. Many female migrants, including those [discussed by] Michele Gamburd . . . , tell of unemployed husbands who drink or gamble their remittances away. Notes one study of Sri Lankan women working as maids in the Persian Gulf: "It is not unusual . . . for the women to find upon their return that their Gulf wages by and large have been squandered on alcohol, gambling and other dubious undertakings while they were away."

To an extent then, the globalization of child care and housework brings the ambitious and independent women of the world together: the career-oriented upper-middle-class woman of an affluent nation and the striving woman from a crumbling Third World or postcommunist economy. Only it does not bring them together in the way that second-wave feminists in affluent countries once liked to imagine—as sisters and allies struggling to achieve common goals. Instead, they come together as mistress and maid, employer and employee, across a great divide of privilege and opportunity.

This trend toward global redivision of women's traditional work throws new light on the entire process of globalization. Conventionally, it is the poorer countries that are thought to be dependent on the richer ones—a dependency symbolized by the huge debt they owe to global financial institutions. What we explore . . . , however, is a dependency that works in the other direction, and it is a dependency of a particularly intimate kind. Increasingly often, as affluent and middle-class families in the First World come to depend on migrants from poorer regions to provide child care, homemaking, and sexual services, a global relationship arises that in some ways mirrors the traditional relationship between the sexes. The First World takes on a role like that of the old-fashioned male in the family—pampered, entitled, unable to cook, clean, or find his socks. Poor countries take on a role like that of the traditional woman within the family—patient, nurturing, and self-denying. A division of labor feminists critiqued when it was "local" has now, metaphorically speaking, gone global.

To press this metaphor a bit further, the resulting relationship is by no means a "marriage," in the sense of being openly acknowledged. In fact, it is striking how invisible the globalization of women's work remains, how little it is noted or discussed in the First World. Trend spotters have had almost nothing to say about the fact that increasing numbers of affluent First World children and elderly persons are tended by immigrant care workers or live in homes cleaned by immigrant maids. Even the political groups we might expect to be concerned about this trend—antiglobalization and feminist activists—often seem to have noticed only the most extravagant abuses, such as trafficking and female enslavement. So if a metaphorically gendered relationship has developed between rich and poor countries, it is less like a marriage and more like a secret affair.

But it is a "secret affair" conducted in plain view of the children. Little Isadora and the other children of the First World raised by "two mommies" may be learning more than their ABC's from a loving surrogate parent. In their own living rooms, they are learning a vast and tragic global politics. Children see. But they also learn how to disregard what they see. They learn how adults make the visible invisible. That is their "early childhood education." . . .

The globalization of women's traditional role poses important challenges to anyone concerned about gender and economic inequity. How can we improve the lives and opportunities of migrant women engaged in legal occupations such as nannies and maids? How can we prevent trafficking and enslavement? More basically, can we find a way to counterbalance the systematic transfer of caring work from poor countries to rich, and the inevitable trauma of the children left behind? [We] do not have easy answers, but . . . [we need to] take that essential first step—to bring the world's most invisible women into the light. Before we can hope to find activist solutions, we need to see these women as full human beings. They are strivers as well as victims, wives and mothers as well as workers—sisters, in other words, with whom we in the First World may someday define a common agenda.

FURTHER READING

Bagley, Bruce, and William Walker (Eds.). 1994. *Drug Trafficking in the Americas.* Miami: University of Miami North-South Center Press.

Bales, Kevin. 2012. *Disposable People: New Slavery in the Global Economy.* Berkeley: University of California Press.

Batstone, David. 2010. *Not For Sale: Return of the Global Slave Trade, and How We Can Fight It.* New York: HarperOne.

Ehrenreich, Barbara, and Arlie Russell Hochschild. 2004. *Global Woman: Nannies, Maids, and Sex Workers in the Global Economy.* New York: Owl Books.

Enloe, Cynthia. 2000. *Bananas, Beaches, and Buses: Making Feminist Sense of International Politics.* Berkeley: University of California Press.

Jeffreys, Sheila. 2008. *The Industrial Vagina: The Political Economy of the Global Sex Trade.* London: Routledge.

Kara, Siddharth. 2010. *Sex Trafficking: Inside the Business of Modern Slavery.* New York: Columbia University Press.

Kenney, Michael. 2007. "The Architecture of Drug Trafficking: Network Forms of Organisation in the Colombian Cocaine Trade," *Global Crime,* 8(3): S.233–259.

Lee, Jin-Kyung. 2010. *Service Economies: Militarism, Sex Work, and Migrant Labor in South Korea.* Minneapolis: University of Minnesota Press.

Malarek, Victor. 2005. *The Natashas: Inside the New Global Sex Trade.* New York: Arcade.

Mares, David. 2005. *Drug Wars and Coffee Houses: The Political Economy of the Global Drug Trade.* Washington, DC: Congressional Quarterly Press

Shirk, David. *The Drug War in Mexico: Confronting a Common Threat.* New York: Council on Foreign Relations.

Watt, Peter, and Roberto Zepeda. 2012. *Drug War Mexico: Politics, Neoliberalism and Violence in the New Narcoeconomy.* London: Zed Books.

Yuh, Ji-Yeon. 2004. *Beyond the Shadow of Camp Town: Korean Military Brides in America.* New York: New York University Press.

17

GLOBAL ENVIRONMENTAL AND HEALTH CRISES

When college students in Santa Barbara toss old plastic chairs off the balconies of their rooms overlooking the Pacific Ocean, they think that the chairs will just disappear. But that's not what happens; they can stay around for years, and currents in the ocean can carry bits of that plastic debris throughout the oceans' ecosystem. Some of it may end up in the Pacific trash vortex—also known as the Great Pacific Garbage Patch—a swirling gyre of oceanborne trash floating on hundreds of square miles of the ocean's surface in the northern central Pacific region.

Perhaps nothing demonstrates the interconnectedness of our world more than situations like this—the environmental and health issues that confront everyone across the globe. An incident in one part of the world can have repercussions on the other side of the planet, just as plastic debris can float across the ocean. Cutting down large swaths of the Amazon rainforest, for instance, can have a global impact; the loss of these trees reduces the ability of the earth to produce sufficient oxygen to offset the rapid accumulation of carbon dioxide in our atmosphere, and this, in turn, creates global warming.

A forest fire in Indonesia in 1997 was so spectacular that it created a cloud of haze that lasted for months and covered much of the Indian Ocean and extended all the way to Africa. The haze combined with smoke to create smog that smothered urban areas, reduced air traffic and endangered the health of those forced to breathe it. The economies of Malaysia and Singapore were damaged. But ultimately it affected everyone on earth since the burning wood produced as much as 2.5 gigatons of carbon dioxide that was released into the atmosphere.

The Indonesian forest fire, therefore, was not just a local disaster. It contributed to the most serious environmental crisis that is currently confronted by the planet: global warming. The planet warms and cools in regular cycles over historical eons, but the current situation of warming is peculiar in two respects: it is rapid, and it is caused by humans.

Scientists have shown that the warming of the earth's surface in the past hundred years has increased at an almost exponential rate. The temperature now is almost one and a half degrees Fahrenheit higher than it was a century ago, and two-thirds of that increase has occurred since 1980. A degree or two might not seem like much, but if the world's temperature increases two or three degrees in the next fifty years—which is almost certain, at the current rates of growth—it will have disastrous results. The ice caps will melt, the ocean will rise, and the weather patterns of the world will be disrupted. As a result, huge storms and droughts will occur, and some seaside real estate will disappear. Lowland areas of seacoast locales such as Miami and Manhattan will be inundated. The crowded country of Bangladesh will become even more densely populated as coastal inhabitants flee inland. Some island nations, such as the Maldives in the Indian Ocean, will simply sink beneath the sea.

What makes this dire situation even worse is the second reason that makes it peculiar: the fact that it is caused by humans. The activities of humans on this planet have created the conditions that have made global warming a horrible reality. What has created this situation is the "greenhouse effect." This occurs when the buildup of carbon dioxide in the atmosphere creates an invisible shield around the earth—somewhat like the glass in a greenhouse—that allows the heat from the sun to penetrate it but does not allow excess heat to filter out.

What produced all of this carbon dioxide is, for the most part, us. The Indonesian forest fire, for example, that dumped all of those tons of carbon dioxide into the atmosphere was likely caused by human activity—the slash and burn clearing of the forests for agriculture. Burning fossil fuels creates even more carbon dioxide. If you go to Beijing during the winter, for instance, you are confronted by a horrible brown-gray sludge of air, which was created by burning wood and coal fires and by the emissions of the gasoline-powered cars, busses, trucks, and motor scooters that crowd the streets of the city. Other things produce other greenhouse gasses such as methane—even the flatulence of cattle is a major producer. We can't do much about cows. We can, however, control the quantity of these gasses that are produced by human activity, including auto emissions and smoke from coal-burning furnaces.

The urgency of the situation and the need for countries around the world to become committed to the reduction of greenhouse gases have led to a series of international climate-change conferences. Alas, none have been very effective. One of the most famous was held in Kyoto, Japan, in 1997; it called for a roughly eight percent reduction of carbon dioxide omissions in highly industrialized nations, but it did not include developing countries such as China and India. Fifty-five countries signed the agreement, but the U.S. Congress showed an unwillingness to commit to it, even though Al Gore, who was vice president at the time, was one of the main negotiators at the conference. Subsequent conferences, including the 2011 meeting in Copenhagen and the 2012 meeting in Qatar, have pledged to continue the agreements made in the Kyoto Protocol and to expand the number of countries committed to it. Yet the response to the requirements has been fairly ineffective. The largest producer of greenhouse gasses, the United States, has failed to sign any of the agreements.

There has been greater international cooperation in response to another transnational threat, however—global pandemics. In a world where high-speed air travel leads to easy mobility from one area to another, diseases can move rapidly from place to place. A small outbreak caused by a rare virus in Africa, for example, can quickly spread to Europe, Asia, and the Americas. An outbreak of influenza type A virus that originated in China in the 1950s and spread throughout the world became known as the "Asian flu." An epidemic spread of cholera in Haiti following the disastrous earthquake in 2010 was attributed to United Nations aid workers who might have unwittingly brought the disease to the island during relief operations. In both of these cases, an international consortium of countries worked together in attempting to contain and ameliorate the spread of the contagion.

International cooperation has also been part of the response to one of the most serious pandemics of the late twentieth and early twenty-first centuries: HIV/AIDS. The acquired immunodeficiency syndrome (AIDS) is a condition in which the body no longer has the natural capability to fight off infections and repel opportunistic diseases. It is caused by the human immunodeficiency virus (HIV), a particularly nasty virus that mutates into different forms and is difficult to identify and destroy. It is also quite contagious, though it is transmitted not by touch or breathing, but through bodily fluids—especially blood, semen, vaginal fluid, and breast milk. For this reason, it is usually transmitted through sexual contact or from a mother to her child through breastfeeding. Although drugs have been developed to stall its progress in the body and to keep the body's immune system from plunging to a dangerous level, these drug cocktails are expensive and not easy to disseminate, especially for the millions who are infected with HIV in poorer countries, such as in sub-Saharan Africa, where AIDS affects a huge proportion of the population, men and women equally. According to statistics maintained by the World Health Organization, there were around 33 million people living with AIDS throughout the world in 2010, many of them in Africa and Asia. The United Nations has set up a special organization solely to deal with the HIV/AIDS epidemic. Thousands of transnational organizations are dedicated to providing AIDS education, distributing condoms, offering other forms of preventive support, and providing less expensive drug treatments. Thus, the bright side of a tragic global epidemic is the way that people throughout the world have joined together to combat the effects of the disease.

The readings in this section cover several aspects of global environmental and health issues. The first reading is a comprehensive survey of climate change and global warming.

It was prepared for the *Encyclopedia of Global Studies* by a scientist who has developed computer modeling programs for climate alterations and predictions. Catherine Gautier was raised in France and received her Ph.D. in physics from the University of Paris. She now teaches in the geography department at the University of California–Santa Barbara. The second reading focuses on the problems of ocean pollution. The author, Ron Fujita, is a California-based oceanographer who is a senior scientist with the Environmental Defense Organization; the excerpt is from his book, *Heal the Ocean: Solutions for Saving Our Seas.* The third reading is an overview of the HIV/AIDS crisis written by Hakan Seckinelgin, a lecturer in international social policy at the London School of Economics. Originally from Turkey, he has been concerned with the politics of international relations, social ethics, global sexualities, and gender studies and has done research specifically on the impact of international HIV/AIDS policies in sub-Saharan Africa.

CLIMATE CHANGE

Catherine Gautier

The global environmental crisis of climate change has resulted from a process called the greenhouse effect. This is a disturbance of the energy balance of the Earth that results in a rise in surface temperature when there is an atmospheric increase in the concentration of greenhouse gases such as carbon dioxide (CO_2).

As humans burn fossil fuels and deforest the land, CO_2 is released, altering for a long time the chemistry of the atmosphere. This change in atmospheric composition has led to a discernible human influence on our planet's climate, to what is referred to as global climate change. It represents changes over time in the averages and variability of surface temperature, precipitation, and wind, as well as associated changes in the Earth's atmosphere, oceans and natural water supplies, snow and ice, land surface, ecosystems, and living organisms. The climate is a complex system evolving under natural and anthropogenic forces; its change produces a variety of impacts felt all over the world. This [essay] discusses the changes and impacts, as well as other concerns, associated with climate change on the Earth.

GLOBAL NATURE OF CLIMATE CHANGE AND THE GREENHOUSE EFFECT

The presence of greenhouse gases (particularly water vapor but also carbon dioxide, ozone, and methane) in the atmosphere leads to an Earth temperature significantly warmer than it would otherwise have been without their greenhouse effect. As human activities add more or new (chlorofluorocarbons for instance) greenhouse gases, the Earth's average temperature increases.

The Earth is naturally warmed by solar (shortwave, SW) radiation absorption and cooled by emission of infrared (longwave, LW) radiation. It is the balance between the warming from SW absorption and the cooling from LW emission that governs the Earth's temperature. When this balance is altered, the Earth's temperature adjusts to the new equilibrium. Such perturbation of the Earth's energy balance is called a radiative forcing, and the greenhouse effect is the main perturbation whereby the presence of greenhouse gases in the atmosphere blocks the emission of LW radiation to space, therefore reducing the cooling this escaping radiation normally causes. This process leads to a warming of the Earth.

Of the CO_2 emitted by human activities, nearly half is quickly taken up by land and ocean, and the remainder is transported by atmospheric motion around the globe. This CO_2 remains in the atmosphere for hundreds of years before being taken up by chemical weathering on land and sediments deposition in the ocean over geological time scales. CO_2 can therefore be considered as having a long lifetime, and the location where it is added to the atmosphere has essentially no influence over where the greenhouse effect will occur. The greenhouse effect occurs globally.

REGIONALIZATION OF THE WARMING

Surface observations averaged over the entire globe show a general temperature increase (~0.8°C) during the last century as is expected from the greenhouse effect. A map of surface temperature changes during the last several decades, however, displays some spatial variations in the warming. . . . In particular, the high latitudes of the Northern Hemisphere display a warming two to three times larger than the globally averaged one. These spatial variations do not result from local greenhouse or other radiative forcing but are the consequence of a regional feedback (a self-reinforcing reaction to a forcing that either enhances or reduces the original forcing) process that tends to regionalize the warming. The so-called snow/ice albedo feedback effect is responsible for the large temperature increase in Northern Hemisphere high latitudes. In regions covered by snow or ice, a large part of the radiation from the sun is reflected (the surface is said to have a high albedo) and little radiation penetrates into the surface. As the surface temperature increases from the greenhouse effect, some snow or ice melts, exposing the surface (whether land or ocean) and allowing solar radiation to penetrate the upper layer where the radiation can be absorbed and warm it. This induces an additional melting of the adjacent snow/ice covered areas, giving rise to more solar radiation absorption. This self-enhancing process is called a positive feedback: Under an initial fluctuation (the warming from increased CO_2 in this case), a domino effect gets established that expands the original melting. The result is a larger temperature increase in these regions than in surrounding regions not covered by snow or ice.

Another source of regionalizing of the temperature change originates from other radiative forcings. One major example is the addition of aerosols (particles suspended in the air) resulting from industrial activities and the burning of wood, or from natural processes such as volcanic eruptions or sand storms. Their impact on climate differs from that of greenhouse gases in two major ways. First, the aerosol lifetime is short (of the order of weeks to months, except for volcanic aerosols that can last a few years in the stratosphere); thus, they do not have time to extend globally, and therefore, their impact remains more regional. A consequence of this short lifetime is that their impact can decrease or even disappear as soon as the source of emission is reduced or eliminated. This is not the case for CO_2 that, once in the atmosphere, can remain there long after the source of emission has disappeared. Second, most aerosols have a cooling effect on the surface. This is particularly true with the prevailing aerosols, including the sulfate aerosols (SO_4) produced through the burning of sulfur-containing coal. The cooling effect of aerosol can in part compensate for the greenhouse warming and therefore mask its real strength. So, as we "clean" our atmosphere from aerosols, for health or other reasons, we might experience a larger warming from the greenhouse effect.

GLOBAL CLIMATE CHANGES

Sea Ice Melting, Glaciers Retreating, and Sea Level Increase   A major aspect of climate change is the melting of sea ice and the retreat of glaciers as a result of the enhanced warming in high latitudes resulting from the snow/ice albedo feedback. These effects have already been observed in most parts of the globe, with varying intensity and timing. Maybe the most compelling example is the rapid melting of Arctic ice. The extent of Arctic ice, at its minimum in September, has generally been decreasing, one year after the next with however some recovery over short periods of time (e.g., in 2008). Ice, however, has been thinning everywhere. The consequences are multiple on humans and natural systems. The animals accustomed to living on sea ice must adjust to smaller ice areas in the summer. For instance, polar bears have to modify their habits as the large ice platforms from which they hunt are reduced to almost nothing and they now have to swim over longer distances to reach their prey. Fishing conditions and catches are also modified, and people have to adapt to those, while they can enjoy longer crop-growing seasons.

Melting glaciers is different in its nature, and it can add large amounts of fresh water to the ocean, increasing the sea level, which is not the case for sea ice. Only a negligible sea level increase occurs when ice already in the water melts. Glacier melt and its associated retreat occurs in both the Arctic and Antarctic. Shorter glaciers flow faster, which results in glaciers breaking up and large icebergs detaching from the ice sheet. Other processes such as melt water percolation through pores and fractures can accelerate the glacier flow through lubrication of its base. Because the Antarctic is a continent covered with a thick layer of ice (in fact the thickest . . . in the world), only glacier retreat occurs. Already, nearly 90% of glaciers have retreated. But the retreat of these glaciers cannot be entirely attributed to global warming, and the slowing down of the retreat in the late 1980s and early 1990s is still unexplained.

Ocean Heat Accumulation, Expansion, and Sea Level Change   The ocean plays a major role in climate, storing heat in the tropical regions, redistributing it toward the poles and exchanging it with the atmosphere. It also plays a role in the carbon cycle as it absorbs a significant part of the CO_2 emitted by human activities, as mentioned. As the greenhouse effect adds heat to the Earth system it is in the ocean that the heat is accumulated and the ocean warms. This has two major effects. First, a warmer ocean evaporates more, therefore putting additional water vapor in the atmosphere. Because water vapor is a greenhouse effect, this leads to an additional warming and therefore this is a positive feedback, possibly the most important one. The second effect of the ocean warming is ocean expansion. This expansion is the second component that induces sea level rise: Ice melting and ocean expansion have contributions nearly similar to this rise.

Temperature Extremes and Extreme Events   Atmospheric temperatures are expected to change in most places in the world, with extremes (both low and high) becoming more common and periods of heat waves occurring more frequently and over longer periods during the summer in many locations. The Northern Hemisphere is more likely to experience these heat waves and, because of the higher population density, their impacts will be more severe. Warmer ocean surface temperatures are expected to lead to increased hurricane intensity and duration, possibly leading to enhanced devastation, particularly in highly populated and more developed coastal regions.

Hydrological Cycle   Despite these major changes in temperature, it is probably the changes in the hydrological cycle that will be affecting human and natural systems the most. Precipitation distribution and intensity have already been modified, and the prediction is for direr changes with, in particular, reduced precipitation in already rain-deficient regions such as the sub-Saharan regions, the Mediterranean surroundings, and the southwestern United States, associated with enhanced likelihood of wild fires. Higher precipitation in northern midlatitudes and in the tropics associated with flooding and landslides are also forecasted. In general, when precipitation falls, it will be more abundant and separated by longer periods of reduced or no rain.

Another major aspect of the hydrological cycle change relates to the nature of precipitation. In a warmer atmosphere, precipitation will fall more often as rain instead of snow. This will lead to a reduction of the snow pack and its ability to store water over long period of times before it is released when it is the most needed in spring and summer. When combined with glaciers melting discussed previously, regions that rely on alpine water sources, such as the countries at the foot of Himalayas, could experience floods followed by water shortages.

Other climatological changes related to shorter scale variability of the atmosphere are expected to occur but are more difficult to predict because of the chaotic nature of atmospheric dynamics. Among them, intense mesoscale wind events are expected to occur more frequently but have limited predictability.

One question often asked is as follows: How do we know that climate change has an anthropogenic origin because climate has always changed? The first thing to note is that the observed temperature change is much faster than any ever observed in the past. Second, the observed increase in carbon dioxide (CO_2) concentration from 280 to nearly 385 parts per million (ppm) has been clearly documented since the beginning of the 20th century as intense industrial activities emitters of CO_2 was ramping up. Moreover, an analysis of carbon isotopes in CO_2 allows us to verify its origin as that produced from burning fossil fuels or burning forests. But because correlation is not causation, the third element of this argumentation is that a theory—the greenhouse effect—links CO_2 (and greenhouse gases) increase with temperature increase. Finally, it has been suggested that the sun could be responsible for a large part of the observed warming. This can be assessed by jointly examining the temperature changes at the surface and in the stratosphere. In the case of a greenhouse-induced change, the stratospheric temperature decreases with increasing CO_2, while for a sun-induced effect, it increases, like at the surface. Observations can therefore help us differentiate an observed warming as a result of the greenhouse effect from one originating mostly from solar variability; the temperature change observed during the last few decades in the stratosphere clearly indicates a decrease.

SOME SIGNIFICANT IMPACTS RESULTING FROM GLOBAL CHANGES

Ocean Acidification   Approximately one third of the CO_2 emitted by human activity has already been taken up by the ocean and thus moderated the atmospheric CO_2 concentration increase and consequently global warming. In addition, as CO_2 dissolves in sea water, carbonic acid is formed. This has the effect of acidifying, or lowering, the pH of the ocean. Although not directly caused by warming, acidification is related to it because, like the greenhouse effect, it is the result of the increase of CO_2 in the atmosphere. Ocean acidification has many impacts on marine ecosystems, most of them highly detrimental to a substantial number of species ranging from corals to lobsters and from sea urchins to mollusks and will eventually affect the entire marine food chain.

Ecosystem Modification and Adaptation and Biodiversity Reduction   The list of impacts of climate change on ecosystems, plants, and animals is long. Combined changes in temperature and precipitation, as well as changes in extremes, can have an impact on the survival of species and lead to a rapid reduction of biodiversity. Ecological niches can disappear or the survival of some species can be at risk because of the appearance of new pests that can survive milder winter, for instance. But not all changes [are bad]: A lengthening growing season in higher latitude, as discussed before, could be beneficial for some crops; increased CO_2 concentration can, up to a certain point, have a fertilizing action.

Overall, however, the modification of ecosystems will affect the services they provide such as the provision of food, clean water production, waste decomposition, regulation of diseases, nutrient cycles, and crop pollination support, or even spiritual and recreational benefits. Those services rely on complex interactions among many species, each species having its unique function and DNA that has evolved to help it respond to natural challenges. Once a species goes extinct, however, it does not come back. And some losses of biodiversity then become irreversible.

Ecosystems can adjust over time to their climatic environment. Individual species making an ecosystem can adapt by moving away from detrimental conditions. To avoid increasing temperatures, they can grow further north in the Northern Hemisphere and/ or at higher altitude. Species that cannot adjust fast enough or have nowhere to go (e.g., alpine ecosystems) will become stressed and at high risk of extinction. Such range shift has happened in the past but during long periods of time. The growing rate of both CO_2 concentration and temperature is now occurring at a faster pace than ever before, and this might be too fast for some species; entire ecosystems might disappear as a result.

CLIMATE CHANGE PREDICTIONS

One question of significance for society is: How much CO_2 in the atmosphere is too much considering that CO_2 concentration is already well outside the envelope of the concentration that has occurred during the past 1 million years? An associated question is: how large a temperature increase is too large? Although no definitive answer can be offered to those questions because of the complexity of the climate system, they can be addressed from a probabilistic perspective using data from paleo-climatological records for guidance based on what has happened in the past and climate models for predictions.

Climate models suggest that if we continue to use fossil fuel energy to fuel our economic growth at the current rate, the global temperature change by the end of the century would be between 2°C and 6°C with a most likely value around 4°C. Most scientists agree that if the temperature increases beyond 2°C, the climate might change in dramatic yet unknown ways. This is why this 2°C figure has been selected as part of recent international discussions. CO_2 emissions that would correspond to a 2°C increase would correspond to releasing approximately twice as much CO_2 as we have done thus far, a far cry from the five times that are predicted if we continue on our current energy usage trajectory. Almost all computations converge to a needed cut of 80% to 85% in CO_2 emissions in highly emitting countries and 50% globally if we want to avoid dangerous climate change.

ADDITIONAL CONCERNS: KNOWN UNKNOWNS

Several unknowns in the climate system can potentially trigger rapid and possibly irreversible global changes. One important one is the possibility of methane release as a result of permafrost—the soil that remains frozen year round in high latitudes—melting. The top layer melts in the summer. This melting has been observed to be expanding with time from rapidly increasing surface temperature. Large amounts of methane are stored under the permafrost, and as it melts, this very powerful greenhouse gas escapes into the atmosphere, significantly adding to the greenhouse effect because it is approximately 25 times more potent than CO_2.

The exact amount of permafrost hydrate methane is not known so this process is among the known unknowns, about which our knowledge might improve over time. However, this is a powerful feedback process that cannot be stopped once it is initiated by a general warming such as that produced by increasing CO_2 concentration. And, naturally, there are unknown unknowns as well, about which not much can be said except that we know they will develop at some point.

CONCLUSION

Global climate change connects people across space by its global nature and time from the long CO_2 lifetime. If unabated, it will be felt by future generations well over the next century. Although climate change is one of the foremost issues of our time that needs immediate attention, it is also the manifestation of another significant concern, that of the overuse of the Earth's resources and their near-term exhaustion that may usher us into unknown territories.

TURNING THE TIDE

Ron Fujita

The ocean is alive. The waves change shape constantly, mesmerizing us with their infinite variations on a theme. The sound of the surf is soothing background music for contemplation. The vast panorama and the roar of breaking waves inspire awe and expansive thoughts.

Changes in perspective offer glimpses of the ocean's nature. At night, the waves sometimes glow with the light of tiny organisms excited by the surf. I leave bioluminescent swirls behind as I swim through warm water in the darkness. Bouncing along in a boat, I am moved by the sight of a pod of dolphins, or of young humpback whales leaping out of the water. But the ocean hides most of its treasures below its mirrored surface.

Putting on a mask and snorkel can induce a startling revelation. Life is everywhere. Clouds of small silvery fishes part as I approach. Tiny damselfish fiercely chase me away from their carefully tended gardens. Elegant sea fans wave in the surge. With the aid of an air tank, I can take the time to return the inquisitive stares of cuttlefish and swim with graceful eagle rays. I meditate on the sound of my breath and the bubbles I leave, and become aware of a school of big tarpon fish cruising by, their beautiful scales gleaming in the sunlight. I have come to know barracudas as individuals, guarding their territories merely by glaring at me.

The ocean seems too immense, its life too vibrant, to be affected by tiny humans and their industries. But scientific papers and data from around the world offer other perspectives. They show that humans have in fact decimated enormous herds of sea cows, sea otters, and sea turtles. The great oyster beds of the Chesapeake and other estuaries have been reduced to pale, sickly vestiges of their former glory. Mind-boggling numbers of fish have been removed from the ocean and as a result, global fish catches are declining, and several major fisheries have collapsed altogether. Some ocean species are already on the verge of extinction—and we have only just begun to explore the ocean's biological diversity.

Beyond all these losses of a precious natural heritage, we have done even worse by the ocean. No living system can function properly without all of its essential components. This is easy to understand in terms of an individual—but it applies also to whole ecosystems. Sea turtles eat seagrasses [which have to be grazed regularly in order to flourish], and so killing off the sea turtles has contributed to the decline of seagrass meadows which are the productive rangelands of the ocean. Hunting southern sea otters to near extinction and killing off lobsters and fish has allowed purple sea urchin populations to explode in the absence of their natural predators. The grazing urchins have then reduced majestic forests of kelps up to 100 feet (about 30 meters) tall to rubble—bare rock covered with hordes of urchins. The excessive harvest of oysters over the decades appears to have interfered with the ability of estuaries like the Chesapeake to cleanse themselves—the oysters were once capable of filtering the entire volume of the bay every three days, but no more.

These are not isolated examples. Because everything is connected, most of our actions have indirect and unintended effects. How can driving a car or using electricity affect the ocean? The burning of coal and oil to propel cars and power our society releases carbon dioxide and other gases that have warmed the world significantly over the last century. As the seas heat up in response to global warming, intensely colorful coral reefs are bleaching, turning a deathly white and starving to death. In 1998, coral reefs suffered their most severe bout of bleaching, associated with unusually warm waters. The great systems of ocean life that we depend on, and are part of, are collapsing—silently, below the waves. . . .

To avoid crisis, we need to think about current trends and the future. Strategic thinking about how scientific, economic, and technological trends may affect the ocean in the future helps us identify threats early. Foreseeing threats may allow us to intervene before large investments of time, energy, money, and ego are made, rendering corrective action more difficult. So, too, will new policies that embody the principles of "do no harm" and precaution. Such policies will reduce the incidence of intractable environmental problems and crises.

But a new way of thinking won't break the cycle of denial and crisis by itself. Even better policies and more comprehensive analyses will not be enough. Behavioral psychology informs us that incentives need to change as well. Institutions and policies aimed at protecting the ocean can thrive only if people get behind them and support them. Consequently, such policies and institutions should provide constant reinforcement and incentives for people. Economic incentives—such as tax breaks for solar power or steep penalties for pollution—can reinforce precautionary behavior and spur technical innovation. Building community around the protection of a special place on land or under the sea can help meet our deep-seated need to relate to one another. At a more profound level, environmental actions can flow from the realization that all of nature is interdependent—ourselves included. Economic incentives, efforts to build community around environmental protection, and a new ocean ethic based on interdependence can reduce the risk of dangerous ecological and economic surprises, as well as inspire acts of healing and restoration.

HIV/AIDS

Hakan Seckinelgin

HIV/AIDS is often referred to as a global disease, and the problems associated with the disease are among the most recognized global issues. It is one of the central global policy problems that are tackled by many actors with a global reach, including international organizations, governments, civil society groups, and others. The disease represents a new stage in thinking about dealing with various diseases at a global level. To deal with its impact, new policy organizations with global mandates have been created. Activism around HIV/AIDS has created a new model of health activism that has inspired people impacted by other diseases.

Acquired immune deficiency syndrome or acquired immunodeficiency syndrome (AIDS) is a disease that results from changes in the human immune system caused by the human immunodeficiency virus (HIV). HIV is a degenerative retrovirus that progressively reduces the effective functioning of the human immune system. It leaves individuals vulnerable to infections that would have otherwise been dealt by their immune system. These infections are called opportunistic infections as they impact the individual's health as a result of their state of HIV infection. The search for the origins of the disease goes on. These origins are still unclear although there are numerous stories that are not conclusively proven. However, despite many controversial debates about its origins, the relationship between HIV and AIDS is clearly established.

The formal definition of AIDS is provided by the U.S. Centers for Disease Control and Prevention (CDC). The initial definition referred to AIDS using associated diseases such as lymphadenopathy. However, in 1993, the CDC revised its definition to use the CD4 T-cell count to define a patient to be in an AIDS state. An individual has AIDS if he or she has less than 200 CD4 T cells per microliter of blood.

HIV is transmitted by HIV-containing bodily fluids of an infected person entering the bloodstream of another person. It is commonly transmitted through sexual contact, blood-transmitting situations such as intravenous drug use, and from mother to child. The means of transmission can be through blood, semen, vaginal fluid, breast milk, and preseminal fluid. Mother-to-child transmission usually happens in the last weeks of the pregnancy and at childbirth. The treatment developed to stop this transmission reduces the chances of this infection. In the absence of treatment, the rate of transmission from mother to child is 25%. The risk of infection is a function of the viral load of the mother at the time of pregnancy and delivery. Therefore, the availability of treatment to the mother to control her viral load is also important for the child. The availability of treatment is central, and the availability of drugs and associated conditions in developing countries present serious challenges in this area.

Sexual transmission of HIV is the most common route. Unprotected sex increases the likelihood of infection between infected and uninfected person. Unprotected sex with multiple partners also increases the possibility of infection and its spread. Another important transmission route is through blood products used by hemophiliacs and others, for example, those receiving blood transfusions. Sharing and reusing syringes that might have been contaminated by HIV is another important transmission route. An example here is the Chinese case where syringes were used multiple times for blood donations, which increased HIV infections in the country. This mode of transmission is particularly important and is often the main mode of transmission where intravenous drug use is prevalent, such as in Eastern Europe and Russia.

The progression of the disease, from HIV infection to AIDS, takes 9 to 10 years. The slow progression stems from the way HIV gradually reduces the production of CD4 T cells that maintain the immune system. If the HIV has reduced CD4 T cells in an individual to less than 200 cells per measure of blood, the individual is deemed to have AIDS.

CLASSIFICATION

In talking about HIV, it is important to be aware of categorizations used in the discussions. There are two types of HIV: HIV-1 and HIV-2. For both types, transmission pathways remain the same and they create clinically indistinguishable AIDS. HIV-2 seems to be different in terms of the period it takes infection to develop into illness. HIV-2 is less common and concentrated in West Africa. Most commonly, HIV refers to HIV-1 as the globally predominant virus. Under this classification, there are four different strains (M-major, O-outlier, and then N and P) identified for HIV-1 indicating four separate introductions of simian immunodeficiency syndrome into humans. Most HIV-1 infections fall under group M. Group O seems to be restricted to west-central Africa. N is a strain that was discovered in Cameroon in 1998 and is very rare, whereas P refers to a new strain discovered in Cameroon in 2009 relating to a gorilla simian immunodeficiency virus.

Within the most common group M, there seems to be nine different subtypes of HIV-1. These are subtypes A, B, C, D, F, G, H, J, and K. This is a changing classification as new subtypes are discovered by scientists. The importance of these classifications is twofold: It is possible at times that two subtype viruses meet in the infected person and mixing of these in their cell creates a new hybrid virus. Although these hybrid viruses may not survive a long time, if they infect more than one person, they are known as circulating recombinant forms (CRFs). Also, different from many other viruses, HIV infection does not generate immunity in the infected person. The infected person can be infected again, particularly if the virus is from a different subtype. In other words, multiple infections are observed.

RESPONSES AND INTERVENTIONS

On June 5, 1981, the CDC reported what is now known as AIDS for the first time. At the time, the CDC recorded a cluster of *Pneumocystis carinii* pneumonia in five homosexual men in Los Angeles and increased cases of Kaposi's sarcoma in New York. As suggested, at that stage, the CDC did not have a formal name for the disease and used the name of the disease associated with it. For instance, they also used Kaposi's sarcoma and opportunistic infections, as the [disease's] name. However, the reaction of the general media is an important component here as they coined the term "gay-related immune deficiency" or GRID. This should be considered as the beginning of the social character of HIV/AIDS. At the same time, the CDC, looking for a name, focused on the initial groups who were considered influenced by the diseases and called it "4H disease"— Haitians, homosexuals, hemophiliacs, and heroin users. In July 1982, the term "AIDS" was introduced and used by the CDC from September of that year onward to overcome the misleading labeling associated with GRID. There were important social implications of using both GRID and 4H. The media attention focused on these groups who were already marginalized in the United States and took their behavior as the cause of the problem. The initial designation of gay men as the cause and the subsequent addition of 4H increased the stigmatization of these groups, further marginalizing them. As gay men were a marginalized community, their needs were also marginal in the overall resource allocations in the country. This created a charged environment where a new movement emerged, led mostly by urban gay men in the United States, to challenge the government, medical profession, and their slow and conventional responses to the crisis at the time. New activists challenged some of these prejudices as people needed to deal with a social stigma that isolated infected people.

The gap between the responses from the health policy establishment and the needs of gay men in the United States meant that people who were suffering from the disease found it very hard to access medical care. Being stigmatized as the cause of the disease in the media stimulated the formation of many self-help groups, both to counter this image through advocacy work and to create a resource base to help those who were in need as a result of their illness. The emergence of the first generation of organizations was very important. These included Gay Men's Health Crisis in New York, San Francisco AIDS Foundation, Bay Area AIDS Consortium, AIDS Project LA, AIDS Foundation Houston, Minnesota AIDS Project, and Boston AIDS. In Europe also, around 1982 similar organizations emerged such as the Terrence Higgins Trust in the United Kingdom and AIDES in France. These organizations were central in thinking about how to deal with the needs of people who were also marginalized from mainstream society. They developed procedures for testing, caring, and dealing with pain with dignity to inform change in the health system that was created for traditional contagious diseases.

In this process, another momentous occasion was the creation of the People with AIDS Coalition (PWA Coalition) in 1983 out of a meeting of HIV/AIDS patients in San Francisco as first of its kind. Subsequent to this event in June 1983, the PWA Coalition issued a statement—the Denver Principles—about the way these patients wanted to be treated and involved in all decisions about their health. The AIDS movement was further radicalized by the establishment of the AIDS Coalition to Unleash Power (ACT UP) in 1987 as a direct action group. They immediately tackled the pharmaceutical industry. As a result of these interventions and general political change in the early 1990s, there was a more welcoming environment for HIV/AIDS debate in the industrialized countries by that time. Also at this time, the problems experienced in Africa began to capture wider attention. Another important point in this process was achieved in the mid-1990s with the introduction of the highly active antiretroviral therapy (HAART) and its use as a multidrug cocktail-therapy method in 1996.

This story is important as people's reactions, in the absence of clear medical response and solutions, also influenced the later response to the disease in developing countries. The model of people's organizations has become one of the important models for international actors focusing on HIV/AIDS in developing countries. Furthermore, the norms and procedures set by the PWA Coalition have become international norms for people living with HIV and AIDS across the globe in policy intervention processes. Some of this influence was related with the way surviving AIDS activists in 1990 moved to work in the international arena. Together with doctors working in Africa, they motivated initial responses from international actors. In 1996, the Joint United Nations Programme on HIV/AIDS became operational as the flagship international organization to coordinate international HIV/AIDS interventions of the UN system and to act as advisor to different countries. At this stage, the focus in the fight against HIV/AIDS was shifting to the developing world and to Africa in particular. As the state of the situation in Africa became clearer, international actors increased their involvement in the region. To increase global awareness and gather more political support, the United Nations General Assembly held a special session on HIV/AIDS on June 25–27, 2001, reaffirming international support for people living with HIV/AIDS. The first decade of the new millennium witnessed the possibility of providing treatment to keep people in developing countries alive. In the first half of the decade, most of the efforts focused on rolling out treatment to those who were in need. However, the financial burden of this made it clear to the international actors that there needed to be increased funding. To facilitate the process, a new form of organization was operationalized in 2002—The Global Fund to Fight HIV/AIDS, Malaria, and Tuberculosis. These steps show how HIV/AIDS has become a global concern and that there are policies that have been developed internationally for implementation in different countries. The intervention strategies, funding bases, and actors involved adopt a global outlook.

FURTHER READING

ACIA. 2005. *Arctic Climate Impacts Assessment Scientific Report*. Cambridge, UK: Cambridge University Press.

Altman, Dennis. 1986. *AIDS and the New Puritanism*. London: Pluto Press.

Altman, Dennis. 1994. *Power and Community: Organizational and Cultural Responses to AIDS*. London: Taylor & Francis.

Archer, David, and Stefan Rahmstorf. 2010. *The Climate Crisis: An Introductory Guide to Climate Change*. Cambridge, UK: Cambridge University Press.

Clapp, Jennifer, and Peter Dauvergne. 2011. *Paths to a Green World: The Political Economy of the Global Environment*. Cambridge, MA: MIT Press.

Farmer, Paul. 1992. *AIDS and Accusation: Haiti and the Geography of Blame*. Berkeley: University of California Press.

Farmer, Paul. 1999. *Infections and Inequalities: The Modern Plagues*. Berkeley: University of California Press.

Fujita, Ron. 2003. *Heal the Ocean: Solutions for Saving Our Seas*. Vancouver, BC: New Society.

Gautier, Catherine, and Jean-Louis Fellous (Eds.). 2008. *Facing Climate Change Together*. Cambridge, UK: Cambridge University Press.

Maslin, Mark. 2009. *Global Warming: A Very Short Introduction*. Oxford, UK: Oxford University Press.

Mathez, Edmond. 2013. *Climate Change: The Science of Global Warming and Our Energy Future*. New York: Columbia University Press.

Patton, Cindy. 2002. *Globalizing AIDS*. Minneapolis: University of Minnesota Press.

Seckinelgin, Hakan. 2008. *International Politics of HIV/AIDS: Global Disease—Local Pain*. London: Routledge.

Schmidt, Gavin, Joshua Wolfe, and Jeffrey Sachs. 2009. *Climate Change: Picturing the Science*. New York: Norton.

18

GLOBAL COMMUNICATIONS AND NEW MEDIA

I have a friend who likes to play chess on the Internet. He's not always sure who he is playing with or where they are from. So he started asking, and was surprised to find out that some of his opponents were in Russia. Others were in Hong Kong, Cairo, and Mexico City. On the Internet you can be anywhere and everywhere, or you can be nowhere, if you want to stay anonymous. A *New Yorker* cartoon that I like shows a dog at a computer terminal, speaking to another dog. "On the Internet," he says, "no one knows that you're a dog."

One of the most dramatic aspects of the global era is the extent to which electronic communications have made it possible for virtually everyone to be in touch with everyone else, either anonymously or not, wherever they are, even if they're a dog. It's true, of course, that global communications are not new. Telephone, telegraph, and international postal services have linked the planet together for more than a century. Movies are distributed worldwide, and television has a global reach, providing a kind of transnational popular culture that affects all corners of the planet.

Most of these media images have in the past been European and American—specifically, Southern Californian—but increasingly there are new centers of media creation and transmission. Al Jazeera television, based in Qatar, rivals CNN and BBC as a global news medium. And Hollywood is not the only global hub of cinema production. It is in fact the third largest producer of films in the world—the first is Bollywood in Mumbai, India, and the second is in Lagos and Enugu, Nigeria. Other global centers of film production are in Hong Kong, Egypt, and Indonesia.

Increasingly, however, people do not watch films solely in movie houses or on television. They see them online on their computers and on mobile Internet devices, where they are part of a broader pattern of Internet information, entertainment, and communication. These new devices replace all of the old forms. Movies and programs are seen online. Telephone calls are made on wireless handheld devices. Postal mail has been replaced by instant e-mail and texting; and Internet services such as Facebook, Tumblr, and Twitter have taken the place of telegraphs in providing quick and inexpensive messaging.

Though Internet use is found everywhere, it is not found everywhere equally. There is what has come to be known as a "digital divide" within and among countries regarding the percentage of the population that has access to computers and the Internet. According to 2011 statistics from the International Telecommunications Union, for instance, only 35 percent of the seven billion people on earth use the Internet. In the United States, over 75 percent of the people are Internet users, whereas in Bangladesh only 5 percent of the people are online. Norway tops the list with 94 percent of the population using the Internet. China has the most Internet users—over 500 million—but China is a huge nation, with over 1.3 billion people, so Internet users make up just 35 percent of its population. In general, access to the Internet's social media is correlated with the wealth of the population, but sometimes the statistics can surprise you. The highest percentage of Facebook users are in Arab emirate nations, followed by Chile and Taiwan, according to 2013 Facebook statistics compiled by Socialbakers. This might explain why so many of your Facebook friends are from Qatar, Taipei, and Santiago. On the other hand, the fact that Facebook is not allowed in China, Russia, North Korea, and Iran may explain why you have so few Facebook friends from Shanghai, Moscow, Pyongyang, and Tehran.

The fact that Facebook is banned in several countries brings up another topic: the attempts to control the Internet. China, which has the largest number of Internet users in the world, is also one of most vigilant in trying to control its population's access to Internet information. When Yahoo and Google tried to bring their Internet search technology to China, they discovered severe limitations regarding what users were allowed to search and find. Information about the struggle for political rights for Tibet, for instance, or the 1989 Tiananmen Square protests are not allowed to appear on Internet searches in China. Sites deemed pornographic or that discuss sensitive political and religious issues are likewise restricted from access. Clever computer users in China know how to get around these restrictions, of course, and most university students in China can gain access to just about everything that an American college student can, but the general public in China finds its Internet use to be limited.

Is it a good idea for a country to be able to control the kinds of information that the public receives? Most people probably think that the Internet should be a free marketplace of ideas and information. Yet most of us would probably also agree that certain kinds of inflammatory racist and hate sites should be banned and that access to child pornography should not be allowed. So the principle of Internet censorship—to some degree—is something that all can affirm. The question is how much censorship.

Should there be a limit on the amount of information available? This was the critical issue with the release of U.S. diplomatic e-mail correspondence by Wikileaks in 2010. Almost 400,000 documents relating to the American military presence in Iraq were released on the Wikileaks site in what became known as the Iraq War Logs. The founder and director of the site, Julian Assange, an Australian Internet activist who based his website in Iceland, claimed that he was doing a public service by revealing the military's illegal and unethical activities. The U.S. government argued that lives would be endangered by revealing secret collaborators. In 2011, additional secret U.S. diplomatic communications were released on the site. In this case, the government claimed that the communications were misleading, since they reflected opinions, gossip, and other tidbits of information that were part of a total information-sharing process and did not reflect official policies. Information that surfaced through these files, however, helped to discredit leaders such as Egypt's Hosni Mubarak and showed that he had less secure U.S. support than had been widely imagined. These leaked dispatches may have helped to spur the protests against Mubarak in 2011, during Arab Spring. The release of massive amounts of secret data and information from the U.S. government's National Security Agency by Edward Snowden in 2013 created a worldwide furor over whether he was a whistle-blower or a treasonous troublemaker. The debate continues regarding whether there can be too much openness on the Internet.

The political impact of Internet communications, however, is undeniable. Whether or not the Wikileaks revelations helped to weaken Mubarak's authority and bring him down, there is no question about the importance of social communications in the Arab Spring uprisings of 2011. The chief organizer of the Tahrir Square protests in Cairo had worked for Google, and the protests were organized through e-mail, texting, Twitter, YouTube, and Facebook. The dramatic confrontations—and the excesses of the Egyptian police in countering the protestors—were broadcast throughout the country and around the world on videos shown on YouTube. It was, arguably, the world's first Internet revolution. For a while Mubarak's regime tried to halt it by closing down the Internet throughout the country. But the crippling economic impact of the loss of computer interaction forced the government to open it again. The Internet revolution continued.

In other countries, the government has also attempted to control the Internet in an endeavor to avert the possibility of political organization. Iran and North Korea have a virtually closed system, though during the Green Revolution in Iran, when thousands of people poured into the streets in 2009 to protest what many felt was an election stolen from the reform candidate, Mir-Hossein Mousavi, Internet communications provided the means for political organization. The protests were dubbed "the Twitter Revolution." In response, the government increasingly tightened Internet freedom and in 2012, the Supreme Leader, Ayatollah Ali Khamenei, instructed the government to create a Supreme Council of Virtual Space to oversee Internet access and censorship.

As mentioned above, China has also attempted to control the availability of information on the Internet, though computer-savvy users can often find a way around the government's controls.

China has often been accused of using its computer sophistication to hack into websites and computer systems around the world. The targets of these hacking attempts have been varied, including supporters of Tibetan rights, corporate production and trade secrets, and governmental information. Though the Chinese government has officially denied that they played a role in these efforts, there is no doubt that China has the ability to launch global raids on information and to disable computer systems. If the new wars of the twenty-first century are computer-based, China will have a significant capability on its side.

Computer interception is also an instrument of other government's military apparatus. During the civil war in Libya that led to the ouster of Muammar Gaddafi, the United States played a significant role in the military efforts of the rebels by helping to disrupt the Internet lines of communication between Gaddafi's regime and its forces in the field. In the Syrian civil war as well, Internet communications interception is an important tactical element.

Other forms of Internet interception are conducted by nongovernmental groups, or by lone hackers. The political group, Anonymous, is famous for being composed of "hactivists"—computer hackers with a political activist agenda. It has hacked into governmental and corporate sites and has also targeted the Scientology religious organization, which it regards as exploitive. Anonymous has hacked into the website of the Westboro Baptist Church, which is notorious for its anti-gay protests, and it has helped to reveal pedophilia computer networks.

Anonymous usually has a political or social agenda, but some other acts of Internet interception are done simply for personal financial gain or for malicious purposes. These acts include malware—computer viruses, worms, Trojan horses, and other virtual devices that can secretly gather information or destroy a computer's capability. In 2000, computers around the world received e-mails with an attachment and "I Love You" in the subject line. When users opened the attachment, however, what they received was not love but a malicious computer worm that destroyed files and sent copies of itself to addresses in the computer's address book. The virus was created by two young hackers in the Philippines as a kind of joke, but it quickly affected more than 50 million computers and caused more than $50 billion of damage. Over 10 percent of all computers around the world were impacted. The damage caused by viruses such as this one has led to major developments in Internet security and global monitoring of the system. In a world that is increasingly maintained through Internet communication and control, everyday life would be difficult to maintain without a functioning Internet.

The readings in this section cover several aspects of global media and communications. The first selection raises the issue of cultural imperialism; it asks whether the content of much of the global media promotes the values and ways of living associated with secular America, and specifically with Southern California, and thereby sets a global standard of what life should be like. The author, Yudhishthir Raj Isar, was raised in India and educated at Delhi University and the Sorbonne in France. He is currently a professor of global communication at the American University in Paris. He explains that the rise of new media production centers in the world and the advent of interactive media are making the "cultural imperialism" accusation less valid in the global era.

The second reading is on the way that globalization affects the development of new centers of media production. The focus of this essay is China. The author, Michael Curtin, is an American specialist on global media who has taught in Hong Kong and at the University of California–Santa Barbara; he was also the director of global studies at the University of Wisconsin–Madison.

The next selection examines the role of new social media in the popular uprisings in Egypt and the Middle East known as Arab Spring. It is written by Natana DeLong-Bas, an American scholar of Middle East studies who received her Ph.D. at Georgetown and teaches at Brandeis University and Boston College. She has written on Wahhabi Islam, the form of Islam that is dominant in Saudi Arabia, and is editor-in-chief of the *Oxford Encyclopedia of Islam and Women*. The final selection, an essay by Harvard political scientist Pippa Norris, is about the inequality created between those who have and those do not have access to the Internet, which creates a worldwide digital divide. She was raised and educated in England and has written on democratic institutions, political communications, and gender politics, as well as having served as consultant to the United Nations and the World Bank.

GLOBAL CULTURE AND MEDIA

Yudhishthir Raj Isar

[There is a] specter of homogenization as the global predicament and of a world culture largely dominated by global media. These perceptions gave rise to the cultural imperialism thesis, which argued that certain "central" cultures exercised hegemony over the rest. This was no doubt the earliest theoretical framework addressing cultural globalization to appear on the world stage; it boiled down to two dystopian visions: the first of a global culture dominated by the commodifying practices of global capitalism; the second of the global dominance of Western—or in many versions—American culture. Both dissolve cultural difference. In some versions, the two are synonymous; in other versions, they together exert hegemony through the diffusion of values, consumer goods, and lifestyles. Although these theories are no longer fashionable in academic circles, they have nevertheless entered the cultural vocabulary across the world and are often invoked in international cultural politics. The argument retains a certain force: The transmission of products and styles from dominant nations to the rest has visibly led to patterns of demand and consumption that in turn are underpinned by and endorse the cultural values, ideals, and practices of their dominant origin. In this manner, it is argued, the integrity of many different dominated cultures has been subverted or at least strongly influenced by the dominant ones.

Ideas such as these underpinned the movement for a New World Information and Communication Order at the United Nations Educational, Scientific and Cultural Organization (UNESCO) that unfolded in the late 1970s and early 1980s regarding imbalances in information flows. Media imperialism was the process whereby the ownership, structure, distribution, or content of the media in any country are singly or together subject to substantial external pressures from the media interests of other countries, without proportionate reciprocation of influence by the country so affected. This thesis assumes a deliberate and active role on the part of the dominating country or group of countries and a deleterious effect on the dominated one. It also takes it for granted that the consumers of the dominant media products will necessarily be influenced by the values inherent in the content. The theory assumes that each person's exposure to these goods and symbols penetrates deeply into the way he or she constructs a phenomenal world and makes sense of his or her life; it makes a leap of inference from the simple presence of cultural goods to the attribution of deeper ideological or cultural effects.

Many other weaknesses in the theory have been identified, but it is useful at this juncture to refer to three alternative frameworks designed to interpret the global dynamic in play. Diana Crane has put forward some of these. The cultural flows or network model considers the transmission process a set of influences that do not necessarily originate in the same place or flow in the same direction. Receivers may also be originators. In this model, cultural globalization corresponds to a network with no clearly defined center or periphery but shifting configurations. Globalization as an aggregation of cultural flows or networks is a less coherent and unitary process than cultural imperialism and one in which cultural influences move in many different directions to bring about more hybridization than homogenization. The reception model argues that audiences vary in the way they respond actively or passively to mass-mediated culture, and that different national, ethnic, and racial groups interpret the same materials differently. Hence, that is why we experience the different responses to cultural globalization by publics in different countries, a phenomenon one observes readily in many developing countries where "cultural pride" is strong. This model does not view globally disseminated culture as a threat to national or local identities. Culture does not transfer in a unilinear way. Movement between cultural areas always involves interpretation, translation, mutation, adaptation, and "indigenization" as the receiving culture brings its own cultural resources to bear, in dialectical fashion, on cultural imports. The cultural imperialism model failed to account for the diverse ways in which audiences make use of foreign media. Finally, a negotiation and competition model is based on the recognition that globalization has stimulated a range of strategies on the part of nations, global cities, and cultural organizations to cope with, counter, or facilitate the culturally globalizing forces. These strategies include preserving or rejuvenating inherited cultural forms, processing and packaging the local for global consumption. In this perspective, for example, globalization is increasingly impelling cities, regions, and nations to not only protect but also position and project their cultures in global space. The cultural imperialism approach overlooked the growing influence of domestic media producers and failed to acknowledge the increasing prominence of transnational media production centers in cities such as Mumbai, Hong Kong, São Paulo, or Lagos. It focused on national cinemas and national broadcasting systems, paying little attention to the increasingly complex and transborder circulations of popular media. Broadening the debate to the cultural industries in general, the global landscape of cultural production has become increasingly polycentric and polysemic, as globalization seems less and less to be resulting in a pattern of mass cultural uniformity. The most evident expression of this state of affairs, as Allen Scott has remarked, is the emergence of a mosaic of cultural production centers tied together in complex relations of competition and collaboration across the globe.

The cultural imperialism model privileged the United States as a central and organizing actor in the international media economy. Instead of dominant power emanating from a single source, however, Michael Curtin among others identifies the complex and contingent forces and flows at work in a multicentric cultural economy, as the number of media producers, distributors, and consumers has grown dramatically, first in Europe and then in Asia, with China and India together adding almost two billion new viewers. Although powerful global media conglomerates were active contributors to these forces and flows, local, national, and regional media firms expanded rapidly as well. In India, Rupert Murdoch's Star TV presumed to displace the government's television monopoly but found itself beleaguered in turn by dozens of new indigenous competitors, many of them telecasting in one of the many subcontinental languages, all of them commercially driven. As a result, Star TV was forced to localize its programming and institutional practices, so as to adapt to competitive forces on the ground. In many other instances, global media corporations have had to adapt to local conditions at the very same time that local film and television enterprises have become more globalized in their perspectives and practices. Rather than exhibiting patterns of domination and subordination, media institutions now seem to be responding to the push-pull dynamic of globalization, as increasing connectivity inspires significant changes in textual and institutional practices.

Hence, the turn away from the idea of Western hegemony and toward the ways in which a larger set of processes operate translocally and interactively. In other words, rather than being an arena of centralized power, the world's increasingly interconnected media environment is more and more the outcome of messy and complicated interactions. These processes, observes Curtin, have led to the use of such adjectives as fractal, disjunctive, or rhizomatic to characterize a complex terrain of textual circulation, reception, and appropriation. This is not to deny that human cultural variety is softening into a paler, and narrower, spectrum, as Clifford Geertz would have put it; yet as this is happening, a new dynamic for the production of new kinds of diversity has emerged, in which the affirmation of cultural difference is a self-conscious project human project.

GLOBAL ARTS, GLOBAL VALUES

Most of the global culture debate addresses the currently dominant notions of culture. Yet there are also strong intimations of globality in regard to the arts. One of the most tenacious clichés of international cultural cooperation has been the idea that artistic expression, probably music in particular, is a "universal" language that needs no translation for it is comprehensible everywhere. This argument makes no allowances for the unequal distribution of "cultural capital," hence, of different cultural codes, which as Pierre Bourdieu and others have shown, still affect the inclusion and exclusion of classes of persons even within the same cultural community. Rather, what is clearly on the increase is communication, exchange, fusion, and hybridization among and between different repertoires and forms. This is clearly the case with regard to popular music, in particular rock, a form that has undoubtedly become a global template for musical expression. It is also characteristic of the increasingly intercultural or transcultural dimension of practice, now increasingly seen in every artistic form, in theater for example through the merging of traditions (including the mixture of actors from different cultures and languages in performance) where audiences are confronted with the specific as well as the universal truth by virtue of performances that blend various cultures. Premonitions of this particular global circumstance came as early as Johann Wolfgang Goethe's vision of the dawning age of Weltliteratur, in which writers and poets should become the first citizens of a global Republic of Letters. At the 2009 Berlin Film Festival, a contemporary take on this process was clearly in evidence, with filmmakers from different countries emulating Alejandro González Iñárritu's deliberately globalist film *Babel,* to explore the thematics of global linkages and interdependencies. Indeed film is among the various media that have made truly global performance possible, while turning, as Albrow observes, the global dimension into a central part of the spectacle; a significant artistic dimension is now that of the world viewing itself.

The latter in turn has become part of a global consciousness that can be understood in terms of the third reading of culture set out at the outset, the general idea of refinement or civilization. One aspect of the global civilization idea, as distinct from earlier ideas of universality, is that the West is once again becoming, as it was earlier in human history, only one element in world society; it will increasingly have to take on board references and constructs that the West itself has played little or no part in making. In the meantime, however, Western-originated ideas have been globally appropriated. The worldwide spread of concerns for human rights, for the environment, for sustainability, for gender issues, for the fight against AIDS, for global governance, for the strengthening of global civil society, and many more, are all manifestations of a shared civilizational project for which the globe is the ethical reference point and action frame. These ideological commitments to certain shared values, an emerging global ethics, are different from the older movements of modernity that affirmed a need for universalistic principles for the sake of international peace and security. Today's globalism is like a categorical imperative, says Albrow, for wherever there are deeds to be done, do them in the light of the needs of the world as a whole.

These needs have to do with coping with massive global risks, linking them to the linked imperative presented by Ulrich Beck, of a new global cosmopolitanism that must unite all in a radically insecure world. So a global culture is also tantamount to a new cosmopolitan sensibility, a planetary awareness, and a political and ethical engagement founded on the ways in which humanity is mixed into increasingly intercultural and transcultural ways of being in the world—a world in which all essential issues and problems are global in nature. Applied to culture in the other two senses as well, this would require us to recognize and contribute toward the elaboration of a true "Culture of cultures"—as a phenomenon both profoundly mixed and essentially plural, and as a way of changing the whole world for the better.

MEDIA CAPITAL IN CHINESE FILM AND TELEVISION

Michael Curtin

At the turn of the twenty-first century, feature films such as *Crouching Tiger, Kung Fu Hustle,* and *Hero*—each of them coproduced with major Hollywood studios—marched out of Asia to capture widespread acclaim from critics, audiences, and industry executives. Taken together they seemed to point to a new phase in Hollywood's ongoing exploitation of talent, labor, and locations around the globe, simply the latest turn in a strategy that has perpetuated American media dominance in global markets for almost a century and contributed to the homogenization of popular culture under the aegis of Western institutions. These movies seem to represent the expanding ambitions of the world's largest movie studios as they begin to refashion Chinese narratives for a Westernized global audience. Yet behind these marquee attractions lies a more elaborate endgame as Hollywood moguls reconsider prior assumptions regarding the dynamics of transnational media institutions and reassess the cultural geographies of media consumption. For increasingly they find themselves playing not only to the Westernized global audience but also to the world's biggest audience: the Chinese audience.

With more than a billion television viewers and a moviegoing public estimated at more than two hundred million, the People's Republic of China (PRC) figures prominently in such calculations. Just as compelling, however, are the sixty million "overseas Chinese" living in such places as Taiwan, Malaysia, and Vancouver. Their aggregate numbers and relative prosperity make them, in the eyes of media executives, a highly desirable audience, one comparable in scale to the audience in France or Great Britain. Taken together, Chinese audiences around the globe are growing daily in numbers, wealth, and sophistication. If the twentieth century was—as *Time* magazine founder Henry Luce put it—the American century, then the twenty-first surely belongs to the people that Luce [as a son of missionaries to China] grew up with, the Chinese. Although dispersed across vast stretches of Asia and around the world, this audience is now connected for the very first time via the intricate matrix of digital and satellite media.

Rupert Murdoch, the most ambitious global media baron of the past twenty years, enthusiastically embraced the commercial potential of Chinese film and television when in 1994 he launched a stunning billion-dollar takeover of Star TV, Asia's first pancontinental telecaster, founded only three years earlier by Li Ka-shing, Hong Kong's richest tycoon. Yet if Western executives are sharpening their focus on Chinese audiences, Asian entrepreneurs have been equally active, expanding and refiguring their media services to meet burgeoning demand, so that today, in addition to Star, hundreds of satellite channels target Chinese audiences in Asia, Europe, Australia, and North America, delivering an elaborate buffet of news, music, sports, and entertainment programming. Among Star's leading competitors is TVB, a Hong Kong-based media conglomerate built on the foundations of a transnational movie studio and now the most commercially successful television station in southern China. Its modern state-of-the-art production facilities and its far-reaching satellite and video distribution platforms position it as a significant cultural force in Europe, Australia, and North America. Equally impressive, Taiwanese and Singaporean media enterprises are extending their operations abroad in hopes of attracting new audiences and shoring up profitability in the face of escalating competition, both at home and abroad. Finally, PRC film and TV institutions, though still controlled by the state and therefore constrained by ideological and infrastructural limitations, are globalizing their strategies, if not yet their operations, regularly taking account of commercial competitors from abroad and aiming to extend their reach as conditions allow. . . .

. . . For several centuries, the imperial powers of the West exercised sway over much of the world by virtue of their economic and military might. In time, cultural influence came to figure prominently in Western hegemony, as the production and distribution of silver screen fantasies helped to disseminate capitalist values, consumerist attitudes, and Anglo supremacy. Likewise, Western news agencies dominated the flow of information, setting the agenda for policy deliberations worldwide. Indeed, throughout the twentieth century, media industries were considered so strategically significant that the U.S. government consistently sought to protect and extend the interests of NBC, Disney, Paramount, and other media enterprises. All of which helps to explain why Hollywood feature films have dominated world markets for almost a century and U.S. television has prevailed since the 1950s. Besides profiting from government favoritism, U.S. media has benefited from access to a large and wealthy domestic market that serves as a springboard for their global operations. By comparison, for most of the twentieth century, the European market was splintered, and the Indian and Chinese markets suffered from government constraints and the relative poverty of their populations. Yet recent changes in trade, industry, politics, and media technologies have fueled the rapid expansion and transformation of media industries in Asia, so that Indian and Chinese centers of film and television production have increasingly emerged as significant competitors of Hollywood in the size and enthusiasm of their audiences, if not yet in gross revenues.

In particular, Chinese film and television industries have changed dramatically since the 1980s with the end of the Cold War, the rise of the World Trade Organization, the modernization policies of the PRC, the end of martial law in Taiwan, the transfer of Hong Kong to Chinese sovereignty, the high-tech liberalization of Singapore, the rise of consumer and youth cultures across the region, and the growing wealth and influence of overseas Chinese in such cities as Vancouver, London, and Kuala Lumpur. Consequently, media executives can, for the very first time, begin to contemplate the prospect of a global Chinese audience that includes more moviegoers and more television households than the United States and Europe combined. Many experts believe this vast and increasingly wealthy Global China market will serve as a foundation for emerging media conglomerates that could shake the very foundations of Hollywood's century-long hegemony.

Despite these changes, Hollywood today is nevertheless very much like Detroit forty years ago, a factory town that produces big, bloated vehicles with plenty of chrome. As production budgets mushroom, quality declines in large part as a result of institutional inertia and a lack of competition. Like Detroit, Hollywood has dominated for so long that many of its executives have difficulty envisioning the transformations now on the horizon. Because of this myopia, the global future is commonly imagined as a world brought together by homogeneous cultural products produced and circulated by American media, a process referred to by some as Disneyfication. Other compelling scenarios must be considered, however. What if, for example, Chinese feature films and television programs began to rival the substantial budgets and lavish production values of their Western counterparts? What if Chinese media were to strengthen and extend their distribution networks, becoming truly global enterprises? That is, what if the future were to take an unexpected detour on the road to Disneyland, heading instead toward a more complicated global terrain characterized by overlapping and at times intersecting cultural spheres served by diverse media enterprises based in media capitals around the world?

THE NEW SOCIAL MEDIA AND THE ARAB SPRING

Natana J. DeLong-Bas

Since January 2011, the eyes of the world have turned to the Arab Spring. Launched by the image of the self-immolation of the Tunisian vegetable vendor Mohamed Bouazizi as an outcry against the humiliation of citizens at the hands of authoritarian states and their security apparatuses, the Arab Spring has so far resulted in a mix of hope for reform and questions about the future of the Middle East and North Africa. Pivotal to the revolutions that peacefully overthrew regimes in Tunisia and Egypt and pressed for change and reform in other countries throughout the region has been the role of the new social media in translating ideas shared in cyberspace into real-life action on the ground.

Given the "youth bulge" in the Middle East—where between 55 and 70 percent of the population of any given country is under the age of thirty—the fact that social media and modern technology have been used to bring about political change should come as no surprise. Because of their experience with heavy-handed government control over the mainstream media, youth tend to be more likely to seek their news from and express themselves on the Internet, generally finding it to be more reliable and accurate and less filled with government propaganda than mainstream resources. Previously dubbed the "Lost Generation," and targeted as a potential source of recruits for jihadist and Islamist groups as they sought a collective identity, the youth are now being hailed as the "Facebook Generation," the "Internet Generation," and the "Miracle Generation" because they have accomplished in less than two months in some places what previous generations had not been able to achieve in over thirty years—and all of it without resorting to violence, terrorism, or appeals to jihad or even necessarily religion. Some of the most striking aspects of these uprisings have been their dedication to peaceful demands and nonviolent protests, their mix of male and female leadership and participation, and their refusal to engage in religious or political rhetoric reminiscent of past movements or more traditional social bases, such as the Muslim Brotherhood in Egypt. Most of the demands have focused on greater personal freedom of expression, expanded rights for political participation, resolution of economic challenges that have led to widespread unemployment and underemployment, and an end to corruption and authoritarianism. All of these are secular demands, rather than calls for an Islamic Revolution or a greater public role for religion.

Although the outcome of such use of social media for political purposes appears to be relatively new, the seeds of activism have been consistently sown for the past two decades with rising access to the Internet, the end of government control over the mainstream media, and the growing availability of new levels of individual freedom of expression. Perhaps the greatest sense of empowerment has come through the ability to use cyberspace as a location for doing what could not otherwise be done in reality: assemble to discuss ideas, concerns, and complaints, and to share frustrations, while also providing the social networking opportunity to unite, strategize, and plan for change. In cyberspace, the social restrictions that exist in reality in some places—such as gender segregation—disappear, providing groups of people who might otherwise never meet and converse the opportunity to connect and recognize what they share in common.

For the past two decades, it has seemed that the jihadis have had somewhat of a monopoly on the use of social media—not only for political purposes, but also to evade detection of their activities, disseminate their ideas, plan terrorist attacks, and both recruit new members and make themselves accessible to self-recruiters. The shift to cyberspace was a deliberate strategic move. During the 1970s, 1980s, and even into the 1990s, radical Islamic preachers made use of cassette tapes to spread their message, often clan-destinely due to their politically subversive messages and the strong presence of police intelligence throughout society. Such cassette tapes existed in the "underground" ter-ritory of individual reproduction and distribution by word of mouth, rather than being made publicly available. During the 1990s and more clearly after 2000, more popular preachers transitioned to satellite television broadcasts and websites to spread their mes-sage, given that these new territories were no longer as strictly controlled by government entities following the introduction of Al-Jazeera in 1996, and given the challenges of placing entirely effective filters on Internet access. Shifting to such a global format am-plified voices that were previously restricted by geography and limited technology to a worldwide audience.

The Internet in particular opened a new communications territory, both in terms of accessing other peoples' ideas and in terms of individual expression. Websites quickly came to be used to generate awareness campaigns of many types, by individuals, orga-nizations, movements, and even governments. In the Gulf, for example, e-government has started to streamline otherwise heavily bureaucratic procedures, such as applying for identification cards and permits, and providing information about how various services operate. In Saudi Arabia, websites like www.saudidivorce.org provide information about divorce laws and women's rights in order to ensure that women are aware of their rights both in Islam and under the law. The hope of website campaigns is that raising public awareness of these rights will result in greater justice.

Organizations further use websites both to proclaim their goals and to compile databases of like-minded individuals. Both organizations and individuals have used web-sites to post petitions requesting changes ranging from expansion of women's rights—particularly with respect to family law and access to the public sphere—to cleaning up the environment. Some of the most prominent Web petitions with respect to women's rights include the One Million Signature campaigns in Morocco and Iran, which seek to garner support for proposed reforms to be presented to the government. These efforts, among many others, demonstrate attempts to use the principles of democracy in new ways and to harness the new social media for social reform.

Perhaps nowhere have the attempts to use social media to promote the principles of democracy in new ways been more visible than in Tunisia and Egypt, where Facebook and Twitter have been used to quickly disseminate information and instructions that the government has not been able to control. Some believe that the new social media have created a new process for revolution. The process begins when someone establishes a page on Facebook, which is seen by various users, who then comment on it and begin interacting with each other. Once the group is solidified, users begin posting pictures, video footage, and links to YouTube. As this happens, news and comments also begin appearing on Twitter, ever expanding the network of people who are linked in to de-bates about these events and images. Since the network is not limited geographically, the scope can quickly become global. While this process can be promising in terms of reaching large numbers of people very quickly and creating instantaneous reactions, it also carries the inherent danger of being used to perpetuate sectarianism, tribalism, regionalism, racism, sexism, and discrimination through the proliferation of extremist or exclusionary content. It must be recalled that Facebook is not the private domain of "enlightened" values or democratic ideals. The reality of an open source is that it is open to everyone and anyone who cares to access and comment on it, whether constructively or destructively. Thus, there is the potential for both democratic change and retrograde reactionism that can have serious political and economic repercussions, and for both building and fracturing social cohesion.

Egypt provides a particularly instructive example of this new model for revolution. The popular protests that ultimately resulted in the 11 February 2011 overthrow of President Hosni Mubarak attribute their origins to a blog written by an Egyptian university student named Kamel. Kamel began writing his blog following an incident in which he fell off a train onto a platform. When policemen approached him, Kamel expected them to offer assistance. Instead, they beat him. Kamel started the blog to protest his public humiliation at the hands of representatives of the authoritarian government. He quickly gained a sympathetic audience, many of whom then turned to Facebook to discuss similarly degrading and brutal experiences, resulting in the creation of an online Facebook community.

The turning point came with the case of a young Egyptian businessman from Alexandria, Khaled Said, who was reportedly beaten to death by two police officers in 2010. Popular outrage against police brutality resulted in the Facebook community responding with a Facebook page titled, "We Are All Khaled Said," which quickly turned into a series of e-mail conversations and, ultimately, a network of wannabe activists. Although he was anonymous at the time, the Facebook administrator was the Google executive Wael Ghonim, who later became the face of the Egyptian revolution. Kamel and Ghonim worked together with others to plan Egypt's first day of protest on 25 January, bringing together activists in Cairo, Alexandria, and Damanhur to end the abuses of the Mubarak regime.

Said's case became a rallying point for the opposition because it shocked the moral conscience of observers—the incident demonstrated the degree to which the state had become abusive. The hope of the activists was to shock, in turn, the moral consciences of both the state and outside observers by juxtaposing the violence and oppression of the regime with the demonstrators' own commitment to nonviolent methods, many of which were met with state violence and repression.

As more and more people joined the Facebook page, dissemination of information about planned gatherings, locations, and goals began. Through Facebook and Twitter, demonstrators were able to garner up-to-the-minute information about events, participants and leaders. In one case, ninety thousand people responded via Facebook and Twitter that they planned to attend particular demonstrations, giving organizers a vision of the intended scope of the event and also clearly showing the power of numbers. When so many respond to a social networking site that they intend to physically participate in an event, others are inspired to join, knowing that they will not be alone. By contrast, in cases where only a few respond to the calls for demonstrations—such as occurred for Saudi Arabia's not very impressive "Day of Rage," in March 2011—those debating whether to attend may have been at least partially discouraged from doing so because of the lack of numbers in the face of an intimidating police presence.

Although use of social media has not been credited with causing the uprisings, it clearly played a role in accelerating the events because of the speed at which communications were transmitted. Social media sites have proven difficult for governments to control, despite Mubarak's efforts to do so early in the protests by shutting the Internet down completely. Rather than having the desired effect of calming the situation, the attempt to regain control appears to have resulted in driving more people onto the streets. Had Mubarak chosen to monitor the social media rather than control it or shut it down, he might have at least come to understand the genuine depth and scope of popular frustration so as to respond to it more productively, or at least by meeting some of the demands of the protesters; instead, his decision to react with shows of strength served only to further inflame the situation.

THE WORLDWIDE DIGITAL DIVIDE: INFORMATION, POVERTY, THE INTERNET, AND DEVELOPMENT

Pippa Norris

There are many reasons why new communications technology, particularly the role of the Internet, may potentially level the playing field allowing nations with moderate levels of development, like Malaysia, Estonia and Brazil, to catch up with post-industrial societies.

Potentially the effect of the Internet in broadening and enhancing access to information and communication may be greatest in poorer nations, because once past the barriers of access the new technology offers a relatively cheap and efficient service. In the global marketplace, small businesses in South Africa and Mexico can sell their products directly to customers in New York, irrespective of the traditional barriers of distance, the costs of advertising, and the intermediate distribution chains. With the travel industry accounting for up to a third of total online revenues in 1997, sales via the Internet are likely to be an important source of growth for developing countries.

The Internet also offers promise in the delivery of basic services like education and health information to far-flung regions, allowing a teacher or doctor in Ghana or Calcutta access to the same database information as one in London or New York. Networks of hospitals and health care professionals in the Ukraine, Mozambique and Senegal can share medical expertise and knowledge. Distance learning can widen access to training and education, such as open universities in India and Thailand and language web sites for schools. In all these regards, in the rosy scenario the Internet promises to level the playing field and strengthen the voice of the voiceless in the developing world.

The global reach of the Internet may also help to integrate the concerns of developing society in the international arena. By connecting disparate social movements, new coalitions can be formed mobilizing global civic society, such as those concerned about the World Trade Organization meeting in Seattle, sweatshop manufacture of Nike shoes, or opposition movements in Burma, linking indigenous groups in developing societies with German greens, Australian trade unionists and EU human rights organizations. This process promises to make international agencies more accountable to grassroots NGOs, a fact that has increased the leverage and networking capacity of the women's movement, human rights activists, and environmentalists. The global reach and speed of connectivity, in particular, allows international mobilization around issues from genetically modified food to the independence movement in East Timor. Foreign policymakers in New York, Brussels and Geneva can no longer assume that the usual diplomatic and political elites can govern international affairs with a passive "permissive consensus" without taking account of the new ability for public information, mobilization, and engagement engendered by the new technology.

Yet basic access is required before the potential benefits of the Internet can flow to poorer societies. How realistic is this? Will the Internet actually strengthen the voice of the voiceless, as some hope, or will it merely produce new forms of cultural imperialism with the major corporate players located in Silicone Valley, Cambridge and Tokyo? In the last few years international agencies like the World Bank, United Nations Development Program, OECD and International Telecommunications Union have expressed growing concern that the explosion of the Internet may leave many nations far behind, producing growing disparities between advanced industrialized and developing societies.

The United Nations Development Report warned that the gains in productivity produced by the new technology may widen differences in economic growth between the most affluent nations and those that lack the skills, resources and infrastructure to invest in the information society: "The network society is creating parallel communications systems: one for those with income, education and literally connections, giving plentiful information at low cost and high speed; the other for those without connections, blocked by high barriers of time, cost and uncertainty and dependent upon outdated information." . . . Echoing these concerns, UNESCO emphasizes that the North-South divide may be exacerbated in a situation where most of the world's population lacks basic access to a telephone, let alone a computer.

As a result, poorer societies can become increasingly marginalized at the periphery of communication networks. Although the Internet is a new technology, there is nothing particularly novel about this pattern. Research on global information flows from north to south have long emphasized the center-periphery distinction, a problem which aroused heated debate in the 1980s centering on UNESCO's New World Information Order.

But the growing importance of the information economy can be expected to exacerbate these divisions.

THE DIFFUSION OF THE INTERNET WORLDWIDE

How far has the Internet diffused around the world? No official data yet exists on how many people go online on a global basis but there is evidence about the penetration of the new technology based on analyzing the location of Internet hosts, web servers and e-commerce sites, as well available surveys of the general population conducted by market researchers. Data remains incomplete, in some countries we have only "guesstimates," but the use of overlapping sources confirms the broad picture of global inequalities of access and use.

The best available evidence on the distribution of users, hosts and hardware indicate that in the emerging Internet Age the information revolution has transformed communications in post-industrial states like Sweden, Australia, and the United States at the cutting edge of technological change, reinforcing their lead in the new economy. But in the early twenty-first century so far the benefits of the Internet have failed to reach most of the poorer nations in Sub-Saharan Africa, South Asia and the Middle East. The gap between the information-rich and poor countries has sharply increased in the emergent years of this new technology.

Nua [an Internet usage statistics provider] provides the most comprehensive unofficial estimates based on combining surveys by different companies, most commonly asking a sample of the general population whether they have access online at home or at work. Reanalysis of this data shows that worldwide the number of Internet users exploded from about 26 million in 1995 to approximately 257 million by Spring 2000. Although a remarkable rise, it remains the case that at present only 4% of the world's population are online. . . .

Globally the regional disparities are marked. The 29 OECD member states, representing post-industrial economies and developed democracies, contain 97% of all Internet hosts, 92% of the market in production and consumption of computer hardware, software and services, and 86% of all Internet users. In contrast the whole of Sub-Saharan Africa contains only 2.5 million Internet users, or less than 1% of the world's online community. Indeed there are more users within affluent Sweden than in the entire continent of Africa.

Growing inequalities are evident even within post-industrial economies. In the European Union, for example, the spring 1999 Eurobarometer survey found that almost two-thirds of the population had access in Sweden, Denmark and Finland, some of the highest levels of penetration worldwide, compared with only one tenth of those living in Mediterranean Europe. . . . Today almost two-thirds of the world's online community is located in just five countries: the United States, Japan, the UK, Canada, and Germany. . . .

Alternative indicators of Internet dispersion can be estimated from the distribution of Internet hosts, which are regularly monitored by agencies such as Netcraft, Network

Wizards, Matrix Information, the Internet Software Consortium, and RIPE (Resceaux Internet-provider Europeens Network coordination service). The most comprehensive estimates for the number of web servers around the globe is provided by Netcraft, who found that by the end of the twentieth century there were about 11.1 million sites worldwide, up from 18,000 in 1995. . . .

The results confirm the North-South division found in surveys of Internet users. Among industrialized societies, the US, Japan, the UK, Canada, Germany and Australia dominate the location of Internet hosts, followed by many Western European countries, with poorer societies like Turkey, Mexico and Poland at the bottom of the ranking. . . . Worldwide the disparities are even greater; there are almost as many hosts in France as in all of Latin America and the Caribbean, and there are more hosts in New York that in all of Africa. . . .

Equally important, many have expressed concern about the development of a social divide, referring to the inequalities of Internet access and use by disadvantaged groups within society, even in countries at the forefront of the information society. In the United States, the Department of Commerce's recent study, *Falling through the Net*, emphasizes the familiar disparities in access found among low-income American households, and the gap among high-school educated, blacks and Hispanics, those in rural areas, and to a lesser extent among women. The 1998 survey found that households with income of $75,000 and above are twenty times as likely to have Internet access as those at the lowest income levels, and more than nine times as likely to have computer access.

In February 2000, President Clinton expressed concern about this situation and proposed a new plan to help bridge the "digital divide," offering private companies a $2bn tax break, new teacher training programs, and the development of Community Technology Centers in low-income neighborhoods to help close the gap so that access to computers eventually becomes as ubiquitous as the availability of the telephone or television (www.digitaldivide.gov). The Department of Commerce has headed this initiative, emphasizing the role of public programs to widen access, promote the skills people need to use the technology, and encourage content that will empower underserved communities. In the private sector too, industry leaders like Steve Case, chairman of AOL-Time Warner, have warned that too many people are being left behind in the information age.

Other countries like Finland, Germany and Sweden have all announced initiatives to address these concerns, often incorporating a mix of private and public resources. The British government has recently introduced new ways to try to expand access to disadvantaged groups, through the distribution of reconditioned computers, there is free email through some ISP providers, companies are planning Internet kiosks allowing free access and email, with revenues generated by advertising and e-commerce, and British Telecom is developing public phones and photo booths with multimedia capabilities on a pay-as-you-go basis (aka "multimedia communication pods"). In south Asia, initiatives have been proposed to extend the Net to rural areas via Internet kiosks, community centers, wireless delivery, and public sector initiatives.

Many factors may have contributed towards the digital divide, including the *structure of opportunities* provided by the public policies within each country, such as public and private initiatives towards IT education and training, investment in science and technology, the costs of ISP services, and the regulation of telecommunications.

Cultural attitudes towards using computers may also contribute towards some of the differences evident between relatively similar societies, like the UK, Germany, France, and Italy, especially familiarity with the English language, since the most comprehensive attempt to map over 1 billion web pages found that 87% of the current contents are published in this tongue.

But in addition to this the role of *resources* can be expected to be particularly important, including levels of socioeconomic development, particularly adult literacy, education and the necessary computer skills. . . .

The regression of per capita $GDP (measured in Purchasing Power Parity) proves a powerful predictor of where countries are located in terms of per capita Internet use (using a scale of the logged mean). There are some outliers of middle-level developing countries that have used an extensive program of government, non-profit and private sector programs to expand Internet access and training in their societies, pulling themselves up by their LAN wires, such as Estonia, Malaysia and Slovenia. Nevertheless in most developing nations the inequalities of resources that continue to produce disparities in health care, longevity and education are also, not surprisingly, evident in the virtual world. Though many hope for a brave new world, access to the Internet is remarkably similar to the diffusion of other forms of information technology that have been available for decades, like telephones and personal computers. . . .

The global digital divide raises many issues for discussion that will be explored further in subsequent research. Will the disparities in Internet access gradually close over time, as the new technology gradually diffuses throughout the world, like the spread of radio? Or will this gap persist or expand? And how can government, non-profit and corporate investment in public access through local centers, Internet cafes and community associations expand access for disadvantaged groups? Recognizing this potential, international agencies have highlighted the need for inclusive strategies in the dispersion of new technologies.

In a speech in October 1999 at Telecom 99 in Geneva, Switzerland, UN Secretary General Kofi Annan warned of the danger of excluding the world's poor from the information revolution in the wired world. "People lack many things: jobs, shelter, food, health care and drinkable water. Today, being cut off from basic telecommunications services is a hardship almost as acute as these other deprivations, and may indeed reduce the chances of finding remedies to them."

Other international organizations echo these concerns. In February 2000 James D. Wolfensohn, president of the World Bank, announced a major new initiative in the attempt to bridge the technological gap between rich and poor nations. "The digital divide is one of the greatest impediments to development," he argued, "and it is growing exponentially."

The available evidence in the emergent era is that, despite its capacity for development, without adequate action by government, non-profits and the corporate sector, the global information gap is likely to widen the North-South divide. In their strategies for overseas aid and development, Western governments need to consider how best to reduce information poverty, complimenting traditional areas of concern such as efforts to improve health, nutrition and literacy. Far from a luxury, access to information has become increasingly essential for the effective delivery of services by professionals like teachers and health care professionals, as well as for small businesses seeking to expand their markets worldwide.

The challenge in the emergent era of the Internet age is to maximize the potential benefits worldwide, while the process of dispersion remains in transition, and before new inequalities become rigidified.

FURTHER READING

Albrow, Martin. 1997. *The Global Age: State and Society beyond Modernity*. Stanford, CA: Stanford University Press.

Anheier, Helmut, and Yudhishthir Raj Isar (Eds.). 2007. *Cultures and Globalization*. 4 vols. London: Sage.

Beck, U. (2006). *The Cosmopolitan Vision*. Cambridge, UK: Polity Press.

Castells, Manuel. 2012. *Networks of Outrage and Hope: Social Movements in the Internet Age*. London: Polity Press

Curtin, Michael. 2007. *Playing to the World's Biggest Audience: The Globalization of Chinese Film and TV*. Berkeley: University of California Press.

Desai, Jigna. 2004. *Beyond Bollywood: The Cultural Politics of South Asian Diasporic Film*. London: Routledge.

Featherstone, Mike (Ed.). 1990. *Global Culture: Nationalism, Globalization and Modernity*. London: Sage.

Friedman, Jonathan. 1994. *Cultural identity and global process*. London: Sage.

Gerbaudo, Paolo. 2012. *Tweets and the Streets: Social Media and Contemporary Activism*. London: Pluto Press.

Jameson, Frederic, and Masao Miyoshi. 1998. *The Cultures of Globalization*. Durham, NC: Duke University Press.

Kaur, Raminder, and Ajay J. Sinha (Eds.). 2005. *Bollyworld: Popular Indian Cinema through a Transnational Lens*. New Delhi: Sage.

Kavoori, Anandam, and Aswin Punathambekar (Eds.). 2008. *Global Bollywood*. New York: New York University Press.

Robertson, Roland. 1992. *Globalization: Social Theory and Global Culture*. London: Sage.

Stevenson, Nick. 2003. *Cultural Citizenship: Cosmopolitan Questions*. Maidenhead, UK: Open University Press.

Tomlinson, John. 1999. *Globalization and Culture*. Chicago: University of Chicago Press.

19

THE GLOBAL MOVEMENT FOR
HUMAN RIGHTS

There may be huge cultural differences among societies from urban Manhattan to tribal Papua New Guinea and from the Amazon rain forests to Sahara oases. But one thing that all societies have in common is that they respect human life; they believe people should be treated with respect and dignity. How this respect is interpreted varies, however, and there is a great deal of disagreement over whether all humans are in fact treated fairly.

Yet there is intuitively a kind of common moral culture—a global ethic—shared by everyone on the planet. This global ethic is the basis for the global movement for human rights—a sentiment and a series of statements and organizations that promote the idea that there are standards of decency in humans' treatment of one another that are shared by all people. Moreover, they feel that it is the responsibility of governments around the world to guarantee those rights and to protect them.

Soon after the United Nations was created in 1945, it began to fashion a statement about human rights that it thought should be binding on every civilized society. Remember that the UN was created at the end of World War II, when the Nazis—the National Socialist regime of Adolf Hitler's Germany—trampled over human rights in the worst way. Toward the end of the war, when it became clear to the world how the Nazi regime had treated Jews, Gypsies, and gay people, the world was horrified. People had been yanked out of their homes, forced to live in substandard conditions or worse in prison camps, where a large percentage of them ultimately perished. Any human being with a conscience would want to make sure that people could never be treated like that again, especially by a government that is supposed to be protecting the safety and security of its citizens.

So in 1947, a group of representatives from around the world convened at Lake Success in New York under UN auspices to draft a Universal Declaration of Human Rights. At the forefront was the widow of deceased American President Franklin Delano Roosevelt. Eleanor Roosevelt made this document her personal cause. During the war, the Allies had articulated "four freedoms" as the goals of the war effort—freedom of speech, freedom of religion, freedom from fear, and freedom from want. The Universal Declaration of Rights was intended to expand upon these basic freedoms and to identify the rights of which all individuals could expect to be assured wherever they lived. They were intended to be "universal."

The full document, which was drafted by a Canadian, John Peters Humphrey, had three parts, the first of which was the Declaration. This was followed by two other documents that were approved later, the International Covenant on Economic, Social, and Cultural Rights, and the International Covenant on Civil and Political Rights. The whole thing was known as the International Bill of Human Rights, and eventually, in 1976, it was implemented as international law, supposedly binding on all countries that signed it.

The Universal Declaration of Human Rights begins with the statement that "recognition of the inherent dignity and of the equal and inalienable rights of all members of the human family is the foundation of freedom, justice and peace in the world." It then lists 30 articles, each of which proclaims a fundamental human right, among them the right of equality regardless of race, ethnicity, sex, religion, or any other reason for discrimination. It also lists the right to be free from slavery and the right of free speech. Article 5 proclaims that no one should be "subject to torture or degrading treatment of punishment." Other rights include freedom from arbitrary arrest and freedom to leave one's country at will and to change one's nationality. It also includes the right to education and to marry whomever one wants to marry.

In December 1948, the Declaration was submitted to the United Nations secretariat, where it passed by a vote of 48 nations in favor and none against. Eight nations abstained, however; most of these were socialist countries that objected to the right to leave one's country and change nationalities at will. Saudi Arabia also abstained, uncomfortable with the notion of individual independence, especially with regard to cultural and marital matters, which the Saudis thought challenged the traditional authority of Islamic Shari'ah law.

Since that time there have been other concerns about the degree to which the Declaration is as "universal" as it proclaims itself to be. Some critics say that it is very Western in its conception of individualism and that it portrays society as constituted of lone individuals united in a social contract to society. Traditional societies, these critics say, are comprised of natural communities, castes, ethnicities, tribes, and religious groups that are bound together by mutual trust and a sense of common duties rather than by individual rights that separate each person from the group. The Islamic Republic of Iran has stated that the UN Declaration and its charters on human rights should not supersede their understanding of Islamic Shari'ah law. At the same, time, however, the constitution of the Islamic Republic of Iran has an extensive list of rights that look quite similar to the articles in the UN Declaration, including the rights to work, to education, to free speech, and to equality before the law. Hence, it would appear that the main features of the UN Declaration continue to be respected as part of a global ethic of dignity and respect toward all human beings.

The organizations and movements for human rights that have been established since the 1948 UN Declaration are dedicated to making certain that governments abide by the principles once they agreed upon them. Among the continuing issues that are prominently discussed are the rights of women, freedom of religion, freedom of speech, ethnic equality, and the ban on political punishment, torture, and holding prisoners without trial. Many people accused the United States, in its conduct of the "war on terror" after 9/11, of having violated human rights in its treatment of al Qaeda prisoners. Some of these violations also contravened another human rights document, the Geneva Convention of 1949, that prescribed appropriate treatment of prisoners of war. Among these agreements is the pledge to treat prisoners with respect and not submit them to torture.

The aim of most movements for human rights is to make violations public when they occur and to shame governments into compliance. Among the leading international organizations are Amnesty International, which is especially concerned about illegally held political prisoners, and Human Rights Watch, which monitors the whole spectrum of human rights issues in countries around the world. There are also legal remedies under international law, although not all countries recognize the authority of international law, of the International Criminal Court, or of the International Court of Justice, located in The Hague, The Netherlands.

The readings in this section cover several aspects related to the protection of human rights in a global context. They begin with a look at the impact of globalization on the concept and practice of human rights. The first reading is from a book on the history of human rights by Micheline Ishay, a professor of international relations at the University of Denver. She notes that economic globalization has been detrimental to labor rights, but that global networks have benefited the movement for women's rights. The second reading focuses specifically on transnational threats to human rights—especially when globalization weakens the authority of nation-states to protect its citizens—along with the possibilities of transnational human rights protection that is possible in the global age. The author of this selection is Alison Brysk, a political scientist who teaches in the global studies program at the University of California–Santa Barbara.

The other two readings in this section place the issue of human rights within the broader scope of global order and ethics. Eve Darian-Smith, an Australian legal studies scholar who teaches at the University of California–Santa Barbara, puts the ideas of human rights within the framework of the development of civilizations and sees it as an ambivalent ethic, at times bringing greater social justice and at times used in ways that are exploitative and counterproductive. The last reading is by David Held, a British political scientist who taught for some years at the London School of Economics, where he established a program in global politics; he now teaches at the University of Durham. In this selection, Held does not deal specifically with human rights, but instead with the changing world order that makes all transnational problems more difficult to solve. He describes how the world is becoming more multipolar in the era of globalization, meaning that the West no longer has unchallenged economic, political, and cultural influence. The paradox of our times, according to Held, is that the problems become more transnational but the means of dealing with them do not.

GLOBALIZATION AND ITS IMPACT: HUMAN RIGHTS FOR WHOM?

Micheline Ishay

This fight remains even more important as the jubilation at the end of the cold war has yielded to a more sobering environment for the pursuit of human rights. Indeed, the pressures of globalization (environmental degradation, the weakening of trade unions, harsh immigration policies, etc.) have further complicated the daunting search for a unified human rights agenda. At the same time, each of these negative aspects of globalization has redirected the specific agenda of various social groups: trade unions, women's groups, children's rights activists, gay rights groups, and advocates for minorities and the disabled. Over time, one may hope that a common understanding of the new challenges presented by globalization will enable each group to unify and to build a more encompassing program.

For over a century and a half, trade unions have fought for workers' rights to decent pay and better working conditions, and for improved social welfare, including health care, education, and social security. Generations of struggle for basic democratic rights, such as the right to organize in the workplace, have culminated in the International Confederation of Free Trade Unions, an organization that now embraces 127 million men and women in 136 countries on five continents. Yet with the decline of trade unions in recent decades, this movement is now under attack on a global scale.

Partly because of the spread of privatization, and partly because of the emergence of post-Fordist globalized production, trade unions in the West have suffered progressive losses in membership and have consequently lost some of the leverage they applied in earlier battles with employers. Despite the optimistic predictions of globalizers, average wages in the United States have been stagnant and have even dropped for the lowest-skilled workers. With growing numbers dependent on social security and welfare benefits, many governments have raised eligibility requirements while cutting payments. In many countries, government spending on education and health has also declined.

In the developing world, for much of the time since independence, trade unions have faced significant interference from governments and even, in some cases, outright control by them. While trade unions in many countries have played a key role in the move toward democratization, they are now facing a new crisis as their former strongholds, sectors like teaching, transport, and civil service, are undermined by privatization and public sector cuts. Worse, as competition becomes global and intensifies, bringing a new level of insecurity to developed nations and increased poverty to much of the developing world, one-fifth of the world's population has been left in conditions of utter poverty as more than 700 million workingmen and workingwomen are not productively employed, let alone properly represented.

While it is true that the Universal Declaration of Human Rights (articles 21–27) and many clauses of the Covenant on Economic, Social and Cultural Rights have codified workers' rights, enforcing a standard international social clause remains, in trade and business summits, a divisive issue. Western labor activists believe that a common social standard would prevent division between workers and dampen capital flight to poorer regions of the world, while rights activists in the developing world, recognizing that lower labor costs are a key incentive for attracting foreign investment, have denounced such measures as dismissive of the needs of poorer societies.

Domestically, trade unions in the southern hemisphere face other difficulties in their fight to secure the rights of their members, to represent workers in the informal sector, and to prevent forced labor. The last problem, little noticed by Western media, in fact represents an alarming reversal for human rights. Despite the banning of slavery in 1926 and in the 1957 Supplementary Convention on the Abolition of Slavery, the practice has not disappeared but has taken on a new form, with the current world total of slaves reaching approximately 27 million. Fifteen to twenty million of those bonded laborers are concentrated in India, Pakistan, Bangladesh, and Nepal. "There are more slaves alive today," argues the British scholar Kevin Bales, "than all the people stolen from Africa in the time of the transatlantic slave trade." That one should never be forced to barter one's freedom for fear of one's life had already been affirmed by Rousseau in the eighteenth century. Slavery remains, despite the Enlightenment's outcry, the nineteenth-century anti-slavery fight, and subsequent abolitionist treaties, a plague for many of the world's poorest people.

Chattel slavery, in which a captured person is born or sold into permanent servitude, still exists in places like Mauritania, yet represents only a very small part of modern slavery. Debt bondage, common in Pakistan and India, is the most prevalent form of slavery today. It occurs when people who are desperately in debt are forced to submit to an agreement in which they (or their children) work without compensation until their employer decides they have paid off their obligations. Another form of modern slavery results when vulnerable people accept (or, as children, are forced by their parents to accept) a contract for guaranteed work and are transported far from home, only to find themselves, in effect, imprisoned and forced to work (child prostitution is a notorious example). That type of slavery is prevalent in Southeast Asia, Brazil, and some Arab states. While these forms of slavery are more widespread in developing countries, immigrants in Western countries, fearing deportation or illegal status, are often exposed to similar forms of bondage. Removed from the public eye, domestic workers, especially women, have remained more vulnerable to exploitative conditions.

Such persistent areas of female exploitation should not obscure the successes of the women's liberation movement in condemning the treatment of women as second-class citizens. In her international best-seller *The Second Sex* (1949), Simone de Beauvoir raised postwar feminist consciousness to a new height. With the emergence of the service sector in the West, women poured into the workforce after World War II, only to remain stigmatized because of their sex. Betty Friedan's *The Feminine Mystique* (1963) captured their tedious domestic lives and degrading daily experiences and, along with Kate Millett's *Sexual Politics* (1969), galvanized the women's movement in the late 1960s. Feminists had concluded that polite requests for change were insufficient and that they needed to develop a new organization to press their demands. The National Organization for Women was established in the United States and, despite a membership that ranged from moderate to radical, found consensus on six measures essential to ensuring women's equality: enforcement of laws banning employment discrimination; maternity leave rights; child-care centers that could enable mothers to work; tax deductions for child-care expenses; equal and unsegregated education; and job-training opportunities for poor women.

As globalization facilitated the erection of transnational social networks, the women's liberation movement spread throughout the world. The goals of feminism, however, varied from country to country, depending upon the level of repression. Western feminists were fighting to change sexist stigma and to achieve social and economic equality, African women were demanding the removal of the bride price, and feminists of the Muslim world were seeking the relaxation of the dress code and regulations enforcing separation of the sexes. Growing awareness of these issues prompted the 1979 adoption of the UN Convention on the Elimination of All Forms of Discrimination against Women (CEDAW), later ratified by 131 countries with the glaring exception of the United States, which stood out as the only industrialized country not to sign it.

TRANSNATIONAL THREATS AND OPPORTUNITIES

Alison Brysk

Globalization—the growing interpenetration of states, markets, communications, and ideas across borders—is one of the leading characteristics of the contemporary world. International norms and institutions for the protection of human rights are more developed than at any previous point in history, while global civil society fosters growing avenues of appeal for citizens repressed by their own states. But assaults on fundamental human dignity continue, and the very blurring of borders and rise of transnational actors that facilitated the development of a global human rights regime may also be generating new sources of human rights abuse. Even as they are more broadly articulated and accepted, the rights of individuals have come to depend ever more on a broad array of global actors and forces, from ministries to multinationals to missionaries.

What are the patterns of the human rights impact of globalization? Are new problems replacing, intensifying, or mitigating state-sponsored repression? Are some dynamics of globalization generating both problems and opportunities? How can new opportunities be used to offset new problems? And how has the idea and practice of human rights influenced the process of globalization?

How does globalization—which liberals claim will promote development, democracy, personal empowerment, and global governance—instead present new challenges for human rights? Globalization is a package of transnational flows of people, production, investment, information, ideas, and authority (not new, but stronger and faster). Human rights are a set of claims and entitlements to human dignity, which the existing international regime assumes will be provided (or threatened) by the state. A more cosmopolitan and open international system should free individuals to pursue their rights, but large numbers of people seem to be suffering from both long-standing state repression and new denials of rights linked to transnational forces. . . . The challenge of globalization is that unaccountable flows of migration and open markets present new threats, which are not amenable to state-based human rights regimes, while the new opportunities of global information and institutions are insufficiently accessible and distorted by persistent state intervention.

The emergence of an "international regime" for human rights, growing transnational social movement networks, increasing consciousness, and information politics have the potential to address both traditional and emerging forms of human rights violations. The United Nations has supervised human rights reform in El Salvador, Cambodia, and Haiti, while creating a new high commissioner for human rights. The first international tribunals since Nuremberg are prosecuting genocide in the former Yugoslavia and Rwanda. Transnational legal accountability and humanitarian intervention promote universal norms and link them to the enforcement power of states. Thousands of nongovernmental organizations monitor and lobby for human rights from Tibet to East Timor. Alongside principled proponents such as Amnesty International, globalization has generated new forms of advocacy such as transnational professional networks (Doctors without Borders), global groups for conflict monitoring, and coalitions across transnational issues (Sierra Club-Amnesty International). New forms of communication allow victims to videotape their plight, advocates to flood governments with faxes, Web sites to mobilize urgent action alerts. But the effectiveness of global consciousness and pressure on the states, paramilitaries, and insurgents responsible for long-standing human rights violations varies tremendously. And access to the new global mechanisms is distributed unevenly, so that some of the neediest victims—such as the illiterate rural poor and refugee women—are the least likely to receive either global or domestic redress.

Beyond this interaction of new solutions with old problems, new human rights problems may result from the integration of markets, the shrinking of states, increased transnational flows such as migration, the spread of cultures of intolerance, and the decision-making processes of new or growing global institutions. The increasing presence of multinational corporations has challenged labor rights throughout Southeast Asia, along the Mexican border, and beyond. Increasing levels of migration worldwide make growing numbers of refugees and undocumented laborers vulnerable to abuse by sending and receiving states, as well as transnational criminal networks. Hundreds of Mexican nationals die each year crossing the U.S. border; in contrast, 450 German migrants were killed during forty years of Europeans crossing the Berlin Wall. International economic adjustment and the growth of tourism are linked to a rise in prostitution and trafficking in women and children, affecting millions in the Caribbean, Southeast Asia, the post-Soviet states and even the United States. The U.S. State Department estimates that one to two million persons each year are trafficked for various forms of forced labor and "modern-day slavery"—including almost 50,000 annually to the United States. The same Internet that empowers human rights activists increases government monitoring, instructs neo-Nazis, and carries transnational death threats against dissenters. Unelected global institutions like the World Bank, international peacekeepers, and environmental NGOs administering protected areas increasingly control the lives of the most powerless citizens of weak states. . . .

HUMAN RIGHTS IN A GLOBAL ARENA

Human rights are a set of universal claims to safeguard human dignity from illegitimate coercion, typically enacted by state agents. These norms are codified in a widely endorsed set of international undertakings: the "International Bill of Human Rights" (Universal Declaration of Human Rights, International Covenant on Civil and Political Rights, and International Covenant on Social and Economic Rights); phenomenon-specific treaties on war crimes (Geneva Conventions), genocide, and torture; and protections for vulnerable groups such as the UN Convention on the Rights of the Child and the Convention on the Elimination of Discrimination against Women. International dialogue on human rights has produced a distinction between three "generations" of human rights, labeled for their historical emergence. Security rights encompass life, bodily integrity, liberty, and sometimes associated rights of political participation and democratic governance. Social and economic rights, highlighted in the eponymous International Covenant, comprise both negative and positive freedoms, enacted by states and others: prominently, rights to food, health care, education, and free labor. More recently discussed collective rights may include rights such as membership in a cultural community and access to a healthy environment. These "generations" of rights often involve different sets of actors and different levels of state accountability.

While the origins of the international human rights regime, U.S. foreign policy, NGO monitoring, and much previous scholarship have focused on security rights, this project will entertain a broader conception of linked political, social, and cultural rights grounded in the Universal Declaration. A focus on security rights may be desirable for clarity and manageability, as well as because security rights of life and freedom are "basic" or enabling rights that make the pursuit of other rights possible. However, human rights claims have an inherently expanding character, which requires the consideration of every type of threat to human dignity under a range of changing social conditions. Thus, both liberty and survival may involve social issues, such as the right to free labor and to organize for better labor conditions. Some vulnerable groups, notably women and indigenous peoples, may face linked threats that emanate from public and private actors, and seek cultural freedoms to meaningfully participate in civic life. Furthermore, the very process of globalization blurs distinctions among categories of rights: humanitarian intervention seeks to rescue ethnic groups, women working as prostitutes are beaten by police for "bothering tourists" to feed their children, and rights to privacy and expression collide on the Internet. . . . These linked rights can be delineated by granting priority to those rights that enable others and those violations that present the greatest harm to victims.

Human rights values derive from and are justified by reference to philosophical constructions of human nature, cultural and religious traditions, demands from civil society, and international influence. In practical importance, the latter two political factors are the most important source of human rights in the contemporary world. Accordingly, despite frequent violations in practice, international consensus has implanted human rights as a nearly universal vocabulary of debate, aspiration, and civic challenges to state legitimacy.

Analysts of human rights have identified a variety of psychological, social, economic, and political patterns that put societies "at risk" of human rights violations. These generally include authoritarian government, civil war, strong ethnic cleavages, weak civil society, power vacuums, critical junctures in economic development, and military dominance. Above all, the study of human rights teaches us that human rights violations usually reflect a calculated (or manipulated) pursuit of political power, not inherent evil or ungovernable passions. One of our first tasks is to analyze the effect of globalization on these risk factors.

The effect of globalization on state-based human rights violations will depend on the type of state and its history. In newly democratizing countries with weak institutions and elite-controlled economies (Russia, Latin America, Southeast Asia), the growth of global markets and economic flows tends to destabilize coercive forces but increase crime, police abuse, and corruption. Global mobility and information flows generally stimulate ethnic mobilization, which may promote self-determination in responsive states but more often produces collective abuses in defense of dominant-group hegemony. On the other hand, the same forces have produced slow institutional openings by less fragmented single-party states (like China and Mexico). In much of Africa, globalization has ironically increased power vacuums, by both empowering substate challengers and providing sporadic intervention, which displaces old regimes without consolidating new ones. Some of the most horrifying abuses of all have occurred in the transnationalized, Hobbesian civil wars of Sierra Leone, Angola, and the Congo.

But the literature on human rights has also moved beyond the conventional wisdom that situated human rights violations and remediation predominantly within the state, to suggest ways in which globalization creates new opportunities to challenge the state "from above and below." Human rights research has produced both evidence of new capabilities for monitoring, pressure, and sanctions, along with reports of new types and venues of abuse. In general, analysts of globalization find that states' international integration improves security rights, but increases inequality and threatens the social rights of citizens. However, neither economic development nor economic growth in and of themselves improve human rights performance. In addition to globalization and growth, findings on the effectiveness of international pressure on state human rights policy suggest that target states must be structurally accessible, internationally sensitive, and contain local human rights activists for linkage.

There is little systematic evidence available on the overall human rights impact of global flows and actors, and that which does exist is often contradictory. For example, quantitative studies that demonstrate improved security rights where MNCs (multinational corporations) are present contrast with case studies documenting multinational reinforcement of state coercion and labor suppression. Other scholars suggest that the impact of multinationals depends more on their type of production, customer base, or sending country than their globalizing nature. Similarly, some studies indicate that even within "economic globalization," different types of global economic flows at different times will have different impacts on democracy and human rights (for example, . . . trade is negative but foreign direct investment is positive). There is some basis for believing that new global human rights mechanisms, such as transnational NGO campaigns, may be particularly effective against transnational actors like multinationals.

HUMAN RIGHTS AS AN ETHICS OF PROGRESS

Eve Darian-Smith

In Europe and the United States, against the turbulent background of the American War of Independence (1776) and the French Revolution (1789), a notion of human rights emerged based on a person's inalienable rights to life, freedom and liberty. . . . Encapsulated in the French Declaration of the Rights of Man and the American Bill of Rights was the idea that all individuals have, by virtue of their humanity, certain inalienable rights that the state is obligated to defend. In practical terms, this meant that a person's human rights were limited to the extent that the state would defend them.

A person's status as citizen was seen as key in determining the degree to which a liberal democratic state would involve itself, or not, in defending any notion of rights and freedoms.

Historically, the concept of rights can be broken down into various categories, such as civil and political rights, as well as cultural, social and economic rights. These different kinds of rights include, to varying degrees, the belief that all people are created equal in nature. Some of these rights, such as the right to vote and the right to be politically represented, are based on a person's status as a citizen of a state. In contrast, cultural, social and economic human rights, at least in theory, are not necessarily linked to a person's status with respect to state institutions but are supposedly determined on the basis of all peoples' intrinsic human dignity.

Despite the lofty principles of human dignity embodied in human rights language, the history of human rights is actually one of violence, oppression, and exploitation. Imperial expansion and colonialism saw the conquest and occupation by European nations of large areas of Africa, the Americas and the Asia-Pacific from the sixteenth to the twentieth centuries. During these centuries of colonial control, classificatory schemas were established whereby people were determined to be Christian or non-Christian, citizens or non-citizens, civilized or savage.

These schemas of mankind were based on hierarchical understandings of race which presumed that different human characteristics, such as intelligence, correlated to a person's ethnic identity and racial characteristics. Hierarchies of race ranked white European males as superior and darker skinned peoples as inferior. In the nineteenth and early twentieth centuries, pseudo-scientific schema based on eugenics lent legitimacy to popular theories about racialized hierarchies of people. Eugenics sought to classify mankind on the basis of genes and improve humanity through selective breeding, sterilization, and other horrifying social policies. On the basis of how a person was classified, certain political, civil, cultural, social and economic rights were granted. Those people considered racially inferior, and less than human, were denied rights and privileges linked to citizenship. As a result, "While the colonizing West brought the constitutive aspects of the human rights tradition—sovereignty, constitutionalism, and ideas of freedom and equality—their beliefs about anthropology effectively excluded non-European peoples from human rights benefits." However, the exclusion of non-European peoples from the benefits of an international human rights discourse began to change with the decolonialization movement after WWII in the mid- to late twentieth century. The decolonization era saw the withdrawal of many European powers from their former colonies and a growth in world attention focused on how best to implement human rights in new self-governing state systems emerging in Africa, Asia and the Pacific. In this context delegates from formerly colonized countries joined the international forum of the United Nations and helped to draft the Universal Declaration of Human Rights. The discussions between representatives from former colonized and colonizing countries were often bitter and tense. After years of heated debate, the end result in the Universal Declaration was to de-link human rights from citizenship by stating that people, as bearers of human rights, were self-determining sovereign actors whether or not a given state recognized them as such. In other words, the Universal Declaration attempted to move human rights discourse away from its former dependence on nation-states as the grantor and enforcer of a person's rights. The Geneva Conventions and Helsinki Agreement of 1975 furthered this agenda, as did the growing international attention to the proliferation of human rights abuses in Latin America and Eastern Europe throughout the 1980s and 1990s. Recent advances have been made on this front through the establishing of the International Criminal Court (ICC) in 2002 which can prosecute any individual for crimes against humanity and is not limited to individuals who have operated in their capacity as state officials. Despite these advances, however, protecting the principle of an individual's right to self-determination has not yet been fully realized in international law.

Implementing a human rights framework has brought empowerment and in some cases actual relief to impoverished peoples and oppressed minorities. International human rights discourse, in conjunction with the rise of local civil society organizations and NGOs such as Human Rights Watch, have been enormously successful in diminishing abuses against women, indigenous peoples, and ethnic and religious minorities in recent decades. At the same time, however, human rights rhetoric can be used in negative ways, create unforeseen results, and may be in fact part of the problem in the seeking of global equality. As sociolegal scholar Bob Nelson reminds us, "The dialectic character of law means that it sometimes is an instrument of social justice, and sometimes is an institution that produces and legitimates hierarchies of race, gender, and class." . . .

Complicating the effectiveness of an international human rights regime is the premise that it is universal in its application. This premise disavows that human rights rhetoric and the human rights movement in general is, at its core, a European project that expresses the "ideology, ethics, aesthetic sensibility and political practice of a particular western eighteenth through twentieth-century liberalism." . . . The human rights premise of universal neutrality is questioned by indigenous and postcolonial scholars who, among others, are deeply skeptical that modern western law as promulgated in the Universal Declaration can operate as a rational and objective enterprise devoid of European cultural assumptions, values and biases. Critical sociolegal scholars point to the liberal ideologies and values embedded in human rights discourse that tend to compromise, and in some instances marginalize, non-western perspectives. Specifically, these scholars are concerned that Euro-American liberal values simplistically envisage individuals as autonomous actors, present states as defenders of an individual's rights, and imply that the concept of justice is fixed and universally recognized.

Indigenous and postcolonial scholars have a sound historical basis for their skepticism about western law and the human rights regime and movement that it engenders. For the past four hundred years, the Enlightenment's triumphant narratives of reason and objectivity were employed by European leaders to argue that western law was universal and therefore applicable to all colonized communities. Euro-American law has been a most effective weapon in institutionalizing colonial oppression and the imperial exploitation of non-European people. Western liberal values—in claiming universal applicability—intrinsically deny historical legacies of colonialism and imperialism that continue to inform and frame discussions of human rights and humanitarian interventions. Accordingly, asks the sociolegal scholar Onuma Yasuaki:

> how should we reconcile human rights with diverse cultures, religions, political and/or economic systems, social practices, as well as criticisms, negative memories and grudges of people in the non-Western world? In other words, what will be, what should be, the relationship between human rights and diverse civilizations and cultures that may have regarded, and still regard, human rights as alien to them? . . .

Balakrishnan Rajagopal adds that this failure to acknowledge legacies of cultural diversity presents long-term consequences. "By ignoring the history of imperialism, by endorsing wars while opposing their consequences, and by failing to link itself with social movements of resistance the main protagonists of the Western human rights discourse are undermining the future of human rights itself." . . .

Against the normative western assumptions embedded in human rights discourse, some critical scholars point out that individuals live in communities and that a person's rights may include relations of collective responsibility and accountability. These scholars also point out that a focus on an individual's relationship to a state is limited given that in many cases state governments are in fact the primary perpetrators of human rights abuses. Moreover, the concept of justice is not a fixed absolute but must be understood in terms of a person's comparative and relational social contexts. Above all, scholars critical of an international human rights regime object to the assumption that such rights embody a modernist ethics of progress that metaphorically positions the global south as the "victim" and the global north as the "savior." In other words, there is a built-in inference in the recognizing and enforcing of human rights that it will automatically bring democratic reform to those people who are "less enlightened." This is an extremely powerful assumption and one that is often difficult to refute.

The western liberal bias built into human rights discourse becomes particularly problematic when naïve presumption of progress and reform are coupled with a focus on oppressed "victims." Such a focus precludes full engagement with the structural socioeconomic inequalities and asymmetries of power within any one society that have historically positioned certain peoples in positions of oppression and "victimhood" in the first place. In human rights discourse, a focus on the relationship of "victim" and "savior" creates a lens through which some histories are prioritized and others are marginalized or even denigrated. This liberal interpretation and representation of particular histories may create, even for the most well-intentioned scholars, activists, policy-makers and bureaucrats, unforeseen political, cultural and economic complications. As noted by the international law scholar David Kennedy, "the remove between human rights professionals and the people they purport to represent can reinforce a global divide of wealth, mobility, information and access to audience. Human rights professionals consequently struggle, ultimately in vain, against a tide of bad faith, orientalism, and self-serving sentimentalism." . . .

For example, in 1991 Colombia introduced a new constitution that recognized minority rights and was viewed by many as a huge breakthrough in institutionalizing democratic reforms. However, as Diana Bocarejo has argued, the new constitution and its open embrace of liberal values also set up a dynamic in which different rights discourses were forced to compete. Today, there is much bitterness between indigenous and peasant communities precisely because the state gives priority to indigenous peoples' rights to undeveloped land over peasant's rights to agrarian land. In this case the native peoples' history of colonial victimization trumped the peasants' history of exploitation irrespective of the fact that both minority groups are largely powerless and oppressed.

In a similar vein, Kristen Drybread compellingly narrates the rising prominence of a universal human rights discourse in Brazil after the fall of the military dictatorship in the 1980s. In an effort to institutionalize reform, the state introduced the Children and Adolescents Act of 1990 which conceded that children were rights-bearing citizens and as a consequence deserving of state support. However, Drybread points out, despite the progressive liberal nature of the legislation, it in effect backfired when applied to Brazilian street children. This was because the state refused to deal with and regulate the structural inequalities and lack of opportunities for poor children that made living on the streets, at least for some, more attractive than being reformed in state-run institutions. The Brazilian government's unwillingness to develop the bureaucratic apparatus and support structures necessary to vindicate children's rights inadvertently contributed to subverting them.

As the above examples from Colombia and Brazil suggest, it cannot always be assumed that state recognition of human rights will automatically bring about reform and progress and rescue those perceived to be victims. Even when states are consciously trying to improve the conditions of their citizens, human rights legislation and the politics of its implementation may not have the desired impact or consequences. The difficulties of implementation are further compounded if racial, ethnic or religious minorities are involved since these are communities typically long oppressed by state systems and are justifiably wary and reluctant to embrace so-called policies and strategies of "reform." In short, while huge advances have been made over the past half decade in the quest for global justice and equality, it is not enough to rely upon the human rights movement which in a variety of ways may be exacerbating social inequities and reinforcing structural inequalities.

CHANGING FORMS OF GLOBAL ORDER

David Held

Until recently, the West has, by and large, determined the rules of the game on the global stage. During the last century, Western countries presided over a shift in world power—from control via territory to control via the creation of governance structures created in the post-1945 era. From the United Nations Charter and the formation of the Bretton-Woods institutions to the Rio Declaration on the environment and the creation of the World Trade Organization, international agreements have invariably served to entrench a well-established international power structure. The division of the globe into powerful nation-states, with distinctive sets of geopolitical interests, and reflecting the international power structure of 1945, is still embedded in the articles and statutes of leading intergovernmental organizations, such as the IMF and the World Bank. Voting rights are distributed largely in relation to individual financial contributions, and geo-economic strength is integrated into decision-making procedures.

The result has been susceptibility of the major international governmental organizations (IGOs) to the agendas of the most powerful states, partiality in enforcement operations (or lack of them altogether), their continued dependency on financial support from a few major states, and weaknesses in the policing of global collective action problems. This has been dominance based on a "club" model of global governance and legitimacy. Policy at the international level has been decided by a core set of powerful countries, above all the "G1," G5 and G7, with the rest largely excluded from the decision-making process.

TOWARDS A MULTIPOLAR WORLD

Today, however, that picture is changing. The trajectory of Western dominance has come to a clear halt with the failure of dominant elements of Western global policy over the past few decades. The West can no longer rule through power or example alone. At the same time, Asia is on the ascent. Over the last half-century, East and Southeast Asia has more than doubled its share of world GDP and increased per capita income at an average growth rate almost two and a half times that in the rest of the world. . . . In the last two decades alone, emerging Asian economies have experienced an average growth rate of almost 8 per cent—3 times the rate in the rich world. . . .

As a result, Asia has been both a stabilizing influence on and a steady contributor to world economic growth. According to the IMF, China alone accounted for around a third of global economic growth in 2008, more than any other nation, and its economy was the only one of the world's 10 biggest which expanded in the wake of the financial crisis. . . . Other Asian economies have bounced back from the financial crisis far more quickly than anyone expected. As an article in the *New York Times* [in 2009] points out, the United States has always led the way out of major global economic crises, but this time the catalyst came from China and the rest of Asia. These countries are no longer simply beholden to the US and other Western countries as recipients of their exports, and this decoupling has to some extent allowed Asian economies to recover more quickly. Boosted by increased consumer spending and massive government-led investment, the region as a whole grew by more than 5 per cent in 2009—at a time when the old G7 contracted by over 3.5 per cent. Simply put, we are seeing a fundamental rebalancing of the world economy, with the centre of gravity shifting noticeably to the East.

The trajectory of change is towards a multipolar world, where the West no longer holds a premium on geopolitical or economic power. Moreover, different discourses and concepts of governance have emerged to challenge the old Western orthodoxy of multilateralism and the post-war order. At the same time, complex global processes, from the ecological to the financial, connect the fate of communities to each other across the world in new ways, requiring effective, accountable and inclusive problem-solving capacity. How this capacity can be ensured is another matter.

THE PARADOX OF OUR TIMES

What I call the paradox of our times refers to the fact that the collective issues we must grapple with are of growing cross-border extensity and intensity, yet the means for addressing these are weak and incomplete. While there is a variety of reasons for the persistence of these problems, at the most basic level the persistence of this paradox remains a problem of governance.

We face three core sets of problems—those concerned with (i) sharing our planet (climate change, biodiversity and ecosystem losses, water deficits); (ii) sustaining our humanity (poverty, conflict prevention, global infectious diseases); and (iii) developing our rulebook (nuclear proliferation, toxic waste disposal, intellectual property rights, genetic research rules, trade rules, finance and tax rules). . . . In our increasingly interconnected world, these global problems cannot be solved by any one nation-state acting alone. They call for collective and collaborative action—something that the nations of the world have not been good at, and which they need to be better at if these pressing issues are to be adequately resolved. Yet, the evidence is wanting that we are getting better at building appropriate governance capacity.

One significant problem is that a growing number of issues span both the domestic and the international domains. The institutional fragmentation and competition between states can lead to these global issues being addressed in an ad hoc and dissonant manner. A second problem is that even when the global dimension of a problem is acknowledged, there is often no clear division of labour among the myriad of international institutions that seek to address it: their functions often overlap, their mandates conflict and their objectives often become blurred. A third problem is that the existing system of global governance suffers from severe deficits of accountability and inclusion. This problem is especially relevant in regard to how less economically powerful states and, hence, their entire populations are marginalized or excluded from decision-making.

FURTHER READING

Brysk, Alison. 2002. *Globalization and Human Rights.* Berkeley: University of California Press.

Darian-Smith, Eve. 2013. *Laws and Societies in Global Contexts: Contemporary Approaches.* Cambridge, UK: Cambridge University Press.

Doswald-Beck, Louise. 2011. *Human Rights in Times of Conflict and Terrorism.* New York: Oxford University Press.

Held, David. 2010. *Cosmopolitanism. Ideals and Realities.* London: Polity Press.

Ishay, Micheline. 2008. *The History of Human Rights: From Ancient Times to the Globalization Era.* Berkeley: University of California Press.

Falk, Richard. 2000. *Human Rights Horizons: The Pursuit of Justice in a Globalizing World.* London: Routledge.

Falk, Richard, Mark Juergensmeyer, and Vesselin Popovski (Eds.). 2012. *Legality and Legitimacy in Global Affairs.* New York: Oxford University Press.

Shaw, Malcolm. 2008. *International Law.* Cambridge, UK: Cambridge University Press.

Shore, Megan. 2009. *Religion and Conflict Resolution: Christianity and South Africa's Truth and Reconciliation Commission.* Burlington, VT: Ashgate.

Trachtman, Joel. 2013. *The Future of International Law: Global Government.* Cambridge, UK: Cambridge University Press.

20

THE FUTURE OF GLOBAL CIVIL SOCIETY

Throughout this book we've been talking about globalization as if it were about things—the economy, the environment, and political and technological changes. But it's not just about things. It's also about people—about us.

How are people changing in the global era? In this chapter, we will consider some new ways in which people are thinking about themselves. Earlier in history, people identified themselves primarily as members of a particular group—an ethnic, religious, or national community. In the global era, sometimes it appears that these traditional identities have become stronger and even strident, as some people desperately want to cling to a meaningful specific association in an era when a uniform sameness seems to be dominant.

But these people are defensive for a reason. The globalization of culture and communications, paired with economic globalization and the ease with which people can travel and relocate around the globe, has changed most other people. It has made most of us less beholden to specific groups—religious or ethnic or nationalistic—even though a few people feel defensive about these changes.

So there is a global wind blowing through the world. It touches everyone, though not always in the same way. In the introduction to an interesting book entitled *Many Globalizations,* editors Samuel Huntington and Peter Berger describe the different ways in which people move beyond their accustomed communities of identity and cultural familiarity in new, transnational networks. People in business often experience these transnational associations in a world in which the partners in a shoe company in

Los Angeles may have to travel frequently to China, Mexico, and Bangladesh to work with the managers of the factories that make their wares and then fly to London, New York, and Buenos Aires to deal with the business leaders who are financing their company and with the retailers who are arranging for their products' distribution. Berger and Huntington call this the "Davos culture," evoking the name of a high-level meeting of business and government leaders every year at Davos, Switzerland, to discuss the state of the world's economy. But the authors also describe a global "faculty club culture" of professors and other scholars who meet regularly at international academic conferences, work together with colleagues around the world on research projects, and are involved in joint publications. Even ethnic communities can become globalized, as members of a group such as Iranians, Filipinos, and Nigerians become dispersed throughout the world. They contact each other through telephone calls, text messages, and Skype, throughout countless e-mails and shared websites. The anthropologist Benedict Anderson describes these as "e-mail ethnicities."

Beyond these particular global cultures, is there a common global culture? This is where the idea of a "global civil society" comes in. The concept of civil society has been a part of Western conversations since the time of the Enlightenment, when *civil society* referred, in general, to the arena for public activity that was neither commercial nor government-related. Religious institutions were sometimes included within civil society and sometimes not, especially if these institutions were seen to be linked closely to the authority of the state.

In an era of globalization, the term *civil society* has been revived to indicate the whole arena of public activity that is not business-oriented or government-controlled. In its most specific sense, global civil society refers to the activities of nongovernmental organizations (NGOs) that provide social services and monitor public concerns such as human rights. In the global era, transnational NGOs have expanded seemingly exponentially, for they fulfill a need as agents for a global concern that no one nation-state can provide. In the case of an organization like Human Rights Watch, for example, the NGO is outside the control of any one nation-state and therefore is free to criticize the human rights shortcomings of the United States as well as those of China, Uganda, Cuba, and every other country on earth.

A somewhat broader concept of global civil society is one that encompasses what the German political scholar Jürgen Habermas calls "the public sphere." This includes not only organizations such as Human Rights Watch and international labor unions, but also social movements such as transnational movements for women's rights and for gay rights. It also includes public conversations through newspapers, journals, radio, television, and electronic media about policy issues that affect everyone in public life.

To some extent, the United Nations helps to nurture this global public sphere. Though it is supported and governed by the nation-states that are members of it, the UN also maintains dozens of agencies and organizations that deal with everything from international postal systems to global environmental problems. Thousands of employees, consultants, and patrons of these entities help to constitute a global community of world order, and the many volunteer UN support groups constitute networks of global citizens.

The broadest way of thinking about global civil society is, indeed, the idea of global citizenship. This is the notion that all people are citizens not only of the particular nation-state with which they are affiliated, but also with the whole human race in a common society that stretches across the planet. (Some of us feel this sense of global citizenship more keenly than others do, however.) When we become aware of our global connections, we are more likely to express active concerns about shared global problems—such as the onset of global warming—and to participate in conversations and actions aimed at making a difference. It is this arena of identity and concern that constitutes a new way of thinking about ourselves as global citizens of planet earth. Some people have described this new way of thinking as "cosmopolitanism," taking the ancient Greek notion of being citizens of the world.

Is the global future a cosmopolitan one? There have been many attempts to chart future scenarios for world order. Not all of them are rosy. Some see the possibilities of strident new nationalisms and fierce religious and ethnic parochialism. Others see a coming confrontation between the North and the South, between the haves and have-nots of an increasingly inequitable world. Still others see the likelihood of great disasters—not just global warming, but possibly nuclear explosions and economic stagnation that will sharply reverse global economic and technological progress. Some predict that globalization could reverse and a new tribalization emerge.

But despite these dire predictions, there is the striking optimism of the possibility of a cosmopolitan future of global citizenship. Increasingly, in a world where everyone wants to live everywhere—and many do—it is hard to maintain the crusty old boundaries of nationhood and ethnic identities. The fact that the United States of America could elect as its president a man like Barack Obama—whose mother's family came from Kansas and whose father came from Kenya and who was himself raised in Indonesia and Hawaii—is a sign that old notions of national identity are breaking down. In a global era, we will increasingly identify with other people across national boundaries and increasingly work together for transnational solutions to problems that are bigger than any one nation-state. In this way, what the German sociologist Ulrich Beck calls "the cosmopolitan vision" may very well be the blueprint for the future. It may be a global future for us all.

The readings in this section cover several aspects of global civil society and the cosmopolitan ideal. The first reading is by Mary Kaldor, a political scientist who at one time worked with the Stockholm International Peace Research Institute and the University of Sussex before becoming the director of the Centre for Study of Global Governance at the London School of Economics. She explores what she regards as a new arena for transnational action—the realm of global civil society. Kaldor regards this as the emergence of a sense of global citizenship and shared action and not simply as a cluster of social service–oriented NGOs. The next reading suggests that the global future will find new sources of power in such transnational movements and organizations, as well as in new regional and local sources of strength in an era when traditional nation-states are less able to act. This excerpt is from an essay by Jan Nederveen Pieterse, a Dutch sociologist who has taught at the University of Illinois and the University of California–Santa Barbara.

The final two readings relate to the cosmopolitan future of global civil society. They explore the notion that there is a shared sense of global citizenship that will be the basis for an emerging global order. Giles Gunn, a professor of English literature who teaches in the global studies program at the University of California–Santa Barbara, provides a nuanced view of cosmopolitanism, explaining that if it is to be effective it has to be more than the intercultural tolerance of multiculturalism. The final reading is by a scholar who embodies globalization; Kwame Anthony Appiah's mother was British and his father was from the Asante region of Ghana. He was raised in Ghana, educated at Cambridge University in England, and teaches at Princeton University in the United States. In this excerpt from his book on cosmopolitanism, Appiah explains why the cosmopolitan ideal is essential for a sense of global citizenship in an increasingly interconnected world.

SOCIAL MOVEMENTS, NGOS, AND NETWORKS

Mary Kaldor

Terms like "global politics" or global civil society signify the domestication of the international. We are accustomed to think of the international as the realm of diplomacy, high-level meetings and military strategy and the domestic, at least in democratic societies, as the realm of debate, discussion and public pressure—in short, the realm of politics; that is the meaning of the Great Divide. The "global scene," says Bauman, was traditionally "the theatre of inter-state" relations. Then after the Second World War, the development of "supra-state integration," the emergence of blocs, not just East and West but also the non-aligned bloc, meant that the "'global scene' was increasingly seen as the theatre of coexistence and competition between groups of states, rather than between states themselves."

The salient characteristic of the world after 1989 is the advent of politics in the "global scene." By global politics, I mean the interaction between the institutions of global governance (international institutions and states) and global civil society—the groups, networks and movements which comprise the mechanisms through which individuals negotiate and renegotiate social contracts or political bargains at a global level. In other words, a system of relations between states or groups of states, characterized by a process of bargaining based on collective interest, in which the threat of armed conflict was an ever-present characteristic of the bargaining, has been supplanted by a much more complex world of politics, involving a range of institutions and individuals and in which there is a place, perhaps small, for individual reason and sentiment, and not just state or bloc interest.

This development is the outcome of changes both from above and below. On the one hand, 1989 marked the end of global conflict, the disintegration of blocs and the end of the prevalent use of ideology to suppress critical voices or even just good-tempered conversation at the international level. This made it possible for states and international institutions to deal with each other in new cooperative and discursive ways that were more receptive to individuals and citizens groups outside the corridors of power. On the other hand, the movements and groups who had struggled for peace and democracy or for human rights and environmental responsibility during the Cold War years were able to take advantage of this new openness as well as the ways in which the new language of global civil society legitimized their activities. . . .

WHO IS GLOBAL CIVIL SOCIETY?

The different contemporary definitions of global civil society outlined in the first chapter tend to correspond to different categories of actors. Thus the neoliberal version of global civil society, where civil society is seen as a substitute for the state, a sort of laissez-faire politics, corresponds to the idea of a civil society composed of a market of NGOs. The very term NGO seems to imply "not" or "instead of" the state. The activist model of civil society corresponds to a civil society composed of social movements and civic networks, while the postmodern version would include the nationalist and fundamentalists as well.

At the end of the 1980s, the energies of the "new" social movements culminated in the wave of democratization that affected not only Eastern Europe but also Africa, Asia and Latin America. I have described the dramatic growth of NGOs in part as the "taming" of the new social movements in the aftermath of democratization and in response to new opportunities offered by international institutions, governments and even global companies. This was also a period when earlier social organizations and civic associations, often the legacy of "old" social movements, were eroded and undermined by economic crisis and structural change. Thus in the 1990s, the sphere of informal politics came to be dominated, on the one hand, by NGOs and, on the other, by "new" nationalist and fundamentalist movements.

This explains the growing disaffection with the term "civil society," the criticism that has been increasingly levelled at the language of "civil society" as being too Eurocentric and, indeed "imperialistic." Neera Chandhoke [a political scientist at Delhi University] says that "civil society" has become a hurrah word, emptied of content and "flattened out." "Witness the tragedy that has visited proponents of the concept: people struggling against authoritarian regimes demanded civil society, what they got were NGOs. . . . If everyone from trades unions, social movements, the UN, the IMF, lending agencies, to states both chauvinistic and democratic hail civil society as the most recent elixir to the ills of the contemporary world, there must be something wrong."

But that is perhaps precisely the advantage of the term. In the late 1990s, new grass roots groups and social organizations and the new anti-capitalist movement began to emerge, offering some renewed hope for creating an emancipatory economic and social agenda. If we think of global civil society, not as NGOs, but as a process through which contracts or agreements are negotiated at global, national and local levels, then it has to include all the various mechanisms through which individual voices can be heard. Civil society provides a legitimizing platform for discordant and radical demands—a name which explains why authorities have to take these demands seriously. Moreover, there are peace and human rights groups still struggling in oppressive regimes like Burma or Zimbabwe or in conflict zones like the Middle East, Kashmir, or the Caucasus, for whom the term "global civil society" holds out some promise of being heard.

Global civil society includes the INGOs and the networks that are the "tamed" successors to the new social movements of the 1970s and 1980s. It also includes the allies of transnational business who promote a market framework at a global level. It includes a new radical anti-capitalist movement which combines both the successors of the new social movements and a new type of labour movement. And to the extent that nationalist and fundamentalist movements are voluntary and participatory, i.e. they provide a mechanism through which individuals can gain access to centres of authority, then they have to be included as well; although in practice, as I have argued, in actually existing civil society, such distinctions may be difficult to draw. The array of organizations and groups through which individuals have a voice at global levels of decision-making represents a new form of global politics that parallels and supplements formal democracy at the national level. These new actors do not take decisions. Nor should they have a formal role in decision-making since they are voluntarily constituted and represent nobody but their own opinions. The point is rather that through access, openness and debate, policy-makers are more likely to act as a Hegelian universal class, in the interests of the human community.

The differentiated character of global civil society can be understood in terms of the complexity of the contemporary world. New Social Movement theorists sometimes talk about a "movement society." The salient feature of globalization is the rapidity of technological and social change. The modern state, in its twentieth-century form, is too top heavy, slow and rigid to find ways of adapting to the myriad of unintended consequences of change. Civil society, a combination of different movements, NGOs and networks, is a way of expressing the reflexivity of the contemporary world.

It is the contestation between these different types of actors, as well as states, international institutions and transnational corporations that will determine the future direction of globalization. Will it be a "civilizing" process in which global politics becomes the normal form of relations at a global level, or can we expect a return to inter-state relations, or, perhaps worse, a wild anarchic process involving inequality and violence?

SHAPING GLOBALIZATION: WHY GLOBAL FUTURES?

Jan Nederveen Pieterse

Why would global futures figure on the agenda? The answer to this question centres on the ramifications of globalization, technological change, and the emergence of global citizenship. Globalization refers to the accelerated worldwide intermeshing of economies, and cross-border traffic and communication becoming ever denser. Technological change is speeding up. Risks and opportunities are globalizing. All this belongs to everyday experience. Accordingly, globalization means global effect and global awareness, and therefore increasingly it also means global engagement.

Citizenship under these circumstances is no longer simply national, or, more precisely, the national domain is now one among several relevant organizational spheres, and citizenship is becoming increasingly national and local, regional, global at the same time. In addition, citizenship is no longer as state-centred as it used to be. The point of democracy is no longer simply influencing the actions of government. National governance has become one institutional sphere among several. Citizenship is not simply "international" either, because the concerns at issue are not simply a multiplication of nation-state or intergovernmental structures. Governance is increasingly a matter of international politics, supranational institutions, international treaties and law, in the process involving macro-regional bodies, transnational corporations, transnational citizen groups, and media—interacting in complex, turbulent, multi-centric ways.

Considered in an evolutionary context, humanity has been growing in capacity, technological accomplishment and reflexivity. Collective awareness of concerns that affect the species and the planet—such as the environment, population, development—has been growing, and so has its public articulation, notably in UN global conferences, so that arguably a global public sphere is emerging. At the same time, technological and political accomplishment and awareness do not "line up" to add up to a condition of collective capacity. Interests are widely dispersed, subjectivities and agendas are diverse, and institutional capacities are relatively feeble.

Why Futures? Anticipation and planning used to be a prerogative and defining feature of government—"gouverner, ç'est prévoir." It extended to business and finance in tandem with the development of instruments of credit (banking, securities, options, derivatives) and insurance, which hinge fundamentally on the capacity to estimate, calculate and hedge outcomes. In both governance and business, forecasting has achieved considerable technical sophistication.

Recently the World Business Council for Sustainable Development initiated a project on Global Scenarios with the following justification:

> Planning for a sustainable future requires business to be able to anticipate and not just react to change. This is the rationale underlying our project on Global Scenarios. This project is designed to help business people reach a shared view of the future and challenge

the "mental maps" they hold about sustainable development. This will allow them to anticipate, not react to, the exposures facing their corporations and ensure that they are fostering sustainable development.

Here the capacity to anticipate is presented as enabling for business people: it puts them ahead in relation to circumstances, technologies, and presumably also public criticism, and enables them to develop a shared agenda.

Capacities to anticipate and plan are crucial to business and financial markets, to governments and international institutions. Accordingly, some futures have already been planned and negotiated, bought and sold several times over before citizens have even begun to think about them. This implies that the horizons and agendas according to which futures are planned and designed reflect limited interests and agendas. Should such capacities to anticipate be reserved to business and government, or should they be a matter of broad public awareness? If they did not become part of civic reflection it would mean that citizen groups would be relegated to a back seat, forever reacting to the futures designed, prepared and communicated piecemeal by governments and corporations.

At the same time, both government and business planning are constrained. Governments increasingly deal with many political and social forces and variables. Corporations are exposed to such flux in the market that they operate with limited time horizons. In the marketplace, contingency is a fact of life: "there is absolutely no way, in the evolving marketplace, that you can know exactly who the suppliers, customers, competitors and collaborators are." . . . A standard quip in business management is: look at how many companies of the Fortune 500 still figure on the list five or ten years hence. It also follows that in government and business planning the command-and-control model no longer applies.

The "colonization of the life world"—commodification, bureaucratization—is a familiar metaphor (although, with the reconfiguration of the state, bureaucratization is to an extent being replaced by informalization). This includes a routinized process of the colonization of futures, because of the concentration of forecasting and planning capabilities in government and corporate hands. The organization of public space, as in urban and infrastructure planning, is an example. What is needed, then, is a decolonization of futures or, to use more general language, a democratization of futures. Gradually it is becoming a common understanding that not only the end stage of public planning but also the design stage needs to be participatory.

There are many forums in which governments, international institutions, banks and corporations compare notes, set agendas and build coalitions. This happens less among citizen groups. "Alternative forums" take place on the periphery of intergovernmental conferences, regional meetings of social organizations, sectoral conferences and academic conferences. Both joint agenda-setting and anticipation are less developed among citizen groups than among corporations and governments. They are not as well endowed with think-tanks, nor do they organize forums aligning their views and agendas. This is happening even less across areas of concern—for example, human rights groups comparing notes with environmental groups, environmental organizations comparing notes with women's groups and indigenous peoples—except locally. Citizen groups concerned with human rights, ecology, women's or community issues, all have their values and preferred futures. But where do they intersect, interconnect? How and to what extent do these various single-issue concerns and futures line up? Thus for citizen groups a preoccupation with futures, local and global, would involve several functions: dialogue across groups; aligning normative concerns; developing a proactive stance and anticipatory sensibilities and capabilities; making futures a matter of public concern.

Another reason why futures thinking is taking on a new relevance is that several modes of anticipation that were available in the past have lost their appeal. Futures used to be packaged and delivered as part of the grand ideologies that framed the social and political movements of the past, particularly nationalism and socialism. The "national question" and the "social question" of the nineteenth century reconverged in twentieth-century social movements, such as the anti-colonial national liberation movements. The ideologies bequeathed by the nineteenth century followed positivist epistemologies and structuralist modes of thinking, relating to macro processes such as imperialism, capitalism and dependency. The future scenarios that emerged from these are now no longer viable or attractive. Nationalism is making place for postnationalism, or at least the reconfiguration of energies in various directions—local, regional, macro-regional, international, global. Delinking or dissociation from capitalism has little meaning in a real world where localities scramble to attract foreign investment. The expectation of a world-scale crisis of capitalism followed by an opening towards socialism has now very few adherents (among the last are the original world-system theorists . . .).

Samuel Huntington's "clash of civilizations" seems so hopelessly static and antiquated that even arguing against it feels like a waste of time. If civilizational destinies or regional projects still seemed relevant a few decades ago, they now sound increasingly quaint. Calls for "the West" to be concerned with this or that . . . are outdated at a time when business is eyeing "emerging markets" across the seas.

Evocations of an "Asian Century" sound outdated even before it has begun. One, the dynamics are Pacific rather than Asian, witness the intercontinental sprawl of the Chinese diaspora. Two, while there is an "Asian Renaissance" . . . , its lineages are not purely Asian (just as the makings of the European Renaissance extended well beyond Europe). Three, much of the talk of "Asian values" is authoritarian in intent, and is often laughed at inside the region. Four, Asian industries, those of Japan included, depend on technology from outside the region, particularly the United States. . . . Five, because of their export orientation, East and Southeast Asian economies depend on markets in the West. Complementarities among Asian economies, while considerable and growing, would not be sufficient to sustain the countries' exports. Intercultural exchange between East and West is so far advanced and so deeply historically layered that in many ways the two can no longer be meaningfully separated. Six, in a 1996 speech in Beijing Prime Minister Mahathir of Malaysia declared the twenty-first century a "Global Century" rather than an "Asian Century." This was a sensible gesture of diplomacy—Western markets would not react well to an upsurge of inward-looking Asian chauvinism; it may also be taken as an expression of an Asian humanism that sets forth a global engagement. Seven, the recent "Asian crisis" shows the frailty of the Tiger economies.

Similar considerations apply to other regional and civilizational projects. Thus interpretations of India centred on "Indian civilization" have historical purchase and thus inform futures, but would they be sufficient to generate relevant future scenarios, or would they rather feed neo-chauvinist Hindutva ideology? This also applies to Islamist projects. The wide world of Islam represents an alternative globalism with considerable historical and civilizational depth, geographical scope and growing economic opportunities. At the cusp of the millennium, however, the Islamic world is dependent in the fields of science and technology, in investments and growth opportunities, armaments and security. Financially and economically, culturally and politically, it is profoundly wired to global centres.

Regional and civilizational projects are most intelligently viewed not as contradictory to but as part of global dynamics. In 2020 Islam will be the second major religion in most of Western Europe (in some countries it already is). Some parts of Europe have been reindustrializing thanks to Korean and Taiwanese investments. Japanese management techniques offer a model to overcome the Taylor model of standardized mass production, from the Pacific to Ireland. . . . Accordingly, regional projects should both inform and be informed by global futures. This is not an argument for going global tout court. Rather, it is to argue for an interdependence and balance of local, national, regional and global engagements.

BEING OTHER-WISE: COSMOPOLITANISM AND ITS DISCONTENTS

Giles Gunn

"Cosmopolitanism" is a word in bad odor in many parts of the world because it is assumed that citizens do, or at any rate should, share a single socio-cultural identity that is based on a common framework of principles, objectives, and biases. Moreover, it is often believed in addition that this common framework of standards and aims, all upheld by a shared structure of rights and privileges, should be reflected in the congruence between the views of their leaders and of the citizens themselves. There is nothing particularly unusual about these ideas since, with several amendments contributed by nationalism, they constitute basic elements of the Westphalian theory of state identity that is taken in most parts of the world to constitute a territorially bounded sovereign community. Yet this same logic has been strongly challenged throughout the world by a contrary set of beliefs that assume that shared identity is not given but constructed, that most people belong to more than one community of identity at a time, that the sovereignty of states is currently declining rather than increasing, and that national communities, and even hegemons like the United States, are locked in webs of regional and global governance and interdependence.

In theoretical terms, cosmopolitanism is situated between these two positions, the first national, the second global. On the one hand, it recognizes the increasing interconnectedness of political communities in various domains—social, economic, environmental, religious, military, cultural—and encourages the development of understanding overlapping problems that require collective if not necessarily identical solutions, whether regional, local, national, or global. On the other, it celebrates difference, diversity, hybridity, and the need to learn how to reason from the perspective of others, while conceding that multiculturalism as presently understood needs to be revised if we are to elude the dangers of essentialism (my identity is primordial and goes all the way down) on the one side or the perils of reductionism (there are only so many identities possible in the nation-state and this isn't one of them) on the other. What cosmopolitanism then offers is a middle path between the two movements that it views with considerable suspicion—ethnocentric nationalism in the first instance and particularistic multiculturalism in the second. What it assumes is the complexity of affiliations, meaningful attachments, and multiple allegiances to issues, people, places, institutions, regions, and traditions that lie beyond the boundaries of resident nation-states, and the need to create a politics commensurate with this vision of things.

In actual terms, however, cosmopolitanism is a good deal more varied and problematic. Its variations are reflected in the ways cosmopolitanism is often qualified, using such adjectival modifiers as "vernacular," "reflexive," "situated," "discrepant," "patriotic," "realistic," "emancipatory," "working-class," "critical," "thick," or "thin." But such qualifiers also reflect a desire to differentiate contemporary cosmopolitanisms from their more universalistic and Eurocentric forbears and to indicate that they do not apply equally to all people in all situations. This is most obvious in the case of those whose cosmopolitanism of whatever kind is not willed but imposed, not selected but suffered, which includes migrants, refugees, exiles, the jobless, the homeless, and others who are displaced by globalizing forces and thus experience cosmopolitanism and all it brings with it as a burden or affliction. It is less obvious, and generally less onerous, for many others who experience cosmopolitanism as related in part to the way their horizons of understanding, not to say the conditions of daily life, are being expanded by an increasing awareness of global perils and problematics. Nuclear proliferation, international terrorism, economic instability, climate change, international drug cartels, transnational sex trafficking, desertification, water shortages, the obsession with sustainability, and even the inability of states to deal with natural calamities of which the world as a whole has been made more aware—Hurricane Katrina, the Asian tsunami, flooding in Pakistan—widen everyone's sense of the new ways they have been made vulnerable in a continuously globalizing world. People now live surrounded by hazards that no longer possess a local habitation or a name. The phrase "community of fate" now refers not only groups of people who suddenly find their futures mutually implicated in the resolution of some temporary social emergency, such as the Severe Acute Respiratory Syndrome (SARS) that broke out in Hong Kong in 2003, but entire global populations, such as those living in low-lying countries or on coastal plains that could easily be threatened within only a matter of decades or less by the continual melting of polar ice caused by the international inability or reluctance to reduce carbon emissions. Horizons have expanded, peoples' sense of the world has broadened and been complicated, because of a deepening realization that they live in something less like a "risk society," than a "risk world."

This global re-thematization of the boundaries of people's lives in many parts of the world is surely one of the forms that cosmopolitanism currently takes. Call it, if you will, cosmopolitanism by default; it is indisputably one of the ways that any who are sensible of a world beyond the framework of their own immediate existence experience its reality. While this is a far cry from the kind of cosmopolitanism that Craig Calhoun dismisses as "the class consciousness of frequent travelers," it is apparent that frequent travelers are no more successful than anyone else in escaping some of its consequences. But the consequences, even when they are acknowledged, are clearly not sensed or suffered equally, which is why many theorists shy away from the blanket use of a term that conceals and sometimes distorts as much as it reveals. Calhoun himself is prepared to use the term but only if it is de-coupled from the neo-liberal capitalist inequities, Western bias, and resistance to radical change with which its many current forms are so often linked. "It needs to approach both cross-cultural relations and the construction of social solidarities with a deeper recognition of diverse starting points and potential outcomes."

David Harvey is suspicious that the new cosmopolitanism is "nothing other than an ethical and humanitarian mask for hegemonic neoliberal practices of class domination and financial and militaristic imperialism," though he is not unsympathetic to the project of a "subaltern cosmopolitanism" if it is informed by geographical, anthropological, and ecological understanding. Timothy Brennan has argued that contemporary cosmopolitanism is in fact inimical to the interests of states still in formation out of the ruins of colonial regimes and often too deeply in thrall to the expansionist policies of the United States and other world powers. Chantal Mouffe finds the whole cosmopolitan project anti-political because it fosters consensuality without contestation, politics without antagonism. While Mouffe does not dispute the fact that any new world order depends on shared ethical-political values such as liberty, equality, and democracy, she is insistent that this consensus reflect the multipolar character of the world where different versions of such a consensus can be can be debated and rejected.

Less severe in their critique about the possibility of a cosmopolitan framework or outlet but no less circumspect in their judgments about the shortcoming of contemporary versions are Homi Bhabha and Paul Gilroy. Bhabha contrasts neoliberal cosmopolitanism with a vernacular cosmopolitanism that focuses on minoritarian perspectives which assert a "right to difference in equality." This is a perspective shaped less by common identities or shared affiliations than by shared practices and ethical commitments—the creation of new forms of representation, accountability, recognition, and cooperation across lines of difference—and is deeply informed by some of the ideas of the American poet Adrienne Rich. Rich argues for the necessity proposed elsewhere in this book of learning how to re-narrativize common histories from the starting points of others, to re-situate ourselves in the geographies and temporalities of different people, indeed, to discover ourselves in their stories as well as our own.

From a perspective no less influenced by the experience of colonialism, Paul Gilroy similarly wonders what kind of alternative cosmopolitanisms will make it possible to live together decently on a deeply divided planet and concludes that it will have to be a vernacular cosmopolitanism from below that sees colonialism as the other side of modernity and replaces the overly exploited and exhausted terms of "multiculturalism" or a West-centric "globalization" with the ideas of conviviality and planetarity. Conviviality is associated with the way the "outside" of, in this case, Europe—"strangers, aliens, and blacks"—have in truth lived on the inside of their societies and helped make them what they are. Far from rendering colonial history external to contemporary European history, Europe's colonial others "can be shown to be alive in the interior spaces through which Europe has come to know and interpret itself." Planetarity is thus for Gilroy a way of challenging the "triumphalism" and sense of "ever-expanding imperialist universals" that so often accompanies the term "global." For him it evokes an indispensible element of estrangement that the term "global" collapses but which is consistent with that form of disloyalty to one's own civilization that Montesquieu first suggested we practice "if we seek either to understand it or to interact equitably with others formed elsewhere." In the present, the planetary therefore involves a "consciousness of the tragedy, fragility, and brevity of indivisible human existence that is all the more valuable as a result of its openness to the damage done by racisms."

Such insights confirm what other cosmopolitan theorists like Peng Cheah and Bruce Robbins have concluded about the necessity to think beyond the national or even the civilizational. They display more interest in the politically transgressive than the epistemologically self-critical character of a cosmopolitan framework for politics, but they insist that cosmopolitanism and cosmopolitics exist at the intersections of culture, politics, and economics, "and that we can conceptualize these phenomena adequately only by working in the volatile zone where ethical philosophy, political theory, cultural anthropology, social theory, critical theory, and cultural studies interact." Jan Nederveen Pieterse tends to agree. While he describes the world as a "global mélange" largely reflective of a hybridity that is almost universal—he also sees the worlds of "East" and "West" as braided in complex ways—Nederveen Pieterse is no less convinced that these perceptions draw from perspectives furnished by everything from cultural anthropology and world history to political economy and development studies.

What all critics of cosmopolitanism seem to agree is that the universalism of what was once assumed to be cosmopolitan has to be radically rethought in relation to a wholly different set of understandings about the way the world actually works in different places, at different times, in relation to different circumstances, through different institutional mechanisms, toward different goals. For another, these changes have brought with them a new set of principles drawing in the West on the Stoic and Kantian cosmopolitan heritages but more circumscribed in nature and application. They are less expansive than the Stoic affirmation of a moral community of humankind in which each person is a citizen and owes a duty to the worldwide community of human beings, and less restricted than the Kantian community of those who are able to step out of their contingent positions and enter a public sphere where they have a right to the free and unrestricted use of their reason.

As David Held rather narrowly articulates them, they are associated with such values as egalitarian individualism, reciprocal recognition, and impartialist reasoning, and where respected, have conspired to create an ethical and political space that not only sets the terms for recognizing peoples' equal worth but also permits them the freedom to determine how, insofar as this does not infringe on similar rights of others, they shall represent and express themselves. Stephen White substitutes for such values his own trinity of human dignity, equality, and respect, but it comes to pretty much the same thing. Cosmopolitanism in the West is defined in relation to a space where people can work out the terms of their liberty, egalitarianism, and autonomy, but there is considerable disagreement about just how successful they can be or for how long.

Nonetheless, Held has managed to put these cosmopolitan principles and justifications into a broader transnational framework involving both short-term and long-term measures that combine to define the directions of less West-centric cosmopolitan politics. Short and long term, there are recommendations that follow from the principles he has elaborated for everything from governance, security, and economy to the environment, and they range from suggestions as specific as making the UN Security Council more representative, enhancing regional and national political infrastructures, strengthening nuclear arms control, regulating global markets and off-shore financial centers, and instituting a tax on carbon and other GHGs to democratizing global governance, taming global markets through correcting and promoting instruments, shifting to a low carbon economy, giving global jurisdiction to a new environment court, and creating permanent peacekeeping and humanitarian emergency forces. Such proposals as these derive their justification from a more potentially global set of convictions having to do with the structure of the moral universe, techniques for generating public action out of private activities, the orientations for public decisions, and the metaprinciples of justification, but they develop certain difficulties not just because of their potentially Euro-American bias but also because of their very specificity.

Seyla Benhabib agrees that cosmopolitanism concerns "norms that ought to govern relations among individuals in a global civil society," but sees it as "a philosophical project of mediations, not of reductions or of totalizations," particularly when considered in relation to the contrasting claims of democratic nationalisms. While convinced that one of the surest indicators of the emergence of cosmopolitan norms derives from the way certain civil, social, and political rights are being unbundled from a sense of national belonging, she is no less confident that the much touted neoliberal weakening of the nation-state has not necessarily hastened the advent of the cosmopolitanism she seeks. Nonetheless she refuses to believe that the emancipatory possibilities of a post-Westphalian cosmopolitanism are purely illusory and thus speaks of "a cosmopolitanism to come."

The most outspoken advocate of the existence of a cosmopolitan outlook or vision is Ulrich Beck who as early as 1998 published a "Cosmopolitan Manifesto" announcing the creation a post-national cosmopolitan world-order as a realistic as well as utopian political project. However, it was not until nearly a decade later that Beck proclaimed that "cosmopolitanism . . . has become the defining feature of a new era . . . of reflexive modernity." For Beck cosmopolitanism is a dialogical perspective "that explores and exploits the creative contradictions of cultures within and between the imagined communities of nation. . . ." A historically novel form of socio-political formation that is to be distinguished from the Westphalian model, Beck offers five principles of a cosmopolitan outlook that has already taken up residence in Europe. They include "the experience of crisis in world society," the "recognition of cosmopolitan differences" and conflict, "cosmopolitan empathy" and "perspective-taking," "the impossibility of living in a world society without borders" and the resulting compulsion to redraw old boundaries and rebuild old walls, and "the mélange principle" that "local, national, ethnic, religious and cosmopolitan cultures and traditions interpenetrate, interconnect, and intermingle." Far from being entirely contemporary, Alexis de Tocqueville, along with Adam Smith before him and John Dewey after him, together with a long list of German thinkers from Kant to Simmel, could detect the early development of these principles and they will continue to undergo important modification and change in the future.

More recently, Beck has sought to play off cosmopolitanism against what he calls "cosmopolitization." The latter refers to the uneven, impure, banal, irregular, asymmetric, coercive process going on all around us beyond the "container of the national space," a result of global institutions and agencies plugging into one another and functioning as a kind of "cosmopolitan realpolitik." This cosmopolitization is further producing a second or reflexive modernity defined by new kinds of world risk whose chief features are de-localization, incalculableness, and non-compensability. In order to conceptualize this new world risk society, Beck believes that we must relinquish the dream of building ever more extensive networks of shared assumptions and laws and accept the fact that we are being more actively integrated into webs of shared threats and menaces. This does not diminish the fact that everyday life has become more cosmopolitan, despite the fact that life is now defined by common dangers as opposed to common ideals; people still have to understand themselves and their lives in relation to those of other people.

Beck's new, somewhat more tempered, position on the subject of cosmopolitization, even if not his pessimistic view of the elements which constitute it, bears some affinities with the way Kwame Anthony Appiah thinks about cosmopolitanism. While Appiah's own preference is for a "rooted" or "partial" cosmopolitanism, he also believes that it is going on all around us in ways both banal or casual and also formal. However, Appiah differs from many cosmopolitan theorists in not finding cosmopolitan allegiances necessarily in contradiction with more local or particularistic, even national, ones, and he furthermore believes that theoretical agreement on principles and values is not always necessary to achieve a workable consensus on policies and practices. Appiah has considerable faith that the intercultural dialogue that is generated from travel as well as from poems, novels, and films also help us identify many points of essential agreement with others that are nonetheless local and contingent. In any case, "the challenge . . . is to take minds and hearts formed over the long millennia of living in local troops and equip them with ideas and institutions that will allow us to live together as the global tribe we have become."

MAKING CONVERSATION

Kwame Anthony Appiah

Our ancestors have been human for a very long time. If a normal baby girl born forty thousand years ago were kidnapped by a time traveler and raised in a normal family in New York, she would be ready for college in eighteen years. She would learn English (along with—who knows?—Spanish or Chinese), understand trigonometry, follow baseball and pop music; she would probably want a pierced tongue and a couple of tattoos. And she would be unrecognizably different from the brothers and sisters she left behind. For most of human history, we were born into small societies of a few score people, bands of hunters and gatherers, and would see, on a typical day, only people we had known most of our lives. Everything our long-ago ancestors ate or wore, every tool they used, every shrine at which they worshipped, was made within that group. Their knowledge came from their ancestors or from their own experiences. That is the world that shaped us, the world in which our nature was formed.

Now, if I walk down New York's Fifth Avenue on an ordinary day, I will have within sight more human beings than most of those prehistoric hunter-gatherers saw in a lifetime. Between then and now some of our forebears settled down and learned agriculture; created villages, towns, and, in the end, cities; discovered the power of writing. But it was a slow process. The population of classical Athens when Socrates died, at the end of the fifth century BC, could have lived in a few large skyscrapers. Alexander set off from Macedon to conquer the world three-quarters of a century later with an army of between thirty and forty thousand, which is far fewer people than commute into Des Moines every Monday morning. When, in the first century, the population of Rome reached a million, it was the first city of its size. To keep it fed, the Romans had had to build an empire that brought home grain from Africa. By then, they had already worked out how to live cheek by jowl in societies where most of those who spoke your language and shared your laws and grew the food on your table were people you would never know. It is, I think, little short of miraculous that brains shaped by our long history could have been turned to this new way of life.

Even once we started to build these larger societies, most people knew little about the ways of other tribes, and could affect just a few local lives. Only in the past couple of centuries, as every human community has gradually been drawn into a single web of trade and a global network of information, have we come to a point where each of us can realistically imagine contacting any other of our six billion conspecifics and sending that person something worth having: a radio, an antibiotic, a good idea. Unfortunately, we could also send, through negligence as easily as malice, things that will cause harm; a virus, an airborne pollutant, a bad idea. And the possibilities of good and of ill are multiplied beyond all measure when it comes to policies carried out by governments in our name. Together, we can ruin poor farmers by dumping our subsidized grain into their markets, cripple industries by punitive tariffs, deliver weapons that will kill thousands upon thousands. Together, we can raise standards of living by adopting new policies on trade and aid, prevent or treat diseases with vaccines and pharmaceuticals, take measures against global climate change, encourage resistance to tyranny and a concern for the worth of each human life.

And, of course, the worldwide web of information—radio, television, telephones, the Internet—means not only that we can affect lives everywhere but that we can learn about life anywhere, too. Each person you know about and can affect is someone to whom you have responsibilities: to say this is just to affirm the very idea of morality. The challenge, then, is to take minds and hearts formed over the long millennia of living in local troops and equip them with ideas and institutions that will allow us to live together as the global tribe we have become.

Under what rubric to proceed? Not "globalization"—a term that once referred to a marketing strategy, and then came to designate a macroeconomic thesis, and now can seem to encompass everything, and nothing. Not "multiculturalism," another shape shifter, which so often designates the disease it purports to cure. With some ambivalence, I have settled on "cosmopolitanism." Its meaning is equally disputed, and celebrations of the "cosmopolitan" can suggest an unpleasant posture of superiority toward the putative provincial. You imagine a Comme des Garçons-clad sophisticate with a platinum frequent-flyer card regarding, with kindly condescension, a ruddy-faced farmer in workman's overalls. And you wince.

Maybe, though, the term can be rescued. It has certainly proved a survivor. Cosmopolitanism dates at least to the Cynics of the fourth century BC, who first coined the expression cosmopolitan, "citizen of the cosmos." The formulation was meant to be paradoxical, and reflected the general Cynic skepticism toward custom and tradition. A citizen—a politēs—belonged to a particular polis, a city to which he or she owed loyalty. The cosmos referred to the world, not in the sense of the earth, but in the sense of the universe. Talk of cosmopolitanism originally signaled, then, a rejection of the conventional view that every civilized person belonged to a community among communities.

The creed was taken up and elaborated by the Stoics, beginning in the third century BC, and that fact proved of critical importance in its subsequent intellectual history. For the Stoicism of the Romans—Cicero, Seneca, Epictetus, and the emperor Marcus Aurelius—proved congenial to many Christian intellectuals, once Christianity became the religion of the Roman Empire. It is profoundly ironic that, though Marcus Aurelius sought to suppress the new Christian sect, his extraordinarily personal Meditations, a philosophical diary written in the second century AD as he battled to save the Roman Empire from barbarian invaders, has attracted Christian readers for nearly two millennia. Part of its appeal, I think, has always been the way the Stoic emperor's cosmopolitan conviction of the oneness of humanity echoes Saint Paul's insistence that "there is neither Jew nor Greek, there is neither bond nor free, there is neither male nor female: for ye are all one in Christ Jesus."

Cosmopolitanism's later career wasn't without distinction. It underwrote some of the great moral achievements of the Enlightenment, including the 1789 "Declaration of the Rights of Man" and Immanuel Kant's work proposing a "league of nations." In a 1788 essay in his journal *Teutscher Merkur,* Christoph Martin Wieland—once called the German Voltaire—wrote, in a characteristic expression of the ideal, "Cosmopolitans . . . regard all the peoples of the earth as so many branches of a single family, and the universe as a state, of which they, with innumerable other rational beings, are citizens, promoting together under the general laws of nature the perfection of the whole, while each in his own fashion is busy about his own well-being." And Voltaire himself—whom nobody, alas, ever called the French Wieland—spoke eloquently of the obligation to understand those with whom we share the planet, linking that need explicitly with our global economic interdependence. "Fed by the products of their soil, dressed in their fabrics, amused by games they invented, instructed even by their ancient moral fables, why would we neglect to understand the mind of these nations, among whom our European traders have traveled ever since they could find a way to get to them?"

So there are two strands that intertwine in the notion of cosmopolitanism. One is the idea that we have obligations to others, obligations that stretch beyond those to whom we are related by the ties of kith and kin, or even the more formal ties of a shared citizenship. The other is that we take seriously the value not just of human life but of particular human lives, which means taking an interest in the practices and beliefs that lend them significance. People are different, the cosmopolitan knows, and there is much to learn from our differences. Because there are so many human possibilities worth exploring, we neither expect nor desire that every person or every society should converge on a single mode of life. Whatever our obligations are to others (or theirs to us) they often have the right to go their own way. As we'll see, there will be times when these two ideals—universal concern and respect for legitimate difference—clash. There's a sense in which cosmopolitanism is the name not of the solution but of the challenge.

A citizen of the world: how far can we take that idea? Are you really supposed to abjure all local allegiances and partialities in the name of this vast abstraction, humanity? Some proponents of cosmopolitanism were pleased to think so; and they often made easy targets of ridicule. "Friend of men, and enemy of almost every man he had to do with," Thomas Carlyle memorably said of the eighteenth-century physiocrat the Marquis de Mirabeau, who wrote the treatise *L'Ami des hommes* when he wasn't too busy jailing his own son. "A lover of his kind, but a hater of his kindred," Edmund Burke said of Jean-Jacques Rousseau, who handed each of the five children he fathered to an orphanage.

Yet the impartialist version of the cosmopolitan creed has continued to hold a steely fascination. Virginia Woolf once exhorted "freedom from unreal loyalties"—to nation, sex, school, neighborhood, and on and on. Leo Tolstoy, in the same spirit, inveighed against the "stupidity" of patriotism. "To destroy war, destroy patriotism," he wrote in an 1896 essay—a couple of decades before the tsar was swept away by a revolution in the name of the international working class. Some contemporary philosophers have similarly urged that the boundaries of nations are morally irrelevant—accidents of history with no rightful claim on our conscience.

But if there are friends of cosmopolitanism who make me nervous, I am happy to be opposed to cosmopolitanism's noisiest foes. Both Hitler and Stalin—who agreed about little else, save that murder was the first instrument of politics—launched regular invectives against "rootless cosmopolitans"; and while, for both, anti-cosmopolitanism was often just a euphemism for anti-Semitism, they were right to see cosmopolitanism as their enemy. For they both required a kind of loyalty to one portion of humanity—a nation, a class—that ruled out loyalty to all of humanity. And the one thought that cosmopolitans share is that no local loyalty can ever justify forgetting that each human being has responsibilities to every other. Fortunately, we need take sides neither with the nationalist who abandons all foreigners nor with the hard-core cosmopolitan who regards her friends and fellow citizens with icy impartiality. The position worth defending might be called (in both senses) a partial cosmopolitanism.

FURTHER READING

Appiah, Kwame Anthony. 2007. *Cosmopolitanism: Ethics in a World of Strangers.* New York: Norton.
Beck, Ulrich, and Cairon Cronin. 2006. *Cosmopolitan Vision.* London: Polity.
Berger, Peter, and Samuel Huntington (Eds.). 2003. *Many Globalizations: Cultural Diversity in the Contemporary World.* New York: Oxford University Press.
Calhoun, Craig. 2007. *Nations Matter: Culture, History, and the Cosmopolitan Dream.* London: Routledge.

Falk, Richard. 1995. *On Humane Governance: Toward a New Global Politics.* University Park: Pennsylvania State University Press.

Gunn, Giles. 2013. *Ideas to Die For: The Cosmopolitan Challenge.* London: Routledge.

Habermas, Jürgen. 1991. *The Structural Transformation of the Public Sphere.* Cambridge, MA: MIT Press.

Kaldor, Mary. 2003. *Global Civil Society: An Answer to War.* London: Polity Press.

Keck, Margaret E., and Kathyrn Sikkink. 1998. *Activists Beyond Borders: Advocacy Networks in International Politics.* Ithaca, NY: Cornell University Press.

Kegley, Charles W., and Gregory A. Raymond. 2011. *The Global Future: A Brief Introduction to World Politics.* Belmont, CA: Wadsworth.

Nederveen Pieterse, Jan. 2000. *Global Futures: Shaping Globalization.* London: Zed Books.

ACKNOWLEDGMENTS

The introductory course in global studies that we began teaching at the University of California, Santa Barbara, in 1995 was quite likely the first such course to be offered in a research university anywhere in the world. I say "we," since it was first taught by myself and my colleague Richard Appelbaum, and later, when we offered it as a two-course series, my colleagues Giles Gunn and Sucheng Chan developed their own versions of it as well. Almost twenty years later there are hundreds of global studies undergraduate programs throughout the United States and around the world, and over sixty graduate courses of study in what is becoming a new academic field. This book has emerged from those courses. It is an attempt to provide clarity about what is encompassed in the field of global studies and to give students a welcoming introduction to its study.

In preparing this book, I am grateful to my colleagues in the global studies program at the University of California, Santa Barbara, and to my far-flung colleagues around the world who are members of the Global Studies Consortium. In places like Leipzig, Shanghai, Tokyo, New York, Roskilde, London, Moscow, Melbourne, Cairo, and New Delhi, a new generation of scholars is shaping an emerging field in innovative and thoughtful ways. I hope that they will find this book to be a congenial companion to their own courses and classrooms.

My thanks to Reed Malcolm, senior editor at the University of California Press, who encouraged me to produce this book, and to my student assistants, Nathan Siegel, Daniel Palm Cisne, and Ian Schechter, for helping to round up all of the missing citations and standardize the format. My colleague and partner, Sucheng Chan, has done more than a spouse should have to do. She has read the introductions for each of the sections, provided suggestions for the reading lists, and saved me from a host of intellectual embarrassments. I value her high standards for scholarship in the field of global history.

Finally, I want to thank all of the students in my classes who have suffered through earlier versions of this reader and helped to improve its quality. Since I teach this class yearly to 300 students, over five thousand have now been introduced to global studies through early versions of this book. I have tried to listen to them, and in turn I hope that this volume will speak to future students in ways that will demonstrate the intellectual excitement and contemporary relevance of the intriguing new field of global studies.

INDEX

Abbasid revolution, 81

Abraham, descendents and ideology of horizons, 79

acidification of ocean by climate change, 343

activist model of civil society, 393

ADRs (African Diaspora religions). *See* Africa: religions

aerosols, impact on climate, 340–41

Afghanistan: drug trade and terrorism, 24–25; segregation of minorities, 95

Africa: colonization and decolonization, 42–44; continent as birthplace of all humanity, 53–54, 56–60; HIV/AIDS, 347–48, 350–51; northern countries as part of Middle East, 75; religions, 55, 63–70; as reminder of other ways of being, 316–17; slave trade, 54, 55, 60–63; social change impeded by infectious diseases, 34; 'state-ethnicity-state' in African politics, 70–72

agriculture: feminization of low-income work, 309; limited opportunities on Arabian Peninsula, 78; and social change, 33–34, 41; women need access to extension services, 312

AIDS (acquired immune deficiency syndrome). *See* HIV/AIDS

Ake, Claude, on violence by the African state, 70–71

Albright, Madeleine K., concern for women in human rights framework, 312–13

Albrow, Martin, on globalization, 6, 21, 359–360

Alexander the Great, 100

Algeria, 247–48

Al Jazeera television company, 8–9, 352, 364

Al Qaeda, 7–10, 199, 236, 244–49

alternative development. *See* post-development and its challenges

Alvarado, Pedro de, 182

Amazon gold mining towns and human trafficking, 328–29

Americas, The: defining, 175–76; development gap between Latin America and U.S., 178, 187–191; discovering new world Columbus created, 178–181; forms of imperial politics in, 39–40; global-in and global-out effects, 176–181; social change dependent on strangers, 34; surviving globalization in three Latin American communities, 178, 191–93; victory of Cortés over Aztecs, 177, 181–87

Amnesty International, 374

Bolivar, Simon, 177

Bolivia: Bechtel water contract annulled after public protests, 314; silver from mountain of Potosí, 176; work of Guaraní Indians with local missionaries, 177, 192

Borobudur as production of Indian genius, 134, 138

boundaries: empire's rule has no territorial or temporal, 207, 208; and false confidence in political identity, 220–23; of former colonies not always along traditional lines, 218

Brazil: Children and Adolescents Act of 1990, 385; impact of 1997 economic crisis, 12–14; as one of BRICS, 177; violence of drug trade, 323; work of rubber tappers with Catholic Church, 177, 192

Brennan, Timothy, on cosmopolitanism, 400

BRICS (Brazil, Russia, India, China, South Africa), 177

British empire: impact of British colonial rule in India, 101, 108–9; slave trade, 61

British government Internet initiatives, 369

Brysk, Alison, on transnational threats to and opportunities for human rights, 374, 377–381

Buddhism: expansion of, 99, 100–101, 103, 115; variety of doctrines, 136–37

Burbank, Jane, and Frederick Cooper, on empire in history, 31–32, 36–41

Burke, Edmund, on Rousseau, 407

Burma, Young Men's Buddhist Association (YMBA), 140

Burundi, genocide, 70

Bush, George W., use of Huntington thesis to declare "War on Terror," 199

business: divide between multinationals and smaller enterprises, 225; midsize companies have overseas factories, 269

Buvinić, Mayra, on women in poverty, 301, 305–13

calendar, Indian lunar-solar year and dating systems, 316

Calhoun, Craig, on cosmopolitanism, 400

California, attempts to keep out Wal-Mart, 264

Canada, Quebec separatist movement, 221

Candomblé (religion), 64–65

Cann, Rebecca, on all humanity from same parents, 57–59

capitalism. *See also* corporate capitalism: capitalist state, as form of transnational state (TNS), 231; and human rights, 379, 381; necessary for new technologies, 223–24; realization of world market as passage within, 206; system at a crossroads, 278

Capone, Al, 321

carbon dioxide (CO_2), 337, 339–345

Carens, Joseph, on borders from standpoint of outsiders, 167–68

Carlisle, Thomas, on cosmopolitan Marquis de Mirabeau, 407

cartographic illusion, nation-state as, 219, 220–23

Case, Steve, on too many people left behind in information age, 369

Castles, Stephen, on "feminization of migration," 316, 332

Catholic Church, role in Latin American democratic transitions, 95

CDC (U.S. Centers for Disease Control and Prevention), naming and responding to HIV/AIDS, 347, 349

CEDAW. *See* United Nations Convention on the Elimination of All Forms of Discrimination against Women (CEDAW):

censorship of the Internet, 353–55

Central Asia. *See* South and Central Asia

central banks and issues of electronic cash, 289

Chaiyasan, Prachuab, Australia and New Zealand as Asian, 152

Chakrabarty, Dipesh, on "hyperreal Europe" and academic historiography, 46

Champa civilization, 134

Chan, Sucheng, on Vietnam, 135–36, 142–49

Chanda, Nayan: on African origin of global humanity, 55, 56–60; DNA associated him with Indian subcontinent, 59

Chandhoke, Neera, criticism of term "civil society," 393

chaos, image transported globally, 31, 75

Chaplin, Charlie, film on assembly line, 275

Chartist movement, 108–9

chattel slavery, 376

Chicago, Capone succeeded by Guzman as "Public Enemy Number One," 321

events, 173; link expatriate groups, 242, 390; role in global culture and politics, 352–56, 378–79, 380; and success of Islamic revolution in Iran, 82–83; and worldwide digital divide, 356, 366–371

communism. *See* Cold War; Marxism/Marx, Karl; Russia/Union of Soviet Socialist Republics (USSR); socialism/socialists; Vietnam, decolonization, war, revolution and refugees

communitarian vs. universal theories of citizenship, 168

"community of fate," 400

comparative methodology limited by preconceptions, 84–85

conflicts, ethnic and religious, 85–91

Congo (DRC), Mobotu's ouster and ensuing violence, 71

consumerism, lure of religion as an antidote to, 250

continental drift, 30–31, 57

conviviality, those "outside" have lived inside their societies, 401

Cooper, Frederick. *See* Burbank, Jane, and Frederick Cooper

coral reefs and global warming, 346

corporate capitalism. *See also* capitalism: commodifying practices, 356; contemporary corporation doomed to disaggregation, 266–67; foreign vs. domestic corporate ownership, 267–270; impact of the transnational economy, 255–57; location of multinationals and labor costs, 274; Wal-Mart as template for 21st century capitalism, 258, 263–67

Cortés, Hernando, conquest of Mexico, 181–87

cosmopolitanism: and global civil society, 392, 398–407; global culture as new sensibility of, 360; Yeats on soul anticipating future, 200

cosmopolitization vs. cosmopolitanism, 403–4

counterfeiting: to counter a superpower, 25; digital, 291

Cox, Bob, on civil society, 226

creation myths and global awareness, 31

creative destruction, 264

Crick, Francis S., and DNA, 56

crime, issues of electronic cash, 291

Critical Theories of Globalization, 20

Crosby, Alfred W., *Ecological Imperialism*, 179–180

cross-country regression analysis, Asian experience in global context, 126–27, 128

Cuauhtemoc, final Aztec emperor, 183

cultural flows model or network model of cultural transmission, 357

culture. *See also* religion: as both divisive and unifying force, 203–4; and communications and new media, 355–360, 370; cultural effects of African diaspora, 54, 55–56, 68–70; idea of human rights alien to some peoples, 383–85; international character of cities, 211–12; now most important distinction among people, 202; vs. political acculturation, 172–73; Third World Cultural Studies perspective, 317–18

currency: China, 125, 283; disappearance as symbol of eroding nation-state, 219; euro, 124, 282–83; issues of electronic cash, 289–290

Curtin, Michael: on Chinese film and television, 356, 360–62; on multicentric cultural economy, 358

Czechoslovakia, breakup of nation-state, 221

dancing as communal activity, 33

Darian-Smith, Eve, on human rights as an ethics of progress, 374–75, 381–85

Darwin, Charles, suggested early progenitors might be from Africa, 56

death and devastation of hot wars during Cold War, 147

debt bondage as most prevalent form of slavery today, 376

debt crises in Latin America, 190

decolonization. *See also* Vietnam, decolonization, war, revolution and refugees: desire for identity based on indigenous values, 241; and human rights, 382; legacy, 149; overseas colonies transformed to nation-states, 142–43

deforestation and global warming, 336

DeLong-Bas, Natana, on new social media and the Arab Spring, 356, 362–66

Delpino, Nena, on rise in female-headed households in Argentina, 309 democracy: citizenship and immigration challenges for Europe, 168; distinction between citizens and residents/aliens central to, 167; electoral, 165; and globalization, 207, 276, 277; in Latin America, 191; religion and transitions, 92–97

Deng Xioping, 117

dependency school of development, 303, 305

deserts, the Arabian Peninsula and ideology of the horizons, 76, 77–79

Deutsch, Karl, on comparative methodology, 84–85

development. *See also* economics; women: alternative conceptualizations to mainstream policy and thought, 317–18; in the Americas, 175–78, 187–191; definition and goals, 299–301; failure of mainstream models, 301–2, 313–15; free market and government's role, 277–79; and Internet access, 366–371; key elements associated with rapid growth, 128; with a more human face, 258, 276–280; post-development and its challenges, 315–17; role of women in the global economy, 301–2, 305–13; schools of research, 301, 302–5; and social change, 302–5; success of countries abiding by own rules, 294–97; toward restructuring China's model of, 130–31

DFI. *See* Direct Foreign Investment (DFI)

Díaz, Bernal: on incorporating some Aztec practices, 186; on Montezuma, 182–83

digital divide, 353, 356, 366–371

digital value units (DVUs), 289–290

Direct Foreign Investment (DFI), 274

discrimination. *See also* ethnicity/ethnic groups; religion: equality of all regardless of any reason for, 373; ethnic, and foreign relations, 151–52; against first groups associated with HIV/AIDS, 349–350; against minorities, 90, 91; perpetuation on Internet, 365; against women, 264, 271, 310, 377, 379

disease. *See* health and disease

DNA, sequences as records of ancestors' journeys, 56–59

Doha round, 278

dollarization, Latin American concerns about, 286

domestic workers treated as slaves, 331–34, 376–77

domino theory proved wrong, 135

Dow Chemical, CEO's dream to base on neutral territory, 229

Drucker, Peter, on corporations, 263–64

drug trade: attempts to control, 320–21, 322; drug war in Mexico, 323–25; failure of war on drugs, 325–28

dualism, rationalistic device creates an illusion of, 252

Durán, Diego, on Aztec treatment of conquered villages, 186

Durkheim, Émile: case studies of tribal societies, 4; influence on Robertson, 21–22

DVUs. *See* digital value units (DVUs)

East Asia: 21st century as Asian, 122–25; African ancestors form majority of current gene pool in, 58; Asian Fund, 125; economic growth in Asia, 125–29; global economic empires, 114–17; Korean and Japanese scholarship in reference to China, 47; more growth and equality without IMF strictures, 276; most dynamic regions same as ones before 1800, 125; success has source in culture, 204

East Timor. *See* Timor-Leste

Ecological Imperialism (Crosby), 179–180

ecology. *See* environmental issues

economics. *See also* capitalism; corporate capitalism; development; labor; poverty: contributions to global studies, 5; development based on manufactured goods, 116; global crises of 1997, 11–14, 123, 278, 279, 282, 398; globalization vs. technical change, 270–76; globalized, but political lines based on states, 220–22; growth in Asia, 117, 123, 125–29, 386–87; Reich on "who is us?," 258, 267–270; religious parties support prosperity, 96; welfare state jeopardized by lack of national control, 224; Westphalian system cannot be separated from market economy, 223–24

ecosystem modification: by climate change, 343–44; by human activities, 346

education: Internet delivery, 366–67; for women, 312
efficiency and outsourcing, 259
Egypt: Arab Spring and new social media, 354, 362–66; Muslim Brotherhood, 92, 93; Nasser's Westernized vision, 241
Ehrenreich, Barbara, and Arlie Russell Hochschild, on domestic workers, 323, 331–34
Eickelman, Dale, on Islamicization of social life, 83
electronic cash, impact on national markets, 283–84, 288–291
El-Hage, Wadih, 248
empire: collapse of European empires after World War II, 36; and global history, 31–32, 36–41; Hardt and Negri on new form of, 199–200, 204–8; West Africa's Manden Kurufaba empire, 53
empirical vs. comparative methodology, 85
employment. *See* jobs
End of History and the Last Man, The (Fukuyama), 16, 17
End of the Nation-State, The (Ohmae), 219
Enlightenment: cosmopolitanism and moral achievements of, 406; foundations, 109; and nation-state, 159, 217, 234, 240–41; and religion, 237–39; and skepticism of science and reason, 249; western law as universal, 383
Enuma Elish, 31
environmental issues. *See also* health and disease: in China, 129, 130; climate change, 339–345; as example of fissures in TCC, 225–26; natural resources exploited by transnational elites, 313–15; ocean challenges, 339, 345–47; sacrificing growth for, 276–77; transcend national boundaries, 336–37, 387; Westphalian system unable to handle, 224
Escobar, Arturo, post-development argument, 316
ethics in resolving issues of future, 250–53
ethnicity/ethnic groups: 55 ethnicities in China, 115; demands for ethnic homelands, 218; discrimination and foreign relations, 151–52; e-mail ethnicities, 242, 390; ethnic

conflicts documented by MAR dataset, 87–89; ethno-religious conflict in the Middle East, 87–91, 95; in Indonesia, 140–43; religion shapes discrimination against ethnic minorities, 86; secondary to revolutionary-democratic point of view, 164; 'state-ethnicity-state' in African politics, 55–56, 70–72; Vietnamese refugees' fear of communist persecution, 148–49
eugenics, 382
Eurasia. *See* South and Central Asia
euro: first attempt to create transnational currency, 282–83; possibility of pricing oil in euros, 124
Europe: 1850s as turning point and birth of globalization, 159, 160–63; citizenship, 166–69, 170–73; colonization and trade, 38–39, 119–122, 134–35, 139, 140; concept of the Middle East, 74–75; emigrants and descendents all over world, 179–180; Eurocentric genealogy of empire, 207–8; initiatives to extend Internet to underserved, 369; nationalism and transnationalism, 157–160, 163–66; no grounds for distinction between western "spenders" and Asia "hoarders," 121–22; often accepted as sole cradle of modern scholarship, 48–49; racist fears elicited by Middle Eastern immigrants, 241; religion and democratic transitions, 95, 96
European Union, 159, 168, 218
Evangelical Protestantism in Latin America, 96
Evans, Gareth, on building stronger relationships between Australia and Asia, 151

Facebook: and Arab Spring, 362–66; global distribution of users, 353
Falk, Richard, on religion and humane global governance, 236–37, 249–253
Fanon, Frantz, on human sufferings paid for colonialism, 314
Feminist Mystique, The (Friedan), 377
film and television: for Chinese audiences at home and abroad, 360–62; Hollywood not only global hub, 352, 360, 361–62

finance: impacts of electronic cash, 283–84, 288–291; money in international affairs, 281–88; possible impact of DFI to countries with cheap labor, 274; U.S. foreign investment grew more than domestic, 269–270; Westphalian system unable to control institutions, 224

financial inequality: "Globalization for Whom?," 293–97; rise of income disparities over the 19th and 20th centuries, 291–93; unequal distribution of wealth, 283, 284

fire, control by humans, 33

Firebaugh, Glenn, on rise of income disparities over 19th and 20th centuries, 284, 291–93

First Indochina War, 145–46

Fitzgerald, Stephen, *Is Australia an Asian Country?* 153

flexible accumulation, 111

Foltz, Richard, on religions of the Silk Road, 101, 102–3

Foran, John. *See* Bhavnani, Kum-Kum, et al

forecasting in governance and business, 395–96

fossil fuels, impact on climate change, 344

Foucauldian thinking, 316

Fox, Jonathan, on Middle Eastern conflicts and religion, 76, 84–92

Foxcomm, 260, 262

France: colonization of Indochina, 143–46; Declaration of the Rights of Man (1795), 163, 381, 406; devolution of power, 221; election of Paine to Republic's National Convention, 164; nation as "one and indivisible," 163; U.S. aid for First Indochina War, 146

Frank, Andre Gunder, on 21st century as Asian, 117, 122–25

freedom, free institutions supported by those accustomed to, 172

frequent flier miles as currency, 283

Friedan, Betty, *The Feminist Mystique,* 377

Friedman, Thomas, shrinking the world to size "small," 6–7, 11–17

Fujita, Ron, on ocean pollution, 339, 345–47

Fukuyama, Francis: on development gap between Latin America and U.S., 178, 187–191; end of Cold War as "end of history," 197; *The End of History and the Last Man,* 16

fundamentalism: Islamic or Christian unlikely alternative for nation-state, 224–25; movements in Islam as one reaction to challenges of West, 80, 81–82; variety in movements in Islam, 83–84

future: dramatically opposed visions, 200–202; planning for a sustainable, 391–92, 395–98

Gamburd, Michele, on unemployed husbands who squander wives' remittances, 333

Garvey, Marcus, 67

Gautier, Catherine, on climate change, 339–345

Geertz, Clifford, on softening of human cultural variety, 358

Gelstein, Rosa, on rise in female-headed households in Argentina, 309

generalizing theory demanded by globalization when in retreat, 18, 22

General Motors, 265–66, 267

Geneva Conference of 1954 on Vietnam, 146

Geneva Conventions, 374, 383

Genghis Khan, 101, 104

geography: of money does matter, 285–88; of production, economic shift toward Asia, 262, 283–84

Gereffi, Gary, producer-driven vs. buyer-driven commodity chains, 260

Germany: horrors of Nazi regime and human rights, 372–73; issues of reunification, 170–71; migrants killed crossing Berlin Wall, 379; outsourcing and job losses, 227–28; power ceded to individual Länder, 221

Gerstacker, Karl A., dream to base Dow Chemical on neutral territory, 229

Ghana, Konkomba-Nanuba war following SAP, 71

Ghonim, Wael, planning of Egypt's first day of protest, 365

Giddens, Anthony: descriptive approach, 22; on "universalization" of nation-state, 233

Gill, Stephen, on Tripartite Commission, 225

Gilroy, Paul, on cosmopolitanism, 401

glaciers, retreat, 341

Global Commission on Drug Policy, 327

Global Fund to Fight AIDS, Tuberculosis and Malaria, The, 351

Helsinki Agreement (1975), 383

Herodotus, on Greco-Persian War, 46

Heyck, Denis Lynn Daly, on surviving
globalization in three Latin American
communities, 178, 191–93

highly active antiretroviral therapy (HAART),
350

Hinduism/Hindus: coexistence of opposites,
251–52; global aspects, 101, 105–8;
influence in Southeast Asia, 134; named
for Indus River, 99

Hirsch, Fred, and One Nation/One Money myth,
284

history: contributions to global studies,
5; of cosmopolitanism, 405–7; and
development of African religion
and culture, 68–70; global cultural
influences on historiography, 32, 45–49;
globalization over time, 30–36, 160–63;
imperial trajectories, 31–32, 36–41; of
Islam, 80–82; new subfields developed,
21; precedents for globalization of
female services, 331–32; in schools of
development research, 304; of slavery,
60–63; from very small societies to global
community, 404–5

Hitchens, Christopher, religion "poisons
everything," 239

Hitler, Adolf, invectives against
cosmopolitanism, 407

HIV/AIDS, 338, 339, 347–351

Hobsbawm, Eric: 1789 to 1914 as "long 19th
century," 161; on the nation, 159, 163–66

Ho Chi Minh, 144–48

Hochschild, Arlie Russell. See Ehrenrech,
Barbara, and Arlie Russell Hochschild

Homo sapiens, travel and colonization by
ancestors of, 56, 57–59

homosexuals, stigma and slow response to HIV/
AIDS, 349–350

Honduras, preference for low-paid female labor,
310

Hong Kong: development strategy, 127; media
enterprises, 361

horizons. See deserts, the Arabian Peninsula and
ideology of the horizons

horizontal integration, 260

horses desired by Chinese, 115

households, poverty and growth of female-
headed, 308–11

Howard, John, favoring of Asian trade but
distaste for multiculturalism, 151–52

Huber, Peter, on market forces, information age
and corporations, 267

Human Development Report, 306, 310

human immunodeficiency virus (HIV). See
HIV/AIDS

human rights: claims in conflict with
sovereignty, 166–68; as an ethics of
progress, 374–75, 381–85; globalization's
impact, 374, 375–381; governments ignore
UN calls for ending slavery, 330–31;
harnessing social media for social reform,
364; International Bill of Human Rights,
372–74; natural resources not just public
good but, 315; reckoned with human being
who seemed to exist nowhere, 167

Human Rights Watch, 374, 383, 390

human settlements, limited opportunities on
Arabian Peninsula, 78–79

human trafficking: attempts to control, 322–23;
migrants as domestic and sex workers,
331–34; as "new slavery," 328–331

Hung, Ho-Fung, on whether rise of China is
sustainable, 117, 129–131

Huntington, Samuel P.: The Clash of
Civilizations and the Remaking of World
Order, 16–17, 198–99, 397; fault lines as
cultural, not political, 222; on a multipolar,
multicivilizational world, 202–4; on
religious conflict and Islam, 85, 91, 243

Huntington, Samuel P., and Peter Berger, Many
Globalizations, 389–390

hybridization, mixing of cultural forms
facilitated by global exchanges, 9–10

hydrological cycle modification by climate
change, 342

hypercards, 288, 289

hyperglobalizer orientation, 21

IBM (International Business Machines
Corporation): and Microsoft as templates
for IT economy, 263; operations abroad,
268–69, 270

Ibn Khaldum, his tolerant ideas, 4

ICC. See International Criminal Court (ICC)

identity: and ethnic and religious conflict, 72, 235; globalization's threat to cultural, 276; national, 170–73, 239–242, 244; from national to global, 391–92, 398–99; people using politics to define, 202; West needs to reconsider, 253; "who is us?" (Reich), 220, 258, 267–270

ideology: doctrines seeking to replace religion, 237; framed social and political movements of past, 397; universality of human rights seen as western, 383

illegal trade. *See* drug trade; human trafficking

immigration: and eliciting of fear in Western nations, 241; and forced labor, 376–77; justification for illiberal policies, 168; of Muslims into West, 82; negligible impact on U.S. wages, 273; some Australians desire to exclude Asians, 150, 152; Vietnam War and global diffusion of cultures, 136

imperialism. *See* colonialism

income: averages in major world regions, 1820, 1950, and 1990, 293*tab.*; creation of wealth as biopolitical production of social life, 206; electronic haves and have-nots, 290–91; gains for women's well-being but decline in, 308–10; global and national distribution of wealth, 283, 284, 293–97, 299–300; redistribution in China, 130; rise in disparities over 19th and 20th centuries, 291–93

India. *See also* Hinduism/Hindus: Bollywood as largest producer of film, 352; cultural influence on Southeast Asia, 135, 136–38; domestic competition for Star TV, 358; and the global information economy, 101, 109–13; impact of British colonial rule, 101, 108–9; mtDNA mutations in Manju line, 57; Nehru's Westernized vision, 241; peaceful relations among diverse cultures, 222; precious metals exchanged for manufactured goods, 120, 121; religions originating in, 99–100; yet to open to world financial markets, 295

Indochina. *See* Vietnam, decolonization, war, revolution and refugees

Indochinese Communist Party, 144, 145

Indo-European (Aryan) culture, 100

Indonesia: development strategy, 128; from Dutch colony to independence, 134, 135, 138–142; *Homo erectus* fossils found in, 56; mildness and tolerance of Islam in Java, 137; reaction to Australia's UN peacekeeping mission in East Timor, 152–53; religion not excluded from political sphere, 94–95, 96; transnational impact of 1997 forest fire, 336; youth organizations, 140

industrialization in long 19th century, 161

inequality. *See also* financial inequality: in concentration of strategic resources between cities, 211; digital divide, 353, 356, 366–371; Latin America's lack of competitiveness due to social, 191

informal sector and employment statistics, 312–13

information technology (IT): city as exemplar of information economy, 209–12; IBM and Microsoft as templates for IT economy, 263; India's leadership, 101, 109–13; technical change rather than globalization as real culprit, 274–76

infrared (longwave, LW) radiation absorption, 339–340

infrastructure investment to support rural men and women, 312

inlanders (Dutch pejorative term for Indonesian natives), 141–42

innovations. *See also* communications and new media; information technology (IT): global city has succeeded factory as site of, 213; mixture of technological dynamism and skepticism, 249–252; Waltons acknowledged debt to other retailers, 266

institutions: of global governance and civil society, 386, 392; international organizations serve existing power structure, 386; local and international coalitions against HIV/AIDS, 349–351; social power grounded in wealth exercised through, 231; unelected forces increasingly control lives of powerless, 379

interdisciplinary study of global issues, 3, 20

International Bill of Human Rights, 372–74, 379

international cooperation: better regarding health than environmental issues, 337–38; and HIV/AIDS, 347–351; needed to solve transnational problems, 387

livestock and social change, 34, 35

local government, resistance to China's central government policies, 130–31

localization of the global, 211, 213

local multicultural neighborhoods in "global cities," 6

local vs. global points of view, 4

Locke, John, nation-state needed for representative government, 217

Long-Term Capital Management (LTCM), faulty computer model forecasts, 13

Los Angeles as global city, 6

LTCM. *See* Long-Term Capital Management (LTCM), faulty computer model forecasts

Luce, Henry, 21st century belongs to Chinese, 361

MacLeod, Celeste Lipow, on Australia's relations with Asia, 136, 149–153

madrasas, very few Al Qaeda members attended, 246

Mahathir Mohamad, 152, 222, 398

Malaysia: barring of Australia and New Zealand from ASEM meetings, 152; development strategy, 128; peaceful relations among diverse cultures, 222; religion not excluded from political sphere, 96

Malay Youth, Union of, 140

malware, extensive damage caused by, 355

Manichaeism, 103

Mann, Charles C., on discovering the new world Columbus created, 177, 178–181

Mansour Jabarah, Mohammed, 248

Many Globalizations (Huntington and Berger), 389–390

Mao Zedong (Mao Tse-Tung), 116–17, 144

Marcus Aurelius, belief in oneness of humanity, 406

marijuana, 321, 326–27

marine ecosystems, 343, 346

markets: easier access as reason for outsourcing, 259; free market and government's role, 277–78; market forces and monetary governance, 286

Marley, Bob, 67

Martyr, Peter, on Montezuma, 184

Marxism/Marx, Karl. *See also* Russia/Union of Soviet Socialist Republics (USSR);

socialism/socialists: attracted politically conscious Vietnamese, 144; neo-Marxist lineage, 22; one of most influential ideologies of 20th century, 158–59; originally dealt with capitalism, not colonialism, 144; theories assumed to be universal, 4

mass media. *See* communications and new media

Matthews, Sally, on African context as reminder of other ways of being, 316–17

McDonald's, local variations, 6

McNeill, William, on globalization as long-term process, 31, 32–36

"McWorld," relationship with jihad, 198, 200–201

Mecca: increased numbers of pilgrims to, 82; as trading center independent of great powers, 78–79

media. *See* communications and new media

Melanesia, Christian population, 154–55

Melucci, Alberto, on supranational organizations and loss of state control, 228

MENA (Middle East and North Africa) region, 93–94, 96–97

Mendes, Chico, 192

Metcalf, Barbara D. and Thomas R., on impact of British colonial rule in India, 101, 108–9

methane and climate change, 337, 339, 344–45

Mexico: conquest by Cortés, 181–87; far more killed crossing U.S. border than Berlin Wall, 379; illegal drug trade, 321, 323–25; migration of educated women, 333

microchips, production of potato chips more advanced than that of, 275

microcredit for women, 312

Micronesia. *See* Pacific Islands, religious communities

Microsoft and IBM as templates for IT economy, 263

Middle East. *See also* Al Qaeda; Arab Spring and the new social media; Islam: battles for control of oil and water, 313–14; contributions to global culture and transnational economy, 74–77; desert terrain and ideology of the horizons, 76, 77–79; mtDNA mutations in Nasrin line, 57; religion and conflicts in, 84–92;

religion and politics in Arab transitions, 92–97; weak or non-existent relations with militants, 249; weak or non-existent state relations with militants, 247–48; "youth bulge," 363

migration. *See* human rights; human trafficking; immigration; refugees

Mikail, Barah, on religion and politics in Arab transitions, 76, 92–97

Mill, John Stewart, definition of nation, 163, 164

Miller, Mark, on "feminization of migration," 332

Millett, Kate, *Sexual Politics*, 377

minorities. *See also* ethnicity/ethnic groups: Minorities at Risk (MAR) dataset, 87–89; risk of segregation when based on religion or ethnicity, 95

Mirabeau, Marquis de (Honoré-Gabriel Riqueti), 407

Miron, Jeffrey, on legalizing illicit drugs, 327

mitochondrial DNA (mtDNA), 57–59

Mobotu Sese Seko, 71

modernization school of development, 302, 305

Modern Times (Charlie Chaplin film), 275

modern world, creation as great watershed of history, 41–45

Mohamed, Ali, 248

Momsen, Janet, on "feminization of migration," 332

money: electronic cash, impact on national markets, 288–291; in international affairs, 283, 284–88; as most traded thing, 281; what is it? 282–83

Mongols, 38, 101, 103–5

Montesquieu, on necessity to think beyond national, 401

Montezuma, role in Spanish victory, 182–84

morality: consideration of all points of view, 172; of open borders, 167

Motolina, Toribio de Benavente, on Tlaxcaltecs, 184

Mouffe, Chantal, on cosmopolitanism, 400

Mousavi, Mir-Hossein, protests organized through Internet, 354

Moussaoui, Zacarias, 246, 247

mtDNA. *See* mitochondrial DNA (mtDNA)

Mubarak, Hosni, 354, 365–66

Mughal dynasty, 101

Muhammad, and history of Islam, 80–82

multicultural societies as different kind of globalization, 241

multidisciplinary approach to development, 318

multi-institutional analysis in schools of development research, 304, 305

multinational corporations. *See* corporate capitalism; transnational corporations (TNCs)

multipolar world, trajectory of change toward, 386–87

Munshi, Debashish. *See* Bhavnani, Kum-Kum, et al

Murdoch, Rupert, competition for Star TV, 358, 361

music not necessarily a universal language, 359

Muslims. *See* Islam

Narayanan, Vasudha, on Hinduism, 101, 105–8

narcotics trade. *See* drug trade

nationalism: in Africa, 43–44, 70–72; movement in Vietnam, 144; Netherlands and Indonesia, 138–142; and religious politics, 235; secular vs. religious, 240; world system as only scheme for social change, 45

National Organization for Women, 377

nation-building: applied only to some nations, 164; and historiography, 46

nation-state: as cartographic illusion, 219, 220–23; as consequence of empire, 40–41; decline of sovereignty, 205–6; defining "nation," 159, 163–66; erosion of, 216–220; as Europe's distinctive contribution to global politics, 142–43, 157, 158, 177; foreign policy must take new media into account, 367; and human rights, 381–82, 383–85; and money, 284–291; as recent phenomenon in history, 37; religion challenges legitimacy of, 239–241; shaped by cultural preferences, 203; 'state-ethnicity-state' in African politics, 55–56, 70–72; and transnational economy, 219–220, 229–233, 378–79, 380–81, 387; weakened by global forces, 197, 214, 374, 394, 399, 402–3; Westphalian system's failure, 219, 223–27; what comes after, 219, 227–29 natural resources. *See* environmental issues

NCR Corporation, 229–230

"negative capability" (Keats), 251

negotiation and competition model of cultural transmission, 357–58

Negri, Antonio, on new form of empire, 204–8

neo-African religions, 64–65

"neo-atheists," 238–39

neoclassical growth model, 126–27

neoliberal version of civil society, 393

neoliberal vs. vernacular cosmopolitanism, 400–401

neo/populist development. *See* post-development and its challenges

Nestorian Christianity, 103

Netherlands, colonization of what became Indonesia, 134–35, 138–142

networks, places between very dangerous, 24–25

"new world disorder," 219, 228

New World Disorder, The (Jowitt), 228

New World Information and Communication Order (UNESCO), 357, 367

new world order. *See also* globalization; transnationalism: 21st century as "God's century," 236, 237–39; Al Qaeda and the new terrorists, 244–49; global cities, 200, 208–14; global forces, 197–200, 204–8; Huntington's multipolar, multicivilizational world, 202–4; "Jihad vs. McWorld," 198, 200–202; and religious politics, 234–37, 239–244, 249–253

Ngo Dinh Diem, 146

NGOs. *See* non-governmental organizations (NGOs)

Nguyen dynasty of Vietnam abdicated throne, 145

Nicaragua, women's cooperatives, 177, 192–93

Nietzsche, Friedrich, "God is dead," 237

Nigeria: confrontation between Christians and Sunni Muslims, 95; direct violence, 70; film production, 352

Nishimizu, Mieko, on educating women, 312

Nnoli, Okwudiba, on 'state-ethnicity-state' in African politics, 55–56, 70–72

non-governmental organizations (NGOs): advantages of futures thinking for citizen groups, 396–97; fear of trade and multinationals, 272; human rights monitoring, 322, 378; making international agencies more accountable, 367; outside control of any one nation-state, 226, 390; social movements and civil society, 383, 392–95

noodles, origin in both Italy and China, 115

normative orientation, globalization in terms of, 20–21

Norris, Pippa, on the worldwide digital divide, 356, 366–371

North-South divide: and access to new media, 367–371; and human rights, 383–85

nuclear threat, 23, 25–26, 143

Obama, Barack, global identity, 391

Oceania. *See* Pacific Islands, religious communities

oceans: and climate, 340, 342, 343; pollution, 336, 339, 345–47

Odeh, Mohamed Saddiq, 245

offshoring. *See* outsourcing/offshoring

Ohmae, Kenichi, on the cartographic illusion, 219, 220–23

oil: death and destruction to control, 313; raising uncertainty to make life harder for U.S., 25; U.S. recovered from crisis much faster than Latin America, 190

Olivier, Roy, on Al Qaeda and the new terrorists, 236, 244–49

Olupona, Jacob, on African religion, 68–70

"The One Big Thing," 17

One Nation, gain in 1998 Queensland election, 152

One Nation/One Money myth, 283, 286–88

opium-producing countries, 321

organizational learning, 261–62

organizations. *See* institutions

Ottoman empire, 38, 39

outsourcing/offshoring: advantages, 256–263; Wal-Mart, 256, 263–67; work and workers in India's knowledge industries, 109–13

Pacific Islands, religious communities, 136, 153–55

Paine, Thomas, 164

Palestine, Al Qaeda members from refugee families, 248

Panagariya, Arvind, on growth and trade, 272

participation and democratization of futures, 396–97

Patten, Chris (Hong Kong), critical role for Australia in Asia, 152

Paul, Saint, on oneness of humanity, 406

Pearl, Daniel, 249

penalties for drug smuggling, 321

Pentecostal school of Christianity, 63, 64, 65–66

permafrost/permafrost hydrate methane, 344–45

Philippines: as former colony of U.S., 135; migration of educated women, 333; silver from Mexico to Manila to China, 116

Philpott, Daniel. *See* Toft, Monica Duffy, et al

Pieterse, Jan Nederveen: on global futures, 391, 395–98; world as "global" mélange," 401

Pinto, Antonia, on prostitutes lured to Amazon towns, 328–29

Pitsuwan, Surin, Australia and New Zealand as Asian, 152

planetarity, 401

Poland, religion not excluded from political sphere, 95

policy. *See* government policy

politics. *See also* autocratic regimes; democracy: failure of political center, 220–22; political acculturation vs. cultural life, 172–73; political economy of Indian IT industry, 111–13; political ideology vs. religion, 92; political subjectivity and cities, 212–14; security and political rights vs. social and economic rights, 379, 380, 381

Polynesia. *See* Pacific Islands, religious communities

Pomeranz, Kenneth, on global silver trade and China, 117–122

population: die-off of native peoples, 35–36; geographical distribution of Hindus, 106; and social change, 32, 34

Porter, Eduardo, on failure of war on drugs, 322, 325–28

Portugal, slave trade allowed by pope, 60

post-development and its challenges, 315–18

potato chips, production more advanced than that of microchips, 275

poverty: alleviation and integration into world economy, 294–97; and human trafficking, 329–330, 376; and Internet access, 366–371; many efforts to fight undercut

by globalization, 191–92; protests brought attention to, 293–94; and women, 301, 305–13, 333

power: cities as places for spatialization of, 210, 213–14; downsides to imbalances in in international politics, 27–28; power politics linked with religious issues, 95–96

Prambanam Hindu Temple, 134

"principle of nationality" different from political nationalism, 165–66

privacy issues of electronic cash, 290

quality of life: as goal of development, 299; indicators of women's, 307*tab.*

racism: of British officials in India, 109; classificatory schemes used to deny rights, 382–83; subhuman negro label, 61–62; worst impacts of development on Black people, 314

Radelat, Steven, et al, on economic growth in Asia, 117, 125–29

radiative forcing, 340

Rajagopal, Balakrishnan, on relationship between human rights and diverse cultures, 384

RAND Corporation, on legalizing marijuana, 327

Rastafarianism, 64, 67

reception model of cultural transmission, 357

refugees. *See also* immigration: "boat people" and "ethnic cleansing," 148–150; contribution to global diffusion of cultures, 136; and human rights, 379; Palestinian Al Qaeda members, 248

Reich, Robert B., "who is us?," 220, 258, 267–270

religion. *See also* Africa: religions; Christianity; Hinduism/Hindus; Islam: 21st century as "God's century," 237–39; and centrist history, 47; challenge to secular state in new world order, 197, 234–240, 242–44; in conquest of Mexico, 186–87; divides people instead of Iron Curtain, 204; faith underlies local strategies, 192; and humane global governance, 249–253; monotheistic God as attack on ideology of the horizons, 79; none emerged unchanged from journey along Silk Road,

religion. *See also* Africa: (*continued*)
101, 102–3, 115; origin of Buddhism,
Hinduism and Sikhism in India, 99–100;
origin of three major religions in Middle
East, 74; and political conflicts, 76, 84–92;
and politics in Arab transitions, 92–97;
role in empire, 37–38; and slavery, 62–69

religious studies: contributions to global studies,
5; Weber's comparative approach, 4–5

resources, role in socioeconomic development,
370–71

Reuter, Peter H., on risks of legalizing drugs,
327

revolutionary ideas and precedence in long 19th
century, 161, 162

Rich, Adrienne, on need to re-narrativize
common histories, 401

richest people in the world, 283

Rise and Fall of the Great Powers, The (Kennedy),
16–17

risk society or risk world, 400, 403–4

Robbins, Bruce, on necessity to think beyond
national, 401

Robbins, Joel, on cultural effects of globalization
on Pacific Islands, 136, 153–55

Robertson, Roland: influenced by Durkheimian-
Weberian tradition, 21–22; recognized
changing history of globalization, 19; on
"universalization" of nation-state, 233; use
of terms globalism and *glocal*, 6

Robinson, William I., on transnational state,
219–220, 229–233

Rodrik, Dani, on unequal distribution of wealth,
284, 293–97

Rome: Christian universal histories, 47; as first
city of a million people, 404–5; linked to
China by trade, 114–15; Roman empire and
its successors, 37–38; slavery in Roman
empire, 60

Roosevelt, Eleanor, and Universal Declaration of
Human Rights, 374

Rosenberg, Justin, criticism of Giddens, 22

Rossabi, Morris, on the Mongols, 101, 103–5

Rousseau, Jean-Jacques, 217, 238, 407

rubber tappers of Brazil, 178, 192, 193

Rushdie, Salman, 83

Russia/Union of Soviet Socialist Republics
(USSR): breakup as last stage of
decolonization, 143; breakup of nation-
state, 218, 221; definition of modernity
compared to U.S., 170; failure of rigid
central planning, 272–73; no longer
deterring nuclear proliferation, 26; as
part of Europe, 157–58; Soviet ideology
and foreign interventions, 159, 169–170;
transmission of Southeast Asian crisis to,
11–13; unresolved fallout from breakup of
Soviet ruble zone, 286

Rwanda, genocide, 70

Sachs, Jeffrey. *See* Radelat, Steven, et al

Sachsenmaier, Dominic, on movements and
patterns in global history, 32, 45–49

Saeed Sheikh, Omar, 249

Said, Khaled, beaten to death by Egyptian police,
365

Salazar Parreñas, Rhacel, on "Philippine
divorce," 333

Salin, Pascal, on money and state sovereignty,
284

Sanskrit enriched native languages in Southeast
Asia, 137

Santería (religion), 65

SAP. *See* structural adjustment program (SAP)
and structural violence

Sassen, Saskia, on global cities, 200, 208–14

Saudi Arabia: abstained from Declaration of
Human Rights, 373; funding of Islamic
centers around the world, 96; websites on
women's rights, 364

"scapes," global perspective from variety of, 4–5,
19–20

sceptic orientation, 21

scholarly disciplines, globalization in terms of,
21

Scholte, Jan Aart, domains worked on, 20

Schumacher, E.F., on appropriate technology,
193

Schumpeter, Joseph, innovations cast social and
political shadows, 264

Scientology sites hacked, 355

Scott, Allen, on mosaic of cultural production
centers, 358

sea level rise, 337, 341, 342

Seckinelgin, Hakan, on international
cooperation and HIV/AIDS, 339, 347–351

Second Sex, The (Beauvoir), 377

secularism: bonding the positive tendencies in religion and, 253; dismay at return of religion to the mainstream of political life, 249; of the modern state in both India and Britain, 108; not necessary to embrace or reject, 92–93; not realistic solution in MENA region, 96–97; secularization thesis as poor guide to global historical reality, 237–39

security and political rights vs. social and economic rights, 379, 380, 381

seigniorage issues of electronic cash, 291

Selassie, Haile ("Ras Tafari") regarded as God, 67

"self-help" programs, based on secularization of Hinduism-based practices, 107

Sen, Amartya: on female disadvantage in survival, 308; goal of development as freedom, 301

Sennett, Richard, on divide between polity and economy, 227

services, globalization of, 111–13

Severino, Jean-Michel, on critical role for Australia in Asia, 152

sex. *See also* discrimination: against women: demand for sex workers, 322–23, 331–32; hidden global economy of drugs and, 322, 323–28

Sexual Politics (Millett), 377

Shah, Timothy Samuel. *See* Toft, Monica Duffy, et al

Shi`ism, 81, 82

Shirk, David, on drug war in Mexico, 322, 323–25

Shiva, Vandana, *Water Wars*, 314

shrinking of the world to size "small," 6–7, 16

Silk Road, 100–101, 102–3, 115

silver, international trade of, 39, 115–122

Singapore, 127, 361

Sklair, Leslie, on three institutional supports of global capitalism, 226

slavery/slave trade. *See also* human trafficking: and coerced labor in Americas and elsewhere, 39; financed by silver trade, 120; forced labor still common in some countries, 376; globalization, and enslavement to economic role, 63; impact on Africa and globally, 54, 55,

60–62; slavery as a matter of control to slaveholders, 329

Sliti, Amor, 248

Snow Crash (Stephenson), 288

Snowden, Edward, 354

So, Alvin Y., on schools of development research, 301, 302–5

social and economic rights vs. security and political rights, 379, 380, 381, 382

social change: agency of subaltern women and men in facilitating, 317; communication and transportation advances promote, 32–33, 35–36, 160; and development, 302–5; thresholds and accelerants of, 32–36; Wallerstein on study of, 32, 41–45

socialism/socialists. *See also* Marxism/Marx, Karl; Russia/Union of Soviet Socialist Republics (USSR): countries abstaining from Universal Declaration of Human Rights, 373; debate on importance of "national question," 165; ethnic group differences seen as secondary, 164; few now see crisis of capitalism as opening toward, 397; most former socialist economies worse off at end of 1990s, 294

social order: empire operates on all registers of, 207; social movements and civil society, 226, 391, 392–94; Westphalian system unable to sustain balance, 224

social sciences: city as strategic site for understanding trends, 208; first major explorations of globalization-as-such, 19; as forerunner of global studies, 3–4; national/international vs. transnational analysis, 232–33; objective and subjective sides of social life, 230–31

social security: in China, 130; growing numbers dependent on, 375; for women, 312

sociopolitical restructuring needed in China, 130–31

solar (shortwave, SW) radiation absorption, 339–340

Sommers, Jeff, on size of Asian market relative to U.S., 124

sophistication of long-ago native societies, 179

South Africa, religion not excluded from political sphere, 95

United States. *See also* Americas, The: Christian militias' fear of global conspiracy, 241; communications and new media, 361, 369; dark side of American predominance, 23–28, 250; definition of modernity compared to that of USSR, 170; development gap between Latin America and, 178, 187–191; economics and finance, 13–14, 123–24, 129, 177, 375; foreign relations, 135–36, 146–49, 168, 355, 374; foreign vs. domestic corporate ownership, 267–270; history, 39–40, 163, 206–7, 217, 296; illegal drug trade and abuse, 321, 324–28; as largest producer of greenhouse gases, 338; no nation-state can form center of an imperial project, 206; Philippines as colony of, 135

Universal Declaration of Human Rights, 373, 374, 379–380, 382–83

universalistic theories of citizenship, 168, 172–73

Upadhya, Carol, and A.R. Vasavi, on outposts of the global information economy, 109–13

upgrading of production firms, 261–62

urban sociology, impact of globalization, 208–9

value added, mostly by design, branding and marketing, 261

values: actions of men and groups justified by ideologies, 42; earlier border-crossing histories written from clear perspective of, 46–47

Vasavi, A.R. *See* Upadhya, Carol, and A.R. Vasavi

Vedic religion, 100

"veil of ignorance" on borders from standpoint of outsiders, 167

vernacular vs. neoliberal cosmopolitanism, 400–401

Vernon, Raymond, *Sovereignty at Bay*, 288

vertical integration, 260

"victim" and "savior" in human rights, 384

Vietnam, decolonization, war, revolution and refugees, 135–36, 142–49

Vilar, Pierre, on common interest against particular interests, 164

violence: of drug wars, 323–28; of Egyptian regime juxtaposed with nonviolent protests, 365; enforcement of slavery by, 328–29; of interethnic disputes, 70–72,

88, 203; religion may bring peace as well as, 239

Voltaire, on planetary obligations, 406

von Wright, G.H., on withering away of nation-state, 228

Voodoo/Vodun, 65, 68

wages: and jobs for women, 264, 271, 310; negligible impacts of globalization, 273, 274; stagnation and decline, 375

Wahhabi movement, 82

Wallerstein, Immanuel, world systems theory, 4, 19, 32, 41–45

Wal-Mart, 256, 258, 260–61, 263–67

Walzer, Michael, on right of immigration, 172

wandering and halting between horizons, 77–79

water: devastating consequences of battles to control, 313–14; impact of climate change on supply, 342

Water Wars (Shiva), 314

Watson, James D., and DNA, 56

WCD. *See* Women, Culture, Development (WCD) paradigm

wealth. *See* income

weapons, Spanish superiority over Aztecs, 187

Weber, Max: charismatic becomes routinized, 68; *The City*, 212; on class struggle, 42; comparative study of religions, 3–4; influence on Robertson, 21–22; on Islam, 79, 80

Weber, Steven, on how globalization went bad, 7, 23–28

Westad, Odd Arne, on Soviet ideology and foreign interventions, 159, 169–170

Westboro Baptist Church site hacked, 355

Western civilizations, power shifting to non-Western civilizations, 204

Westernization: of Al Qaeda militants, 245–49; "McWorld" as term for consumer culture, 198; recognizing nationalization at least partly as, 48–49; visions of Nasser, Nehru and the Shah, 241

Westphalia, Treaty of, as beginning of idea of nation-state, 217

Westphalian model of monetary geography, 287–88

Westphalian system: theory of state identity

challenged, 398–99; as "Westfailure" system, 219, 223–27

Whirlpool, foreign employees, 269

White, Stephen, on values and cosmopolitan principles, 402

"who is us?" (Reich), 220, 258, 267–270

Wieland, Christoph Martin, on cosmopolitanism, 406

Wikileaks, 354

Williamson, Gilbert, NCR as global company headquartered in U.S., 229–230

Wilson, Allan, mtDNA research, 57–59

Wilson, Charles E., comment on what's good for GM is good for America, 265

Wolfensohn, James D., World Bank initiatives to extend Internet to underserved, 370–71

women: global redivision of traditional domestic work, 331–34; history contained in cells of modern, 56–57; and human rights, 364, 377; human trafficking, 322, 328–331; Nicaraguan cooperatives, 178, 192–93; in poverty as new global underclass, 305–13; role in the global economy, 301–2, 313–18; UN Convention on the Elimination of Discrimination against Women, 379; wages, 264, 271, 310

Women, Culture, Development (WCD) paradigm, 317

Woolf, Virginia, on "freedom from unreal loyalties," 407

Woollacott, Martin, on economy's emancipation from space and job loss, 227

World Bank: called on Australia to help in East Asian economic crisis, 152; initiatives to extend Internet to underserved, 370–71

World Business Council for Sustainable Development, Global Scenarios, 395–96

world citizenship, 173

world-system perspective school of development, 303, 305

world systems theory, 4, 19, 32, 41–45

"world time," as world context of any given era, 44–45

World Trade Center: 1993 bombing as initial action of Al Qaeda, 244–45, 246–47; 2001 attacks, 7–8, 247

World Trade Organization (WTO): development successes with rules prohibited by, 295–96; Doha round, 278; Seattle protests brought attention to globalization, 181, 270–71; weak enforcement of standards, 256–57

World War I, role in impact of globalization, 162

World War II: as end of an era, 161–62; Nazi invasion of France and Japan's activities in Southeast Asia, 144–45

WTO. See World Trade Organization (WTO)

Yasuaki, Onuma, on relationship between human rights and diverse cultures, 384

Y chromosome: M52 Y chromosome shared by many Indians, 59; tracing African ancestry through father, 58

Yeats, William Butler: "the center will not hold," 202, 222; on two eternities of race and soul, 200

Yemen, agriculture and interest in Arabian Peninsula, 78

YMBA. See Burma, Young Men's Buddhist Association (YMBA)

yoga and other Hindu traditions, 105, 107–8

Yoruba religious traditions, 65

Yousef, Ramzi Ahmed, 245

youth, nationalism often promoted by youthful intelligentsias, 139–140

YouTube and Arab Spring, 354, 364

Yue Yuen (subsidiary of Taiwanese company Pou Chen), 261–62

Yugoslavia: breakup of nation-state, 221; peaceful relations among diverse cultures, 222; religious identities fueled mutual animosity, 94

Zeiler, Thomas, on process of globalization, 160

Ziai, Aram, on post-development, 316